Principles
of
Data
Mining

Adaptive Computation and Machine Learning

Thomas Dietterich, Editor
Christopher Bishop, David Heckerman, Michael Jordan, and Michael Kearns, Associate Editors

Bioinformatics: The Machine Learning Approach, Pierre Baldi and Søren Brunak
Reinforcement Learning: An Introduction, Richard S. Sutton and Andrew G. Barto
Graphical Models for Machine Learning, Brendan J. Frey
Learning in Graphical Models, Michael I. Jordan
Causation, Prediction, and Search, second edition, Peter Spirtes, Clark Glymour, and Richard Scheines
Principles of Data Mining, David J. Hand, Heikki Mannila, and Padhraic Smyth

Principles
of
Data
Mining

David Hand

Heikki Mannila

Padhraic Smyth

A Bradford Book
The MIT Press
Cambridge, Massachusetts
London, England

This book was typeset in Palatino by the authors and was printed and bound in the United States of America.

Library of Congress Cataloging-in-Publication Data

Hand, D. J.
    Principles of data mining / David Hand, Heikki Mannila, Padhraic Smyth.
        p.   cm.—(Adaptive computation and machine learning)
    Includes bibliographical references and index.
    ISBN 0-262-08290-X (hc. : alk. paper)
    1. Data Mining.   I. Mannila, Heikki.   II. Smyth, Padhraic.   III. Title.   IV. Series.

QA76.9.D343 H38 2001
006.3—dc21   2001032620

To Crista, Aidan, and Cian

To Paula and Elsa

To Shelley, Rachel, and Emily

Brief Contents

Contents

List of Tables

List of Figures

Series Foreword

The rapid growth and integration of databases provides scientists, engineers, and business people with a vast new resource that can be analyzed to make scientific discoveries, optimize industrial systems, and uncover financially valuable patterns. To undertake these large data analysis projects, researchers and practitioners have adopted established algorithms from statistics, machine learning, neural networks, and databases and have also developed new methods targeted at large data mining problems. *Principles of Data Mining* by David Hand, Heikki Mannila, and Padhraic Smyth provides practioners and students with an introduction to the wide range of algorithms and methodologies in this exciting area. The interdisciplinary nature of the field is matched by these three authors, whose expertise spans statistics, databases, and computer science. The result is a book that not only provides the technical details and the mathematical principles underlying data mining methods, but also provides a valuable perspective on the entire enterprise.

Data mining is one component of the exciting area of machine learning and adaptive computation. The goal of building computer systems that can adapt to their environments and learn from their experience has attracted researchers from many fields, including computer science, engineering, mathematics, physics, neuroscience, and cognitive science. Out of this research has come a wide variety of learning techniques that have the potential to transform many scientific and industrial fields. Several research communities have converged on a common set of issues surrounding supervised, unsupervised, and reinforcement learning problems. The MIT Press series on Adaptive Computation and Machine Learning seeks to unify the many diverse strands of machine learning research and to foster high quality research and innovative applications.

Thomas Dietterich

Preface

The science of extracting useful information from large data sets or databases is known as data mining. It is a new discipline, lying at the intersection of statistics, machine learning, data management and databases, pattern recognition, artificial intelligence, and other areas. All of these are concerned with certain aspects of data analysis, so they have much in common—but each also has its own distinct flavor, emphasizing particular problems and types of solution.

Because data mining encompasses a wide variety of topics in computer science and statistics it is impossible to cover all the potentially relevant material in a single text. Given this, we have focused on the topics that we believe are the most fundamental.

From a teaching viewpoint the text is intended for undergraduate students at the senior (final year) level, or first or second-year graduate level, who wish to learn about the basic principles of data mining. The text should also be of value to researchers and practitioners who are interested in gaining a better understanding of data mining methods and techniques. A familiarity with the very basic concepts in probability, calculus, linear algebra, and optimization is assumed—in other words, an undergraduate background in any quantitative discipline such as engineering, computer science, mathematics, economics, etc., should provide a good background for reading and understanding this text.

There are already many other books on data mining on the market. Many are targeted at the business community directly and emphasize specific methods and algorithms (such as decision tree classifiers) rather than general principles (such as parameter estimation or computational complexity). These texts are quite useful in providing general context and case studies, but have limitations in a classroom setting, since the underlying foundational principles are often missing. There are other texts on data mining that have a more academic flavor, but to date these have been written largely from a computer science viewpoint, specifically from either a database viewpoint (Han and Kamber, 2000), or from a machine learning viewpoint (Witten and Franke, 2000).

This text has a different bias. We have attempted to provide a foundational view of data mining. Rather than discuss specific data mining applications at length (such as, say, collaborative filtering, credit scoring, and fraud detection), we have instead focused on the underlying theory and algorithms that provide the "glue" for such applications. This is not to say that we do not pay attention to the applications. Data mining is fundamentally an applied discipline, and with this in mind we make frequent references to case studies and specific applications where the basic theory can (or has been) applied.

In our view a mastery of data mining requires an understanding of both statistical and computational issues. This requirement to master two different areas of expertise presents quite a challenge for student and teacher alike. For the typical computer scientist, the statistics literature is relatively impenetrable: a litany of jargon, implicit assumptions, asymptotic arguments, and lack of details on how the theoretical and mathematical concepts are actually realized in the form of a data analysis algorithm. The situation is effectively reversed for statisticians: the computer science literature on machine learning and data mining is replete with discussions of algorithms, pseudocode, computational efficiency, and so forth, often with little reference to an underlying model or inference procedure. An important point is that *both* approaches are nonetheless essential when dealing with large data sets. An understanding of both the "mathematical modeling" view, and the "computational algorithm" view are essential to properly grasp the complexities of data mining.

In this text we make an attempt to bridge these two worlds and to explicitly link the notion of statistical modeling (with attendant assumptions, mathematics, and notation) with the "real world" of actual computational methods and algorithms.

With this in mind, we have structured the text in a somewhat unusual manner. We begin with a discussion of the very basic principles of modeling and inference, then introduce a systematic framework that connects models to data via computational methods and algorithms, and finally instantiate these ideas in the context of specific techniques such as classification and regression. Thus, the text can be divided into three general sections:

1. **Fundamentals**: Chapters 1 through 4 focus on the fundamental aspects of data and data analysis: introduction to data mining (chapter 1), mea-

surement (chapter 2), summarizing and visualizing data (chapter 3), and uncertainty and inference (chapter 4).

2. **Data Mining Components**: Chapters 5 through 8 focus on what we term the "components" of data mining algorithms: these are the building blocks that can be used to systematically create and analyze data mining algorithms. In chapter 5 we discuss this systematic approach to algorithm analysis, and argue that this "component-wise" view can provide a useful systematic perspective on what is often a very confusing landscape of data analysis algorithms to the novice student of the topic. In this context, we then delve into broad discussions of each component: model representations in chapter 6, score functions for fitting the models to data in chapter 7, and optimization and search techniques in chapter 8. (Discussion of data management is deferred until chapter 12.)

3. **Data Mining Tasks and Algorithms**: Having discussed the fundamental components in the first 8 chapters of the text, the remainder of the chapters (from 9 through 14) are then devoted to specific data mining tasks and the algorithms used to address them. We organize the basic tasks into density estimation and clustering (chapter 9), classification (chapter 10), regression (chapter 11), pattern discovery (chapter 13), and retrieval by content (chapter 14). In each of these chapters we use the framework of the earlier chapters to provide a general context for the discussion of specific algorithms for each task. For example, for classification we ask: what models and representations are plausible and useful? what score functions should we, or can we, use to train a classifier? what optimization and search techniques are necessary? what is the computational complexity of each approach once we implement it as an actual algorithm? Our hope is that this general approach will provide the reader with a "roadmap" to an understanding that data mining algorithms are based on some very general and systematic principles, rather than simply a cornucopia of seemingly unrelated and exotic algorithms.

In terms of using the text for teaching, as mentioned earlier the target audience for the text is students with a quantitative undergraduate background, such as in computer science, engineering, mathematics, the sciences, and more quantitative business-oriented degrees such as economics. From the instructor's viewpoint, how much of the text should be covered in a course will depend on both the length of the course (e.g., 10 weeks versus 15 weeks) and the familiarity of the students with basic concepts in statistics and machine learning. For example, for a 10-week course with first-year graduate students who have some exposure to basic statistical concepts, the instructor might wish to move quickly through the early chapters: perhaps covering chapters 3, 4, 5, and 7 fairly rapidly; assigning chapters 1, 2, 6, and 8 as background/review reading; and then spending the majority of the 10 weeks covering chapters 9 through 14 in some depth.

Conversely many students and readers of this text may have little or no formal statistical background. It is unfortunate that in many quantitative disciplines (such as computer science) students at both undergraduate and graduate levels often get only a very limited exposure to statistical thinking in many modern degree programs. Since we take a fairly strong statistical view of data mining in this text, our experience in using draft versions of the text in computer science departments has taught us that mastery of the entire text in a 10-week or 15-week course presents quite a challenge to many students, since to fully absorb the material they must master quite a broad range of statistical, mathematical, and algorithmic concepts in chapters 2 through 8. In this light, a less arduous path is often desirable. For example, chapter 11 on regression is probably the most mathematically challenging in the text and can be omitted without affecting understanding of any of the remaining material. Similarly some of the material in chapter 9 (on mixture models for example) could also be omitted, as could the Bayesian estimation framework in chapter 4. In terms of what is essential reading, most of the material in chapters 1 through 5 and in chapters 7, 8, and 12 we consider to be essential for the students to be able to grasp the modeling and algorithmic ideas that come in the later chapters (chapter 6 contains much useful material on the general concepts of modeling but is quite long and could be skipped in the interests of time). The more "task-specific" chapters of 9, 10, 11, 13, and 14 can be chosen in a "menu-based" fashion, i.e., each can be covered somewhat independently of the others (but they do assume that the student has a good working knowledge of the material in chapters 1 through 8).

An additional suggestion for students with limited statistical exposure is to have them review some of the basic concepts in probability and statistics *before* they get to chapter 4 (on uncertainty) in the text. Unless students are comfortable with basic concepts such as conditional probability and expectation, they will have difficulty following chapter 4 and much of what follows in later chapters. We have included a brief appendix on basic probability and definitions of common distributions, but some students will probably want to go back and review their undergraduate texts on probability and statistics before venturing further.

On the other side of the coin, for readers with substantial statistical background (e.g., statistics students or statisticians with an interest in data mining) much of this text will look quite familiar and the statistical reader may be inclined to say "well, this data mining material seems very similar in many ways to a course in applied statistics!" And this is indeed somewhat correct, in that data mining (as we view it) relies very heavily on statistical models and methodologies. However, there are portions of the text that statisticians will likely find quite informative: the overview of chapter 1, the algorithmic viewpoint of chapter 5, the score function viewpoint of chapter 7, and all of chapters 12 through 14 on database principles, pattern finding, and retrieval by content. In addition, we have tried to include in our presentation of many of the traditional statistical concepts (such as classification, clustering, regression, etc.) additional material on algorithmic and computational issues that would not typically be presented in a statistical textbook. These include statements on computational complexity and brief discussions on how the techniques can be used in various data mining applications. Nonetheless, statisticians will find much familiar material in this text. For views of data mining that are more oriented towards computational and data-management issues see, for example, Han and Kamber (2000), and for a business focus see, for example, Berry and Linoff (2000). These texts could well serve as complementary reading in a course environment.

In summary, this book describes tools for data mining, splitting the tools into their component parts, so that their structure and their relationships to each other can be seen. Not only does this give insight into what the tools are designed to achieve, but it also enables the reader to design tools of their own, suited to the particular problems and opportunities facing them. The book also shows how data mining is a process—not something which one does, and then finishes, but an ongoing voyage of discovery, interpretation, and re-investigation. The book is liberally illustrated with real data applications, many arising from the authors' own research and applications work. For didactic reasons, not all of the data sets discussed are large—it is easier to explain what is going on in a "small" data set. Once the idea has been communicated, it can readily be applied in a realistically large context.

Data mining is, above all, an exciting discipline. Certainly, as with any scientific enterprise, much of the effort will be unrewarded (it is a rare and perhaps rather dull undertaking which gives a guaranteed return). But this is more than compensated for by the times when an exciting discovery—a gem or nugget of valuable information—is unearthed. We hope that you as a reader of this text will be inspired to go forth and discover your own gems!

We would like to gratefully acknowledge Christine McLaren for granting permission to use the red blood cell data as an illustrative example in chapters 9 and 10. Padhraic Smyth's work on this text was supported in part by the National Science Foundation under Grant IRI-9703120.

We would also like to thank Niall Adams for help in producing some of the diagrams, Tom Benton for assisting with proof corrections, and Xianping Ge for formatting the references. Naturally, any mistakes which remain are the responsibility of the authors (though each of the three of us reserves the right to blame the other two).

Finally we would each like to thank our respective wives and families for providing excellent encouragement and support throughout the long and seemingly never-ending saga of "the book"!

mining exercise play no role in the data collection strategy. This is one way in which data mining differs from much of statistics, in which data are often collected by using efficient strategies to answer specific questions. For this reason, data mining is often referred to as "secondary" data analysis.

The definition also mentions that the data sets examined in data mining are often large. If only small data sets were involved, we would merely be discussing classical exploratory data analysis as practiced by statisticians. When we are faced with large bodies of data, new problems arise. Some of these relate to housekeeping issues of how to store or access the data, but others relate to more fundamental issues, such as how to determine the representativeness of the data, how to analyze the data in a reasonable period of time, and how to decide whether an apparent relationship is merely a chance occurrence not reflecting any underlying reality. Often the available data comprise only a sample from the complete population (or, perhaps, from a hypothetical superpopulation); the aim may be to *generalize* from the sample to the population. For example, we might wish to predict how future customers are likely to behave or to determine the properties of protein structures that we have not yet seen. Such generalizations may not be achievable through standard statistical approaches because often the data are not (classical statistical) "random samples," but rather "convenience" or "opportunity" samples. Sometimes we may want to summarize or *compress* a very large data set in such a way that the result is more comprehensible, without any notion of generalization. This issue would arise, for example, if we had complete census data for a particular country or a database recording millions of individual retail transactions.

The relationships and structures found within a set of data must, of course, be novel. There is little point in regurgitating well-established relationships (unless, the exercise is aimed at "hypothesis" confirmation, in which one was seeking to determine whether established pattern also exists in a new data set) or necessary relationships (that, for example, all pregnant patients are female). Clearly, novelty must be measured relative to the user's prior knowledge. Unfortunately few data mining algorithms take into account a user's prior knowledge. For this reason we will not say very much about novelty in this text. It remains an open research problem.

While novelty is an important property of the relationships we seek, it is not sufficient to qualify a relationship as being worth finding. In particular, the relationships must also be understandable. For instance simple relationships are more readily understood than complicated ones, and may well be preferred, all else being equal.

1 *Introduction*

1.1 Introduction to Data Mining

Progress in digital data acquisition and storage technology has resulted in the growth of huge databases. This has occurred in all areas of human endeavor, from the mundane (such as supermarket transaction data, credit card usage records, telephone call details, and government statistics) to the more exotic (such as images of astronomical bodies, molecular databases, and medical records). Little wonder, then, that interest has grown in the possibility of tapping these data, of extracting from them information that might be of value to the owner of the database. The discipline concerned with this task has become known as *data mining*.

Defining a scientific discipline is always a controversial task; researchers often disagree about the precise range and limits of their field of study. Bearing this in mind, and accepting that others might disagree about the details, we shall adopt as our working definition of data mining:

> Data mining is the analysis of (often large) observational data sets to find unsuspected relationships and to summarize the data in novel ways that are both understandable and useful to the data owner.

The relationships and summaries derived through a data mining exercise are often referred to as *models* or *patterns*. Examples include linear equations, rules, clusters, graphs, tree structures, and recurrent patterns in time series.

The definition above refers to "observational data," as opposed to "experimental data." Data mining typically deals with data that have already been collected for some purpose other than the data mining analysis (for example, they may have been collected in order to maintain an up-to-date record of all the transactions in a bank). This means that the objectives of the data

Data mining is often set in the broader context of *knowledge discovery in databases,* or KDD. This term originated in the artificial intelligence (AI) research field. The KDD process involves several stages: selecting the target data, preprocessing the data, transforming them if necessary, performing data mining to extract patterns and relationships, and then interpreting and assessing the discovered structures. Once again the precise boundaries of the data mining part of the process are not easy to state; for example, to many people data transformation is an intrinsic part of data mining. In this text we will focus primarily on data mining algorithms rather than the overall process. For example, we will not spend much time discussing data preprocessing issues such as data cleaning, data verification, and defining variables. Instead we focus on the basic principles for modeling data and for constructing algorithmic processes to fit these models to data.

The process of seeking relationships within a data set— of seeking accurate, convenient, and useful summary representations of some aspect of the data—involves a number of steps:

- determining the nature and structure of the representation to be used;

- deciding how to quantify and compare how well different representations fit the data (that is, choosing a "score" function);

- choosing an algorithmic process to optimize the score function; and

- deciding what principles of data management are required to implement the algorithms efficiently.

The goal of this text is to discuss these issues in a systematic and detailed manner. We will look at both the fundamental principles (chapters 2 to 8) and the ways these principles can be applied to construct and evaluate specific data mining algorithms (chapters 9 to 14).

Example 1.1 Regression analysis is a tool with which many readers will be familiar. In its simplest form, it involves building a predictive model to relate a *predictor* variable, X, to a *response* variable, Y, through a relationship of the form $Y = aX + b$. For example, we might build a model which would allow us to predict a person's annual credit-card spending given their annual income. Clearly the model would not be perfect, but since spending typically increases with income, the model might well be adequate as a rough characterization. In terms of the above steps listed, we would have the following scenario:

- The representation is a model in which the response variable, spending, is linearly related to the predictor variable, income.

- The score function most commonly used in this situation is the sum of squared discrepancies between the predicted spending from the model and observed spending in the group of people described by the data. The smaller this sum is, the better the model fits the data.

- The optimization algorithm is quite simple in the case of linear regression: a and b can be expressed as explicit functions of the observed values of spending and income. We describe the algebraic details in chapter 11.

- Unless the data set is very large, few data management problems arise with regression algorithms. Simple summaries of the data (the sums, sums of squares, and sums of products of the X and Y values) are sufficient to compute estimates of a and b. This means that a single pass through the data will yield estimates.

Data mining is an interdisciplinary exercise. Statistics, database technology, machine learning, pattern recognition, artificial intelligence, and visualization, all play a role. And just as it is difficult to define sharp boundaries between these disciplines, so it is difficult to define sharp boundaries between each of them and data mining. At the boundaries, one person's data mining is another's statistics, database, or machine learning problem.

1.2   The Nature of Data Sets

We begin by discussing at a high level the basic nature of data sets.

A *data set* is a set of measurements taken from some environment or process. In the simplest case, we have a collection of objects, and for each object we have a set of the same p measurements. In this case, we can think of the collection of the measurements on n objects as a form of $n \times p$ *data matrix*. The n rows represent the n objects on which measurements were taken (for example, medical patients, credit card customers, or individual objects observed in the night sky, such as stars and galaxies). Such rows may be referred to as *individuals, entities, cases, objects,* or *records* depending on the context.

The other dimension of our data matrix contains the set of p measurements made on each object. Typically we assume that the same p measurements are made on each individual although this need not be the case (for example, different medical tests could be performed on different patients). The p columns of the data matrix may be referred to as *variables*, *features*, *attributes*, or *fields*; again, the language depends on the research context. In all situations the idea is the same: these names refer to the measurement that is represented by each column. In chapter 2 we will discuss the notion of measurement in much more detail.

ID	Age	Sex	Marital Status	Education	Income
248	54	Male	Married	High school graduate	100000
249	??	Female	Married	High school graduate	12000
250	29	Male	Married	Some college	23000
251	9	Male	Not married	Child	0
252	85	Female	Not married	High school graduate	19798
253	40	Male	Married	High school graduate	40100
254	38	Female	Not married	Less than 1st grade	2691
255	7	Male	??	Child	0
256	49	Male	Married	11th grade	30000
257	76	Male	Married	Doctorate degree	30686

Table 1.1 Examples of data in Public Use Microdata Sample data sets.

Example 1.2 The U.S. Census Bureau collects information about the U.S. population every 10 years. Some of this information is made available for public use, once information that could be used to identify a particular individual has been removed. These data sets are called PUMS, for Public Use Microdata Samples, and they are available in 5 % and 1 % sample sizes. Note that even a 1 % sample of the U.S. population contains about 2.7 million records. Such a data set can contain tens of variables, such as the age of the person, gross income, occupation, capital gains and losses, education level, and so on. Consider the simple data matrix shown in table 1.1. Note that the data contains different types of variables, some with continuous values and some with categorical. Note also that some values are *missing*—for example, the **Age** of person 249, and the **Marital Status** of person 255. Missing measurements are very common in large real-world data sets. A more insidious problem is that of measurement noise. For example, is person 248's income really $100,000 or is this just a rough guess on his part?

A typical task for this type of data would be finding relationships between different variables. For example, we might want to see how well a person's income could be predicted from the other variables. We might also be interested in seeing if there are naturally distinct groups of people, or in finding values at which variables often coincide. A subset of variables and records is available online at the Machine Learning Repository of the University of California, Irvine, www.ics.uci.edu/~mlearn/MLSummary.html.

Data come in many forms and this is not the place to develop a complete taxonomy. Indeed, it is not even clear that a complete taxonomy can be developed, since an important aspect of data in one situation may be unimportant in another. However there are certain basic distinctions to which we should draw attention. One is the difference between quantitative and categorical measurements (different names are sometimes used for these). A quantitative variable is measured on a numerical scale and can, at least in principle, take any value. The columns Age and Income in table 1.1 are examples of quantitative variables. In contrast, categorical variables such as Sex, Marital Status and Education in 1.1 can take only certain, discrete values. The common three point severity scale used in medicine (mild, moderate, severe) is another example. Categorical variables may be ordinal (possessing a natural order, as in the Education scale) or nominal (simply naming the categories, as in the Marital Status case). A data analytic technique appropriate for one type of scale might not be appropriate for another (although it does depend on the objective—see Hand (1996) for a detailed discussion). For example, were marital status represented by integers (e.g., 1 for single, 2 for married, 3 for widowed, and so forth) it would generally not be meaningful or appropriate to calculate the arithmetic mean of a sample of such scores using this scale. Similarly, simple linear regression (predicting one quantitative variable as a function of others) will usually be appropriate to apply to quantitative data, but applying it to categorical data may not be wise; other techniques, that have similar objectives (to the extent that the objectives can be similar when the data types differ), might be more appropriate with categorical scales.

Measurement scales, however defined, lie at the bottom of any data taxonomy. Moving up the taxonomy, we find that data can occur in various relationships and structures. Data may arise sequentially in time series, and the data mining exercise might address entire time series or particular segments of those time series. Data might also describe spatial relationships, so that individual records take on their full significance only when considered in the context of others.

Consider a data set on medical patients. It might include multiple measurements on the same variable (e.g., blood pressure), each measurement taken at different times on different days. Some patients might have extensive image data (e.g., X-rays or magnetic resonance images), others not. One might also have data in the form of *text*, recording a specialist's comments and diagnosis for each patient. In addition, there might be a hierarchy of relationships between patients in terms of doctors, hospitals, and geographic locations. The more complex the data structures, the more complex the data mining models, algorithms, and tools we need to apply.

For all of the reasons discussed above, the $n \times p$ data matrix is often an oversimplification or idealization of what occurs in practice. Many data sets will not fit into this simple format. While much information can in principle be "flattened" into the $n \times p$ matrix (by suitable definition of the p variables), this will often lose much of the structure embedded in the data. Nonetheless, when discussing the underlying principles of data analysis, it is often very convenient to assume that the observed data exist in an $n \times p$ data matrix; and we will do so unless otherwise indicated, keeping in mind that for data mining applications n and p may both be very large. It is perhaps worth remarking that the observed data matrix can also be referred to by a variety names including *data set, training data, sample, database,* (often the different terms arise from different disciplines).

Example 1.3 Text documents are important sources of information, and data mining methods can help in retrieving useful text from large collections of documents (such as the Web). Each document can be viewed as a sequence of words and punctuation. Typical tasks for mining text databases are classifying documents into predefined categories, clustering similar documents together, and finding documents that match the specifications of a query. A typical collection of documents is "Reuters-21578, Distribution 1.0," located at `http://www.research.att.com/~lewis`. Each document in this collection is a short newswire article.

A collection of text documents can also be viewed as a matrix, in which the rows represent documents and the columns represent words. The entry (d, w), corresponding to document d and word w, can be the number of times w occurs in d, or simply 1 if w occurs in d and 0 otherwise.

With this approach we lose the ordering of the words in the document (and, thus, much of the semantic content), but still retain a reasonably good representation of the document's contents. For a document collection, the number of rows is the number of documents, and the number of columns is the number of distinct words. Thus, large multilingual document collections may have millions of rows and hundreds of thousands of columns. Note that such a data matrix will be very sparse; that is, most of the entries will be zeroes. We discuss text data in more detail in chapter 14.

Example 1.4 Another common type of data is *transaction data,* such as a list of purchases in a store, where each purchase (or transaction) is described by the date, the customer ID, and a list of items and their prices. A similar example is a Web transaction log, in which a sequence of triples (user id, web page, time), denote the user accessing a particular page at a particular time. Designers and owners of Web sites often have great interest in understanding the patterns of how people navigate through their site.

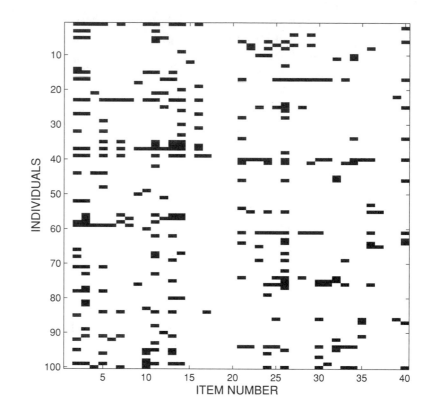

Figure 1.1 A portion of a retail transaction data set displayed as a binary image, with 100 individual customers (rows) and 40 categories of items (columns).

As with text documents, we can transform a set of transaction data into matrix form. Imagine a very large, sparse matrix in which each row corresponds to a particular individual and each column corresponds to a particular Web page or item. The entries in this matrix could be binary (e.g., indicating whether a user had ever visited a certain Web page) or integer-valued (e.g., indicating how many times a user had visited the page).

Figure 1.1 shows a visual representation of a small portion of a large retail transaction data set displayed in matrix form. Rows correspond to individual customers and columns represent categories of items. Each black entry indicates that the customer corresponding to that row purchased the item corresponding to that column. We can see some obvious patterns even in this simple display. For example, there is considerable variability in terms of which categories of items customers purchased and how many items they purchased. In addition, while some categories were purchased by quite a few customers (e.g., columns 3, 5, 11, 26) some were not purchased at all (e.g., columns 18 and 19). We can also see pairs of categories which that were frequently purchased together (e.g., columns 2 and 3).

Note, however, that with this "flat representation" we may lose a significant portion of information including sequential and temporal information (e.g., in what order and at what times items were purchased), any information about structured relationships between individual items (such as product category hierarchies, links between Web pages, and so forth). Nonetheless, it is often useful to think of such data in a standard $n \times p$ matrix. For example, this allows us to define distances between users by comparing their p-dimensional Web-page usage vectors, which in turn allows us to cluster users based on Web page patterns. We will look at clustering in much more detail in chapter 9.

1.3 Types of Structure: Models and Patterns

The different kinds of representations sought during a data mining exercise may be characterized in various ways. One such characterization is the distinction between a global *model* and a local *pattern*.

A *model structure*, as defined here, is a *global* summary of a data set; it makes statements about any point in the full measurement space. Geometrically, if we consider the rows of the data matrix as corresponding to p-dimensional vectors (i.e., points in p-dimensional space), the model can make a statement about any point in this space (and hence, any object). For example, it can assign a point to a cluster or predict the value of some other variable. Even when some of the measurements are missing (i.e., some of the components of the p-dimensional vector are unknown), a model can typically make some statement about the object represented by the (incomplete) vector.

A simple model might take the form $Y = aX + c$, where Y and X are variables and a and c are parameters of the model (constants determined during the course of the data mining exercise). Here we would say that the functional form of the model is *linear*, since Y is a linear function of X. The conventional statistical use of the term is slightly different. In statistics, a model is linear if it is a linear function of the *parameters*. We will try to be clear in the text about which form of linearity we are assuming, but when we discuss the *structure* of a model (as we are doing here) it makes sense to consider linearity as a function of the variables of interest rather than the parameters. Thus, for example, the model structure $Y = aX^2 + bX + c$, is considered a linear model in classic statistical terminology, but the functional form of the model relating Y and X is *nonlinear* (it is a second-degree polynomial).

In contrast to the global nature of models, *pattern structures* make statements only about restricted regions of the space spanned by the variables. An example is a simple probabilistic statement of the form if $X > x_1$ then $\text{prob}(Y > y_1) = p1$. This structure consists of *constraints* on the values of the variables X and Y, related in the form of a probabilistic rule. Alternatively we could describe the relationship as the conditional probability $p(Y > y_1 | X > x_1) = p1$, which is semantically equivalent. Or we might notice that certain classes of transaction records do not show the peaks and troughs shown by the vast majority, and look more closely to see why. (This sort of exercise led one bank to discover that it had several open accounts that belonged to people who had died.)

Thus, in contrast to (global) models, a (local) pattern describes a structure relating to a relatively small part of the data or the space in which data could occur. Perhaps only some of the records behave in a certain way, and the pattern characterizes which they are. For example, a search through a database of mail order purchases may reveal that people who buy certain combinations of items are also likely to buy others. Or perhaps we identify a handful of "outlying" records that are very different from the majority (which might be thought of as a central cloud in p-dimensional space). This last example illustrates that global models and local patterns may sometimes be regarded as opposite sides of the same coin. In order to detect unusual behavior we need a description of usual behavior. There is a parallel here to the role of *diagnostics* in statistical analysis; local pattern-detection methods have applications in anomaly detection, such as fault detection in industrial processes, fraud detection in banking and other commercial operations.

Note that the model and pattern structures described above have parameters associated with them; a, b, c for the model and x_1, y_1 and $p1$ for the pattern. In general, once we have established the structural form we are interested in finding, the next step is to estimate its parameters from the available data. Procedures for doing this are discussed in detail in chapters 4, 7, and 8. Once the parameters have been assigned values, we refer to a particular model, such as $y = 3.2x + 2.8$, as a "fitted model," or just "model" for short (and similarly for patterns). This distinction between model (or pattern) structures and the actual (fitted) model (or pattern) is quite important. The structures represent the general functional forms of the models (or patterns), with unspecified parameter values. A fitted model or pattern has specific values for its parameters.

The distinction between models and patterns is useful in many situations. However, as with most divisions of nature into classes that are convenient for human comprehension, it is not hard and fast: sometimes it is not clear whether a particular structure should be regarded as a model or a pattern. In such cases, it is best not to be too concerned about which is appropriate; the distinction is intended to aid our discussion, not to be a proscriptive constraint.

1.4 Data Mining Tasks

It is convenient to categorize data mining into types of *tasks*, corresponding to different objectives for the person who is analyzing the data. The categorization below is not unique, and further division into finer tasks is possible, but it captures the types of data mining activities and previews the major types of data mining algorithms we will describe later in the text.

1. **Exploratory Data Analysis (EDA)** (chapter 3): As the name suggests, the goal here is simply to explore the data without any clear ideas of what we are looking for. Typically, EDA techniques are *interactive* and *visual*, and there are many effective graphical display methods for relatively small, low-dimensional data sets. As the dimensionality (number of variables, p) increases, it becomes much more difficult to visualize the cloud of points in p-space. For p higher than 3 or 4, projection techniques (such as principal components analysis) that produce informative low-dimensional projections of the data can be very useful. Large numbers of cases can be difficult to visualize effectively, however, and notions of scale and detail come into play: "lower resolution" data samples can be displayed or summarized at the cost of possibly missing important details. Some examples of EDA applications are:

   - Like a pie chart, a *coxcomb* plot divides up a circle, but whereas in a pie chart the angles of the wedges differ, in a coxcomb plot the radii of the wedges differ. Florence Nightingale used such plots to display the mortality rates at military hospitals in and near London (Nightingale, 1858).

   - In 1856 John Bennett Lawes laid out a series of plots of land at Rothamsted Experimental Station in the UK, and these plots have remained untreated by fertilizers or other artificial means ever since. They provide a rich source of data on how different plant species develop and compete, when left uninfluenced. Principal components analysis has been used to display the data describing the relative yields of different species (Digby and Kempton, 1987, p. 59).

- More recently, Becker, Eick, and Wilks (1995) described a set of intricate spatial displays for visualization of time-varying long-distance telephone network patterns (over 12,000 links).

2. **Descriptive Modeling** (chapter 9): The goal of a descriptive model is describe all of the data (or the process generating the data). Examples of such descriptions include models for the overall probability distribution of the data (*density estimation*), partitioning of the p-dimensional space into groups (*cluster analysis and segmentation*), and models describing the relationship between variables (*dependency modeling*). In segmentation analysis, for example, the aim is to group together similar records, as in market segmentation of commercial databases. Here the goal is to split the records into homogeneous groups so that similar people (if the records refer to people) are put into the same group. This enables advertisers and marketers to efficiently direct their promotions to those most likely to respond. The number of groups here is chosen by the researcher; there is no "right" number. This contrasts with cluster analysis, in which the aim is to discover "natural" groups in data—in scientific databases, for example. Descriptive modelling has been used in a variety of ways.

- Segmentation has been extensively and successfully used in marketing to divide customers into homogeneous groups based on purchasing patterns and demographic data such as age, income, and so forth (Wedel and Kamakura, 1998).

- Cluster analysis has been used widely in psychiatric research to construct taxonomies of psychiatric illness. For example, Everitt, Gourlay and Kendell (1971) applied such methods to samples of psychiatric inpatients; they reported (among other findings) that "all four analyses produced a cluster composed mainly of patients with psychotic depression."

- Clustering techniques have been used to analyze the long-term climate variability in the upper atmosphere of the Earth's Northern hemisphere. This variability is dominated by three recurring spatial pressure patterns (clusters) identified from data recorded daily since 1948 (see Cheng and Wallace [1993] and Smyth, Ide, and Ghil [1999] for further discussion).

3. **Predictive Modeling: Classification and Regression** (chapters 10 and 11): The aim here is to build a model that will permit the value of one variable to be predicted from the known values of other variables. In classification, the variable being predicted is categorical, while in regression the variable is quantitative. The term "prediction" is used here in a general sense, and no notion of a time continuum is implied. So, for example, while we might want to predict the value of the stock market at some future date, or which horse will win a race, we might also want to determine the diagnosis of a patient, or the degree of brittleness of a weld. A large number of methods have been developed in statistics and machine learning to tackle predictive modeling problems, and work in this area has led to significant theoretical advances and improved understanding of deep issues of inference. The key distinction between prediction and description is that prediction has as its objective a unique variable (the market's value, the disease class, the brittleness, etc.), while in descriptive problems no single variable is central to the model. Examples of predictive models include the following:

- The SKICAT system of Fayyad, Djorgovski, and Weir (1996) used a tree-structured representation to learn a classification tree that can perform as well as human experts in classifying stars and galaxies from a 40-dimensional feature vector. The system is in routine use for automatically cataloging millions of stars and galaxies from digital images of the sky.

- Researchers at AT&T developed a system that tracks the characteristics of all 350 million unique telephone numbers in the United States (Cortes and Pregibon, 1998). Regression techniques are used to build models that estimate the probability that a telephone number is located at a business or a residence.

4. **Discovering Patterns and Rules** (chapter 13): The three types of tasks listed above are concerned with model building. Other data mining applications are concerned with pattern detection. One example is spotting fraudulent behavior by detecting regions of the space defining the different types of transactions where the data points significantly different from the rest. Another use is in astronomy, where detection of unusual stars

or galaxies may lead to the discovery of previously unknown phenomena. Yet another is the task of finding combinations of items that occur frequently in transaction databases (e.g., grocery products that are often purchased together). This problem has been the focus of much attention in data mining and has been addressed using algorithmic techniques based on *association rules*.

A significant challenge here, one that statisticians have traditionally dealt with in the context of outlier detection, is deciding what constitutes truly unusual behavior in the context of normal variability. In high dimensions, this can be particularly difficult. Background domain knowledge and human interpretation can be invaluable. Examples of data mining systems of pattern and rule discovery include the following:

- Professional basketball games in the United States are routinely annotated to provide a detailed log of every game, including time-stamped records of who took a particular type of shot, who scored, who passed to whom, and so on. The *Advanced Scout* system of Bhandari et al. (1997) searches for rule-like patterns from these logs to uncover interesting pieces of information which might otherwise go unnoticed by professional coaches (e.g., "When Player X is on the floor, Player Y's shot accuracy decreases from 75% to 30%.") As of 1997 the system was in use by several professional U.S. basketball teams.

- Fraudulent use of cellular telephones is estimated to cost the telephone industry several hundred million dollars per year in the United States. Fawcett and Provost (1997) described the application of rule-learning algorithms to discover characteristics of fraudulent behavior from a large database of customer transactions. The resulting system was reported to be more accurate than existing hand-crafted methods of fraud detection.

5. **Retrieval by Content** (chapter 14): Here the user has a pattern of interest and wishes to find similar patterns in the data set. This task is most commonly used for text and image data sets. For text, the pattern may be a set of keywords, and the user may wish to find relevant documents within a large set of possibly relevant documents (e.g., Web pages). For images, the user may have a sample image, a sketch of an image, or a description of an image, and wish to find similar images from a large set of images. In both cases the definition of similarity is critical, but so are the details of the search strategy.

There are numerous large-scale applications of retrieval systems, including:

- Retrieval methods are used to locate documents on the Web, as in the Google system (`www.google.com`) of Brin and Page (1998), which uses a mathematical algorithm called PageRank to estimate the relative importance of individual Web pages based on link patterns.

- QBIC ("Query by Image Content"), a system developed by researchers at IBM, allows a user to interactively search a large database of images by posing queries in terms of content descriptors such as color, texture, and relative position information (Flickner et al., 1995).

Although each of the above five tasks are clearly differentiated from each other, they share many common components. For example, shared by many tasks is the notion of *similarity* or *distance* between any two data vectors. Also shared is the notion of score functions (used to assess how well a model or pattern fits the data), although the particular functions tend to be quite different across different categories of tasks. It is also obvious that different model and pattern structures are needed for different tasks, just as different structures may be needed for different kinds of data.

1.5   Components of Data Mining Algorithms

In the preceding sections we have listed the basic categories of tasks that may be undertaken in data mining. We now turn to the question of how one actually accomplishes these tasks. We will take the view that data mining algorithms that address these tasks have four basic components:

1. **Model or Pattern Structure**: determining the underlying structure or functional forms that we seek from the data (chapter 6).

2. **Score Function**: judging the quality of a fitted model (chapter 7).

3. **Optimization and Search Method**: optimizing the score function and searching over different model and pattern structures (chapter 8).

4. **Data Management Strategy**: handling data access efficiently during the search/optimization (chapter 12).

We have already discussed the distinction between model and pattern structures. In the remainder of this section we briefly discuss the other three components of a data mining algorithm.

1.5.1   Score Functions

Score functions quantify how well a model or parameter structure fits a given data set. In an ideal world the choice of score function would precisely reflect the utility (i.e., the true expected benefit) of a particular predictive model. In practice, however, it is often difficult to specify precisely the true utility of a model's predictions. Hence, simple, "generic" score functions, such as least squares and classification accuracy are commonly used.

Without some form of score function, we cannot tell whether one model is better than another or, indeed, how to choose a good set of values for the parameters of the model. Several *score functions* are widely used for this purpose; these include likelihood, sum of squared errors, and misclassification rate (the latter is used in supervised classification problems). For example, the well-known squared error score function is defined as

$$\sum_{i=1}^{n} \left(y(i) - \hat{y}(i) \right)^2 \tag{1.1}$$

where we are predicting n "target" values $y(i)$, $1 \leq i \leq n$, and our predictions for each are denoted as $\hat{y}(i)$ (typically this is a function of some other "input" variable values for prediction and the parameters of the model).

Any views we may have on the theoretical appropriateness of different criteria must be moderated by the practicality of applying them. The model that we consider to be most likely to have given rise to the data may be the ideal one, but if estimating its parameters will take months of computer time it is of little value. Likewise, a score function that is very susceptible to slight changes in the data may not be very useful (its utility will depend on the objectives of the study). For example if altering the values of a few extreme cases leads to a dramatic change in the estimates of some model parameters caution is warranted; a data set is usually chosen from a number of possible data sets, and it may be that in other data sets the value of these extreme cases would have differed. Problems like this can be avoided by using *robust* methods that are less sensitive to these extreme points.

1.5.2   Optimization and Search Methods

The score function is a measure of how well aspects of the data match proposed models or patterns. Usually, these models or patterns are described in terms of a structure, sometimes with unknown parameter values. The goal of optimization and search is to determine the structure and the parameter values that achieve a minimum (or maximum, depending on the context) value of the score function. The task of finding the "best" values of parameters in models is typically cast as an optimization (or estimation) problem. The task of finding interesting patterns (such as rules) from a large family of potential patterns is typically cast as a combinatorial search problem, and is often accomplished using heuristic search techniques. In linear regression, a prediction rule is usually found by minimizing a least squares score function (the sum of squared errors between the prediction from a model and the observed values of the predicted variable). Such a score function is amenable to mathematical manipulation, and the model that minimizes it can be found algebraically. In contrast, a score function such as misclassification rate in supervised classification is difficult to minimize analytically. For example, since it is intrinsically discontinuous the powerful tool of differential calculus cannot be brought to bear.

Of course, while we can produce score functions to produce a good match between a model or pattern and the data, in many cases this is not really the objective. As noted above, we are often aiming to generalize to new data which might arise (new customers, new chemicals, etc.) and having too close a match to the data in the database may prevent one from predicting new cases accurately. We discuss this point later in the chapter.

1.5.3   Data Management Strategies

The final component in any data mining algorithm is the data management strategy: the ways in which the data are stored, indexed, and accessed. Most well-known data analysis algorithms in statistics and machine learning have been developed under the assumption that all individual data points can be accessed quickly and efficiently in random-access memory (RAM). While main memory technology has improved rapidly, there have been equally rapid improvements in secondary (disk) and tertiary (tape) storage technologies, to the extent that many massive data sets still reside largely on disk or tape and will not fit in available RAM. Thus, there will probably be a price to pay for accessing massive data sets, since not all data points can be simultaneously close to the main processor.

Many data analysis algorithms have been developed without including any explicit specification of a data management strategy. While this has worked in the past on relatively small data sets, many algorithms (such as classification and regression tree algorithms) scale very poorly when the "traditional version" is applied directly to data that reside mainly in secondary storage.

The field of databases is concerned with the development of indexing methods, data structures, and query algorithms for efficient and reliable data retrieval. Many of these techniques have been developed to support relatively simple counting (aggregating) operations on large data sets for reporting purposes. However, in recent years, development has begun on techniques that support the "primitive" data access operations necessary to implement efficient versions of data mining algorithms (for example, tree-structured indexing systems used to retrieve the neighbors of a point in multiple dimensions).

1.6   The Interacting Roles of Statistics and Data Mining

Statistical techniques alone may not be sufficient to address some of the more challenging issues in data mining, especially those arising from massive data sets. Nonetheless, statistics plays a very important role in data mining: it is a necessary component in any data mining enterprise. In this section we discuss some of the interplay between traditional statistics and data mining.

With large data sets (and particularly with very large data sets) we may simply not know even straightforward facts about the data. Simple eyeballing of the data is not an option. This means that sophisticated search and examination methods may be required to illuminate features which would be readily apparent in small data sets. Moreover, as we commented above, often the object of data mining is to make some inferences beyond the available database. For example, in a database of astronomical objects, we may want to make a statement that "all objects like this one behave thus," perhaps with an attached qualifying probability. Likewise, we may determine that particular regions of a country exhibit certain patterns of telephone calls. Again, it is probably not the calls in the database about which we want to make a statement. Rather it will probably be the pattern of future calls which we want to be able to predict. The database provides the set of objects which will be used to construct the model or search for a pattern, but the ultimate objective will not generally be to describe those data. In most cases the objective is to describe the general process by which the data arose, and other data sets which could have arisen by the same process. All of this means that it is necessary to avoid models or patterns which match the available database too closely: given that the available data set is merely one set from the sets of data which could have arisen, one does not want to model its idiosyncrasies too closely. Put another way, it is necessary to avoid *overfitting* the given data set; instead one wants to find models or patterns which *generalize* well to potential future data. In selecting a score function for model or pattern selection we need to take account of this. We will discuss these issues in more detail in chapter 7 and chapters 9 through 11. While we have described them in a data mining context, they are fundamental to statistics; indeed, some would take them as the defining characteristic of statistics as a discipline.

Since statistical ideas and methods are so fundamental to data mining, it is legitimate to ask whether there are really any differences between the two enterprises. Is data mining merely exploratory statistics, albeit for potentially huge data sets, or is there more to data mining than exploratory data analysis? The answer is yes—there *is* more to data mining.

The most fundamental difference between classical statistical applications and data mining is the size of the data set. To a conventional statistician, a "large" data set may contain a few hundred or a thousand data points. To someone concerned with data mining, however, many millions or even billions of data points is not unexpected—gigabyte and even terabyte databases are by no means uncommon. Such large databases occur in all walks of life. For instance the American retailer Wal-Mart makes over 20 million transactions daily (Babcock, 1994), and constructed an 11 terabyte database of customer transactions in 1998 (Piatetsky-Shapiro, 1999). AT&T has 100 million customers and carries on the order of 300 million calls a day on its long distance network. Characteristics of each call are used to update a database of models for every telephone number in the United States (Cortes and Pregibon, 1998). Harrison (1993) reports that Mobil Oil aims to store over 100 terabytes of data on oil exploration. Fayyad, Djorgovski, and Weir (1996) describe the Digital Palomar Observatory Sky Survey as involving three terabytes of data. The ongoing Sloan Digital Sky Survey will create a raw observational data set of 40 terabytes, eventually to be reduced to a mere 400 gigabyte catalog containing 3×10^8 individual sky objects (Szalay et al., 1999). The NASA Earth Observing System is projected to generate multiple gigabytes of raw data per hour (Fayyad, Piatetsky-Shapiro, and Smyth, 1996). And the human genome project to complete sequencing of the entire human genome will likely generate a data set of more than 3.3×10^9 nucleotides in the process (Salzberg, 1999). With data sets of this size come problems beyond those traditionally considered by statisticians.

Massive data sets can be tackled by sampling (if the aim is modeling, but not necessarily if the aim is pattern detection) or by adaptive methods, or by summarizing the records in terms of *sufficient statistics*. For example, in standard least squares regression problems, we can replace the large numbers of scores on each variable by their sums, sums of squared values, and sums of products, summed over the records—these are sufficient for regression coefficients to be calculated no matter how many records there are. It is also important to take account of the ways in which algorithms scale, in terms of computation time, as the number of records or variables increases. For example, exhaustive search through all subsets of variables to find the "best" subset (according to some score function), will be feasible only up to a point. With p variables there are $2^p - 1$ possible subsets of variables to consider. Efficient search methods, mentioned in the previous section, are crucial in pushing back the boundaries here.

Further difficulties arise when there are many variables. One that is important in some contexts is the *curse of dimensionality*; the exponential rate of growth of the number of unit cells in a space as the number of variables increases. Consider, for example, a single binary variable. To obtain reasonably accurate estimates of parameters within both of its cells we might wish to have 10 observations per cell; 20 in all. With two binary variables (and four cells) this becomes 40 observations. With 10 binary variables it becomes 10240 observations, and with 20 variables it becomes 10485760. The curse of dimensionality manifests itself in the difficulty of finding accurate estimates of probability densities in high dimensional spaces without astronomically large databases (so large, in fact, that the gigabytes available in data mining applications pale into insignificance). In high dimensional spaces, "nearest" points may be a long way away. These are not simply difficulties of manipulating the many variables involved, but more fundamental problems of what can actually be done. In such situations it becomes necessary to impose additional restrictions through one's prior choice of model (for example, by assuming linear models).

Various problems arise from the difficulties of accessing very large data sets. The statistician's conventional viewpoint of a "flat" data file, in which rows represent objects and columns represent variables, may bear no resemblance to the way the data are stored (as in the text and Web transaction data sets described earlier). In many cases the data are distributed, and stored on many machines. Obtaining a random sample from data that are split up in this way is not a trivial matter. How to define the sampling frame and how long it takes to access data become important issues.

Worse still, often the data set is constantly evolving—as with, for example, records of telephone calls or electricity usage. Distributed or evolving data can multiply the size of a data set many-fold as well as changing the nature of the problems requiring solution.

While the size of a data set may lead to difficulties, so also may other properties not often found in standard statistical applications. We have already remarked that data mining is typically a secondary process of data analysis; that is, the data were originally collected for some other purpose. In contrast, much statistical work is concerned with primary analysis: the data are collected with particular questions in mind, and then are analyzed to answer those questions. Indeed, statistics includes subdisciplines of experimental design and survey design—entire domains of expertise concerned with the best ways to collect data in order to answer specific questions. When data are used to address problems beyond those for which they were originally collected, they may not be ideally suited to these problems. Sometimes the data sets are entire populations (e.g., of chemicals in a particular class of chemicals) and therefore the standard statistical notion of inference has no relevance. Even when they are not entire populations, they are often *convenience* or *opportunity* samples, rather than random samples. (For instance, the records in question may have been collected because they were the most easily measured, or covered a particular period of time.)

In addition to problems arising from the way the data have been collected, we expect other distortions to occur in large data sets—including missing values, contamination, and corrupted data points. It is a rare data set that does not have such problems. Indeed, some elaborate modeling methods include, as part of the model, a component describing the mechanism by which missing data or other distortions arise. Alternatively, an estimation method such as the EM algorithm (described in chapter 8) or an imputation method that aims to generate artificial data with the same general distributional properties as the missing data might be used. Of course, all of these problems also arise in standard statistical applications (though perhaps to a lesser degree with small, deliberately collected data sets) but basic statistical texts tend to gloss over them.

In summary, while data mining does overlap considerably with the standard exploratory data analysis techniques of statistics, it also runs into new problems, many of which are consequences of size and the non traditional nature of the data sets involved.

1.7   Data Mining: Dredging, Snooping, and Fishing

An introductory chapter on data mining would not be complete without reference to the historical use of terms such as "data mining," "dredging," "snooping," and "fishing." In the 1960s, as computers were increasingly applied to data analysis problems, it was noted that if you searched long enough, you could always find some model to fit a data set arbitrarily well. There are two factors contributing to this situation: the complexity of the model and the size of the set of possible models.

Clearly, if the class of models we adopt is very flexible (relative to the size of the available data set), then we will probably be able to fit the available data arbitrarily well. However, as we remarked above, the aim may be to generalize beyond the available data; a model that fits well may not be ideal for this purpose. Moreover, even if the aim is to fit the data (for example, when we wish to produce the most accurate summary of data describing a complete population) it is generally preferable to do this with a simple model. To take an extreme, a model of complexity equivalent to that of the raw data would certainly fit it perfectly, but would hardly be of interest or value.

Even with a relatively simple model structure, if we consider enough different models with this basic structure, we can eventually expect to find a good fit. For example, consider predicting a response variable, Y from a predictor variable X which is chosen from a very large set of possible variables, $X_1, \ldots, X_p$, none of which are related to Y. By virtue of random variation in the data generating process, although there are no underlying relationships between Y and any of the X variables, there will appear to be relationships in the data at hand. The search process will then find the X variable that appears to have the strongest relationship to Y. By this means, as a consequence of the large search space, an apparent pattern is found where none really exists. The situation is particularly bad when working with a small sample size n and a large number p of potential X variables. Familiar examples of this sort of problem include the spurious correlations which are popularized in the media, such as the "discovery" that over the past 30 years when the winner of the Super Bowl championship in American football is from a particular league, a leading stock market index historically goes up in the following months. Similar examples are plentiful in areas such as economics and the social sciences, fields in which data are often relatively sparse but models and theories to fit to the data are relatively plentiful. For instance, in economic time-series prediction, there may be a relatively short time-span of historical data available in conjunction with a large number of economic indicators (potential predictor variables). One particularly humorous example of this type of prediction was provided by Leinweber (personal communication) who achieved almost perfect prediction of annual values of the well-known Standard and Poor 500 financial index as a function of annual values from previous years for butter production, cheese production, and sheep populations in Bangladesh and the United States.

The danger of this sort of "discovery" is well known to statisticians, who have in the past labelled such extensive searches "data mining" or "data dredging"—causing these terms to acquire derogatory connotations. The problem is less serious when the data sets are large, though dangers remain even then, if the space of potential structures examined is large enough. These risks are more pronounced in pattern detection than model fitting, since patterns, by definition, involve relatively few cases (i.e., small sample sizes): if we examine a billion data points, in search of an unusual configuration of just 50 points, we have a good chance of detecting this configuration.

There are no easy technical solutions to this problem, though various strategies have been developed, including methods that split the data into subsamples so that models can be built and patterns can be detected using one part, and then their validity can be tested on another part. We say more about such methods in later chapters. The final answer, however, is to regard data mining not as a simple technical exercise, divorced from the meaning of the data. Any potential model or pattern should be presented to the data owner, who can then assess its interest, value, usefulness, and, perhaps above all, its potential reality in terms of what else is known about the data.

1.8 Summary

Thanks to advances in computers and data capture technology, huge data sets—containing gigabytes or even terabytes of data—have been and are being collected. These mountains of data contain potentially valuable information. The trick is to extract that valuable information from the surrounding mass of uninteresting numbers, so that the data owners can capitalize on it. Data mining is a new discipline that seeks to do just that: by sifting through these databases, summarizing them, and finding patterns.

Data mining should not be seen as a simple one-time exercise. Huge data collections may be analyzed and examined in an unlimited number of ways. As time progresses, so new kinds of structures and patterns may attract interest, and may be worth seeking in the data.

Data mining has, for good reason, recently attracted a lot of attention: it is a new technology, tackling new problems, with great potential for valuable commercial and scientific discoveries. However, we should not expect it to provide answers to all questions. Like all discovery processes, successful data mining has an element of serendipity. While data mining provides useful tools, that does not mean that it will inevitably lead to important, interesting, or valuable results. We must beware of over-exaggerating the likely outcomes. But the potential is there.

1.9   Further Reading

Brief, general introductions to data mining are given in Fayyad, Piatetsky-Shapiro, and Smyth (1996), Glymour et al. (1997), and a special issue of the *Communications of the ACM*, Vol. 39, No. 11. Overviews of certain aspects of predictive data mining are given by Adriaans and Zantige (1996) and Weiss and Indurkhya (1998). Witten and Franke (2000) provide a very readable, applications-oriented account of data mining from a machine learning (artificial intelligence) perspective and Han and Kamber (2000) is an accessible textbook written from a database perspective data mining. There are many texts on data mining aimed at business users, notably Berry and Linoff (1997, 2000) that contain extensive practical advice on potential business applications of data mining.

Leamer (1978) provides a general discussion of the dangers of data dredging, and Lovell (1983) provides a general review of the topic. From a statistical perspective. Hendry (1995, section 15.1) provides an econometrician's view of data mining. Hand et al. (2000) and Smyth (2000) present comparative discussions of data mining and statistics. Casti (1990, 192–193 and 439) provides a briefly discusses "common folklore" stock market predictors and coincidences.

2 *Measurement and Data*

2.1 Introduction

Our aim is to discover relationships that exist in the "real world," where this may be the physical world, the business world, the scientific world, or some other conceptual domain. However, in seeking such relationships, we do not go out and look at that domain firsthand. Rather, we study data describing it. So first we need to be clear about what we mean by *data*.

Data are collected by mapping entities in the domain of interest to symbolic representation by means of some measurement procedure, which associates the value of a variable with a given property of an entity. The relationships between objects are represented by numerical relationships between variables. These numerical representations, the data items, are stored in the data set; it is these items that are the subjects of our data mining activities.

Clearly the measurement process is crucial. It underlies all subsequent data analytic and data mining activities. We discuss this process in detail in section 2.2.

We remarked in chapter 1 that the notion of "distance" between two objects is fundamental. Section 2.3 outlines distance measures between two objects, based on the vectors of measurements taken on those objects. The raw results of measurements may or may not be suitable for direct data mining. Section 2.4 briefly comments on how the data might be transformed before analysis.

We have already noted that we do not want our data mining activities simply to discover relationships that are mere artifacts of the way the data were collected. Likewise, we do not want our findings to be properties of the way the data are defined: discovering that people with the same surname often live in the same household would not be a major breakthrough. In section 2.5 we briefly introduce notions of the *schema* of data—the a priori structure imposed on the data.

No data set is perfect, and this is particularly true of large data sets. Measurement error, missing data, sampling distortion, human mistakes, and a host of other factors corrupt the data. Since data mining is concerned with detecting unsuspected patterns in data, it is very important to be aware of these imperfections—we do not want to base our conclusions on patterns that merely reflect flaws in data collection or of the recording processes. Section 2.6 discusses quality issues in the context of measurements on cases or records and individual variables or fields. Section 2.7 discusses the quality of aggregate collections of such individuals (i.e., samples).

Section 2.8 presents concluding remarks, and section 2.9 gives pointers to more detailed reading.

2.2   Types of Measurement

Measurements may be categorized in many ways. Some of the distinctions arise from the nature of the properties the measurements represent, while others arise from the use to which the measurements are put.

To illustrate, we will begin by considering how we might measure the property WEIGHT. In this discussion we will denote a property by using uppercase letters, and the variable corresponding to it (the result of the mapping to numbers induced by the measurement operation) by lowercase letters. Thus a measurement of WEIGHT yields a value of weight. For concreteness, let us imagine we have a collection of rocks.

The first thing we observe is that we can rank the rocks according to the WEIGHT property. We could do this, for example, by placing a rock on each pan of a weighing scale and seeing which way the scale tipped. On this basis, we could assign a number to each rock so that larger numbers corresponded to heavier rocks. Note that here only the ordinal properties of these numbers are relevant. The fact that one rock was assigned the number 4 and another was assigned the number 2 would not imply that the first was in any sense twice as heavy as the second. We could equally have chosen some other number, provided it was greater than 2, to represent the WEIGHT of the first rock. In general, any monotonic (order preserving) transformation of the set of numbers we assigned would provide an equally legitimate assignment. We are only concerned with the order of the rocks in terms of their WEIGHT property.

We can take the rocks example further. Suppose we find that, when we place a large rock on one pan of the weighing scale and two small rocks on the other pan, the pans balance. In some sense the WEIGHT property of the two small rocks has combined to be equal to the WEIGHT property of the large rock. It turns out (this will come as no surprise!) that we can assign numbers to the rocks in such a way that not only does the order of the numbers correspond to the order observed from the weighing scales, but the sum of the numbers assigned to the two smaller rocks equals the number assigned to the larger rock. That is, the total weight of the two smaller rocks equals the weight of the larger rock. Note that even now the assignment of numbers is not unique. Suppose we had assigned the numbers 2 and 3 to the smaller rocks, and the number 5 to the larger rock. This assignment satisfies the ordinal and additive property requirements, but so too would the assignment of 4, 6, and 10 respectively. There is still some freedom in how we define the variable weight corresponding to the WEIGHT property.

The point of this example is that *our numerical representation reflects the empirical properties of the system we are studying.* Relationships between rocks in terms of their WEIGHT property correspond to relationships between values of the measured variable weight. This representation is useful because it allows us to make inferences about the physical system by studying the numerical system. Without juggling sacks of rocks, we can see which sack contains the largest rock, which sack has the heaviest rocks on average, and so on.

The rocks example involves two empirical relationships: the order of the rocks, in terms of how they tip the scales, and their *concatenation* property— the way two rocks together balance a third. Other empirical systems might involve less than or more than two relationships. The order relationship is very common; typically, if an empirical system has only one relationship, it is an order relationship. Examples of the order relationship are provided by the SEVERITY property in medicine and the PREFERENCE property in psychology.

Of course, not even an order relationship holds with some properties, for example, the properties HAIR COLOR, RELIGION, and RESIDENCE OF PROGRAMMER, do not have a natural order. Numbers can still be used to represent "values" of the properties, (blond = 1, black = 2, brown = 3, and so on), but the only empirical relationship being represented is that the colors are different (and so are represented by different numbers). It is perhaps even more obvious here that the particular set of numbers assigned is not unique. Any set in which different numbers correspond to different values of the property will do.

Given that the assignment of numbers is not unique, we must find some way to restrict this freedom—or else problems might arise if different researchers use different assignments. The solution is to adopt some convention. For the rocks example, we would adopt a basic "value" of the property WEIGHT, corresponding to a basic value of the variable **weight**, and defined measured values in terms of how many copies of the basic value are required to balance them. Examples of such basic values for the WEIGHT/**weight** system are the gram and pound.

Types of measurement may be categorized in terms of the empirical relationships they seek to preserve. However, an important alternative is to categorize them in terms of the transformations that lead to other equally legitimate numerical representations. Thus, a numerical severity scale, in which only order matters, may be represented equally well by any numbers that preserve the order—numbers derived through a monotonic or ordinal transformation of the original ones. For this reason, such scales are termed *ordinal scales*.

In the rocks example, the only legitimate transformations involved multiplying by a constant (for example, converting from pounds to grams). Any other transformation (squaring the numbers, adding a constant, etc.) would destroy the ability of the numbers to represent the order and concatenation property by addition. (Of course, other transformations may enable the empirical relationships to be represented by different mathematical operations. For example, if we transformed the values 2, 3, and 5 in the rocks example to e^2, e^3, and e^5, we could represent the empirical relationship by multiplication: $e^2 e^3 = e^5$. However, addition is the most basic operation and is a favored choice.) Since with this type of scale multiplying by a constant leaves the ratios of values unaffected, such scales are termed *ratio scales*.

In the other case we outlined above (the hair color example) any transformation was legitimate, provided it preserved the unique identity of the different numbers—it did not matter which of two numbers was larger, and addition properties were irrelevant. Effectively, here, the numbers were simply used as labels or names; such scales are termed *nominal scales*.

There are other scale types, corresponding to different families of legitimate (or admissible) transformations. One is the *interval scale*. Here the family of legitimate transformations permit changing the units of measurement by multiplying by a constant, plus adding an arbitrary constant. Thus, not only is the unit of measurement arbitrary, but so also is the origin. Classic examples of such scales are conventional measures of temperature (Fahrenheit,

Centigrade, etc.) and calendar time.

It is important to understand the basis for different kinds of measurement scale so we can be sure that any patterns discovered during mining operations are genuine. To illustrate the dangers, suppose that two groups of three patients record their pain on an ordinal scale that ranges from 1 (no pain) to 10 (severe pain); one group of patients yields scores of 1, 2, and 6, while the other yields 3, 4, and 5. The mean of the first three is $(1 + 2 + 6)/3 = 3$, while that of the second three is 4. The second group has the larger mean. However, since the scale is purely ordinal any order-preserving transformation will yield an equally legitimate numerical representation. For example, a transformation of the scale so that it ranged from 1 to 20, with (1, 2, 3, 4, 5, 6) transformed to (1, 2, 3, 4, 5, 12) would preserve the order relationships between the different levels of pain—if a patient A had worse pain than a patient B using the first scale, then patient A would also have worse pain than patient B using the second scale. Now, however, the first group of patients would have a mean score $(1 + 2 + 12)/3 = 5$, while the second group would still have a mean score 4. Thus, two equally legitimate numerical representations have led to opposite conclusions. The pattern observed using the first scale (one mean being larger than the other) was an artifact of the numerical representation adopted, and did not correspond to any true relationship among the objects (if it had, two equally legitimate representations could not have led to opposite conclusions). To avoid such problems we must be sure to only make statistical statements for which the truth value will be invariant under legitimate transformations of the measurement scales. In this example, we could make the statement that the median of the scores of the second group is larger than the median of the scores of the first group; this would remain true, whatever order-preserving transformation we applied.

Up to this point, we have focussed on measurements that provide mappings in which the relationships between numbers in the empirical system being studied correspond to relationships between numbers in a numerical system. Because the mapping serves to represent relationships in an empirical system, this type of measurement is called *representational*.

However, not all measurement procedures fit easily into this framework. In some situations, it is more natural to regard the measurement procedure as *defining* a property in question, as well as assigning a number to it. For example, the property QUALITY OF LIFE in medicine is often measured by identifying those components of human life that one regards as important, and then defining a way of combining the scores corresponding to the separate components (e.g., a weighted sum). EFFORT in software engineering is sometimes defined in a similar way, combining measures of the number of program instructions, a complexity rating, the number of internal and external documents and so forth. Measurement procedures that define a property as well as measure it are called *operational* or *nonrepresentational* procedures. The operational perspective on measurement was originally conceived in physics, around the start of the century, amid uneasiness about the reality of concepts such as atoms. The approach has gone on to have larger practical implications for the social and behavioral sciences. Since in this method the measurement procedure also defines the property, no question of legitimate transformations arises. Since there are no alternative numerical representations any statistical statements are permissible.

> **Example 2.1** One early attempt at measuring programming effort is given by Halstead (1977). In a given program if a is the number of unique operators, b is the number of unique operands, n is the number of total operator occurrences, and m is the total number of operand occurrences, then the programming effort is
>
> $$e = am(n + m)\log(a + b)/2b.$$
>
> This is a nonrepresentational measurement, since it defines programming effort, as well as providing a way to measure it.

One way of describing the distinction between representational and operational measurement is that the former is concerned with *understanding* what is going on in a system, while the latter is concerned with *predicting* what is going on. The difference between understanding (or describing) a system and predicting its behavior crops up elsewhere in this book. Of course, the two aims overlap, but the distinction is a useful one. We can construct effective and valuable predictive systems that make no reference to the mechanisms underlying the process. For instance most people successfully drive automobiles or operate video recorders, without any idea of their inner workings.

In principle, the mappings defined by the representational approach to measurement, or the numbers assigned by the operational approach, can take any values from the continuum. For example, a mapping could tell us that the length of the diagonal of a unit square is the square root of 2. However, in practice, recorded data are only approximations to such mathematical ideals. First, there is often unavoidable error in measurement (e.g., if you repeatedly measure someone's height to the nearest millimeter you will observe a distribution of values). Second, data are recorded to a finite number of decimal places. We might record the length of the diagonal of a unit square as 1.4, or 1.41, or 1.414, or 1.4142, and so on, but the measure will never be exact. Occasionally, this kind of approximation can have an impact on an analysis. The effect is most noticeable when the approximation is crude (when the data are recorded to only very few decimal places).

The above discussion provides a theoretical basis for measurement issues. However, it does not cover all descriptive measurement terms that have been introduced. Many other taxonomies for measurement scales have been described, sometimes based not on the abstract mathematical properties of the scales but rather on the sorts of data analytic techniques used to manipulate them. Examples of such alternatives include counts versus measurements; nominal, ordinal, and numerical scales; qualitative versus quantitative measurements; metrical versus categorical measurements; and grades, ranks, counted fractions, counts, amounts, and balances. In most cases it is clear what is intended by these terms. Ranks, for example, correspond to an operational assignment of integers to the particular entities in a given collection on the basis of the relative "size" of the property in question: the ranks are integers which preserve the order property.

In data mining applications (and in this text), the scale types that occur most frequently are categorical scales in which any one-to-one transformation is allowed (nominal scales), ordered categorical scales, and numerical (quantitative or real-valued) scales.

2.3 Distance Measures

Many data mining techniques (for example, nearest neighbor classification methods, cluster analysis, and multidimensional scaling methods) are based on similarity measures between objects. There are essentially two ways to obtain measures of similarity. First, they can be obtained directly from the objects. For example, a marketing survey may ask respondents to rate pairs of objects according to their similarity, or subjects in a food tasting experiment may be asked to state similarities between flavors of ice-cream. Alternatively, measures of similarity may be obtained indirectly from vectors of measurements or characteristics describing each object. In the second case it is necessary to define precisely what we mean by "similar," so that we can calculate formal similarity measures.

Instead of talking about how similar two objects are, we could talk about how dissimilar they are. Once we have a formal definition of either "similar" or "dissimilar," we can easily define the other by applying a suitable monotonically decreasing transformation. For example, if $s(i, j)$ denotes the similarity and $d(i, j)$ denotes the dissimilarity between objects i and j, possible transformations include $d(i, j) = 1 - s(i, j)$ and $d(i, j) = \sqrt{2(1 - s(i, j))}$. The term *proximity* is often used as a general term to denote either a measure of similarity or dissimilarity.

Two additional terms—*distance* and *metric*—are often used in this context. The term distance is often used informally to refer to a dissimilarity measure derived from the characteristics describing the objects—as in *Euclidean distance*, defined below. A *metric*, on the other hand, is a dissimilarity measure that satisfies three conditions:

1. $d(i, j) \geq 0$ for all i and j, and $d(i, j) = 0$ if and only if $i = j$;

2. $d(i, j) = d(j, i)$ for all i and j; and

3. $d(i, j) \leq d(i, k) + d(k, j)$ for all i, j, and k.

The third condition is called the *triangle inequality*.

Suppose we have n data objects with p real-valued measurements on each object. We denote the vector of observations for the ith object by $\mathbf{x}(i) = (x_1(i), x_2(i), \ldots, x_p(i)), 1 \leq i \leq n$, where the value of the kth variable for the ith object is $x_k(i)$. The *Euclidean distance* between the ith and jth objects is defined as

$$d_E(i, j) = \left(\sum_{k=1}^{p} (x_k(i) - x_k(j))^2 \right)^{\frac{1}{2}}. \tag{2.1}$$

This measure assumes some degree of *commensurability* between the different variables. Thus, it would be effective if each variable was a measure of length (with the number p of dimensions being 2 or 3, it would yield our standard physical measure of distance) or a measure of weight, with each variable measured using the same units. It makes less sense if the variables are noncommensurate. For example, if one variable were length and another were weight, there would be no obvious choice of units; by altering the choice of units we would change which variables were most important as far as the distance was concerned.

Since we often have to deal with data sets in which the variables are not commensurate, we must find some way to overcome the arbitrariness of the choice of units. A common strategy is to standardize the data by dividing each of the variables by its sample standard deviation, so that they are all regarded as equally important. (But note that this does not resolve the issue—treating the variables as equally important in this sense is still making an arbitrary assumption.) The standard deviation for the kth variable X_k can be estimated as

$$\hat{\sigma}_k = \left(\frac{1}{n} \sum_{i=1}^{n} (x_k(i) - \mu_k)^2 \right)^{\frac{1}{2}} \tag{2.2}$$

where μ_k is the mean for variable X_k, which (if unknown) can be estimated using the *sample mean* $\bar{x}_k = \frac{1}{n} \sum_{i=1}^{n} x_k(i)$. Thus, $x'_k = x_k / \hat{\sigma}_k$ removes the effect of scale as captured by $\hat{\sigma}_k$.

In addition, if we have some idea of the relative importance that should be accorded to each variable, then we can weight them (after standardization), to yield the weighted Euclidean distance measure

$$d_{WE}(i, j) = \left(\sum_{k=1}^{p} w_k \left(x_k(i) - x_k(j) \right)^2 \right)^{\frac{1}{2}}. \tag{2.3}$$

The Euclidean and weighted Euclidean distances are both additive, in the sense that the variables contribute independently to the measure of distance. This property may not always be appropriate. To take an extreme case, suppose that we are measuring the heights and diameters of a number of cups. Using commensurate units, we could define similarities between the cups in terms of these two measurements. Now suppose that we measured the height of each cup 100 times, and the diameter only once (so that for any given cup we have 101 variables, 100 of which have almost identical values). If we combined these measurements in a standard Euclidean distance calculation, the height would dominate the apparent similarity between the cups. However, 99 of the height measurements do not contribute anything to what we really want to measure; they are very highly correlated (indeed, perfectly, apart from measurement error) with the first height measurement. To eliminate such redundancy we need a data-driven method. One approach is to standardize the data, not just in the direction of each variable, as with weighted Euclidean distance, but also taking into account the *covariances* between the variables.

Example 2.2 Consider two variables X and Y, and assume we have n objects, with X taking the values $x(1), \ldots, x(n)$ and Y taking the values $y(1), \ldots, y(n)$.

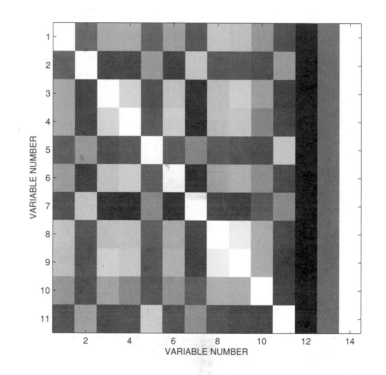

Figure 2.1   A sample correlation matrix plotted as a pixel image. White corresponds to +1 and black to -1. The three rightmost columns contain values of -1, 0, and +1 (respectively) to provide a reference for pixel intensities. The remaining 11 × 11 pixels represent the 11 × 11 correlation matrix. The data come from a well-known data set in the regression research literature, in which each data vector is a suburb of Boston and each variable represents a certain general characteristic of a suburb. The variable names are (1) per-capita crime rate, (2) proportion of area zoned for large residential lots, (3) proportion of non-retail business acres, (4) nitric oxide concentration, (5) average number of rooms perdwelling, (6) proportion of pre-1940 homes, (7) distance to retail centers index, (8) accessibility to highways index, (9) property tax rate, (10) pupil-to-teacher ratio, and (11) median value of owner-occupied homes.

Then the *sample covariance* between X and Y is defined as

$$Cov(X, Y) = \frac{1}{n} \sum_{i=1}^{n} (x(i) - \bar{x})(y(i) - \bar{y}), \qquad (2.4)$$

where $\bar{x}$ is the sample mean of the X values and $\bar{y}$ is the sample mean of the Y values.

The covariance is a measure of how X and Y vary together: it will have a large positive value if large values of X tend to be associated with large values of Y and small values of X with small values of Y. If large values of X tend to be associated with small values of Y, it will take a negative value.

More generally, with p variables we can construct a $p \times p$ matrix of covariances, in which the element (k, l) is the covariance between the kth and lth variables. From the definition of covariance above, we can see that such a matrix (a covariance matrix) must be symmetric.

The value of the covariance depends on the ranges of X and Y. This dependence can be removed by standardizing, dividing the values of X by their standard deviation and the values of Y by their standard deviation. The result is the *sample correlation coefficient* $\rho(X, Y)$ between X and Y:

$$\rho(X, Y) = \frac{\sum_{i=1}^{n} (x(i) - \bar{x})(y(i) - \bar{y})}{\left(\sum_{i=1}^{n} (x(i) - \bar{x})^2 \sum_{i=1}^{n} (y(i) - \bar{y})^2 \right)^{\frac{1}{2}}}. \qquad (2.5)$$

In the same way that a covariance matrix can be formed if there are p variables, a $p \times p$ correlation matrix can be formed in the same manner. Figure 2.1 shows a pixel image of a correlation matrices for an 11-dimensional data set on housing-related variables across different Boston suburbs. From the matrix we can clearly see structure in terms of how different variables are correlated. For example, variables 3 and 4 (relating to business acreage and presence of nitrous oxide) are each highly negatively correlated with variable 2 (the percent of large residential lots in the suburb) and positively correlated with each other. Variable 5 (average number of rooms) is positively correlated with variable 11 (median home value) (i.e., larger houses tend to be more valuable). Variables 8 and 9 (tax rates and highway accessibility) are also highly correlated.

Note that covariance and correlation capture *linear dependencies* between variables (they are more accurately termed *linear covariance* and *linear correlation*). Consider data points that are uniformly distributed around a circle in two dimensions (X and Y), centered at the origin. The variables are clearly *dependent*, but in a nonlinear manner and they will have zero linear correlation. Thus, independence implies a lack of correlation, but the reverse is not generally true. We will have more to say about independence in chapter 4.

Recall again our coffee cup example with 100 measurements of height and one measurement of width. We can discount the effect of the 100 correlated variables by incorporating the covariance matrix in our definition of distance. This leads to the Mahalanobis distance between two p-dimensional measurements $\mathbf{x}(i)$ and $\mathbf{x}(j)$, defined as:

$$d_{MH}(i,j) = \left((\mathbf{x}(i) - \mathbf{x}(j))^T \Sigma^{-1} (\mathbf{x}(i) - \mathbf{x}(j)) \right)^{\frac{1}{2}} \qquad (2.6)$$

where T represents the transpose, Σ is the $p \times p$ sample covariance matrix, and Σ^{-1} standardizes the data relative to Σ. Note that although we have been thinking about our p-dimensional measurement vectors $\mathbf{x}(i)$ as *rows* in our data matrix, the convention in matrix algebra is to treat these as $p \times 1$ *column vectors* (we can still visualize our data matrix as being an $n \times p$ matrix). Entry (k, l) of Σ is defined between variable X_k and X_l, as in equation 2.5. Thus, we have a $p \times 1$ vector transposed (to give a $1 \times p$ vector), multiplied by the $p \times p$ matrix Σ^{-1}, multiplied by a $p \times 1$ vector, yielding a scalar distance. Of course, other matrices could be used in place of Σ. Indeed, the statistical frameworks of canonical variates analysis and discriminant analysis use the average of the covariance matrices of different groups of cases.

The Euclidean metric can also be generalized in other ways. For example, one obvious generalization is to the Minkowski or L_λ metric:

$$\left(\sum_{k=1}^{p} (x_k(i) - x_k(j))^\lambda \right)^{\frac{1}{\lambda}}, \qquad (2.7)$$

where $\lambda \geq 1$. Using this, the Euclidean distance is the special case of $\lambda = 2$. The L_1 metric (also called the *Manhattan* or *city-block metric*) can be defined as

$$\sum_{k=1}^{p} \mid x_k(i) - x_k(j)) \mid . \qquad (2.8)$$

The case $\lambda \to \infty$ yields the L_∞ metric

$$\max_k |x_k(i) - x_k(j)| .$$

There is a huge number of other metrics for quantitative measurements, so the problem is not so much defining one but rather deciding which is most appropriate for a particular situation.

For multivariate *binary data* we can count the number of variables on which two objects take the same or take different values. Consider table 2.1, in

	$j = 1$	$j = 0$
$i = 1$	$n_{1,1}$	$n_{1,0}$
$i = 0$	$n_{0,1}$	$n_{0,0}$

Table 2.1   A cross-classification of two binary variables.

which all p variables defined for objects i and j take values in $\{0, 1\}$; the entry $n_{1,1}$ in the box for $i = 1$ and $j = 1$ denotes that there are $n_{1,1}$ variables such that i and j both have value 1.

With binary data, rather than measuring the dissimilarities between objects, we often measure the similarities. Perhaps the most obvious measure of similarity is the simple matching coefficient, defined as

$$\frac{n_{1,1} + n_{0,0}}{n_{1,1} + n_{1,0} + n_{0,1} + n_{0,0}}, \tag{2.9}$$

the proportion of the variables on which the objects have the same value, where $n_{1,1} + n_{1,0} + n_{0,1} + n_{0,0} = p$, the total number of variables. Sometimes, however, it is inappropriate to include the (0,0) cell (or the (1,1) cell, depending on the meaning of 0 and 1). For example, if the variables are scores of the presence (1) or absence (0) of certain properties, we may not care about all the irrelevant properties had by neither object. (For instance, in vector representations of text documents it may be not be relevant that two documents *do not* contain thousands of specific terms). This consideration leads to a modification of the matching coefficient, the *Jaccard coefficient*, defined as

$$\frac{n_{1,1}}{n_{1,1} + n_{1,0} + n_{0,1}}. \tag{2.10}$$

The *Dice coefficient* extends this argument. If (0,0) matches are irrelevant, then (0,1) and (1,0) mismatches should lie between (1,1) matches and (0,0) matches in terms of relevance. For this reason the number of (0,1) and (1,0) mismatches should be multiplied by a half. This yields $2n_{1,1}/(2n_{1,1}+n_{1,0}+n_{0,1})$. As with quantitative data, there are many different measures for multivariate binary data—again the problem is not so much defining such measures but choosing one that possesses properties that are desirable for the problem at hand.

For categorical data in which the variables have more than two categories, we can score 1 for variables on which the two objects agree and 0 otherwise, expressing the sum of these as a fraction of the possible total p. If we know about the categories, we might be able to define a matrix giving values for the different kinds of disagreement.

Additive distance measures can be readily adapted to deal with mixed data types (e.g., some binary variables, some categorical, and some quantitative) since we can add the contributions from each variable. Of course, the question of relative standardization still arises.

2.4   Transforming Data

Sometimes raw data are not in the most convenient form and it can be advantageous to modify them prior to analysis. Note that there is a duality between the form of the model and the nature of the data. For example, if we speculate that a variable Y is a function of the square of a variable X, then we either could try to find a suitable function of X^2, or we could square X first, to $U = X^2$, and fit a function to U. The equivalence of the two approaches is obvious in this simple example, but sometimes one or other can be much more straightforward.

> **Example 2.3** Clearly variable V_1 in figure 2.2 is nonlinearly related to variable V_2. However, if we work with the reciprocal of V_2, that is, $V_3 = 1/V_2$, we obtain the linear relationship shown in figure 2.3.

Sometimes, especially if we are concerned with formal statistical inferences in which the shape of a distribution is important (as when running statistical tests, or calculating confidence intervals), we might want to transform the data so that they approximate the requisite distribution more closely. For example, it is common to take logarithms of positively skewed data (such as bank account sizes or incomes) to make the distribution more symmetric (so that it more closely approximates a normal distribution, on which many inferential procedures are based).

> **Example 2.4** In figure 2.4 not only are the two variables nonlinearly related, but the variance of V_2 increases as V_1 increases. Sometimes inferences are based on an assumption that the variance remains constant (for example, in the basic model for regression analysis). In the case of these (artificial) data, a square root transformation of V_2 yields the transformed data shown in figure 2.5.

Since our fundamental aim in data mining is exploration, we must be prepared to contemplate and search for the unsuspected. Certain transformations of the data may lead to the discovery of structures that were not at all

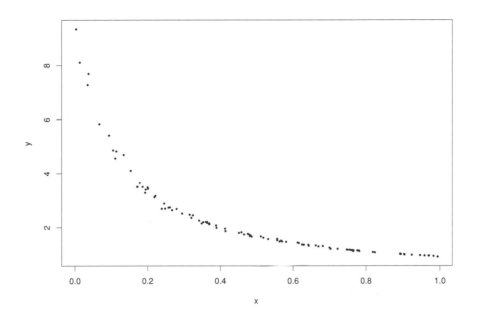

Figure 2.2   A simple nonlinear relationship between variable V_1 and V_2. (In these and subsequent figures V_1 and V_2 are on the X and Y axes respectively).

obvious on the original scale. On the other hand, it is possible to go too far in this direction: we must be wary of creating structures that are simply artifacts of a peculiar transformation of the data (see the example of the ordinal pain scale in section 2.2). Presumably, when this happens in a data mining context, the domain expert responsible for evaluating an apparent discovery will soon reject the structure.

Note also that in transforming data we may sacrifice the way it represents the underlying objects. As described in section 2.2 the standard mapping of rocks to weights maps a physical concatenation operation to addition. If we nonlinearly transform the numbers representing the weights, using logarithms or taking square roots for example, the physical concatenation operation is no longer preserved. Caution—and common sense—must be exercised.

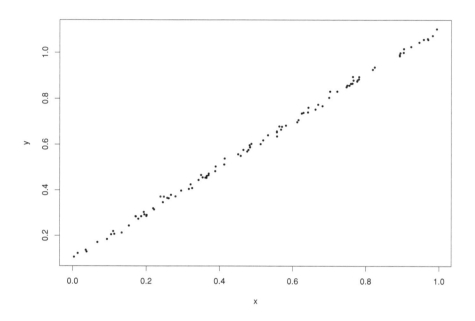

Figure 2.3   The data of figure 2.2 after the simple transformation of V_2 to $1/V_2$.

Common data transformations include taking square roots, reciprocals, logarithms, and raising variables to positive integral powers. For data expressed as proportions, the *logit transformation*, $f(p) = \frac{p}{1-p}$, is often used.

Some classes of techniques assume that the variables are categorical—that only a few (ordered) responses are possible. At an extreme, some techniques assume that responses are binary, with only two possible outcome categories. Of course continuous variables (those that can, at least in principle, take any value within a given interval) can be split at various thresholds to reduce them to categories. This sacrifices information, with the information loss increasing as the number of categories is reduced, but in practice this loss can be quite small.

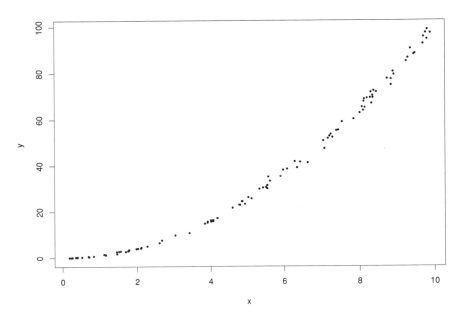

Figure 2.4 Another simple nonlinear relationship. Here the variance of V_2 increases as V_1 increases.

2.5 The Form of Data

We mentioned in chapter 1 that data sets come in different forms; these forms are known as *schemas*. The simplest form of data (and the only form we have discussed in any detail) is a set of vector measurements on objects $o(1), \ldots, o(n)$. For each object we have measurements of p variables $X_1, \ldots, X_p$. Thus, the data can be viewed as a matrix with n rows and p columns. We refer to this standard form of data as a *data matrix*, or simply *standard data*. We can also refer to the data set as a *table*.

Often there are several types of objects we wish to analyze. For example, in a payroll database, we might have data both about employees, with variables name, department-name, age, and salary, and about departments with variables department-name, budget and manager. These data matrices are con-

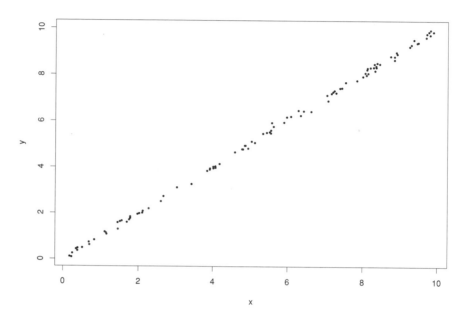

Figure 2.5   The data of figure 2.4 after a simple square root transformation of V_2. Now the variance of V_2 is relatively constant as V_1 increases.

nected to each other by the occurrence of the same (categorical) values in the department-name fields and in the fields name and manager. Data sets consisting of several such matrices or tables are called *multirelational data*.

In many cases multirelational data can be mapped to a single data matrix or table. For example, we could join the two data tables using the values of the variable department-name. This would give us a data matrix with the variables name, department-name, age, salary, budget (of the department), and manager (of the department). The possibility of such a transformation seems to suggest that there is no need to consider multirelational structures at all since in principle we could represent the data in one large table or matrix. However, this way of joining the data sets is not the only possibility: we could also create a table with as many rows as there are departments (this would be useful if we were interested in getting information about the departments, e.g., determining whether there was a dependence between the budget of a department and the age of the manager). Generally no single table best captures all the information in a multirelational data set. More important, from the point of view of efficiency in storage and data access, "flattening" multirelational data to form a single large table may involve the needless replication of numerous values.

Some data sets do not fit well into the matrix or table form. A typical example is a time series, in which consecutive values correspond to measurements taken at consecutive times, (e.g., measurements of signal strength in a waveform, or of responses of a patient at a series of times after receiving medical treatment). We can represent a time series using two variables, one for time and one for the measurement value at that time. This is actually the most natural representation to use for storing the time series in a database. However, representing the data as a two-variable matrix does not take into account the ordered aspect of the data. In analyzing such data, it is important to recognize that a natural order does exist. It is common, for example, to find that neighboring observations are more closely related (more highly correlated) than distant observations. Failure to account for this factor could lead to a poor model.

A *string* is a sequence of symbols from some finite alphabet. A sequence of values from a categorical variable is a string, and so is standard English text, in which the values are alphanumeric characters, spaces, and punctuation marks. Protein and DNA/RNA sequences are other examples. Here the letters are individual proteins (note that a string representation of a protein sequence is a 2-dimensional view of a 3-dimensional structure). A string is another data type that is ordered and for which the standard matrix form is not necessarily suitable.

A related ordered data type is the *event-sequence*. Given a finite alphabet of categorical event types, an event-sequence is a sequence of pairs of the form {*event, occurrence time*}. This is quite similar to a string, but here each item in the sequence is tagged with an occurrence time. An example of an event-sequence is a telecommunication alarm log, which includes a time of occurrence for each alarm. More complicated event-sequences include transaction data (such as records of retail or financial transactions), in which each transaction is time-stamped and the events themselves can be relatively complex (e.g., listing all purchases along with prices, department names, and so forth). Furthermore, there is no reason to restrict the concept of event sequences to categorical data; for example we could extend it to real-valued events occurring asynchronously, such as data from animal behavioral experiments or bursts of energy from objects in deep space.

Of course, order may be imposed simply for logistic convenience: placing patient records in alphabetical order by name assists retrieval, but the fact that Jones precedes Smith is unlikely to have any impact on most data mining activities. Still, care must always be exercised in data mining. For example, records of members of the same family (with the same last name) would probably occur near one another in a data set, and they may have related properties. (We may find that a contagious disease tends to infect groups of people whose names are close together in the data set.)

Ordered data are spread along a unidimensional continuum (per individual variable), but other data often lie in higher dimensions. *Spatial, geographic*, or *image* data are located in two and three dimensional spaces. It is important to recognize that some of the variables are part of the defining data schema in these examples: that is, some of the variables merely specify the coordinates of observations in the spaces. The discovery that geographical data lies in a two-dimensional continuum would not be very profound.

A *hierarchical* structure is a more complex data schema. For example, a data set of children might be grouped into classes, which are grouped into years, which are grouped into schools, which are grouped into counties, and so on. This structure is obvious in a multirelational representation of the data, but can be harder to see in a single table. Ignoring this structure in data analysis can be very misleading. Research on statistical models for such multi-level data has been particularly active in recent years. A special case of hierarchical structures arises when responses to certain items on a questionnaire are contingent on answers to other questions: for instance the relevance of the question "Have you had a hysterectomy?" depends on the answer to the question "Are you male or female?"

To summarize, in any data mining application it is crucial to be aware of the schema of the data. Without such awareness, it is easy to miss important patterns in the data or, perhaps worse, to rediscover patterns that are part of the fundamental design of the data. In addition, we must be particularly careful about data schemas when sampling, as we will discuss in more detail in chapter 4.

2.6   Data Quality for Individual Measurements

The effectiveness of a data mining exercise depends critically on the quality of the data. In computing this idea is expressed in the familiar acronym

GIGO—*Garbage In, Garbage Out*. Since data mining involves secondary analysis of large data sets, the dangers are multiplied. It is quite possible that the most interesting patterns we discover during a data mining exercise will have resulted from measurement inaccuracies, distorted samples or some other unsuspected difference between the reality of the data and our perception of it.

It is convenient to characterize data quality in two ways: the quality of the individual records and fields, and the overall quality of the collection of data. We deal with each of these in turn.

No measurement procedure is without the risk of error. The sources of error are infinite, ranging from human carelessness, and instrumentation failure, to inadequate definition of what it is that we are measuring. Measuring instruments can lead to errors in two ways: they can be inaccurate or they can be imprecise. This distinction is important, since different strategies are required for dealing with the different kinds of errors.

A *precise* measurement procedure is one that has small variability (often measured by its variance). Using a precise process, repeated measurements on the same object under the same conditions will yield very similar values. Sometimes the word precision is taken to connote a large number of digits in a given recording. We do not adopt this interpretation, since such "precision" can all too easily be spurious, as anyone familiar with modern data analysis packages (which sometimes give results of calculations to eight or more decimal places) will know.

An *accurate* measurement procedure, in contrast, not only possesses small variability, but also yields results close to what we think of as the true value. A measurement procedure may yield precise but inaccurate measurements. For example repeated measurements of someone's height may be precise, but if these were made while the subject was wearing shoes, the result would be inaccurate. In statistical terms, the difference between the mean of repeated measurements and the true value is the *bias* of a measurement procedure. Accurate procedures have small bias as well as small variance.

Note that the concept of a "true value" is integral to the concept of accuracy. But this concept is rather more slippery than it might at first appear. Take a person's height, for example. Not only does it vary slightly from moment to moment—as the person breathes and as his or her heart beats—but it also varies over the course of a day (gravity pulls us down). Astronauts returning from extended tours in space, are significantly taller than when they set off (though they soon revert to their former height). Mosteller (1968) remarked that "Today some scientists believe that true values do not

exist separately from the measuring process to be used, and in much of social science this view can be amply supported. The issue is not limited to
social science; in physics, complications arise from the different methods of
measuring microscopic and macroscopic quantities such as lengths. On the
other hand, because it suggests ways of improving measurement methods,
the concept of true value is useful; since some methods come much nearer
to being ideal than others, the better ones can provide substitutes for true
values."

Other terms are also used to express these concepts. The *reliability* of a measurement procedure is the same as its precision. The former term is typically
used in the social sciences whereas the latter is used in the physical sciences.
This use of two different names for the same concept is not as unreason-
able as it might seem, since the process of determining reliability is quite
different from that of determining precision. In measuring the precision of
an instrument, we can use that instrument repeatedly: assuming that during the course of the repeated applications the circumstances will not change
much. Furthermore, we assume that the measurement process itself will not
influence the system being measured. (Of course, there is a grey area here:
as Mosteller noted, very small or delicate phenomena may indeed be per-
turbed by the measurement procedure.) In the social and behavioral sciences,
however, such perturbation is almost inevitable: for instance a test asking a
subject to memorize a list of words could not usefully be applied twice in
quick succession. Effective retesting requires more subtle techniques, such
as alternative-form testing (in which two alternative forms of the measuring
instrument are used), split-halves testing (in which the items on a single test
are split into two groups), and methods that assess internal consistency (giving the expected correlation of one test with another version that contains
the same number of items).

Earlier we described two factors contributing to the inaccuracy of a measurement. One was basic precision—the extent to which repeated measurements of the same object gave similar results. The other was the extent
to which the distribution of measurements was centered on the true value.
While precision corresponds to reliability, the other component corresponds
to *validity*. Validity is the extent to which a measurement procedure measures what it is supposed to measure. In many areas—including software
engineering and economics—careful thought is required to construct metrics
that tap the underlying concepts we want to measure. If a measurement procedure has poor validity, any conclusions we draw from it about the target
phenomena will be at best dubious and at worst positively misleading. This

is especially true in feedback situations, where action is taken on the basis of measurements. If the measurements are not tapping the phenomenon of interest, such actions could lead the system to depart even further from its target state.

2.7   Data Quality for Collections of Data

In addition to the quality of individual observations, we need to consider the quality of collections of observations. Much of statistics and data mining is concerned with inference from a sample to a population, that is, how, on the basis of examining just a fraction of the objects in a collection, one can infer things about the entire population. Statisticians use the term *parameter* to refer to descriptive summaries of populations or distributions of objects (more generally, of course, a parameter is a value that indexes a family of mathematical functions). Values computed from a sample of objects are called *statistics,* and appropriately chosen statistics can be used as estimates of parameters. Thus, for example, we can use the average of a sample as an estimate of the mean (parameter) of an entire population or distribution.

Such estimates are useful only if they are accurate. As we have just noted, inaccuracies can occur in two ways. Estimates from different samples might vary greatly, so that they are unreliable: using a different sample might have led to a very different estimate. Or the estimates might be biased, tending to be too large or too small. In general, the precision of an estimate (the extent to which it would vary from sample to sample) increases with increasing sample size; as resources permit, we can reduce this uncertainty to an acceptable value. Bias, on the other hand, is not so easily diminished.

Some estimates are intrinsically biased, but do not cause a problem because the bias decreases with increasing sample size. Of more significance in data mining are biases arising from an inappropriate sample. If we wanted to calculate the average weight of people living in New York, it would obviously be inadvisable to restrict our sample to women. If we did this, we would probably underestimate the average. Clearly, in this case, the population from which our sample is drawn (women in New York) is not the population to which we wish to generalize (everyone in New York). Our sampling frame, the list of people from which we will draw our sample, does not match the population about which we want to make an inference. This is a simple example—we were able to clearly identify the population from which the sample was drawn (women in New York). Difficulties arise when it is less obvious what the effect of the incorrect sampling frame will be. Suppose, for example, that we drew our sample from people working in offices. Would this lead to biased estimates? Maybe the sexes are disproportionately represented in offices. Maybe office workers have a tendency to be heavier than average because of their sedentary occupation. There are many reasons why such a sample might not be representative of the population we aim to study. The concept of representativeness is key to the ability to make valid inferences, as is the concept of a random sample. We discuss the need for random samples, as well as strategies for drawing such samples, in chapter 4.

Because we often have no control over the way the data are collected, quality issues are particularly important in data. Our data set may be a distorted sample of the population we wish to describe. If we know the nature of this distortion then we might be able to allow for it in our inferences, but in general this is not the case and inferences must be made with care. The terms *opportunity sample* and *convenience sample* are sometimes used to describe samples that are not properly drawn from the population of interest. The sample of office workers above would be a convenience sample—it is much more convenient to sample from them than to sample from the whole population of New York. Distortions of a sample can occur for many reasons, but the risk is especially grave when humans are involved. The effects can be subtle and unexpected: for instance, in large samples, the distribution of stated ages tends to cluster around integers ending with 0 or 5—just the sort of pattern that data mining would detect as potentially interesting. Interesting it may be, but will probably be of no value in our analysis.

A different kind of distortion occurs when customers are selected through a chain of selection steps. With bank loans, for example, an initial population of potential customers is contacted (some reply and some do not), those who reply are assessed for creditworthiness (some receive high scores and some do not), those with high scores are offered a loan (some accept and some do not), those who take out a loan are followed up (some are good customers, paying the installments on time, and others are not), and so on. A sample drawn at any particular stage would give a distorted perspective on the population at an earlier stage.

In this example of candidates for bank loans, the selection criteria at each step are clearly and explicitly stated but, as noted above, this is not always the case. For example, in clinical trials samples of patients are selected from across the country, having been exposed to different diagnostic practices and perhaps different previous treatments in different primary care facilities.

Here the notion of taking a "random sample from a well-defined population" makes no sense. This problem is compounded by the imposition of inclusion/exclusion criteria: perhaps the patients must be male, aged between 18 and 50, with a primary diagnosis of the disease in question made no longer than two years ago, and so on. (It is hardly surprising in this context, that the sizes of effects recorded in clinical trials are typically larger than those found when the treatments are applied more widely. On the other hand it is reassuring that the *directions* of the effects do normally generalize in this way.)

In addition to sample distortion arising from a mismatch between the sample population and the population of interest other kinds of distortion arise. The aim of many data mining exercises is to make some prediction of what will happen in the future. In such cases it is important to remember that populations are not static. For instance the nature of a customers shopping at a certain store will change over time, perhaps because of changes in the social culture of the surrounding neighborhood, or in response to a marketing initiative, or for many other reasons. Much work on predictive methods has failed to take account of such *population drift*. Typically, the future performance of such methods is assessed using data collected at the same time as the data used to build the model—implicitly assuming that the distribution of objects used to construct the model is the same as that of future objects. Ideally, a more sophisticated model is required that can allow for evolution over time. In principle, population drift can be modeled, but in practice this may not be easy.

An awareness of the risks of using distorted samples is vital to valid data mining, but not all data sets are samples from the population of interest. Often the data set comprises the entire population, but is so large that we wish to work with a sample from it. We can formulate valid descriptions of the population represented in such a data set, to any degree of accuracy, provided the sample is properly chosen. Of course, technical difficulties may arise, as we discuss in more detail in chapter 4, when working with data sets that have complex structures and that might be dispersed over many different databases. In chapter 4, we explain how to draw samples from a data set in such a way that we can make accurate inferences about the overall population of values in the data set, but we restrict our discussion to the cases in which the actual drawing of a sample is straightforward, once we know which cases should be included.

Distortion of samples can be viewed as a special case of incomplete data, one in which entire records are missing from what would otherwise be a representative sample. Data can also be missing in other ways. In particular, individual fields may be missing from records. In some ways this is not as serious as the situation described above. (At least here, one can see that the data are missing!) Still, significant problems may arise from incomplete data. The fundamental question is "Why are the data missing?" Was there information in the missing data that is not present in the data that have been recorded? If so, inferences based on the observed data are likely to be biased. In any incomplete data problem, it is crucial to be clear about the objectives of the analysis. In particular, if the aim is to make an inference only about the cases that have complete records, inferences based only on the complete cases is entirely valid.

Outliers or anomalous observations represent another, quite different aspect of data quality. In many situations the objective of the data mining exercise is to detect anomalies: in fraud detection and fault detection those records that differ from the majority are precisely the ones that are of interest. In such cases we would use a pattern detection process (see chapters 6 and 13). On the other hand, if the aim is model building—constructing a global model to aid understanding of, or prediction from, the data—outliers may simply obscure the main points of the model. In this case we might want to identify and remove them before building our model.

When observing only one variable, we can detect outliers simply by plotting the data—as a histogram, for example. Points that are far from the others will lie out in the tails. However, the situation becomes more interesting—and challenging—when multiple variables are involved. In this case, it is possible that each variable for a particular record has perfectly normal values, but the overall pattern of scores is abnormal. Consider the distribution of points shown in figure 2.6. Clearly there is an unusual point here, one that would immediately arouse suspicion if such a distribution were observed in practice. But the point stands out only because we produced the two dimensional plot. A one dimensional examination of the data would indicate nothing unusual at all about the point in question.

Furthermore, there may be highly unusual cases whose abnormality becomes apparent only when large numbers of variables are examined simultaneously. In such cases, a computer is essential to detection.

Every large data set includes suspect data. Rather than promoting relief, a large data set that appears untarnished by incompleteness, distortion, measurement error, or other problems should invite suspicion. Only when we recognize and understand the inadequacies of the data can we take steps to alleviate their impact. Only then can we be sure that the discovered struc-

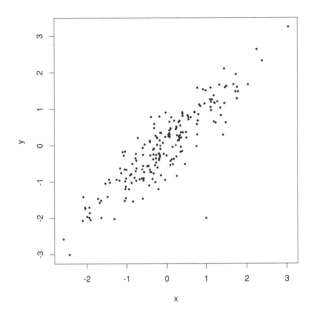

Figure 2.6 A plot of 200 points from highly positively correlated bivariate data (from a bivariate normal distribution), with a single easily identifiable outlier.

tures and patterns reflect what is really going on in the world. Since data miners rarely have control over the data collection processes, an awareness of the dangers that can arise from poor data is crucial. Hunter (1980) stated the risks succinctly:

> Data of a poor quality are a pollutant of clear thinking and rational decisionmaking. Biased data, and the relationships derived from such data, can have serious consequences in the writing of laws and regulations.

And, we might add, they can have serious consequences in developing scientific theories, in unearthing commercially valuable information, in improving quality of life, and so on.

2.8   Conclusion

In this chapter we have restricted our discussion to numeric data. However, other kinds of data also arise. For example, text data is an important class of non-numeric data, which we discuss further in chapter 14. Sometimes the definition of an individual data item (and hence whether it is numeric or non-numeric) depends on the objectives of our analysis: in economic contexts, in which hundreds of thousands of time series are stored in databases, the data items might be entire time series, rather than the individual numbers within those series.

Even with non-numeric data, numeric data analysis plays a fundamental role. Often non-numeric data items, or the relationships between them, are reduced to numeric descriptions, which are subject to standard methods of analysis. For example, in text processing we might measure the number of times a particular word occurs in each document, or the probability that certain pairs of words appear in documents.

2.9   Further Reading

The magnum opus on representational measurement theory is the three volume work of Krantz et al. (1971), Suppes et al. (1989), and Luce et al. (1990). Roberts (1979) also outlines this approach. Dawes and Smith (1985) and Michell (1986, 1990) describe alternative approaches, including the operational approach. Hand (1996) explores the relationship between measurement theory and statistics. Some authors place their discussions of software metrics in a formal measurement theoretical context—see, for example, Fenton (1991). Anderberg (1973) includes a good discussion of similarity and dissimilarity measures.

Issues of reliability and validity are often discussed in treatments of measurement issues in the social, behavioral, and medical sciences—see, for example, Dunn (1989) and Streiner and Norman (1995). Carmines and Zeller (1979) also discuss such issues. A key work on incomplete data and different types of missing data mechanisms is Little and Rubin (1987). The bank loan example of distorted samples is taken from Hand, McConway, and Stanghellini (1997). Goldstein (1995) is a key work on multilevel modeling.

3 *Visualizing and Exploring Data*

3.1 Introduction

This chapter explores visual methods for finding structures in data. Visual methods have a special place in data exploration because of the power of the human eye/brain to detect structures—the product of aeons of evolution. Visual methods are used to display data in ways that capitalize upon the particular strengths of human pattern processing abilities. This approach lies at quite the opposite end of the spectrum from methods for formal model building and for testing to see whether observed data could have arisen from a hypothesized data generating structure. Visual methods are important in data mining because they are ideal for sifting through data to find unexpected relationships. On the other hand, they do have their limitations, particularly, as we illustrate below, with very large data sets.

Exploratory data analysis can be described as *data-driven hypothesis generation*. We examine the data, in search of structures that may indicate deeper relationships between cases or variables. This process stands in contrast to *hypothesis testing* (we use the phrase here in an informal and general sense; more formal methods are described in chapter 4) which begins with a proposed model or hypothesis and undertakes statistical manipulations to determine the likelihood that the data arose from such a model. The phrase *data based* in the above description indicates that it is the patterns in the data that give rise to the hypotheses—in contrast to situations in which hypotheses are generated from theoretical arguments about underlying mechanisms. This distinction has implications for the legitimacy of subsequent testing of the hypotheses. It is closely related to the issues of overfitting discussed in chapter 7 (and again in 10 and 11). A simple example will illustrate the problem.

If we take 10 random samples of size 20 from the same population, and measure the values of a single variable, the random samples will have different means (just by virtue of random variability). We could compare the means using formal tests. Suppose, however, we took only the two samples giving rise to the smallest and largest means, ignoring the others. A test of the difference between these means might well show significance. If we took 100 samples, instead of 10, then we would be even more likely to find a significant difference between the largest and the smallest means. By ignoring the fact that these are the largest and smallest in a set of 100, we are biasing the analysis toward detecting a difference—even though the samples were generated from the same population.

In general, when searching for patterns, we cannot test whether a discovered pattern is a real property of the underlying distribution (as opposed to a chance property of the sample) without taking into account the size of the search—the number of possible patterns we have examined. The informal nature of exploratory data analysis makes this very difficult—it is often impossible to say how many patterns have been examined. For this reason researchers often use a separate data set, obtained from the same source as the first, to conduct formal testing for the existence of any pattern. (Alternatively, they may use some kind of sophisticated method such as cross-validation and sample re-use, as described in chapter 7.)

This chapter examines informal graphical data exploration methods, which have been widely used in data analysis down through the ages. Early books on statistics contain many such methods. They were often more practical than lengthy, number crunching alternatives in the days before computers. However, something of a revolution has occurred in recent years, and now such methods are even more widely used. As with the bulk of the methods decribed in this book, the revolution has been driven by the computer: computers enable us to view data in many different ways, both quickly and easily, and have led to the development of extremely powerful data visualization tools.

We begin the discussion in section 3.2 with a description of simple summary statistics for data. Section 3.3 discusses visualization methods for exploring distributions of values of single variables. Such tools, at least for small data sets, have been around for centuries, but even here progress in computer technology has led to the development of novel approaches. Moreover, even when using univariate displays, we often want simultaneous univariate displays of many variables, so we need concise displays that readily convey the main features of distributions.

Section 3.4 moves on to methods for displaying the relationships between pairs of variables. Perhaps the most basic form is the scatterplot. Due to the sizes of the data sets often encountered in data mining applications, scatterplots are not always enlightening—the diagram may be swamped by the data. Of course, this qualification can also apply to other graphical displays.

Moving beyond variable pairs, section 3.5 describes some of the tools used to examine relationships between multiple variables. No method is perfect, of course: unless a very rare relationship holds in the data, the relationship between multiple variables cannot be completely displayed in two dimensions.

Principal components analysis is illustrated in section 3.6. This method can be regarded as a special (indeed, the most basic) form of multidimensional scaling analysis. These are methods that seek to represent the important structure of the data in a reduced number of dimensions. Section 3.7 discusses additional multidimensional scaling methods.

There are numerous books on data visualization (see section 3.8) and we could not hope to examine all of the possibilities thoroughly in a single chapter. There are also several software packages motivated by an awareness of the importance of data visualization that have very powerful and flexible graphics facilities.

3.2 Summarizing Data: Some Simple Examples

We mentioned in earlier chapters that the *mean* is a simple summary of the average of a collection of values. Suppose that $x(1), \ldots, x(n)$ comprise a set of n data values. The *sample mean* is defined as

$$\hat{\mu} = \sum_i x(i)/n. \tag{3.1}$$

(Note that we use μ to refer to the true mean of the population, and $\hat{\mu}$ to refer to a sample-based *estimate* of this mean). The sample mean has the property that it is the value that is "central" in the sense that it minimizes the sum of squared differences between it and the data values. Thus, if there are n data values, the mean is the value such that the sum of n copies of it equals the sum of the data values.

The mean is a measure of *location*. Another important measure of location is the *median*, which is the value that has an equal number of data points above and below it. (Easy if n is an odd number. When there is an even number it is usually defined as halfway between the two middle values.)

The most common value of the data is the *mode*. Sometimes distributions have more than one mode (for example, there may be 10 objects which take the value 3 on some variable, and another 10 which take the value 7, with all other values taken less often than 10 times) and are therefore called *multimodal*.

Other measures of location focus on different parts of the distribution of data values. The first *quartile* is the value that is greater than a quarter of the data points. The third quartile is greater than three quarters. (We leave it to you to discover why we have not mentioned the second quartile.) Likewise, *deciles* and *percentiles* are sometimes used.

Various measures of *dispersion* or *variability* are also common. These include the *standard deviation* and its square, the *variance*. The variance is defined as the average of the squared differences between the mean and the individual data values:

$$\hat{\sigma}^2 = \sum_i (x(i) - \mu)^2 / n. \tag{3.2}$$

Note that since the mean minimizes the sum of these squared differences, there is a close link between the mean and the variance. If μ is unknown, as is often the case in practice, we can replace μ above with $\hat{\mu}$, our data based estimate. When μ is replaced with $\hat{\mu}$, to get an unbiased estimate (as discussed in chapter 4), the variance is estimated as

$$\sum_i (x(i) - \hat{\mu})^2 / (n - 1). \tag{3.3}$$

The standard deviation is the square root of the variance:

$$\hat{\sigma} = \sqrt{\sum_i (x(i) - \mu)^2 / n}. \tag{3.4}$$

The *interquartile range*, common in some applications, is the difference between the third and first quartile. The *range* is the difference between the largest and smallest data point.

Skewness measures whether or not a distribution has a single long tail and is commonly defined as

$$\frac{\sum (x(i) - \hat{\mu})^3}{\left(\sum (x(i) - \hat{\mu})^2\right)^{3/2}}. \tag{3.5}$$

For example, the distribution of peoples' incomes typically shows the vast majority of people earning small to moderate amounts, and just a few people earning large sums, tailing off to the very few who earn astronomically large sums—the Bill Gateses of the world. A distribution is said to be *right-skewed* if the long tail extends in the direction of increasing values and *left-skewed* otherwise. Right-skewed distributions are more common. Symmetric distributions have zero skewness.

3.3   Tools for Displaying Single Variables

One of the most basic displays for univariate data is the histogram, showing the number of values of the variable that lie in consecutive intervals. With small data sets, histograms can be misleading: random fluctuations in the values or alternative choices for the ends of the intervals can give rise to very different diagrams. Apparent multimodality can arise, and then vanish for different choices of the intervals or for a different small sample. As the size of the data set increases, however, these effects diminish. With large data sets, even subtle features of the histogram can represent real aspects of the distribution.

Figure 3.1 shows a histogram of the number of weeks during 1996 in which owners of a particular credit card used that card to make supermarket purchases (the label on the vertical axis has been removed to conceal commercially sensitive details). There is a large mode to the left of the diagram: most people did not use their card in a supermarket, or used it very rarely. The number of people who used the card a given number of times decreases rapidly with increases in the number of times. However, the relatively large number of people represented in this diagram allows us to detect another, much smaller mode toward the right hand end of the diagram. Apparently there is a tendency for people to make regular weekly trips to a supermarket, though this is reduced from 52 annual transactions, probably by interruptions such as holidays.

Example 3.1

Figure 3.2 shows a histogram of diastolic blood pressure for 768 females of Pima Indian heritage. This is one variable out of eight that were collected for the purpose of building classification models for forecasting the onset of diabetes. The documentation for this data set (available online at the UCI Machine Learning data archive) states that there are no missing values in the data. However, a cursory glance at the histogram reveals that about 35 subjects have a blood pressure value of zero, which is clearly impossible if these subjects were alive when the measurements were taken (presumably they were). A

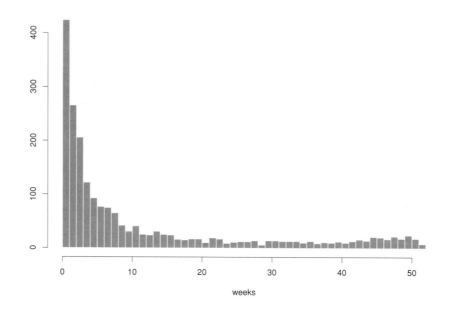

Figure 3.1   Histogram of the number of weeks of the year a particular brand of credit card was used.

plausible explanation is that the measurements for these 35 subjects are in fact missing, and that the value "0" was used in the collection of the data to code for "missing." This seems likely given that a number of the other variables (such as `triceps-fold-skin-thickness`) also have zero-values that are physically impossible.

The point here is that even though the histogram has limitations it is nonetheless often quite valuable to plot data before proceeding with more detailed modeling. In the case of the Pima Indians data, the histogram clearly reveals some suspicious values in the data that are incompatible with the physical interpretations of the variables being measured. Performing such simple checks on the data is always advisable before proceeding to use a data mining algorithm. Once we apply an algorithm it is unlikely that we will notice such data quality problems, and these problems may distort our analysis in an unpredictable manner.

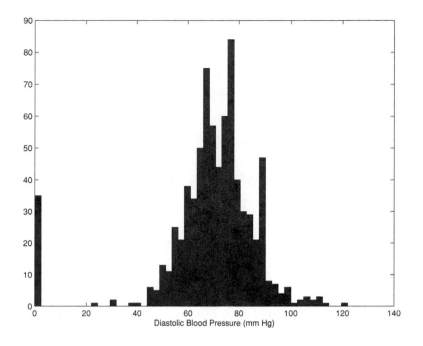

Figure 3.2   Histogram of diastolic blood pressure for 768 females of Pima Indian descent.

The disadvantages of histograms have also been tackled by smoothing estimates. One of the most widely used types is the kernel estimate.

Kernel estimates smooth out the contribution of each observed data point over a local neighborhood of that point (we will revisit the kernel method again in chapter 9). Consider a single variable X for which we have measured values $\{x(1), \ldots, x(n)\}$. The contribution of data point $x(i)$ to the estimate at some point x^* depends on how far apart $x(i)$ and x^* are. The extent of this contribution is dependent upon on the shape of the *kernel function* adopted and the width accorded to it. Denoting the kernel function by K and its width (or bandwidth) by h, the estimated density at any point x is

$$\hat{f}(x) = \frac{1}{n} \sum_{i=1}^{n} K\left(\frac{x - x(i)}{h}\right), \tag{3.6}$$

where $\int K(t)dt = 1$ to ensure that the estimate $f(x)$ itself integrates to 1 (i.e., is a proper density) and where the kernel function K is usually chosen to be a smooth unimodal function with a peak at 0. The quality of a kernel estimate depends less on the shape of K than on the value of h.

A common form for K is the Normal (Gaussian) curve, with h as its spread parameter (standard deviation), i.e.,

$$K(t, h) = Ce^{-\frac{1}{2}(\frac{t}{h})^2} \tag{3.7}$$

where C is a normalization constant and $t = x - x(i)$ is the distance of the query point x to data point $x(i)$. The bandwidth h is equivalent to σ, the standard deviation (or width) of the Gaussian kernel function.

There are formal methods for optimizing the fit of these estimates to the unknown distribution that generated the data, but here our interest is in graphical procedures. For our purposes the attraction of such estimates is that by varying h, we can search for peculiarities in the shape of the sample distribution. Small values of h lead to very spiky estimates (not much smoothing at all), while large values lead to oversmoothing. The limits at each extreme of h are the empirical distribution of the data points (i.e., "delta functions" on each data point $x(i)$) as $h \to 0$, and a uniform flat distribution as $h \to \infty$. These limits correspond to the extremes of total commitment to the data (with no mass anywhere except at the observed data points), versus completely ignoring the observed data.

Figure 3.3 shows a kernel estimate of the density of the weights of 856 elderly women who took part in a study of osteoporosis. The distribution is clearly right skewed and there is a hint of multimodality. Certainly the assumption often made in classical statistical work that distributions are normal does not apply in this case. (This is not to say that statistical techniques nominally based on that assumption might not still be valid. Often the arguments are asymptotic—based on normality arising from the central limit theorem. In this case, the assumption that the sample *mean* of 856 subjects would vary from sample to sample according to a normal distribution would be reasonable for practical purposes.)

Figure 3.4 shows what happens when a larger value is used for the smoothing parameter h. Which of the two kernel estimates is "better" is a difficult question to answer. Figure 3.4 is more conservative in that less credence is given to local (potentially random) fluctuations in the observed data values.

Although this section focuses on displaying single variables, it is often desirable to display different groups of scores on a single variable separately, so that the groups may be compared. (Of course, we can think of this as a two-variable situation, in which one of the variables is the grouping factor.)

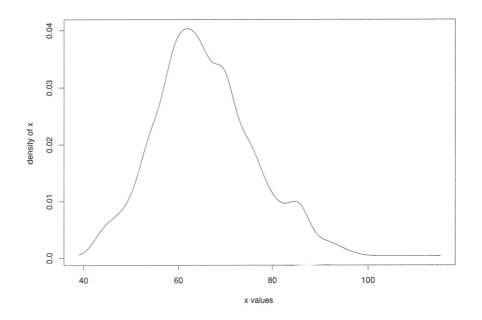

Figure 3.3 Kernel estimate of the weights (in kg) of 856 elderly women.

Histograms, kernel plots, and other unidimensional displays can be used separately for each group. However, this can become unwieldy if there are more than two or three groups. In such cases a useful alternative display is the box and whisker plot.

Although various versions of box and whisker plots exist, the essential ideas are the same. A *box* containing which the bulk of the data is defined—for example, the interval between the first and third quartiles. A line across this box indicates some measure of location—often the median of the data. Whiskers project from the ends of the box to indicate the spread of the tails of the empirical distribution.

We illustrate the boxplot using a subset of the diabetes data set from figure 3.2. Figure 3.5 shows four panels of box plots, each containing a separate boxplot for each of the two classes in the data, *healthy* (1) and *diabetic* (2).The diagrams show clearly how mean, dispersion, and skewness vary with val-

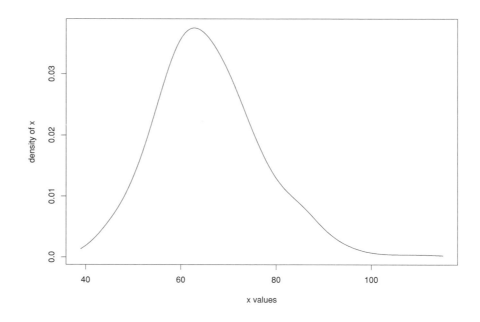

Figure 3.4   As figure 3.3, but with more smoothing.

ues of the grouping variable.

3.4   Tools for Displaying Relationships between Two Variables

The scatterplot is a standard tool for displaying two variables at a time. Figure 3.6 shows the relationship between two variables describing credit card repayment patterns (the details are confidential). It is clear from this diagram that the variables are strongly correlated—when one value has a high (low) value, the other variable is likely to have a high (low) value. However, a significant number of people depart from this pattern; showing high values on one of the variables and low values on the other. It might be worth investigating these individuals to find out why they are unusual.

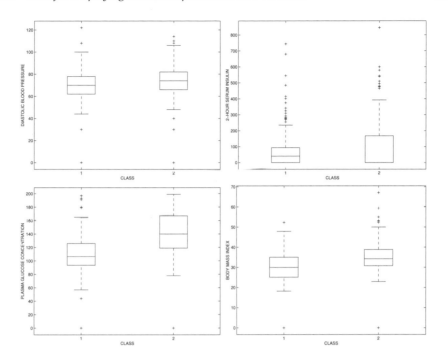

Figure 3.5 Boxplots on four different variables from the Pima Indians diabetes data set. For each variable, a separate boxplot is produced for the healthy subjects (labeled 1) and the diabetic subjects (labeled 2). The upper and lower boundaries of each box represent the upper and lower quartiles of the data respectively. The horizontal line within each box represents the median of the data. The whiskers extend 1.5 times the interquartile range from the end of each box. All data points outside the whiskers are plotted individually (although some overplotting is present, e.g., for values of 0).

Unfortunately, in data mining, scatterplots are not always so useful. If there are too many data points we will find ourselves looking at a purely black rectangle. Figure 3.7 illustrates this sort of problem. This shows a scatterplot of 96,000 points from a study of bank loans. Little obvious structure is discernible, although it might appear that later applicants in general are older. On the other hand, the apparent greater vertical dispersion toward the right end of the diagram could equally be caused by a greater number of samples on the right side. In fact, the linear regression fit to these data has a very small but highly significant *downward* slope.

Even when the situation is not quite so extreme, scatterplots with large

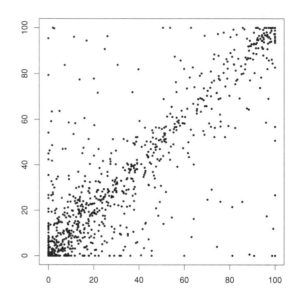

Figure 3.6   A standard scatterplot for two banking variables.

numbers of points can conceal more than they reveal. Figure 3.8 plots the number of weeks a particular credit card was used to buy petrol (gasoline) in a given year against the number of weeks the card was used in a supermarket (each data point represents an individual credit card). There is clearly some correlation, but the actual correlation 0.482 is much higher than it appears here. The diagram is deceptive because it conceals a great deal of overprinting in the bottom left corner—there are 10,000 customers represented here altogether. The bimodality shown in figure 3.1 can also be discerned in this figure, though not as easily as in figure 3.1.

Another curious phenomenon is also apparent in figure 3.8. The distribution of the number of weeks the card was used in a petrol station is skewed for low values of the supermarket variable, but fairly uniform for high values. What could explain this? (Of course, bearing in mind the point above, this apparent phenomenon needs to be checked for overprinting.)

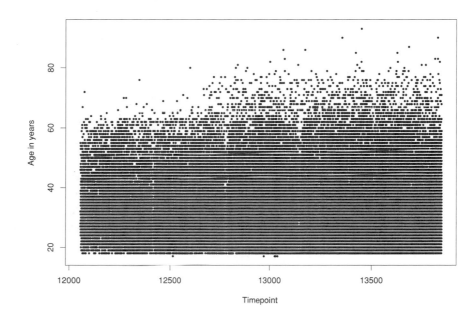

Figure 3.7   A scatterplot of 96,000 cases, with much overprinting. Each data point represents an individual applicant for a loan. The vertical axis shows the age of the applicant, and the horizontal axis indicates the day on which the application was made.

Contour plots can help overcome some of these problems. Note that creating a contour plot in two dimensions effectively requires us to construct a two-dimensional density estimate, using something like a two-dimensional generalization of the kernel method of equation 3.6, again raising the issue of bandwidth selection but now in a two-dimensional context. A contour plot of the 96,000 points shown in figure 3.7 is given in figure 3.9. Certain trends are clear from this display that cannot be discerned in figure 3.7. For instance the density of points increases toward the right side of the diagram; the apparent increasing dispersion of the vertical axis is due to there being a greater concentration of points in that area. The vertical skewness of the data is also very evident in this diagram. The unimodality of the data, and

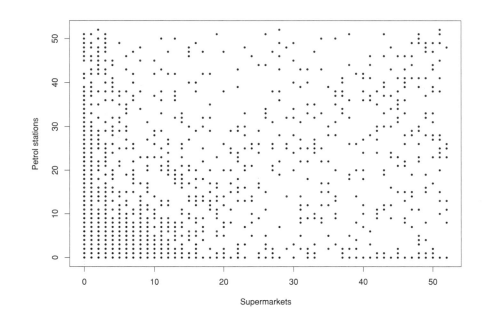

Figure 3.8   Overprinting conceals the actual strength of the correlation.

the position of the single mode cannot be seen at all in figure 3.7 but is quite clear in figure 3.9. Note that since the horizontal axis in these plots is time, an alternative way to display the data is to plot contours of constant conditional probability density, as time progresses.

Other standard forms of display can be used when one of the two variables is time, to show the value of the other variable as time progresses. This can be a very effective way of detecting trends and departures from expected or standard behaviour. Figure 3.10 shows a plot of the number of credit cards issued in the United Kingdom from 1985 to 1993 inclusive. A smooth curve has been fitted to the data to place emphasis on the main features of the relationship. It is clear that around 1990 something caused a break in a growth pattern that had been linear up to that point. In fact, what happened was that in 1990 and 1991 annual fees were introduced for credit cards, and many users reduced their holding to a single card.

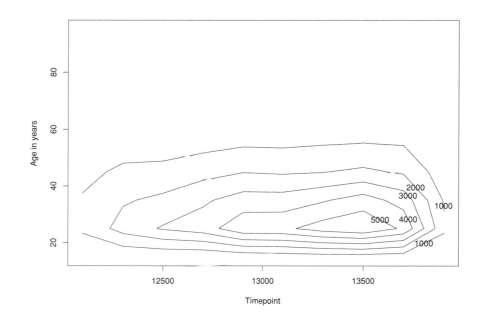

Figure 3.9 A contour plot of the data from figure 3.7.

Figure 3.11 shows a plot of the number of miles flown by UK airlines, during each month from January 1963 to December 1970. There are several patterns immediately apparent from this display that conform with what one might expect to observe, such as the gradually increasing trend and the periodicity (with large peaks in the summer and small peaks around the new year). The plot also reveals an interesting bifurcation of the summer peak, suggesting a tendency for travelers to favor the early and late summer over the middle period.

Figure 3.12 provides a third example of the power of plots in which time is one of the two variables. From February to June 1930, an experiment was carried out in Lanarkshire, Scotland to investigate whether adding milk to children's diets had an effect on "physique, general health and increasing mental alertness" (Leighton and McKinlay, 1930). In this study 20,000 children were allocated to one of three groups; 5000 of the children received

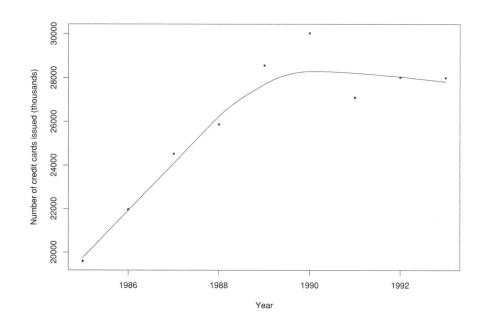

Figure 3.10   A plot of the number of credit cards in circulation in the United Kingdom, by year.

three-quarters of a pint of raw milk per day, 5000 received three-quarters of a pint of pasteurized milk per day, and 10,000 formed a control group receiving no dietary milk supplement. The children were weighed at the start of the experiment and again four months later. Interest lay in whether there was differential growth between the three groups.

Figure 3.12 plots the mean weight of the control group of girls against the mean age of the group they are in. The first point corresponds to the youngest age group (mean age 5.5 years) at the start of the experiment, and the second point corresponds to this group four months later. The third and fourth points correspond to the second age group, and so on. The points are connected by lines to make the shape easier to discern. Similar shapes are apparent for all groups in the experiment.

The plot immediately reveals an unexpected pattern that cannot be seen

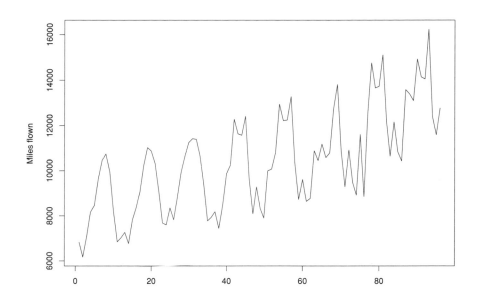

Figure 3.11 Patterns of change over time in the number of miles flown by UK airlines in the 1960s.

from a table of the data. We would expect a smooth plot, but there are clear steps evident here. It seems that each age group does not gain as much weight as expected. There are various possible explanations for this shape. Perhaps children grow less during the early months of the year than during the later ones. However, similar plots of heights show no such intermittent growth, so we need a more elaborate explanation in which height increases uniformly but weight increases in spurts. Another possible explanation arises from the fact that the children were weighed in their clothes. The report does say, "All of the children were weighed without their boots or shoes and wearing only their ordinary outdoor clothing. The boys were made to turn out the miscellaneous collection of articles that is normally found in their pockets, and overcoats, mufflers, etc., were also discarded. Where a child was found to be wearing three or four jerseys—a not uncom-

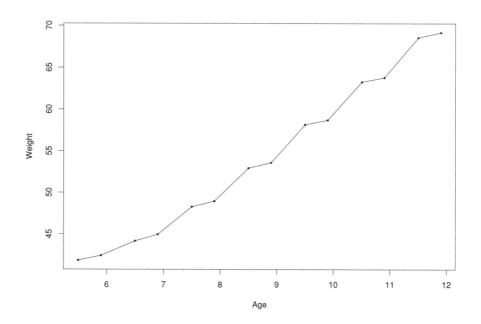

Figure 3.12 Weight changes over time in a group of 10,000 school children in the 1930s. The steplike pattern in the data highlights a problem with the measurement process.

mon experience—all in excess of one were removed." It still seems likely, however, that the summer garb was lighter than the winter garb. This example illustrates that the patterns discovered by data mining may not shed much light on the phenomena under investigation, but finding data anomalies and shortcomings may be just as valuable.

3.5   Tools for Displaying More Than Two Variables

Since sheets of paper and computer screens are flat, they are readily suited for displaying two-dimensional data, but are not effective for displaying higher dimensional data. We need some kind of projection, from the higher dimensional data to a two dimensional plane, with modifications to show (aspects of) the other dimensions. The most obvious approach along these lines is to examine the relationships between all pairs of variables, extending the basic scatterplot described in section 3.3 to a *scatterplot matrix*.

Figure 3.13 illustrates a scatterplot matrix for characteristics, performance measures, and relative performance measures of 209 computer CPUs dating from over 10 years ago. The variables are cycle time, minimum memory (kb), maximum memory (kb), cache size (kb), minimum channels, maximum channels, relative performance, and estimated relative performance (relative to an IBM 370/158-3). While some pairs of variables appear to be unrelated, others are strongly related. *Brushing* allows us to highlight points in a scatterplot matrix in such a way that the points corresponding to the same objects in each scatterplot are highlighted. This is particularly useful in interactive exploration of data.

Of course, scatterplot matrices are not really multivariate solutions: they are multiple bivariate solutions, in which the multivariate data are projected into multiple two-dimensional plots (and in each two-dimensional plot all other variables are ignored). Such projections necessarily sacrifice information. Picture a cube formed from eight smaller cubes. If data points are uniformly distributed in alternate subcubes, with the others being empty, all three one-dimensional and all three two-dimensional projections show uniform distributions. (This "exclusive-or" structure caused great difficulty with perceptrons—the precursors of today's neural networks which we will discuss in chapters 5 and 11.)

Interactive graphics come into their own when more than two variables are involved, since then we can rotate ("spin") the direction of projection in a search for structure. Some systems even let the software follow random rotations, while we watch and wait for interesting structures to become apparent. While this is a good idea in principle, the excitement of watching a cloud of points shift relative position as the direction of viewing changes can quickly pall, and more structured methods are desirable. Projection pursuit, described in chapter 11, is one such method.

Trellis plotting also utilizes multiple bivariate plots. Here, however, rather than displaying a scatterplot for each pair of variables, they fix a particular pair of variables that is to be displayed and produce a series of scatterplots conditioned on levels of one or more other variables.

Figure 3.14 shows a trellis plot for data on epileptic seizures. The horizontal axis of each plot gives the number of seizures that 58 patients experienced over a certain two week period, and the vertical axis gives the number of seizures experienced over a later two week period. The two left hand graphs

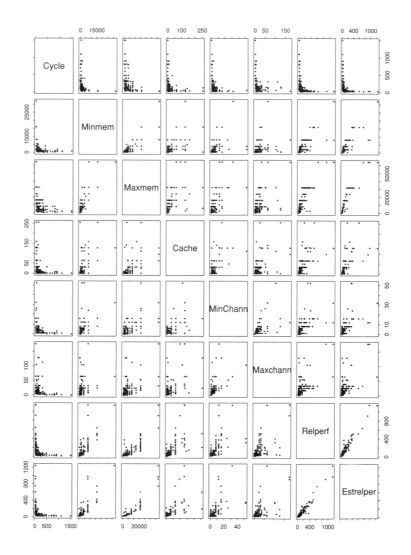

Figure 3.13   A scatterplot matrix for the computer CPU data.

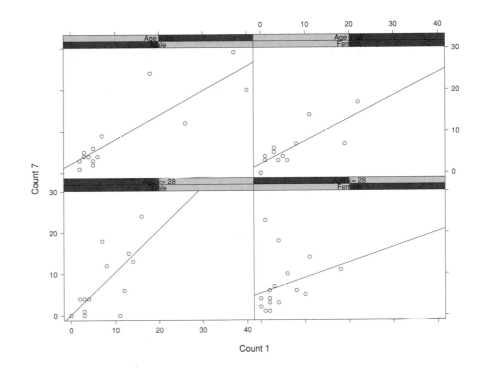

Figure 3.14   A trellis plot for the epileptic seizures data.

show the figures for males, and the two right hand graphs the figures for females. The two upper graphs show ages 29 to 42 while the two lower graphs
show ages 18 to 28. (The original data set included the record of another
subject who had much higher counts. We have removed this subject here so
that we can more clearly see the relationships between the scores of the other
subjects.) From these plots, we can see that the younger group show lower
average counts than the older group. The figures also hint at some possible
differences between the slopes of the estimated best fitting lines relating the
y and x axes, though we would need to carry out formal tests to be confident
that these differences were real.

Trellis plots can be produced with any kind of component graph. Instead
of scatterplots in each cell, we could have histograms, time series plots, con-

tour plots, or any other types of plots.

An entirely different way to display multivariate data is through the use of *icons*, small diagrams in which the sizes of different features are determined by the values of particular variables. Star icons are among the most popular. In these, different directions from the origin correspond to different variables, and the lengths of radii projecting in these directions correspond to the magnitudes of the variables. Figure 3.15 shows an example. The data displayed here come from 12 chemical properties that were measured on 53 mineral samples equally spaced along a long drill into the Earth's surface.

Another type of icon plot, Chernoff's faces, is discussed frequently in introductory texts on the subject. In these plots, the sizes of features in cartoon faces (length of nose, degree of smile, shape of eyes, etc.) represent the values of the variables. The method is based on the principle that the human eye is particularly adept at recognizing and distinguishing between faces. Although they are entertaining, plots of this type are seldom used in serious data analysis since the idea does not work very well in practice with more than a handful of cartoon faces. In general, iconic representations are effective only for relatively small numbers of cases since they require the eye to scan each case separately.

Parallel coordinates plots show variables as parallel axes, representing each case as a piecewise linear plot connecting the measured values for that case. Figure 3.16 shows such a plot for four repeated measurements of the number of epileptic seizures experienced by 58 patients during successive two week periods. The data are clearly skewed and might be modeled by a Poisson distribution (see Appendix). Since the data set is not too large, we can follow the trajectories of individual patients.

Another way of representing dimensions is through the use of color. Line styles, as in the parallel coordinates plot above, can serve the same purpose.

No single method of representing multivariate data is a universal solution. Which method is most useful in a given situation will depend on the data and on the structures being sought.

3.6   Principal Components Analysis

Scatterplots project multivariate data into a two-dimensional space defined by just two of the variables. This allows us to examine pairwise relationships between variables, but such simple projections might conceal more complicated relationships. To detect these relationships we can use projec-

Figure 3.15   An example of a star plot.

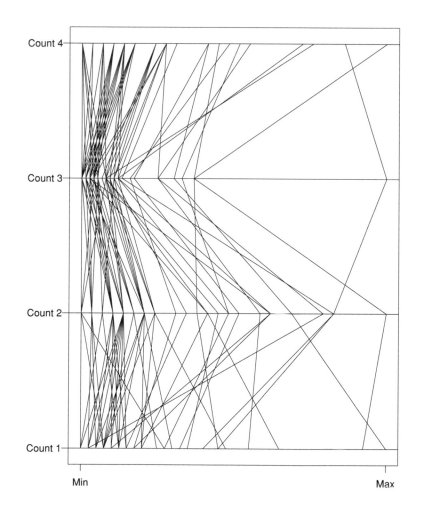

Figure 3.16   A parallel coordinates plot for the epileptic seizure data.

tions along different directions, defined by any weighted linear combination of variables (e.g., along the direction defined by $2x_1 + 3x_2 + x_3$).

With only a few variables, it might be feasible to search for such interesting spaces manually, rotating the distribution of the data. With more than a few variables, however, it is best to let the computer loose to search by itself. To do this, we need to define what an "interesting" projection might look like, so that the computer knows when it has found one. *Projection pursuit methods* are based on this general principle of allowing the computer to search for interesting directions. (Such techniques, however, are computationally quite intensive: we will return to projection pursuit in chapter 11 when we discuss regression.)

However, in one special case—for one specific definition of what constitutes an "interesting" direction—a computationally efficient explicit solution can be found. This is when we seek the projection onto the two-dimensional plane for which the sum of squared differences between the data points and their projections onto this plane is smaller than when any other plane is used. (We use two-dimensional projections here for convenience, but in general we can use any k-dimensional projection, $1 \leq k \leq p - 1$). This two-dimensional plane can be shown to be spanned by (1) the linear combination of the variables that has maximum sample variance and (2) the linear combination that has maximum variance subject to being uncorrelated with the first linear combination. Thus "interesting" here is defined in terms of the *maximum variability* in the data.

Of course, we can take this process further, seeking additional linear combinations that maximize the variance subject to being uncorrelated with all those already selected. In general, if we are lucky, we find a set of just a few such linear combinations ("components") that describes the data fairly accurately. The mathematics of this process is described below. Our aim here is to capture the intrinsic variability in the data. This is a useful way of reducing the dimensionality of a data set, either to ease interpretation or as a way to avoid overfitting and to prepare for subsequent analysis.

Suppose that $\mathbf{X}$ is an $n \times p$ data matrix in which the rows represent the cases (each row is a data vector $\mathbf{x}(i)$) and the columns represent the variables. Strictly speaking, the ith row of this matrix is actually the transpose $\mathbf{x}^T$ of the ith data vector $\mathbf{x}(i)$, since the convention is to consider data vectors as being $p \times 1$ column vectors rather than $1 \times p$ row vectors. In addition, assume that $\mathbf{X}$ is mean-centered so that the value of each variable is relative to the sample mean for that variable (i.e., the estimated mean has been subtracted from each column).

Let $\mathbf{a}$ be the $p \times 1$ column vector of projection weights (unknown at this point) that result in the largest variance when the data $\mathbf{X}$ are projected along $\mathbf{a}$. The projection of any particular data vector $\mathbf{x}$ is the linear combination $\mathbf{a}^T\mathbf{x} = \sum_{j=1}^{p} a_j x_j$. Note that we can express the projected values onto $\mathbf{a}$ of all data vectors in $\mathbf{X}$ as $\mathbf{Xa}$ ($n \times p$ by $p \times 1$, yielding an $n \times 1$ column vector of projected values). Furthermore, we can define the *variance* along $\mathbf{a}$ as

$$
\begin{aligned}
\sigma_{\mathbf{a}}^2 &= \left(\mathbf{Xa}\right)^T \left(\mathbf{Xa}\right) \\
&= \mathbf{a}^T \mathbf{X}^T \mathbf{Xa} \\
&= \mathbf{a}^T V \mathbf{a},
\end{aligned}
\tag{3.8}
$$

where $V = \mathbf{X}^T\mathbf{X}$ is the $p \times p$ covariance matrix of the data (since $\mathbf{X}$ has zero mean), as defined in chapter 2. Thus, we can express $\sigma_{\mathbf{a}}^2$ (the variance of the projected data (a scalar) that we wish to maximize) as a function of both $\mathbf{a}$ and the covariance matrix of the data $\mathbf{V}$.

Of course, maximizing $\sigma_{\mathbf{a}}^2$ directly is not well-defined, since we can increase $\sigma_{\mathbf{a}}^2$ without limit simply by increasing the size of the components of $\mathbf{a}$. Some kind of constraint must be imposed, so we impose a normalization constraint on the $\mathbf{a}$ vectors such that $\mathbf{a}^T\mathbf{a} = 1$.

With this normalization constraint we can rewrite our optimization problem as that of maximizing the quantity

$$
u = \mathbf{a}^T \mathbf{Va} - \lambda(\mathbf{a}^T\mathbf{a} - 1),
\tag{3.9}
$$

where λ is a Lagrange multiplier. Differentiating with respect to $\mathbf{a}$ yields

$$
\frac{\partial u}{\partial \mathbf{a}} = 2\mathbf{Va} - 2\lambda\mathbf{a} = 0,
\tag{3.10}
$$

which reduces to the familiar eigenvalue form of

$$
(\mathbf{V} - \lambda\mathbf{I})\mathbf{a} = 0.
\tag{3.11}
$$

Thus, the first principal component $\mathbf{a}$ is the eigenvector associated with the largest eigenvalue of the covariance matrix $\mathbf{V}$. Furthermore, the second principal component (the direction orthogonal to the first component that has the largest projected variance) is the eigenvector corresponding to the second largest eigenvalue of $\mathbf{V}$, and so on (the eigenvector for the kth largest eigenvalue corresponds to the kth principal component direction).

In practice of course we may be interested in projecting to more than two-dimensions. A basic property of this projection scheme is that if the data are

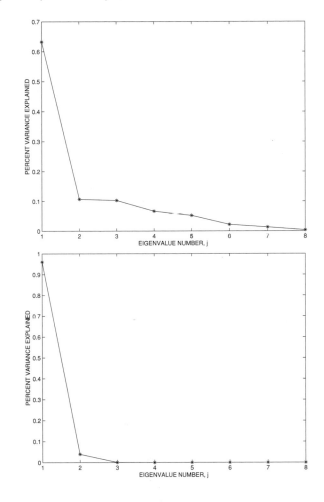

Figure 3.17   Scree plots for the computer CPU data set. The upper plot displays the eigenvalues from the correlation matrix, and the lower plot is for the covariance matrix.

projected into the first k eigenvectors, the variance of the projected data can be expressed as $\sum_{j=1}^{k} \lambda_j$, where λ_j is the jth eigenvalue. Equivalently, the squared error in terms of approximating the true data matrix X using only the first k eigenvectors can be expressed as

$$\frac{\sum_{j=k+1}^{p} \lambda_j}{\sum_{l=1}^{p} \lambda_l}.$$

(3.12)

Thus, in choosing an appropriate number k of principal components, one approach is to increase k until the squared error quantity above is smaller than some acceptable degree of squared error. For high-dimensional data sets, in which the variables are often relatively well-correlated, it is not uncommon for a relatively small number of principal components (say, 5 or 10) to capture 90% or more of the variance in the data.

A useful visual aid in this context is the *scree plot*—which shows the amount of variance explained by each consecutive eigenvalue. This is necessarily nonincreasing with the number of the component, and the hope is that it demonstrates a sudden dramatic fall toward zero. A principal components analysis of the correlation matrix of the computer CPU data described earlier gives rise to eigenvalues proportional to 63.26, 10.70, 10.30, 6.68, 5.23, 2.18, 1.31, and 0.34 (see figure 3.17). The fall from the first to the second eigenvalue is dramatic, but after that the decline is gradual. (The weights that the first component puts on the eight variables are (0.199, -0.365, -0.399, -0.336, -0.331, - 0.298, -0.421, -0.423). Note that, it gives them all roughly similar weights, but gives the first variable (cycle time) a weight opposite in sign to those of the other variables.) If, instead of the correlation matrix, we analyzed the covariance matrix, the variables with larger ranges of values would tend to dominate. In the case of these data, the values given for memory are much larger than those for the other variables. (This is because they are given in kilobytes. Had they been given in megabytes, this would not be the case—an example of the arbitrariness of the scaling of noncommensurate variables (see chapter 2)). Principal components analysis of the covariance matrix gives proportions of variation attributable to the different components as 96.02, 3.93, 0.04, 0.01, 0.00, 0.00, 0.00, and 0.00 (see figure 3.17). Here the fall from the first component is very striking—the variability in the data can, indeed, be explained almost entirely by the differences in memory capacity. Often, however, there is no obvious fall such as this—no point at which the remaining variance in the data can be attributed to random variation. Then the choice of how many components to extract is fairly arbitrary. The proportion of the total variance that we regard as providing an adequate simplified description of the data depends on the field of application. In some cases it might be sufficient for the first few components to describe 60% of the variance, but in other fields one might hope for 95% or more.

When conducting principal components analysis prior to further analyses, it is risky to choose a small number of components that fail to explain the variability in the data very well. Information is lost, and there is no guarantee that the sacrificed information is not relevant to the aims of further analyses. (Indeed, this is true even if the retained components do explain the variability well, short of 100%.) For example, we might perform principal components analysis prior to classifying our data. Since the aims of dimension reduction and classification are somewhat different, it is possible that the reduction to a few spanning components may lose valuable information about the differences between the classes—we will see an example of this at the end of chapter 9. Likewise, for many multivariate data sets in which the points fall into two (or more) classes, a prior principal components analysis may completely obliterate the differences between the distributions of the classes. On the other hand, in regression problems (chapter 11) with many explanatory variables, unless the data set is large, there may be problems of instability of the estimated coefficients. A principal components analysis is sometimes performed to reduce the large number of explanatory variables to a few linear combinations prior to carrying out the regression analysis.

Despite the risks of failing to extract relevant information, principal components analysis is a powerful and valuable tool. Because it is based on linear projections and minimizing the variance (or sum of squared errors), numerical manipulations can be carried out explicitly, without any iterative searches. Computing the principal component solutions directly from the eigenvector equations will scale roughly as $O(np^2 + p^3)$ (np^2 to calculate $\mathbf{V}$ and p^3 to solve the eigenvalue equations for the $p \times p$ matrix). This means that it can be applied to data sets with large numbers of records n (but does not scale so well as a function of dimensionality p). As illustrated above when we applied principal components analysis to both correlation and covariance matrices, the method is not invariant under rescalings of the original variables. The appropriate steps to take will depend on the objectives of the analysis. Typically we rescale the data if different variables measure different attributes (e.g., height, weight, and lung capacity) since otherwise the results of a direct principal components analysis depend on the arbitrary choice of units used for each attribute.

To illustrate the simple graphical use of principal components analysis, figure 3.18 shows the projections (indicated by the numbers) of 17 pills onto the space spanned by the first two principal components. The six measurements

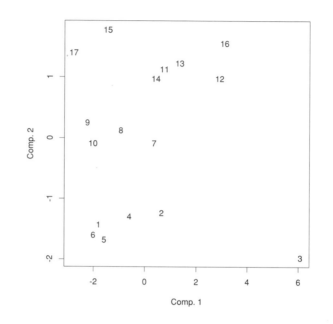

Figure 3.18 Projection onto the first two principal components.

on each pill are the times at which a specified proportion (10%, 30%, 50%, 70%, 75%, and 90%) of the pill has dissolved. It is clear from this diagram that one of the pills is very different from the others, lying in the bottom right corner, far from the other points.

Sometimes we can gain insights from the pattern of weights (or loadings, as they are sometimes called) defining the components of a principal components analysis. Huba et al. (1981) collected data on 1684 students in Los Angeles showing consumption of each of thirteen legal and illegal psychoactive substances: cigarettes, beer, wine, spirits, cocaine, tranquilizers, drug store medications used to get high, heroin and other opiates, marijuana, hashish, inhalants (such as glue), hallucinogenics, and amphetamines. They scored each as 1 (never tried), 2 (tried only once), 3 (tried a few times), 4 (tried many times), 5 (tried regularly). Taking these variables in order, the weights of the first component from a principal components analysis were (0.278, 0.286,

0.265, 0.318, 0.208, 0.293, 0.176, 0.202, 0.339, 0.329, 0.276, 0.248, 0.329). This component assigns roughly equal weights to each of the variables and can be regarded as a general measure of how often students use such substances. Thus, the biggest difference between the students is in terms of how often they use psychoactive substances, regardless of which substances they use.

The second component had weights (0.280, 0.396, 0.392, 0.325, -0.288, -0.259, -0.189, -0.315, 0.163, -0.050, -0.169, -0.329, -0.232). This is interesting because it gives positive weights to the legal substances and negative weights to the illegal ones: therefore, once we have controlled for overall substance use, the major difference between the students lies in their use of legal versus illegal substances. This is just the sort of relationship one would hope to discover from a data mining exercise.

Another statistical technique, *factor analysis,* is often confused with principal components analysis, but the two have very different aims. As described above, principal components analysis is a transformation of the data to new variables. We can then select just some of these as providing an adequate description of the data. Factor analysis, on the other hand, is a *model* for data, based on the notion that we can define the measured variables $X_1, \ldots, X_p$ as linear combinations of a smaller number m ($m < p$) of "latent" (unobserved) factors—variables that cannot be measured explicitly. The objective of factor analysis is to unearth information about these latent variables.

We can define $\mathbf{F} = (F_1, \ldots, F_m)^T$ as the $m \times 1$ column vector of unknown latent variables, taking values $\mathbf{f} = (f_1, \ldots, f_m)$. Then a measured data vector $\mathbf{x} = (x_1, \ldots, x_p)^T$ (defined here as a $p \times 1$ column vector) is regarded as a linear function of $\mathbf{f}$ defined by

$$\mathbf{x} = \Lambda \mathbf{f} + \mathrm{e}. \tag{3.13}$$

Here Λ is a $p \times m$ matrix of *factor loadings* giving the weights with which each factor contributes to each manifest variable. The components of the $p \times 1$ vector e are uncorrelated random variables, sometimes termed *specific factors* since they contribute only to single manifest (observed) variables, $X_j, 1 \leq j \leq p$. Factor analysis is a special case of structural linear relational models described in chapter 9, so we will not dwell on estimation procedures here. However, since factor analysis was the earliest model structure of this form to be developed, it has a special place, not only because of its history, but also because it continues to be among the most widely used of such models.

Factor analysis has not had an entirely uncontroversial history, partly because its solutions are not invariant to various transformations. It is easy to see that new factors can be defined from equation 3.13 via $m \times m$ orthogonal matrices $\mathbf{M}$, such that $\mathbf{x} = (\mathbf{\Lambda M})\,(\mathbf{Mf}) + $e. This corresponds to rotating the factors in the space they span. Thus, the extracted factors are essentially non-unique, unless extra constraints are imposed. There are various constraints in general use, including methods that seek to extract factors for which the weights are as close to 0 or 1 as possible, defining the variables as clearly as possible in terms of a subset of the factors.

3.7   Multidimensional Scaling

In the preceding section we described how to use principal components analysis to project a multivariate data set onto the plane in which the data has maximum dispersion. This allows us to examine the data visually, while sacrificing the minimum amount of information. Such a method is effective only to the extent that the data lie in a two-dimensional linear subspace of the area spanned by the measured variables. But what if the data forms a set that is intrinsically two-dimensional, but instead of being "flat," is curved or otherwise distorted in the space spanned by the original variables? (Imagine a crumpled piece of paper, intrinsically two-dimensional, but occupying three dimensions.) In this event it is quite possible that principal components analysis might fail to detect the underlying two-dimensional structure. In such cases, multidimensional scaling can be helpful. Multidimensional scaling methods seek to represent data points in a lower dimensional space while preserving, as far as is possible, the distances between the data points. Since, we are mostly concerned with two-dimensional representations, we shall restrict most of our discussion to such cases. The extension to higher dimensional representations is immediate.

Many multidimensional scaling methods exist, differing in how they define the distances that are being preserved, the distances they map to, and how the calculations are performed. Principal components analysis may be regarded as a basic form. In this approach the distances between the data points are taken as Euclidean (or Pythagorean), and they are mapped to distances in a reduced space that are also measured using the Euclidean metric. The sum of squared distances between the original data points and their projections provides a measure of quality of the representation. Other methods of multidimensional scaling also have associated measures of the quality of the representation.

Since multidimensional scaling methods seek to preserve interpoint distances, such distances can serve as the starting point for an analysis. That is, we do not need to know any measured values of variables for the objects being analyzed, only how similar the objects are, in terms of some distance measure. For example, the data may have been collected by asking respondents to rate the similarity between pairs of objects. (A classic example of this is a matrix showing the number of times the Morse codes for different letters are confused. There are no "variables" here, simply a matrix of "similarities" measuring how often is letter was mistaken for another.) The end point of the process is the same—a configuration of data points in a two–dimensional space. In a sense, the objects and the raters are used to determine on what dimensions "similarity" is to be measured. Multidimensional scaling methods are widely used in areas such as psychometrics and market research, in attempts to understand perceptions of relationships and similarities between objects.

From an $n \times p$ data matrix $\mathbf{X}$ we can compute an $n \times n$ matrix $\mathbf{B} = \mathbf{X}\mathbf{X}^T$. (Since this scales as $O(n^2)$ in both time and memory, it is clear that this approach is not practical for very large numbers of objects n). It is straightforward to see from this that the Euclidean distance between the ith and jth objects is given by

$$d_{ij}^2 = b_{ii} + b_{jj} - 2b_{ij}. \tag{3.14}$$

If we could invert this relationship, then, given a matrix of distances $\mathbf{D}$ (derived from original data points by computing Euclidean distances or obtained by other means), we could compute the elements of $\mathbf{B}$. $\mathbf{B}$ could then be factorized to yield the coordinates of the points. One factorization of $\mathbf{B}$ would be in terms of the eigenvectors. If we chose those associated with the two largest eigenvalues, we would have a two-dimensional representation that preserved the structure of the data as well as possible.

The feasibility of this procedure hinges upon our ability to invert equation 3.14. Unfortunately, this is not possible without imposing some extra constraints. Because shifting the mean and rotating a configuration of points does not affect the interpoint distances, for any given a set of distances there is an infinite number of possible solutions, differing in the location and orientation of the point configuration.

A sufficient constraint to impose is the assumption that the means of all the variables are 0. That is, we assume $\sum_i x_{ik} = 0$ for all $k = 1, ..., p$. This means that $\sum_i b_{ij} = \sum_j b_{ij} = 0$. Now, by summing equation 3.14 first over i, then over j, and finally over both i and j, we obtain

$$\sum_i d_{ij}^2 \;\; = \;\; tr(\mathbf{B}) + nb_{jj}$$

$$\sum_j d_{ij}^2 \;=\; tr(\mathbf{B}) + nb_{ii}$$

$$\sum_{ij} d_{ij}^2 \;=\; 2ntr(\mathbf{B}) \qquad\qquad (3.15)$$

where $tr(\mathbf{B})$ is the trace of the matrix $\mathbf{B}$. The third equation expresses $tr(\mathbf{B})$ in terms of the d_{ij}^2, the first and second express b_{jj} and b_{ii} in terms of d_{ij}^2 and $tr(\mathbf{B})$, and hence in terms of d_{ij}^2 alone. Plugging these into equation 3.14 expresses b_{ij} as a function of d_{ij}^2, yielding the required inversion.

This process is known as the *principal coordinates* method. It can be shown that the scores on the components calculated from a principal components analysis of a data matrix $\mathbf{X}$ (and hence a factorization of the matrix $\mathbf{X}^T$) are the same as the coordinates of the above scaling analysis.

Of course, if the matrix $\mathbf{B}$ does not arise not as a product $\mathbf{X}\mathbf{X}^T$, but by some other route (such as simple subjective differences between pairs of objects), then there is no guarantee that all the eigenvalues will be non-negative. If the negative eigenvalues are small in absolute value, they can be ignored.

Classical multidimensional scaling into two dimensions finds the projection into two dimensions that is most accurate in the sense that it minimizes

$$\sum_i \sum_j (\delta_{ij} - d_{ij})^2, \qquad\qquad (3.16)$$

where δ_{ij} is the observed distance between points i and j in the p-dimensional space and d_{ij} is the distance between the points representing these objects in the two-dimensional space. Expressed this way the process permits ready generalization. Given distances or dissimilarities, derived in one way or another, we can seek a distribution of points in a two-dimensional space that minimizes the sum of squared differences $\sum_i \sum_j (\delta_{ij} - d_{ij})^2$. Thus, we relax the restriction that the configuration must be found by projection. With this relaxation an exact algebraic solution will generally not be possible, so numerical methods must be used: we simply have a function of $2n$ parameters (the coordinates of the points in the two-dimensional space) that is to be minimized.

The score function $\sum_i \sum_j (\delta_{ij} - d_{ij})^2$, measuring how well the interpoint distances in the derived configuration match those originally provided, is invariant with respect to rotations and translations. However, it is not invariant to rescalings: if the δ_{ij} were multiplied by a constant, we would end up with the same solution, but a different value of $\sum_i \sum_j (\delta_{ij} - d_{ij})^2$. To permit different situations to be properly compared we divide $\sum_i \sum_j (\delta_{ij} - d_{ij})^2$

by $\sum_{i,j} d_{ij}^2$, yielding the standardized residual sum of squares. A common score function is the square root of this quantity, the *stress*. A variant on the stress is the *sstress*, defined as

$$\sqrt{\sum_i \sum_j (\delta_{ij}^2 - d_{ij}^2)^2 / \sum_i \sum_j d_{ij}^4}. \qquad (3.17)$$

These measures effectively assume that the differences between the original dissimilarities and the distances in the two-dimensional configuration are due to random discrepancies and arbitrary distortions—that is, that $d_{ij} = \delta_{ij} + \epsilon_{ij}$. More sophisticated models can also be built. For example, we might assume that $d_{ij} = a + b\delta_{ij} + \epsilon_{ij}$. Now a two-stage procedure is necessary. Beginning with a proposed configuration, we regress the distances d_{ij} in the two-dimensional space on the given dissimilarities, yielding estimates for a and b. We then find new values of the d_{ij} that minimize the stress

$$\sqrt{\sum_i \sum_j (d_{ij} - a - b\delta_{ij})^2 / \sum_i \sum_j d_{ij}^2}, \qquad (3.18)$$

and repeat this process until we achieve satisfactory convergence.

Multidimensional scaling methods such as the above, which attempt to model the dissimilarities as given, are called metric methods. Sometimes, however, a more general approach is required. For example, we may not be given the precise similarities, only their rank order (objects A and B are more similar than B and C, and so on); or we may not be prepared to assume that the relationship between d_{ij} and δ_{ij} has a particular form, just that some monotonic relationship exists. This requires a two-stage approach similar to that described in the preceding paragraph, but with a technique known as monotonic regression replacing simple linear regression, yielding non-metric multidimensional scaling. The term non-metric here indicates that the method seeks to preserve only ordinal relationships.

Multidimensional scaling is a powerful method for displaying data to reveal structure. However, as with the other graphical methods described in this chapter, if there are too many data points the structure becomes obscured. Moreover, since multidimensional scaling involves applying highly sophisticated transformations to the data (more so than a simple scatterplot or principal components analysis) there is a possibility that artifacts may be introduced. In particular, in some situations the dissimilarities between objects can be determined more accurately when the objects are similar than

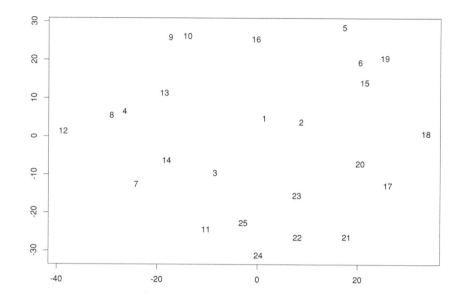

Figure 3.19   A multidimensional scaling plot of the village dialect similarities data.

when they are quite different. Consider the evolution of the style of a man-ufactured object. Those objects that are produced within a short time of each other will probably have much in common, while those separated by a greater time gap may have very little in common. The consequence will be an induced curvature in the multidimensional scaling plot, where we might have hoped to achieve a more or less straight line. This phenomenon is known as the *horseshoe effect*.

Figure 3.19 shows a plot produced using nonmetric scaling to minimize the sstress score function of equation 3.17. The data arose from a study of English dialects. Each pair of a group of 25 villages was rated according to the percentages of 60 items for which the villages used different words. The villages, and the counties in which they are located, are listed in table 3.1. The figure shows that villages from the same county (and hence that are relatively close geographically) tend to use the same words.

1	North Wheatley	Nottinghamshire
2	South Clifton	Nottinghamshire
3	Oxton	Nottinghamshire
4	Eastoft	Lincolnshire
5	Keelby	Lincolnshire
6	Wiloughton	Lincolnshire
7	Wragby	Lincolnshire
8	Old Bolingbroke	Lincolnshire
9	Fulbeck	Lincolnshire
10	Sutterton	Lincolnshire
11	Swinstead	Lincolnshire
12	Crowland	Lincolnshire
13	Harby	Leicestershire
14	Packington	Leicestershire
15	Goadby	Leicestershire
16	Ullesthorpe	Leicestershire
17	Empingham	Rutland
18	Warmington	Northamptonshire
19	Little Harrowden	Northamptonshire
20	Kislingbury	Northamptonshire
21	Sulgrave	Northamptonshire
22	Warboys	Huntingdonshire
23	Little Downham	Cambridgeshire
24	Tingewick	Buckinghamshire
25	Turvey	Bedfordshire

Table 3.1   Numerical codes, names, and counties for the 25 villages with dialect similarities displayed in figure 3.19.

Multidimensional scaling methods typically display the data points in a two-dimensional space. If the variables are also described in this space (provided the data are in vector form) the relationships between data points and variables may be clearly seen. Given the complicated nonlinear relationship between the space defined by the original variables and the space used to display the data, representing the original variables is a non-trivial task. Plots that display both data points and variables are known as *biplots*. The "bi" here signifies that there are two modes being displayed—the points and the variables—not that the display is two-dimensional. Indeed, three-dimensional biplots have also been developed. Forms of multidimensional scaling that involve nonlinear transformations produce nonlinear biplots. Biplots have even been produced for categorical data, and in this case the levels of the variables are represented by regions in the plot. Effective interpretation of multidimensional and biplot displays requires practice and experience.

3.8   Further Reading

Exploratory data analysis achieved an identity and respectability with the publication of John Tukey's book *Exploratory Data Analysis* (Tukey, 1977). Since then, as progress in computer technology facilitated rapid and straightforward production of accurate graphical displays, such methods have blossomed. Modern data visualization techniques can be very powerful ways of discovering structure. Books on graphical methods include those of Tufte (1983), Chambers et al. (1983), and Jacoby (1997). Wilkinson (1999) is a particularly interesting recent addition to the visualization literature, introducing a novel and general purpose language for analyzing and synthesizing a wide variety of data visualization techniques.

Interactive dynamic methods are emphasized by Asimov (1985), Becker, Cleveland, and Wilks (1987), Cleveland and McGill (1988), and Buja, Cook, and Swayne (1996). Books that describe smoothing approaches to displaying univariate distributions, as well as multivariate extensions, include those of Silverman (1986), Scott (1992), and Wand and Jones (1995). Carr et al. (1987) discuss scatterplot techniques for large data sets. Wegman (1990) discusses parallel coordinates. Categorical data is somewhat more difficult to visualize than quantitative real-valued data, and for this reason, visualization techniques for categorical data are not as widely developed or used. Still, Blasius and Greenacre (1998) provide a useful and broad review of recent developments in the visualization and exploratory data analysis of categorical data. Cook and Weisberg (1994) describe the use of graphical techniques for the task of regression modeling.

Card, MacKinlay, and Shneiderman (1999) contains a collection of papers on a variety of topics entitled "information visualization" and describe a number of techniques for displaying complex heterogeneous data sets in a useful manner. Keim and Kriegel (1994) describe a system specifically designed for database exploration.

Multidimensional scaling has become a large field in its own right. Books on this include those by Davidson (1983) and Cox and Cox (1994). Biplots are discussed in detail by Gower and Hand (1996).

The CPU data is from Ein-Dor and Feldmesser (1987), and is reproduced in Hand et al. (1994), dataset 325. The data on English dialects is from Morgan (1981) and is reproduced in Hand et al. (1994), dataset 145. The data on epileptic seizures is given in Thall and Vail (1990) and also in Hand et al. (1994). The mineral core data shown in the icon plot is described in Chernoff (1973).

4 *Data Analysis and Uncertainty*

4.1 Introduction

In this chapter, we focus on uncertainty and how to cope with it. Not only is the process of mapping from the real world to our databases seldom perfect, but the domain of the mapping—the real world itself—is beset with ambiguities and uncertainties. The basic tool for dealing with uncertainty is probability, and we begin by defining the concept and showing how it is used to construct statistical models. Section 4.2 provides a brief discussion of the distinction between probability calculus and the interpretation of probability, focusing on the two main interpretations: the frequentist and the subjective (Bayesian). Section 4.3 extends this discussion to define the concept of a random variable, with a particular focus on the relationships that can exist between multiple random variables.

Fundamental to many data mining activities is the notion of a sample. Sometimes the database contains only a sample from the universe of possible records; section 4.4 explores this situation, explaining why samples are often sufficient to work with. Section 4.5 describes *estimation,* the process of moving beyond a data sample to develop parameter estimates for a model describing the data. In particular, we review in some detail the basic principles of the maximum likelihood and Bayesian approaches to estimation. Section 4.6 discusses the closely related topic of how to evaluate the quality of a hypothesis on the basis of observed data. Section 4.7 outlines various systematic methods for drawing samples from data. Section 4.8 presents some concluding remarks, and section 4.9 gives pointers to more detailed reading.

4.2   Dealing with Uncertainty

The ubiquity of the idea of uncertainty is illustrated by the rich variety of words used to describe it and related concepts. *Probability, chance, randomness, luck, hazard,* and *fate* are just a few examples. The omnipresence of uncertainty requires us to be able to cope with it: modeling uncertainty is a necessary component of almost all data analysis. Indeed, in some cases our primary aim is to model the uncertain or random aspects of data. It is one of the great achievements of science that we have developed a deep and powerful understanding of uncertainty. The capricious gods that were previously invoked to explain the lack of predictability in the world have been replaced by mathematical, statistical, and computer-based models that allow us to understand and manipulate uncertain events. We can even attempt the seemingly impossible and predict uncertain events, where prediction for a data miner either can mean the prediction of future events (where the notion of uncertainty is very familiar) or prediction in a nontemporal sense of a variable whose true value is somehow hidden from us (for example, diagnosing whether a person has cancer, based on only descriptive symptoms).

We may be uncertain for various reasons. Our data may be only a sample from the population we wish to study, so that we are uncertain about the extent to which different samples differ from each other and from the overall population. Perhaps our interest lies in making a prediction about tomorrow, based on the data we have today, so that our conclusions are subject to uncertainty about what the future will bring. Perhaps we are ignorant and cannot observe some value, and have to base our ideas on our "best guess" about it. And so on.

Many conceptual bases have been formulated for handling uncertainty and ignorance. Of these, by far the most widely used is probability. Fuzzy logic is another that has a moderately large following, but this area—along with closely related areas such as possibility theory and rough sets—remains rather controversial: it lacks the sound theoretical backbone and widespread application and acceptance of probability. These ideas may one day develop solid foundations, and become widely used, but because of their current uncertain status we will not consider them further in this book.

It is useful to distinguish between *probability theory* and *probability calculus*. The former is concerned with the interpretation of probability while the latter is concerned with the manipulation of the mathematical representation of probability. (Unfortunately, not all textbooks make this distinction between the two terms—often books on probability calculus are given titles such as

"Introduction to the Theory of Probability.") The distinction is an important one because it permits the separation of those areas about which there is universal agreement (the calculus) from those areas about which opinions differ (the theory). The calculus is a branch of mathematics, based on well-defined and generally accepted axioms (stated by the Russian mathematician Kolmogorov in the 1930s); the aim is to explore the consequences of those axioms. (There are some areas in which different sets of axioms are used, but these are rather specialized and generally do not impinge on problems of data mining.) The theory, on the other hand, leaves scope for perspectives on the mapping from the real world to the mathematical representation— i.e., on what probability is.

A study of the history and philosophy of probability theory reveals that there are as many perspectives on the meaning of probability as there are thinkers. However, the views can be grouped into variants of a few different types. Here we shall restrict ourselves to discussing the two most important types (in terms of their impact on data mining practice). More philosophically inclined readers may wish to consult section 4.9 for references to material containing broader discussions.

The *frequentist view* of probability takes the perspective that probability is an objective concept. In particular, the probability of an event is defined as the limiting proportion of times that the event would occur in repetitions of essentially identical situations. A simple example is the proportion of times a head comes up in repeatedly tossing a coin. This interpretation restricts our application of probability: for instance we cannot assess the probability that a particular athlete will win a medal in the next Olympics because this is a one-off event, where the notion of a "limiting proportion" makes no sense. On the other hand, we can certainly assess the probability that a customer in a supermarket will purchase a certain item, since we can use a large number of similar customers as the basis for a limiting proportion argument. It is clear in this last example that some *idealization* is going on: different customers are not really the same as repetitions of a single customer. As in all scientific modeling we need to decide what aspects are important for our model to be sufficiently accurate. In predicting customer behavior we might decide that the differences between customers do not matter.

The frequentist view was the dominant perspective on probability throughout most of the last century, and hence it underpins most widely used statistical software. However, in the last decade or so, a competing view has acquired increasing importance. This view, that of *subjective probability*, has been around since people first started formalizing probabilistic notions, but until recently it was primarily of theoretical interest. What revived the approach was the development of the computer and of powerful algorithms for manipulating and processing subjective probabilities. The principles and methodologies for data analysis that derive from the subjective point of view are often referred to as *Bayesian statistics*. A central tenet of Bayesian statistics is the explicit characterization of *all* forms of uncertainty in a data analysis problem, including uncertainty about any parameters we estimate from the data, uncertainty as to which among a set of model structures are best or closest to "truth," uncertainty in any forecast we might make, and so on. Subjective probability is a very flexible framework for modeling such uncertainty in different forms.

From the perspective of subjective probability, probability is an individual degree of belief that a given event will occur. Thus, probability is not an objective property of the outside world, but rather an internal state of the individual—and may differ from individual to individual. Fortunately it turns out that if we adopt certain tenets of rational behaviour the set of axioms underlying subjective probability is the same as that underlying the frequentist view. The *calculus* is the same for the two viewpoints, even though the underlying *interpretation* is quite different.

Of course, this does not imply that the conclusions drawn using the two approaches are necessarily the same. At the very least, subjective probability can make statements about areas that frequentist probability cannot address. Moreover, statistical inferences based on subjective probability necessarily involve a subjective component—the initial or prior belief that an event will happen. As noted above, this factor is likely to differ from person to person.

Nonetheless, the frequentist and subjective viewpoints in many cases lead to roughly the same answers, particularly for simple hypotheses and large data sets. Rather than committing to one viewpoint or the other, many practitioners view both as useful in their own right, with each appropriate in different situations. The methodologies for data analysis that derive from the frequentist view tend to be computationally simpler, and thus (to date at least) have dominated in the development of data mining techniques where the size of the data sets do not favor the application of complex computational methods. However, when applied with care the Bayesian (subjective) methodology has the ability to tease out more subtle information from the data. Just as applied statistics has seen increased interest in Bayesian methods in recent years, we can expect to see more Bayesian ideas being applied in data mining in the future. In the rest of this book we will refer to both frequentist and Bayesian views where appropriate. As we will see later in this chapter, in a certain sense the two viewpoints can be reconciled: the frequentist methodology of fitting models and patterns to data can be implemented as a special case of a more general Bayesian methodology. For the practitioner this is quite useful, since it means that the same general modeling and computational apparatus can be used.

4.3 Random Variables and Their Relationships

We introduced the notion of a variable in chapter 2. In this chapter we introduce the concept of a *random variable*. A random variable is a mapping from a property of objects to a variable that can take one of a set of possible values, via a process that appears to the observer to have some element of unpredictability to it. The possible values of a random variable X are called the domain of X. We use uppercase letters such as X to refer to a random variable and lowercase letters such as x to refer to a value of a random variable.

An example of a random variable is the outcome of a coin toss (the domain is the set {heads, tails}). Less obvious examples of random variables include the number of times we have to toss a coin to obtain the first head (the domain is the set of positive integers) and the flying time of a paper aeroplane in seconds (the domain is the set of positive real numbers).

The appendix defines the basic properties of univariate (single) random variables, including both probability mass functions $p(X)$ when the domain of X is finite and probability density functions $f(x)$ when the domain of X is the real-line or any interval defined on it. Basic properties of the expectation of X, $E[X] = \int x f(x) dx$, for real-valued X, are also reviewed, noting for example that since E is a linear operator we have that $E[X + Y] = E[X] + E[Y]$. These basic properties are extremely useful in allowing us to derive general principles for data analysis in a statistical context and we will refer to distributions, densities, expectation, etc., frequently throughout the remainder of this chapter.

4.3.1 Multivariate Random Variables

Since data mining often deals with multiple variables, we must also introduce the concept of a *multivariate random variable*. A multivariate random variable $\mathbf{X}$ is a set $X_1, \ldots, X_p$ of random variables. We use the m-dimensional vector $\mathbf{x} = \{x_1, \ldots, x_p\}$ to denote a set of values for $\mathbf{X}$. The *density function* $f(\mathbf{X})$ of the multivariate random variable $\mathbf{X}$ is called the *joint density func-*

tion of $\mathbf{X}$. We denote this as $f(\mathbf{X}) = f(X_1 = x_1, \ldots, X_p = x_p)$, or simply $f(x_1, \ldots, x_p)$. Similarly, we have joint probability distributions for variables taking values in a finite set. Note that $f(\mathbf{X})$ is a scalar function of p variables.

The density function of any single variable in the set $\mathbf{X}$ (or, more generally, any subset of the complete set of variables) is called a *marginal density* of the joint density. Technically, it is derived from the joint density by summing or integrating across the variables not included in the subset. For example, for a tri-variate random variable $\mathbf{X} = (X_1, X_2, X_3)$ the marginal density of $f(X_1)$ is given by $f(x_1) = \int \int f(x_1, x_2, x_3) dx_2 dx_3$.

The density of a single variable (or a subset of the complete set of variables) given (or "conditional on") particular values of the other variables is a *conditional density*. Thus we can speak of the conditional density of variable X_1 given that X_2 takes the value 6, denoted $f(x_1 \mid x_2 = 6)$. In general, the conditional density of X_1 given some value of X_2 is denoted by $f(x_1 \mid x_2)$, and is defined as

$$f(x_1 \mid x_2) = \frac{f(x_1, x_2)}{f(x_2)}. \tag{4.1}$$

For discrete-valued random variables we have equivalent definitions ($p(a_1 \mid a_2)$, etc.). We can also use mixtures of the two—e.g., a conditional probability density function $f(x_1 \mid a_1)$ for a continuous variable conditioned on a categorical variable, and a conditional probability mass function $p(a_1 \mid x_1)$ for the reverse case.

Example 4.1 Suppose we have data on purchases of products from supermarkets, with each observation (row) in the data matrix representing the products bought by one customer. Let each column represent a particular product, and associate a random variable with each column so that there is one variable per product. An observation in a given row and column has value 1 if the customer corresponding to that row bought the product from that column, and has value 0 otherwise.

Denote by A the binary random variable for a particular column, corresponding to the event "purchase of product A." A data-driven estimate of the probability that A takes value 1 is simply the fraction of customers who bought product A—i.e., n_A/n, where n is the total number of customers and n_A is the number of customers who bought product A. For example, if $n = 100,000$ and $n_A = 10,000$, an estimate of the probability that a randomly selected customer bought product A is 0.1.

Now consider a second product (a second column in the data matrix), with random variable B defined in the same way as A. Let n_B be the number of customers who bought product B; assume $n_B = 5000$ and therfore $p(B = 1) =$

0.05. Now let n_{AB} be the number of customers who purchased *both* A and B. Following the same argument as above, an estimate of $p(A = 1, B = 1)$ is given by n_{AB}/n. We can now estimate $p(B = 1|A = 1)$ as n_{AB}/n_A. Thus, for example, if $n_{AB} = 10$, we estimate $p(B = 1|A = 1)$ as $10/10,000 = 0.001$. We see from this that, while the estimated probability of a customer buying product B is 0.05, this reduces to 0.001 if we know that this customer bought product A as well. For the people in our database, the proportion of people buying B is far smaller among those who also bought A than among the people in the database as a whole (and thus smaller than among those who did not buy A). This prompts the question of whether buying A makes the purchase of B less likely in general, or whether this finding is simply an accident true only of the data we happen to have in our database. This is precisely the sort of question that we will address in the remainder of this chapter, particularly in section 4.6 on *hypothesis testing*.

Note that particular variables in the multivariate set **X** may well be related to each other in some manner. Indeed, a generic problem in data mining is to find relationships between variables. Is purchasing item A likely to be related to purchasing item B? Is detection of pattern A in the trace of a measuring instrument likely to be followed shortly afterward by a particular fault? Variables are said to be *independent* if there is no relationship between the occurrence of values of the variables; otherwise they are *dependent*. More formally, variables X and Y are independent if and only if $p(x, y) = p(x)p(y)$ for all values of X and Y. An equivalent formulation is that X and Y are independent if and only if $p(x \mid y) = p(x)$ or $p(y \mid x) = p(y)$ for all values of X and Y. (Note that these definitions hold whether each p in the expression is a probability mass function or a density function—in the latter case the variables are independent if and only if $f(x, y) = f(x)f(y)$). The second form of the definition shows that when X and Y are independent the distribution of X is the same whether or not the value of Y is known. Thus, Y carries no information about X, in the sense that the value taken by Y does not influence the probability of X taking any value. The random variables A and B in example 4.3.1 describing supermarket purchases are likely to be dependent, given the data as stated.

We can generalize these ideas to more than two variables. For example, we say that X is *conditionally independent* of Y given Z if for all values of X, Y, and Z we have that $p(x, y \mid z) = p(x \mid z)p(y \mid z)$, or equivalently $p(x \mid y, z) = p(x \mid z)$. To illustrate, suppose a person purchases **bread** (so that a random variable Z takes the value 1). Then subsequent purchases of **butter** (random variable X takes the value 1) and **cheese** (random variable

Y takes the value 1) might be modeled as being conditionally independent—the probability of purchasing cheese is unaffected by whether or not butter was purchased, once we know that bread has been purchased.

Note that conditional independence need not imply marginal (unconditional) independence. That is, the conditional independence relations above do not imply $p(x, y) = p(x)p(y)$. For example, in our illustration we might reasonably expect purchases of butter and cheese to be dependent in general (since they are both dependent on bread purchases). The reverse also applies: X and Y may be (unconditionally) independent, but conditionally dependent given a third variable Z. The subtleties of these dependence and independence relations have important consequences for data miners. In particular, even though two observed variables (such as butter and cheese) may appear to be dependent given the data, their true relationship may be masked by a third (potentially unobserved) variable (such as bread in our illustration).

> **Example 4.2** Care is needed when studying and interpreting conditional independence statements. Consider the following hypothetical example. A and B represent two different treatments, and the fractions shown in the table are the fraction of patients who recover (thus, at the top left, 2 out of 10 "old" patients receiving treatment A recover). The data have been partitioned into "old" and "young" groups, according to whether the patients were older or younger than 30.
>
> | | A | B |
> |-------|-------|-------|
> | Old | 2/10 | 30/90 |
> | Young | 48/90 | 10/10 |
>
> For each of the two age strata, treatment B appears superior to treatment A. However, now consider the overall results—obtained by aggregating the rows of the above table:
>
> | | A | B |
> |-------|--------|--------|
> | Total | 50/100 | 40/100 |
>
> Overall, in this aggregate table, treatment A seems superior to treatment B. At first glance this result seems rather mysterious (in fact, it is known as *Simpson's paradox* (Simpson, 1951)).

The apparent contradiction between the two sets of results is explained by the fact that the first set is conditional on particular age strata, while the second is unconditional. When the two conditional statements are combined, the differences in sample sizes of the four groups cause the proportions based on the larger samples (Old B and Young A) to dominate the other two proportions.

The assumption of conditional independence is widely used in the context of sequential data, for which the next value in the sequence is often independent of all of the past values in the sequence given only the current value in the sequence. In this context, conditional independence is known as the *first-order Markov* property.

The notions of independence and conditional independence (which can be viewed as a generalization of independence) are central to many of the key concepts in data analysis, as we shall see in later chapters. The assumptions of independence and conditional independence enable us to factor the joint densities of many variables into much more tractable products of simpler densities, e.g.,

$$f(x_1, \ldots, x_n) = f(x_1) \prod_{j=2}^{n} f(x_j | x_{j-1}), \tag{4.2}$$

where each variable x_j is conditionally independent of variables $x_1, \ldots, x_{j-2}$, given the value of x_j (this is an example of a first-order Markov model). In addition to the computational benefits provided by such simplifications, it also provides important modeling gains by allowing us to construct more understandable models with fewer parameters. Nonetheless, independence is a very strong assumption that is frequently violated in practice (for example, assuming sequences of letters in text are first-order Markov may not be realistic). Still, keeping in mind that our models are inevitably approximations to the real world, the benefits of appropriate independence assumptions often outweigh the alternative of building more complex but less stable models. We will return to this theme of modeling in chapter 6.

A special case of dependency is correlation, or linear dependency, as introduced in chapter 2. (Note that statistical dependence is not the same as correlation: two variables may be dependent but not linearly correlated). Variables are said to be positively correlated if high values of one variable tend to be associated with high values of the other, and to be negatively correlated if high values of one tend to be associated with low values of the other. It is important not to confuse correlation with *causation*. Two variables may be highly positively correlated without any causal relationship between them. For example, yellow-stained fingers and lung cancer may be correlated, but are causally linked only via a third variable, namely whether a person smokes or not. Similarly, human reaction time and earned income may be negatively correlated, but this does not mean that one causes the other. In this case a more convincing explanation is that a third variable, age, is causally related to both of these variables.

> **Example 4.3** A paper published in the *Journal of the American Medical Association* in 1987 (volume 257, page 785) examined the in-hospital mortality for 18,986 coronary bypass graft operations that were carried out at 77 hospitals in the United States. A regression analysis (see chapter 11) showed that hospitals that carried out more operations tended to have lower in-hospital mortality rates (even adjusting for different types of cases at different hospitals). From this pattern it was concluded that average in-hospital mortality following this type of operation would be reduced if the low-volume surgery units were closed.
>
> However, determining the relationship between quality of outcome and number of treated cases in a hospital requires a longitudinal analysis in which the sizes are deliberately manipulated. The results of large-volume hospitals might degrade if their volume was increased. The correlation between outcome and size might have arisen not because larger size induces superior performance, but because superior performance attracts more cases, or because both the number of cases and the outcome are related to some other factor.

4.4   Samples and Statistical Inference

As we noted in chapter 2, many data mining problems involve the entire population of interest, while others involve just a sample from this population. In the latter case, the samples may arise at the start—perhaps only a sample of tax-payers is selected for detailed investigation; perhaps a complete census of the population is carried out only occasionally, with just a sample being selected in most years; or perhaps the data set consists of market research results. In other cases, even though the complete data set is available, the data mining operation is carried out on a sample. This is entirely legitimate if the aim is *modeling* (see chapter 1), which seeks to represent the prominent structures of the data, and not small idiosyncratic deviations. Such structures will be preserved in a sample, provided it is not too small. However, working with a small sample of a large data set may be less appropriate if the aim is *pattern detection*: in this case the aim may be to detect small deviations from the bulk of the data, and if the sample is too small such deviations may be excluded. Moreover, if the aim is to detect records that show anomalous behavior, the analysis must be based on the entire sample.

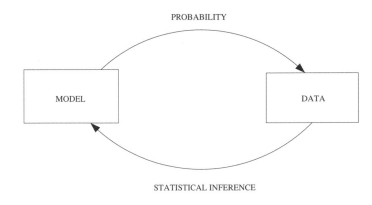

Figure 4.1 An illustration of the dual roles of probability and statistics in data analysis. Probability specifies how observed data can be generated from models. Statistical inference allows us to infer models from observed data.

It is when a sample is used that the power of inferential statistics comes into play. *Statistical inference* allows us to make statements about population structures, to estimate the size of these structures, and to state our degree of confidence in them, all on the basis of a sample. (See figure 4.1 for a simple illustration of the roles of probability and statistics). Thus, for example, we could say that our best estimate of a population value is 6.3, and that one is 95% confident that the true population value lies between 5.9 and 6.7. (Definition and interpretation of intervals such as these is a delicate point, and depends on what philosophical basis we adopt—frequentist or Bayesian, for example. We shall say more about such intervals later in this chapter.) Note the use of the word *estimate* for the population value here. If we were basing our analysis on the entire population, we would use the word *calculate*: if all the constituent numbers are known, we can actually calculate the population value, and no notion of estimation arises.

In order to make an inference about a population structure, we must have a model or pattern structure in mind: we would not be able to assess the evidence for some structure underlying the data if we never contemplated the existence of such a structure. So, for example, we might hypothesize that the value of some variable Z depends on the values of two other variables X and Y. Our model is that Z is related to X and Y. Then we can estimate the strength of these relationships in the population. (Of course, we may conclude that one or both of the relationships are of strength zero—that there is no relationship.)

Statistical inference is based on the premise that the sample has been drawn from the population in a random manner—that each member of the population had a particular probability of appearing in the sample. The model will specify the distribution function for the population—the probability that a particular value for the random variable will arise in the sample. For example, if the model indicates that the data have arisen from a Normal distribution with a mean of 0 and a standard deviation of 1, it also tells us that the probability of observing a value as large as +20 is very small. Indeed, under the assumption that the model is correct, a precise probability can be put on observing a value greater than +20. Given the model, we can generally compute the probability that an observation will fall within any interval. For samples from categorical distributions, we can estimate the probability that values equal to each of the observed values would have arisen. In general, if we have a model M for the data we can state the probability that a random sampling process would lead to the data $D = \{\mathbf{x}(1), \ldots, \mathbf{x}(n)\}$, here $\mathbf{x}(i)$ is the ith p-dimensional vector of measurements (the ith row in our $n \times p$ data matrix). This probability is expressed as $p(D \mid M)$. Often we do not make dependence on the model M explicit and simply write $p(D)$, relying on the context to make it clear. (As noted in the appendix the probability of observing any *particular* value of a variable that has a continuous cumulative distribution function is zero—particular values refer to intervals of length zero, and therefore the area under the probability density function across such an interval is zero. However, all real data actually refer to finite (if small) intervals (e.g., if someone is said to be 5 feet 11 inches tall, they are known to have a height in the interval between 5 feet 10.5 inches and 5 feet 11.5 inches). Thus it does make sense to talk of the probability of any particular data value being observed in practice.)

Let $p(\mathbf{x}(i))$ be the probability of individual i having vector measurement $\mathbf{x}(i)$ (here p could be a probability mass function or a density function, depending on the nature of $\mathbf{x}$). If we further assume that the probability of each member of the population being selected for inclusion in the sample has no effect on the probability of other members being selected (that is, that the separate observations are independent, or that the data are drawn "at random"), the overall probability of observing the entire distribution of values in the sample is simply the product of the individual probabilities:

$$p(D \mid \theta, M) = \prod_{i=1}^{n} p\left(\mathbf{x}(i) \mid \theta, M\right), \tag{4.3}$$

where M is the model and θ are the parameters of the model (assumed fixed at this point). (When regarded as a function of the parameters θ in the model M, this is called the *likelihood function*. We discuss it in detail below.) Methods have been developed to cope with situations in which observing one value alters the chance of observing another, but independence is by far the most commonly used assumption, even when it is only approximately true.

Based on this probability, we can decide how realistic the assumed model is. If our calculations suggest it is very unlikely that the assumed model would have given rise to the observed data, we might feel justified in rejecting the model; this is the principle underlying hypothesis tests (section 4.6). In hypothesis testing we decide to reject an assumed model (the null hypothesis) if the probability of the observed data arising under that model is less than some pre-specified value (often 0.01 or 0.05—the *significance level* of the test).

A similar principle is used in estimating population values for the parameters of the model. Suppose that our model indicates that the data arise from a Normal distribution with unit variance but unknown mean μ. We could propose various values for the mean, for each one calculating the probability that the observed data would have arisen if the population mean had that value. We could carry out hypothesis tests for each value, rejecting those with a low probability of having given rise to the observed data. Or we can short-cut this process and simply use the estimate of the mean with the highest probability of having generated the observed data. This value is called the maximum likelihood estimate of the mean, and the process we have described is maximum likelihood estimation (see section 4.5). The probability that a particular model would give rise to the observed data, when expressed as a function of the parameters, is called the likelihood function. This function can also be used to define an interval of likely values; we can say, for example, that, assuming our model is correct, 90% of intervals generated from a data sample in this way will contain the true value of the parameter.

4.5 Estimation

In chapter 3 we described several techniques for summarizing a given set of data. When we are concerned with inference, we want to make more general statements, statements about the entire population of values that *might* have been drawn. These are statements about the probability distribution or probability density function (or, equivalently, about the cumulative distribution function) from which the data are assumed to have arisen.

4.5.1   Desirable Properties of Estimators

In the following subsections we describe the two most important methods of estimating the parameters of a model: maximum likelihood estimation and Bayesian estimation. It is important to be aware of the differing properties of different methods so that we can adopt a method suited to our problem. Here we briefly describe some attractive properties of *estimators*. Let $\hat{\theta}$ be an estimator of a parameter θ. Since $\hat{\theta}$ is a number derived from the data, if we were to draw a different sample of data, we would obtain a different value for $\hat{\theta}$. Thus, $\hat{\theta}$ is a random variable. Therefore, it has a distribution, with different values arising as different samples are drawn. We can obtain descriptive summaries of that distribution. It will, for example, have a mean or expected value, $E[\hat{\theta}]$. Here the expectation function E is taken with respect to the true (unknown) distribution from which the data are assumed to be sampled— that is, over all possible data sets of size n that could occur weighted by their probability of occurrence.

The *bias* of $\hat{\theta}$ (a concept we introduced informally in chapter 2) is defined as

$$Bias(\theta) = E[\hat{\theta}] - \theta, \tag{4.4}$$

the difference between the expected value of the estimator $E[\hat{\theta}]$ and the true value of the parameter θ. Estimators for which $E[\hat{\theta}] = \theta$ have bias 0 are said to be *unbiased*. Such estimators show no *systematic* departure from the true parameter value on average, although for any particular single data set D we might have that $\hat{\theta}$ is far away from θ. Note that since both the sampling distribution and the true value of θ are unknown in practice, we cannot typically calculate the actual bias for a given data set. Nonetheless, the general concept of bias (and variance, below) is of fundamental importance in estimation.

Just as the bias of an estimator can be used as a measure of its quality, so also can its variance:

$$Var(\hat{\theta}) = E[\hat{\theta} - E[\hat{\theta}]]^2. \tag{4.5}$$

The variance measures the random, data-driven component of error in our estimation procedure; it reflects how sensitive our estimator will be to the idiosyncrasies of individual data sets. Note that the variance does not depend on the true value of θ—it simply measures how much our estimates will vary across different observed data sets. Thus, although the true sampling distribution is unknown, we can in principle get a data-driven estimate of the variance of an estimator, for a given value of n, by repeatedly sub-sampling our original data set and calculating the variance of the estimated $\hat{\theta}$s across these simulated samples. We can choose between estimators that have the same bias by choosing one with minimum variance. Unbiased estimators that have minimum variance are called, unsurprisingly, *best unbiased estimators*.

As an extreme example, if we were to completely ignore our data D and simply say arbitrarily that $\hat{\theta} = 1$ for every data set, then $var(\hat{\theta})$ is zero since the estimate $\hat{\theta}$ never changes as D changes—however this would be a very ineffective estimator in practice since unless we made a very lucky guess we are almost certainly wrong in our estimate of θ, i.e., there will be a non-zero (and potentially very large) bias.

The *mean squared error* of $\hat{\theta}$ is $E[(\hat{\theta}-\theta)^2]$, the mean of the squared difference between the value of the estimator and the true value of the parameter. Mean squared error has a natural decomposition as the sum of the squared bias of $\hat{\theta}$ and its variance:

$$
\begin{aligned}
E\left[(\hat{\theta} - \theta)^2\right] &= E\left[(\hat{\theta} - E[\hat{\theta}] + E[\hat{\theta}] - \theta)^2\right] \\
&= \left(E[\hat{\theta}] - \theta\right)^2 + E\left[(\hat{\theta} - E[\hat{\theta}])^2\right] \\
&= \left(Bias(\hat{\theta})\right)^2 + Var(\hat{\theta}),
\end{aligned}
\tag{4.6}
$$

where in going from the first to second lines above we took advantage of the fact that various cross-terms in the squared expression cancel out, noting (for example) that $E[\theta] = \theta$ since θ is a constant, etc. Mean squared error is a very useful criterion since it incorporates both systematic (bias) and random (variance) differences between the estimated and true values. (Of course it too is primarily of theoretical interest, since to calculate it we need to know θ, which we don't in practice). Unfortunately, bias and variance often work in different directions: modifying an estimator to reduce its bias increases its variance, and vice versa. The trick is to arrive at the best compromise. Balancing bias and variance is a central issue in data mining and we will return to this point in chapter 6 in a general context and in later chapters in more specific contexts.

There are also more subtle aspects to the use of mean squared error in estimation. For example, mean squared error treats equally large departures from θ as equally serious, regardless of whether they are above or below θ. This is appropriate for measures of location, but may not be appropriate for measures of dispersion (which, by definition, have a lower bound of zero) or for estimates of probabilities or probability densities.

Suppose that we have a sequence $\hat{\theta}_{n_1}, \ldots, \hat{\theta}_{n_m}$ of estimators, based on increasing sample sizes $n_1 \ldots, n_m$. The sequence is said to be *consistent* if the probability of the difference between $\hat{\theta}$ and the true value θ being greater than any given value tends to 0 as the sample size increases. This is clearly an attractive property (especially in data mining contexts, with large samples) since the larger the sample is the closer the estimator is likely to be to the true value (assuming that the data are coming from a particular distribution—as discussed in chapters 1 and 2, for very large databases this may not be a reasonable assumption).

4.5.2   Maximum Likelihood Estimation

Maximum likelihood estimation is the most widely used method of parameter estimation. Consider a data set of n observations $D = \{\mathbf{x}, \ldots, \mathbf{x}(n)\}$, independently sampled from the same distribution $f(\mathbf{x} \mid \theta)$ (as statisticians say, *independently and identically distributed* or *iid*). The *likelihood function* $L(\theta \mid \mathbf{x}(1), \ldots, \mathbf{x}(n))$ is the probability that the data would have arisen, for a given value of θ, regarded as a function of θ, i.e., $p(D \mid \theta)$. Note that although we are implicitly assuming a particular model M here, as defined by $f(\mathbf{x} \mid \theta)$, for convenience we do not explicitly condition on M in our likelihood definitions below—later, when we consider multiple models we will need to explicitly keep track of which model we are talking about.

Since we have assumed that the observations are independent we have

$$
\begin{aligned}
L(\theta \mid D) &= L(\theta \mid \mathbf{x}(1), \ldots, \mathbf{x}(n)) \\
&= p(\mathbf{x}(1), \ldots, \mathbf{x}(n) \mid \theta) \\
&= \prod_{i=1}^{n} f(\mathbf{x}(i) \mid \theta),
\end{aligned} \tag{4.7}
$$

which is a scalar function of θ (where θ itself may be a vector of parameters rather than a single parameter). The *likelihood of a data set* $L(\theta \mid D)$, the probability of the actual observed data D for a particular model, is a fundamental concept in data analysis. Defining a likelihood for a given problem amounts to specifying a probabilistic model for how the data were generated. It turns out that once we can state such a likelihood, the door is opened to the application of many general and powerful ideas from statistical inference. Note that since likelihood is defined as a function of θ the convention is that we

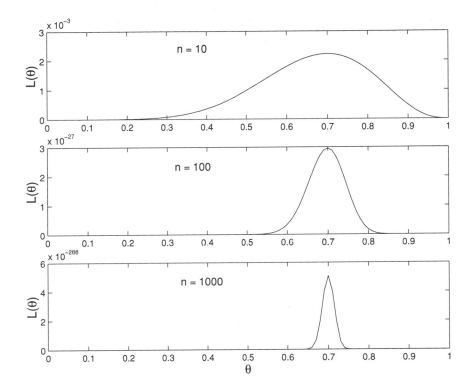

Figure 4.2 The likelihood function for three hypothetical data sets under a Binomial model: $r = 7, n = 10$ (top), $r = 70, n = 100$ (center), and $r = 700, n = 1000$ (bottom).

can drop or ignore any terms in $p(D \mid \theta)$ that do not contain θ, i.e., likelihood is only defined within an arbitrary scaling constant, so it is the shape as a function of θ that matters and not the actual values that it takes. Note also that the idd assumption above is not necessary to define a likelihood: for example, if our n observations had a Markov dependence (where each $\mathbf{x}(i)$ depends on $\mathbf{x}(i-1)$, we would define the likelihood as a product of terms such as $f(\mathbf{x}(i) \mid \mathbf{x}(i-1), \theta)$.

The value for θ for which the data has the highest probability of having arisen is the *maximum likelihood estimator* (or MLE). We will denote the maximum likelihood estimator for θ as $\hat{\theta}_{ML}$.

Example 4.4 Customers in a supermarket either purchase or do not purchase milk. Suppose we want an estimate of the proportion of customers purchasing milk, based on a sample $x(1), \ldots, x(1000)$ of 1000 randomly drawn observations from the database. Here $x(i)$ takes the value 1 if the ith customer in the sample does purchase milk and 0 if he or she does not. A simple model here would be the observations independently follow a Binomial distribution (described in the appendix) with unknown parameter $0 \leq \theta \leq 1$; that is, θ is the probability that milk is purchased by a random customer. Under the usual assumption of conditional independence given the model, the likelihood can be written as

$$L(\theta \mid x(1), \ldots, x(1000)) = \prod_i \theta^{x(i)}(1-\theta)^{1-x(i)} = \theta^r(1-\theta)^{1000-r},$$

where r is the number among the 1000 who do purchase milk. Taking logs of this yields

$$l(\theta) = \log L(\theta) = r \log \theta + (1000 - r) \log(1 - \theta),$$

which, after differentiating and setting to zero, yields

$$\frac{r}{\theta} - \left(\frac{1000 - r}{1 - \theta}\right) = 0,$$

from which we obtain $\hat{\theta}_{ML} = r/1000$. Thus, the proportion purchasing milk is in fact also the maximum-likelihood estimate of θ under this Binomial model.

In figure 4.2 we plot the likelihood as a function of θ for three hypothetical data sets under this Binomial model. The data sets correspond to 7 milk purchases, 70 milk purchases, and 700 milk purchases out of $n = 10$, $n = 100$, and $n = 1000$, total purchases respectively. The peak of the likelihood function is at the same value, $\theta = 0.7$ in each case, but the uncertainty about the true value of θ (as reflected in the "spread" of the likelihood function) becomes much smaller as n increases (i.e., as we obtain a large customer database). Note that the absolute value of the likelihood function is not relevant; only its shape is of importance.

Example 4.5 Suppose we have assumed that our sample $x(1), \ldots, x(n)$ of n data points has arisen independently from a Normal distribution with unit variance and unknown mean θ. This sort of situation can arise when the source of uncertainty is measurement error; we may know that the results have a certain variance (here rescaled to 1), but not know the mean value for the object that is being repeatedly measured. Then the likelihood function for θ is

$$
\begin{aligned}
L(\theta \mid x(1), \ldots, x(n)) &= \prod_{i=1}^{n} (2\pi)^{-1/2} \exp\left(-\frac{1}{2}(x(i) - \theta)^2\right) \\
&= (2\pi)^{-n/2} \exp\left(-\frac{1}{2} \sum_{i=1}^{n}(x(i) - \theta)^2\right),
\end{aligned}
$$

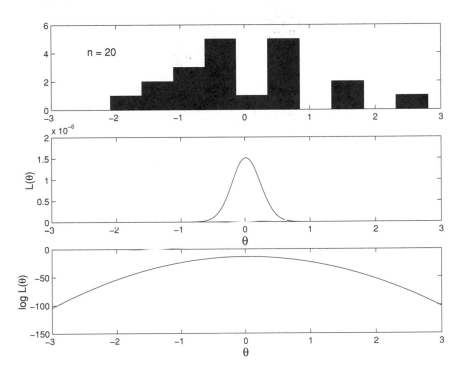

Figure 4.3 The likelihood as a function of θ for a sample of 20 data points from a Normal density with a true mean of 0 and a known standard deviation of 1: (a) a histogram of 20 data points generated from the true model (top), (b) the likelihood function for θ (center), and (c) the log-likelihood function for θ (bottom).

with log-likelihood defined as

$$l(\theta \mid x(1), \ldots, x(n)) = -\frac{n}{2} \log 2\pi - \frac{1}{2} \sum_{i=1}^{n} (x(i) - \theta)^2, \qquad (4.8)$$

To find the MLE we set the derivative $\frac{d}{d\theta} l(\theta \mid x(1), \ldots, x(n))$ to 0 and get

$$\sum_{i=1}^{n} (x(i) - \theta) = 0.$$

Hence, the maximum likelihood estimator $\hat{\theta}_{ML}$ for θ is $\hat{\theta}_{ML} = \sum_i x(i)/n$, the sample mean.

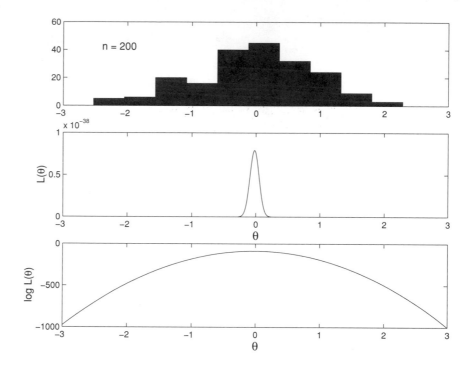

Figure 4.4   The likelihood function for the same model as in figure 4.3 but with 200 data points: (a) a histogram of the 200 data points generated from the true model (top), (b) the likelihood function for θ (center), and (c) the log-likelihood function for θ (bottom).

Figure 4.3 shows both the likelihood function $L(\theta)$ and the log-likelihood $l(\theta) = \log L(\theta)$ as a function of θ for a sample of 20 data points from a Normal density with a true mean of 0 and a known standard deviation of 1. Figure 4.4 shows the same type of plot but with 200 data points. Note how the likelihood function is peaked around the value of the true mean at 0. Also note (as in the Binomial example) how the likelihood function narrows as more data becomes available, reflecting decreasing support from the data for values of θ that are not close to 0.

Example 4.6 A useful general concept in statistical estimation is the notion of a *sufficient statistic*. Loosely speaking, we can define a quantity $s(D)$ as a sufficient statistic for θ if the likelihood $L(\theta)$ only depends on the data through $s(D)$. Thus, in the Binomial model above, the total number of "successes" r

(the number of people who purchase milk) is a sufficient statistic for the Binomial parameter θ. It is sufficient in the sense that the likelihood is only a function of r (assuming n is known already). Knowing which particular customers purchased milk (which particular rows in the data matrix have 1's in the milk column) is irrelevant from the point of view of our Binomial model, once we know the sum total r. Similarly, for the example above involving the estimation of the mean of a Normal distribution, the sum of the observations $\sum_{i=1}^{n} x(i)$ is a sufficient statistic for the likelihood of the mean (keeping in mind that the likelihood is only defined as a function of θ and all other terms can be dropped).

For massive data sets this idea of sufficient statistics can be quite useful in practice—instead of working with the full data set we can simply compute and store the sufficient statistics, knowing that these are sufficient for likelihood-based estimation. For example, if we are gathering large volumes of data on a daily basis (e.g., Web logs) we can in principle just update the sufficient statistics nightly and throw the raw data away. Unfortunately, however, sufficient statistics often do not exist for many of the more flexible model forms that we like to use in data mining applications, such as trees, mixture models, and so forth, that are discussed in detail later in this book. Nonetheless, for simpler models, sufficient statistics are a very useful concept.

Maximum likelihood estimators are intuitively and mathematically attractive; for example, they are consistent estimators in the sense defined earlier. Moreover, if $\hat{\theta}_{ML}$ is the MLE of a parameter θ, then $g(\hat{\theta}_{ML})$ is the MLE of the function $g(\theta)$, though some care needs to be exercised if g is not a one-to-one function. On the other hand, nothing is perfect—maximum likelihood estimators are often biased (depending on the parameter and the underlying model), although this bias may be extremely small for large data sets, often scaling as $O(1/n)$.

For simple problems (where "simple" refers to the mathematical structure of the problem, and not to the number of data points, which can be large), MLEs can be found using differential calculus. In practice, the log-likelihood $l(\theta)$ is usually maximized (as in the Binomial and Normal density examples above), since this replaces the awkward product in the definition with a sum; this process leads to the same result as maximizing $L(\theta)$ directly because the logarithm is a monotonic function. Of course we are often interested in models that have more than one parameter (models such as neural networks (chapter 11) can have hundreds or thousands of parameters). The univariate definition of likelihood generalizes directly to the multivariate case, but in this situation the likelihood is a *mulutivariate function* of d parameters (that is, a scalar-valued function defined on a d-dimensional parameter space). Since d can be large, finding the maximum of this d-dimensional function can be quite challenging if no closed-form solution exists. We will return to this topic of *optimization* in detail in chapter 8 where we discuss iterative search methods. Multiple maxima can present a difficult problem (which is why stochastic optimization methods are often necessary), as can situations in which optima occur at the boundaries of the parameter space.

> **Example 4.7** *Simple linear regression* is widely used in data mining. This was mentioned briefly in chapter 1 and is discussed again in detail in chapter 11. In its simplest form it relates two variables: X, a *predictor* or *explanatory* variable, and Y, a *response* variable. The relationship is assumed to take the form $Y = a + bX + e$, where a and b are parameters and e is a random variable assumed to come from a Normal distribution with a mean of 0 and a variance of σ^2, and we can write $e = Y - (a + bX)$. Here the data consists of a set of pairs $D = \{(x(1), y(1)), \ldots, (x(n), y(n))\}$ and the probability density function of the response data given the explanatory data is $f(y(1), \ldots, y(n) \mid x(1), \ldots, x(n), a, b)$. We are interested not in modeling the distribution of the xs, but rather in modeling $f(y|x)$.
>
> Thus, the likelihood (or more precisely, conditional likelihood) function for this model can be written as
>
> $$L(a, b|D) = \prod_{i=1}^{n} \frac{1}{\sigma\sqrt{2\pi}} \exp\left(-0.5(y(i) - (a + bx(i))/\sigma)^2\right)$$
>
> $$= \frac{1}{(2\pi\sigma^2)^{n/2}} \exp\left(-0.5/\sigma^2 \sum_{i=1}^{n} (y(i) - (a + bx(i)))^2\right).$$
>
> To find the maximum likelihood estimators of a and b, we can take logs and discard terms that do not involve either a or b. This yields
>
> $$\sum_{i}^{n} (y(i) - (a + bx(i)))^2.$$
>
> Thus, we can estimate a and b by finding those values that minimize the sum of squared differences between the predicted values $a + bx(i)$ and the observed values $y(i)$. Such a procedure—minimizing a sum of squares—is ubiquitous in data mining, and goes under the name of the *least squares method*. The sum of squares criterion is of great historical importance, with roots going back to Gauss and beyond. At first it might seem arbitrary to choose a sum of squares (why not a sum of absolute values, for example?), but the above shows how the least squares choice arises naturally from the choice of a Normal distribution for the error term in the model.

Up to this now we have been discussing *point estimates,* single number esti-mates of the parameter in question. A point estimate is "best" in some sense, but it conveys no idea of the uncertainty associated with it—perhaps there was a large number of almost equally good estimates, or perhaps this esti-mate was by far the best. Interval estimates provide this sort of information. In place of a single number they give an interval with a specified degree of confidence that this interval contains the unknown parameter. Such an in-terval is called a *confidence interval,* and the upper and lower limits of the interval are called *confidence limits.* Interpretation of confidence intervals is rather subtle. Here, since we are assuming that θ is unknown but fixed, it does not make sense to say that θ has a certain probability of lying within a given interval: it either does or it does not. However, it does make sense to say that an interval calculated by the given procedure contains θ with a certain probability: after all, the interval is calculated from the sample, and is thus a random variable.

Example 4.8 The following example is deliberately artificial to keep the expla-nation simple. Suppose the data consist of 100 independent observations from a Normal distribution with unknown mean μ and known variance σ^2, and we want a 95% confidence interval for μ. That is, given the data $x(1), \ldots, x(n)$, we want to find a lower limit $l(x)$ and an upper limit $u(x)$ such that $P(\mu \in [l(x), u(x)]) = 0.95$.

The distribution of the sample mean $\bar{x}$ in this situation (which is also the max-imum likelihood estimate of the mean, $\hat{\mu}_{ML}$) is known to follow a Normal distribution with a mean of μ and a variance of $\sigma^2/100$, and hence standard deviation of $\sigma/10$. We also know, from the properties of the Normal distribu-tion (see the appendix), that 95% of the probability lies within 1.96 standard deviations of the mean. Hence,

$$P(\mu - 1.96\sigma/10 \leq \bar{x} \leq \mu + 1.96\sigma/10) = 0.95.$$

This can be rewritten as

$$P(\bar{x} - 1.96\sigma/10 \leq \mu \leq \bar{x} + 1.96\sigma/10) = 0.95.$$

Thus, $l(x) = \bar{x} - 1.96\sigma/10$ and $u(x) = \bar{x} + 1.96\sigma/10$ define a suitable 95% confidence interval.

Frequently confidence intervals are based on the assumption that the sam-ple statistic has a roughly Normal distribution. This is often realistic: the *central limit theorem* tells us that the distribution of many statistics can be ap-proximated well by a Normal distribution, especially if the sample size is large. Using this approximation, we find an interval in which the statistic has a known probability of lying, given the unknown true parameter value, θ, and invert it to find an interval for the unknown parameter. In order to apply this approach, we need an estimate of the standard deviation of the estimator $\hat{\theta}$. One way to derive such an estimate is the *bootstrap* method.

Example 4.9

Many bootstrap methods, of gradually increasing sophistication and complexity, have been developed over the last two decades. The basic idea is as follows. The data originally arose from a distribution $F(X)$, and we wish to make some statement about this distribution. However, we have only a sample of data $(x(1), ..., x(n))$, which we may denote by $\hat{F}(X)$. What we do is draw a subsample, $\breve{F}(X)$, from $\hat{F}(X)$, and act as if $\hat{F}(X)$ were the real distribution. We can repeat this many times, computing a statistic for each of these subsamples. This process gives us information on the sampling properties of statistics calculated from samples drawn from $\hat{F}(X)$, which we hope are similar to the sampling properties of statistics calculated from samples drawn from $F(X)$.

To illustrate, consider an early approach to estimating the performance of a predictive classification rule. As we have discussed above, evaluating performance of a classification rule simply by reclassifying the data used to design it is unwise—it is likely to lead to optimistically biased estimates. Suppose that e_A is the estimate of misclassification rate obtained by the simple resubstitution process of estimating the classification error on the same data as was used to estimate the parameters of the classification model. We really want to estimate e_C, the "true" misclassification rate which we expect to achieve on future objects. The difference between these is $(e_C - e_A)$. If we could estimate this difference, we could adjust e_A to yield a better estimate. In fact, we can estimate this difference, as follows. Suppose we regard $\hat{F}(X)$ as the true distribution and draw from it a subsample—$\breve{F}(X)$. Now, acting as if $\hat{F}(X)$ were the true distribution, we can build a rule based on the data in the subsample $\breve{F}(X)$ and apply it both to $\hat{F}(X)$ and to $\breve{F}(X)$. The difference in performance in these two situations will give us an estimate of the difference $(e_C - e_A)$. To reduce any effects arising from the randomness of the sampling procedure, we repeat the subsampling many times and average the results. The final result is an estimate of the difference $(e_C - e_A)$ that can be added to the value of e_A obtained by resubstituting the data $\hat{F}(X)$ into the rule based on $\hat{F}(X)$, to yield an estimate of the true misclassification rate e_C.

4.5.3   Bayesian Estimation

In the frequentist approach to inference described so far the parameters of a population are fixed but unknown, and the data comprise a random sample from that population (since the sample was drawn in a random way). The intrinsic variability thus lies in the data $D = \{\mathbf{x}(1), \ldots, \mathbf{x}(n)\}$. In contrast, Bayesian statistics treats the data as known—after all, they have been observed and recorded—and the parameters θ as random variables. Thus, whereas frequentists regard a parameter θ as a fixed but unknown quantity, Bayesians regard θ as having a distribution of possible values and see the observed data as possibly shedding light on this distribution. $p(\theta)$ reflects our degree of belief on where the true (unknown) parameters θ may be. If $p(\theta)$ is very peaked about some value of θ then we are very sure about our convictions (although of course we may be entirely wrong!). If $p(\theta)$ is very broad and flat (and this is the more typical case) then we are expressing a prior belief that is less certain on the location of θ.

Note that while the term *Bayesian* has a fairly precise meaning in statistics, it has sometimes been used in a somewhat looser manner in the computer science and pattern recognition literature to refer to the use of any form of probabilistic model in data analysis. In this text we adopt the more standard and widespread statistical definition, which is described below.

Before the data are analyzed, the distribution of the probabilities that θ will take different values is known as the *prior* distribution $p(\theta)$. Analysis of the data D leads to modification of this distribution to take into account the information in the empirical data, yielding the *posterior* distribution, $p(\theta \mid D)$. The modification from prior to posterior is carried out by means of a theorem named after Thomas Bayes:

$$p(\theta \mid D) = \frac{p(D \mid \theta)p(\theta)}{p(D)} = \frac{p(D \mid \theta)p(\theta)}{\int_{\psi} p(D \mid \psi)p(\psi)d\psi}. \tag{4.9}$$

Note that this updating procedure leads to a *distribution*, rather than a single value, for θ. However, the distribution can be used to yield a single value estimate. We could, for example, take the mean of the posterior distribution, or its mode (the latter technique is known as the *maximum a posteriori* method, or MAP). If we choose the prior $p(\theta)$ in a specific manner (e.g., $p(\theta)$ is uniform over some range), the MAP and maximum likelihood estimates of θ may well coincide (since in effect the prior is "flat" and prefers no one value of θ over any other). In this sense, maximum likelihood can be viewed as a special case of the MAP procedure, which in turn is a restricted ("point estimate") form of Bayesian estimation.

For a given set of data D and a particular model, the denominator in equation 4.9 is a constant, so we can alternatively write the expression as

$$p(\theta \mid D) \propto p(D \mid \theta)p(\theta).$$ (4.10)

Here we see that the posterior distribution of θ given D (that is, the distribution conditional on having observed the data D) is proportional to the product of the prior $p(\theta)$ and the likelihood $p(D \mid \theta)$. If we have only weak beliefs about the likely value of the parameter before collecting the data, we will want to choose a prior that spreads the probability widely (for example, a Normal distribution with large variance). In any case, the larger the set of observed data, the more the likelihood dominates the posterior distribution, and the lower the importance of the particular shape of the prior.

Example 4.10 Consider example 4.4 once again involving the proportion of customers who purchase milk, where we consider a single binary variable X and wish to estimate $\theta = p(X = 1)$. A widely used prior for a parameter θ that varies between 0 and 1 is the *Beta* distribution, defined as

$$p(\theta) \propto \theta^{\alpha-1}(1 - \theta)^{\beta-1}$$ (4.11)

where $\alpha > 0, \beta > 0$ are the two parameters of this model. It is straightforward to show that $E[\theta] = \frac{\alpha}{\alpha+\beta}$, that the mode of θ is $\frac{\alpha-1}{\alpha+\beta-2}$, and the variance is $var(\theta) = \frac{\alpha\beta}{(\alpha+\beta)^2(\alpha+\beta+1)}$. Thus, if we assume for example that α and β are chosen to be both greater than 1, we can see that the relative sizes of α and β control the location of both the mean and the mode: if $\alpha = \beta$ then the mean and the mode are at 0. If $\alpha < \beta$ then the mode is less than 0.5, and so forth.

Similarly, the variance is inversely proportional to $\alpha + \beta$: the size of the sum $\alpha+\beta$ controls the "narrowness" of the prior $p(\theta)$. If α and β are relatively large, we will have a relatively narrow peaked prior about the mode. In this manner, we can choose α and β to reflect any prior beliefs we might have about the parameter θ.

Recall from example 4.4 that the likelihood function for θ under the Binomial model can be written as

$$L(\theta \mid D) = \theta^r(1 - \theta)^{n-r},$$ (4.12)

where r is the number of 1's in the n total observations. We see that the Beta and Binomial likelihoods are similar in form: the Beta looks like a Binomial likelihood with $\alpha - 1$ prior successes and $\beta - 1$ prior failures. Thus, in effect, we can think of $\alpha + \beta - 2$ as the equivalent sample size for the prior, i.e., it is as if our Beta prior is based on this many prior observations.

Combining the likelihood and the prior, we get

$$
\begin{aligned}
p(\theta|D) \quad &\propto \quad p(D|\theta)p(\theta) \\
&= \quad \theta^r(1-\theta)^{n-r}\theta^{\alpha-1}(1-\theta)^{\beta-1} \\
&= \quad \theta^{r+\alpha-1}(1-\theta)^{n-r+\beta-1}.
\end{aligned}
\tag{4.13}
$$

This is conveniently in the form of another Beta distribution, i.e., the posterior on θ, $p(\theta|D)$, is itself another Beta distribution but with parameters $r+\alpha$ and $n-r+\beta$.

Thus, for example, the mean of this posterior distribution $p(\theta|D)$ is $\frac{r+\alpha}{n+\alpha+\beta}$. This is very intuitive. If $\alpha=\beta=0$ we get the standard MLE of $\frac{r}{n}$. Otherwise, we get a modified estimate, where not all weight is placed on the data alone (on r and n). For example, in data mining practice, it is common to use the heuristic estimate of $\frac{r+1}{n+2}$ for estimates of probabilities, rather than the MLE, corresponding in effect to using a point estimate based on posterior mean and a Beta prior with $\alpha=\beta=1$. This has the effect of "smoothing" the estimate away from the extreme values of 0 and 1. For example, consider a supermarket where we wanted to estimate the probability of a particular product being purchased, but in the available sample D we had $r=0$ (perhaps the product is purchased relatively rarely and no-one happened to buy it in the day we drew a sample). The MLE estimate in this case would be 0, whereas the posterior mean would be $\frac{1}{n+2}$, which is close to 0 for large n but allows for a small (but non-zero) probability in the model for that the product is purchased on an average day.

In general, with high-dimensional data sets (i.e., large p) we can anticipate that certain events will not occur in our observed data set D. Rather than committing to the MLE estimate of a probability $\theta=0$, which is equivalent to stating that the event is impossible according to the model, it is often more prudent to use a Bayesian estimate of the form described here. For the supermarket example, the prior $p(\theta)$ might come from historical data at the same supermarket, or from other stores in the same geographical location. This allows information from other related analyses (in time or space) to be leveraged, and leads to the more general concept of Bayesian hierarchical models (which is somewhat beyond the scope of this text).

One of the primary distinguishing characteristics of the Bayesian approach is the avoidance of so-called *point-estimates* (such as a maximum likelihood estimate of a parameter) in favor of retaining full knowledge of all uncertainty involved in a problem (e.g., calculating a full posterior distribution on θ).

As an example, consider the Bayesian approach to making a prediction about a new data point $\mathbf{x}(n+1)$, a data point not in our training data set D.

Here x might be the value of the Dow-Jones financial index at the daily closing of the stock-market and $n + 1$ is one day in the future. Instead of using a point estimate for $\hat{\theta}$ in our model for prediction (as we would in a maximum likelihood or MAP framework), the Bayesian approach is to average over all possible values of θ, weighted by their posterior probability $p(\theta \mid D)$:

$$
\begin{aligned}
p(\mathbf{x}(n+1) \mid D) &= \int p(\mathbf{x}(n+1), \theta \mid D)d\theta \\
&= \int p(\mathbf{x}(n+1) \mid \theta)p(\theta \mid D)d\theta, \qquad (4.14)
\end{aligned}
$$

since $\mathbf{x}(n + 1)$ is conditionally independent of the training data D, given θ, by definition. In fact, we can take this further and also average over different models, using a technique known as Bayesian model averaging. Naturally, all of this averaging can entail considerably more computation than the maximum likelihood approach. This is a primary reason why Bayesian methods have become practical only in recent years (at least for small-scale data sets). For large-scale problems and high-dimensional data, fully Bayesian analysis methods can impose significant computational burdens.

Note that the structure of equations 4.9 and 4.10 enables the distribution to be updated sequentially. For example, after we build a model with data D_1, we can update it with further data D_2:

$$
p(\theta \mid D_1, D_2) \propto p(D_2 \mid \theta)p(D_1 \mid \theta)p(\theta). \qquad (4.15)
$$

This sequential updating property is very attractive for large sets of data, since the result is independent of the order of the data (provided, of course, that D_1 and D_2 are conditionally independent given the underlying model p).

The denominator in equation 4.9, $p(D) = \int_{\psi} p(D \mid \psi)p(\psi)d\psi$, is called the *predictive distribution* of D, and represents our predictions about the value of D. It includes our uncertainty about θ, via the prior $p(\theta)$, and our uncertainty about D when θ is known, via $p(D \mid \theta)$. The predictive distribution changes as new data are observed, and can be useful for model checking: if observed data D have only a small probability according to the predictive distribution, that distribution is unlikely to be correct.

Example 4.11 Suppose we believe that a single data point x comes from a Normal distribution with unknown mean θ and known variance α—that is, $x \sim N(\theta, \alpha)$. Now suppose our prior distribution for θ is $\theta \sim N(\theta_0, \alpha_0)$, with known θ_0 and α_0. Then

$$
\begin{aligned}
p(\theta \mid x) &\propto p(x \mid \theta)p(\theta) \\
&= \frac{1}{\sqrt{2\pi\alpha}} \exp(\frac{-1}{2\alpha}(x - \theta)^2) \frac{1}{\sqrt{2\pi\alpha_0}} \exp(\frac{-1}{2\alpha_0}(\theta - \theta_0)^2) \\
&\propto \exp(-\frac{1}{2}\theta^2(1/\alpha_0 + 1/\alpha) + \theta(\theta_0/\alpha_0 + x/\alpha)).
\end{aligned}
$$

The mathematics here looks horribly complicated (a fairly common occurrence with Bayesian methods), but consider the following reparameterization. Let

$$
\alpha_1 = (\alpha_0^{-1} + \alpha^{-1})^{-1}
$$

and

$$
\theta_1 = \alpha_1(\theta_0/\alpha_0 + x/\alpha).
$$

After some algebraic manipulations we get

$$
p(\theta \mid x) \propto \exp(-\frac{1}{2}\theta^2/\alpha_1 + \theta\theta_1/\alpha_1) \propto \exp(-\frac{1}{2}(\theta - \theta_1)^2/\alpha_1).
$$

Since this is a probability density function for θ, it must integrate to unity. Hence the posterior on θ has the form

$$
p(\theta \mid x) = \frac{1}{\sqrt{2\pi\alpha_1}} \exp(-\frac{1}{2}(\theta - \theta_1)^2/\alpha_1).
$$

This is a Normal distribution $N(\theta_1, \alpha_1)$. Thus the Normal prior distribution has been updated to yield a Normal posterior distribution and therefore the complicated mathematics can be avoided. Given a Normal prior for the mean and data arising from a Normal distribution as above, we can obtain the posterior merely by computing the updated parameters. Moreover, the updating of the parameters is not as messy as it might at first seem.

Reciprocals of variances are called *precisions*. Here $1/\alpha_1$, the precision of the updated distribution, is simply the sum of the precisions of the prior and the data distributions. This is perfectly reasonable: adding data to the prior should decrease the variance, or increase the precision. Likewise, the updated mean, θ_1, is simply a weighted sum of the prior mean and the datum x, with weights that depend on the precisions of those two values.

When there are n data points, with the situation described above, the posterior is again Normal, now with updated parameter values

$$
\alpha_1 = (1/\alpha_0 + n/\alpha)^{-1}
$$

and

$$
\theta_1 = \alpha_1(\theta_0/\alpha_0 + \bar{x}n/\alpha).
$$

The choice of prior distribution can play an important role in Bayesian analysis (more for small samples than for large samples as mentioned earlier). The prior distribution represents our initial belief that the parameter takes different values. The more confident we are that it takes particular values, the more closely the prior will be bunched around those values. The less confident we are, the larger the dispersion of the prior. In the case of a Normal mean, if we had no idea of the true value, we would want to use a prior that gave equal probability to each possible value, i.e., a prior that was perfectly flat or that had infinite variance. This would not correspond to any *proper* density function (which must have some non-zero values and which must integrate to unity). Still, it is sometimes useful to adopt *improper* priors that are uniform throughout the space of the parameter. We can think of such priors as being essentially flat in all regions where the parameter might conceivably occur. Even so, there remains the difficulty that priors that are uniform for a particular parameter are not uniform for a nonlinear transformation of that parameter.

Another issue, which might be seen as either a difficulty or a strength of Bayesian inference, is that priors show an individual's prior belief in the various possible values of a parameter—and individuals differ. It is entirely possible that your prior will differ from mine and therefore we will probably obtain different results from an analysis. In some circumstances this is fine, but in others it is not. One way to overcome this problem is to use a so-called *reference* prior, a prior that is agreed upon by convention. A common form of reference prior is *Jeffrey's* prior. To define this, we first need to define the *Fisher information*:

$$I(\theta \mid \mathbf{x}) = -E\left[\frac{\partial^2 \log L(\theta \mid x)}{\partial \theta^2}\right] \tag{4.16}$$

for a scalar parameter θ—that is, the negative of the expectation of the second derivative of the log-likelihood. Essentially this measures the curvature or flatness of the likelihood function. The flatter a likelihood function is, the less the information it provides about the parameter values. Jeffrey's prior is then defined as

$$p(\theta) \propto \sqrt{I(\theta \mid \mathbf{x})}. \tag{4.17}$$

This is a convenient reference prior since if $\phi = \phi(\theta)$ is some function of θ, this has a prior proportional to $\sqrt{I(\phi \mid \mathbf{x})}$. This means that a consistent prior will result no matter how the parameter is transformed.

The distributions in the examples display began with a Beta or Normal prior and ended with a Beta or Normal posterior. *Conjugate families* of distributions satisfy this property in general: the prior distribution and posterior distribution belong to the same family. The advantage of using conjugate families is that the complicated updating process can be replaced by a simple updating of the parameters.

We have already remarked that it is straightforward to obtain single point estimates from the posterior distribution. Interval estimates are also easy to obtain—integration of the posterior distribution over a region gives the estimated probability that the parameter lies in that region. When a single parameter is involved and the region is an interval, the result is a *credibility interval*. The shortest possible credibility interval is the interval containing a given probability (say 90%) such that the posterior density is highest over the interval. Given that one is prepared to accept the fundamental Bayesian notion that the parameter is a random variable, the interpretation of such intervals is much more straightforward than the interpretation of frequentist confidence intervals.

Of course, it is a rare model that involves only one parameter. Typically models involve several or many parameters. In this case we can find joint posterior distributions for all parameters simultaneously or for individual (sets of) parameters alone. We can also study conditional distributions for some parameters given fixed values of the others. Until recently, Bayesian statistics provided an interesting philosophical viewpoint on inference and induction, but was of little practical value; carrying out the integrations required to obtain marginal distributions of individual parameters from complicated joint distributions was too difficult (only in rare cases could analytic solutions be found, and these often required the imposition of undesirable assumptions). However, in the last 10 years or so this area has experienced something of a revolution. Stochastic estimation methods, based on drawing random samples from the estimated distributions, enable properties of the distributions of the parameters to be estimated and studied. These methods, called Markov chain Monte Carlo (MCMC) methods are discussed again briefly in chapter 8.

It is worth repeating that the primary characteristic of Bayesian statistics lies in its treatment of uncertainty. The Bayesian philosophy is to make all uncertainty explicit in any data analysis, including uncertainty about the estimated parameters as well as any uncertainty about the model. In the maximum likelihood approach, a point estimate of a parameter is often considered the primary goal, but a Bayesian analyst will report a full posterior distribution on the parameter as well as a posterior on model structures. Bayesian prediction consists of taking weighted averages over parameter values and model structures (where the weights are proportional to the likelihood of the parameter or model given the data, times the prior). In principle, this weighted averaging can provide more accurate predictions than the alternative (and widely used) approach of conditioning on a single model using point estimates of the parameters. However, in practice, the Bayesian approach requires estimation of the averaging weights, which in high-dimensional problems can be difficult. In addition, a weighted average over parameters or models is less likely to be interpretable if description is a primary goal.

4.6 Hypothesis Testing

Although data mining is primarily concerned with looking for unsuspected features in data (as opposed testing specific hypotheses that are formed before we see the data), in practice we often do want to test specific hypotheses (for example, if our data mining algorithm generates a potentially interesting hypothesis that we would like to explore further).

In many situations we want to see whether the data support some idea about the value of a parameter. For example, we might want to know if a new treatment has an effect greater than that of the standard treatment, or if two variables are related in a population. Since we are often unable to measure these for an entire population, we must base our conclusions on a samples. Statistical tools for exploring such hypotheses are called *hypothesis tests*.

4.6.1 Classical Hypothesis Testing

The basic principle of hypothesis tests is as follows. We begin by defining two complementary hypotheses: the *null hypothesis* and the *alternative hypothesis*. Often the null hypothesis is some point value (e.g., that the effect in question has value zero—that there is no treatment difference or regression slope) and the alternative hypothesis is simply the complement of the null hypothesis. Suppose, for example, that we are trying to draw conclusions about a parameter θ. The null hypothesis, denoted by H_0, might state that $\theta = \theta_0$, and the alternative hypothesis (H_1) might state that $\theta \neq \theta_0$. Using the observed data, we calculate a statistic (what form of statistic is best depends on the nature of the hypothesis being tested; examples are given below). The statistic would vary from sample to sample—it would be a random variable. If we assume that the null hypothesis is correct, then we can determine the expected distribution for the chosen statistic, and the observed value of the statistic would be one point from that distribution. If the observed value were way out in the tail of the distribution, we would have to conclude either that an unlikely event had occurred or that the null hypothesis was not, in fact, true. The more extreme the observed value, the less confidence we would have in the null hypothesis.

We can put numbers on this procedure. Looking at the top tail of the distribution of the statistic (the distribution based on the assumption that the null hypothesis is true), we can find those potential values that, taken together, have a probability of 0.05 of occurring. These are extreme values of the statistic—values that deviate quite substantially from the bulk of the values, assuming the null hypothesis is true. If this extreme observed value did lie in this top region, we could *reject* the null hypothesis "at the 5% level": only 5% of the time would we expect to see a result in this region—as extreme as this—if the null hypothesis were correct. For obvious reasons, this region is called the *rejection region* or *critical region*. Of course, we might not merely be interested in deviations from the null hypothesis in one direction. That is, we might be interested in the lower tail, as well as the upper tail of the distribution. In this case we might define the rejection region as the union of the test statistic values in the lowest 2.5% of the probability distribution and the test statistic values in the uppermost 2.5% of the probability distribution. This would be a *two-tailed* test, as opposed to the previously described *one-tailed* test. The size of the rejection region, known as the *significance level* of the test, can be chosen at will. Common values are 1%, 5%, and 10%.

We can compare different test procedures in terms of their *power*. The power of a test is the probability that it will correctly reject a false null hypothesis. To evaluate the power of a test, we need a specific alternative hypothesis so we can calculate the probability that the test statistic will fall in the rejection region if the alternative hypothesis is true.

A fundamental question is how to find a good test statistic for a particular problem. One strategy is to use the *likelihood ratio*. The likelihood ratio statistic used to test the hypothesis $H_0 : \theta = \theta_0$ against the alternative $H_1 : \theta \neq \theta_0$ is defined as

$$\lambda = \frac{L(\theta_0 \mid D)}{\sup_\psi L(\psi \mid D)}, \tag{4.18}$$

where $D = \{\mathbf{x}(1), \ldots, \mathbf{x}(n)\}$. That is, the ratio of the likelihood when $\theta = \theta_0$ to the largest value of the likelihood when θ is unconstrained. Clearly, the null hypothesis should be rejected when λ is small. This procedure can easily be generalized to situations in which the null hypothesis is not a point hypothesis but includes a set of possible values for θ.

Example 4.12 Suppose that we have a sample of n points independently drawn from a Normal distribution with unknown mean and unit variance, and that we wish to test the hypothesis that the mean has a value of 0. The likelihood under this (null hypothesis) assumption is

$$L\left(0 \mid x(1), \ldots, x(n)\right) = \prod_i p(x(i) \mid 0) = \prod_i \frac{1}{\sqrt{2\pi}} \exp\left(-\frac{1}{2}(x(i) - 0)^2\right).$$

The maximum likelihood estimator of the mean of a Normal distribution is the sample mean, so the unconstrained maximum likelihood is

$$L\left(\mu \mid x(1), \ldots, x(n)\right) = \prod_i p(x(i) \mid \mu) = \prod_i \frac{1}{\sqrt{2\pi}} \exp\left(-\frac{1}{2}(x(i) - \bar{x})^2\right).$$

The ratio of these simplifies to

$$\lambda = \exp\left(-n(\bar{x} - 0)^2/2\right).$$

Therefore, our rejection region is thus $\{\lambda \mid \lambda \leq c\}$ for a suitably chosen value of c. This expression can be rewritten as

$$\bar{x} \geq \sqrt{-\frac{2}{n} \ln c},$$

where $\bar{x} = \frac{1}{n}\sum_i x(i)$ is the sample mean. Thus, the test statistic $\bar{x}$ has to be compared with a constant.

Certain types of tests are used very frequently. These include tests of differences between means, tests to compare variances, and tests to compare an observed distribution with a hypothesized distribution (so-called *goodness-of-fit tests*). The common *t*-test of the difference between the means of two independent groups is described in the display below. Descriptions of other tests can be found in introductory statistics texts.

Example 4.13 Let $x(1), \ldots, x(n)$ be a sample of n observations randomly drawn from a Normal distribution $N(\mu_x, \sigma^2)$, and let $y(1), \ldots, y(m)$ be an independent sample of m observations randomly drawn from a Normal distribution $N(\mu_y, \sigma^2)$. Suppose we wish to test the hypothesis that the means are equal, $H_0 : \mu_x = \mu_y$. The likelihood ratio statistic under these circumstances reduces to

$$t = \frac{\bar{x} - \bar{y}}{\sqrt{s^2(1/n + 1/m)}},$$

with

$$s = s_x^2 \frac{n-1}{n+m-2} + s_y^2 \frac{m-1}{n+m-2},$$

where

$$s_x^2 = \sum (s - \bar{x})^2 / (n-1)$$

is the estimated variance for the x sample and s_y^2 is the same coefficient for the ys. The quantity s is thus a simple weighted sum of the sample variances of the two samples, and the test statistic is merely the difference between the two sample means adjusted by the estimated standard deviation of that difference. Under the null hypothesis, t follows a t distribution (see the appendix) with $n + m - 2$ degrees of freedom.

Although the two populations being compared here are assumed to be Normal, this test is fairly robust to departures from Normality, especially if the sample sizes and the variances are roughly equal. This test is very widely used.

Example 4.14 Relationships between variables are often of central interest in data mining. At an extreme, we might want to know if two variables are not related at all, so that the distribution of the value taken by one is the same regardless of the value taken by the other. A suitable test for independence of two categorical variables is the chi-squared test. This is essentially a goodness-of-fit test in which the data are compared with a model based on the null hypothesis of independence.

Suppose we have two variables, x and y, with x taking the values x_i, $i = 1, ..., r$ with probabilities $p(x_i)$ and y taking the values y_j, $j = 1, ..., s$ with probabilities $p(y_j)$. Suppose that the joint probabilities are $p(x_i, y_j)$. Then, if x and y are independent, $p(x_i, y_j) = p(x_i) p(y_j)$. The data permit us to estimate the distributions $p(x_i)$ and $p(y_j)$ simply by calculating the proportions of the observations that fall at each level of x and the proportions that fall at each level of y. Let the estimate of the probability of the x variable taking value x_i be $n(x_i)/n$ and $n(x_i)/n$ the estimate of the probability of the y variable taking value y_j. Multiplying these together gives us estimates of the probabilities we would expect in each cell, under the independence hypothesis; thus, our estimate of $p(x_i, y_j)$ under the independence assumption is $n(x_i) n(y_j)/n^2$. Since there are n observations altogether, this means we would expect, under the null hypothesis, to find $n(x_i) n(y_j)/n$ observations in the (x_i, y_j)th cell. For convenience, number the cells sequentially in some order from 1 to t (so $t = r.s$) and let E_k represent the expected number in the kth cell. We can compare this with the observed number in the kth cell, which we shall denote as O_k. Somehow, we need to aggregate this comparison over all t cells. A suitable aggregation is given by

$$X^2 = \sum_{k=1,t} \frac{(E_k - O_k)^2}{E_k}. \tag{4.19}$$

The squaring here avoids the problem of positive and negative differences canceling out, and the division by E_k prevents large cells dominating the measure. If the null hypothesis of independence is correct, X^2 follows a χ^2 distribution with $(r-1)(s-1)$ degrees of freedom, so that significance levels can either be found from tables or be computed directly.

We illustrate using medical data in which the outcomes of surgical operations (no improvement, partial improvement, and complete improvement) are classified according to the kind of hospital in which they occur ("referral" or "non-referral"). The data are illustrated below, and the question of interest is whether the outcome is independent of hospital type (that is, whether the outcome distribution is the same for both types of hospital).

	Referral	Non-referral
No improvement	43	47
Partial improvement	29	120
Complete improvement	10	118

The total number of patients from referral hospitals is $(43 + 29 + 10) = 82$, and the total number of patients who do not improve at all is $(43 + 47) = 90$. The overall total is 367. From this it follows that the expected number in the top left cell of the table, under the independence assumption, is $82 \times 90/367 = 20.11$. The observed number is 43, so this cell contributes a value of $(20.11 - 43)^2/20.11$ to X^2. Performing similar calculations for each of the six cells, and adding the results yields $X^2 = 49.8$. Comparing this with a χ^2 distribution with $(3-1)(2-1) = 2$ degrees of freedom reveals a very high level of significance, suggesting that the outcome of surgical operations does depend on hospital type.

The hypothesis testing strategy outlined above is based on the assumption that a random sample has been drawn from some distribution, and the aim of the testing is to make a probability statement about a parameter of that distribution. The ultimate objective is to make an inference from the sample to the underlying population of potential values. For obvious reasons, this is sometimes described as the *sampling paradigm*. An alternative strategy is sometimes appropriate, especially when we are not confident that the sample has been obtained though probability sampling (see chapter 2), and therefore inference to the underlying population is not possible. In such cases, we can still sometimes make a probability statement about some effect under a null hypothesis. Consider, for example, a comparison of a treatment and a control group. We might adopt as our null hypothesis that there is no treatment effect, so the distribution of scores of people who received the treatment should be the same as that of those who did not. If we took a sample of people (possibly not randomly drawn) and randomly assign them to the treatment and control groups, we would expect the difference of mean scores between the groups to be small if the null hypothesis was true. Indeed, under fairly general assumptions, it is not difficult to work out the distribution of the difference between the sample means of the two groups we would expect if there were no treatment effect, and if such difference were just a consequence of an imbalance in the random allocation. We can then explore how unlikely it is that a difference as large or larger than that actually obtained would be seen. Tests based on this principle are termed *randomization tests* or *permutation tests*. Note that they make no statistical inference from the sample to the overall population, but they do enable us to make conditional probability statements about the treatment effects, conditional on the observed values.

Many statistical tests make assumptions about the forms of the population distributions from which the samples are drawn. For example, in the two-sample *t*-test, illustrated above, an assumption of Normality was made. Often, however, it is inconvenient to make such assumptions. Perhaps we have little justification for the assumption, or perhaps we know that the data do not to follow the form required by a standard test. In such circumstances we can adopt *distribution-free tests*. Tests based on ranks fall into this class. Here the basic data are replaced by the numerical labels of the positions in which they occur. For example, to explore whether two samples arose from the same distribution, we could replace the actual numerical values by their ranks. If they did arise from the same distribution, we would expect the ranks of the members of the two samples to be well mixed. If, however, one distribution had a larger mean than the other, we would expect one sample to tend to have large ranks and the other to have small ranks. If the distributions had the same means but one sample had a larger variance than the other, we would expect one sample to show a surfeit of large and small ranks and the other to dominate the intermediate ranks. Test statistics can be constructed based on the average values or some other measurements of the ranks, and their significance levels can be evaluated using randomization arguments. Such test statistics include the sign test statistic, the rank sum test statistic, the Kolmogorov-Smirnov test statistic, and the Wilcoxon test statistic. Sometimes the term *nonparametric test* is used to describe such tests—the rationale being that these tests are not testing the value of a parameter of any assumed distribution.

Comparison of hypotheses H_0 and H_1 from a Bayesian perspective is achieved by comparing their posterior probabilities:

$$p\left(H_i|x\right) \propto p\left(x|H_i\right)p\left(H_i\right) \tag{4.20}$$

Taking the ratio of these leads to a factorization in terms of the prior odds and the likelihood ratio, or *Bayes factor*:

$$\frac{p\left(H_0|x\right)}{p\left(H_1|x\right)} \propto \frac{p\left(H_0\right)}{p\left(H_1\right)}\cdot\frac{p\left(x|H_0\right)}{p\left(x|H_1\right)}. \tag{4.21}$$

There are some complications here, however. The likelihoods are *marginal likelihoods* obtained by integrating over parameters not specified in the hypotheses, and the prior probabilities will be zero if the H_i refer to particular values from a continuum of possible values (e.g., if they refer to values of a parameter θ, where θ can take any value between 0 and 1). One strategy for dealing with this problem is to assign a discrete non-zero prior probability to the given values of θ.

4.6.2   Hypothesis Testing in Context

This section has so far described the classical (frequentist) approach to statistical hypothesis testing. In data mining, however, analyses can become more complicated.

Firstly, because data mining involves large data sets, we should *expect* to obtain statistical significance: even slight departures from the hypothesized model form will be identified as significant, even though they may be of no practical importance. (If they are of practical importance, of course, then well and good.) Worse, slight departures from the model arising from contamination or data distortion will show up as significant. We have already remarked on the inevitability of this problem.

Secondly, sequential model fitting processes are common. Beginning in chapters 8 we will describe various *stepwise* model fitting procedures, which gradually refine a model by adding or deleting terms. Running separate tests on each model, as if it were *de novo*, leads to incorrect probabilities. Formal sequential testing procedures have been developed, but they can be quite complex. Moreover, they may be weak because of the multiple testing going on.

Thirdly, the fact that data mining is essentially an exploratory process has various implications. One is that many models will be examined. Suppose we test m true (though we will not know this) null hypotheses at the 5% level, each based on its own subset of the data, independent of the other tests. For each hypothesis separately, there is a probability of 0.05 of incorrectly rejecting the hypothesis. Since the tests are independent, the probability of incorrectly rejecting at least one is $p = 1 - (1 - 0.05)^m$. When $m = 1$ we have $p = 0.05$, which is fine. But when $m = 10$ we obtain $p = 0.4013$, and when $m = 100$ we obtain $p = 0.9941$. Thus, if we test as few as even 100 true null hypotheses, we are almost certain to incorrectly reject at least one. Alternatively, we could control the overall *family* error rate, setting the probability of incorrectly rejecting one of more of the m true null hypotheses to 0.05. In this case we use $0.05 = 1 - (1 - \alpha)^m$ for each given m to obtain the level α at which each of the separate null hypotheses is tested. With $m = 10$ we obtain $\alpha = 0.0051$, and with $m = 100$ we obtain $\alpha = 0.0005$. This means that we have a very small probability of incorrectly rejecting any of the separate component hypotheses.

Of course, in practice things are much more complicated: the hypotheses are unlikely to be completely independent (at the other extreme, if they are completely dependent, accepting or rejecting one implies the acceptance or rejection of all), with an essentially unknowable dependence structure, and there will typically be a mixture of true (or approximately true) and false null hypotheses.

Various *simultaneous test procedures* have been developed to ease these difficulties (even though the problem is not really one of inadequate methods, but is really more fundamental). A basic approach is based on the *Bonferroni* inequality. We can expand the probability $(1 - \alpha)^m$ that none of the true null hypotheses are rejected to yield $(1 - \alpha)^m \geq 1 - m\alpha$. It follows that $1 - (1 - \alpha)^m \leq m\alpha$—that is, the probability that one or more true null hypotheses is incorrectly rejected is less than or equal to $m\alpha$. In general, the probability of incorrectly rejecting one or more of the true null hypotheses is smaller than the sum of probabilities of incorrectly rejecting each of them. This is a first-order *Bonferroni inequality*. By including other terms in the expansion, we can develop more accurate bounds—though they require knowledge of the dependence relationships between the hypotheses.

With some test procedures difficulties can arise in which a global test of a family of hypotheses rejects the null hypothesis (so we believe at least one to be false), but no single component is rejected. Once again strategies have been developed for overcoming this in particular applications. For example, in multivariate analysis of variance, which compares several groups of objects that have been measured on multiple variables, test procedures have been developed that overcome these problems by comparing each test statistic with a single threshold value.

It is obvious from the above discussion that while attempts to put probabilities on statements of various kinds, via hypothesis tests, do have a place in data mining, they are not a universal solution. However, they can be regarded as a particular type of a more general procedure that maps the data and statement to a numerical value or *score*. Higher scores (or lower scores, depending upon the procedure) indicate that one statement or model is to be preferred to another, without attempting any absolute probabilistic interpretation. The penalized goodness-of-fit score functions described in chapter 7 can be thought of in this context.

4.7   Sampling Methods

As mentioned earlier, data mining can be characterized as secondary analysis, and data miners are not typically involved directly with the data collection process. Still, if we have information about that process that might be useful for our analysis, we should take advantage of it. Traditional statistical data collection is usually carried out with a view to answering some particular question or questions in an efficient and effective manner. However, since data mining is a process seeking the unexpected or the unforeseen, it does not try to answer questions that were specified before the data were collected. For this reason we will not be discussing the sub-discipline of statistics known as *experimental design*, which is concerned with optimal ways to collect data. The fact that data miners typically have no control over the data collection process may sometimes explain poor data quality: the data may be ideally suited to the purposes for which it was collected, but not adequate for its data mining uses.

We have already noted that when the database comprises the entire population, notions of statistical inference are irrelevant: if we want to know the value of some population parameter (the mean transaction value, say, or the largest transaction value), we can simply calculate it. Of course, this assumes that the data describe the population perfectly, with no measurement error, missing data, data corruption, and so on. Since, as we have seen, this is an unlikely situation, we may still be interested in making an inference from the data as recorded to the "true" underlying population values.

Furthermore, the notions of populations and samples can be deceptive. For example, even when values for the entire population have been captured in the database, often the aim is not to describe that population, but rather to make some statement about likely future values. For example, we may have available the entire population of transactions made in a chain of supermarkets on a given day. We may well wish to make some kind of inferential statement—statement about the mean transaction value for the next day or some other future day. This also involves uncertainty, but it is of a different kind from that discussed above. Essentially, here, we are concerned with *forecasting*. In market basket analysis we do not really wish to describe the purchasing patterns of last month's shoppers, but rather to forecast how next month's shoppers are likely to behave.

We have distinguished two ways in which samples arise in data mining. First, sometimes the database itself is merely a sample from some larger population. In chapter 2 we discussed the implications of this situation and the dangers associated with it. Second the database contains records for every object in the population, but the analysis of the data is based on only a sample from it. This second technique is appropriate only in modeling situations and certain pattern detection situations. It is not appropriate when we are seeking individual unusual records.

Our aim is to draw a sample from the database that allows us to construct a model that reflects the structure of the data in the database. The reason for using just a sample, rather than the entire data set, is one of efficiency. At an extreme, it may be infeasible, in terms of time or computational requirements, to use the entirety of a large database. By basing our computations solely on a sample, we make the computations quicker and easier. It is important, however, that the sample be drawn in such a way that it reflects the structure of the complete set—i.e., that it is representative of the entire database.

There are various strategies for drawing samples to try to ensure representativeness. If we wanted to take just 1 in 2 of the records (a *sampling fraction* of 0.5), we could simply take every other record. Such a direct approach is termed *systematic sampling*. Often it is perfectly adequate. However, it can also lead to unsuspected problems. For instance, if the database contained records of married couples, with husbands and wives alternating, systematic sampling could be disastrous—the conclusions drawn would probably be entirely mistaken. In general, in any sampling scheme in which cases are selected following some regular pattern there is a risk of interaction with an unsuspected regularity in the database. Clearly what we need is a selection pattern that avoids regularities—a random selection pattern.

The word random is used here in the sense of avoiding regularities. This is slightly different from the usage employed previously in this chapter, where the term referred to the mechanism by which the sample was chosen. There it described the probability that a record would be chosen for the sample. As we have seen, samples that are random in this second sense can be used as the basis for statistical inference: we can, for example, make a statement about how likely it is that the sample mean will differ substantially from the population mean.

If we draw a sample using a random process, the sample will satisfy the second meaning and is likely to satisfy the first as well. (Indeed, if we specify clearly what we mean by "regularities" we can give a precise probability that a randomly selected sample will not match such regularities.) To avoid biasing our conclusions, we should design our sample selection mechanism in such a way that that each record in the database has an equal chance of being chosen. A sample with equal probability of selecting each member of the population is known as an *epsem* sample. The most basic form of epsem sampling is simple random sampling, in which the n records comprising the sample are selected from the N records in the database in such a way that each set of n records has an equal probability of being chosen. The estimate of the population mean from a simple random sample is just the sample mean.

At this point we should note the distinction between sampling with replacement and sampling without replacement. In the former, a record selected for inclusion in the sample has a chance of being drawn again, but in the latter, once a record is drawn it cannot be drawn a second time. In data mining since the sample size is often small relative to the population size, the differences between the results of these two procedures are usually negligible.

Figure 4.5 illustrates the results of a simple random sampling process used in calculating the mean value of a variable for some population. It is based on drawing samples from a population with a true mean of 0.5. A sample of a specified size is randomly drawn and its mean value is calculated; we have repeated this procedure 200 times and plotted histograms of the results. Figure 4.5shows the distribution of sample mean values (a) for samples of size 10, (b) size 100, and (c) size 1000. It is apparent from this figure that the larger the sample, the more closely the values of the sample mean are distributed around about the true mean. In general, if the variance of a population of size N is σ^2, the variance of the mean of a simple random sample of size n

from that population, drawn without replacement, is

$$\frac{\sigma^2}{n}\left(1 - \frac{n}{N}\right). \tag{4.22}$$

Since we normally deal with situations in which N is large relative to n (i.e., situations that involve a small sampling fraction), we can usually ignore the second factor, so that, a good approximation of the variance is σ^2/n. From this it follows that the larger the sample is the less likely it is that the sample mean will deviate significantly from the population mean—which explains why the dispersion of the histograms in figure 4.5 decreases with increasing sample size. Note also that this result is independent of the population size. What matters here is the size of the sample, not the size of the sampling fraction, and not the proportion of the population that is included in the sample. We can also see that, when the sample size is doubled, the standard deviation is reduced not by a factor of 2, but only by a factor of $\sqrt{2}$—there are diminishing returns to increasing the sample size. We can estimate σ^2 from the sample using the standard estimator

$$\sum (x(i) - \bar{x})/(n - 1), \tag{4.23}$$

where $x(i)$ is the value of the ith sample unit and $\bar{y}$ is the mean of the n values in the sample.

The simple random sample is the most basic form of sample design, but others have been developed that have desirable properties under different circumstances. Details can be found in books on survey sampling, such as those cited at the end of this chapter. Here we will briefly describe two important schemes.

In *stratified random sampling*, the entire population is split into nonoverlapping subpopulations or strata, and a sample (often, but not necessarily, a simple random sample) is drawn separately from within each stratum. There are several potential advantages to using such a procedure. An obvious one is that it enables us to make statements about each of the subpopulations separately, without relying on chance to ensure that a reasonable number of observations come from each subpopulation. A more subtle, but often more important, advantage is that if the strata are relatively homogeneous in terms of the variable of interest (so that much of the variability between values of the variable is accounted for by differences between strata), the variance of the overall estimate may be smaller than that arising from a simple random sample. To illustrate, one of the credit card companies we work with categorizes transactions into 26 categories· supermarket, travel agent, gas station,

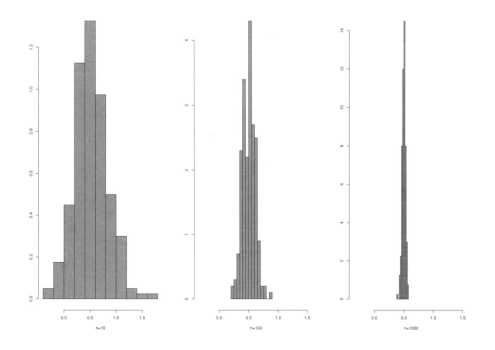

Figure 4.5 Means of samples of size 10(a), 100(b), and 1000(c) drawn from a population with a mean of 0.5.

and so on. Suppose we wanted to estimate the average value of a transaction. We could take a simple random sample of transaction values from the database of records, and compute its mean, using this as our estimate. However, with such a procedure some of the transaction types might end up being underrepresented in our sample, and some might be overrepresented. We could control for this by forcing our sample to include a certain number of each transaction type. This would be a stratified sample, in which the transaction types were the strata. This example illustrates why the strata must be relatively homogeneous internally, with the heterogeneity occurring between strata. If all the strata had the same dispersion as the overall population, no advantage would be gained by stratification.

In general, suppose that we want to estimate the population mean for some variable, and that we are using a stratified sample, with simple random sampling within each stratum. Suppose that the kth stratum has N_k elements in it, and that n_k of these are chosen for the sample from this stratum. Denoting the sample mean within the kth stratum by $\bar{x}_k$, the estimate of the overall population mean is given by

$$\sum \frac{N_k \bar{x}_k}{N}, \tag{4.24}$$

where N is the total size of the population. The variance of this estimator is

$$\frac{1}{N^2} \sum N_k^2 var(\bar{x}_k), \tag{4.25}$$

where $var(\bar{x}_k)$ is the variance of the simple random sample of size n_k for the kth stratum, computed as above.

Data often have a hierarchical structure. For example, letters occur in words, which lie in sentences, which are grouped into paragraphs, which occur in chapters, which form books, which sit in libraries. Producing a complete sampling frame and drawing a simple random sample may be difficult. Files will reside on different computers at a site within an organization, and the organization may have many sites; if we are studying the properties of those files, we may find it impossible to produce a complete list from which we can draw a simple random sample. In cluster sampling, rather than drawing a sample of the individual elements that are of interest, we draw a sample of units that contain several elements. In the computer file example, we might draw a sample of computers. We can the examine all of the files on each of the chosen computers, or move on to a further stage of sampling.

Clusters are often of unequal sizes. In the above example we can view a computer as providing a cluster of files, and it is very unlikely that all computers in an organization would have the same number of files. But situations with equal-sized clusters do arise. Manufacturing industries provide many examples: six-packs of beer or packets of condoms, for instance. If all of the units in each selected cluster are chosen (if the subsampling fraction is 1) each unit has the probability a/K of being selected, where a is the number of clusters chosen from the entire set of K clusters. If not all the units are chosen, but the sampling fraction in each cluster is the same, each unit will have the same probability of being included in the sample (it will be an epsem sample). This is a common design. Estimating the variance of a statistic based on such a design is less straightforward than the cases described above since the sample size is also a random variable (it is dependent upon which clusters happen to be included in the sample). The estimate of the mean of a variable is a ratio of two random variables: the total sum for the units included in the sample and the total number of units included in the sample. Denoting the size of the simple random sample chosen from the kth cluster by n_k, and the total sum for the units chosen from the kth cluster by s_k, the sample mean r is

$$\sum x_k / \sum n_k.$$
(4.26)

If we denote the overall sampling fraction by f (often this is small and can be ignored) the variance of r is

$$\frac{1-f}{(\sum n_k)^2} \frac{a}{1-a} \left(\sum s_k^2 + r^2 \sum n_k^2 - 2r \sum s_k n_k \right).$$
(4.27)

4.8   Conclusion

Nothing is certain. In the data mining context, our objective is to make discoveries from data. We want to be as confident as we can that our conclusions are correct, but we often must be satisfied with a conclusion that could be wrong—though it will be better if we can also state our level of confidence in our conclusions. When we are analyzing entire populations, the uncertainty will creep in via less than perfect data quality: some values may be incorrectly recorded, some values may be missing, some members of the population be omitted from the database entirely, and so on. When we are working with samples, our aim is often to draw a conclusion that applies to the broader population from which the sample was drawn. The fundamental tool in tackling all of these issues is probability. This is a universal language for handling uncertainty, a language that has been refined throughout this century and has been applied across a vast array of situations. Application of the ideas of probability enables us to obtain "best" estimates of values, even in the face of data inadequacies, and even when only a sample has been measured. Moreover, application of these ideas also allows us to quantify our confidence in the results.

Later chapters of this book make heavy use of probabilistic arguments. They underlie many—perhaps even most—data mining tools, from global modeling to pattern identification.

4.9 Further Reading

Books containing discussions of different schools of probability, along with the consequences for inference, include those by DeFinetti (1974, 1975), Barnett (1982), and Bernardo and Smith (1994). References to other work on statistics and particular statistical models are given at the ends of chapters 6, 9, 10, and 11.

There are many excellent basic books on the calculus of probability, including those by Grimmett and Stirzaker (1992) and Feller (1968, 1971). The text by Hamming (1991) is oriented towards engineers and computer scientists (and contains many interesting examples), and Applebaum (1996) is geared toward undergraduate mathematics students. Probability calculus is a dynamic area of applied mathematics, and has benefited substantially from the different areas in which it has been applied. For example, Alon and Spencer (1992) give a fascinating tour of the applications of probability in modern computer science.

The idea of randomness as departure from the regular or predictable is discussed in work on Kolmogorov complexity (e.g., Li and Vitanyi, 1993).

Whittaker (1990) provides an excellent treatment of the general principles of conditional dependence and independence in graphical models. Pearl (1988) is a seminal work in this area from the the artificial intelligence perspective.

There are numerous introductory texts on inference, such as those by Daly et al. (1995), as well as more advanced texts that contain a deeper discussion of inferential conscepts, such as Cox and Hinkley (1974), Schervish (1995), Lindsey (1996), and Lehmann and Casella (1998), and Knight (2000). A broad discussion of likelihood and its applications is provided by Edwards (1972). Bayesian methods are now the subjects of entire books. Gelman et al. (1995) provides an excellent general text on Bayesian approach. A comprehensive reference is given by Bernardo and Smith (1994) and a lighter introduction is give by Lee (1989). Nonparametric methods are described by Randles and Wolfe (1979) and Maritz (1981). Bootstrap methods are described by Efron and Tibshirani (1993).

Miller (1980) describes simultaneous test procedures. The methods we have outlined above are not the only approaches to the problem of inference about multiple parameters; Lindsey (1999) describes another.

Books on survey sampling discuss efficient strategies for drawing samples— see, for example, Cochran (1977) and Kish (1965).

5 *A Systematic Overview of Data Mining Algorithms*

5.1 Introduction

This chapter will examine what we mean in a general sense by a *data mining algorithm* as well as what components make up such algorithms. A working definition is as follows:

> A data mining algorithm is a well-defined procedure that takes data as input and produces output in the form of models or patterns.

We use the term *well-defined* indicate that the procedure can be precisely encoded as a finite set of rules. To be considered an *algorithm*, the procedure must always terminate after some finite number of steps and produce an output.

In contrast, a *computational method* has all the properties of an algorithm except a method for guaranteeing that the procedure will terminate in a finite number of steps. While specification of an algorithm typically involves defining many practical implementation details, a computational method is usually described more abstractly. For example, the search technique *steepest descent* is a computational method but is not in itself an algorithm (this search method repeatedly moves in parameter space in the direction that has the steepest decrease in the score function relative to the current parameter values). To specify an algorithm using the steepest descent method, we would have to give precise methods for determining where to begin descending, how to identify the direction of steepest descent (calculated exactly or approximated?), how far to move in the chosen direction, and when to terminate the search (e.g., detection of convergence to a local minimum).

As discussed briefly in chapter 1, the specification of a data mining algorithm to solve a particular task involves defining specific *algorithm components*:

1. the data mining *task* the algorithm is used to address (e.g., visualization, classification, clustering, regression, and so forth). Naturally, different types of algorithms are required for different tasks.

2. the *structure* (functional form) of the model or pattern we are fitting to the data (e.g., a linear regression model, a hierarchical clustering model, and so forth). The structure defines the boundaries of what we can approximate or learn. Within these boundaries, the data guide us to a particular model or pattern. In chapter 6 we will discuss in more detail forms of model and pattern structures most widely used in data mining algorithms.

3. the *score function* we are using to judge the quality of our fitted models or patterns based on observed data (e.g., misclassification error or squared error). As we will discuss in chapter 7, the score function is what we try to maximize (or minimize) when we fit parameters to our models and patterns. Therefore, it is important that the score function reflects the relative practical utility of different parameterizations of our model or pattern structures. Furthermore, the score function is critical for learning and generalization. It can be based on goodness-of-fit alone (i.e., how well the model can describe the observed data) or can try to capture *generalization* performance (i.e., how well will the model describe data we have not yet seen). As we will see in later chapters, this is a subtle issue.

4. the *search* or *optimization method* we use to search over parameters and structures, i.e., computational procedures and algorithms used to find the maximum (or minimum) of the score function for particular models or patterns. Issues here include computational methods used to optimize the score function (e.g., steepest descent) and search-related parameters (e.g., the maximum number of iterations or convergence specification for an iterative algorithm). If the model (or pattern) structure is a single fixed structure (such as a kth-order polynomial function of the inputs), the search is conducted in parameter space to optimize the score function relative to this fixed structural form. If the model (or pattern) structure consists of a set (or family) of different structures, there is a search over both structures and their associated parameter spaces. Optimization and

Table 5.1 Three well-known data mining algorithms broken down in terms of their algorithm components.

	CART	Backpropagation	A Priori
Task	Classification and Regression	Regression	Rule Pattern Discovery
Structure	Decision Tree	Neural Network (Nonlinear functions)	Association Rules
Score Function	Cross-validated Loss Function	Squared Error	Support/ Accuracy
Search Method	Greedy Search over Structures	Gradient Descent on Parameters	Breadth-First with Pruning
Data Management Technique	Unspecified	Unspecified	Linear Scans

search are traditionally at the heart of any data mining algorithm, and will be discussed in much more detail in chapter 8.

5. the *data management technique* to be used for storing, indexing, and retrieving data. Many statistical and machine learning algorithms do not specify any data management technique, essentially assuming that the data set is small enough to reside in main memory so that random access of any data point is free (in terms of time) relative to actual computational costs. However, massive data sets may exceed the capacity of available main memory and reside in secondary (e.g., disk) or tertiary (e.g., tape) memory. Accessing such data is typically orders of magnitude slower than accessing main memory, and thus, for massive data sets, the physical location of the data and the manner in which it is accessed can be critically important in terms of algorithm efficiency. This issue of data management will be discussed in more depth in chapter 12.

Table 5.1 illustrates how three well-known data mining algorithms (CART, backpropagation, and the A Priori algorithm) can be described in terms of these basic components. Each of these algorithms will be discussed in detail later in this chapter. (One of the differences between statistical and data mining perspectives is evident from this table. Statisticians would regard CART as a model, and backpropagation as a parameter estimation algorithm. Data miners tend to see things more in terms of algorithms: processing the data using the algorithm to yield a result. The difference is really more one of perspective than substance.)

Specification of the model (or pattern) structures and the score function typically happens "off-line" as part of the human-centered process of setting up the data mining problem. Once the data, the model (or pattern) structures, and the score function have been decided upon, the remainder of the problem—optimizing the score function—is largely computational. (In practice there may be several iterations of this process as models and score functions are revised in light of earlier results). Thus, the algorithmic core of a data mining algorithm lies in the computational methods used to implement the search and data management components.

The component-based description presented in this chapter provides a general high-level framework for both *analysis* and *synthesis* of data mining algorithms. From an analysis viewpoint, describing existing data mining algorithms in terms of their components clarifies the role of each component and makes it easier to compare competing algorithms. For example, do two algorithms differ in terms of their model structures, their score functions, their search techniques, or their data management strategies? From a synthesis viewpoint, by combining different components in different combinations we can build data mining algorithms with different properties. In chapters 9 through 14 we will discuss each of the components in much more detail in the context of specific algorithms. In this chapter we will focus on how the pieces fit together at a high level. The primary theme here is that the component-based view of data mining algorithms provides a parsimonious and structured "language" for description, analysis, and synthesis of data mining algorithms.

For the most part we will limit the discussion to cases in which we have a single form of model or pattern structure (e.g., trees, polynomials, etc.), rather than those in which we are considering multiple types of model structures for the same problem. The component viewpoint can be generalized to handle such situations, but typically the score functions, the search method, and the data management techniques all become more complex.

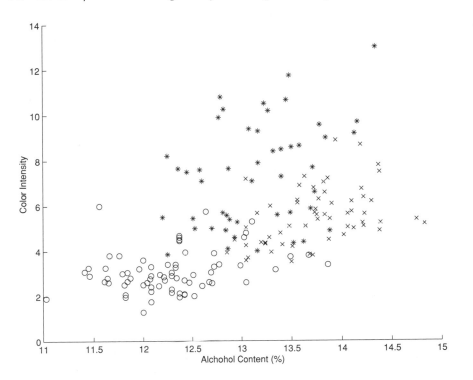

Figure 5.1 A scatterplot of data showing color intensity versus alcohol content for a set of wines. The data mining task is to classify the wines into one of three classes (three different cultivars), each shown with a different symbol in the plot. The data originate from a 13-dimensional data set in which each variable measures of a particular characteristic of a specific wine.

5.2 An Example: The CART Algorithm for Building Tree Classifiers

To clarify the general idea of viewing algorithms in terms of their components, we will begin by looking at one well-known algorithm for classification problems.

The CART (Classification And Regression Trees) algorithm is a widely used statistical procedure for producing classification and regression models with a tree-based structure. For the sake of simplicity we will consider

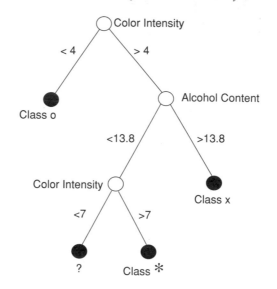

Figure 5.2 A classification tree for the data in figure 5.1 in which the tests consist of thresholds (shown beside the branches) on variables at each internal node and leaves contain class decisions. Note that one leaf is denoted ? to illustrate that there is considerable uncertainty about the class labels of data points in this region of the space.

only the classification aspect of CART, that is, mapping an input vector **x** to a categorical (class) output label y (see figure 5.1). (A more detailed discussion of CART is provided in chapter 10.) In the context of the components discussed above, CART can be viewed as the "algorithm-tuple" consisting of the following:

1. *task = prediction (classification)*

2. *model structure = tree*

3. *score function = cross-validated loss function*

4. *search method = greedy local search*

5. *data management method = unspecified*

The fundamental distinguishing aspect of the CART algorithm is the *model structure* being used; the classification tree. The CART tree model consists of a hierarchy of univariate binary decisions. Figure 5.2 shows a simple example of such a classification tree for the data in figure 5.1. Each internal node in the tree specifies a binary test on a single variable, using thresholds on real and integer-valued variables and subset membership for categorical variables. (In general we use b branches at each node, $b \geq 2$.) A data vector $\mathbf{x}$ descends a unique path from the root node to a leaf node depending on how the values of individual components of $\mathbf{x}$ match the binary tests of the internal nodes. Each leaf node specifies the class label of the most likely class at that leaf or, more generally, a probability distribution on class values conditioned on the branch leading to that leaf.

The structure of the tree is derived from the data, rather than being specified *a priori* (this is where data mining comes in). CART operates by choosing the best variable for splitting the data into two groups at the root node. It can use any of several different splitting criteria; all produce the effect of partitioning the data at an internal node into two disjoint subsets (branches) in such a way that the class labels in each subset are as homogeneous as possible. This splitting procedure is then recursively applied to the data in each of the child nodes, and so forth. The size of the final tree is a result of a relatively complicated "pruning" process, outlined below. Too large a tree may result in overfitting, and too small a tree may have insufficient predictive power for accurate classification.

The hierarchical form of the tree structure clearly separates algorithms like CART from classification algorithms based on non-tree structures (e.g., a model that uses a linear combination of all variables to define a decision boundary in the input space). A tree structure used for classification can readily deal with input data that contain *mixed* data types (i.e., combinations of categorical and real-valued data), since each internal node depends on only a simple binary test. In addition, since CART builds the tree using a single variable at a time, it can readily deal with large numbers of variables. On the other hand, the representational power of the tree structure is rather coarse: the decision regions for classifications are constrained to be hyperrectangles, with boundaries constrained to be parallel to the input variable axes (as an example, see figure 5.3).

The score function used to measure the quality of different tree structures is a general misclassification loss function, defined as

$$\sum_{i=1}^{n} C\left(y(i), \hat{y}(i)\right), \tag{5.1}$$

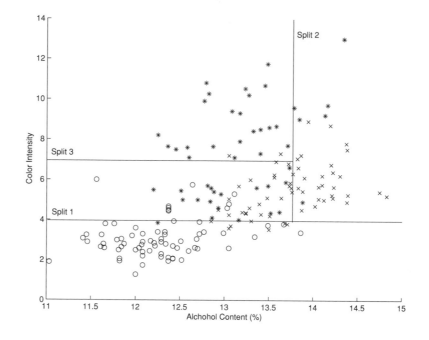

Figure 5.3   The decision boundaries from the classification tree in figure 5.2 are superposed on the original data. Note the axis-parallel nature of the boundaries.

where $C\left(y(i), \hat{y}(i)\right)$ is the loss incurred (positive) when the class label for the ith data vector, $y(i)$, is predicted by the tree to be $\hat{y}(i)$. In general, C is specified by an $m \times m$ matrix, where m is the number of classes. For the sake of simplicity we will assume here a loss of 1 is incurred whenever $\hat{y}(i) \neq y(i)$, and the loss is 0 otherwise. (This is known as the "0-1" loss function, or the misclassification rate if we normalize the sum above by dividing by n.)

CART uses a technique known as *cross-validation* to estimate this misclassification loss function. We will explain cross-validation in more detail in chapter 7. Basically, this method partitions the training data into a subset for building the tree and then estimates the misclassification rate on the remaining *validation* subset. This partitioning is repeated multiple times on different subsets, and the misclassification rates are then averaged to yield a *cross-validation estimate* of how well a tree of a particular size will perform on new, unseen data. The size of tree that produces the smallest cross-validated

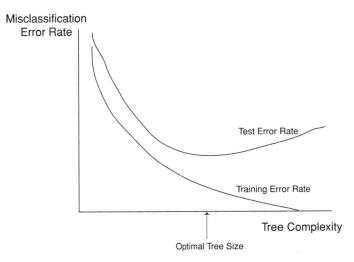

Figure 5.4   A hypothetical plot of misclassification error rates for both training and test data as a function of tree complexity (e.g., number of leaves in the tree).

misclassification estimate is selected as the appropriate size for the final tree model. (This description captures the essence of tree selection via cross-validation, but in practice the process is a little more complex.)

Cross-validation allows CART to estimate the performance of any tree model on data not used in the construction of the tree—i.e., it provides an estimate of generalization performance. This is critical in the tree-growing procedure, since the misclassification rate on the training data (the data used to construct the tree) can often be reduced by simply making the tree more complex; thus, the training data error is not necessarily indicative of how the tree will perform on new data.

Figure 5.4 illustrates this point with a hypothetical plot of typical error rates as a function the size of the tree. The error rate on the training data decreases monotonically (to an error rate of zero if the variables can produce leaves that each contain data from a only single class). The test error rate on new data (which is what we are typically interested in for prediction) also decreases at first. Very small trees (to the left) do not have sufficient predictive power to make accurate predictions. However, unlike the training error, the test error "bottoms out" and begins to increase again as the algorithm overfits the data and adds nodes that are merely predicting noise or random variation in the training data, and which is irrelevant to the predictive task. The goal of an algorithm like CART is to find a tree close to the optimal tree size (which is of course unknown ahead of time); it tries to find a model that is complex enough to capture any structure that exists, but not so complex that it overfits. For small to medium amounts of data it is preferable to do this without having to reserve some of our data to estimate this out-of-sample error. For very large data sets we can sometimes afford to simply partition the data into training and validation data sets and to monitor performance on the validation data.

The use of a cross-validated score function distinguishes CART from most other data mining algorithms based on tree models. For example, the C4.5 algorithm (a widely used alternative to CART for building classification trees) judges individual tree structures by heuristically adjusting the estimated error rate on the training data to approximate the test error rate (in an attempt to correct for the fact that the training error rate is generally an underestimate of the out-of-sample error rate). The adjusted error rate is then used in a pruning phase to search for the tree that maximizes this score.

CART uses a greedy local search method to identify good candidate tree structures, recursively expanding the tree from a root node, and then gradually "pruning" back specific branches of this large tree. This heuristic search method is dictated by the combinatorially large search space (i.e., the space of all possible binary tree structures) and the lack of any tractable method for finding the single optimal tree (relative to a given score function). The folk wisdom in tree learning is that greedy local search in tree building works just about as well as any more sophisticated heuristic, and is much simpler to implement than more complex search methods. Thus, greedy local search is the method of choice in most practical tree learning algorithms.

In terms of data management, CART implicitly assumes that the data are all in main memory. To be fair to CART, very few algorithms published outside the database literature provide any explicit guidance on data management for large data sets. For some algorithms, adding an appropriate data management technique is straightforward and can be done in a relatively modular fashion. For example, if each data point needs to be visited only once and the order does not matter, data management is trivial (just read the data points sequentially in subsets into main memory).

For tree algorithms, however, the model, the score function, and the search method are complex enough to make data management quite nontrivial. To understand why this is so, remember that a tree algorithm recursively partitions the observations (the rows of our data matrix) into subsets in a data-driven manner, requiring us to repeatedly find different subsets of observations in our database and determine various properties of these subsets. In a naive implementation of the algorithm for data sets too large to fit in main memory, this will involve many repeated scans of the secondary storage medium (such as a disk), leading to very poor time performance. Scalable versions of tree algorithms have been developed recently that use special purpose data structures to deal efficiently with data outside main memory.

To summarize our reductionist view of CART, we note that the algorithm consists of (1) a tree model structure, (2) a cross-validated score function, and (3) a two-phase greedy search over tree structures ("growing" and "pruning"). In this sense, CART is relatively straightforward to understand once one grasps the key ideas involved. Clearly, we could develop alternative algorithms that use the same tree structure, cross-validated score function, and search techniques, and that are similar in spirit to CART, but that are application-specific in details of implementation (such as how missing data are handled in both training and prediction). For a given data mining application, customizing the algorithm in this fashion might be well worth pursuing. In short, the power of an algorithm such as CART is in the fundamental concepts that it embodies, rather than in the specific details of implementation.

5.3 The Reductionist Viewpoint on Data Mining Algorithms

Repeating the basic mantra of this chapter, once we have a data set and a specific data mining task, a data mining algorithm can be thought of as a "tuple" consisting of {*model structure, score function, search method, data management technique*}. While this is a simple observation, it has some fairly profound implications. First, the number of different algorithms we can generate is very large! By combining different model structures with different score functions, different search methods, and different data management techniques, we can generate a potentially infinite number of different algorithms. (This point has not escaped academic researchers.)

However, the complexity of "algorithm space" is manageable once we realize the second implication: while there is a very large number of possible algorithms, there is only a relatively small number of fundamental "values" for each component in the tuple. Specifically, there are well-defined categories of models and patterns that we can use for problems such as regression, classification, or clustering; we will discuss these in detail in chapter 6. Similarly, as we will see in chapter 7, there are relatively few score functions (such as likelihood, sum-of-squared-errors, and classification rate) that have broad appeal. There are also just a few general classes of search and optimization methods that have wide applicability, and the essential principles of data management can be reduced to a relatively small number of different techniques (as discussed in chapters 8 and 12, respectively).

Thus, many well-known data mining algorithms are composed of a combination of well-defined components. In other words algorithms tend to be relatively tightly clustered in "algorithm space" (as spanned by the "dimensions" of model structure, score function, search method, and data management technique).

The *reductionist* (i.e., a component-based) view for data mining algorithms is quite useful in practice. It clarifies the underlying operation of a particular data mining algorithm by reducing it to its essential components. In turn, this makes it easier to compare different algorithms, since we can clearly see similarities and differences at the component level (e.g., we were able to distinguish between CART and C4.5 primarily in terms of what score functions they use).

Even more important, this view places an emphasis on the fundamental properties of an algorithm avoiding the tendency to think of lists of algorithms. When faced with a data mining application, a data miner should think about which *components* fit the specifics of his or her problem, rather than which specific "off-the-shelf" algorithm to choose. In an ideal world, the data miners would have available a software environment within which they could *compose* components (from a library of model structures, score functions, search methods, etc.) to synthesize an algorithm customized for their specific applications. Unfortunately this remains a ideal state of affairs rather than the practical norm; current data analysis software packages often provide only a list of algorithms, rather than a component-based toolbox for algorithm synthesis. This is understandable given the aim of providing usable tools for data miners who do not have the background or the time to understand the underlying details at a component level. However these software tools may not be ideal for more skilled practitioners who wish to customize and synthesize problem-specific algorithms. The "cookbook" approach is also somewhat dangerous, since naive users of data mining tools may not fully understand the limitations (and underlying assumptions) of the particular black-box algorithms they are using. In contrast, a description

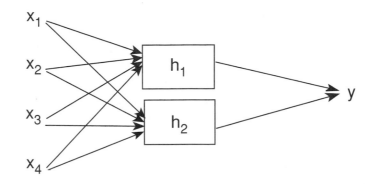

Figure 5.5 A diagram of a simple multilayer perceptron (or neural network) model with two hidden nodes ($d_1 = 2$) and a single output node ($d_2 = 1$).

based on components makes it relatively clear what is inside the black box.

To illustrate the general utility of the reductionist viewpoint, in the next three sections we will look at three well-known algorithms in terms of their components. These and related algorithms will addressed in more detail in chapters 9 through 14, where we discuss a more complete range of solutions for different data mining tasks.

5.3.1   Multilayer Perceptrons for Regression and Classification

Feedforward multilayer perceptrons (MLPs) are the most widely used models in the general class of artificial neural network models. The MLP structure provides a nonlinear mapping from a real-valued input vector **x** to a real-valued output vector **y**. As a result, an MLP can be used as a nonlinear model for regression problems, as well as for classification, through appropriate interpretation of the outputs. The basic idea is that a vector of p input values is multiplied by a $p \times d_1$ weight matrix, and the resulting d_1 values are each individually transformed by a nonlinear function to produce d_1 "hidden node" outputs. The resulting d_1 values are then multiplied by a $d_1 \times d_2$ weight matrix (another "layer" of weights), and the d_2 values are each put through a non-linear function. The resulting d_2 values can either be used as the outputs of the model or be put through another layer of weight multiplications and non-linear transformations, and so on (hence, the "multilayer" nature of the model; the term *perceptron* refers to the original model of this form proposed in the 1960s, consisting of a single layer of weights followed by a threshold nonlinearity).

As an example, consider the simple network model in figure 5.5 with a single "hidden" layer. Two inner products, $s_1 = \sum_{i=1}^{4} \alpha_i x_i$ and $s_2 = \sum_{i=1}^{4} \beta_i x_i$, are calculated via the first layer of weights (the αs and the βs), and each in turn transformed by a nonlinear function at the hidden nodes to produce two scalar values: h_1 and h_2. The nonlinear logistic function, i.e., $h_1 = h(s_1) = 1/(1 + e^{-s_1})$, is widely used. Next h_1 and h_2 are weighted and combined to produce the output value $y = \sum_{i=1}^{2} w_i h_i$ (we could in principle perform a nonlinear transformation on y also). Thus, y is a *nonlinear function* of the input vector $\mathbf{x}$. The hs can be viewed as nonlinear transformations of the four-dimensional input, a new set of two "basis functions," h_1 and h_2. The parameters of this model to be estimated from the data are the eight weights on the input layer ($\alpha_1, \ldots, \alpha_4, \beta_1, \ldots, \beta_4$) and the two weights on the output layer (w_1 and w_2). In general, with p inputs, a single hidden layer with h hidden nodes, and a single output, there are $(p+1)h$ parameters (weights) in all to be estimated from the data. In general we can have multiple layers of such weight multiplications and nonlinear transformations, but a single hidden layer is used most often since multiple hidden layer networks can be slow to train. The weights of the MLP are the parameters of the model and must be determined from the data.

Note that if the output $\mathbf{y}$ is a scalar y (i.e., $d_2 = 1$) and is bounded between 0 and 1 (we can just choose a nonlinear transformation of the weighted values coming from the previous layer to ensure this condition), we can use y as an indicator of class membership for two-class problems and (for example) threshold at 0.5 to decide between class 1 and class 2. Thus, MLPs can easily be used for classification as well as for regression. Because of the nonlinear nature of the model, the decision boundaries between different classes produced by a network model can also be quite non-linear. Figure 5.6 provides an example of such decision boundaries. Note that they are highly nonlinear, in contrast to those produced by the classification tree in figure 5.3. Unlike the classification tree in figure 5.2, however, there is no simple summary form we can use to describe the workings of the neural network model.

The reductionist view of an MLP learning algorithm yields the following "algorithm-tuple":

1. *task = prediction: classification or regression*

2. *structure = multiple layers of nonlinear transformations of weighted sums of the inputs*

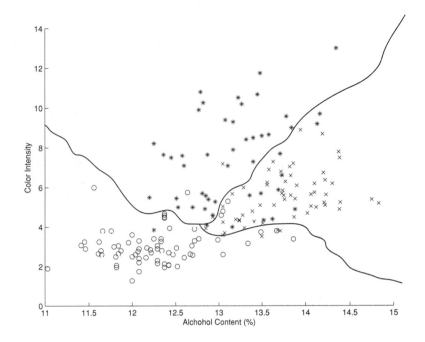

Figure 5.6 An example of the type of decision boundaries that a neural network model would produce for the two-dimensional wine data of figure 5.2(a).

3. *score function = sum of squared errors*

4. *search method = steepest-descent from randomly chosen initial parameter values*

5. *data management technique = online or batch*

The distinguishing feature of this algorithm is the multilayer, nonlinear nature of its model structure (note both that the output y is a nonlinear function of the inputs and that the parameters θ (the weights) appear nonlinearly in the score function). This clearly sets a neural network apart from more traditional linear and polynomial functional forms for regression and from tree-based models for classification.

The sum of squared errors (SSE), the most widely used score function for MLPs, is defined as:

$$S_{SSE} = \sum_{i}^{n} \Big(y(i) - \hat{y}(i) \Big)^2, \tag{5.2}$$

where $y(i)$ and $\hat{y}(i)$ are the true target value and the output of the network, respectively, for the ith data point, and where $\hat{y}(i)$ is a function of the input vector $\mathbf{x}(i)$ and the MLP parameters (weights) θ. It is sometimes assumed that squared error is the *only* score function that can be used with a neural network model. In fact, as long as it is differentiable as a function of the model parameters (allowing us to determine the direction of steepest descent), *any* score function can be used as the basis for a steepest-descent search method such as backpropagation. For example, if we view squared error as just a special case of a more general log-likelihood function (as discussed in chapter 4), we can use a variety of other likelihood-based score functions in place of squared error, tailored for specific applications.

Training a neural network consists of minimizing S_{SSE} by treating it as a function of the unknown parameters θ (i.e., parameter estimation of θ given the data). Given that each $\hat{y}(i)$ is typically a highly nonlinear function of the parameters θ, the score function S_{SSE} is also highly nonlinear as a function of θ. Thus, there is no closed-form solution for finding the parameters θ that minimize S_{SSE} for an MLP. In addition, since there can be many local minima on the surface of S_{SSE} as a function of θ, training a neural network (i.e., finding the parameters that minimize S_{SSE} for a particular data set and model structure) is often a highly non-trivial multivariate optimization problem. Iterative local search techniques are required to find satisfactory local minima.

The original training method proposed for MLPs, known as backpropagation, is a relatively simple optimization method. It essentially performs steepest-descent on the score function (the sum of squared errors) in parameter space, solving this nonlinear optimization problem by descending to a local minimum given a randomly chosen starting point in parameter space. (In practice we usually descend from multiple starting points and select the best local minimum found overall.) In a more general context, there is a large family of optimization methods for such nonlinear optimization problems. It is often assumed that steepest-descent is the only optimization method that can be used to train an MLP, but in fact more powerful nonlinear optimization techniques such as conjugate gradient techniques can be brought to bear on this problem. We discuss some of these techniques in chapter 8.

In terms of data management, a neural network can be trained either online (updating the weights based on cycling through one data point at a time) or in batch mode (updating the weights after seeing all of the data points). The online updating version of the algorithm is a special case of a more general class of online estimation algorithms (see chapter 8 for further discussion of the trade-offs involved in using such algorithms).

An important practical distinction between MLPs and classification trees is that a tree algorithm (such as CART) searches through models of different complexities in a relatively automated manner (e.g., finding the right-sized tree is a basic feature of the CART algorithm). In contrast, there is no widely accepted procedure for determining the appropriate structure for an MLP (i.e., determining how many layers and how many hidden nodes to include in the model). Numerous algorithms exist for constructing network structures automatically, including methods that start with small networks and add nodes and weights in an incremental "growing" manner, as well as methods that start with large networks and "prune" away weights and nodes that appear to be irrelevant. Incrementally growing a network structure can be subject to local minima problems (the best network with k hidden nodes may be quite different in parameter space from the best network with $k - 1$ hidden nodes). On the other hand, training an overly large network can be prohibitively expensive, especially when the model structure is large (e.g., with a large input dimensionality p). In practice, network structures are often determined by a trial-and-error procedure of manually adjusting the number of hidden nodes until satisfactory performance is reached on a validation data set (a set of data points not used in training).

The component-based view of MLPs illustrates that the general approach is not very far removed from more traditional statistical estimation and optimization techniques. Many of these techniques (e.g., the incorporation of Bayesian priors into the score function to drive small weights to zero (to "regularize" the model) or the use of more sophisticated multivariate optimization procedures such as conjugate gradient techniques during weight search) can be used in training network models. In the 1980s, when neural network models were first introduced, the connections to the statistical literature were not at all obvious (although they seem quite clear in retrospect). There is no doubt that the primary contribution of the neural modeling approach lies in the nonlinear multilayer nature of the underlying model structure.

5.3.2   The A Priori Algorithm for Association Rule Learning

Association rules are among the most popular representations for local patterns in data mining. Chapter 13 provides a more in-depth description, but here we sketch the general idea and briefly describe a generic association rule algorithm in terms of its components. (This description is loosely based on the well-known A Priori algorithm, which was one of the earliest algorithms for finding association rules.)

An association rule is a simple probabilistic statement about the co-occurrence of certain events in a database, and is particularly applicable to sparse transaction data sets. For the sake of simplicity we assume that all variables are binary. An association rule takes the following form:

$$\text{IF } A = 1 \text{ AND } B = 1 \text{ THEN } C = 1 \text{ with probability } p \qquad (5.3)$$

where A, B, and C are binary variables and $p = p(C = 1 | A = 1, B = 1)$, i.e., the conditional probability that $C = 1$ given that $A = 1$ and $B = 1$. The conditional probability p is sometimes referred to as the "accuracy" or "confidence" of the rule, and $p(A = 1, B = 1, C = 1)$ is referred to as the "support." This *pattern structure* or *rule structure* is quite simple and interpretable, which helps explain the general appeal of this approach. Typically the goal is to find all rules that satisfy the constraint that the accuracy p is greater than some threshold p_a and the support is greater than some threshold p_s (for example, to find all rules with support greater than 0.05 and accuracy greater than 0.8). Such rules comprise a relatively weak form of knowledge; they are really just summaries of co-occurrence patterns in the observed data, rather than strong statements that characterize the population as a whole. Indeed, in the sense that the term "rule" usually implies a causal interpretation (from the left to the right hand side), the term "association rule" is strictly speaking a misnomer since these patterns are inherently correlational but need not be causal.

The general idea of finding association rules originated in applications involving "market-basket data." These data are usually recorded in a database in which each observation consists of an actual basket of items (such as grocery items), and the variables indicate whether or not a particular item was purchased. We can think of this type of data in terms of a data matrix of n rows (corresponding to baskets) and p columns (corresponding to grocery items). Such a matrix can be very large, with n in the millions and p in the tens of thousands, and is generally very sparse, since a typical basket contains only a few items. Association rules were invented as a way to find simple patterns in such data in a relatively efficient computational manner.

In our reductionist framework, a typical data mining algorithm for association rules has the following components:

1. *task = description: associations between variables*

2. *structure = probabilistic "association rules" (patterns)*

3. *score function = thresholds on accuracy and support*

4. *search method = systematic search (breadth-first with pruning)*

5. *data management technique = multiple linear scans*

The score function used in association rule searching is a simple binary function. There are two thresholds: p_s is a lower bound on the support of the rule (e.g., $p_s = 0.1$ when we want only those rules that cover at least 10% of the data) and p_a is a lower bound on the accuracy of the rule (e.g., $p_a = 0.9$ when we want only rules that are at least 90% accurate). A pattern gets a score of 1 if it satisfies both of the threshold conditions, and gets a score of 0 otherwise. The goal is find all rules (patterns) with a score of 1.

The search problem is formidable given the exponential number of possible association rules—namely, $O(p2^{p-1})$ for binary variables if we limit our attention to rules with positive propositions (e.g., $A = 1$) in the left and right-hand sides. Nonetheless, by taking advantage of the nature of the score function, we can reduce the average run-time of the algorithm to much more manageable proportions. Note that if either $p(A = 1) \leq p_s$ or $p(B = 1) \leq p_s$, clearly $p(A = 1, B = 1) \leq p_s$. We can use this observation in our search for association rules by first finding all of the individual events (such as $A = 1$) that have a probability greater than the threshold p_s (this takes one linear scan of the entire database). An event (or set of events) is called "frequent" if the probability of the event(s) is greater than the support threshold p_s. We consider all possible pairs of these frequent events to be candidate frequent sets of size 2.

In the more general case of going from frequent sets of size $k-1$ to frequent sets of size k, we can *prune* any sets of size k that contain a subset of $k-1$ items that themselves are not frequent at the $k-1$ level. For example, if we had only frequent sets $\{A = 1, B = 1\}$ and $\{B = 1, C = 1\}$, we could combine them to get the candidate $k = 3$ frequent set $\{A = 1, B = 1, C = 1\}$. However, if the subset of items $\{A = 1, C = 1\}$ was not frequent (i.e., this item set were not on the list of frequent sets of size $k = 2$), then $\{A = 1, B = 1, C = 1\}$ could not be frequent either, and it could safely be pruned. Note that this pruning can take place without searching the data directly, resulting in a considerable computational speedup for large data sets.

Given the pruned list of candidate frequent sets of size k, the algorithm performs another linear scan of the database to determine which of these sets are in fact frequent . The confirmed frequent sets of size k (if any) are combined to generate all possible frequent sets containing $k + 1$ events, followed by pruning, and then another scan of the database, and so on—until no more frequent sets can be generated. (In the worst case, all possible sets of events are frequent and the algorithm takes exponential time. However, since in practice the data are often very sparse for the types of transaction data sets analyzed by these algorithms, the cardinality of the largest frequent set is usually quite small (relative to n), at least for relatively large support values.) The algorithm then makes one final linear scan through the data set, using the list of all frequent sets that have been found. It determines which subset combinations of the frequent sets also satisfy the accuracy threshold when expressed as a rule, and then returns the corresponding association rules.

Association rule algorithms comprise an interesting class of data mining algorithms in that the search and data management components are their most critical components. In particular, association rule algorithms use a systematic breadth-first, general-to-specific search method that explicitly tries to minimize the number of linear scans through the database. While there exist numerous other rule-finding algorithms in the machine learning literature (with similar rule-based representations), association rule algorithms are designed specifically to operate on very large data sets in a relatively efficient manner. Thus, for example, research papers on association rule algorithms tend to emphasize computational efficiency rather than interpretation of the rules that the algorithms produce.

5.3.3 Vector-Space Algorithms for Text Retrieval

The general task of "retrieval by content" is loosely described as follows: we have a query object and a large database of objects, and we would like to find the k objects in the database that are most similar to the query object. We are all familiar with this problem in the context of searching through online collections of text. For example, our query could be a short set of keywords and the "database" could correspond to a large set of Web pages. Our task in this case would be to find the Web pages that are most relevant to our keywords.

Chapter 14 discusses this retrieval task in greater depth. Here we look at a generic text retrieval algorithm in terms of its components. One of the most important aspects of this problem is how similarity is defined. Text documents are of different lengths and structure. How can we compare such diverse documents? A key idea in text retrieval is to reduce all documents to a uniform vector representation, as follows. Let $t_1, \ldots, t_p$ be p *terms* (words, phrases, etc.). We can think of these as variables, or columns in our data matrix. A document (a row in our data matrix) is represented by a vector of length p, where the ith component contains the count of how often term t_i appears in the document. As with market-basket data, in practice we can have a very large data matrix (n in the millions, p in the tens of thousands) that is very sparse (most documents will have many zeros). Again, of course, we normally would not actually store the data as a large $n \times p$ matrix: a more efficient representation is to store a list for each term t_i of all the documents containing that term.

Given this "vector-space" representation, we can now readily define similarity. One simple definition is to make the similarity distance a function of the angle between the two vectors in p-space. The angle measures similarity in a given direction in "term-space" and factors out any differences arising from the fact that large documents tend to have more occurrences of a word than small documents. The vector-space representation and the angle similarity measure may seem relatively primitive, but in practice this scheme works surprisingly well, and there exists a multitude of variations on this basic theme in text retrieval.

With this information, we are ready to define the components of a simple generic text-retrieval algorithm that takes one document and finds the k most similar documents:

1. *task = retrieval of the k most similar documents in a database relative to a given query*

2. *representation = vector of term occurrences*

3. *score function = angle between two vectors*

4. *search method = various techniques*

5. *data management technique = various fast indexing strategies*

There are many variations on the specific definitions of the components given above. For example, in defining the score function, we can specify similarity metrics more general than the angle function. In specifying the search method, various heuristic search techniques are possible. Note that search in this context is *real-time search*, since the algorithm has to retrieve the patterns in realtime for a user (unlike the data mining algorithms we looked at earlier, for which search meant off-line searching for the optimal parameters and model structures).

Different applications may call for different components to be used in a retrieval algorithm. For example, in searching through legal documents, the absence of particular terms might be significant, and we might want to reflect this in our definition of a score function. In a different context we might want the opposite effect, i.e., to downweight the fact that two documents do *not* contain certain terms (relative to the terms they have in common).

It is clear, however, that the model representation is really the key idea here. Once the use vector representation has been established, we can define a wide range of similarity metrics in vector-space, and we can use standard search and indexing techniques to find near neighbors in sparse p-dimensional space. Different retrieval algorithms may vary in the details of the score function or search methods, but most share the same underlying vector representation of the data. Were we to define a different representation for a document (say a generative model for the data based on some form of grammar), we would probably have to come up with fundamentally different score functions and search methods.

5.4   Discussion

For the novice and the seasoned researcher alike, wandering through the jungle of data mining algorithms can be somewhat bewildering. We hope that the component-based view presented in this chapter provides a useful practical tool for the reader in evaluating algorithms. The process is as follows: try to strip away the jargon and marketing spin that are inevitable in any research paper or product literature, and reduce the algorithm to its basic components. The component-based description provides a well-defined and "calibrated" framework on which to base comparisons—e.g., we can compare a new algorithm to other well-known algorithms and see precisely how it differs in terms of its components, if it differs at all.

It is interesting to note the different emphases placed on algorithmic aspects of data mining in different research communities. A cursory glance through most statistical journals will reveal plenty of equations specifying models, score functions, and computational methods, with relatively few detailed algorithmic specifications of how the models will be fit in practice. Conversely, computer science journals on machine learning and pattern recognition often emphasize the computational methods and algorithms, with little emphasis on the appropriateness of either the structure of the model or the score function being used to fit it. For example, it is not uncommon to see empirical comparisons being made among *algorithms*, rather than among the underlying models or score functions. In the context of data mining, the different emphases in the two research areas have led to the development of quite different (and often complementary) methodologies. Statistical approaches often place significant emphasis on theoretical aspects of inference procedures (e.g., parameter estimation and model selection) and less emphasis on computational issues. Computer science approaches to data mining tend to do the reverse, focusing more on efficient search and data management and less on the appropriateness of the model (and pattern) structures, or on the relevance of the score function. This "cultural" difference is worth keeping in mind throughout this text, as it helps to explain the factors that motivated the development of specific models, inference methods, and algorithms within these two research communities.

For both the statistical and the computer science schools of thought, it is probably fair to say that the typical research paper is not very clear on what the underlying components of a particular algorithm are. The literature is replete with fancy-sounding names and acronyms for different algorithms. In many papers, the descriptions of the model structure, the score function, and the search method are abstrusely intertwined.

In practice, *all* components of a data mining algorithm are essential. The *relative* importance of the model, the score function, and the computational implementation varies from problem to problem. For small data sets, the interpretability and predictive power of the model may be (relatively speaking) a much more important factor than any computational concerns. However, as data sets become larger (in terms of both the number of measurements and the number of variables), the role of computation becomes increasingly important. For example, while a clustering algorithm with time complexity $O(n^2)$ may be tractable with $n = 100$, it will be completely intractable for $n = 10^8$ (and will likely remain intractable in our lifetime!). Furthermore, the time complexity is typically stated assuming that all of the data reside in main memory. If for each computational step in the algorithm, instead of a data point being retrieved from main memory, it must be retrieved from disk (for example), there will be an additional large multiplicative constant time factor involved in the expression for time complexity.

For very large data sets there are clear trade-offs between the sophistication of the modeling we wish to carry out and the computational expense (i.e., time taken) to achieve a certain quality of fit. For massive data sets, the computational methodology directly influences what types of model structures can be fit to the data. Computational issues tend to play a much more prominent role in data mining than in traditional statistical modeling.

Of course, the model structures and the score functions should always be carefully chosen and explicitly acknowledged in any data mining problem. There is little advantage in being able to handle vast data sets efficiently if the underlying models that are returned are not useful. Thus, data miners need to carefully evaluate the trade-offs between searching for sophisticated model/pattern structures and the computational resources required to find and fit such structures reliably.

5.5   Further Reading

There are very few papers that promote a systematic component-based view of data mining algorithms. An exception is Buntine, Fischer, and Pressburger (1999), who provide an interesting discussion (with examples) of how to achieve rapid automatic prototyping of data mining algorithms from high-level algorithmic specifications. Classic general texts on algorithms are Cormen, Leiserson and Rivest (1990) and Knuth (1997).

The principles of CART were first described in Breiman et al. (1984), and C4.5 is described in detail in Quinlan (1993). Buntine (1992) and Chipman, George, and McCulloch (1998) discuss Bayesian extensions to CART. Crawford (1989) describes methods for constructing classification trees in an incremental manner, and Gehrke et al. (1999) describe related ideas for scalable tree construction algorithms for massive data sets. Ballard (1997) is a very readable introductory text on modern neural network algorithms and their relation to actual brain modeling. Geman, Bienenstock, and Doursat (1992) provide an excellent discussion of the connections between statistical ideas and neural network learning algorithms. Ripley (1996) gives a thorough survey of both neural network algorithms (chapter 5) and tree learning algorithms (chapter 7) from a statistical perspective, while the text by Bishop (1995) is devoted entirely to a statistical treatment of neural network learning algorithms.

Agrawal et al. (1996) provide a review of association rule algorithms, as well as an in-depth look at the search method and its efficiency. Salton and McGill (1983) give a useful introduction to information retrieval, and Witten, Moffatt, and Bell (1999) include a detailed and thorough discussion of the various issues involved in retrieval algorithms for massive text and image databases.

6 *Models and Patterns*

6.1 Introduction

We have introduced the distinction between *models* and *patterns* in earlier chapters. Here we explore these ideas in more depth, and examine some of the major classes of models and patterns used in data mining, in preparation for a detailed examination in subsequent chapters.

A model is a high-level, global description of a data set. It takes a large sample perspective. It may be descriptive—summarizing the data in a convenient and concise way—or it may be inferential, allowing one to make some statement about the population from which the data were drawn or about likely future data values. In this chapter we will discuss a variety of basic model forms such as linear regression models, mixture models, and Markov models.

In contrast, a pattern is a local feature of the data, perhaps holding for only a few records or a few variables (or both). An example of a pattern would be a local "structural" feature in our p-dimensional variable space such as a mode (or a gap) in a density function or an inflexion point in a regression curve. Often patterns are of interest because they represent departures from the general run of the data: a pair of variables that have a particularly high correlation, a set of items that have exceptionally high values on some variables, a group of records that always score the same on some variables, and so on. As with models, we may want to find patterns for descriptive reasons or for inferential reasons. We may want to identify members of the existing database that have unusual properties, or we may want to predict which future records are likely to have unusual properties. Examples of patterns are transient waveforms in an EEG trace, unusual combinations of products that are frequently purchased together by retail customers, and outliers in a database of semiconductor manufacturing data.

Data compression can provide a useful way to illustrate the concept of a patterns versus a model. Consider transmitter T that has an image I that is to be sent to a receiver R (though the principle holds for data sets that are not images). There are two main strategies: (a) send all of the data (the pixels in the image I) exactly, or (b) transmit some compressed version of the image—that is, some summary of the image I. Data mining to a large extent corresponds to the second approach, the compression being achieved either by representing the original data as a model, or by identifying unusual features of the data through patterns.

In modeling, some loss in fidelity is likely to be incurred when we summarize the data—this means that the receiver R will not be able to reconstruct the data precisely. An example of a model for the image data might be replacing each square of 16×16 pixels in the original image by the average values of these pixels. The "model" in this case would just be a set of smaller and lower resolution (1/16th) images. A more sophisticated model might adaptively partition each image into local regions of different sizes and shapes, where the pixel values can be fairly accurately described by a constant pixel intensity within each such region. The "model" (or message) in this case would be both the values of the constants within each region and the description of the boundaries of the regions for each. For both types of models (the average-pixel model and the locally constant model) it is clear that the complexity of the image model (the number of pixels being averaged, the average size of the locally constant regions) can be traded for the amount of information being transmitted (or equivalently, the amount of information being lost in the transmission—that is, the compression rate).

From a pattern detection viewpoint, a pattern in an image is some structure in the image that is purely local: for example, a partially obscured circular object in the upper-left corner of the image. This is clearly a different form of compression from the global compression models above. The receiver R can no longer reconstruct a summary of the *whole image*, but it does have a description of some *local part* of the image. Depending on the problem and objectives, local structure may be much more relevant than a global model. Rather than sending a summary model description of a vast noisy "sea" of pixel values, the transmitter T instead "focuses" the receiver R's attention on the important aspects. We can think of association rules from chapter 5 in this context: they try to focus attention on potentially interesting associations among subsets of variables.

The analogy between image coding and data analysis is not perfect (for example, compression, as we have described it, does not take into account the idea of generalization to unseen data), but nonetheless, it allows us to grasp the essential trade-offs between representing local structure at a fairly high resolution and lower-resolution global structure.

This chapter is organized as follows: section 6.2 discusses some of the fundamental properties of models and the choices we have to make in building a model. Section 6.3 focuses on the general principles behind models in which one of the variables is singled out as a "response" to be predicted from the others. This includes regression and supervised classification models. Many data mining problems involve large numbers of variables, and these present particular challenges, which are discussed in section 6.5. Descriptive models are discussed in section 6.4. Many data sets contain data that have been collected to conform to some schema (such as time series or image data), and they typically require special consideration in modeling. Section 6.6 discusses issues associated with such structured data. Finally, section 6.7 describes patterns for both multivariate and sequential data.

6.2   Fundamentals of Modeling

A model is an abstract representation of a real-world process. For example, $Y = 3X + 2$ is a very simple model of how the variable Y might relate to the variable X. This particular model can be thought of as an instance of the more general *model structure* $Y = aX + c$, where for this particular model we have set $a = 3$ and $c = 2$. More generally still, we could put $Y = aX + c + e$, where e is a random variable accounting for a random component of the mapping from X to Y (we will return to this later). We often refer to a and c as the *parameters* of the model, and will often use the notation θ to refer to a generic parameter or a set (or vector) of parameters, as we did in chapter 4. In this example, $\theta = \{a, c\}$. Given the form or structure of a model, we choose appropriate values for its parameters by estimation—that is, by minimizing or maximizing an appropriate score function measuring the fit of the model to the data. Procedures for this were described in chapter 4 and are described further in later chapters.

However, before we can estimate the parameters of a model, we must first choose an appropriate functional form of the model itself. The aim of this section is to present a high-level overview of the main classes of models used in data mining.

Model building in data mining is data-driven. It is usually not driven by the notion of any underlying mechanism or "reality," but simply seeks to capture the relationships in the data. Even in those cases in which there is a postulated true generative mechanism for the data, we should bear in mind that, as George Box put it, "All models are wrong but some are useful." For example, while we might postulate the existence of a linear model to explain the data, it is likely to be a fiction, since even in the best of circumstances there will be small nonlinear effects that we will be unable to capture in the model. We are looking for a model that encapsulates the main aspects of the data generating process.

Since data mining is data-driven, the discovery of a highly predictive model (for example) should not be taken to mean that there is a causal relationship. For example, an analysis of customer records may show that customers who buy high-quality wines are also more likely to buy designer clothes. Clearly one propensity is not causally related to the other propensity (in either direction). Rather, they are both more likely to be the consequence of a relatively high income. However, the fact that neither the wine nor the clothes variable causes the other does not mean that they are not useful for predictive purposes. Predicting the likely clothes-buying behavior from observed wine-buying behavior would be entirely legitimate (if the relationship were found in the data), from a marketing perspective. Since no causal relationship has been established, however, it would be false to conclude that *manipulating* one of the variables would lead to a change in the other. That is, inducing people to buy high-quality wines would be unlikely to lead them also to buy designer clothes, even if the relationship existed in the data.

6.3   Model Structures for Prediction

In a predictive model, one of the variables is expressed as a function of the others. This permits the value of the *response* variable to be predicted from given values of the others (the *explanatory* or *predictor* variables). The response variable in general predictive models is often denoted by Y, and the p predictor variables by $X_1, \ldots, X_p$. Thus, for example, we might want to construct a model for predicting the probability that an applicant for a loan will default, based on application forms and the behavior of past customers contained in a database. The record for the ith past customer can be conveniently represented as $\{(\mathbf{x}(i), y(i))\}$. Here $y(i)$ is the outcome class (good or bad) of the ith customer, and $\mathbf{x}(i)$ is the vector $\mathbf{x} = (x_1(i), \ldots, x_p(i))$ of application form values for the ith customer. The model will yield predictions, $\hat{y} = f(x_1, \ldots, x_p; \theta)$ where $\hat{y}$ is the prediction of the model and θ represents the parameters of the model structure. When Y is quantitative, this task of estimating a mapping from the p-dimensional $\mathbf{X}$ to Y is known as *regression*. When Y is categorical, the task of learning a mapping from $\mathbf{X}$ to Y is called *classification learning* or *supervised classification*. Both of these tasks can be considered *function approximation* problems in that we are learning a mapping from a p-dimensional variable $\mathbf{X}$ to Y. For simplicity of exposition in this chapter we will focus primarily on the regression task, since many of the same general principles carry over directly to the classification task. Chapters 10 and 11 deal, respectively, with supervised classification and regression in detail.

6.3.1   Regression Models with Linear Structure

We begin our discussion of predictive models with models in which the response variable is a linear function of the predictor variables:

$$\hat{Y} = a_0 + \sum_{j=1}^{p} a_j X_j \tag{6.1}$$

where $\theta = \{a_0, \ldots, a_p\}$. Again we note that the model is purely empirical, so that the existence of a well-fitting and highly predictive model does not imply any causal relationship. We have used $\hat{Y}$ rather than simply Y on the left of this expression because it is a *model*, which has been constructed from the data. That is, the values of $\hat{Y}$ are values predicted from the $\mathbf{X}$, and not values actually observed. This distinction is discussed in more detail in chapter 11.

Geometrically, this model describes a p-dimensional hyperplane embedded in a $(p+1)$-dimensional space with slope determined by the a_j's and intercept by a_0. The aim of parameter estimation is to choose the a values to locate and angle this hyperplane so as to provide the best fit to the data $\{(\mathbf{x}(i), y(i))\}, i = 1, \ldots, n$, where the quality of fit is measured in terms of the differences between observed y values and the values $\hat{y}$ predicted from the model.

Models with this type of linear structure hold a special place in the history of data analysis, partly because estimation of parameters is straightforward with appropriate score functions, and partly because the structure of the model is simple and easy to interpret. For example, the *additive* nature of the model means that the parameters tell us the effect of changing any one of the predictor variables "keeping the others constant." Of course, there are circumstances in which the notion of *individual contribution* makes little sense. In particular, if two variables are highly correlated, then it is not meaningful to talk of the contribution from changing one while "holding the other constant." Such issues are discussed in more detail in later chapters.

We can retain the additive nature of the model, while generalizing beyond linear functions of the predictor variables. Thus

$$\hat{Y} = a_0 + \sum_{j=1}^{p} a_j f_j(X_j) \tag{6.2}$$

where the f_j functions are smooth (but possibly nonlinear) functions of the X_js. For example, the f_js could be log, square-root, or related transformations of the original X variables. This model still assumes that the dependent variable Y depends on the independent variables in the model (the Xs) in an additive fashion. Again, this may be a strong assumption in practice, but it will lead to a model in which it may be easy to interpret the contribution of each individual X variable. The simplicity of the model also means that there are relatively few parameters ($p + 1$) to estimate from the data, making the estimation problem relatively straightforward.

We can also generalize this linear model structure to allow general polynomials in the Xs with cross-product terms to allow interaction among the X_js in the model. The one-dimensional case is again familiar—we can imagine a 2nd or 3rd or kth order polynomial interpolating the observed y values. The multidimensional case generalizes this so that we have a smooth surface defined on p variables in the $(p + 1)$-dimensional space.

Note in passing that even though these predictive models are *nonlinear* in the variables X, they are still *linear* in the parameters. This makes estimation of these parameters much easier than in the case where the parameters enter in a nonlinear fashion, as we will see in chapter 11.

> **Example 6.1** In figure 6.1(a) we show a set of 50 data points that are simulated from the equation $y = 0.001x^3 - 0.05x^2 + x^3 + e$, where e is additive Gaussian noise (zero mean, standard deviation $\sigma = 3$), over the range $x \in [1, 50]$. A linear fit to the data is shown in figure 6.1(b) and a second-order polynomial fit is shown in figure 6.1(c). Although the linear fit captures the general upward trend in Y as a function of X (over this particular range), the second-order fit is clearly better. Neither fit fully captures the underlying curvature of the true structure, as can be seen from the structure in the errors for each model (that

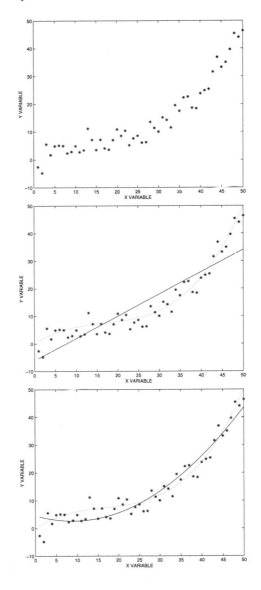

Figure 6.1 (a) Fifty data points that are simulated from a third-order polynomial equation with additive Gaussian (Normal) noise, (b) the fit of the model $aX + b$ (solid line), (c) the fit of the model $aX^2 + bX + c$ (solid line). The dotted lines in (b) and (c) indicate the true model from which the data points were generated (see text). The model parameters in each case were estimated by minimizing the sum of squared errors between model predictions and observed data.

is, the errors for each model have systematic structure as a function of x). Both fits were determined by minimizing a sum of squares score function.

Note that by allowing models with higher order terms and interactions between the components of **X** we can in principle estimate a more complex surface than with a simple linear model (a hyperplane). However, note that as p (the dimensionality of the input space) increases, the number of possible interaction terms in our model (such as $X_j X_k$) increases as a combinatorial function of p. Since each term has a weight coefficient (a parameter) in the additive model, the number of parameters to be estimated for the full model (with all possible interaction terms of order k among p variables) increases dramatically as p increases. The interpretation and understanding of such a model makes the estimation problem more difficult, and it also becomes increasingly difficult as p increases. A practical alternative is to select some small subset of the overall set of possible interactions to participate in the model. However, if the selection is carried out in a data-driven fashion (as is typically the fashion in a data mining application), the number of all possible interaction terms (the size of the search space) scales as 2^p, making the search problem exponentially more difficult as dimensionality p increases. We will return to this issue of how to handle dimensionality later in this chapter.

The generalization to polynomials brings up an important point, namely the *complexity* of the model. The more complex models contain the simpler models as special cases (so-called *nesting*). For example, the first-order $\alpha_1 X_1 + \alpha_0$ model can be viewed as a special case of the 2nd order polynomial model $\alpha_2 X_1^2 + \alpha_1 X_1 + \alpha_0$ by setting α_2 to zero. Thus, it is clear that a complex model (a high-order polynomial in the **X** variables) can always fit the observed data at least as well any simpler model can (since it includes any simpler model as a special case). In turn, this raises the complicated issue of how we should choose one model over another when the complexity (or expressive power) of each is different. This is a subtle question: we may want the model that is closest to some hypothesized unknown "truth"; we may want to find a model that captures the main features of the data without being too complicated; we may want to find the model that has the best predictive performance on data that it has not seen; and so on. We will return to this in later chapters. For now, however, we return to focus on the expressive capabilities of the models themselves without thinking yet of how we will choose among such models given observed data.

Transforming the predictor variables is one way to generalize a linear structure. Another way is to transform the response variable. $sqrt(Y)$ may be

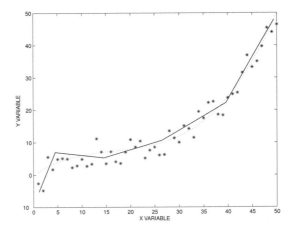

Figure 6.2 An example of a piecewise linear fit to the data of figure 6.1 with $k = 5$ linear segments.

perfectly related to a linear combination of the **X** variables, so that rather than fitting Y directly we may want to transform it by taking the square root first, and then use a linear combination of the **X** variables to predict $sqrt(Y)$. Of course, we will not know beforehand that the square root is an appropriate transformation. We have to experiment, trying different transformations (and bearing in mind the constraints implied by the nature of the measurements involved, as discussed in chapter 2). This is why data mining is an exciting voyage of discovery, and not a mere exercise in applying standard tools in standard ways.

As we show in chapter 11, the simple linear regression model can be thought of as seeking to predict the expected value of the Y distribution at each value of the **X** predictors, namely $E[Y|X]$. That is, the regression model provides a prediction of a *parameter* of the conditional distribution of Y, where the parameter is the mean. More generally, of course, we can seek to predict other parameters of the conditional Y distribution from a linear combination of the **X** variables. This leads to the ideas of *generalized linear models* and *neural networks,* discussed in chapter 11.

We see that, although linear models are simple and easy to interpret (and, we will also see, their parameters can be easily estimated), they permit ready generalization to very powerful and flexible families of models. Any idea that the word *linear* implies a narrow class of models is illusory.

6.3.2   Local Piecewise Model Structures for Regression

Yet further generalizations of the basic linear model can be achieved if we assume that Y is *locally* linear in the X's, with a different local dependence in various regions of the $\mathbf{X}$ space—that is, a piecewise linear model. Geometrically, our model structure consists of a *set* of different p-dimensional hyperplanes, each covering a region of the input ($\mathbf{X}$) space disjoint from the others. The parameters of this model structure include both the local parameters for each hyperplane as well as the locations (boundaries) of the hyperplanes. For a one-dimensional X the picture is quite easy to visualize: a curve is approximated by k different line segments (see figure 6.2 for an example). Note that, in this figure, the line is continuous, with the line segments joining up. We could define a model structure that relaxes this, not requiring continuity at the ends of the line segments. This can be a useful model form, but sometimes the discontinuities can be problematic and undesirable because they imply a sudden jump in the predicted value of the response variable for an infinitesimal change in a predictor variable. To take an example, if a split between two line segments occurs at the value $50,000 for the variable income, we might get widely varying $\hat{y}$ predictions of the response variable, probability of loan default, for two applicants who are identical except that one earns $50,001 and the other earns $49,999. If the discontinuities are regarded as undesirable, one can go further and enforce continuity of derivatives of various orders at the end of the segments (which would clearly no longer be straight lines). Such curve segments are termed *splines*, with the whole model being a *spline function*. Typically, each line segment is taken to be a low-degree (quadratic or cubic) polynomial. The result is a smooth curve, but one that may change direction many times—the model would be highly flexible.

These ideas can be generalized to more than one predictor variable. Again the local segments (which will now be (hyper)surfaces, not merely lines) may, but need not, join at their edges. Tree structures (described for supervised classification problems in chapter 10) provide an example of models of this form.

The piecewise linear model is a good example of how we can build relatively complex models for nonlinear phenomena by piecing together simple components (in this case hyperplanes). This is a recurring theme in data mining, the idea of composing complex global structures from relatively simple local components—and it also provides a link between ideas of modeling and ideas of pattern detection. That is, the locality also provides a framework for decomposing a complex model into simpler local patterns. For example, a "peak" in $\hat{Y}$ as a function of X will be reflected by two appropriately sloped line segments that adjoin each other.

This subsection and the preceding one together serve to show how complex models are built up from simpler ones, either by combining the simpler ones into more complex ones, or by generalizing them in various ways. No model used in data mining exists in splendid isolation. Rather, all such models are linked by a variety of connections, each being generalizations, special cases, or variants of others. The trick in effective model building in data mining is to choose a model form that is well suited to answer the question being posed. This is not simply an exercise in choosing one model form, applying it, and presenting the conclusion. Rather, we fit a model, modify it or extend it in the light of the results, and repeat the exercise. Data mining, like data analysis in general, is an iterative process.

6.3.3 Nonparametric "Memory-Based" Local Models

In the preceding subsection we gave some examples of how models that are based on local characteristics of the data are related to, indeed are on a continuum including, broad global models. In this subsection we develop the ideas of local modeling further. (We recall that patterns, while also local, are isolated structures, and are not components of a global summary of the data. Thus we can talk of local modeling techniques as distinct from patterns.)

Roughly speaking, the spline and tree models briefly described above replace the data points by a function estimated from a neighborhood of data points. An alternative strategy is to retain the data points, and to leave the estimation of the predicted value of Y until the time at which a prediction is actually required. No longer are the data replaced by a function and its estimated parameters. For example, to estimate the value of a response variable Y for a new case, we could take the average of the Y values of the most similar k objects in the data set, where most similar is defined in terms of the predictor variables.

This idea has been extended to include all of the data set objects, but to weight them according to how similar they are to the new object—dissimilar ones will have small weight, similar ones large weight. The weight determines just how much their Y value contributes to the final estimate. An example of such an estimator is the *locally weighted regression* or *loess regression* model.

Although we have described the local smoothing ideas in a predictive modeling context, they can also be applied in a descriptive and density estimation context—which is the domain for which they were in fact first developed. Indeed, we have already seen an example of such methods for graphical display of a single variable in chapter 3 (where we used the ideas to estimate a probability density function), and we shall see more of them in later chapters. In this context, the so-called *kernel* estimators introduced in chapter 3 are common.

The obvious question with such estimators is how to determine the form of the weight function. A weight function that decays only slowly with decreasing similarity will lead to a smooth estimate, while one that decays rapidly will lead to a jagged estimate. A compromise must be found that is best suited to the aims of the analysis.

The weight function can be decomposed into two parts. One is its precise functional form, and the other is its "bandwidth." Thus, suppose that $K\left(\frac{x-z}{h}\right)$ is a smoothing function, which determines the contribution to the estimate at a new point z from a data set point at x. The size of this contribution will depend on the form of K and also on the size of the bandwidth h. A larger bandwidth h leads to a smoother function estimate, and a smaller bandwidth leads to a rougher, more jagged estimate. In practice, the precise form of the weight function turns out to be less important than the "bandwidth."

> **Example 6.2** Figure 6.3 shows an example of a regression function constructed with a triangular kernel using three different bandwidths. Here we are estimating the proportion of Nitrous oxide (NOx) in emissions as a function of ethanol (E), based on measurements taken on 81 automotive engines under different conditions. The widest bandwidth ($h = 0.5$) is clearly too broad, leading to an oversmoothed estimate that "misses" the central peak and the two tails. The narrowest bandwidth ($h = 0.02$) yields a very "spiky" estimate that appears to follow the noise in the observed data. The intermediate-valued bandwidth ($h = 0.1$) represents a reasonable trade-off, where the major features of the relationship between NOx and E are retained without overfitting. Subjective visual inspection can be useful technique for choosing bandwidths for simple one-dimensional problems, but does not generalize well to the multidimensional case. One can also use more automated methods such as cross-validation for choosing h in a data-driven manner.

Kernel methods are closely related to *nearest neighbor methods*. Indeed, both classes of methods have now been extended and developed so that in some cases they are identical. Whereas kernel methods define the degree of smoothing in terms of a kernel function and bandwidth, nearest neighbor

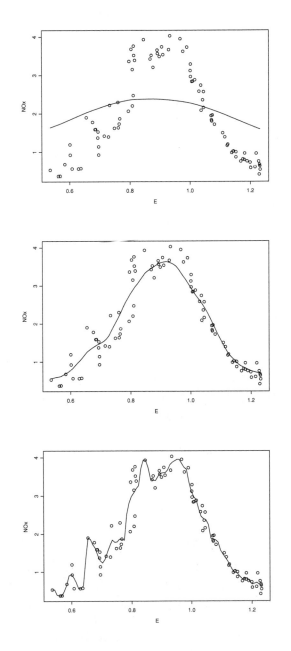

Figure 6.3   Nitrous oxide (NOx) as a function of ethanol (E) using kernel regression with triangular kernels, with bandwidths $h = 0.5, 0.1$, and 0.02, in clockwise order.

methods let the data determine the bandwidth by defining it in terms of the *number* of nearest neighbors. For example, the basic single nearest neighbor classifier (where Y is a class identifier) assigns a new object to the same class as its most similar object in the data set, and the k-nearest neighbor classifier assigns a new object to the most common class amongst the most similar k objects in the data set. More sophisticated nearest neighbor methods weight the contribution of according to distance from the point to be classified, and more sophisticated kernel methods let the bandwidth h depend on the data—so that they can be seen to be almost identical in terms of model structure.

Local model structures such as kernel models are often described as *nonparametric* because the model is largely data-driven with no parameters in the conventional sense (except for the bandwidth h). Such data-driven smoothing techniques (such as the kernel models) are useful for data interpretation, at least in one or two dimensions.

It will be clear that local models have their attractions. However, no model provides an answer to all problems, and local models have weaknesses. In particular, as the number of variables in the predictor space increases, so the number of data points required to obtain accurate estimates increases exponentially (a consequence of the "curse of dimensionality"—see section 6.5 below). This means that these "local neighborhood" models tend to scale poorly to high dimensions.

Another drawback, particularly from a data mining viewpoint, is the lack of interpretability of the model. In low dimensions ($p \leq 3$ or so), we can plot the estimates. In high dimensions this is not possible, and there is no direct manner by which to summarize the model. Indeed, it is stretching the definition of a model to even call these representations models at all, since they are never explicitly defined as functions but instead are implicitly defined by the data.

6.3.4 Stochastic Components of Model Structures

Until this point, apart from a few brief references, we have ignored the fact that, with real data, we generally cannot find a perfect functional relationship between the predictor variables $\mathbf{X}$ and the response variable Y. That is, for any given vector of predictor variables $\mathbf{x}$, more than one value of Y can be observed. The distribution of the values y at each value of $\mathbf{X}$ represents an aspect of variation that cannot be reduced by more sophisticated model building using just the variables in $\mathbf{X}$. For this reason it is sometimes termed the *unexplainable* or *nonsystematic* or *random* component of the variation, with the variation in Y that can be explained in terms of the $\mathbf{X}$ variables being termed the *explainable* or *systematic* variation. (Of course merely because the systematic variation can be explained in principle by the variables in $\mathbf{X}$, does not mean that we can necessarily build a model that will be able to do it).

In most of our discussion we have focused on the systematic component of the models, but we also need to consider the random component. The random component of models can arise from many sources. It can arise from simple measurement error—repeated measurements of Y will give different results, as discussed in chapter 2. The random component can also arise because our set of $\mathbf{X}$ variables does not include all of the variables that are required to make a perfect prediction of Y (for example, predicting whether a customer will purchase a particular product or not based only on past purchasing behavior will ignore potentially relevant demographic information about them such as age, income, and so on). Indeed, we should expect this usually to be the case—it would be a rare situation in which *all* of the variability in a variable was perfectly explained by just a handful of other variables, down to the finest detail.

> **Example 6.3** We can extend the regression modeling framework discussed earlier to include a stochastic component. We will assume that for any $\mathbf{x}$ we will observe a particular y but with some noise added; that is, there is some inherent uncertainty in the relationship between $\mathbf{x}$ and y:
>
> $$y = g(\mathbf{x}; \theta) + e \qquad (6.3)$$
>
> where $g(\mathbf{x}; \theta))$ is a deterministic function of the inputs $\mathbf{x}$, and e is often assumed to be a random variable (which is independent of $\mathbf{x}$) with constant variance σ^2 and zero-mean. The random term e can reflect noise in the measurement process (that is, we don't observe the "true" value for y but instead get a measurement of y which has random noise added). More generally, the random component e can reflect the fact that there are hidden variables (that are not being measured or are "hidden" from observation) that affect y in a manner that cannot be accounted for by the dependence of Y on the variables $\mathbf{X}$ alone.
>
> The zero-mean assumption on e is fairly harmless, since if the noise has a constant non-zero mean it can be absorbed into g without loss of generality. If, for example, we make the common assumption that e has a Normal distribution with zero mean and constant variance σ^2, then
>
> $$y|\mathbf{x} \sim N(\mu_{y|\mathbf{x}}, \sigma^2), \quad \mu_{y|\mathbf{x}} = E[y|\mathbf{x}] = g(\mathbf{x}; \theta). \qquad (6.4)$$

The constant σ^2 assumption may require closer scrutiny in practice: for example, if Y represents the variable annual credit card spending, and X is income, it is plausible that the *variability* in Y will grow as a function of X. If this were the case, then to model this effect, σ would need to be a function of x in the model above.

Note that the functional form of g is left free in these equations; that is, it could be chosen to be any of the various model structures we discussed earlier. We have already seen in chapter 4 that the Normal assumption on e above leads naturally to the principle of least-squares regression—that is, finding the parameters θ that determine g such that $g(\mathbf{x}; \theta)$ minimizes the sum of squares of between $f(\mathbf{x}; \theta)$ and the observed y values.

The random component is important when it comes to choosing suitable score functions for estimating parameters and choosing between models. The likelihood score function, for example, introduced in chapter 4 and also discussed elsewhere, is based on assumptions about the form of the distribution of the random component. Extensions of the likelihood function that include a smoothness penalty so that too complex a model is not fitted also require assumptions about the distribution of the random component. More advanced methods based on likelihood concepts (for example, so-called *quasi-likelihood methods*) relax detailed distributional assumptions, but still base their choice of parameter estimates on aspects of the distribution of the random component.

6.3.5   Predictive Models for Classification

So far we have concentrated on predictive models in which the variable to be predicted, Y, was quantitative. We now briefly consider the case of a categorical variable Y, taking only a few possible categorical values. This is a *(supervised) classification* problem, with the aim being to assign a new object to its correct class (that is, the correct Y category) on the basis of its observed $\mathbf{X}$ values.

In classification we are essentially interested in modeling the boundaries between classes. As with regression, we can could make simple parametric assumptions about the functional form of the boundaries. For example, a classic approach is to use a linear hyperplane in the p-dimensional $\mathbf{X}$ space to define a decision boundary between two classes. That is, the model partitions the $\mathbf{X}$-space into disjoint decision regions (one for each class), where the decision regions are separated by linear boundaries (see figure 6.4 for an example). A more complex model might allow higher-order polynomial

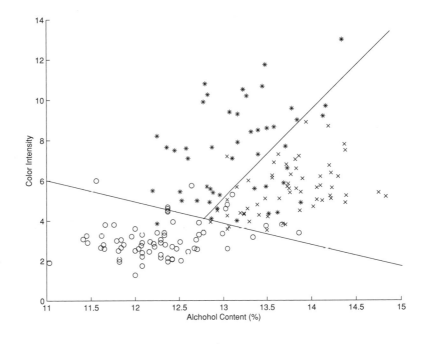

Figure 6.4   An example of linear decision boundaries for the two-dimensional wine classification data set of chapter 5 (See figure 5.1).

terms, yielding smooth polynomial decision boundaries. If we allow very flexible non-linear forms for our boundaries we arrive at models such as the neural network classifiers discussed in chapter 5.

Just as in regression modeling, another way to allow more flexibility is to combine multiple simple local models, e.g., combinations of piecewise linear decision boundaries, as in figure 6.5. For example, the classification tree models of chapter 5 define a particular class of local linear decision boundaries that are hierarchical and axis-parallel in structure. As mentioned earlier, the nearest-neighbor classifier is one where the class label of the nearest-neighbor from the training data set of a new unclassified data point is used for prediction. Although this technique is generally thought of as a method rather than a model per se, it does in fact implicitly define a piecewise linear decision boundary (at least when using Euclidean distance to define neighbors).

There are a large number of different classification techniques, provid-

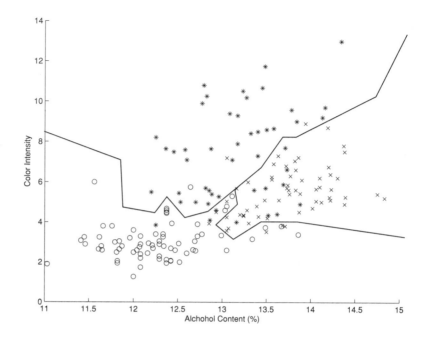

Figure 6.5 An example of *piecewise linear* decision boundaries for the two-dimensional wine classification data set of chapter 5 (see figure 5.1).

ing different ways to model decision boundaries. Something like nearest-neighbor is very flexible (allowing multiple local disjoint decision regions for each class, with flexible boundaries) whereas a single global hyperplane is a much simpler model.

From a practical modeling standpoint, prior knowledge about the shape of classification boundaries may not be as readily available as knowledge we may have about how Y is related to $\mathbf{X}$ in a regression problem. Nonetheless, the functional forms used successfully for discrimination models are quite similar to those we discussed earlier for regression modeling, and the same general themes emerge. We will return to classification models in much more detail in chapter 10 on classification.

6.3.6 An Aside: Selecting a Model of Appropriate Complexity

In our discussion so far we have seen that model structures range from the relatively simple to the complex. For example, in regression we saw that the complexity of a "piecewise-local" model structure is controlled by the number k of local regions (assuming that the complexity of the local function in each region is fixed). As we make k larger, we can obtain a curve that "follows" the observed data more closely. Put another way, the *expressive power* of the model structure increases in that it can represent more complex functions.

As we increase the expressive power of a model it is clear that we can in general continue to get a better fit to the available data. However, we need to be careful. While our score function on the training data may be improving, our model may actually be getting worse in terms of generalizing to new data. (Recall our discussion of this "overfitting" phenomenon in the context of classification trees in chapter 5, and figure 5.4 in particular). On the other hand, if we go the other direction and over-simplify our model structure, it may end being too simple. This issue of selecting a model of the appropriate complexity is always a key concern in any data analysis venture where we consider models of different complexities. In fact we will look at this from a theoretical viewpoint in chapter 7, using a generalization of the bias-variance trade-off that we first introduced in chapter 4.

In practice how can we choose a suitable compromise between simplicity and complexity? From a data-driven viewpoint (i.e., data mining) we can define a score function that tries to estimate how well a model will perform on new data and not just on the training data. A commonly used approach is to combine both the usual goodness-of-fit term (on the training data) with an explicit second term to penalize model complexity. Another widely used approach is to partition the training data into two or more subsets (e.g., via cross-validation as described in chapter 5 for trees) and to train models on one subset and select models using a different validation data set.

Since the focus of this chapter is on the representational capabilities of different model and pattern structures (rather than on how they are scored relative to the data), we defer detail discussion of score functions to chapter 7. However, for the reader who up to this point was wondering how we would be able to select among the many different models being discussed here, the answer is that there do indeed exist well-defined data-driven score functions that allow us to search over different model structures in a principled manner to find what appears to be the best model for a given task (with some caveats as we will see in chapter 7).

6.4   Models for Probability Distributions and Density Functions

The previous section provided an overview of predictive problems, in which one of the variables (we labeled it Y) was singled out as special, to be predicted from the others. Many modeling problems in data mining fall into this class. However, many others are "descriptive," with the aim being simply to produce a summary or description of the data. If the available data are the complete data (for example, all chemical compounds of a certain type), then no notion of inference is relevant, and the aim is merely simplifying description. On the other hand, if the available data are a sample, or have been measured with error (so that collecting them again could yield slightly different values), then the aim is really one of inference—inferring the "true," or at least a good, model structure. In this latter case it is useful to think of the data as having been produced from an underlying probability function.

6.4.1   General Concepts

In this section we focus on some of the general classes of models used for density estimation (a more detailed discussion is given in chapter 9). While the functional form of the underlying models tend to be somewhat different from those we have seen earlier (for example, unimodal "bump" functions versus the linear and polynomial functions we saw for regression), several of the main concepts such as linear combinations of simpler models are once again widely applicable.

There are two general classes of distribution and density models:

1. **Parametric Models:** where a particular functional form is assumed. For real-valued variables the function is often characterized by a *location* parameter (the mean) and a *scale* parameter (characterizing the variability)—for example, the Normal density function and Binomial distribution. Parametric models have the advantage of simplicity (easy to estimate and interpret) but may have relatively high bias because real data may not obey the assumed functional form. The appendix contains a brief review of some of the more well-known parametric density and distribution models.

2. **Nonparametric Models:** where the distribution or density estimate is data-driven and relatively few assumptions are made a priori about the functional form. For example, we can use the kernel estimates introduced in chapter 3 and section 6.3.3: the local density at x is defined as a weighted average of points near to x.

Taking the above as the extremes, we can also define intermediate models that lie between these parametric and nonparametric extremes: *mixture models*. These are discussed below.

6.4.2 Mixtures of Parametric Models

A mixture density for **x** is defined as

$$p(\mathbf{x}) = \sum_{k=1}^{K} p_k(\mathbf{x}|\theta_k)\pi_k. \tag{6.5}$$

This model decomposes the overall density (or distribution) for **x** into a weighted linear combination of K *component* or *class* densities (or distributions). Each of the component densities $p_k(\mathbf{x}|\theta_k)$ typically consists of a relatively simple parametric model (such as a Normal distribution) with parameters θ_k. π_k represents the probability that a randomly chosen data point was generated by component k, $\sum_k \pi_k = 1$.

To illustrate, consider a single Normal distribution used as a model for a two-dimensional data set. This distribution can be thought of as a "symmetric bump function," whose location and shape we can to try to locate in the 2-space to model the density of the data as well as possible (see figure 6.6 for a simple example). An intuitive interpretation of the mixture model is that it allows us to place k of these bumps (or components) in the two-dimensional space to approximate the true density. The locations and shapes of the k bump functions can be fixed independently of each other. In addition, we are allowed to attach weights to the components. If the weights are positive and sum to 1 the overall function is still a probability density (see equation 6.5).

As k increases, the mixture model allows for quite flexible functional forms, as *local* bumps can be placed to capture local characteristics of the density (this is reminiscent of the local modeling ideas in regression). Clearly k plays the role of controlling complexity: for larger k we get a more flexible model but also one that is more complicated to interpret and more difficult to fit.

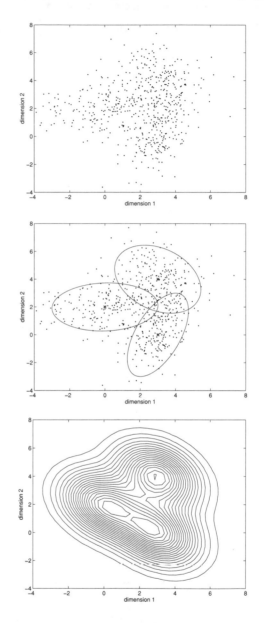

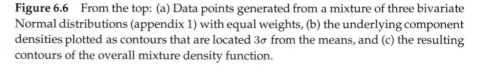

Figure 6.6   From the top: (a) Data points generated from a mixture of three bivariate Normal distributions (appendix 1) with equal weights, (b) the underlying component densities plotted as contours that are located 3σ from the means, and (c) the resulting contours of the overall mixture density function.

Table 6.1   A simple contingency table for two-dimensional categorical data for a hypothetical data set of medical patients who have been diagnosed for dementia.

		Dementia		
		None	Mild	Severe
Smoker	No	426	66	132
	Yes	284	44	88

The usual bias-variance trade-offs again apply. Of course, we are not constrained to use only Normal components (although these tend to be quite popular in practice). Mixtures of exponentials and other densities could equally well be used. The details of how the locations, shapes, and value of k are determined from the data are deferred until chapter 9. The important point here is that mixtures provide a natural generalization of the simple parametric density model (which is global) to a weighted sum of these models, allowing local adaptation to the density of the data in p-space.

The general principles underlying a mixture model are broadly applicable, and the general idea occurs in many guises in probabilistic model building. For example, the idea of hierarchical structure can be nicely captured using mixture models. In chapter 8 we will discuss the mechanics of how mixtures are fitted to data, and in chapter 9 we will see how they can be usefully employed for detecting clusters in data.

In terms of interpretability, either mixture models can be used simply as "black boxes" that provide a flexible model form, or the individual mixture components can be given an explicit interpretation. For example, components of a mixture model fitted to customer data could be interpreted as characterizing different types of customers. One interpretation of a mixture model (particularly in a clustering context) is that the components are generated by a *hidden variable* taking K values, and the location and shapes in p-space of the components are unknown to us a priori, but may be revealed by the data. Thus, mixture models share with projection pursuit and related methods the general idea of hypothesizing a relatively simple latent or hidden structure that may be generating the observed data. In chapter 8 and 10 we will discuss the use of the expectation-maximization (EM) algorithm for learning the parameters of mixture models from data.

6.4.3   Joint Distributions for Unordered Categorical Data

For categorical data we have a joint distribution function defined in the cross-product of all possible values of the p individual ariables. For example, if A is a variable taking values $\{a_1, a_2, a_3\}$ and B is a variable taking values $\{b_1, b_2\}$, then there are six possible values for the joint distribution of A and B. We will assume here (for simplicity) that the values are truly categorical and that there is (for example) no notion of scale or order.

For small values of p, and for small numbers of variable values, it is convenient to display the values of the distribution in the form of a *contingency table* of cells, one cell per joint value, as shown in the example of table 6.1. This becomes impractical as the number of variables and values get beyond four or five. In addition, the contingency table does not really allow us to see any potential structure that might be in the data. For example, the data in table 6.1 have been constructed so that the variables are independent: however, this fact is not immediately apparent from looking at the table.

In contrast to the case of quantitative variables, with categorical variables in which the categories are unordered there is no notion of a smooth probability function. Thus, if for example all variables each have m possible values, one would have to specify $m^p - 1$ independent probability values to specify the model fully (the -1 comes from the constraint that they sum to 1). Clearly this quickly becomes impractical as p and m increase. In the next section we look at systematic techniques for structuring both distribution and density functions to find parsimonious ways to describe high-dimensional data.

6.4.4   Factorization and Independence in High Dimensions

Dimensionality is a fundamental challenge in density and distribution estimation. As the dimensions of the $\mathbf{x}$, space grow it rapidly becomes more difficult to construct fully specified model structures since model complexity tends to grow exponentially with dimension (the curse of dimensionality referred to earlier in this chapter).

Factorization of a density function into simpler component parts provides a general technique for constructing simple models for multivariate data. This is a simple yet powerful idea that recurs throughout multivariate modeling. For example, if we assume that the individual variables are *independent*, we can write the joint density function as

$$p(\mathbf{x}) = p(x_1, \ldots, x_p) = \prod_{k=1}^{p} p_k(x_k) \qquad (6.6)$$

where $\mathbf{x} = (x_1, \ldots, x_p)$ and p_k is the one-dimensional density function for X_k. Typically it is much simpler to model the one-dimensional densities separately, than to model their joint density. Note that the independence model for $\log p(\mathbf{x})$ has an *additive* form, reminiscent of the linear and additive model structures we discussed for regression.

This factorization certainly simplifies things, but it has come at a modeling cost. The assumption that the variables are independent will not be even approximately true for many real problems. Thus, a full independence assumption is in essence one extreme end of a spectrum (the low-complexity end), a spectrum that extends to the fully specified joint density model at the other end (the high-complexity end). Of course, we do not have to choose models solely from the extremes of this complexity continuum, and can, instead, try to find something in between. The joint probability function $p(\mathbf{x})$ can be written in general as

$$p\left(\mathbf{x}\right) = p_1\left(x_1\right) \prod_{k=2}^{p} p\left(x_k | x_1, \ldots, x_{k-1}\right) \tag{6.7}$$

The right-hand side factorizes the joint function into a sequence of conditional distributions. Now we can try to model each of those conditional distributions separately. Often considerable simplification results because each variable X_k is dependent on only a few of its predecessors. That is, in the conditional distribution for the kth variable, we can often ignore some of variables $X_1, \ldots, X_{k-1}$. Such factorizations permits a natural representation of the model as a directed graph, with the nodes corresponding to variables, and the edges showing dependencies between the variables. Thus the edges directed *into* the node for the kth variable will be coming from (a subset of) the variables $x_1, \ldots, x_{k-1}$. These variables are, naturally enough, called the *parents* of variable x_1.

Sometimes we have to experiment by fitting different models to the data to seek such simplifying factorizations. In other cases such simplifications will be evident from the structure of the data—for example, if the variables represent the same property measured sequentially (for instance, at different times). In this case, a *Markov chain* model is often appropriate—in which all of the previous information relevant to the kth variable is contained in the immediately preceding variable (so that the terms in this factorization simplify to $p\left(x_k | x_1, \ldots, x_{k-1}\right) = p\left(x_k | x_{k-1}\right)$). The model structure for a first-order Markov model is shown in figure 6.7.

Graphs that are used represent probability models, such as that in fig-

Figure 6.7 A graphical model structure corresponding to a first-order Markov assumption.

ure 6.7 are often referred to as *graphical models*. In the discussion below we focus specifically on the widely-used subclass of acyclic directed graphs (also sometimes known in computer science as belief networks when used as probability models). Note that this graph representation emphasizes the independence structure of the model (e.g., see figure 6.7 again) and leaves the actual functional and numeric parametrization of parent-child relationships unspecified.

For another example of a graphical model, consider the variables age, education (level of education a person has) and baldness (whether a person is bald or not). Clearly age cannot depend on either of the other two variables. Conversely, both education and baldness are directly dependent on age. Furthermore, it is quite implausible that education and baldness are directly dependent on each other given age—that is, once we know the person's age, knowing whether or not they are bald tells us nothing about their education level (and vice versa). On the other hand, if we do not know a person's age, then baldness may provide information about education (for example, a bald person is more likely to be older, and hence, in turn, more likely to have a university degree). Thus, a plausible graphical model is the one in figure 6.8.

These ideas can be taken further, by the postulation of the existence of unobserved hidden or *latent* variables, which explain many of the observed relationships in the data. Figure 6.9 provides such an example. In this model structure a single latent variable has been introduced as an intermediate variable that simplifies the relationship between the observed data (in this case, medical symptoms) and the underlying causal factors (here, two independent diseases). The introduction of hidden variables in a manner such as this can serve to simplify the relationships in a model structure; for example, given the values here of the intermediate variable, the symptoms become independent. However, we must exercise discretion in practice in terms of how many hidden variables we introduce into the model structure to avoid introducing spurious structure into the fitted model. In addition, as we will discuss in chapters 8 and 9, parameter estimation and model selection with

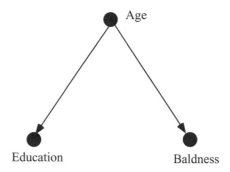

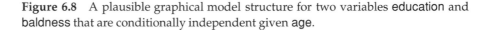

Figure 6.8   A plausible graphical model structure for two variables education and baldness that are conditionally independent given age.

hidden variables is quite nontrivial.

In the context of classification and clustering, it is often convenient to assume that the variables are *conditionally independent* of each other given the value of the class variable. That is,

$$p(\mathbf{x}|y) = \prod_{j=1}^{p} p_j(x_j|y), \qquad (6.8)$$

where y is a particular (categorical) class value. This is simply the conditional independence ("naive") Bayes model introduced in the context of classification modeling in section 6.3.5. The graphical representation for such a model is shown in figure 6.10.

Equation 6.8 can also be used in the case where Y is an unobserved (hidden, latent) variable that is introduced to simplify the modeling of $p(\mathbf{x})$, i.e., we have a finite mixture of the form

$$p(\mathbf{x}) = \sum_{k=1}^{K} \left(\prod_{j=1}^{p} p_j(x_j|y = k) \right) p(y = k), \qquad (6.9)$$

where Y takes K values, and each component $p(\mathbf{x}|y = k)$ is modeled using the conditional independence assumption of equation 6.8. As an example, we might model the joint distribution of how customers purchase p products in this fashion, where (for example) if a customer belongs to a specific component k then the likelihood of purchasing certain subsets of products, i.e., $p_j(x_j|y = k)$, is increased for certain subsets of products x_j. Thus, although

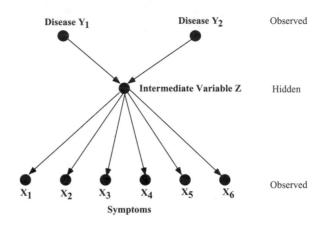

Figure 6.9   The graphical model structure for a problem with two diseases that are marginally (unconditionally) independent, a single intermediate variable Z that directly depends on both diseases, and six symptom variables that are conditionally independent given Z.

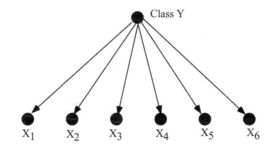

Figure 6.10   The first-order Bayes graphical model structure, with a single class Y and 6 conditionally independent feature variables $X_1, \ldots, X_6$.

the products (the x_j) are modeled as being conditionally independent given $y = k$, the mixture model induces an unconditional (marginal) independence by virtue of the fact that certain products co-occur with higher probability in certain components k. In effect, the hidden Y variable acts to group the variables x_j together into equivalence classes, where within each equivalence class the variables are modeled as being conditionally independent. The use of hidden variables in this manner can be a powerful modeling technique, and it is one we return to in more detail in chapter 9.

6.5   The Curse of Dimensionality

We have noted in various places that what works well in a one-dimensional setting may not scale up very well to multiple dimensions. In particular, the amount of data we need often increases exponentially with dimensionality if we are to maintain a specific level of accuracy in our parameter or function estimates. This is sometimes referred to as the "curse of dimensionality." This can be important, since data miners are often interested in finding models and patterns in high-dimensional problems. Note that "high-dimensional" can be as few as $p = 10$ variables or as many as $p = 1000$ variables or beyond—it depends on the complexity of the models concerned and on the size of the available data.

> **Example 6.4** The following example is taken from Silverman (1986) and illustrates emphatically the difficulties of density estimation in high dimensions. Consider data that is simulated from a multivariate Normal density with unit covariance matrix and mean $(0,0,\ldots,0)$ (see the appendix for a definition of the multivariate Normal density). Assume that the bandwidth h, in a kernel density estimate, is chosen such that it minimizes the mean square error at the mean. Silverman calculated the number of data points required to ensure that the relative mean square error at zero is less than 0.1—that is, that $E[(\hat{p}(\mathbf{x}) - p(\mathbf{x}))^2]/p(\mathbf{x})^2 < 0.1$—at $\mathbf{x} = 0$ and where $p(\mathbf{x})$ is the true Normal density, and $\hat{p}(\mathbf{x})$ is a kernel estimate using a Normal kernel with the optimal bandwidth parameter. Thus, we are looking at the relatively "easy" problem of estimating (within 10% relative accuracy) a Normal density at the mode of this density (where the points will be most dense on average) by using a Normal kernel: what could be easier? Silverman showed (analytically) that the number of data points grows exponentially. In 1 dimension we need 4 points, in 2 we need 19, 3 we need 67, in 6 we need 2790, and by 10 dimensions we need about 842,000. This is an inordinate number of data points for such a simple problem! The lesson to be learned is that density estimation tasks (and indeed most other data mining tasks) rapidly become very difficult as dimensionality increases.

There are two basic (and fairly obvious) strategies for coping with high-dimensional problems. The first is simply to use a subset of relevant variables to construct the model. That is, to find a subset of p' variables where $p' << p$. The second is to transform the original p variables into a new set of p' variables, where again $p' << p$. Examples of this approach include principal component analysis, projection pursuit, and neural networks.

6.5.1   Variable Selection for High-Dimensional Data

Variable selection is a fairly general (and sensible) strategy when dealing with high-dimensional problems. Consider for example the problem of predicting Y using $X_1, \ldots, X_p$. It is often plausible that not all of the p variables are necessary for accurate prediction. Some X variables may be completely unrelated to the predictor variable Y (for example, the month of a person's birth is unlikely to be related to their creditworthiness). Others may be *redundant* in the sense that two or more X variables contain essentially the same predictive information. (For example, the variables income before tax and income after tax are likely to be highly correlated.)

We can use the notion of independence (introduced in chapter 3) to gauge *relevance* in a quantitative manner. For example, if $p(y|x_1) = p(y)$ for all values of y and x_1, then the target variable Y is independent of input variable X_1. If $p(y|x_1, x_2) = p(y|x_2)$, then Y is independent of X_1 if the value of X_2 is already known. In practice, of course, we are not necessarily able to identify from a finite sample which variables are independent and which are not; that is, we must estimate this effect. Furthermore, we are interested not only in strict independence or dependence, but also in the degree of dependence. Thus, we could (for example) rank individual X variables in terms of their estimated linear correlation coefficient with Y: that would tell us about estimated individual *linear* dependence. If Y is categorical (as in classification), we could measure the average mutual information between Y and X':

$$I(Y; X') = \sum_{i,j} p(y_i, x_j') \log \frac{p(y_i, x_j')}{p(y_i)p(x_j')} \tag{6.10}$$

to provide an estimate of the dependence of X and Y, where X' here is a categorical variable (for example, a quantized version of a real-valued X). Other measures of the relationship between Y and the Xs can also be used.

However, the interaction of *individual* X variables with Y does not necessarily tell us anything about how *sets of variables* may interact with Y. The classic example, for Boolean variables, is the parity function, where Y is defined to be 1 if the sum of the (binary) values of the $X_1, \ldots, X_p$ variables in the set is an even integer, and Y is 0 otherwise. Y is independent of any individual X variable, yet is a deterministic function of the full set. While this is something of an extreme example, it nonetheless illustrates that such *non-linear non-additive* interactions can be masked if we only look at individual pair-wise interactions between Xs and Y. Thus, in the general case, the set of k *best individual* X variables (as ranked by correlation for example) is not the same as the *best set* of X variables of size k. Since one can have $2^p - 1$ different nonempty subsets of p variables, exhaustive search is not feasible except for very small p. Worse still, for many prediction problems, there is no optimal search algorithm (in the sense of being guaranteed to find the best set of variables) that has worst-case time complexity any better than $O(2^p)$.

This means that, in practice, subset selection methods tend to rely on heuristic search to find good model structures. Many algorithms are based on the simple heuristic of greedy selection, such as adding or deleting one variable at a time. We will return to this issue of search in chapter 8.

6.5.2   Transformations for High-Dimensional Data

The second general category of ideas is based on *transforming* the predictor variables. The intuitive idea here is to search for a set of p' variables (let us call them $Z_1, \ldots, Z_{p'}$), where typically p' is much smaller than p, where the Z variables are defined as functions of the original X variables, and where the Zs are chosen in some sense to be the "best" set of p' variables for our task.

This general theme, of replacing the observed variables with a smaller set of variables that are somehow more fundamental to the task at hand, shows up repeatedly in different branches of data analysis. The Zs are variously referred to as *basis functions*, *factors*, *latent variables*, *principal components*, and so forth, depending on the specific goals and methods used to derive them. We will examine some of these models (and their associated fitting algorithms) in detail in later chapters, but for now we illustrate the general idea with just two specific examples:

- *Projection Pursuit Regression* uses a model structure of the form

$$\hat{y} = \sum_{j=1}^{p'} w_j h_j(\alpha_j^T \mathbf{x}) \qquad (6.11)$$

where $\alpha_j^T \mathbf{x}$ is the projection of the vector $\mathbf{x}$ onto the jth weight vector α_j (both vectors being p-dimensional, resulting in a scalar inner product), h_j is a nonlinear function of this scalar projection, and the w_j are scalar weights for the resulting nonlinear functions. The procedures for determining the w_j, the form of the h_j, and the "projection directions" α_j can be rather complex and algorithm-dependent, but the underlying idea is quite general.

For example, this is essentially the form of the model structure that underlies neural networks (to be discussed later in chapter 11), where for such networks the functional forms of the h_j are usually chosen to be something like $h_j(t) = 1/(1 + e^{-t})$. One limitation of this class of models is the fact that they are quite difficult to interpret unless $p' = 1$. Another limitation is that the algorithms for estimating the parameters of these models can be computationally quite complex and may not be practical for very large data sets. We will return to this model family in chapter 11.

- *Principal Components Analysis:* We introduced principal components analysis (PCA) in chapter 3. This is a classic technique in which the original p predictor variables are replaced by another set of p variables $(Z_1, \ldots, Z_p)$ that are formed from linear combinations of the original variables. The data vectors comprising the original data set map to new vectors in the **Z** space and, as explained in chapter 3, the sets of weights defining the Zs are chosen so as to maximize the variance of the original data set when expressed in terms of these new variables. Principal components analysis is thus a special case of projection pursuit, where the projection index in this case is the variance along the projected direction. Principal components has two merits as a data reduction technique. Firstly, it sequentially extracts most of the variance of the data in the X space, so we might hope that only the first few components (far fewer than the full number p of original X variables) contain most of the information in the data. Secondly, by virtue of the way in which the components are extracted (see chapter 3) they are orthogonal, so that interpretation is eased. However, one should be aware that the principal component vectors in the **X** space may not necessarily be the ideal projection directions for optimizing *predictive* performance on a different variable Y (for example). For example, when we try to model differences among groups (or classes) in the data (for classification and clustering), the principal component projections need not emphasize group differences and indeed can even hide them. (Similar remarks can be made about more general projection pursuit methods.) Nonetheless, PCA is widely used in data analysis and can be a very useful dimension-reduction tool. There are a wide number of other techniques (each with different properties) available for dimension reduction, including factor analysis (chapter 4), projection pursuit (chapter 11, and above), independent component analysis, and so forth.

6.6   Models for Structured Data

In many situations either the individuals, the variables, or both, possess some well-defined relationships that are known a priori. Examples include linear chains or sequences (where the measurements are ordered—for example, protein sequences), time series (where the measurements are ordered in time, perhaps on a uniform time scale), and spatial or image data (where the measurements are defined on a spatial grid). Even more complex structure is possible. For example, in medicine one can have imaging data of the brain measured on a three-dimensional grid, with repeated measurements over time.

Such structured data is inherently different from the types of measurements we have discussed in most places in this chapter. Up to this point we have implicitly assumed that the n individual objects (the patients, the customers) in our data set are a random sample from an underlying population. Specifically, we have assumed that the measurement vectors $\mathbf{x}(i), 1 \leq i \leq n$, are conditionally independent of each other given a particular fitted model (that is, that the likelihood of the data can be expressed as the product of individual $p(\mathbf{x}(i))$. For example, if we have a Normal density model for the variable weight, then we are assuming that knowing the weight of one person tells us nothing about the weight of any other person in the data set. (We are, of course, here ignoring subtle dependencies that may exist such as having members of the same family appear sequentially in our data set, where such family members might be predisposed to having similar overweight or underweight tendencies.) Thus, although it may be an approximation, we have been working with this assumption on the basis that it is a useful assumption for many practical situations.

However, there are problems for which the dependence is explicit and needs to be modeled. For example, if we take measurements of a person's blood pressure every five minutes over a 24-hour period, then clearly there is very likely to be some significant dependence between the successive values. How should we model such dependence?

One approach is to reduce the multiple observations on each object to one or a few variables (that is, a fixed multivariate description $\mathbf{x}$), using ideas about the expected relationships between them (we referred to this possibility above). This is sometimes called the *feature extraction* approach. For example, we might expect blood pressure to decrease over the 24-hour period as a medication begins to take effect, so we might replace the 5 times 12 times 24 observations for each person by just two numbers showing a starting value and the decreasing slope of a linear trend. Or we might use the same principle and fit a curve in which the rate of decrease reduces over time. The numbers describing the curves for each subject (which are often called *derived variables*) can then be analyzed in the standard way.

Note that this general approach (of converting sequential measurements into a non-sequential vector representation) may be sufficient for a given data mining task, but in general there is a loss of information in this process, in that we lose the timing and order information present in the original measurements. For certain applications this sequential information may be critical. As an example, we may have a population of Web users, among whom are a group who navigate from Web page A, to page B, to page C, repeatedly in that order, in a cyclic fashion. If we were to reduce this information to a histogram of which pages were visited (yielding a histogram with three roughly equal bins), we would lose the ability to discover the dynamic cyclic pattern underlying the data.

Let us consider an example of a sequential data model, namely a first-order Markov model for T data points observed sequentially, $y_1, \ldots, y_T$. Note that for even moderately large values of T, a full joint density for $p(y_1, y_2, \ldots, y_T)$ will be a very complex object (for example, if Y takes m discrete values, it will require the specification of $O(m^T)$ numbers). Thus, in modeling data with structure, we can take direct advantage of the ideas presented in the last section on factorization; that is, the structure of the data will suggest a natural structuring for any models we will build. Thus, we return to our first-order Markov model, again defined as:

$$p(y_1, \ldots, y_T) = p_1(y_1) \prod_{t=2}^{T} p_t(y_t \,|\, y_{t-1}) \qquad (6.12)$$

We can simplify this model considerably if we make the assumption of *stationarity*, namely that the probability functions in the model do not depend on the specific time t, that is, $p_t(y_t|y_{t-1}) = p(y_t|y_{t-1})$. Thus, the *same* conditional probability function is used in different parts of the sequence. This drastically cuts down on the number of parameters we need for the model. For example, if Y is m-ary, the nonstationary model would require $O(m^2 T)$ parameters (a matrix of $m \times m$ conditional probabilities for each time point in the sequence), while the stationary model only requires $O(m^2)$ probabilities (one matrix of $m \times m$ conditional probabilities that is used throughout the sequence). The notion of stationarity can be applied to much more general Markov models than the first-order model above, and indeed extends naturally to spatial data models as well (for which we would assume stationarity in space, rather than in time). If we assume stationarity, then we cannot account for *changes* in the statistical model as a function of time or space. However, stationarity is advantageous from a parametrization standpoint, making it a very useful and practical assumption in model building—we will assume it throughout our discussion unless specifically stated otherwise.

The Markov model in equation 6.12 has a simple generative interpretation (see figure 6.7, with ys instead of xs). The first value in the sequence y_1 is chosen by drawing a y_1 value randomly according to some initial distribution $p(y_1)$. The value at time $t = 2$ is randomly chosen according to the conditional density function $p(y_2|y_1)$, where the value y_1 is known and fixed. Once y_2 has been chosen in this manner, y_3 is now generated according to $p(y_3|y_2)$ where the value y_2 is now fixed, and so on until time T.

However, the Markov model assumption is rather strong (as we discussed in section 6.4.4). In words, it says that the influence of the past is completely summarized by the value of Y at time $t-1$. Specifically, Y_t does not have any "long-range" dependencies other than its immediate dependence on Y_{t-1}. Clearly there are many situations in which this model may not be accurate. For example, consider modeling the grammatical structure of English text, where Y takes values such as `verb`, `adjective`, `noun`, and so on. The first-order Markov assumption is inadequate here since (for example) deciding whether a verb is singular or plural will depend on the subject of the verb, that in turn may be much further back in the sentence than just one word back.

For real-valued Ys, the Markov model is often specified as a conditional Normal distribution:

$$p(y_t|y_{t-1}) = \frac{1}{\sqrt{2\pi}\sigma} exp - \frac{1}{2}\left(\frac{y_t - g(y_{t-1})}{\sigma}\right)^2 \qquad (6.13)$$

where $g(y_{t-1})$ plays the role of the mean of the Normal (it is a deterministic function linking the past y_{t-1} to the present y_t) and σ is the noise in the model (assumed stationary here). A common choice for the function g is to make it a linear function of y_{t-1}, $g(y_{t-1}) = \alpha_0 + \alpha_1 y_{t-1}$, leading to the well-known *first-order autoregressive model*,

$$y_t = \alpha_0 + \alpha_1 y_{t-1} + e \qquad (6.14)$$

where e is zero-mean Gaussian noise with standard deviation σ and the αs are the parameters of the model. Note that equation 6.14 can be expressed in the form of equation 6.13 under these assumptions.

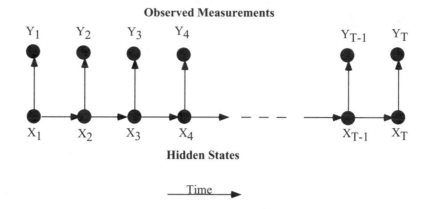

Figure 6.11   A graphical model structure corresponding to a first-order hidden Markov assumption.

The model in equation 6.14 has a simple interpretation from a generative viewpoint; the value y_t at time t in the sequence is generated by taking the previous value y_{t-1}, multiplying it by a constant α_1, adding an offset α_0, and adding some amount of random noise e. For y to remain stable (bounded as $t \to \infty$) it is necessary that $-1 < \alpha_1 < 1$. Values of $|\alpha_1|$ closer to 1 imply stronger dependence among successive y values; values of $|\alpha_1|$ closer to 0 imply weaker dependence. This model structure is clearly closely related to the standard regression model structures of section 6.3. Instead of regressing on independent X values, here Y is regressed on "lagged" values of itself. Thus, from our knowledge of regression model structures, we can immediately think of a multitude of generalizations of the simple first-order model above. For example, y_t can depend on earlier lags in the sequence; that is, we can replace the mean at time t by $g(y_{t-1})$ in equation 6.13 with $g(y_{t-1}, y_{t-2}, \ldots, y_{t-k})$, known as a *kth order Markov model*. Again, a common choice for $g(y_{t-1}, y_{t-2}, \ldots, y_{t-k})$ is a simple linear model of the form $\alpha_0 + \sum \alpha_i y_i$. In principle, however, rather than just linear regression, we could use any of the general functional forms discussed in section 6.3, such as additive models, polynomial models, local linear models, data-driven local models, and so forth.

A further important generalization of the Markov model structures we have discussed so far is to explicitly model the notion of a hidden *state variable*. The general notion of hidden state for sequential and spatial models is prevalent in engineering and the sciences and recurs in a variety of functional model forms. Specific examples of such structures include hidden Markov models (HMMs) and Kalman filters. The HMM structure is easily explained by looking at its corresponding graphical model structure, shown in figure 6.11. From a generative viewpoint a first-order HMM operates as follows (picture the observations being generated by moving from left to right along the chain). The hidden state variable X is categorical (corresponding to m discrete states) and is first-order Markov. Thus, x_t is generated by sampling a value from the conditional distribution function $p(x_t|x_{t-1})$ in the usual Markov chain fashion, where $p(x_t|x_{t-1})$ is an $m \times m$ matrix of conditional probabilities. Once the state at time t is generated (with value x_t), an observation y_t is now generated with probability $p(y_t|x_t)$. Here y_t could be univariate or multivariate, or real-valued or categorical, or a combination of both. Thus, in a HMM, the observations y_t only depend on the state at time t, and the state sequence is a first-order Markov chain. The state sequence is unobserved or hidden, and the ys are directly observed: thus, there is uncertainty (given a model structure and a set of observed y's) about which particular state sequence generated the data.

We can think of the HMM structure as a form of mixture model (m different density functions for the Y variable), where we have now added Markov dependence between "adjacent" mixture components x_t and x_{t+1}. For the record, the joint probability of an observed sequence and any particular hidden state sequence for a first-order HMM can be written as:

$$p(y_1,\ldots,y_T,x_1,\ldots,x_T) = p(x_1)p(y_1|x_1)\prod_{t=2}^{T}p(y_t|x_t)p(x_t|x_{t-1}). \qquad (6.15)$$

The factorization on the right-hand side is apparent from the graphical model structure in figure 6.11. When regarded as a function of the parameters of the distributions, this is the likelihood of the variables $(Y_1,\ldots,Y_T,X_1,\ldots,X_T)$. The likelihood of the observed ys is useful for fitting such model structures to data (that is, learning the parameters of $p(y_t|x_t)$ and $p(x_t|x_{t-1})$). To calculate $p(y_1,\ldots,y_T)$ (the likelihood of the *observed* data) one has to sum the left-hand side terms over the m^T possible state sequences, that appears at first glance to involve a sum over an exponential number of terms. Fortunately there is a convenient recursive way to perform this calculation in time proportional to $O(m^2T)$.

Again, it is clear that we can generalize the first-order HMM structure in different directions. A kth order Markov model corresponds to having x_t

depend on the previous k states. The dependence of the ys can also be generalized, allowing for example y_t to have a linear dependence on the k previous ys (as in an autoregressive model) as well as direct dependence on x_t. This yields a natural generalization of the usual autoregressive model structure to a *mixture of autoregressive models,* which we can think of generatively as switching (in Markov fashion) among m different autoregressive models. *Kalman filters* are a closely related cousin of the HMM, where now the hidden states are *real-valued* (such as the unknown velocity or momentum of a vehicle, for example), but the independence structure of the model is essentially the same as we have described it for an HMM.

Computer scientists will recognize in our generative description of a hidden Markov model that it is quite reminiscent of a finite state machine (FSM). In fact, as we have described it here, a first-order HMM is directly equivalent to a stochastic FSM with m states; that is, the choice of the next state is governed by $p(x_{t+1}|x_t)$. This naturally suggests a generalization of model structures in terms of different *grammars*. Finite-state machines are simple forms of grammar known as *regular grammars*. The next level up (in the so-called Chomsky hierarchy of grammars) is the *context-free grammar*, which can be thought of as augmenting the finite-state machine with a *stack*, permitting the model structure to "remember" long-range dependencies such as closing parentheses at the ends of clauses, and so forth. As we ascend the grammar hierarchy, our model structures become more expressive, but also become much more difficult to fit to data. Thus, despite the fact that regular grammars (or HMMs) are relatively simple in structure, this form of model structure has dominated the application of Markov models to sequential data (over other more complex grammar structures), due to the difficulties of fitting such complex structures to real data.

Finally, although we have only described simple data structures where the Ys exist in an ordered sequence, it is clear that for more general data dependencies (such as data on a two-dimensional grid) we can think of equivalent generalizations of the Markov model structures to model such dependence. For example, *Markov random fields* are essentially the multidimensional analogs of Markov chains (for example, in two dimensions we would have a grid structure rather than a chain for our graphical model).

It turns out that such models are much more difficult to analyze and work with than chain models. For example, problems such as summing out the hidden variables in the likelihood (as we mentioned for equation 6.15) do not typically admit tractable solutions and must be approximated. Thus, spatial data can be more difficult to work with than sequential data, although conceptually the ideas of stationarity, Markovianity, linear models, and so forth, can all still be applied. One common approach with gridded data, which may or may not make sense depending on the application, is to "shape" the two-dimensional grid data (say $n \times n$ grid points) into a single vector of length n^2, perform PCA on these vectors, project each set of grid measurements onto a small set of PCA vectors, and model the data using standard multivariate models in this reduced dimensional space. This approach ignores much of the inherent spatial information in the original grid, but nonetheless can be quite practical in many situations. Similarly, for *multivariate time series or sequences,* where we have p different time series or sequences measured over the same time frame (corresponding for example to different biomedical monitors on the same patient), we can use PCA to reduce the p original time series to a much smaller number of "component" series for further analysis.

6.7   Pattern Structures

Throughout this book, we have characterized a model as describing the whole (or a large part of the) data set, and a pattern as characterizing some local aspect of the data. A pattern can be considered to be a predicate that returns `true` for those objects or parts of objects in the data for which the pattern occurs, and `false` otherwise. To define a class of patterns we need to specify two things: the syntax of the patterns (the language specifying how they are defined) and their semantics (our interpretation of what they tell us about data to which they are applied). In this section we consider patterns for two different types of discrete-valued data: data in standard matrix form and data described as strings.

6.7.1   Patterns in Data Matrices

A generic approach for building patterns is to start from primitive patterns and combine them using logical connectives. (An alternative is to build a special class of patterns for a particular application.) Returning again to our data matrix notation, assume we have p variables $X_1, \ldots, X_p$. Let $\mathbf{x} = (x_1, \ldots, x_p)$ be a p-dimensional vector of measurements of these variables. We denote the ith individual in the data set as $\mathbf{x}(i)$, where $1 \leq i \leq n$. The entire data set $D = \{\mathbf{x}(1), \ldots, \mathbf{x}(n)\}$. In turn, $x_k(i)$ is the value of the kth measurement on the ith individual.

In general, a *pattern* for the variables $X_1, \ldots, X_p$ identifies a subset of all possible observations over these variables. A general language for expressing patterns can be built by starting from *primitive patterns*. These are simply conditions on the values of the variables. For example, if c is a possible value of X_k, then $X_k = c$ is a primitive pattern. If the values of X_k are ordered (for example, numbers on the real line), we can also include inequalities such as $X_k \leq c$ as primitive conditions. If needed, the primitive patterns could also include multivariate conditions such as $X_k X_j > 2$ for numeric data or $X_k = X_j$ for discrete data.

Given a set of primitive patterns, we can form more complex patterns by using logical connectives such as *AND* ($\wedge$) and *OR* ($\vee$). For example, we can form a pattern

$$(\text{age} \leq 40) \wedge (\text{income} \leq 10)$$

that describes a certain subset of the input records in a payroll database. Note, for example, that each branch of a classification tree (as described in chapter 5) forms a conjunctive pattern of this form. Another example is the pattern

$$(\text{chips} = 1) \wedge (\text{beer} = 1 \vee \text{soft drink} = 1)$$

describing a subset of rows in a market basket database.

A *pattern class* is a set of legal patterns. A pattern class $\mathcal{C}$ is defined by specifying the collection of primitive patterns and the legal ways of combining primitive patterns. For example, if the variables $X_1, \ldots, X_p$ all range over $\{0, 1\}$, we can define a class of patterns $\mathcal{C}$ consisting of all possible conjunctions of the form

$$(X_{j_1} = 1) \wedge (X_{j_2} = 1) \wedge \cdots \wedge (X_{j_k} = 1).$$

Patterns in this class that occur frequently in a data set D are called *frequent sets* (of variables), since each such pattern is uniquely determined by a subset of the variables: this pattern could be written just as $\{X_{i_1}, X_{i_2}, \ldots, X_{i_k}\}$. Conjunctive patterns such as frequent sets are relatively easy to discover from data, and we consider them in detail in chapter 13.

Given a pattern class and a dataset D, one of the important properties of a pattern is its frequency in the data set. The frequency $fr(\rho)$ of a pattern ρ can be defined as the relative number of observations in the dataset about which ρ is true. In some cases, only patterns that occur reasonably often are of interest in data mining. However, having a frequency of a pattern close to 0 can also be quite informative in its own right. (Indeed, sometimes it is the rare but unusual pattern that is of particular interest.) Of course, the frequency of a pattern is not the only important property of the pattern. Properties such as semantic simplicity, understandability, and the novelty or surprise of the pattern are obviously also of interest. As an example, for any particular observation $(x_1, \ldots, x_p)$ in the data set we can write a conjunctive pattern $(X_1 = x_1) \wedge \cdots \wedge (X_p = x_p)$ that matches exactly that observation. The disjunction of all of such conjunctive patterns forms a pattern that has frequency 1 for the data set. However, the pattern would be just a bloated way of writing out the entire data set and would be quite uninteresting.

Given a class of patterns, *a pattern discovery task* is to find all patterns from that class that satisfy certain conditions with respect to the data sets. For example, we might be interested in finding all the frequent set patterns whose frequency is at least 0.1 and where the variable X_7 occurs in the pattern. More generally, the definition of the pattern discovery task might include also conditions on the informativeness, novelty, and understandibility of the pattern. In defining the pattern class and the pattern discovery task the challenge is to find the right balance between expressivity of the patterns, their comprehensibility, and the computational complexity of solving the discovery task.

Given a class of patterns $\mathcal{C}$, we can easily define rules. A *rule* is simply an expression $\rho \Rightarrow \varphi$, where ρ and φ are patterns from a pattern class $\mathcal{C}$. The semantics of a logical rule are that if the expression ρ is true for an object, then φ is also true. We can relax this definition to allow for uncertainty in the mapping from ρ to φ, where φ is true with some probability if ρ is true. The *accuracy* of such a rule is defined as $p(\varphi|\rho)$, the conditional probability that φ is true for an object, given that ρ is true. As is described in chapter 4, we can easily estimate such probabilities from a data set using appropriate frequency counts; that is

$$\hat{p}(\varphi|\rho) = \frac{fr(\rho \wedge \varphi)}{fr(\rho)}.$$

The *support* $fr(\rho \Rightarrow \varphi)$ of the rule $\rho \Rightarrow \varphi$ can be defined either as $fr(\rho)$ (the fraction of objects to which the rule applies) or $fr(\rho \wedge \varphi)$ (the fraction of objects for which both the left- and right-hand sides of the rule are true).

For example, if our patterns are frequent sets, then a rule would have the form

$$\{A_1, \ldots, A_k\} \Rightarrow \{B_1, \ldots, B_h\},$$

where each of the A_ks and B_js are binary variables. Written out in full, the rule would be

$$(A_1 = 1) \wedge \cdots \wedge (A_k = 1) \Rightarrow (B_1 = 1) \wedge \cdots \wedge (B_h - 1).$$

Such rules are called *association rules*, a widely used pattern structure in data mining (we will discuss in detail the algorithmic principles behind finding such rules in chapter 13).

Here we have described patterns that define subsets of the original data set. That is, each pattern was defined by a formula that referred only to the variables of a single observation. In certain cases, however, we need to use patterns defined by referring to several observations. For example, we might wish to identify all those points in a geographical database that form the vertices of an equilateral triangle. As a more formal example, consider a data set with discrete variables $A_1, \ldots, A_p$. A *functional dependency* is an expression of the form

$$A_{i_1} A_{i_2} \cdots A_{i_k} \rightarrow A_{i_{k+1}},$$

where $1 \leq i_j \leq p$ for $i = 1, \ldots, k+1$. Note the syntactic similarity to the definition of association rules. However, the *functional dependency* defined by this expression is true in a data set if, for all pairs of observations $\mathbf{x} = (a_1, \ldots, a_p)$ and $\mathbf{y} = (b_1, \ldots, b_p)$ in the data set, we have that if $\mathbf{x}$ and $\mathbf{y}$ agree on all the variables A_{i_j} for $j = 1, \ldots, k$, then $\mathbf{x}$ and $\mathbf{y}$ agree also on $A_{i_{k+1}}$. That is, if $a_{i_j} = b_{i_j}$ for all $i = 1, \ldots, k$, then also $a_{i_{k+1}} = b_{i_{k+1}}$. Functional dependencies have their roots in database design, and they are also of interest in query optimization. Knowing the functional dependencies that hold in a data set may be important for understanding the structure of the data.

The patterns or conditions written in these refer only to the values occurring in a single record in the database. Sometimes we are also interested in describing patterns that refer to other observations, such as those that arise in "the employees whose income is the smallest in their department." Such conditions can also be described using logical formalisms. For example,

$$\{\mathbf{x}_k \mid \mathsf{age} \leq 40 \wedge \mathsf{income} \leq 10\}.$$

6.7.2 Patterns for Strings

In the last section we discussed examples of patterns for data in the traditional matrix form. Other types of data require other types of patterns. To illustrate, we consider patterns for strings. Formally, a *string* over alphabet S is a sequence $a_1 \ldots a_n$ of elements (also called *letters*) of S. The alphabet S can be the binary alphabet $\{0, 1\}$, the set of all ASCII codes, the DNA alphabet $\{\mathsf{A}, \mathsf{C}, \mathsf{G}, \mathsf{T}\}$, or the set of all words consisting of ASCII characters. The set of all strings built from letters from S is denoted by S^*.

Note how string data differs from data in standard matrix form: for a string, there is no fixed set of variables. If and when we want to use the notions of probability to describe string data, we typically consider each of the letters of the string to be a random variable.

The data can be one or several strings, and in most cases we are interested in finding out how many times a certain pattern occurs in the strings. (For example, we might want to compute the number of exact occurrences of a certain DNA sequence in a large collection of sequences.) The simplest string pattern is a substring: the pattern $b_1 \ldots b_k$ occurs in the string $a_1 \ldots a_n$ at position i, if $a_{i+j-1} = b_j$ for all $j = 1, \ldots, k$. For example, for DNA sequences we might be interested in finding occurrences of the substring pattern ATTATTAA, and for strings over the ASCII alphabet we might be interested in whether or not the pattern data mining occurs in a given string.

For strings we might, however, be interested in a larger class of patterns. A *regular expression* E is an expression that defines a set $L(E)$ of strings. The expression E is one of

1. a string s; then $L(s) = \{s\}$

2. a concatenation $E_1 E_2$; in this case the set $L(E_1 E_2)$ consists of all strings that are a concatenation of a string in $L(E_1)$ and a string in $L(E_2)$

3. a choice $E_1 \mid E_2$; then $L(E_1 \mid E_2) = L(E_1) \cup L(E_2)$

4. an iteration E^*; then $L(E^*)$ consists of all strings that can be written as a concatenation of 0 or more strings from $L(E)$

Thus, $10(00|11)^*01$ is a regular expression that describes all strings that start with 10 and end with 01 and in between contain a sequence of pairs 00 and 11.

Regular expressions are a form of patterns that are quite well suited to describing interesting classes of strings. While there are simple classes of strings that cannot be described by regular expressions (such as the set of strings consisting of all balanced sequences of parentheses), many quite complicated phenomena of strings can still be captured by using them.

While regular expressions are fine for defining patterns over strings, they are not sufficiently expressive for expressing variations in the occurrence times of events. A simple class of patterns that can take the occurrence times into account is the *episode*. At a high level, an episode is a partially ordered collection of events occurring together. The events may be of different types, and may refer to different variables. For example, in biostatistical data an event might be a headache followed by a sense of disorientation occurring within a given time period. It is also useful for them to be insensitive to intervening events—as with, for example, alarms in a telecommunications network, logs of user interface actions, and so on. Episodes can also be incorporated into the type of rules discussed earlier.

6.8   Further Reading

There are many books on regression modeling. Draper and Smith (1981) and Cook and Weisberg (1999) each provide excellent overviews. McCullagh and Nelder (1989) is the definitive text on generalized linear models and Hastie and Tibshirani (1990) is equally definitive on generalized additive models. Fan and Gijbels (1996) provide a very extensive discussion of local polynomial methods and Wand and Jones (1995) contains a more theoretically oriented treatment of kernel estimation methods (both for regression and density estimation). Hand (1982) contains a detailed description of kernel methods in supervised classification problems.

Fairly recent treatments of advances in classification modeling are provided by McLachlan (1992), Ripley (1996), Bishop (1996), Mitchell (1996), Hand (1997), and Cherkassky and Muller (1998). The McLachlan text and the Ripley text are aimed primarily at a statistical audience. A notable feature of Ripley's text is the illustration of basic concepts using a variety of different data sets. The Bishop text and the Cherkassky and Muller texts are more focused on neural networks and related developments, and each contains many ideas that have yet to make their way into the mainstream statistical literature. Duda and Hart (1973) remains a classic in the classification literature with a very clear and comprehensive treatment of essential ideas involved in building classification models. Reviews of Bishop (1996), Ripley (1996), Looney (1997), Nakhaeizadeh and Taylor (1997), and Mitchell (1997) are provided in *Statistics and Computing*, volume 8, number 1.

The most comprehensive texts on mixture models are those of Titterington, Makov, and Smith (1985) and McLachlan and Basford (1988), and McLachlan and Peel (2000). Other general discussions of the area include Redner and Walker (1984) and Everitt and Hand (1981). Silverman's 1992 text on density estimation contains a wealth of insight, while Scott's (1992) text on the same topic is notable for its discussion of "average-shifted histogram" models that share some of the properties of both histograms and kernel estimators, and that might be of interest for models based on "binning" of massive data sets.

The text by Jolliffe (1986) is completely devoted to principal component methods. Huber (1985) provides a detailed discussion of projection pursuit, and Hyvarinen (1999) contains a thorough survey of independent component analysis and related techniques for dimension reduction.

Hidden Markov models are discussed in Elliott et al. (1995) and MacDonald and Zucchini (1997). A very readable introduction to the vast literature on autoregressive and related time-series models is Chatfield (1996). Harvey (1989), Box, Jenkins, and Reinsel (1994), and Hamilton (1994) provide more in-depth mathematical treatment of time-series modeling and its application to forecasting. Switching models are covered in depth in Kim and Nelson (1999). Cressie (1991) is a well-known text on spatial data analysis and the text by Dryden and Mardia (1998) provides a broad discussion on modeling of 2-dimensional shapes. Grenander's 1996 book on generative models for sequences and spatial data is a fascinating read, linking many ideas from statistics and computer science.

Ramsey and Silverman (1996) discuss a general approach to modeling of data that are functions of time and/or space, e.g., modeling of time-series from different weather stations. Books on modeling of repeated measures analysis include Crowder and Hand (1990), Hand and Crowder (1996), Diggle, Liang, and Zeger (1994), and Lindsey (1999).

The idea of using logical formulas to describe patterns is used widely in database systems. See for example Ramakrishnan and Gehrke (1999) or Ullman and Widom (1997) for introductory texts. Frequent sets were introduced by Agrawal, Imielinski, and Swami (1993). Regular expressions are treated in many textbooks on theory of computation such as Lewis and Papadimitriou (1998). Text patterns are discussed also in Gusfield (1997). Episodes are considered in Mannila, Toivonen, and Verkamo (1997).

7 Score Functions for Data Mining Algorithms

7.1 Introduction

In chapter 6 we focused on different representations and structures that are available to us for fitting models and patterns to data. Now we are ready to consider how we will match these structures to data. Recall that a model or pattern structure is the functional form, with the parameters left "floating." For example, $Y = aX + b$ might be one such model structure, with a and b the parameters. Given a model or pattern structure, we must score different settings of the parameter values with respect to data, so that we can choose a good set (or even "the best"). In the simple linear regression example in chapter 1, we saw how a *least squares* principle could be used to choose between different parameter values. This involved finding the values of the parameters a and b that minimized the sum of squared differences between the predicted values of y (from the model) and the observed (data) values of y. In this case, the *score function* is thus the sum of squared errors between model predictions and actual target measurements. Our goal in this chapter is to broaden the reader's horizon in terms of the score functions that can be used for data mining. We will see that the venerable squared error score function is but one of many, and indeed can be viewed as a special case arising from more general principles.

It is important to bear in mind why we are interested in score functions in the first place. Ultimately the purpose of a score function should be to rank models as a function of how useful the models are to the data miner. Unfortunately in practice it can be quite difficult to measure "utility" in terms of direct practical usefulness to the person building the model. For example, in predicting stock market returns one might use squared error between predictions and actual data as a score function to train one's model. However, if the model is then used in a real financial environment, a host of other factors such as trading costs, risks, diversity, and so forth, come into play to determine the true utility of the model. This illustrates that we often settle for simpler "generic" score functions (such as squared error) that have many desirable well-understood properties and are relatively easy to work with. Of course, one should not take this to an extreme: the score function being used should reflect the overall goals of the data mining task as far as is possible. One should try to avoid the situation, unfortunately all too common in practice, of using a convenient score function (perhaps because it is the default score function in the software package being used) that is completely inappropriate for the task.

Different score functions have different properties, and are useful in different situations. One of the goals of this chapter is to make the reader aware of these differences and of the implications of using one score function rather than another. Just as there are a few fundamental principles underlying model and pattern structures, so there are some basic principles underlying the different score functions. These are outlined in this chapter.

It is useful to make three distinctions at the outset. The first is between score functions for models, and score functions for patterns. The second is between score functions for *predictive* structures, and score functions for *descriptive* structures. And the third is between score functions for models of fixed complexity, and score functions for models of different complexity. These distinctions will be illustrated below.

A minor comment on the terminology used below is in order. In some places we will refer to score functions (such as error) that we clearly wish to *minimize,* whereas in other places we will refer to score functions (such as log-likelihood) that we clearly wish to *maximize.* The general concept is the same in either case, since the negative (or "inverse") of an "error-based" score function can always be maximized, and vice versa.

7.2 Scoring Patterns

Since the whole idea of searching for local patterns in data is relatively recent, there is a far smaller toolbox of techniques available for scoring patterns compared to the plethora of techniques for scoring models. Indeed, there is really no general consensus on how patterns should be scored. This is largely a result of the fact that the usefulness of a pattern lies in the eye of the beholder. One person's noisy outlier may be another person's Nobel Prize. Fundamentally, patterns might be evaluated in terms of how interesting or unexpected they are to the data analyst. But we could only hope to quantify this if somehow we had a precise model of what the user actually knows already. We are all familiar with the experience that the first time we learn something surprising is a lot more informative than the fifth or tenth time we hear the same information again. Thus, the degree to which a pattern is interesting to a person must be a function of their prior knowledge.

In practice, however, we cannot hope (except in simple situations) to be able to model a person's prior knowledge. Faced with a data set, a scientist or a marketing expert would have difficulty in precisely formulating what it is that they already know about the problem. Even subjective Bayesians can have problems choosing priors for complex multiparameter models—and evade them by choosing standard forms for the priors, that are only very simplistic representations of prior knowledge. We have found that, once certain patterns begin to emerge from the data (via visualization, descriptive statistics, or rules found by a data mining algorithm), database owners often say "Ah yes, but of course we knew that already," changing their minds about what they claim to have expected once they have seen the data.

Having said all of this, the fact remains that most techniques currently used in data mining for scoring patterns essentially assume that they are measuring degree of informativeness relative to a *completely uninformed prior model*; that is, it is effectively assumed that the data analyst has no prior information at all about the problem, beyond perhaps a few simple marginal and descriptive statistics. The hope is that this will eliminate the very obvious patterns (by focusing attention on patterns that are different from the known simple ones) and that the user can effectively "post-prune" the remaining patterns found by the algorithm to retain the truly interesting ones. The danger, of course, is that for some data sets and some forms of pattern searches, almost all patterns that are found by the data mining algorithm will essentially be uninteresting to the data analyst.

To illustrate these ideas we choose one simple (but widely used) pattern structure, the *probabilistic rule* (as discussed in chapter 5 under association rules) and explored in detail later in chapter 13. This has the form

$$\text{IF } a \text{ THEN } b \text{ with probability } p$$

where a and b are Boolean propositions (events) defined on a subset of the variables of interest and $p = p(b|a)$. How can we measure how interesting or informative this rule is to an uninformed observer? One simple approach is to assume that the observer already knows the marginal (unconditional) probability for the event b, $p(b)$.

For example, suppose that we are studying a population of data miners. Let b represent the event that a randomly chosen person in this population is a data mining researcher, and let a be the event that such a person has read this book. Suppose we find that $p(b) = 0.25$ and that $p(b|a) = 0.75$; that is, 25% of this population are researchers and 75% of people who have read this book are researchers. This is interesting because it tells us that the proportion of people who undertake research is higher among those who have read the book than it is in this population of data miners in general (and hence, by implication, it is higher than among the people who have not read the book). Note, as an aside, that there are no causal implications to this. It could be that the book inspired a reader to take up research, or that a person involved in research hoped the book would help them.

The types of simple score functions that are used to capture the informativeness of such a rule rely in general on how "far" the posterior probability $p(b|a)$ is (after learning that event a is true), from the prior probability $p(b)$. Thus, for example, one could simply measure absolute distance between the probabilities $|p(b|a) - p(b)|$, or perhaps measure distance on log-odds scale, $\log \frac{p(b|a)}{p(\bar{b}|a)}$ where $\bar{b}$ represents the event that a person is not a researcher.

When we compare *different* patterns, such as $p(b|a)$ and $p(b|c)$, it is also useful to take into account the *coverage* of a pattern—that is, the proportion of the data to which it applies. To continue our example above, let c be the condition that the a randomly chosen data miner is one of the three authors of this book. A second pattern might be "if c then b" ("if a data miner is an author of this book then they are a researcher"), with $p(b|c) = 1$ since the three authors are all researchers. However, the condition c only applies to three data miners, which is a very small fraction of the universe of data miners. On the other hand, (we hope that) the coverage of event a will be much larger; that is, $p(a)$ is significantly greater than $p(c)$. To illustrate, suppose that $p(a) = 0.2$ and $p(c) = 0.003$. Then, although the second pattern is very accurate ($p(b|c) = 1$) it is not particularly useful since it only applies to a very small fraction of the population (0.3%), whereas the first pattern is not as accurate ($p(b|a) = 0.75$) but it has much broader applicability (to 20% of the population). It is easy to develop a variety of measures that augment the score function to take coverage into account. For example, we could multiply the previously defined scores by the probability of the conditioning event; $p(a)|p(b|a) - p(b)| = |p(b, a) - p(b)p(a)|$ that can be interpreted as measuring the difference in probability between an independence assumption and the observed joint probability for the two events a and b. Alternatively, the approach used in association rule mining (chapters 5 and 13) defines a threshold p_t, and only seeks patterns with coverage greater than p_t.

There are numerous other score functions for patterns that have been proposed in the data mining literature. None have gained widespread acceptance or general use, largely because judging the novelty and utility of a pattern is often quite subjective and application-specific. Thus, human interpretation by a domain expert remains the most practical way to evaluate patterns at present (e.g., having a human search through and interpret a set of candidate patterns produced by a data mining algorithm).

7.3   Predictive versus Descriptive Score Functions

We now turn to score functions for models, where there is a much greater selection of useful methods available compared to patterns.

7.3.1   Score Functions for Predictive Models

A convenient place to begin is by considering the distinction between prediction and description. Score functions for predictive problems are relatively straightforward. In a prediction task, our training data comes with a "target" value Y, this being a quantitative variable for regression or a categorical variable for classification, and our data set $D = \{(\mathbf{x}(1), y(1)), \ldots, (\mathbf{x}(n), y(n))\}$ consists of pairs of input vectors and target values. Let $\hat{f}(\mathbf{x}(i); \theta)$ be the prediction generated by the model for individual i, $1 \leq i \leq n$, using parameter values θ. Let $y(i)$ be the actual observed value (or "target") for the ith individual in the training data set.

Clearly our score function should be a function of the difference between the predictions $\hat{f}(\mathbf{x}(i); \theta)$ and the targets $y(i)$. Commonly used score functions include the sum of squared errors,

$$S_{SSE}(\theta) = \frac{1}{N} \sum_{i=1}^{N} \left(\hat{f}(\mathbf{x}(i); \theta) - y(i) \right)^2 \tag{7.1}$$

for quantitative Y, and the misclassification rate (or error rate or "zero-one" score function) for categorical Y, namely,

$$S_{0/1}(\theta) = \frac{1}{N} \sum_{i=1}^{N} I \left(\hat{f}(\mathbf{x}(i); \theta), y(i) \right) \tag{7.2}$$

where $I(a, b) = 1$ if a is not equal to b and 0 otherwise. These are the two most widely-used score functions for regression and classification respectively. They are simple to understand and (in the case of squared error at least) often lead to straightforward optimization problems.

However, note that we have made some strong assumptions in how these score functions are defined above. For example, by summing over the individual errors we are assuming that errors for all individuals may be treated equally. This is a very common assumption and generally useful. However, if (for example) we have a data set in which the measurements were taken at different times, we might want to assign higher weight in the score function to predictions on more recent items. Similarly, we might have different subsets of items in the data set where the target values are more reliable in some subsets than others (for example, some quantification of measurement error in a subset). Here we might wish to assign lower weight in the score function to predictions on the items with less reliable measurements.

Furthermore, both are functions *only* of the difference between the predictions and targets—in particular, they do not depend on the *values* of the target $y(i)$. This is something we might want to take account of. For example, if Y were a categorical variable indicating whether or not a person had cancer, we might wish to give more weight to the error of not detecting a true cancer and less weight to errors that correspond to false alarms. For real-valued Y, *squared*-error may not be appropriate—perhaps the quality of the model is more appropriately reflected in *absolute error* (squared-error gives greater weight to extreme differences between the observed and predicted Y values than does absolute error). And, as a third example, in an investment scenario, we might want be more tolerant (from a risk-taking standpoint) of predictions of Y that *underestimate* the true value than we are to predictions that *overestimate*, suggesting that an asymmetric function might be more appropriate.

The basic score functions above are rather simple. Thus, we may need in practice to adjust them to reflect the aims of our data mining project more accurately. Sometimes this is not easy (defining the "real aims" may be difficult, especially in data mining contexts, where problems are often open ended). In other cases, even if one cannot state the aims precisely, one might be able to improve on the basic score function. For example, for the cancer problem, instead of using the zero-one loss function it might be more appropriate to define a score function based on a *cost matrix*. Thus, let $\hat{k}$ be the predicted class, k the true class, and define a matrix of "costs" $c(\hat{k}, k), 1 \leq \hat{k}, k \leq K$ that reflects the severity of classifying a patient with true class k into class $\hat{k}$.

In selecting a score function for a particular predictive data mining task there is always a trade-off between choosing a simple score function (such as sum of squared errors) and a much more complex one. The simpler score function will usually be more convenient to work with computationally and will be easier to define. However, more complex score functions (such as those mentioned above) may reflect better the actual reality of the prediction problem. An important point is that many data mining algorithms (such as tree models, linear regression models, and so forth) can in principle handle fairly general score functions—e.g., an algorithm based on cross-validation can use any well-defined score function. Of course, even though this is true in theory, in practice not all software implementations allow the data miner to define their own application-specific score function.

7.3.2 Score Functions for Descriptive Models

For descriptive models, in which there is no "target" variable to be predicted, it is less clear how to define a score function. A fundamental approach is through the likelihood function, which we introduced in chapter 4, but which we here describe from a slightly different perspective. Let $\hat{p}(\mathbf{x}; \theta)$ be the estimated probability of observing a data point at $\mathbf{x}$, as defined by our model $\hat{p}$ with parameters θ, where X is categorical (the extension to continuous variables is straightforward, and $\hat{p}$ would then be a probability density function). If the model is a good one, then it might be expected to place a high probability at those values of X where a data point is observed. Thus $\hat{p}(\mathbf{x})$ itself can be taken as a measure of quality of the model—a score function—at the point $\mathbf{x}$. This is the basic idea of maximum likelihood (chapter 4) once again: better models assign higher probability to observed data. (This is fine actually as long as we can assume that all the models we are considering have equal functional complexity, so that the comparison is "fair"—the case in which we are comparing models of different complexities will be discussed later in this chapter.)

If we assume that the data points have arisen independently, we can define an overall score function for the model by combining these score functions for the individual data points simply by multiplying them together:

$$L(\theta) = \prod_{i=1}^{n} \hat{p}(\mathbf{x}(i); \theta). \tag{7.3}$$

This is again the likelihood function of chapter 4, for a set of data points, that we maximize to find an estimate of θ. As we noted there, it is typically more convenient to work with the log-likelihood. Now the contribution of an individual data point to the overall score function is $\log \hat{p}(\mathbf{x}(i); \theta)$, and the overall function is the sum of these:

$$\log L(\theta) = \sum_{i=1}^{n} \log \hat{p}(\mathbf{x}(i); \theta). \tag{7.4}$$

If we work with the negative of the $\log \hat{p}(\mathbf{x}(i); \theta)$, as is often done, then this function needs to be *minimized*. We define

$$S_L(\theta) = -\log L(\theta) = -\sum_{i=1}^{n} \log \hat{p}(\mathbf{x}(i); \theta). \tag{7.5}$$

Note again the intuitive interpretation: $-\log \hat{p}$ is our error term (it gets larger as $\hat{p}$ gets smaller), and we are summing this over all of our data points. The largest possible value for $\hat{p}$ is 1 (for categorical data) and, hence, $S_L(\theta)$ is lower bounded by 0. Thus, we can think of $S_L(\theta)$ as a type of entropy term that measures how well the parameters θ can compress (or predict) the training data.

A particularly useful feature of the likelihood (or, equivalently, the negative log-likelihood) is that it is very general. It can be defined for any problem in which the model or pattern being examined is expressed in terms of probability functions. For example, one might assume that Y in a predictive model is a perfect linear function of some predictor variable X, as well as extra randomly distributed errors, as discussed in the last section. If one can postulate a parametric form for the probability distribution of these errors, then one can compute the likelihood of the data for any proposed parameters in the model. In fact, as we saw in chapter 4, if the error terms are supposed to be Normally distributed with mean 0 about a deterministic function of X then the likelihood score function is equivalent to the sum of squared errors score function.

Although (negative log-)likelihood is a powerful and useful score function, it too has its limitations. In particular, if a parameterization assigns any data point a probability near 0, the log-likelihood will approach $-\infty$. Thus, the overall error can be dominated by extreme points. If the true probability of that same point is also very small, then the model is being penalized for a prediction in the tails of the density function (very unlikely events), that may have little relation to the practical utility of the model. Conversely, there may be problems (such as predicting the occurrence of rare events) in which it is precisely in the tails of the density that we are most interested in accurate prediction. Thus, while likelihood is based on strong theoretical foundations and is generally useful for scoring probabilistic models, it is important to realize that it may not necessarily reflect the true utility of a model for a particular task. Other score functions for determining the quality of probabilistic predictions are also possible, each with its own particular characteristics. For example we can define the integrated squared error between our estimate $\hat{p}(\mathbf{x}; \theta)$ and the true probability $p(\mathbf{x})$, $\int (\hat{p}(\mathbf{x}; \theta) - p(\mathbf{x}))^2 d\mathbf{x}$. By completing the square, and ignoring terms not depending on θ, we get a score function of the form $\int \hat{p}(\mathbf{x}; \theta)^2 d\mathbf{x} - 2E[\hat{p}(\mathbf{x}; \theta)]$, where each term can be empirically approximated to provide an estimate of the true integrated squared error as a function of θ.

For *nonprobabilistic* descriptive models, such as partition-based clustering, it is quite easy to come up with all sorts of score functions based on how well separated the clusters are, how compact they are, and so forth. For example, for simple prototype-based clustering (the k-means model discussed in chapter 9), a simple and widely used score function is the sum of square errors within each cluster

$$S_{KSSE}(\theta) = \sum_{k=1}^{K} e_k, \quad e_k = \sum_{i \in cluster_k} ||\mathbf{x}(i) - \mu_k||^2 \qquad (7.6)$$

where θ is the parameter vector for the cluster model, $\theta = \{\mu_1, \ldots, \mu_K\}$, and the μ_ks are the cluster centers. However, it is quite difficult to formulate any score function for cluster models that reflect how close the clusters are to "truth" (if this is regarded as meaningful). The ultimate judgment on the utility of a given clustering depends on how useful the clustering is in the context of the particular application. Does it provide new insight into the data? Does it permit a meaningful categorization of the data? And so on. These are questions that typically can only be answered in the context of a particular problem and cannot be captured by a single score metric. To put it another way, once again the score functions for tasks such as clustering are not necessarily very closely related to the true utility function for the problem. We will return to the issue of score functions for clustering tasks in chapter 9.

To summarize, there are simple "generic" score functions for tasks such as classification, regression, and density estimation, that are all useful in their own right. However, they do have limitations, and it is perhaps best to regard them as starting points from which to generalize to more application-specific score functions.

7.4   Scoring Models with Different Complexities

In the preceding sections we described score functions as minimizing some measure of discrepancy between the observed data and the proposed model. One might expect models that are close to the data (in the sense embodied in the score function) to be "good" models. However, we need to be clear about why we are building the model.

7.4.1   General Concepts in Comparing Models

We can distinguish between two types of situations (as we have in earlier chapters). In one type of situation we are merely trying to build a summarizing descriptive model of a data set that captures its main features. Thus, for example, we might want to summarize the main chemical compounds among the members of a particular family of compounds, where our database contains records for all possible members of this family. In this case, accuracy of the model is paramount—though it will be mediated by considerations of comprehensibility. The best accuracy is given by a model that exactly reproduces the data, or describes the data in some equivalent form, but the whole point of the modeling exercise in this case is to reduce the complexity of the data to something that is more comprehensible. In situations like this, simple goodness of fit of the model to the data will be one part of an overall score measure, with comprehensibility being another part (and this part will be subjective). An example of a general technique in this context is based on data compression and information-theoretic arguments, where our score function is generally decomposed as

$$S_I(\theta, M) \;\; = \;\; \text{number of bits to describe the data given the model}$$
$$+ \text{ number of bits to describe the model (and parameters)}$$

where the first term measures the goodness of fit to the data and the second measures the complexity of the model M and its parameters θ. In fact, for the first term ("number of bits to describe the data given the model) we can use $S_L = -\log p(D|\theta, M)$ (negative log-likelihood, log base 2). For the second term ("number of bits to describe the model") we can use $-\log p(\theta, M)$ (this is in effect just taking negative logs of the general Bayesian score function discussed in chapter 4). Intuitively, we can think of $-\log p(\theta, M)$ (the second term) as the communication "cost" in bits to transmit the model structure and its parameters from some hypothetical transmitter to a hypothetical receiver, and S_L (the first term) as the cost of transmitting the portion of the data (the errors) that the model and its parameters do not account for. These two parts will tend to work in opposite directions—a good fit to the data will be achieved by a complicated model, while comprehensibility will be achieved by a simple model. The overall score function trades off what is meant by an acceptable model.

In the other general situation our aim is really to generalize from the available data to new data that could arise. For example, we might want to infer how new customers are likely to behave or infer the likely properties of new sky objects not yet observed. Once again, while goodness of fit to the observed data is clearly a part of what we will mean by a good model, it is not the whole story. In particular, since the data do not represent the whole population (there would be no need for generalization if they did) there will be aspects of the observed data ("noise") that are not characteristic of the entire population and vice versa. A model that provided a very good fit to the observed data would also fit these aspects—and, hence, would not provide the best possible predictions. Once again, we need to modify the simple goodness of fit measure in order to define an overall score function. In particular, we need to modify it by a component that prevents the model from becoming too complex, and fitting all the idiosyncrasies of the observed data.

In both situations, an ideal score function strikes some sort of compromise between how well the model fits the data and the simplicity of the model, although the theoretical basis for the compromise is different. This difference is likely to mean that different score functions are appropriate for the different situations. Since the compromise when the aim is simply to summarize the main features of a data set necessarily involves a subjective component ("what does the data miner regard as an acceptably simple model?"), we will concentrate here on the other situation: our aim is to determine, from the data we have available, which model will perform best on data we have not yet seen.

7.4.2 Bias-Variance Again

Before examining score functions that we might hope will provide a good fit to data as yet unseen, it will be useful to look in more detail at the need to avoid modeling the available data too closely. We discussed bias and variance in the context of estimates of parameters θ in chapter 4 and we discuss it again here in the more general context of score functions.

As we have mentioned in earlier chapters, it is extremely unlikely that one's chosen model structure will be "correct." There are too many features of the real world for us to be able to model them exactly (and there are also deep questions about just what "correct" means). This implies that the chosen model form will provide only an approximation to the "truth." Let us take a predictive model to illustrate. Then, at any given value of X (which we take to be univariate for simplicity—exactly the same argument holds for multivariate X), the model is likely to provide predicted values of Y that are not exactly right. More formally, suppose we draw many different data sets, fit a model of the specified structure (for example, a piecewise local model with given number of components, each of given complexity; a polynomial function of X of given degree; and so on) to each of them, and determine the expected value of the predicted Y at any X. Then this expected predicted value is unlikely to coincide exactly with the true value. That is, the model is likely to provide a biased prediction of the true Y at any given X. (Recall that bias of an estimate was defined in chapter 4 as the difference between the expected value of the estimate and the true value.) Thus, perfect prediction is too much to hope for!

However, we can make the difference between the expected value of the predictions and the unknown true value smaller (indeed, we can make it as small as we like for some classes of models and some situations) by increasing the complexity of the model structure. In the examples above, this means increasing the number of components in the piecewise linear model, or increasing the degree of the polynomial.

At first glance, this looks great—we can obtain a model that is as accurate as we like, in terms of bias, simply by taking a complicated enough model structure. Unfortunately, there is no such thing as a free lunch, and the increased accuracy in terms of bias is only gained at a loss in other terms.

By virtue of the very flexibility of the model structure, its predictions at any fixed X could vary dramatically between different data sets. That is, although the average of the predictions at any given X will be close to the true Y (this is what small bias means), there may be substantial variation between the predictions arising from the different data sets. Since, in practice, we will only ever observe one of these predictions (we really have only one data set to use to estimate the model's parameters) the fact that "on average" things are good will provide little comfort. For all we know we have picked a data set that yields predictions far from the average. There is no way of telling.

There is another way of looking at this. Our very flexible model (with, for example, a large number of piecewise components or a high degree) has led to one that closely follows the data. Since, at any given X, the observed value of Y will be randomly distributed about its mean, our flexible model is also modeling this random component of the observed Y value. That is, the flexible model is *overfitting* the data.

Finally (though, yet again, it is really just another way of looking at the same thing), increasing the complexity of the model structure means increasing the number of parameters to be estimated. Generally, if more parameters are being estimated, then the accuracy of each estimate will decrease (its variance, from data set to data set, will increase).

The complementarity of bias and variance in the above, is termed the *bias-variance trade-off*. We want to choose a model in which neither is too large—but reducing either one tends to increase the other. They can be combined to yield an overall measure of discrepancy between the data and the model to yield the *mean squared error* (MSE). Consider the standard regression setting we have discussed before, where we are assuming that y is a deterministic function of $\mathbf{x}$ (where we now generalize to the vector case) with additive noise, that is, $y = f(\mathbf{x}; \theta) + e$, where e is (for example) Normal with zero-mean. Thus, $\mu_y = E[y|\mathbf{x}]$ represents the true (and unknown) expected value for any data point $\mathbf{x}$ (where here the expectation E is with respect to the noise e), and $\hat{y} = f(\mathbf{x}; \theta)$ is the estimate provided by our model and fitted parameters θ. The MSE at $\mathbf{x}$ is then defined as:

$$
\begin{aligned}
MSE(\mathbf{x}) &= E\left[\hat{y} - \mu_y\right]^2 \\
&= E\left[\hat{y} - E\left(\hat{y}\right)\right]^2 + E\left[E\left(\hat{y}\right) - \mu_y\right]^2
\end{aligned}
\tag{7.7}
$$

or *MSE = Variance + Bias²*. (The expectation E here is taken with respect to $p(D)$, the probability distribution over all possible data sets for some fixed size n). This equation bears close inspection. We are treating our prediction $\hat{y}$ here as a random quantity, where the randomness arises from the random sampling that generated the training data D. Different data sets D would lead to different models and parameters, and different predictions $\hat{y}$. The expectation, E, is over different data sets of the same size n, each randomly chosen from the population in question. The variance term $E\left[\hat{y} - E\left(\hat{y}\right)\right]^2$ tell us how much our estimate $\hat{y}$ will vary across different potential data sets of size n. In other words, it measures the sensitivity of $\hat{y}$ to the particular data set being used to train our model. As an extreme example, if we always picked a constant y_1 as our prediction, without regard to the data at all, then this variance would be zero. At the other extreme, if we have an extremely complex model with many parameters, our predictions $\hat{y}$ may vary greatly depending from one individual training data set to the next.

The bias term $E\left[E\left(\hat{y}\right) - \mu_y\right]$ reflects the systematic error in our prediction—

that is how far away our average prediction is, $E(\hat{y})$, from truth μ_y. If we use a constant y_1 as our prediction, ignoring the data, we may have large bias (that is, this difference may be large). If we use a more complex model, our average prediction may get closer to the truth, but our variance may be quite large. The bias-variance quantifies the tension between simpler models (low variance, but potentially high bias) and more complex ones (potentially low bias but typically high variance).

In practice, of course, we are interested in the average MSE over the entire domain of the function we are estimating, so we might define the expected MSE (with respect to the input distribution $p(\mathbf{x})$) as $\int MSE(\mathbf{x})p(\mathbf{x})d\mathbf{x}$, that again has the same additive decomposition (since expectation is linear).

Note that while we can in principle measure the variance of our predictions $\hat{y}$ (for example, by some form of resampling such as the bootstrap method), the bias will always be unknown since it involves μ_y that is itself unknown (this is after all what we are trying to learn). Thus, the bias-variance decomposition is primarily of theoretical interest since we cannot measure the bias component explicitly, and in turn it does not provide a practical score function combining these two aspects of estimation error. Nonetheless, the practical implications in general are clear: we need to choose a model that is not too inflexible (because its predictions will then have substantial bias) but not too flexible (since then its predictions will have substantial variance). That is, we need a score function that can handle models of different complexities and take into account this compromise, and one that can be implemented in practice. This is the focus of the next section.

We should note that in certain data mining applications, the issue of variance may not be too important, particularly when the models are relatively simple compared to the amount of data being used to fit them. This is because variance is a function of sample size (as we discussed in chapter 4). Increasing the sample size decreases the variance of an estimator. Unfortunately, no general statements can be made about when variance and overfitting will be important issues. It depends on both the sample size of the training data D and the complexity of the model being fit.

7.4.3 Score Functions That Penalize Complexity

How, then, can we choose a suitable compromise between flexibility (so that a reasonable fit to the available data is obtained) and overfitting (in which the model fits chance components in the data)? One way is to choose a score function that encapsulates the compromise. That is, we choose an overall score function that is explicitly composed of two components: a component that measures the goodness of fit of the model to the data, and an extra component that puts a premium on simplicity. This yields an overall score function of the form

$$\text{score(model)} = \text{error(model)} + \text{penalty-function(model)},$$

where we want want to minimize this score. We have discussed several different ways to define the error component of the score in the preceding sections. What might the additional penalty component look like?

In general (though there are subtleties that mean that this is something of a simplification), the complexity of a model M will be related to the number of parameters, d, under consideration. We will adopt the following notation in this context. Consider that there are K different model structures, $M_1, \ldots, M_K$, from which we wish to choose one (ideally the one that predicts best on future data). Model M_k has d_k parameters. We will assume that for each model structure $M_k, 1 \leq k \leq K$, the best fitting parameters $\hat{\theta}_k$ for that model (those that maximize goodness-of-fit to the data) have already been chosen; that is, we have already determined point estimates of these parameters for each of these K model structures and now we wish to choose among these fitted models.

The widely used *Akaike information criterion* or *AIC* is defined as

$$S_{AIC}(M_k) = 2S_L(\hat{\theta}_k; M_k) + 2d_k, \quad 1 \leq k \leq K. \tag{7.8}$$

where S_L is the negative log-likelihood as defined in equation 7.5 and the penalty term is $2d_k$. This can be derived formally using asymptotic arguments.

An alternative, based on Bayesian arguments, also takes into account the sample size, n. This *Bayesian Information Criterion* or *BIC* is defined as

$$S_{BIC}(M_k) = 2S_L(\hat{\theta}_k; M_k) + d_k \log n \tag{7.9}$$

where S_L is again the negative log-likelihood of 7.5. Note the effect of the additive penalty term $d_k \log n$. For fixed n, the penalty term grows linearly in number of parameters d_k, which is quite intuitive. For a fixed number of parameters d_k, the penalty term increases in proportion to $\log n$. Note that this logarithmic growth in n is offset by the potentially linear growth in S_L as a function of n (since it is a sum of n terms). Thus, asymptotically as n gets very large, for relatively small values of d_k, the error term S_L (linear in n) will dominate the penalty term (logarithmic in n). Intuitively, for very large numbers of data points n, we can "trust" the error on the training data and the penalty function term is less relevant. Conversely, for small numbers of data points n, the penalty function term $d_k \log n$ will play a more influential role in model selection.

There are many other penalized score functions with similar additive forms to those above (namely an error-based term plus a penalty term) include the adjusted R^2 and C_p scores for regression, the minimum description length (MDL) method (which is closely related to the MAP score of chapter 4), and Vapnik's structural risk minimization approach (SRM).

Several of these penalty functions can be derived from fairly fundamental theoretical arguments. However, in practice these types of penalty functions are often used under far broader conditions than the assumptions used in the derivation of the theory justify. Nonetheless, since they are easy to compute they are often quite convenient in practice in terms of giving at least a general idea of what the appropriate complexity for a model is, given a particular data set and data mining task.

A different approach is provided by the Bayesian framework of chapter 4. We can try to compute the posterior probability of each model given the data directly, and select the one with the highest posterior probability; that is,

$$
\begin{aligned}
p(M_k|D) \quad &\propto \quad p(D|M_k)p(M_k) \\
&= \quad \int p(D, \theta_k|M_k)p(M_k)d\theta_k \\
&= \quad \int p(D|\theta_k)p(\theta_k|M_k)d\theta_k \; p(M_k)
\end{aligned}
\tag{7.10}
$$

where the integral represents calculating the expectation of the likelihood of the data over parameter space (also known as *marginal likelihood*), relative to a prior in parameter space $p(\theta_k|M_k)$, and the term $p(M_k)$ is a prior probability for each model. This is clearly quite different from the "point estimate" methods—the Bayesian philosophy is to fully acknowledge uncertainty and, thus, average over our parameters (since we are unsure of their exact values) rather than "picking" point estimates such as $\hat{\theta}_k$. Note that this Bayesian approach implicitly penalizes complexity, since higher dimensional parameter spaces (more complex models) will mean that the probability mass in $p(\theta_k|M_k)$ is spread more thinly than in simpler models.

Of course, in practice explicit integration is often intractable for many parameter spaces and models of interest and Monte Carlo sampling techniques are used. Furthermore, for large data sets, the $p(D|\theta_k)$ function may in fact be quite "peaked" about a single value $\hat{\theta}_k$ (recall the maximum likelihood estimation examples in chapter 4), in which case we can reasonably approximate the Bayesian expression above by the value of the peak plus some estimate of the surrounding volume (for example, a Taylor series type of expansion around the posterior mode of $p(D|\theta)p(\theta)$)—this type of argument can be shown to lead to approximations such as BIC above).

7.4.4 Score Functions Using External Validation

A different strategy for choosing models is sometimes used, not based on adding a penalty term, but instead based on external validation of the model. The basic idea is to (randomly) split the data into two mutually exclusive parts, a *design* part D_d, and a *validation* part D_v. The design part is used to construct the models and estimate the parameters. Then the score function is recalculated using the validation part. These validation scores are used to select models (or patterns). An important point here is that our estimate of the score function for a particular model, say $S(M_k)$, is itself a random variable, where the randomness comes from both the data set being used to train (design) the model and the data set being used to validate it. For example, if our score is some error function between targets and model predictions (such as sum of squared errors), then ideally we would like to have an *unbiased estimate* of the value of this score function on future data, for each model under consideration. In the validation context, since the two data sets are independently and randomly selected, for a given model the validation score provides an unbiased estimate of the score value of that model for new ("out-of-sample") data points. That is, the bias in estimates, that inevitably arises with the design component, is absent from the independent validation estimate. It follows from this (and the linearity of expectation) that the difference between the scores of two models evaluated on a validation set will have an expected value in the direction favoring the better model. Thus, the difference in validation scores can be used to choose between models. Note that we have previously discussed unbiased estimates of parameters θ (chapter 4), unbiased estimates of what we are trying to predict μ_y (earlier in this chapter), and now unbiased estimates of our score function S. The same principles of bias and variance underly all three contexts, and indeed all three contexts are closely interlinked (accuracy in parameter estimates will affect accuracy of our predictions, for example)—it is important, however, to understand the distinction between them.

This general idea of validation has been extended to the notion of *cross-validation*. The splitting into two independent sets is randomly repeated many times, each time estimating a new model (of the given form) from the design part of the data and obtaining an unbiased estimate the out-of-sample performance of each model from the validation component. These unbiased estimates are then averaged to yield an overall estimate. We described the use of cross-validation to choose between CART recursive partitioning models in chapter 5. Cross-validation is popular in practice, largely because it is simple and reasonably robust (in the sense that it relies on relatively few assumptions). However, if the partitioning is repeated m times it does come at a cost of (on the order of) m times the complexity of a method based on just using a single validation set. (There are exceptions in special cases. For example, there is an algorithm for the leave-one-out special case of cross-validation applied to linear discriminant analysis that has the same order of computational complexity as the basic model construction algorithm.)

For small data sets, the process of selecting validation subsets D_v can lead to significant variation across data sets, and thus, the *variance* of the cross-validation score also needs to be monitored in practice to check whether or not the variation may be unreasonably high. Finally, there is a subtlety in cross-validation scoring in that we are averaging over models that have potentially different parameters but the same complexity. It is important that we are actually averaging over essentially the *same* basic model each time. If, for example, the fitting procedure we are using can get trapped at different local maxima in parameter space, on different subsets of training data, it is not clear that it is meaningful to average over the validation scores for these models.

It is true, as stated above, that the estimate of performance obtained from such a process for a given model is unbiased. This is why such methods are very widely used and have been extensively developed for performance assessment (see Further Reading). However, some care needs to be exercised. If the validation measures are subsequently used to choose between models (for example, to choose between models of different complexity), then the validation score of the model that is finally selected will be a biased estimate of this model's performance. To see this, imagine that, purely by chance some model did exceptionally well on a validation set. That is, by the accidental way the validation set happened to have fallen, this model did well. Then this model is likely to be chosen as the "best" model. But clearly, this model will not do so well with new out-of-sample data sets. What this means in practice is that, if an assessment of the likely future performance of a (predictive) model is needed, then this must be based on yet a third data set, the *test set*, about which we shall say more in the next subsection.

7.5 Evaluation of Models and Patterns

Once we have selected a model or pattern, based on its score function, we will often want to know (in a predictive context) how well this model or pattern will perform on new unseen data. For example, what error rate, on future unseen data, would we expect from a predictive classification model we have built using a given training set? We have already referred to this issue when discussing the validation set method of model selection above.

Again we note that if any of the same data that have been used for selecting a model or used for parameter estimation are then also used again for performance evaluation, then the evaluation will be optimistically biased. The model will have been chosen precisely because it does well on this particular data set. This means that the *apparent* or *resubstitution* performance, as the estimate based on reusing the training set is called, will tend to be optimistically biased.

If we are only considering a single model structure, and not using validation to select a model, then we can use subsampling techniques such as validation or cross-validation, splitting the data into training and test sets, to obtain an unbiased estimate of our model's future performance. Again this can be repeated multiple times, and the results averaged. At an extreme, the test set can consist of only one point, so that the process is repeated N times, with an average of the N single scores yielding the final estimate. This principle of leaving out part of the data, so that it can provide an independent test set, has been refined and developed to a great degree of technical depth and sophistication, notably in jackknife and bootstrap methods, as well as the leaving-one-out cross-validation method (all of these are different, though related and sometimes confused). The further reading section below gives pointers to publications containing more details.

The essence of the above is that, to obtain unbiased estimates of likely future performance of a model we must assess its performance using a data set which is independent of the data set used to construct and select the model. This also applies if validation data sets are used. Suppose, for example, we chose between K models by partitioning the data into two subsets, where we fit parameters on the first subset, and select the single "best" model using the model scores on the second (validation) subset . Then, since we will choose that model which does best on the validation data set, the model will be selected so that it fits the idiosyncrasies of this validation data set. In effect, the validation data set is being used as part of the design process and performance as measured on the validation data will be optimistic. This be-

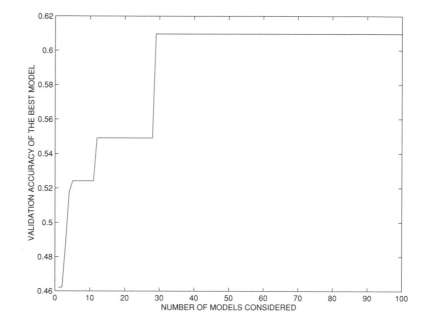

Figure 7.1   Classification accuracy of the best model selected on a validation data set from a set of K models, $1 \leq K \leq 100$, where each model is making random predictions.

comes more severe, the larger is the set of models from which the final model is chosen.

> **Example 7.1** The problem of optimistic performance on validation data is illustrated by a hypothetical two-class classification problem where we have selected the best of K models using a validation data set of 100 data points. We have taken the two classes to have equal prior probabilities of 0.5 and, to take an extreme situation, have arranged things so that none of the "predictor" variables in our models have any predictive power at all; that is, all the input variables are independent of the class variable Y. This means that each model is in fact generating purely random predictions so that the long-run accuracy on new unseen data for any of the models will be 0.5 (although of course we would not be aware of this fact). Figure 7.1 shows the cross-validation accuracy obtained from a simple simulation of this scenario, where we increased the number of models K being considered from 1 to 100. When we chose from a small number of models (fewer than 10) the proportion of validation

set points correctly classified by the best of them is close enough to 0.5. However, by $K = 15$ the "best" model, selected using the validation set, correctly classifies a proportion 0.55 of the validation set points, and by $k = 30$ the best model classifies a proportion 0.61 of the validation set correctly.

The message here is that if one uses a validation set to choose between models, one cannot also use it to provide an estimate of likely future performance. The very fact that one is choosing models which do well on the validation set means that performance estimates on this set are biased as estimates of performance on other unseen data. As we said above, the validation set, being used to choose between models, has really become part of the design process. This means that to obtain unbiased estimates of likely future performance we ideally need access to yet another data set (a "hold-out" set) that has not been used in any way in the estimation or model selection so far. For very large data sets this is usually not a problem, in that data is readily available, but for small data sets it can be problematic since it effectively reduces the data available for training.

7.6   Robust Methods

We have pointed out elsewhere that the notion of a "true" model is nowadays regarded as a weak one. Rather, it is assumed that all models are approximations to whatever is going on in nature, and our aim is to find a model that is close enough for the purpose to hand. In view of this, it would be reassuring if our model did not change too dramatically as the data on which it was based changed. Thus, if a slight shift in value of one data point led to radically different parameter estimates and predictions in a model, one might be wary of using it. Put another way, we would like our models and patterns to be insensitive to small changes in the data. Likewise, the score functions and models may be based on certain assumptions (for example, about underlying probability distributions). Again it would be reassuring if, if such assumptions were relaxed slightly, the fitted model and its parameters and predictions did not change dramatically.

Score functions aimed at achieving these aims have been developed. For example, in a *trimmed* mean a small proportion of the most extreme data points are dropped, and the mean of the remainder used. Now the values of outlying points have no effect on the estimate. The extreme version of this (assuming a univariate distribution with equal numbers being dropped from each tail), arising as a higher and higher proportion is dropped from the tails, is the median—which is well known to be less sensitive to changes in outlying points than is the arithmetic mean. As another example, the Winsorized mean involves reducing the most extreme points to have the same values as the next most extreme points, before computing the usual mean.

Although such modifications can be thought of as robust forms of score functions, it is sometimes easier to describe them (and, indeed think of them) in terms of the algorithms used to compute them.

7.7   Further Reading

Piatetsky-Shapiro (1991), Silberschatz and Tuzhilin (1996), and Bayardo and Agrawal (1999) contain general discussions on score functions for patterns and probabilistic rules.

Hand (1997) discuss score functions for classification problems in great detail. Bishop (1995) discusses score functions in the context of neural networks. Breiman et al. (1984) discuss how general misclassification costs can be used as score functions for tree classifiers. Domingos (1999) provides a flexible methodology for converting any classification algorithm that operates on the assumption of 0-1 classification loss into a more general algorithm that can use any classification cost-matrix.

Devroye (1984) argues for the use of L1 distance measures as score functions for density estimation problems, while Silverman (1986) describes more conventional squared-error (L2) score functions in the same context.

The topics of bias and variance are discussed in a general learning context in the paper by Geman, Bienenstock, and Doursat (1992). Friedman (1997) develops a bias-variance decomposition for classification problems that turns out to have fundamentally different properties to classical squared-error bias-variance.

Linhart and Zucchini (1986) provide an overview of statistical model selection techniques. Chapter 2 of Ripley (1996) provides a comprehensive overview of score functions for model selection in classification and regression. The first general treatment of cross-validation was provided by Stone (1974) while Hjort (1993) outlines more recent ideas on cross-validation and related sampling techniques for model selection. Books on statistical theory (for example Lindsey, 1996) include discussions of penalized model selection in general, including measures such as AIC and BIC. Akaike (1973) introduced the AIC principle and Schwarz (1978) contains the original discussion on BIC. Burnham and Anderson (1998) provide a recent detailed treatment of

BIC and related approaches. Vapnik (1995) contains a detailed account of the structural risk minimization (SRM) approach to model selection and Rissanen (1987) provides a detailed discussion of stochastic complexity, minimum description length (MDL) and related concepts. Lehmann (1986) discusses the more classical statistical approach of comparing two models at a time within a hypothesis-testing framework.

Bernardo and Smith (1994) has a detailed theoretical account of Bayesian approaches to score functions and model selection in general (see also Dawid (1984) and Kass and Raftery (1995)).

Ripley (1996, chapter 2) and Hand (1997) provide detailed discussions of evaluating the performance of classification and regression models. Salzberg (1997) and Dietterich (1998) discuss the specific problem of assessing statistical significance in differences of performance among multiple classification models and algorithms.

Huber (1980) is an important book on robust methods.

8 *Search and Optimization Methods*

8.1 Introduction

In chapter 6 we saw that there are broad classes of *model structures* or *representations* that can be used to represent knowledge in structured form. Subsequently, in chapter 7 we discussed the principles of how such structures (in the form of models and patterns) can be *scored* in terms of how well they match the observed data. This chapter focuses on the *computational methods* used for model and pattern-fitting in data mining algorithms; that is, it focuses on the procedures for searching and optimizing over parameters and structures guided by the available data and our score functions. The importance of effective search and optimization is often underestimated in the data mining, statistical and machine learning algorithm literatures, but successful applications in practice depend critically on such methods.

We recall that a *score function* is the function that numerically expresses our preference for one model or pattern over another. For example, if we are using the sum of squared errors, S_{SSE}, we will prefer models with lower S_{SSE}—this measures the error of our model (at least on the training data). If our algorithm is searching over multiple models with different representational power (and different complexities), we may prefer to use a penalized score function such as S_{BIC} (as discussed in chapter 7) whereby more complex models are penalized by adding a penalty term related to the number of parameters in the model.

Regardless of the specific functional form of our score function S, once it has been chosen, our goal is to optimize it. (We will usually assume without loss of generality in this chapter that we wish to *minimize* the score function, rather than maximize it). So, let $S(\theta|D, M) = S(\theta_1, \ldots, \theta_d|D, M)$ be the score function. It is a scalar function of a d-dimensional parameter vector θ and a model structure M (or a pattern structure ρ), conditioned on a specific set of observed data D.

This chapter examines the fundamental principles of how to go about finding the values of parameter(s) that minimize a general score function S. It is useful in practical terms, although there is no high-level conceptual difference, to distinguish between two situations, one referring to parameters that can only take discrete values (discrete parameters) and the other to parameters that can take values from a continuum (continuous parameters).

Examples of discrete parameters are those indexing different classes of models (so that 1 might correspond to trees, 2 to neural networks, 3 to polynomial functions, and so on) and parameters that can take only integral values (for example, the number of variables to be included in a model). The second example indicates the magnitude of the problems that can arise. We might want to use, as our model, a regression model based on a subset of variables chosen from a possible p variables. There are $K = 2^p$ such subsets, which can be very large, even for moderate p. Similarly, in a pattern context, we might wish to examine patterns that are probabilistic rules involving some subset of p binary variables expressed as a conjunction on the left-hand side (with a fixed right-hand side). There are $J = 3^p$ possible conjunctive rules (each variable takes value 1, 0, or is not in the conjunction at all). Once again, this can easily be an astronomically large number. Clearly, both of these examples are problems of *combinatorial optimization*, involving *searching* over a set of possible solutions to find the one with minimum score.

Examples of continuous parameters are a parameter giving the mean value of a distribution or a parameter vector giving the centers of a set of clusters into which the data set has been partitioned. With continuous parameter spaces, the powerful tools of differential calculus can be brought to bear. In some special but very important special cases, this leads to closed form solutions. In general, however, these are not possible and iterative methods are needed. Clearly the case in which the parameter vector θ is unidimensional is very important, so we shall examine this first. It will give us insights into the multidimensional case, though we will see that other problems also arise in this situation. Both unidimensional and multidimensional situations can be complicated by the existence of local minima: parameter vectors with values smaller than any other similar vectors, but are not the smallest values that can be achieved. We shall explore ways in which such problems can be overcome.

Very often, the two problems of searching over a set of possible model structures and optimizing parameters within a given model go hand in hand;

that is, since any single model or pattern structure typically has unknown parameters then, as well as finding the best model or pattern structure, we will also have to find the best parameters for each structure considered during the search. For example, consider the set of models in which $\hat{y}$ is predicted as a simple linear combination of some subset of the three predictor variables x_1, x_2, and x_3. One model would be $\hat{y}(i) = ax_1(i) + bx_2(i) + cx_3(i)$, and others would have the same form but merely involving pairs of the predictor variables or single predictor variables. Our search will have to roam over all possible subsets of the x_j variables, as noted above, but for each subset, it will also be necessary to find the values of the parameters (a, b, and c in the case with all three variables) that minimize the score function.

This description suggests that one possible design choice, for algorithms that minimize score functions over both model structures and parameter estimates, is to nest a loop for the latter in a loop for the former. This is often used since it is relatively simple, though it is not always the most efficient approach from a computational viewpoint.

It is worth remarking at this early stage that in some data mining algorithms the focus is on finding *sets* of models, patterns, or regions within parameter space, rather than just the single *best* model, pattern, or parameter vector, according to the chosen score function. This occurs, for example, in Bayesian averaging techniques and in searching for sets of patterns. Usually (although, as always, there are exceptions) in such frameworks similar general principles of search and optimization will arise as in the single model/pattern/parameter case and, so in the interests of simplicity of presentation we will focus primarily on the problem of finding the single best model, pattern, and/or parameter-vector.

Section 2 focuses on general search methods for situations where there is no notion of continuity in the model space or parameter space being searched. This section includes discussion of the combinatorial problems that typically prevent exhaustive examination of all solutions, the general state-space representation for search problems, discussion of particular search strategies, as well as methods such as branch and bound that take advantage of properties of the parameter space or score function to reduce the number of parameter vectors that must be explicitly examined. Section 3 turns to optimization methods for continuous parameter spaces, covering univariate and multivariate cases, and problems complicated by constraints on the permissible parameter values. Section 4 describes a powerful class of methods that apply to problems that involve (or can usefully be regarded as involving) missing values. In many data mining situations, the data sets are so large that multiple passes through the data have to be avoided. Section 5 describes algorithms aimed at this. Finally, since many problems involve score functions that have multiple minima (and maxima), stochastic search methods have been developed to improve the chances of finding the global optimum (and not merely a rather poor local optimum). Some of these are described in section 6.

8.2 Searching for Models and Patterns

8.2.1 Background on Search

This subsection discusses some general high level issues of search. In many practical data mining situations we will not know ahead of time what particular model structure M or pattern structure ρ is most appropriate to solve our task, and we will search over a *family* of model structures $\mathcal{M} = \{M_1, \ldots, M_K\}$ or pattern structures $\mathcal{P} = \{\rho_1, \ldots, \rho_J\}$. We gave some examples of this earlier: finding the best subset of variables in a linear regression problem and finding the best set of conditions to include in the left-hand side of a conjunctive rule. Both of these problems can be considered "best subsets" problems, and have the general characteristic that a combinatorially large number of such solutions can be generated from a set of p "components" (p variables in this case). Finding "best subsets" is a common problem in data mining. For example, for predictive classification models in general (such as nearest neighbor, naive Bayes, or neural network classifiers) we might want to find the subset of variables that produces the lowest classification error rate on a validation data set.

A related model search problem, that we used as an illustration earlier in chapter 5, is that of finding the best tree-structured classifier from a "pool" of p variables. This has even more awesome combinatorial properties. Consider the problem of searching over all possible binary trees (that is, each internal node in the tree has two children). Assume that all trees under consideration have depth p so that there are p variables on the path from the root node to any leaf node. In addition, let any variable be eligible to appear at any node in the tree, remembering that each node in a classification tree contains a test on a single variable, the outcomes of which define which branch is taken from that node. For this family of trees there are on the order of p^{2^p} different tree structures—that is, p^{2^p} classification trees that differ from each other in the specification of at least one internal node. In practice, the number of possible tree structures will in fact be larger since we also want to consider various subtrees of the full-depth trees. Exhaustive search over all possible trees is clearly infeasible!

We note that from a purely mathematical viewpoint one need not necessarily distinguish between different model structures in the sense that all such model structures could be considered as special cases of a single "full" model, with appropriate parameters set to zero (or some other constant that is appropriate for the model form) so that they disappear from the model. For example, the linear regression model $y = ax_1 + b$ is a special case of $y = ax_1 + cx_2 + dx_3 + b$ with $c = d = 0$. This would reduce the model structure search problem to the type of parameter optimization problem we will discuss later in this chapter. Although mathematically correct, this viewpoint is often not the most useful way to think about the problem, since it can obscure important structural information about the models under consideration.

In the discussion that follows we will often use the word *models* rather than the phrase *models or patterns* to save repetition, but it should be taken as referring to both types of structure: the same general principles that are outlined for searching for models are also true for the problem of searching for patterns.

Some further general comments about search are worth making here:

- We noted in the opening section that finding the model or structure with the optimum score from a family $\mathcal{M}$ necessarily involves finding the best parameters θ_k for each model structure M_k within that family. This means that, conceptually and often in practice, a nested loop search process is needed, in which an optimization over parameter values is nested within a search over model structures.

- As we have already noted, there is typically no notion of the score function S being a "smooth" function in "model space," and thus, many of the traditional optimization techniques that rely on smoothness information (for example, gradient descent) are not applicable. Instead we are in the realm of *combinatorial optimization* where the underlying structure of the problem is inherently discrete (such as an index over model structures) rather than a continuous function. Most of the combinatorial optimization problems that occur in data mining are inherently intractable in the sense that the only way to guarantee that one will find the best solution is to visit all possible solutions in an exhaustive fashion.

- For some problems, we will be fortunate in that we will not need to perform a full new optimization of parameter space as we move from one model structure to the next. For example, if the score function is *decomposable*, then the score function for a new structure will be an additive function of the score function for the previous structure as well as a term accounting for the change in the structure. For example, adding or deleting an internal node in a classification tree only changes the score for data points belonging to the subtree associated with that node. However, in many cases, changing the structure of the model will mean that the old parameter values are no longer optimal in the new model. For example, suppose that we want to build a model to predict y from x based on two data points $(x, y) = (1, 1)$ and $(x, y) = (3, 3)$. First let us try very simple models of the form $y = a$, that is y is a constant (so that all our predictions are the same). The value of a that minimizes the sum of squared errors $(1 - a)^2 + (3 - a)^2$ is 2. Now let us try the more elaborate model $y = bx + a$. This adds an extra term into the model. Now the values of a and b that minimize the sum of squared errors (this is a standard regression problem, although a particularly simple example) are, respectively, 0 and 1. We see that the estimate of a depends upon what else is in the model. It is possible to formalize the circumstances in which changing the model will leave parameter estimates unaltered, in terms of *orthogonality* of the data. In general, it is clearly useful to know when this applies, since much faster algorithms can then be developed (for example, if variables are orthogonal in a regression case, we can just examine them one at a time). However, such situations tend to arise more often in the context of designed experiments than in the secondary data occurring in data mining situations. For this reason, we will not dwell on this issue here.

For linear regression, parameter estimation is not difficult and so it is straightforward (if somewhat time-consuming) to recalculate the optimal parameters for each model structure being considered. However, for more complex models such as neural networks, parameter optimization can be both computationally demanding as well as requiring careful "tuning" of the optimization method itself (as we will see later in this chapter). Thus, the "inner loop" of the model search algorithm can be quite taxing computationally. One way to ease the problem is to leave the existing parameters in the model fixed to their previous values and to estimate only the values of parameters added to the model. Although this strategy is clearly suboptimal, it permits a trade-off between highly accurate parameter estimation of just a few models or approximate parameter estimation of a much larger set of models.

- Clearly for the best subsets problem and the best classification tree problem, exhaustive search (evaluating the score function for all candidate models in the model family $\mathcal{M}$) is intractable for any nontrivial values of p since there are 2^p and p^{2^p} models to be examined in each case. Unfortunately, this combinatorial explosion in the number of possible model and pattern structures will be the norm rather than the exception for many data mining problems involving search over model structure. Thus, without even taking into account the fact that for each model one may have to perform some computationally complex parameter optimization procedure, even simply enumerating the models is likely to become intractable for large p. This problem is particularly acute in data mining problems involving very high-dimensional data sets (large p).

- Faced with inherently intractable problems, we must rely on what are called *heuristic search* techniques. These are techniques that experimentally (or perhaps provably on average) provide good performance but that cannot be guaranteed to provide the best solution always. The *greedy heuristic* (also known as *local improvement*) is one of the better known examples. In a model search context, greedy search means that, given a current model M_k we look for other models that are "near" M_k (where we will need to define what we mean by "near") and move to the best of these (according to our score function) if indeed any are better than M_k.

8.2.2   The State-Space Formulation for Search in Data Mining

A general way to describe a search algorithm for discrete spaces is to specify the problem as follows:

1. **State Space Representation:** We view the search problem as one of moving through a discrete set of states. For model search, each model structure M_k consists of a state in our state space. It is conceptually useful to think of each state as a vertex in a graph (which is potentially very large). An abstract definition of our search problem is that we start at some particular node (or state), say M_1, and wish to move through the state space to find the node corresponding to the state that has the highest score function.

2. **Search Operators:** Search operators correspond to legal "moves" in our search space. For example, for model selection in linear regression the operators could be defined as either adding a variable to or deleting a

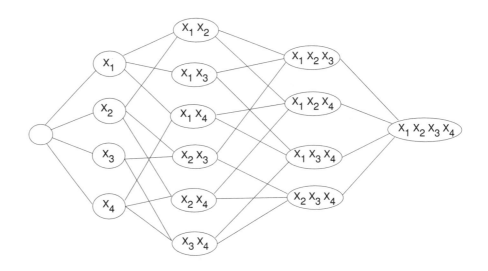

Figure 8.1 An example of a simple state-space involving four variables X_1, X_2, X_3, X_4. The node on the left is the null set—i.e., no variables in the model or pattern.

variable from the current model. The search operators can be thought of as defining directed edges in the state space graph. That is, there is a directed edge from state M_i to M_j if there is an operator that allows one to move from one model structure M_i to another model structure M_j.

A simple example will help illustrate the concept. Consider the general problem of selecting the best subset from p variables for a particular classification model (for example, the nearest neighbor model). Let the score function be the cross-validated classification accuracy for any particular subset. Let M_k denote an individual model structure within the general family we are considering, namely all $K = 2^p - 1$ different subsets containing at least one variable. Thus, the state-space has $2^p - 1$ states, ranging from models consisting of subsets of single variables $M_1 = \{x_1\}, M_2 = \{x_2\}, \ldots$ all the way through to the full model with all p variables, $M_K = \{x_1, \ldots, x_p\}$. Next we define our operators. For subset selection it is common to consider simple operators such as adding one variable at a time and deleting one variable at a time. Thus, from any state with p' variables (model structure) there are two "directions" one can "move" in the model family: add a variable to move to a state with $p' + 1$ variables, or delete a variable to move to a state with $p' - 1$ variables (figure 8.1 shows a state-space for subset selection for 4 variables with these two operators). We can easily generalize these operators to adding or deleting r variables at a time. Such "greedy local" heuristics are embedded in many data mining algorithms. Search algorithms using this idea vary in terms of what state they start from: *forward selection* algorithms work "forward" by starting with a minimally sized model and iteratively adding variables, whereas *backward selection* algorithms work in reverse from the full model. Forward selection is often the only tractable option in practice when p is very large since working backwards may be computationally impractical.

It is important to note that by representing our problem in a state-space with limited connectivity we have *not* changed the underlying intractability of the general model search problem. To find the optimal state it will still be necessary to visit all of the exponentially many states. What the state-space/operator representation does is to allow us to define systematic methods for *local exploration* of the state-space, where the term "local" is defined in terms of which states are adjacent in the state-space (that is, which states have operators connecting them).

8.2.3   A Simple Greedy Search Algorithm

A general iterative greedy search algorithm can be defined as follows:

1. **Initialize:** Choose an initial state $M^{(0)}$ corresponding to a particular model structure M_k.

2. **Iterate:** Letting $M^{(i)}$ be the current model structure at the ith iteration, evaluate the score function at all possible adjacent states (as defined by the operators) and move to the best one. Note that this evaluation can consist of performing parameter estimation (or the change in the score function) for each neighboring model structure. The number of score function evaluations that must be made is the number of operators that can be applied to the current state. Thus, there is a trade-off between the number of operators available and the time taken to choose the next model in state-space.

3. **Stopping Criterion:** Repeat step 2 until no further improvement can be

attained in the local score function (that is, a local minimum is reached in state-space).

4. **Multiple Restarts:** (optional) Repeat steps 1 through 3 from different initial starting points and choose the best solution found.

This general algorithm is similar in spirit to the local search methods we will discuss later in this chapter for parameter optimization. Note that in step 2 that we must explicitly evaluate the effect of moving to a neighboring model structure in a discrete space, in contrast to parameter optimization in a continuous space where we will often be able to use explicit gradient information to determine what direction to move. Step 3 helps avoid ending at a local minimum, rather than the global minimum (though it does not guarantee it, a point to which we return later). For many structure search problems, greedy search is provably suboptimal. However, in general it is a useful heuristic (in the sense that for many problems it will find quite good solutions on average) and when repeated with multiple restarts from randomly chosen initial states, the simplicity of the method makes it quite useful for many practical data mining applications.

8.2.4 Systematic Search and Search Heuristics

The generic algorithm described above is often described as a "hill-climbing" algorithm because (when the aim is to maximize a function) it only follows a single "path" in state-space to a local maximum of the score function. A more general (but more complex) approach is to keep track of multiple models at once rather than just a single current model. A useful way to think about this approach is to think of a *search tree*, a data structure that is dynamically constructed as we search the state-space to keep track of the states that we have visited and evaluated. (This has nothing to do with classification trees, of course.) The search tree is not equivalent to the state-space; rather, it is a representation of how a particular search algorithm moves through a state-space.

An example will help to clarify the notion of a search tree. Consider again the problem of finding the best subset of variables to use in a particular classification model. We start with the "model" that contains no variables at all and predicts the value of the most likely class in the training data as its prediction for all data points. This is the *root node* in the search tree. Assume that we have a forward-selection algorithm that is only allowed to add variables one at a time. From the root node, there are p variables we can add to

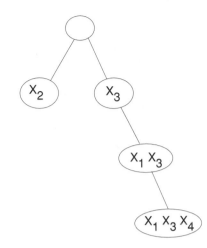

Figure 8.2   An example of a simple search tree for the state-space of figure 8.1.

the model with no variables, and we can represent these p new models as p children of the original root node. In turn, from each of these p nodes we can add p variables, creating p children for each, or p^2 in total (clearly, $p^2 - \binom{p}{2}$ are redundant, and in practice we need to implement a duplicate-state detection scheme to eliminate the redundant nodes from the tree).

Figure 8.2 shows a simple example of a search tree for the state space of figure 8.1. Here the root node contains the empty set (no variables) and only the two best states so far are considered at any stage of the search. The search algorithm (at this point of the search) has found the two best states (as determined by the score function) to be X_2 and X_1, X_3, X_4.

Search trees evolve dynamically as we search the state-space, and we can imagine (hypothetically) keeping track of all of the leaf nodes (model structures) as candidate models for selection. This quickly becomes infeasible since at depth k in the tree there will be p^k leaf nodes to keep track of (where the root node is at depth zero and we have branching factor p). We will quickly run out of memory using this brute-force method (which is essentially *breadth-first* search of the search tree). A memory-efficient alternative is *depth-first* search, which (as its name implies) explores branches in the search tree to some maximum depth before backing up and repeating the depth-first search in a recursive fashion on the next available branch.

Both of these techniques are examples of *blind search*, in that they simply order the nodes to be explored lexicographically rather than by the score function. Typically, improved performance (in the sense of finding higher quality models more quickly) can be gained by exploring the more promising nodes first. In the search tree this means that the leaf node with the highest score is the one whose children are next considered; after the children are added as leaves, the new leaf with the highest score is examined. Again, this strategy can quickly lead to many more model structures (nodes in the tree) being generated than we will be feasibly able to keep in memory. Thus, for example, one can implement a *beam search* strategy that uses a *beam width* of size b to "track" only the b best models at any point in the search (equivalently to only keep track of the b best leaves on the tree). (In figure 8.2 we had $b = 2$.) Naturally, this might be suboptimal if the only way to find the optimal model is to first consider models that are quite suboptimal (and thus, might be outside the "beam"). However, in general, beam search can be quite effective. It is certainly often much more effective than simple hill-climbing, which is similar to depth-first search in the manner in which it explores the search tree: at any iteration there is only a single model being considered, and the next model is chosen as the child of the current model with the highest score.

8.2.5   Branch-and-Bound

A related and useful idea in a practical context is the notion of *branch-and-bound*. The general idea is quite simple. When exploring a search tree, and keeping track of the best model structure evaluated so far, it may be feasible to calculate analytically a lower bound on the best possible score function from a particular (as yet unexplored) branch of the search tree. If this bound is greater than the score of the best model so far, then we need not search this subtree and it can be pruned from further consideration. Consider, for example, the problem of finding the best subset of k variables for classification from a set of p variables where we use the training set error rate as our score function. Define a tree in which the root node is the set of all p variables, the immediate child nodes are the p nodes each of which have a single variable dropped (so they each have $p - 1$ variables), the next layer has two variables dropped (so there are $\binom{p}{2}$ unique such nodes, each with $p - 2$ variables), and so on down to the $\binom{p}{k}$ leaves that each contain subsets of k variables (these are the candidate solutions). Note that the training set error rate cannot *decrease* as we work down any branch of the tree, since lower nodes are based on fewer variables.

Now let us begin to explore the tree in a depth-first fashion. After our depth-first algorithm has descended to visit one or more leaf nodes, we will have calculated scores for the models (leaves) corresponding to these sets of k variables. Clearly the smallest of these is our best candidate k-variable model so far. Now suppose that, in working down some other branch of the tree, we encounter a node that has a score larger than the score of our smallest k-variable node so far. Since the score cannot decrease as we continue to work down this branch, there is no point in looking further: nodes lower on this branch cannot have smaller training set error rate than the best k-variable solution we have already found. We can thus save the effort of evaluating nodes further down this branch. Instead, we back up to the nearest node above that contained an unexplored branch and begin to investigate that. This basic idea can be improved by ordering the tree so that we explore the most promising nodes first (where "promising" means they are likely to have low training set error rate). This can lead to even more effective pruning. This type of general branch and bound strategy can significantly improve the computational efficiency of model search. (Although, of course, it is not a guaranteed solution—many problems are too large even for this strategy to provide a solution in a reasonable time.)

These ideas on searching for model structure have been presented in a very general form. More effective algorithms can usually be designed for specific model structures and score functions. Nonetheless, general principles such as iterative local improvement, beam search, and branch-and-bound have significant practical utility and recur commonly under various guises in the implementation of many data mining algorithms.

8.3 Parameter Optimization Methods

8.3.1 Parameter Optimization: Background

Let $S(\theta) = S(\theta|D, M)$ be the score function we are trying to optimize, where θ are the parameters of the model. We will usually suppress the explicit dependence on D and M for simplicity. We will now assume that the model structure M is fixed (that is, we are temporarily in the inner loop of parameter estimation where there may be an outer loop over multiple model structures). We will also assume, again, that we are trying to minimize S, rather than maximize it. Notice that S and $g(S)$ will be minimized for the same value of θ if g is a monotonic function of S (such as $\log S$).

In general θ will be a d-dimensional vector of parameters. For example, in a regression model θ will be the set of coefficients and the intercept. In a tree model, θ will be the thresholds for the splits at the internal nodes. In an artificial neural network model, θ will be a specification of the weights in the network.

In many of the more flexible models we will consider (neural networks being a good example), the dimensionality of our parameter vector can grow very quickly. For example, a neural network with 10 inputs and 10 hidden units and 1 output, could have $10 \times 10 + 10 = 110$ parameters. This has direct implications for our optimization problem, since it means that in this case (for example) we are trying to find the minimum of a nonlinear function in 110 dimensions.

Furthermore, the shape of this potentially high-dimensional function may be quite complicated. For example, except for problems with particularly simple structure, S will often be multimodal. Moreover, since $S = S(\theta|D, M)$ is a function of the observed data D, the precise structure of S for any given problem is data-dependent. In turn this means that we may have a completely different function S to optimize for each different data set D, so that (for example) it may be difficult to make statements about how many local minima S has in the general case.

As discussed in chapter 7, many commonly used score functions can be written in the form of a sum of local error functions (for example, when the training data points are assumed to be independent of each other):

$$S(\theta) = \sum_{i=1}^{N} e\left(y(i), \hat{y}_\theta(i) \right) \tag{8.1}$$

where $\hat{y}_\theta(i)$ is our model's estimate of the target value $y(i)$ in the training data, and e is an error function measuring the distance between the model's prediction and the target (such as square error or log-likelihood). Note that the complexity in the functional form S (as a function of θ) can enter both through the complexity of the model structure being used (that is, the functional form of $\hat{y}$) and also through the functional form of the error function e. For example, if $\hat{y}$ is linear in θ and e is defined as squared error, then S will be quadratic in θ, making the optimization problem relatively straightforward since a quadratic function has only a single (global) minimum or maximum. However, if $\hat{y}$ is generated by a more complex model or if e is more complex as a function of θ, S will not necessarily be a simple smooth function of θ with a single easy-to-find extremum. In general, finding the parameters

θ that minimize $S(\theta)$ is usually equivalent to the problem of minimizing a complicated function in a high-dimensional space.

Let us define the gradient function of S as

$$\mathbf{g}(\theta) = \nabla_\theta S(\theta) = \left(\frac{\partial S(\theta)}{\partial \theta_1}, \frac{\partial S(\theta)}{\partial \theta_2}, \ldots, \frac{\partial S(\theta)}{\partial \theta_d} \right), \tag{8.2}$$

which is a d-dimensional vector of partial derivatives of S evaluated at θ. In general, $\nabla_\theta S(\theta) = 0$ is a necessary condition for an extremum (such as a minumum) of S at θ. This is a set of d simultaneous equations (one for each partial derivative) in d variables. Thus, we can search for solutions θ (that correspond to extrema of $S(\theta)$) of this set of d equations.

We can distinguish two general types of parameter optimization problems:

1. The first is when we can solve the minimization problem in *closed form*. For example, if $S(\theta)$ is quadratic in θ, then the gradient $\mathbf{g}(\theta)$ will be linear in θ and the solution of $\nabla S(\theta) = 0$ involves the solution of a set of d linear equations. However, this situation is the exception rather than the rule in practical data mining problems.

2. The second general case occurs when $S(\theta)$ is a smooth nonlinear function of θ such that the set of d equations $\mathbf{g}(\theta) = 0$ does not have a direct closed form solution. Typically we use iterative improvement search techniques for these types of problems, using local information about the curvature of S to guide our local search on the surface of S. These are essentially hill-climbing or descending methods (for example, steepest descent). The backpropagation technique used to train neural networks is an example of such a steepest descent algorithm.

Since the second case relies on local information, it may end up converging to a local minimum rather than the global minimum. Because of this, such methods are often supplemented by a stochastic component in which, to take just one example, the optimization procedure starts several times from different randomly chosen starting points.

8.3.2   Closed Form and Linear Algebra Methods

Consider the special case when $S(\theta)$ is a *quadratic* function of θ. This is a very useful special case since now the gradient $\mathbf{g}(\theta)$ is linear in θ and the minimum of S is the unique solution to the set of d linear equations $\mathbf{g}(\theta) = 0$ (assuming the matrix of second derivatives of S at these solutions satisfies the condition of being positive definite). This is illustrated in the context of multiple regression (which usually uses a sum of squared errors score function) in chapter 11. We showed in chapter 4 how the same result was obtained if likelihood was adopted as the score function, assuming Normal error distributions. In general, since such problems can be framed as solving for the inverse of an $d \times d$ matrix, the complexity of solving such linear problems tends to scale in general as $O(nd^2 + d^3)$, where it takes order of nd^2 steps to construct the original matrix of interest and order of d^3 steps to invert it.

8.3.3   Gradient-Based Methods for Optimizing Smooth Functions

In general of course, we often face the situation in which $S(\theta)$ is not a simple function of θ with a single minimum. For example, if our model is a neural network with nonlinear functions in the hidden units, then S will be a relatively complex nonlinear function of θ with multiple local minima. We have already noted that many approaches are based on iteratively repeating some local improvement to the model.

   The typical iterative local optimization algorithm can be broken down into four relatively simple components:

1. **Initialize:** Choose an initial value for the parameter vector $\theta = \theta^0$ (this is often chosen randomly).

2. **Iterate:** Starting with $i = 0$, let

$$\theta^{i+1} = \theta^i + \lambda^i \mathbf{v}^i \tag{8.3}$$

   where $\mathbf{v}$ is the direction of the next step (relative to θ^i in parameter space) and λ^i determines the distance. Typically (but not necessarily) $\mathbf{v}^i$ is chosen to be in a direction of improving the score function.

3. **Convergence:** Repeat step 2 until $S(\theta^i)$ appears to have attained a local minimum.

4. **Multiple Restarts:** Repeat steps 1 through 3 from different initial starting points and choose the best minimum found.

   Particular methods based on this general structure differ in terms of the chosen direction $\mathbf{v}^i$ in parameter space and the distance λ^i moved along the chosen direction, amongst other things. Note that this is this algorithm has essentially the same design as the one we defined in section 8.2 for local search among a set of discrete states, except that here we are moving in continuous d-dimensional space rather than taking discrete steps in a graph.

The direction and step size must be determined from local information gathered at the current point of the search—for example, whether first derivative or second derivative information is gathered to estimate the local curvature of S. Moreover, there are important trade-offs between the quality of the information gathered and the resources (time, memory) required to calculate this information. No single method is universally superior to all others; each has advantages and disadvantages.

All of the methods discussed below require specification of initial starting points and a convergence (termination) criterion. The exact specifications of these aspects of the algorithm can vary from application to application. In addition, all of the methods are used to try to find a *local extremum* of $S(\theta)$. One must check in practice that the found solution is in fact a minimum (and not a maximum or saddlepoint). In addition, for the general case of a nonlinear function S with multiple minima, little can be said about the quality of the local minima relative to the global minima without carrying out a brute-force search over the entire space (or using sophisticated probabilistic arguments that are beyond this text). Despite these reservations, the optimization techniques that follow are extremely useful in practice and form the core of many data mining algorithms.

8.3.4   Univariate Parameter Optimization

Consider first the special case in which we just have a single unknown parameter θ and we wish to minimize the score function $S(\theta)$ (for example, figure 8.3). Although in practical data mining situations we will usually be optimizing a model with more than just a single parameter, the univariate case is nonetheless worth looking at, since it clearly illustrates some of the general principles that are relevant to the more general multivariate optimization problem. Moreover, univariate search can serve as a *component* in a multivariate search procedure, in which we first find the *direction* of search using the gradient and then decide how far to move in that direction using univariate search for a minimum along that direction.

Letting $g(\theta) = S'(\theta) = \frac{\partial S(\theta)}{\partial \theta}$, the minimum of S occurs wherever $g(\theta) = 0$ and the second derivative $g'(\theta) > 0$. If a closed form solution is possible, then we can find it and we are done. If not, then we can use one of the methods below.

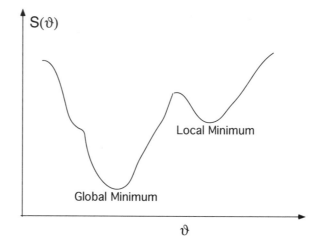

Figure 8.3 An example of a score function $S(\theta)$ of a single univariate parameter θ with both a global minimum and a local minimum.

The Newton-Raphson Method

Suppose that the solution occurs at some unknown point θ^s; that is, $g(\theta^s) = 0$. Now, for points θ^* not too far from θ^s we have, by using a Taylor series expansion

$$g(\theta^s) \approx g(\theta^*) + (\theta^s - \theta^*)g'(\theta^*), \tag{8.4}$$

where this linear approximation ignores terms of order $(\theta^s - \theta^*)^2$ and above. Since θ^s satisfies $g(\theta^s) = 0$, the left-hand side of this expression is zero. Hence, by rearranging terms we get

$$\theta^s \approx \theta^* - \frac{g(\theta^*)}{g'(\theta^*)}. \tag{8.5}$$

In words, this says that given an initial value θ^*, then an approximate solution of the equation $g(\theta^s) = 0$ is given by adjusting θ^* as indicated in equation 8.5. By repeatedly iterating this, we can in theory get as close to the solution as we like. This iterative process is the *Newton-Raphson* (NR) iterative update for univariate optimization based on first and second derivative information. The ith step is given by

$$\theta^{i+1} = \theta^i - \frac{g(\theta^i)}{g'(\theta^i)}. \tag{8.6}$$

The effectiveness of this method will depend on the quality of the linear approximation in equation 8.4. If the starting value is close to the true solution θ^s then we can expect the approximation to work well; that is, we can locally approximate the surface around $S(\theta^*)$ as parabolic in form (or equivalently, the derivative $g(\theta)$ is linear near θ^* and θ^s). In fact, when the current θ is close to the solution θ^s, the convergence rate of the NR method is *quadratic* in the sense that the error at step i of the iteration $e_i = |\theta^i - \theta^s|$ can be recursively written as

$$e_i \propto e_{i-1}^2. \tag{8.7}$$

To use the Newton-Raphson update, we must know both the derivative function $g(\theta)$ and the second derivative $g'(\theta)$ in closed form. In practice, for complex functions we may not have closed-form expressions, necessitating numerical approximation of $g(\theta)$ and $g'(\theta)$, which in turn may introduce more error into the determination of where to move in parameter space. Generally speaking, however, if we can evaluate the gradient and second derivative accurately in closed form, it is advantageous to do so and to use this information in the course of moving through parameter space during iterative optimization.

The drawback of NR is, of course, that our initial estimate θ^i may not be sufficiently close to the solution θ^s to make the approximation work well. In this case, the NR step can easily overshoot the true minimum of S and the method need not converge at all.

The Gradient Descent Method

An alternative approach, which can be particularly useful early in the optimization process (when we are potentially far from θ^s), is to use only the gradient information (which provides at least the correct direction to move in for a 1-dimensional problem) with a heuristically chosen step size λ:

$$\theta^{i+1} = \theta^i - \lambda g(\theta^i). \tag{8.8}$$

The multivariate version of this method is known as *gradient* (or *steepest*) descent. Here λ is usually chosen to be quite small to ensure that we do not step too far in the chosen direction. We can view gradient descent as a special case of the NR method, whereby the second derivative information $\frac{1}{g'(\theta^i)}$ is replaced by a constant λ.

Momentum-Based Methods

There is a practical trade-off in choosing λ. If it is too small, then gradient descent may converge very slowly indeed, taking very small steps at each iteration. On the other hand, if λ is too large, then the guarantee of convergence is lost, since we may overshoot the minimum by stepping too far. We can try to accelerate the convergence of gradient descent by adding a *momentum* term:

$$\theta^{i+1} = \theta^i + \triangle^i \tag{8.9}$$

where $\triangle^i$ is defined recursively as

$$\triangle^i = -\lambda g(\theta^i) + \mu \triangle^{i-1} \tag{8.10}$$

and where μ is a "momentum" parameter, $0 \le \mu \le 1$. Note that $\mu = 0$ gives us the standard gradient descent method of equation 8.8, and $\mu > 0$ adds a "momentum" term in the sense that the current direction $\triangle^i$ is now also a function of the previous direction $\triangle^{i-1}$. The effect of μ in regions of low curvature in S is to accelerate convergence (thus, improving standard gradient descent, which can be very slow in such regions) and fortunately has little effect in regions of high curvature. The momentum heuristic and related ideas have been found to be quite useful in practice in training models such as neural networks.

Bracketing Methods

For functions which are not well behaved (if the derivative of S is not smooth, for example) there exists a different class of scalar optimization methods that do not rely on any gradient information at all (that is, they work directly on the function S and not its derivative g). Typically these methods are based on the notion of *bracketing*—finding a bracket $[\theta_1, \theta_2]$ that provably contains an extremum of the function. For example, if there exists a "middle" θ value θ_m, such that $\theta_1 > \theta_m > \theta_2$ and $S(\theta_m)$ is less than both $S(\theta_1)$ and $S(\theta_2)$, then clearly a local minimum of the function S must exist between θ_1 and θ_2 (assuming that S is continuous). One can use this idea to fit a parabola through the three points θ_1, θ_m, and θ_2 and evaluate $S(\theta_p)$ where θ_p is located at the minimum value of parabola. Either θ_p is the desired local minimum, or else we can narrow the bracket by eliminating θ_1 or θ_2 and iterating with another parabola. A variety of methods exist that use this idea with varying degrees of sophistication (for example, a technique known as Brent's method is widely used). It will be apparent from this outline that bracketing methods are really a search strategy. We have included them here, however, partly because of their importance in finding optimal values of parameters, and partly because they rely on the parameter space having a connected structure (for example, ordinality) even if the function being minimized is not continuous.

8.3.5 Multivariate Parameter Optimization

We now move on to the much more difficult problem we are usually faced with in practice, namely, finding the minimum of a scalar score function S of a *multivariate* parameter vector θ in d-dimensions. Many of the methods used in the multivariate case are analogous to the scalar case. On the other hand, d may be quite large for our models, so that the multidimensional optimization problem may be significantly more complex to solve than its univariate cousin. It is possible, for example, that local minima may be much more prevalent in high dimensional spaces than in lower-dimensional spaces. Moreover, a problem similar (in fact, formally equivalent) to the combinatorial explosion that we saw in the discussion of search also manifests itself in multidimensional optimization; this is the curse of dimensionality that we have already encountered in chapter 6. Suppose that we wish to find the d dimensional parameter vector that minimizes some score function, and where each parameter is defined on the unit interval, $[0, 1]$. Then the multivariate parameter vector θ is defined on the unit d-dimensional hypercube. Now suppose we know that at the optimal solution none of the components of θ lie in $[0, 0.5]$. When $d = 1$, this means that half of the parameter space has been eliminated. When $d = 10$, however, only $\left(\frac{1}{2}\right)^{10} \simeq \frac{1}{1000}$ of the parameter space has been eliminated, and when $d = 20$ only $\left(\frac{1}{2}\right)^{20} \simeq \frac{1}{1000000}$ of the parameter space has been eliminated. Readers can imagine—or do the arithmetic themselves—to see what happens when really large numbers of parameters are involved. This shows clearly why there is a real danger of missing a global minimum, with the optimization ending on some (suboptimal) local minimum.

Following the pattern of the previous subsection, we will first describe methods for optimizing functions continuous in the parameters (extensions of the Newton-Raphson method, and so on) and then describe methods that can be applied when the function is not continuous (analogous to the bracketing method).

The iterative methods outlined in the preceding subsection began with some initial value, and iteratively improved it. So suppose that the parameter vector takes the value θ^i at the ith step. Then, to extend the methods outlined in the preceding subsection to the multidimensional case we have to answer two questions:

1. In which direction should we move from θ^i?

2. How far should we step in that direction?

The local iterations can generally be described as

$$\theta^{i+1} = \theta^i + \lambda^i \mathbf{v}^i \tag{8.11}$$

where θ^i is the parameter estimate at iteration i and $\mathbf{v}$ is the d-dimensional vector specifying the next direction to move (specified in a manner dependent on the particular optimization technique being used).

For example, the *multivariate gradient descent* method is specified as

$$\theta^{i+1} = \theta^i - \lambda \mathbf{g}(\theta^i) \tag{8.12}$$

where λ is the scalar *learning rate* and $\mathbf{g}(\theta)$ is a d-dimensional gradient function (as defined in equation 8.2). This method is also known as *steepest descent*, since $-\mathbf{g}(\theta^i)$ will point in the direction of steepest slope from θ^i. Provided λ is chosen to be sufficiently small then gradient descent is guaranteed to converge to a local minimum of the function S.

The *backpropagation* method for parameter estimation popular with neural networks is really merely a glorified steepest descent algorithm. It is somewhat more complicated than the standard approach only because of the multiple layers in the network, so that the derivatives required above have to be derived using the chain rule.

Note that the gradient in the steepest descent algorithm need not necessarily point directly towards the minimum. Thus, as shown in figure 8.4, being limited to take steps only in the direction of the gradient can be an extremely inefficient way to find the minimum of a function. A more sophisticated class of multivariate optimization methods uses local second derivative information about θ to decide where in the parameter space to move to next. In particular, *Newton's method* (the multivariate equivalent of univariate NR) is defined as:

$$\theta^{i+1} = \theta^i - H^{-1}(\theta^i) g(\theta^i) \tag{8.13}$$

where $H^{-1}(\theta^i)$ is the inverse of the $d \times d$ matrix of second derivatives of S (known as the *Hessian matrix*) evaluated at θ^i. The Hessian matrix has entries defined as:

$$h_{lm} = \frac{\partial S(\theta)}{\partial \theta_l \partial \theta_m}, \qquad 1 \le l, m \le d. \tag{8.14}$$

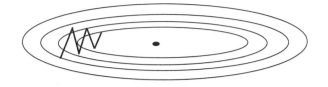

Figure 8.4 An example of a situation in which we minimize a score function of two variables and the shape of the score function is a parabolic "bowl" with the minimum in the center. Gradient descent does not point directly to the minimum but instead tends to point "across" the bowl (solid lines on the left), leading to a series of indirect steps before the minimum is reached.

As in the univariate case, if S is quadratic the step taken by the Newton iteration in parameter space points directly toward the minimum of S. We might reasonably expect that for many functions the shape of the function is approximately locally quadratic in θ about its local minima (think of approximating the shape of the top of a "smooth" mountain by a parabola), and hence, that at least near the minima, the Newton strategy will be making the correct assumption about the shape of S. In fact, this assumption is nothing more than the multivariate version of Taylor's series expansion. Of course, since the peak will usually not be exactly quadratic in shape, it is necessary to apply the Newton iteration recursively until convergence. Again, as in the univariate case, the use of the Newton method may diverge rather than converge (for example, if the Hessian matrix $H(\theta^i)$ is singular; that is, the inverse H^{-1} does not exist at θ^i).

The Newton scheme comes at a cost. Since H is a $d \times d$ matrix, there will be $O(nd^2 + d^3)$ computations required per step to estimate H and invert it. For models with large numbers of parameters (such as neural networks) this may be completely impractical. Instead, we could, for example, approximate H by its diagonal (giving $O(nd)$ complexity per step). Even though the diagonal approximation will clearly be incorrect (since we can expect that parameters will exhibit dependence on each other), the approximation may nonetheless be useful as a linear cost alternative to the full Hessian calculation.

An alternative approach is to build an approximation to H^{-1} iteratively based on gradient information as we move through parameter space. These techniques are known as *quasi-Newton* methods. Initially we take steps in the direction of the gradient (assuming an initial estimate of $\hat{H} = I$ the identity matrix) and then take further steps in the direction $-\hat{H}_i^{-1}(\theta^i)g(\theta^i)$, where

$\hat{H}_i^{-1}(\theta^i)$ is the estimate of H^{-1} at iteration i. The BFGS (Broyden-Fletcher-Goldfarb-Shanno) method is a widely used technique based on this general idea.

Of course, sometimes special methods have been developed for special classes of models and score functions. An example is the *iteratively weighted least squares method* for fitting generalized linear models, as described in chapter 11.

The methods we have just described all find a "good" direction for the step at each iteration. A simple alternative would be merely to step in directions parallel to the axes. This has the disadvantage that the algorithm can become stuck—if, for example there is a long narrow valley diagonal to the axes. If the shape of the function in the vicinity of the minimum is approximated by a quadratic function, then the principal axes of this will define directions (probably not parallel to the axes). Adopting these as an alternative coordinate system, and then searching along these new axes, will lead to a quicker search. Indeed, if the function to be minimized really is quadratic, then this procedure will find the minimum exactly in d steps. These new axes are termed *conjugate directions*.

Once we have determined the direction **v** in which we are to move, we can adopt a "line search" procedure to decide how far to move; that is, we simply apply one of the one-dimensional methods discussed above, in the chosen direction. Often a fast and approximate method of choosing the size of the univariate steps may be sufficient in multivariate optimization problems, since the choice of direction itself will itself be based on various approximations.

The methods described so far are all based on, or at least derived from, finding the local direction for the "best" step and then moving in that direction. The *simplex search* method (not to be confused with the *simplex algorithm* of linear programming) evaluates $d+1$ points arranged in a simplex (a "hypertetrahedron") in the d-dimensional parameter space and uses these to define the best direction in which to step. To illustrate, let us take the case of $d=2$. The function is evaluated at three $(=d+1$ when $d=2)$ points, arranged as the vertices of an equilateral triangle, which is the simplex in two dimensions. The triangle is then reflected in the side opposite the vertex with the largest function value. This gives a new vertex, and the process is repeated using the triangle based on the new vertex and the two that did not move in the previous reflection. This is repeated until oscillation occurs (the triangle just flips back and forth, reflecting about the same side). When this happens the sides of the triangle are halved, and the process continues.

This basic simplex search method has been extended in various ways. For example, the Nelder and Mead variant allows the triangle to increase as well as decrease in size so as to accelerate movement in appropriate situations. There is evidence to suggest that, despite its simplicity, this method is comparable to the more sophisticated methods described above in high-dimensional spaces. Furthermore, the method does not require derivatives to be calculated (or even to exist).

A related search method, called *pattern search,* also carries out a local search to determine the direction of step. If the step reduces the score function, then the step size is increased. If it does poorly, the step size is decreased (until it hits a minimum value, at which point the search is terminated). (The word *pattern* in the phrase *pattern search* has nothing to do with the patterns of data mining as discussed earlier.)

8.3.6   Constrained Optimization

Many optimization problems involve constraints on the parameters. Common examples include problems in which the parameters are probabilities (which are constrained to be positive and to sum to 1), and models that include the variance as a parameter (which must be positive). Constraints often occur in the form of inequalities, requiring that a parameter θ satisfy $c_1 \leq \theta \leq c_2$, for example, with c_1 and c_2 being constants, but more complex constraints are expressed as functions: $g(\theta_1, ..., \theta_d) \leq 0$ for example. Occasionally, constraints have the form of equalities. In general, the region of parameter vectors that satisfy the constraints is termed the *feasible region.*

Problems that have linear constraints and convex score functions can be solved by methods of *mathematical programming.* For example, *linear programming* methods have been used in supervised classification problems, and *quadratic programming* is used in suport vector machines. Problems in which the score functions and constraints are nonlinear are more challenging.

Sometimes constrained problems can be converted into unconstrained problems. For example, if the feasible region is restricted to positive values of the parameters $(\theta_1, ..., \theta_d)$, we could, instead, optimize over $(\phi_1, ..., \phi_d)$, where $\theta_i = \phi_i^2$, $i = 1, ..., d$. Other (rather more complicated) transformations can remove constraints of the form $c_1 \leq \theta \leq c_2$.

A basic strategy for removing equality constraints is through *Lagrange multipliers.* A necessary condition for θ to be a local minimum of the score function $S = S(\theta)$ subject to constraints $h_j(\theta) = 0$, $j = 1, ..., m$, is that it satisfies $\nabla S(\theta) + \sum_j \lambda_j \nabla h_j(\theta) = 0$, for some scalars, λ_j. These equations and the constraints yield a system of $(d + m)$ simultaneous (nonlinear) equations, that can be solved by standard methods (often by using a least squares routine to minimize the sum of squares of the left hand sides of the $(d + m)$ equations). These ideas are extend to inequality constraints in the *Kuhn-Tucker conditions* (see Further Reading).

Unconstrained optimization methods can be modified to yield constrained methods. For example, penalties can be added to the score function so that the parameter estimates are repelled if they should approach boundaries of the feasible region during the optimization process.

8.4   Optimization with Missing Data: The EM Algorithm

In this section we consider the special but important problem of maximizing a likelihood score function when some of the data are missing, that is, there are variables in our data set whose values are unobserved for some of the cases. It turns out that a large number of problems in practice can effectively be modeled as missing data problems. For example, measurements on medical patients where for each patient only a subset of test results are available, or application form data where the responses to some questions depends on the answers to others.

More generally, any model involving a hidden variable (i.e., a variable that cannot be directly observed) can be modeled as a missing data problem, in which the values of this variable are unknown for all n objects or individuals. Clustering is a specific example; in effect we assume the existence of a discrete-valued hidden cluster variable C taking values $\{c_1, \ldots, c_k\}$ and the goal is to estimate the values of C (that is, the cluster labels) for each observation $\mathbf{x}(i)$, $1 \leq i \leq n$.

The Expectation-Maximization (EM) algorithm is a rather remarkable algorithm for solving such missing data problems in a likelihood context. Specifically, let $D = \{\mathbf{x}(1), \ldots, \mathbf{x}(n)\}$ be a set of n observed data vectors. Let $H = \{z(1), \ldots, z(n)\}$ represent a set of n values of a hidden variable Z, in one-to-one correspondence with the observed data points D; that is, $z(i)$ is associated with data point $\mathbf{x}(i)$. We can assume Z to be discrete (this is not necessary, but is simply convenient for our description of the algorithm), in which case we can think of the unknown $z(i)$ values as class (or cluster) labels for the data, that are hidden.

We can write the log-likelihood of the observed data as

$$l(\theta) = \log p(D|\theta) = \log \sum_H p(D, H|\theta) \tag{8.15}$$

where the term on the right indicates that the observed likelihood can be expressed as the likelihood of both the observed and hidden data, summed over the hidden data values, assuming a probabilistic model in the form $p(D, H|\theta)$ that is parametrized by a set of unknown parameters θ. Note that our optimization problem here is doubly complicated by the fact that *both* the parameters θ and the hidden data H are unknown.

Let $Q(H)$ be any probability distribution on the missing data H. We can then write the log-likelihood in the following fashion:

$$
\begin{aligned}
l(\theta) &= \log \sum_H p(D, H|\theta) \\
&= \log \sum_H Q(H) \frac{p(D, H|\theta)}{Q(H)} \\
&\geq \sum_H Q(H) \log \frac{p(D, H|\theta)}{Q(H)} \\
&= \sum_H Q(H) \log p(D, H|\theta) + \sum_H Q(H) \log \frac{1}{Q(H)} \\
&= F(Q, \theta) \tag{8.16}
\end{aligned}
$$

where the inequality is a result of the concavity of the log function (known as Jensen's inequality).

The function $F(Q, \theta)$ is a lower bound on the function we wish to maximize (the likelihood $l(\theta)$). The EM algorithm alternates between maximizing F with respect to the distribution Q with the parameters θ fixed, and then maximizing F with respect to the parameters θ with the distribution $Q = p(H)$ fixed. Specifically:

$$\text{E-step:} \qquad Q^{k+1} = \arg\max_Q F(Q^k, \theta^k) \tag{8.17}$$

$$\text{M-step:} \qquad \theta^{k+1} = \arg\max_\theta F(Q^{k+1}, \theta^k) \tag{8.18}$$

It is straightforward to show that the maximum in the E-step is achieved when $Q^{k+1} = p(H|D, \theta^k)$, a term that can often be calculated explicitly in a relatively straightforward fashion for many models. Furthermore, for this value of Q the bound becomes tight, i.e., the inequality becomes an equality above and $l(\theta^k) = F(Q, \theta^k)$.

The maximization in the M-step reduces to maximizing the first term in F (since the second term does not depend on θ), and can be written as

$$\theta^{k+1} = \arg \max_{\theta} \sum_{H} p(H|D, \theta^k) \log p(D, H|\theta^k). \qquad (8.19)$$

This expression can also fortunately often be solved in closed form.

Clearly the E and M steps as defined cannot decrease $l(\theta)$ at each step: at the beginning of the M-step we have that $l(\theta^k) = F(Q^{k+1}, \theta^k)$ by definition, and the M-step further adjusts θ to maximize this F.

The EM steps have a simple intuitive interpretation. In the E-step we estimate the distribution on the hidden variables Q, conditioned on a particular setting of the parameter vector θ^k. Then, keeping the Q function fixed, in the M-step we choose a new set of parameters θ^{k+1} so as to maximize the expected log-likelihood of observed data (with expectation defined with respect to $Q = p(H)$). In turn, we can now find a new Q distribution given the new parameters θ^{k+1}, then another application of the M-step to get θ^{k+2}, and so forth in an iterative manner. As sketched above, each such application of the E and M steps is guaranteed not to decrease the log-likelihood of the observed data, and under fairly general conditions this in turn implies that the parameters θ will converge to at least a local maximum of the log-likelihood function.

To specify an actual algorithm we need to pick an initial starting point (for example, start with either an initial randomly chosen Q or θ) and a convergence detection method (for example, detect when any of Q, θ, or $l(\theta)$ do not change appreciably from one iteration to the next). The EM algorithm is essentially similar to a form of local hill-climbing in multivariate parameter space (as discussed in earlier sections of this chapter) where the direction and distance of each step is implicitly (and automatically) specified by the E and M steps. Thus, just as with hill-climbing, the method will be sensitive to initial conditions, so that different choices of initial conditions can lead to different local maxima. Because of this, in practice it is usually wise to run EM from different initial conditions (and then choose the highest likelihood solution) to decrease the probability of finally settling on a relatively poor local maximum. The EM algorithm can converge relatively slowly to the final parameter values, and for example, it can be combined with more traditional optimization techniques (such as Newton-Raphson) to speed up convergence in the later iterations. Nonetheless, the standard EM algorithm is widely used given the broad generality of the framework and the relative ease with which an EM algorithm can be specified for many different problems.

The computational complexity of the EM algorithm is dictated by both the number of iterations required for convergence and the complexity of each of the E and M steps. In practice it is often found that EM can converges relatively slowly as it approaches a solution, although the actual rate of convergence can depend on a variety of different factors. Nonetheless, for simple models at least, the algorithm can often converge to the general vicinity of the solution after only a few (say 5 or 10) iterations. The complexity of the E and M steps at each iteration depends on the nature of the model being fit to the data (that is, the likelihood function $p(D, H|\theta)$). For many of the simpler models (such as the mixture models discussed below) the E and M steps need only take time linear in n, i.e., each data point need only be visited once during each iteration.

Examples 8.1 and 8.2 illustrate the application of the EM algorithm in estimating the parameters of a normal mixture and a Poisson mixture (respectively) for one-dimensional measurements x. In each case, the data are assumed to have arisen from a mixture of K underlying component distributions (normal and Poisson, respectively). However, the component labels are unobserved, and we do not know which component each data point arose from. We will discuss the estimation of these types of mixture models in more detail again in chapter 9.

Example 8.1 We wish to fit a normal mixture distribution

$$f(x) = \sum_{k=1}^{K} \pi_k f_k(x; \mu_k, \sigma_k) \tag{8.20}$$

where μ_k is the mean of the kth component, σ_k is the standard deviation of the kth component, and π_k is the prior probability of a data point belonging to component k ($\sum_K \pi_k = 1$). Hence, for this problem, we have that the parameter vector $\theta = \{p_1, \ldots, p_K, \mu_1, \ldots, \mu_K, \sigma_1, \ldots, \sigma_K\}$. Suppose for the moment that we knew the values of θ. Then, the probability that an object with measurement vector x arose from the kth class would be

$$\hat{P}(k \mid x) = \frac{\pi_k f_k(x; \mu_k, \sigma_k)}{f(x)} \tag{8.21}$$

This is the basic E-step.

From this, we can then estimate the values of π_k, μ_k, and σ_k as

$$\hat{\pi}_k = \frac{1}{n} \sum_{i=1}^{n} \hat{P}(k \mid x(i)) \tag{8.22}$$

$$\hat{\mu}_k = \frac{1}{n\hat{\pi}_k} \sum_{i=1}^{n} \hat{P}(k \mid x(i))x(i) \qquad (8.23)$$

$$\hat{\sigma}_k = \frac{1}{n\hat{\pi}_k} \sum_{i=1}^{n} \hat{P}(k \mid x(i))(x(i) - \hat{\mu}_k)^2 \qquad (8.24)$$

where the summations are over the n points in the data set. These three equations are the M-steps. This set of equations leads to an obvious iterative procedure. We pick starting values for μ_k, σ_k, and π_k, plug them into equation 8.21 to yield estimates $\hat{P}(k \mid x)$, use these estimates in equations 8.22, 8.23, and 8.24, and then iterate back using the updated estimates of μ_k, σ_k, and π_k, cycling around until a convergence criterion (usually convergence of the likelihood or model parameters to a stable point) has been satisfied.

Note that equations 8.23 and 8.24 are very similar to those involved in estimating the parameters of a single normal distribution, except that the contribution of each point are split across the separate components, in proportion to the estimated size of that component at the point. In essence, each data point is weighted by the probability that it belongs to that component. If we actually knew the class labels the weights for data point $x(i)$ would be 1 for the class to which the data point belongs and 0 for the other $K - 1$ components (in the standard manner).

Example 8.2 The Poisson model can be used to model the rate at which individual events occur, for example, the rate at which a consumer uses a telephone calling card. For some cards, there might be multiple individuals (within a single family for example) on the same account (with copies of the card), and in theory each may have a different rate at which they use it (for example, the teenager uses the card frequently, the father much less frequently, and so on). Thus, with K individuals, we would observe event data generated by a mixture of K Poisson processes:

$$f(x) = \sum_{k=1}^{K} \pi_k \frac{(\lambda_k)^x e^{-\lambda_k}}{x!}, \qquad (8.25)$$

the equations for the iterative estimation procedure analogous to example 8.4 take the form

$$\hat{P}(k \mid x(i)) = \frac{\pi_k P(x(i) \mid k)}{f(x(i))} = \frac{\pi_k \frac{(\lambda_k)^{x(i)} e^{-\lambda_k}}{x(i)!}}{f(x(i))} \qquad (8.26)$$

$$\hat{\pi}_k = \frac{1}{n} \sum_{i=1}^{n} \hat{P}(k \mid x(i)) \qquad (8.27)$$

$$\hat{\lambda}_k = \frac{1}{n\hat{\pi}_k} \sum_{i=1}^{n} \hat{P}(k \mid x\,(i))x\,(i) \qquad (8.28)$$

8.5 Online and Single-Scan Algorithms

All of the optimization methods we have discussed so far implicitly assume that the data are all resident in main memory and, thus, that each data point can be easily accessed multiple times during the course of the search. For very large data sets we may be interested in optimization and search algorithms that see each data point only once at most. Such algorithms may be referred to as *online* or *single-scan* and clearly are much more desirable than "multiple-pass" algorithms when we are faced with a massive data set that resides in secondary memory (or further away).

In general, it is usually possible to modify the search algorithms above directly to deal with data points one at a time. For example, consider simple gradient descent methods for parameter optimization. As discussed earlier, for the "offline" (or batch) version of the algorithm, one finds the gradient $g(\theta)$ in parameter space, evaluates it at the current location θ^k, and takes a step proportional to distance λ in that direction. Now moving in the direction of the gradient $g(\theta)$ is only a heuristic, and it may not necessarily be the optimal direction. In practice, we may do just as well (at least, in the long run) if we move in a direction approximating that of the gradient. This idea is used in practice in an *online approximation* to the gradient, that uses the current best estimate based both on the current location and the current and (perhaps) "recent" data points. The online estimates can be viewed as *stochastic* (or "noisy") estimates of the full gradient estimate that would be produced by the batch algorithm looking at all of the data points. There exists a general theory in statistics for this type of search technique, known as *stochastic approximation*, which is beyond the scope of this text but that is relevant to online parameter estimation. Indeed, in using gradient descent to find weight parameters for neural networks (for example) stochastic online search has been found to be useful in practice. The stochastic (data-driven) nature of the search is even thought to sometimes improve the quality of the solutions found by allowing the search algorithm to escape from local minima in a manner somewhat reminiscent of simulated annealing (see below).

More generally, the more sophisticated search methods (such as multivariate methods based on the Hessian matrix) can also be implemented in an online manner by appropriately defining online estimators for the required search directions and step-sizes.

8.6   Stochastic Search and Optimization Techniques

The methods we have presented thus far on model search and parameter optimization rely heavily on the notion of taking local greedy steps near the current state. The main disadvantage is the inherent myopia of this approach. The quality of the solution that is found is largely a function of the starting point. This means that, at least with a single starting position, there is the danger that the minimum (or maximum) one finds may be a nonglobal local optimum. Because of this, methods have been developed that adopt a more global view by allowing large steps away from the current state in a nondeterministic (stochastic) manner. Each of the methods below is applicable to either the parameter optimization or model search problem, but for simplicity we will just focus here on model search in a state-space.

- **Genetic Search:** Genetic algorithms are a general set of heuristic search techniques based on ideas from evolutionary biology. The essential idea is to represent states (models in our case) as chromosomes (often encoded as binary strings) and to "evolve" a *population* of such chromosomes by selectively pairing chromosomes to create new offspring. Chromosomes (states) are paired based on their "fitness" (their score function) to encourage the fitter chromosomes to survive from one generation to the next (only a limited number of chromosomes are allowed to survive from one generation to the next). There are many variations on this general theme, but the key ideas in genetic search are:

  - Maintenance of a set of candidate states (chromosomes) rather than just a single state, allowing the search algorithm to explore different parts of the state space simultaneously

  - Creating new states to explore based on combinations of existing states, allowing in effect the algorithm to "jump" to different parts of the state-space (in contrast to the local improvement search techniques we discussed earlier)

  Genetic search can be viewed as a specific type of heuristic, so it may work well on some problems and less well on others. It is not always clear that it provides better performance on specific problems than a simpler method such as local iterative improvement with random restarts. A practical drawback of the approach is the fact that there are usually many *algorithm parameters* (such as the number of chromosomes, specification of how chromosomes are combined, and so on) that must be specified and it may not be clear what the ideal settings are for these parameters for any given problem.

- **Simulated Annealing:** Just as genetic search is motivated by ideas from evolutionary biology, the approach in *simulated annealing* is motivated by ideas from physics. The essential idea is to not to restrict the search algorithm to moves in state-space that decrease the score function (for a score function we are trying to minimize), but to also allow (with some probability) moves that can *increase* the score function. In principle, this allows a search algorithm to escape from a local minimum. The probability of such non-decreasing moves is set to be quite high early in the process and gradually decreased as the search progresses. The decrease in this probability is analogous to the process of gradually decreasing the *temperature* in the physical process of annealing a metal with the goal of obtaining a low-energy state in the metal (hence the name of the method).

  For the search algorithm, higher temperatures correspond to a greater probability of large moves in the parameter space, while lower temperatures correspond to greater probability of only small moves that decrease the function being taken. Ultimately, the *temperature schedule* reduces the temperature to zero, so that the algorithm by then only moves to states that decrease the score function. Thus, at this stage of the search, the algorithm will inevitably converge to a point at which no further decrease is possible. The hope is that the earlier (more random) moves have led the algorithm to the deepest "basin" in the score function surface. In fact, one of the appeals of the approach is that it can be mathematically proved that (under fairly general conditions) this will happen if one is using the appropriate temperature schedule. In practice, however, there is usually no way to specify the optimal temperature schedule (and the precise details of how to select the possible nondecreasing moves) for any specific problem. Thus, the practical application of simulated annealing reduces to (yet another) heuristic search method with its own set of algorithm parameters that are often chosen in an ad hoc manner.

  We note in passing that the idea of *stochastic search* is quite general, where the next set of parameters or model is chosen stochastically based on a probability distribution on the quality of neighboring states conditioned on the current state. By exploring state-space in a stochastic fashion, a search algorithm can in principle spend more time (on average) in the higher quality states and build up a model on the distribution of the quality (or score) function across the state-space. This general approach has become very popular in Bayesian statistics, with techniques such as Monte Carlo Markov Chain (MCMC) being widely used. Such methods can be viewed as generalizations of the basic simulated annealing idea, and again, the key ideas originated in physics. The focus in MCMC is to find the *distribution* of scores in parameter or state-space, weighted by the probability of those parameters or models given the data, rather than just finding the location of the single global minimum (or maximum).

It is difficult to make general statements about the practical utility of methods such as simulated annealing and genetic algorithms when compared to a simpler approach such as iterative local improvement with random restarts, particularly if we want to take into account the amount of time taken by each method. It is important when comparing different search methods to compare not only the *quality* of the final solution but also the *computational resources* expended to find that solution. After all, if time is unlimited, we can always use exhaustive enumeration of all models to find the global optimum. It is fair to say that since stochastic search techniques typically involve considerable extra computation and overhead (compared to simpler alternatives) that they tend to be used in practice on specialized problems involving relatively small data sets, and are often not practical from a computational viewpoint for very large data sets.

8.7   Further Reading

Papadamitriou and Steiglitz (1982) is a classic (although now a little outdated) text on combinatorial optimization. Cook et al. (1998) is an authoritative and more recent text on the topic. Pearl (1984) deals specifically with the topic of search heuristics. The CN2 rule-finding algorithm of Clark and Niblett (1989) is an example of beam search in action.

Press et al. (1988) is a useful place to start for a general introduction and some sound practical advice on numerical optimization techniques, particularly chapters 9 and 10. Other texts such as Gill, Murray, and Wright (1981) and Fletcher (1987) are devoted specifically to optimization and provide a wealth of practical advice as well as more details on specific methods. Luenberger (1984) and Nering and Tucker (1993) discuss linear programming and related constrained optimization techniques in detail. Mangasarian (1997) describes the application of constrained optimization techniques to a variety problems in data mining, including feature selection, clustering, and robust model selection. Bradley, Fayyad, and Mangasarian (1999) contain further discussion along these lines.

Thisted (1988) is a very useful and comprehensive reference on the application of optimization and search methods specifically to statistical problems. Lange (1999) is more recent text on the same topic (numerical methods for statistical optimization) with a variety of useful techniques and results. Bishop (1995, chapter 7) has an extensive and well-written account of optimization in the context of parameter estimation for neural networks, with specific reference to online techniques.

The seminal paper on the EM algorithm is Dempster, Laird, and Rubin (1977) which first established the general theoretical framework for the procedure. This paper had been preceded by almost a century of work in the general spirit of EM, including Newcomb (1886) and McKendrick (1926). The work of Baum and Petrie (1966) was an early development of a specific EM algorithm in the context of hidden Markov models. McLachlan and Krishnan (1998) provide a comprehensive treatment of the many recent advances in the theory and application of EM. Meilijson (1989) introduced a general technique for speeding up EM convergence, and Lange (1995) discusses the use of gradient methods in an EM context. A variety of computational issues concerning EM in a mixture modeling context are discussed in Redner and Walker (1984). Neal and Hinton (1998) discuss online versions of EM that can be particularly useful in the context of massive data sets.

Online learning in a regression context can be viewed theoretically as a special case of the general technique of stochastic approximation of Robbins and Monro (1951)—see Bishop (1995, chapter 2) for a discussion in the context of neural networks.

Mitchell (1997) is a comprehensive introduction to the ideas underlying genetic algorithms. Simulated annealing was introduced by Kirkpatrick, Gelatt, and Vecchi (1983) but has its origins in much earlier work in statistical physics. Van Laarhoven and Aarts (1987) provide a general overview of the field. Brooks and Morgan (1995) contains a systematic comparison between simulated annealing and more conventional optimization techniques (such as Newton-based methods), as well as hybrids of the two. They conclude that hybrid methods appear better than either traditional methods or simulated annealing on their own. Gilks, Richardson, and Spiegelhalter (1996) is an edited volume containing a good sampling of recent work in statistics using stochastic search and MCMC methods in a largely Bayesian context.

9 *Descriptive Modeling*

9.1   Introduction

In earlier chapters we explained what is meant, in the context of data mining, by the terms *model* and *pattern*. A model is a high-level description, summarizing a large collection of data and describing its important features. Often a model is *global* in the sense that it applies to all points in the measurement space. In contrast, a pattern is a local description, applying to some subset of the measurement space, perhaps showing how just a few data points behave or characterizing some persistent but unusual structure within the data. Examples would be a mode (peak) in a density function or a small set of outliers in a scatter plot.

Earlier chapters distinguished between models and patterns, and also between descriptive and predictive models. A descriptive model presents, in convenient form, the main features of the data. It is essentially a summary of the data, permitting us to study the most important aspects of the data without their being obscured by the sheer size of the data set. In contrast, a predictive model has the specific objective of allowing us to predict the value of some target characteristic of an object on the basis of observed values of other characteristics of the object.

This chapter is concerned with descriptive models, presenting outlines of several algorithms for finding descriptive models that are important in data mining contexts. Chapters 10 and 11 will describe predictive models, and chapter 13 will describe descriptive patterns.

We have already noted that data mining is usually concerned with building empirical models—models that are not based on some underlying theory about the mechanism through which the data arose, but that are simply a description of the observed data. The fundamental objective is to produce insight and understanding about the structure of the data, and to enable us to see its important features. Beyond this, of course, we hope to discover unsuspected structure as well as structure that is interesting and valuable in some sense. A good model can also be thought of as *generative* in the sense that data generated according to the model will have the same characteristics as the real data from which the model was produced. If such synthetically generated data have features not possessed by the original data, or do not possess features of the original data (such as, for example, correlations between variables), then the model is a poor one: it is failing to summarize the data adequately.

This chapter focuses on specific techniques and algorithms for fitting descriptive models to data. It builds on many of the ideas introduced in earlier chapters: the principles of uncertainty (chapter 4), decomposing data mining algorithms into basic components (chapter 5), and the general principles underlying model structures, score functions, and parameter and model search (chapters 6, 7, and 8, respectively).

There are, in fact, many different types of model, each related to the others in various ways (special cases, generalizations, different ways of looking at the same structure, and so on). We cannot hope to examine all possible models types in detail in a single chapter. Instead we will look at just some of the more important types, focusing on methods for density estimation and cluster analysis in particular. The reader is alerted to the fact that are other descriptive techniques in the literature (techniques such as structural equation modeling or factor analysis for example) that we do not discuss here.

One point is worth making at the start. Since we are concerned here with global models, with structures that are representative of a mass of objects in some sense, then we do not need to worry about failing to detect just a handful of objects possessing some property; that is, in this chapter we are not concerned with patterns. This is good news from the point of view of scalability: as we discussed in chapter 4, we can, for example, take a (random) sample from the data set and still hope to obtain good results.

9.2   Describing Data by Probability Distributions and Densities

9.2.1   Introduction

For data that are drawn from a larger population of values, or data that can be regarded as being drawn from such a larger population (for example, because the measurements have associated measurement error), describing data in terms of their underlying distribution or density function is a fundamental *descriptive* strategy. Adopting our usual notation of a p-dimensional data matrix, with variables $X_1, \ldots, X_p$, our goal is to model the joint distribution or density $f(X_1, \ldots, X_p)$ as first encountered in chapter 4. For convenience, we will refer to "densities" in this discussion, but the ideas apply to discrete as well as to continuous X variables.

The joint density in a certain sense provides us with complete information about the variables $X_1, \ldots, X_p$. Given the joint density, we can answer any question about the relationships among any subset of variable; for example, are X_3 and X_7 independent? Thus, we can answer questions about the conditional density of some variables given others; for example, what is the probability distribution of X_3 given the value of X_7, $f(x_3 \mid x_7)$?.

There are many practical situations in which knowing the joint density is useful and desirable. For example, we may be interested in the *modes* of the density (for real-valued Xs). Say we are looking at the variables income and credit-card spending for a data set of n customers at a particular bank. For large n, in a scatterplot we will just see a mass of points, many overlaid on top of each other. If instead we estimate the joint density f(income, spending) (where we have yet to describe how this would be done), we get a density function of the two dimensions that could be plotted as a contour map or as a three-dimensional display with the density function being plotted in the third dimension. The estimated joint density would in principle impart useful information about the underlying structure and patterns present in the data. For example, the presence of peaks (modes) in the density function could indicate the presence of subgroups of customers. Conversely, gaps, holes, or valleys might indicate regions where (for one reason or another) this particular bank had no customers. And the overall shape of the density would provide an indication of how income and spending are related, for this population of customers.

A quite different example is given by the problem of generating approximate answers to queries for large databases (also known as *query selectivity estimation*). The task is the following: given a query (that is, a condition that the observations must satisfy), estimate the fraction of rows that satisfy this condition (the *selectivity* of the query). Such estimates are needed in query optimization in database systems, and a single query optimization task might need hundreds of such estimates. If we have a good approximation for the joint distribution of the data in the database, we can use it to obtain approximate selectivities in a computationally efficient manner.

Thus, the joint density is fundamental and we will need to find ways to estimate and conveniently summarize it (or its main features).

9.2.2   Score Functions for Estimating Probability Distributions and Densities

As we have noted in earlier chapters, the most common score function for estimating the parameters of probability functions is the *likelihood* (or, equivalently by virtue of the monotonicity of the log transform, the *log-likelihood*). As a reminder, if the probability function of random variables $\mathbf{X}$ is $f(\mathbf{x}; \theta)$, where θ are the parameters that need to be estimated, then the log-likelihood is $\log f(D|\theta)$ where $D = \{\mathbf{x}(1), \ldots, \mathbf{x}(n)\}$ is the observed data. Making the common assumption that that the separate rows of the data matrix have arisen independently, this becomes

$$S_L(\theta) = - \sum_{i=1}^{n} \log f(\mathbf{x}(i); \theta). \tag{9.1}$$

If f has a simple functional form (for example, if it has the form of the single univariate distributions outlined in the appendix) then this score function can usually be minimized explicitly, producing a closed form estimator for the parameters θ. However, if f is more complex, iterative optimization methods may be required.

Despite its importance, the likelihood may not always be an adequate or appropriate measure for comparing models. In particular, when models of different complexity (for example, Normal densities with covariance structures parameterized in terms of different numbers of parameters) are compared then difficulties may arise. For example, with a nested series of models in which higher-level models include lower-level ones as special cases, the more flexible higher level models will always have a greater likelihood. This will come as no surprise. The likelihood score function is a measure of how well the model fits the data, and more flexible models necessarily fit the data no worse (and usually better) than a nested less flexible model. This means that likelihood will be appropriate in situations in which we are using it as a score function to summarize a complete body of data (since then our aim is simply closeness of fit between the simplifying description and the raw data) but not if we are using it to select a single model (from a set of candidate model structures) to apply it to a sample of data from a larger population (with the implicit aim being to generalize beyond the data actually observed). In the latter case, we can solve the problem by modifying the likelihood to take the complexity of the model into account. We discussed this in detail in chapter 7, where we outlined several score functions based on adding an extra term to the likelihood that penalizes model complexity. For example, the BIC (Bayesian Information Criterion) score function was defined as:

$$S_{BIC}(M_k) = 2S_L(\hat{\theta}_k; M_k) + d_k \log n, \quad 1 \leq k \leq K, \tag{9.2}$$

where d_k is the number of parameters in model M_k and $S_L(\hat{\theta}_k; M_k)$ is the minimizing value of the negative log-likelihood (achieved at $\hat{\theta}_k$).

Alternatively, also as discussed in chapter 7, we can calculate the score using an independent sample of data, producing an "out-of-sample" evaluation. Thus the *validation log-likelihood* (or "holdout log-likelihood") is defined as

$$S_{vl}(M_k) = \sum_{\mathbf{x} \in D_v} \log f_{M_k}(\mathbf{x}|\hat{\theta}), 1 \leq k \leq K, \tag{9.3}$$

where the points $\mathbf{x}$ are from the validation data set D_v, the parameters $\hat{\theta}$ were estimated (for example, via maximum likelihood) on the disjoint training data $D_t = D \setminus D_v$, and there are K models under consideration.

9.2.3 Parametric Density Models

We pointed out, in chapter 6, that there are two general classes of density function model structures: parametric and nonparametric. *Parametric models* assume a particular functional form (usually relatively simple) for the density function, such as a uniform distribution, a Normal distribution, an exponential distribution, a Poisson distribution, and so on (see Appendix A for more details on some of these common densities and distributions). These distribution functions are often motivated by underlying causal models of generic data-generating mechanisms. Choice of what might be an appropriate density function should be based on knowledge of the variable being measured (for example, the knowledge that a variable such as income can only be positive should be reflected in the choice of the distribution adopted to model it). Parametric models can often be characterized by a relatively small number of parameters. For example, the p-dimensional Normal distribution is defined as

$$f(\mathbf{x}) = \frac{1}{(2\pi)^{\frac{p}{2}} |\Sigma|^{\frac{1}{2}}} e^{-\frac{1}{2}(\mathbf{x}-\mu)^T \Sigma^{-1}(\mathbf{x}-\mu)}, \tag{9.4}$$

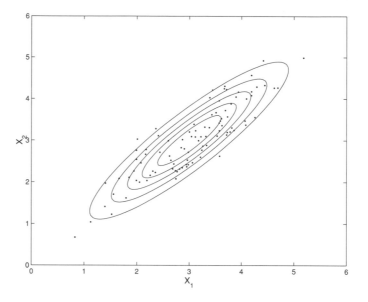

Figure 9.1 Illustration of the density contours for a two-dimensional Normal density function, with mean $[3, 3]$ and covariance matrix $\Sigma = \left(\begin{smallmatrix} 1.0 & 0.9 \\ 0.9 & 1.0 \end{smallmatrix} \right)$. Also shown are 100 data points simulated from this density.

where Σ is the $p \times p$ covariance matrix of the X variables, $|\Sigma|$ is the determinant of this matrix, and μ is the p-dimensional vector mean of the Xs. The *parameters* of the model are the mean vector and the covariance matrix (thus, $p + p(p + 1)/2$ parameters in all).

The multivariate Normal (or Gaussian) distribution is particularly important in data analysis. For example, because of the central limit theorem, under fairly broad assumptions the mean of N independent random variables (each from any distribution) tends to have a Normal distribution. Although the result is asymptotic in nature, even for relatively small values of N (e.g., $N = 10$) the sample mean will typically be quite Normal. Thus, if a measurement can be thought of as being made up of the sum of multiple relatively independent causes, the Normal model is often a reasonable model to adopt.

The functional form of the multivariate Normal model in equation 9.4 is less formidable than it looks. The exponent, $(\mathbf{x} - \mu)^T \Sigma^{-1} (\mathbf{x} - \mu)$, is a scalar value (a quadratic form) known as the *Mahalanobis distance* between the data point $\mathbf{x}$ and the mean μ, denoted as $r^2_\Sigma(\mathbf{x}, \mu)$. This is a generalization of standard Euclidean distance that takes into account (through the covariance matrix Σ) correlations in p-space when distance is calculated. The denominator in equation 9.4 is simply a normalizing constant (call it C) to ensure that the function integrates to 1 (that is, to ensure it is a true probability density function). Thus, we can write our Normal model in significantly simplified form as

$$f(\mathbf{x}) = \frac{1}{C} e^{-r_\Sigma^2(\mathbf{x}, \mu)/2} . \tag{9.5}$$

If we were to plot (say for $p = 2$) all of the points $\mathbf{x}$ that have the same fixed values of $r_\Sigma^2(\mathbf{x}, \mu)$, (or equivalently, all of the points $\mathbf{x}$ that like on iso-density contours $f(\mathbf{x}) = c$ for some constant c), we would find that they trace out an ellipse in 2-space (more generally, a hyperellipsoid in p-space), where the ellipse is centered at μ. That is, the contours describing the multivariate Normal distribution are ellipsoidal, with height falling exponentially from the center as a function of $r_\Sigma^2(\mathbf{x}, \mu)$. Figure 9.1 provides a simple illustration in two dimensions. The eccentricity and orientation of the elliptical contours is determined by the form of Σ. If Σ is a multiple of the identity matrix (all variables have the same variance and are uncorrelated) then the contours are circles. If Σ is a diagonal matrix, but with different variance terms on the diagonals, then the axes of the elliptical contours are parallel to the variable axes and the contours are elongated along the variable axes with greater variance. Finally, if some of the variables are highly correlated, the (hyper) elliptical contours will tend to be elongated along vectors defined as linear combinations of these variables. In figure 9.1, for example, the two variables X_1 and X_2 are highly correlated, and the data are spread out along the line defined by the linear combination $X_1 + X_2$.

For high-dimensional data (large p) the number of parameters in the Normal model will be dominated by the $O(p^2)$ covariance terms in the covariance matrix. In practice we may not want to model all of these covariance terms explicitly, since for large p and finite n (the number of data points available) we may not get very reliable estimates of many of the covariance terms. We could, for example, instead assume that the variables are independent, which is equivalent in the Normal case to assuming that the covariance matrix has a diagonal structure (and, hence, has only p parameters). (Note that if we assume that Σ is diagonal it is easy to show that the p-dimensional multivariate Normal density factors into a product of p univariate Normal distributions, a necessary and sufficient condition for independence of the p variables.) An even more extreme assumption would be to assume that

$\Sigma = \sigma^2 I$, where I is the identity matrix—that is, that the data has the same variance for all p variables as well as being independent.

Independence is a highly restrictive assumption. A less restrictive assumption would be that the covariance matrix had a block diagonal structure: we assume that there are groups of variables (the "blocks") that are dependent, but that variables are independent across the groups. In general, all sorts of assumptions may be possible, and it is important, in practice, to test the assumptions. In this regard, the multivariate Normal distribution has the attractive property that two variables are conditionally independent, given the other variables, if and only if the corresponding element of the inverse of the covariance matrix is zero. This means that the inverse covariance matrix Σ^{-1} reveals the pattern of relationships between the variables. (Or, at least, it does in principle: in fact, of course, it will be necessary to decide whether a small value in the inverse covariance matrix is sufficiently small to be regarded as zero.) It also means that we can hypothesize a graphical model in which there are no edges linking the nodes corresponding to variables that have a small value in this inverse matrix (we discussed graphical models in chapter 6).

It is important to test the assumptions made in a model. Specific statistical goodness-of-fit tests are often available, but even simple eyeballing can be revealing. The simple histogram, or one of its more sophisticated cousins outlined in chapter 3, can immediately reveal constraints on permissible ranges (for example, the non-negativity of income noted above), lack of symmetry, and so on. If the assumptions are not justified, then analysis of some transformation of the raw scores may be appropriate. Unfortunately, there are no hard-and-fast rules about whether or not an assumption is justified. Slight departures may well be unimportant—but it will depend on the problem. This is part of the art of data mining. In many situations in which the distributional assumptions break down we can obtain perfectly legitimate estimates of parameters, but statistical tests are invalid. For example, we can physically fit a regression model using the least squares score function, whether or not the errors are Normally distributed, but hypothesis tests on the estimated parameters may well not be accurate. This might matter during the model building process—in helping to decide whether or not to include a variable—but it may not matter for the final model. If the final model is good for its purpose (for example, predictive accuracy in regression) that is sufficient justification for it to be adopted.

Fitting a p-dimensional Normal model is quite easy. Maximum likelihood (or indeed Bayesian) estimation of each of the means and the covariance terms can be defined in closed form (as discussed in chapter 4), and takes only $O(n)$ steps for each parameter, so $O(np^2)$ in total. Other well-known parametric models (such as those defined in the appendix) also usually possess closed-form parameter solutions that can be calculated by a single pass through the data.

The Normal model structure is a relatively simple and constrained model. It is unimodal and symmetric about the axes of the ellipse. It is parametrized completely in terms of its mean vector and covariance matrix. However, it follows from this that nonlinear relationships cannot be captured, nor can any form of multimodality or grouping. The mixture models of the next section provide a flexible framework for modeling such structures. The reader should also note that although the Normal model is probably the most widely-used parametric model in practice, there are many other density functions with different "shapes" that are very useful for certain applications (e.g., the exponential model, the log-normal, the Poisson, the Gamma: the interested reader is referred to the appendix). The multivariate t-distribution is similar in form to the multivariate Normal but allows for longer tails, and is found useful in practical problems where more data can often occur in the tails than a Normal model would predict.

9.2.4   Mixture Distributions and Densities

In chapter 6 we saw how simple parametric models could be generalized to allow *mixtures* of components—that is, linear combinations of simpler distributions. This can be viewed as the next natural step in complexity in our discussion of density modeling: namely, the generalization from parametric distributions to weighted linear combinations of such functions, providing a general framework for generating more complex density and distribution models as combinations of simpler ones. Mixture models are quite useful in practice for modeling data when we are not sure what specific parametric form is appropriate (later in this chapter we will see how such mixture models can also be used for the task of *clustering*).

It is quite common in practice that a data set is *heterogeneous* in the sense that it represents multiple different subpopulations or groups, rather than one single homogeneous group. Heterogeneity is particularly prevalent in very large data sets, where the data may represent different underlying phenomena that have been collected to form one large data set. To illustrate this point, consider figure 3.1 in chapter 3. This is a histogram of the number of weeks owners of a particular credit card used that card to make supermarket purchases in 1996. As we pointed out there, the histogram appears to be bimodal, with a large and obvious mode to the left and a smaller, but nevertheless possibly important mode to the right. An initial stab at a model for such data might be that it follows a Poisson distribution (despite being bounded above by 52), but this would not have a sufficiently heavy tail and would fail to pick up the right-hand mode. Likewise, a binomial model would also fail to follow the right-hand mode. Something more sophisticated and flexible is needed. An obvious suggestion here is that the empirical distribution should be modeled by a theoretical distribution that has two components. Perhaps there are two kinds of people: those who are unlikely to use their credit card in a supermarket and those who do so most weeks. The first set of people could be modeled by a Poisson distribution with a small probability. The second set could be modeled by a reversed Poisson distribution with its mode around 45 or 46 weeks (the position of the mode would be a parameter to be estimated in fitting the model to the data). This leads us to an overall distribution of the form

$$f(x) = \pi \frac{(\lambda_1)^x e^{-\lambda_1}}{x!} + (1 - \pi) \frac{(\lambda_2)^{52-x} e^{-\lambda_2}}{(52 - x)!}, \qquad (9.6)$$

where x is the value of the random variable X taking values between 0 and 52 (indicating how many weeks a year a person uses their card in a supermarket), and $\lambda_1 > 0, \lambda_2 > 0$ are parameters of the two component Poisson models. Here π is the probability that a person belongs to the first group, and, given this, the expression $\lambda_1^x e^{-\lambda_1}/x!$ gives the probability that this person will use their card x times in the year. Likewise, $1 - \pi$ is the probability that this person belong to the second group and $\lambda_2^{52-x} e^{-\lambda_2}/(52 - x)!$ is the conditional probability that such a person will use their card x times in the year.

One way to think about this sort of model is as a two-stage generative process for a particular individual. In the first step there is a probability π (and $1 - \pi$) that the individual comes from one group or the other. In the second step, an observation x is generated for that person according to the component distribution he or she was assigned to in the first step.

Equation 9.6 is an example of a *finite mixture distribution,* where the overall model $f(x)$ is a weighted linear combination of a finite number of component distributions (in this case just two). Clearly it leads to a much more flexible model than a simple single Poisson distribution—at the very least, it involves three parameters instead of just one. However, by virtue of the argument that led to it, it may also be a more realistic description of what is underlying the data. These two aspects—the extra flexibility of the models consequent on the larger number of parameters and arguments based on suspicion of a heterogeneous underlying population—mean that mixture models are widely used for modeling distributions that are more complicated than simple standard forms.

The general form of a mixture distribution (for multivariate **x**) is

$$f(\mathbf{x}) = \sum_{k=1}^{K} \pi_k f_k(\mathbf{x}; \theta_k), \tag{9.7}$$

where π_k is the probability that an observation will come from the kth component (the so-called kth *mixing proportion* or *weight*), K is the number of components, $f_k(x; \theta_k)$ is the distribution of the kth component, and θ_k is the vector of parameters describing the kth component (in the Poisson mixture example above, each θ_k consisted of a single parameter λ_k). In most applications the component distributions f_k have the same form, but there are situations where this is not the case. The most widely used form of mixture distribution has Normal components. Note that the mixing proportions π_k must lie between 0 and 1 and sum to 1.

Some examples of the many practical situations in which mixture distributions might be expected on theoretical grounds are the length distribution of fish (since they hatch at a specific time of the year), failure data (where there may be different causes of failure, and each cause results in a distribution of failure times), time to death, and the distribution of characteristics of heterogeneous populations of people (e.g., heights of males and females).

9.2.5   The EM Algorithm for Mixture Models

Unlike the simple parametric models discussed earlier in this chapter, there is generally no direct closed-form technique for maximizing the likelihood score function when the underlying model is a mixture model, given a data set $D = \{\mathbf{x}(1), \ldots, \mathbf{x}(n)\}$. This is easy to see by writing out the log-likelihood for a mixture model—we get a sum of terms such as $\log(\sum_k \pi_k f_k(\mathbf{x}; \theta_k))$, leading to a nonlinear optimization problem (unlike, for example, the closed form solutions for the multivariate Normal model).

Over the years, many different methods have been applied in estimating the parameters of mixture distributions given a particular mixture form. One of the more widely used modern methods in this context is the EM approach. As discussed in chapter 8, this can be viewed as a general iterative optimization algorithm for maximizing a likelihood score function given a probabilistic model with missing data. In the present case, the mixture model can be regarded as a distribution in which the class labels are missing. If we knew these labels, we could get closed-form estimates for the parameters of each component by partitioning the data points into their respective groups. However, since we do not know the origin of each data point, we must simultaneously try to learn which component a data point originated from and the parameters of these components. This "chicken-and-egg" problem is neatly solved by the EM algorithm; it starts with some guesses at the parameter values for each component, then calculates the probability that each data point came from one of the K components (this is known as the E-step), calculates new parameters for each component given these probabilistic memberships (this is the M-step, and can typically be carried out in closed form), recalculates the probabilistic memberships, and continues on in this manner until the likelihood converges. As discussed in chapter 8, despite the seemingly heuristic nature of the algorithm, it can be shown that for each EM-step the likelihood can only increase, thus guaranteeing (under fairly broad conditions) convergence of the method to at least a local maximum of the likelihood as a function of the parameter space.

The complexity of the EM algorithm depends on the complexity of the E and M steps at each iteration. For multivariate normal mixtures with K components the computation will be dominated by the calculation of the K covariance matrices during the M-step at each iteration. In p dimensions, with K clusters, there are $O(Kp^2)$ covariance parameters to be estimated, and each of these requires summing over n data points and membership weights, leading to a $O(Kp^2n)$ time-complexity per step. For univariate mixtures (such as the Poisson above) we get $O(Kn)$. The space-complexity is typically $O(Kn)$ to store the K membership probability vectors for each of the n data points $\mathbf{x}(i)$. However, for large n, we often need not store the $n \times K$ membership probability matrix explicitly, since we may be able to calculate the parameter estimates during each M-step *incrementally* via a single pass through the n data points.

EM often provides a large increase in likelihood over the first few iterations and then can slowly converge to its final value; however the likelihood function as a function of iterations need not be concave. For example, figure 9.2 illustrates the convegence of the log-likelihood as a function of the EM iteration number, for a problem involving fitting Gaussian mixtures to a two-dimensional medical data set (that we will later discuss in more detail in section 9.6). For many data sets and models we can often find a reasonable

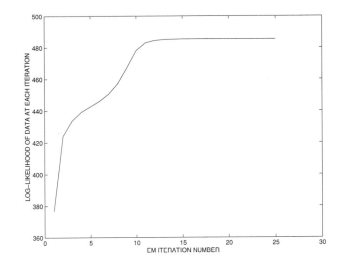

Figure 9.2   The log-likelihood of the red-blood cell data under a two-component Normal mixture model (see figure 9.11) as a function of iteration number.

solution in only 5 to 20 iterations of the algorithm. Each solution provided by EM is of course a function of where one started the search (since it is a local search algorithm), and thus, multiple restarts from randomly chosen starting points are a good idea to try to avoid poor local maxima. Note that as either (or both) K and p increase, the number of local maxima of the likelihood can increase greatly as the dimensionality of the parameter space scales accordingly.

Sometimes caution has to be exercised with maximum likelihood estimates of mixture distributions. For example, in a normal mixture, if we put the mean of one component equal to one of the sample points and let its standard deviation tend to zero, the likelihood will increase without limit. The maximum likelihood solution in this case is likely to be of limited value. There are various ways around this. The largest finite value of the likelihood might be chosen to give the estimated parameter values. Alternatively, if the standard deviations are constrained to be equal, the problem does not arise. A more general solution is to set up the problem in a Bayesian context, with priors on the parameters, and maximize the MAP score function (for example) instead of the likelihood. Here the priors provide a framework for "biasing" the score function (the MAP score function) away from problematic regions in parameter space in a principled manner. Note that the EM algorithm generalizes easily from the case of maximizing likelihood to maximizing MAP (for example, we replace the M-step with an MAP-step, and so forth).

Another problem that can arise is due to lack of identifiability. A family of mixture distributions is said to be *identifiable* if and only if the fact that two members of the family are equal,

$$\sum_{k=1}^{c} \pi_k f(x; \theta_k) = \sum_{j=1}^{c'} \pi'_j f(x; \theta'_j), \tag{9.8}$$

implies that $c = c'$, and that for all k there is some j such that $\pi_k = \pi'_j$ and $\theta_k = \theta'_j$. If a family is not identifiable, then two different members of it may be indistinguishable, which can lead to problems in estimation.

Nonidentifiability is more of a problem with discrete distributions than continuous ones because, with m categories, only $m - 1$ independent equations can be set up. For example, in the case of a mixture of several Bernoulli components, there is effectively only a single piece of information available in the data, namely, the proportion of 1s that occur in the data. Thus, there is no way of estimating the proportions that are separately due to each component Bernoulli, or the parameters of those components.

9.2.6 Nonparametric Density Estimation

In chapter 3 we briefly discussed the idea of estimating a density function by taking a local data-driven weighted average of x measurements about the point of interest (the so-called "kernel density" method). For example, a *histogram* is a relatively primitive version of this idea, in which we simply count the number of points that fall in certain bins. Our estimate for the density is the number of points in a given bin, appropriately scaled. The histogram is problematic as a model structure for densities for a number of reasons. It provides a nonsmooth estimate of what is often presumed to be truly a smooth function, and it is not obvious how the number of bins, bin locations, and widths should be chosen. Furthermore, these problems are exacerbated when we move beyond the one-dimensional histogram to a p-dimensional histogram. Nonetheless, for very large data sets and small p (particularly $p = 1$), the bin widths can be made quite small, and the resulting density estimate may still be relatively smooth and insensitive to the exact location or width of the bins. With large data sets it always a good idea to look at the histograms (with a large number of bins) for each variable, since the histogram can provide a wealth of information on outliers, multimodality, skewness, tail behavior, and so forth (recall the example of the Pima Indians blood pressure data in chapter 3, where the histogram clearly indicated the presence of some rather suspicious values at zero).

A more general model structure for local densities is to define the density at any point **x** as being proportional to a weighted sum of all points in the training data set, where the weights are defined by an appropriately chosen *kernel function*. For the one-dimensional case we have (as defined in chapter 3)

$$f(x) = \frac{1}{n} \sum_{i=1}^{n} w_i, \quad w_i = K\left(\frac{x - x(i)}{h}\right), \tag{9.9}$$

where $f(x)$ is the kernel density estimate at a query point x, $K(t)$ is the kernel function (for example, $K(t) = 1 - |t|, t \leq 1; K(t) = 0$ otherwise) and h is the *bandwidth* of the kernel. Intuitively, the density at x is proportional to the sum of weights evaluated at x, which in turn depend on the proximity of the n points in the training data to x. As with nonparametric regression (discussed in chapter 6), the model is not defined explicitly, but is determined implicitly by the data and the kernel function. The approach is "memory-based" in the sense that all of the data points are retained in the model; that is, no summarization occurs. For very large data sets of course this may be impractical from a computational and storage viewpoint.

In one dimension, the kernel function K is usually chosen as a smooth unimodal function (such as a Normal or triangular distribution) that integrates to 1; the precise shape is typically not critical. As in regression, the bandwidth h plays the role of determining how smooth the model is. If h is relatively large, then the kernel is relatively wide so that many points receive significant weight in the sum and the estimate of the density is very smooth. If h is relatively small, the kernel estimate is determined by the small number of points that are close to x, and the estimate of the density is more sensitive locally to the data (more "spiky" in appearance). Estimating a good value of h in practice can be somewhat problematic. There is no single objective methodology for finding the bandwidth h that has wide acceptance. Techniques based on cross-validation can be useful but are typically computationally complex and not always reliable. Simple "eyeballing" of the resulting density along specific dimensions is always recommended to check whether or not the chosen values for h appear reasonable.

Under appropriate assumptions these kernel models are flexible enough to approximate *any* smooth density function, if h is chosen appropriately, which

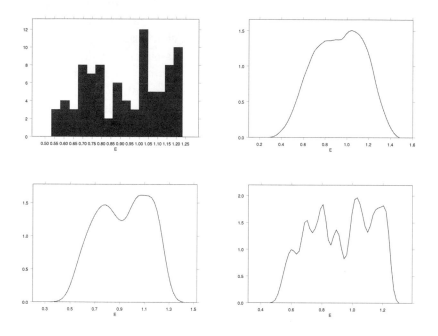

Figure 9.3   Density estimates for the variable ethanol (E) using a histogram (top left) and Gaussian kernel estimates with three different bandwidths: $h = 0.5$ (top right), $h = 0.25$ (lower left), and $h = 0.1$ (lower right).

adds to their appeal. However, this approximation result holds in the limit as we get an infinite number of data points, making it somewhat less relevant for the finite data sets we see in practice. Nonetheless, kernel models can be very valuable for low-dimensional problems as a way to determine structure in the data (such as local peaks or gaps) in a manner that might not otherwise be visible.

Example 9.1 Figure 9.3 shows an example of different density estimates for measurements of ethanol (E) from a data set involving air pollution measurements at different geographic locations. The histogram (top left) is quite "rough" and noisy, at least for this particular choice of bin widths and bin locations. The Normal kernel with bandwidth $h = 0.5$ is probably too smooth (top right). Conversely, the estimate based on a bandwidth of $h = 0.1$ (lower right) is probably too noisy, and introduces modes in the density that are likely to be spurious. The $h = 0.25$ estimate (lower left) is quite plausible and appears to have a better trade-off between over-and undersmoothing than the other estimates; it would suggest that the ethanol measurements have a definite bimodal characteristic. While visual inspection can be useful technique for determining bandwidths interactively, once again, it is largely limited to one-dimensional or two-dimensional problems.

Density estimation with kernel models becomes much more difficult as p increases. To begin with, we now need to define a p-dimensional kernel function. A popular choice is to define the p-dimensional kernel as a product of one-dimensional kernels, each with its own bandwidth, which keeps the number of parameters (the bandwidths $h_1, \ldots, h_p$ for each dimension) linear in the number of dimensions. A less obvious problem is the fact that in high dimensions it is natural for points to be farther away from each other than we might expect intuitively (the "curse of dimensionality" again). In fact, if we want to keep our approximation error constant as p increases, the number of data points we need grows exponentially with p. (Recall the example in chapter 6 where we would need 842,000 data points to get a reliable estimate of the density value at the mean of a 10-dimensional Normal distribution.) This is rather unfortunate and means in practice that kernel models are really practical only for relatively low-dimensional problems.

Kernel methods are often complex to implement for large data sets. Unless the kernel function $K(t)$ has compact support (that is, unless it is zero outside some finite range on t) then calculating the kernel estimate $f(x)$ at some point x potentially involves summing over contributions from all n data points in the database. In practice of course since most of these contributions will be negligible (that is, will be in the tails of the kernel) there are various ways to speed up this calculation. Nonetheless, this "memory-based" representation can be a relatively complex one to store and compute with (it can be $O(n)$ to compute the density at just one query data point).

9.2.7 Joint Distributions for Categorical Data

In chapter 6 we discussed the problem of constructing joint distributions for multivariate categorical data. Say we have p variables each taking m values. The joint distribution requires the specification of $O(m^p)$ different probabilities. This exponential growth is problematic for a number of reasons.

First there is the problem of how to estimate such a large number of probabilities. As an example, let $\{p_1, \ldots, p_{m^p}\}$ represent a list of all the joint probability terms in the unknown distribution we are trying to estimate from a data set with n p-dimensional observations. Hence, we can think of m^p different "cells," $\{c_1, \ldots, c_{m^p}\}$ each containing n_i observations, $1 \leq i \leq m^p$. The expected number of data points in cell i, given a random sample from $p(\mathbf{x})$ of size n, can be written as $E_{p(\mathbf{x})}[n_i] = np_i$. Assuming (for example) that $p(\mathbf{x})$ is approximately uniform (that is, $p_i \approx 1/m^p$) we get that

$$E_{p(\mathbf{x})}[n_i] \approx \frac{n}{m^p}. \tag{9.10}$$

Thus, for example, if $n < 0.5m^p$, the expected number of data points falling in any given cell is closer to 0 than to 1. Furthermore, if we use straightforward frequency counts (the maximum likelihood estimate—see chapter 4) as our method for estimating probabilities, we will estimate $\hat{p}_i = 0$ for each empty cell, whether or not $p_i = 0$ in truth. Note that if $p(\mathbf{x})$ is nonuniform the problem is actually worse since there will be more cells with smaller p_i (that is, less chance of any data falling in them). The fundamental problem here is the m^p exponential growth in the number of cells. With $p = 20$ binary variables ($m = 2$) we get $m^p \approx 10^6$. By doubling the number of variables to $p = 40$ we now get $m^p \approx 10^{12}$. Say that we had n data points for the case of $p = 20$ and that we wanted to add some new variables to the analysis while still keeping the expected number of data points per cell to be constant (that is, the same as it was with n data points). If we added extra 20 variables to the problem we would need to increase the data set from n to $n' = 10^6 n$, an increase by a factor of a million.

A second practical problem is that even if we can reliably estimate a full joint distribution from data, it is exponential in both space and time to work with directly. A full joint distribution will have a $O(m^p)$ memory requirement; for example, $O(10^{12})$ real-valued probabilities would need to be stored for a full distribution on 40 binary variables. Furthermore, many computations using this distribution will also scale exponentially. Let the variables be $\{X_1, \ldots, X_p\}$, each taking m values. If we wanted to determine the marginal distribution on any single variable X_j (say), we could calculate it as

$$p(x_j) = \sum_{X_1, \ldots, X_{j-1}, X_{j+1}, \ldots, X_p} p(X_1, \ldots, X_{j-1}, x_j, X_{j+1} \ldots, X_p), \tag{9.11}$$

that is, by summing over all the other variables in the distribution. The sum on the right involves $O(m^{p-1})$ summations—for example, $O(10^{39})$ summations when $p = 40$ and $m = 2$. Clearly this sort of exercise is intractable except for relatively small values of m and p.

The practical consequence is that we can only reliably estimate and work with *full* joint distributions for relatively low-dimensional problems. Although our examples were for categorical data, essentially the same problems also arise of course for ordered or real-valued data.

As we have seen in chapter 6, one of the key ideas for addressing this curse of dimensionality is to impose *structure* on the underlying distribution $p(\mathbf{x})$—for example, by *assuming* independence:

$$p(\mathbf{x}) = p(x_1, \ldots, x_p) = \prod_{j=1}^{p} p_j(x_j). \qquad (9.12)$$

Instead of requiring $O(m^p)$ separate probabilities here we now only need p "marginal" distributions $p_1(x_1), \ldots, p_p(x_p)$, each of which can be specified by m numbers, for a total of mp probabilities. Of course, as discussed earlier, the independence assumption is just that, an *assumption,* and typically it is far too strong an assumption for most real-world data mining problems.

As described earlier in chapter 6, a somewhat weaker assumption is to presume that there exists a hidden ("latent") variable C, taking K values, and that the measurements $\mathbf{x}$ are *conditionally independent* given C. This is equivalent to the mixture distributions discussed earlier, with an additional assumption of conditional independence within each component; that is,

$$p(\mathbf{x}) = \sum_{k=1}^{K} \pi_k p_k(\mathbf{x}) = \sum_{k-1}^{K} \pi_k \left(\prod_{j=1}^{p} p_{k,j}(x_j) \right). \qquad (9.13)$$

This model requires mp probabilities per component, times K components, in addition to the K component weights $\pi_1, \ldots, \pi_K$. Thus, it scales linearly in K, m, and p, rather than exponentially. The EM algorithm can again be used to estimate the parameters for each component $p_k(\mathbf{x})$ (and the weights π_k), where the conditional independence assumption is enforced during estimation. One way to think about this "mixture of independence models" is that we are trying to find K different groups in the data such that for each group the variables are at least approximately conditionally independent. In fact, given a fixed K value, EM will try to find K component distributions (each of conditional independence form) that maximize the overall likelihood of the data. This model can be quite useful for modeling large sparse transactional data sets or sets of text documents represented as binary vectors. Finding a suitable value of K depends on our goal: from a descriptive viewpoint we can vary K in accordance with how complex we wish our fitted model to be. Note also that this form of model is equivalent to the first-order "naive"

Bayes model discussed in chapter 6 (and again in chapter 10 in the context of classification), whereas here the class variable C is unobserved and must be learned from the data. We will see later in this chapter that this also forms a useful basis for clustering the data, where we interpret each component $p_k(\mathbf{x})$ as a cluster.

A somewhat different way to structure a probability distribution parsimoniously is to model conditional independence in a general manner. We have described one such general framework (known as *belief networks*, or equivalently, *acyclic directed graphical models*) back in chapter 6. Recall that the basic equation for such models can be written as

$$p(\mathbf{x}) = \prod_{j=1}^{p} p_j(x_j | pa(x_j)), \qquad (9.14)$$

which is a *factorization* of the overall joint distribution function into a product of conditional distributions. In fact, such a factorization can always be defined by the chain rule, but this model gains its power when the dependencies can be assumed to be relatively sparse. Recall that the graphical formalism associates each variable X_j with a single node in a graph. A directed edge from X_i to X_j indicates that X_j depends directly on X_i. $pa(x_j)$ indicates values taken from the *parent set* $pa(X_j)$ of variables for variable X_j. The connectivity structure of a graph implies a set of conditional independence relationships for $p(\mathbf{x})$. These independence relationships can be summarized by the fact that, given the values of the parents of X_j, $pa(X_j)$, a node X_j is independent of all other variables in the graph that are non-descendants of X_j.

If the sizes of the parent sets in the graph are relatively small compared to p, then we will have a much simpler representation for the joint distribution (compared to the full model). In this context, the independence model corresponds to a graph with no edges at all, and the complete graph corresponds to the full joint distribution with no independence structure being assumed. Another well-known graph structure is the Markov chain model, in which the variables are ordered in some manner (for example, temporally) and each variable X_j depends only on X_{j-1}. Here each variable is linked to just two others, so that the overall graph is a single line of connected nodes (see figure 6.7 in chapter 6).

A primary attraction of the graphical formalism is that it provides a systematic and mathematically precise language for describing and communicating the structure of independence relationships in probability distributions.

Perhaps more importantly it also provides a systematic framework for *computational methods* in handling probability calculations with the associated joint distribution. For example, if the underlying graph is singly-connected (that is, when directionality of the edges is ignored the graph has no loops), one can show that the time to compute any marginal or conditional probability of interest is upper bounded by pm^{d+1}, where p is the number of variables, m is the number of values for each variable (assumed the same for all variables for simplicity), and d is the number of variables in the largest parent set in the graph. For example, for a Markov chain model we have $d = 1$ leading to the well-known $O(pm^2)$ complexity for such models. For graphs that have loops, there is an equivalent complexity bound of $pm^{d'+1}$, where d' is the size of the largest parent set in an equivalent singly connected graph (obtained from the original graph in a systematic manner).

From a data mining perspective there are two aspects to learning graphical models from data: learning the parameters given a fixed graphical structure, and the more difficult problem of learning parameters and structure together. Note that in the categorical case the parameters of the model are simply the conditional probability tables for each variable, $p(x_j|pa(X_j)), 1 \leq j \leq p$.

Given a fixed structure, there is no need to perform structure-search, and the simple maximum likelihood or MAP score functions work fine. If there are no hidden variables, the problem of learning reduces to estimating the conditional probability tables for each variable X_j given its parents $pa(X_j)$: in either the maximum likelihood or MAP case this reduces to simple counting (see chapter 4). With hidden variables, and assuming that the connectivity of these hidden variables in the graph is known, the EM algorithm (chapter 8) is again directly applicable under fairly broad conditions. The estimation of the conditional probability tables is now iterative (rather than closed-form as in the nonhidden case), and as usual care must be taken with initial conditions and detection of convergence. The mixture models discussed earlier can be viewed as graphical models with a single hidden variable. Hidden Markov models (as used in speech) can be viewed as graphical models with a discrete hidden time-dependent variable that is assumed to be Markov.

It is worth emphasizing that if we have strong prior belief that a particular graphical model structure is appropriate for our data mining problem, then it is usually worth taking advantage of this knowledge (assuming it is reliable) either as a fixed model or as a starting point for the structure learning methods described below.

Learning the structure of a directed graphical model from data has been a topic of research interest recently, and there now exist numerous algorithms for this purpose. Consider, first, the problem of learning structure with no hidden variables. The score function is typically some form of penalized likelihood: the BIC score function (see section 9.2.2), for example, is fairly widely used because it is easy to compute. Given a score function, the problem reduces to searching in graph space for the graph structure (with estimated parameters) that produces the maximum score. The general problem of finding the maximum score has been shown to be NP-hard (as seems to be the case with most nontrivial structure-finding problems in data mining). Thus, iterative local search methods are used: starting with some "prior" structure such as the empty graph and then adding and deleting edges until no further local improvement in the score function is possible. One useful feature from a computational viewpoint is that because the distribution can be expressed in *factored form* (equation 9.14), the likelihood and penalty terms can also be factored into expressions that are local in terms of the graph structure—for example, terms that only involve X_j and its parents. Thus, we can calculate the effect of local changes to the model (such as adding or deleting an edge) with local computations (since the impact of the change affects only one factor in the score function).

Learning structure with hidden variables is still considered to be something of a research problem. Clearly it is more difficult than learning structure with no hidden variables (which is itself NP-hard). The EM algorithm is again applicable, but the search problem is typically quite complex since there are so many different ways that one can introduce hidden variables into a multivariate model.

The family of *log-linear models* is a further generalization of acyclic directed graphical models, which characterize dependence relations in a more general form. Discussion of this class of models is beyond the scope of this text (references are provided in the section on further reading). Markov random fields are another class of graphical models, where an *undirected* graph is used to represent dependence, e.g., to represent correlational effects between pixels in an image. These random field models have seen wide application in image analysis and spatial statistics, where they are used to define a joint distribution over measurements on a grid or image.

9.3 Background on Cluster Analysis

We now move beyond probability density and distribution models to focus on the related descriptive data mining task of *cluster analysis*—that is, decomposing or partitioning a (usually multivariate) data set into groups so that the points in one group are similar to each other and are as different as possible from the points in other groups. Although the same techniques may often be applied, we should distinguish between two different objectives. In one, which we might call *segmentation* or *dissection,* the aim is simply to partition the data in a way that is convenient. "Convenient" here might refer to administrative convenience, practical convenience, or any other kind. For example, a manufacturer of shirts might want to choose just a few sizes and shapes so as to maximize coverage of the male population. He or she will have to choose those sizes in terms of collar size, chest size, arm length, and so on, so that no man has a shape too different from that of a well-fitting shirt. To do this, he or she will partition the population of men into a few groups in terms of the variables collar, chest, and arm length. Shirts of one size will then be made for each group.

In contrast to this, we might want to see whether a sample of data is composed of natural subclasses. For example, whiskies can be characterized in terms of color, nose, body, palate, and finish, and we might want to see whether they fall into distinct classes in terms of these variables. Here we are not partitioning the data for practical convenience, but rather are hoping to discover something about the nature of the sample or the population from which it arose—to discover whether the overall population is, in fact, heterogeneous.

Technically, this second exercise is what *cluster analysis* seeks to do—to see whether the data fall into distinct groups, with members within each group being similar to other members in that group but different from members of other groups. However, the term "cluster analysis" is often used in general to describe both segmentation and cluster analysis problems (and we shall also be a little lax in this regard). In each case the aim is to split the data into classes, so perhaps this is not too serious a misuse. It is resolved, as we shall see below, by the fact that there is a huge number of different algorithms for partitioning data in this way. The important thing is to match our method with our objective. This way, mistakes will not arise, whatever we call the activity.

Example 9.2 Owners of credit cards can be split into subgroups according to how they use their card—what kind of purchases they make, how much money they spend, how often they use the card, where they use the card, and so on. It can be very useful for marketing purposes to identify the group to which a card owner belongs, since he or she can then be targeted with promotional material that might be of interest (this clearly benefits the owner of the card, as well as the card company). Market segmentation in general is, in fact, a heavy user of the kinds of techniques discussed in this section. The segmentation may be in terms of lifestyle, past purchasing behavior, demographic characteristics, or other features.

A chain store might want to study whether outlets that are similar, in terms of social neighborhood, size, staff numbers, vicinity to other shops, and so on, have similar turnovers and yield similar profits. A starting point here would be to partition the outlets, in terms of these variables, and then to examine the distributions of turnover within each group.

Cluster analysis has been heavily used in some areas of medicine, such as psychiatry, to try to identify whether there are different subtypes of diseases lumped together under a single diagnosis.

Cluster analysis methods are used in biology to see whether superficially identical plants or creatures in fact belong to different species. Likewise, geographical locations can be split into subgroups on the basis of the species of plants or animals that live there.

As an example of where the difference between dissection and clustering analysis might matter, consider partitioning the houses in a town. If we are organizing a delivery service, we might want to split them in terms of their geographical location. We would want to dissect the population of houses so that those within each group are as close as possible to each other. Delivery vans could then be packed with packages to go to just one group. On the other hand, a company marketing home improvement products might want to split the houses into naturally occurring groups of similar houses. One group might consist of small starter homes, another of three-and four-bedroom family homes, and another (presumably smaller) of executive mansions.

It will be obvious from this that such methods (cluster and dissection techniques) hinge on the notion of *distance*. In order to decide whether a set of points can be split into subgroups, with members of a group being closer to other members of their group than to members of other groups, we need to say what we mean by "closer to." The notion of "distance," and different measures of it, has already been discussed in chapter 2. Any of the measures described there, or indeed any other distance measure, can be used as the basis for a cluster or dissection analysis. As far as these techniques are concerned, the concept of distance is more fundamental than the coordinates of the points. In principle, to carry out a cluster analysis all we need to know is the set of interpoint distances, and not the values on any variables. However, some methods make use of "central points" of clusters, and so require that the raw coordinates be available.

Cluster analysis has been the focus of a huge amount of research effort, going back for several decades, so that the literature is now vast. It is also scattered. Considerable portions of it exist in the statistical and machine learning literatures, but other many other publications on cluster analysis may be found elsewhere. One of the problems is that new methods are constantly being developed, sometimes without an awareness of what has already been developed. More seriously, a proper understanding of their properties and the way they behave with different kinds of data is available for very few of the methods. One of the reasons for this is that it is difficult to tell whether a cluster analysis has been successful. Contrast this with predictive modeling, in which we can take a test data set and see how accurately the value of the target variable is predicted in this set. For a clustering problem, unfortunately, there is no direct notion of *generalization* to a test data set, although, as we will see in our discussion of probabilistic clustering (later in this chapter), it is possible in some situations to pose the question of whether or not the cluster structure discovered in the training data is genuinely present in the underlying population. Generally speaking, however, the validity of a clustering is often in the eye of the beholder; for example, if a cluster produces an interesting scientific insight, we can judge it to be useful. Quantifying this precisely is difficult, if not impossible, since the interpretation of how interesting a clustering is will inevitably be application-dependent and subjective to some degree.

As we shall see in the next few sections, different methods of cluster analysis are effective at detecting different *kinds* of clusters, and we should consider this when we choose a particular algorithm. That is, we should consider what we mean or intend to mean by a "cluster." In effect, different clustering algorithms will be biased toward finding different types of cluster structures (or "shapes") in the data, and it is not always easy to ascertain precisely what this bias is from the description of the clustering algorithm.

To illustrate, we might take a "cluster" as being a collection of points such that the maximum distance between all pairs of points in the cluster is as small as possible. Then each point will be similar to each other point in the cluster. An algorithm will be chosen that seeks to partition the data so as to minimize this maximum interpoint distance (more on this below). We would clearly expect such a method to produce compact, roughly spherical, clusters. On the other hand, we might take a "cluster" as being a collection of points such that each point is as close as possible to some other member of the cluster—although not necessarily to all other members. Clusters discovered by this approach need not be compact or roughly spherical, but could have long (and not necessarily straight) sausage shapes. The first approach would simply fail to pick up such clusters. The first approach would be appropriate in a segmentation situation, while the second would be appropriate if the objects within each hypothesized group were measured at different stages of some evolutionary process. For example, in a cluster analysis of people suffering from some illness, to see whether there were different subtypes, we might want to allow for the possibility that the patients had been measured at different stages of the disease, so that they had different symptom patterns even though they belonged to the same subtype.

The important lesson to be learned from this is that we must match the method to the objectives. In particular, we must adopt a cluster analytic tool that is effective at detecting clusters that conform to the definition of what is meant by "cluster" in the problem at hand. It is perhaps worth adding that we should not be too rigid about it. Data mining, after all, is about discovering the *unexpected,* so we must not be too determined in imposing our preconceptions on the analysis. Perhaps a search for a different kind of cluster structure will throw up things we have not previously thought of.

Broadly speaking, we can identify three different general types of cluster analysis algorithms: those based on an attempt to find the optimal partition into a specified number of clusters, those based on a hierarchical attempt to discover cluster structure, and those based on a probabilistic model for the underlying clusters. We discuss each of these in turn in the next three sections.

9.4   Partition-Based Clustering Algorithms

In chapter 5 we described how data mining algorithms can often be conveniently thought of in five parts: the *task,* the *model,* the *score function,* the *search* method, and the *data management* technique. In partition-based clustering the *task* is to partition a data set into k disjoint sets of points such that the points within each set are as homogeneous as possible, that is, given the set of n data points $D = \{\mathbf{x}(1), \ldots, \mathbf{x}(n)\}$, our task is to find K clusters $\mathcal{C} = \{C_1, \ldots, C_K\}$ such that each data point $\mathbf{x}(i)$ is assigned to a unique cluster C_k.

Homogeneity is captured by an appropriate *score function* (as discussed below), such as minimizing the distance between each point and the centroid of the cluster to which it is assigned. Partition-based clustering typically places more emphasis on the score function than on any formal notion of a model. Often the *centroid* or *average* of the points belonging to a cluster is considered to be a representative point for that cluster, and there is no explicit statement of what sort of shape of cluster is being sought. For cluster representations based on the notion of a single "center" for each cluster, however, the boundaries between clusters will be implicitly defined. For example, if a point **x** is assigned to a cluster according to which cluster center is closest in a Euclidean-distance sense, then we will get linear boundaries between the clusters in **x** space.

We will see that maximizing (or minimizing) the score function is typically a computationally intractable *search* problem, and thus, iterative improvement heuristic search methods, such as those described in chapter 8, are often used to optimize the score function given a data set.

9.4.1 Score Functions for Partition-Based Clustering

A large number of different score functions can be used to measure the quality of clustering and a wide range of algorithms has been developed to search for an optimal (or at least a good) partition.

In order to define the clustering score function we need to have a notion of distance between input points. Denote by $d(\mathbf{x}, \mathbf{y})$ the distance between points $\mathbf{x}, \mathbf{y} \in D$, and assume for simplicity that the function d defines a metric on D. Most score functions for clustering stress two aspects: clusters should be compact, and clusters should be as far from each other as possible. A straightforward formulation of these intuitive notions is to look at *within cluster variation* $wc(\mathcal{C})$ and *between cluster variation* $bc(\mathcal{C})$ of a clustering $\mathcal{C}$. The within cluster variation measures how compact or tight the clusters are, while the between cluster variation looks at the distances between different clusters.

Suppose that we have selected *cluster centers* $\mathbf{r}_k$ from each cluster. This can be a designated representative data point $\mathbf{x}(i) \in C_k$ that is defined to be "central" in some manner. If the input points belong to a space where taking means makes sense, we can use the centroid of the points in the cluster C_k as the cluster center, where $\mathbf{r}_k$ will then be defined as

$$\mathbf{r}_k = \frac{1}{n_k} \sum_{\mathbf{x} \in C_k} \mathbf{x}, \tag{9.15}$$

with n_k the number of points in the kth cluster. A simple measure of *within-cluster variation* is to look at the sum of squares of distances from each point to the center of the cluster it belongs to:

$$wc(\mathcal{C}) = \sum_{k=1}^{K} wc(C_k) = \sum_{k=1}^{K} \sum_{\mathbf{x}(i) \in C_k} d\left(\mathbf{x}, \mathbf{r}_k\right)^2 . \tag{9.16}$$

For the case in which $d(\mathbf{x}, \mathbf{r}_k)$ is defined as Euclidean distance, $wc(\mathcal{C})$ is referred to as the *within-cluster sum-of-squares*.

Between-cluster variation can be measured by the distance between cluster centers:

$$bc(\mathcal{C}) = \sum_{1 \le j < k \le K} d\left(\mathbf{r}_j, \mathbf{r}_k\right)^2 . \tag{9.17}$$

The overall quality (or score function) of a clustering $\mathcal{C}$ can then be defined as a monotone combination of the factors $wc(\mathcal{C})$ and $bc(\mathcal{C})$, such as the ratio $bc(\mathcal{C})/wc(\mathcal{C})$.

The within cluster measure above is in a sense global: for the cluster C_k to make a small contribution to it, all points of C_k have to be relatively close to the cluster center. Thus the use of this measure of cluster tightness leads to spherical clusters. The well-known K-means algorithm, discussed in the next section, uses the means within each group as cluster centers and Euclidean distance for d to search for the clustering $\mathcal{C}$ that minimizes the within cluster variation of equation 9.16, for measurements $\mathbf{x}$ in a Euclidean space $\mathcal{R}^p$.

If we are given a candidate clustering, how difficult is it to evaluate $wc(\mathcal{C})$ and $bc(\mathcal{C})$? Computing $wc(\mathcal{C})$ takes $O(\sum_i |C_i|) = O(n)$ operations, while $bc(\mathcal{C})$ can be computed in $O(k^2)$ operations. Thus computing a score function for a single clustering requires (at least in principle) a pass through the whole data.

A different notion of within cluster variation is to consider for each point in the cluster the distance to the nearest point in the same cluster, and take the maximum of these distances:

$$wc(C_k) = \max_i \min_{\mathbf{y}(j) \in C_k} \{d\left(\mathbf{x}(i), \mathbf{y}(j)\right) \mid x(i) \in C_k, x \neq y\}. \tag{9.18}$$

This *minimum distance* or *single-link* criterion for cluster distance leads to elongated clusters. We will return to this score function in the context of hierarchical agglomerative clustering algorithms in section 9.5.

We can use the notion of covariance to develop more general score functions for clusterings $\mathcal{C}$ in a Euclidean space. For points within a particular cluster C_k, we can define a $p \times p$ matrix

$$\mathbf{W}_k = \sum_{\mathbf{x} \in C_k} (\mathbf{x} - \mathbf{r}_k)(\mathbf{x} - \mathbf{r}_k)^T \tag{9.19}$$

that is an (unnormalized) *covariance matrix* for the points in cluster C_k. The within-cluster sum-of-squares for a particular cluster is then the trace (sum of diagonal elements) of this matrix, $tr(\mathbf{W}_k)$, and thus the total within-cluster sum-of-squares of equation 9.16 can be expressed as

$$wc(\mathcal{C}) = \sum_k tr(\mathbf{W}_k). \tag{9.20}$$

In this context, letting $\mathbf{W} = \sum_k \mathbf{W}_k$, we can see that a score function that tries to make $\mathbf{W}$ "smaller" (for example, minimize the trace or the determinant of $\mathbf{W}$) will tend to encourage a more compact clustering of the data.

We can define a matrix $\mathbf{B}$ that summarizes the squared differences between the cluster centers as

$$\mathbf{B} = \sum_{k=1}^{c} n_k (\mathbf{r}_k - \hat{\mu})(\mathbf{r}_k - \hat{\mu})^T, \tag{9.21}$$

where $\hat{\mu}$ is the estimated global mean of all data points in D. This is a $p \times p$ matrix that characterizes the covariance of the cluster means (weighted by n_k) with respect to each other. For example, $tr(\mathbf{B})$ is the weighted sum of squared distances of the cluster means relative to the estimated global mean of the data. Thus, having a score function that emphasizes a "larger" $\mathbf{B}$ will tend to encourage the cluster means to be more separated.

We stress again the important, but often overlooked, point that the nature of the score function has a very important influence on what types of clusters will be found in the data. Different score functions (for example, different combinations of $\mathbf{W}$ and $\mathbf{B}$) can express significantly different preferences in terms of cluster structure.

Traditional score functions based on $\mathbf{W}$ and $\mathbf{B}$ are $tr(\mathbf{W})$, the trace of $\mathbf{W}$, the determinant $|\mathbf{W}|$ of $\mathbf{W}$, and $tr(\mathbf{BW}^{-1})$. A disadvantage of $tr(\mathbf{W})$ is that it depends on the scaling adopted for the separate variables. Alter the units of one of them and a different cluster structure may result. Of course, this can be overcome by standardizing the variables prior to analysis, but this is often just as arbitrary as any other choice. The $tr(\mathbf{W})$ criterion tends to yield compact spherical clusters, and it also has a tendency to produce roughly equal groups. Both of these properties may make this score function useful in a segmentation context, but they are less attractive for discovering natural clusters (for example, in astronomy the discovery of a distinct very small cluster may represent a major advance).

The $|\ \mathbf{W}\ |$ score function does not have the same scale dependence as $tr(\mathbf{W})$, so it also detects elliptic structures as clusters, but it also favors equal-sized clusters. Adjustments that take cluster size into account have been suggested (for example, dividing by $\prod n_k^{2n_k}$), so that the equal-sized cluster tendency is counteracted, but it might be better to go for a different criterion altogether than adjust an imperfect one. Note also that the original score function, $|\ \mathbf{W}\ |$, has optimality properties if the data are thought to arise from a mixture of multivariate normal distributions, and this is sacrificed by the modification. (Of course, if our data are thought to be generated in that way, we might contemplate fitting a formal mixture model, as outlined in section 9.2.4.)

The $tr(\mathbf{B}\mathbf{W}^{-1})$ score function also has a tendency to yield equal-sized clusters, and this time of roughly equal shape. Note that since this score function is equivalent to summing the eigenvalues of $\mathbf{B}\mathbf{W}^{-1}$ it will place most emphasis on the largest eigenvalue and hence will tend to yield collinear clusters.

The property that the clusters obtained from using these score functions tend to have similar shape is not attractive in all situations (indeed, it is probably rarely attractive). Score functions based on other ways of combining the separate within-cluster matrices $\mathbf{W}_k$ can relax this—for example, $\prod |\ \mathbf{W}_k\ |^{n_k}$ and $\prod |\ \mathbf{W}_k\ |^{1/p}$, where p is the number of variables. Even these score functions, however, have a tendency to favor similarly-sized clusters. (A modification to the $\prod |\ \mathbf{W}_k\ |^{n_k}$ score functions, analogous to that of the $|\ \mathbf{W}\ |$ score function, that can help to overcome this property, is to divide each $|\ \mathbf{W}_k\ |$ by $\prod n_k^{2n_k}$. This is equivalent to letting the distance vary between different clusters.)

A variant of these methods uses the sum of squared distances not from the cluster means, but from particular members of the cluster. The search (see below) then includes a search over cluster members to find the one that minimizes the score function. In general, of course, measures other than the sum of squared distances from the cluster "center" can be used. In particular, the influence of the outlying points of a cluster can be reduced by replacing the sum of squared distances by robust estimates of distance. The L_1 norm has also been proposed as a measure of distance. Typically this will be used with the vector of medians as the cluster "center."

Methods based on minimizing a within cluster matrix of sums of squares can be regarded as minimizing deviations from the centroids of the groups. A technique known as *maximal predictive classification* (developed for use with binary variables in taxonomy but more widely applicable) can also be regarded as minimizing deviations from group "centers," though with a different definition of centers. Suppose that each component of the measurement vector is binary—that is, each object has given rise to a binary vector—and suppose we have a proposed grouping into clusters. For each group we can define a binary vector that consists of the most common value, within the group, of each variable. This vector of modes (instead of means) will serve as the "center" of the group. Distance of a group member from this center is then measured in terms of the number of variables that have values that differ from those in this central vector. The score function optimized is then the total number of differences between the objects and the centers of the groups they belong to. The "best" grouping is the one that minimizes the overall number of such differences.

Hierarchical methods of cluster analysis, described in the next section, do not construct a single partition of the data, but rather construct a hierarchy of (typically) nested clusters. We can then decide where to cut the hierarchy so as to partition the data in such a way as to obtain the most convincing partition. For partition-based methods, however, it is necessary to decide at the start how many clusters we want. Of course, we can rerun the analysis several times, with different numbers of clusters, but this still requires us to be able to choose between competing numbers. There is no "best" solution to this problem. We can, of course, examine how the clustering score function changes as we increase the number of clusters, but this may not be comparable across different numbers; for example, perhaps the score shows apparent improvement as the number increases, regardless of whether there is really a better cluster structure (for example, the sum of within cluster squared distances is guaranteed to not increase with K). For a multivariate uniform distribution divided optimally into K clusters, the score function $K^2 \mid \mathbf{W} \mid$ asymptotically takes the same value for all K; results such as this can be used as the basis for comparing partitions with different K values.

It is apparent that cluster analysis is very much a data-driven tool, with relatively little formal model-building underlying it. However, some researchers have attempted to put it on a sounder model-based footing. For example, we can supplement the procedures by assuming that there is also a random process generating sparsely distributed points uniformly across the whole space, in addition to whatever mechanism generates clusters of points.

This makes the methods less susceptible to outliers. A further assumption is to model the distribution of the data parametrically within each cluster using specific distributional assumptions—we will return to this in our discussion of probabilistic model-based clustering in section 9.6.

9.4.2 Basic Algorithms for Partition-Based Clustering

We saw in the previous section that a large variety of score functions can be used to determine the quality of clustering. Now what about the algorithms to optimize those score functions? In principle, at least, the problem is straightforward. We simply search through the space of possible assignments $\mathcal{C}$ of points to clusters to find the one that minimizes the score (or maximizes it, depending on the chosen score function).

The nature of the search problem can be thought of as a form of combinatorial optimization, since we are searching for the allocation of n objects into K classes that maximizes (or minimizes) our chosen score function. The number of possible allocations (different clusterings of the data) is approximately K^n. For example, there are some $2^{100} \approx 10^{10}$ possible allocations of 100 objects into two classes. Thus, as we have seen with other data mining problems, direct exhaustive search methods are certainly not applicable unless we are dealing with tiny data sets. Nonetheless, for some clustering score functions, methods have been developed that permit exhaustive coverage of all possible clusterings without actually carrying out an exhaustive search. These include branch and bound methods, which eliminate potential clusterings on the grounds that they have poorer scores than alternatives already found, without actually evaluating the scores for the potential clusterings. Such methods, while extending the range over which exhaustive evaluation can be made, still break down for even moderately-sized data sets. For this reason, we do not examine them further here.

Unfortunately, neither do there exist closed-form solutions for any score function of interest; that is, there is usually no direct method for finding a specific clustering $\mathcal{C}$ that optimizes the score function. Thus, since closed form solutions do not exist and exhaustive search is infeasible, we must resort to some form of systematic *search* of the space of possible clusters (such search methods were discussed in chapter 8). It is important to emphasize that given a particular score function, the problem of clustering has been reduced to an optimization problem, and thus there are a large variety of choices available in the optimization literature that are potentially applicable.

Iterative-improvement algorithms based on local search are particularly popular for cluster analysis. The general idea is to start with a randomly chosen clustering of the points, then to reassign points so as to give the greatest increase (or decrease) in the score function, then to recalculate the updated cluster centers, to reassign points again, and so forth until there is no change in the score function or in the cluster memberships. This greedy approach has the virtue of being simple and guaranteeing at least a local maximum (minimum) of the score function. Of course it suffers the usual drawback of greedy search algorithms in that we do not know how good the clustering $\mathcal{C}$ that it converges to is relative to the best possible clustering of the data (the global optimum for the score function being used).

Here we describe one well known example of this general approach, namely, the K-means algorithm (which has close connection to the EM algorithm discussed in chapter 8 and was mentioned in section 9.2.4). The number K of clusters is fixed before the algorithm is run (this is typical of many clustering algorithms). There are several variants of the K-means algorithm. The basic version begins by randomly picking K cluster centers, assigning each point to the cluster whose mean is closest in a Euclidean distance sense, then computing the mean vectors of the points assigned to each cluster, and using these as new centers in an iterative approach. As an algorithm, the method is as follows: assuming we have n data points $D = \{\mathbf{x}_1, \ldots, \mathbf{x}_n\}$, our task is to find K clusters $\{C_1 \ldots, C_K\}$:

> **for** $k = 1, \ldots, K$ let $\mathbf{r}(k)$ be a randomly chosen point from D;
> **while** changes in clusters C_k happen **do**
>   form clusters:
>   **for** $k = 1, \ldots, K$ **do**
> $C_k = \{\mathbf{x} \in D \mid d(\mathbf{r}_k, \mathbf{x}) \leq d(\mathbf{r}_j, \mathbf{x})$ for all $j = 1, \ldots, K, j \neq k\}$;
>   **end**;
>   compute new cluster centers:
>   **for** $k = 1, \ldots, K$ **do**
> $\mathbf{r}_k$ = the vector mean of the points in C_k
>   **end**;
> **end**;

Example 9.3 Electromechanical control systems for large 34m and 70m antennas are an important component in NASA's Deep Space Network for tracking and communicating with deep-space spacecraft. The motor-currents of the an-

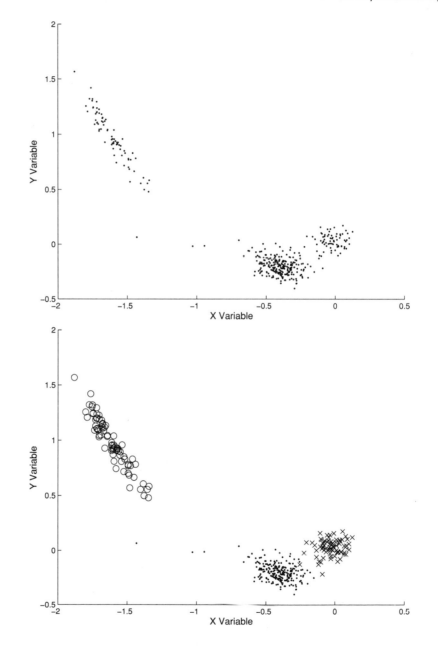

Figure 9.4   Antenna data. On top the data points are shown without class labels, and on the bottom different symbols are used for the three known classes (dots are normal, circles are tachometer noise, and x's are short circuit.)

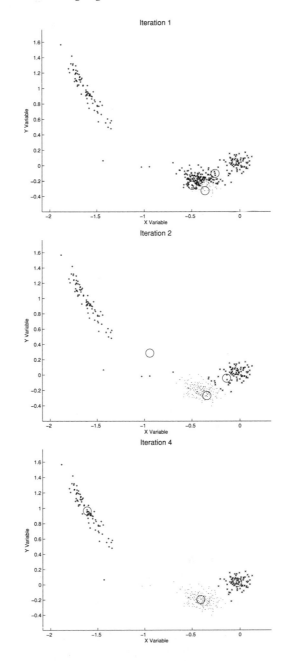

Figure 9.5   Example of running the K-means algorithm on the two-dimensional antenna data. The plots show the locations of the means of the clusters (large circles) at various iterations of the K-means algorithm, as well as the classification of the data points at each iteration according to the closest mean (dots, circles, and xs for each of the three clusters).

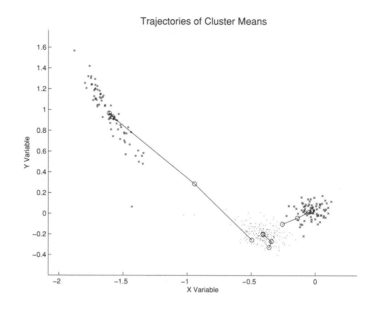

Figure 9.6 A summary of the trajectories of the three cluster means during the K-means iterations of figure 9.5.

tenna control systems are quite sensitive to subtle changes in operating behavior and can be used for online health monitoring and fault detection. Figure 9.4 shows sample data from a 34m Deep Space Network antenna. Each bivariate data point corresponds to a two-second window of motor-current measurements, that have been modeled by a simple autoregressive (linear) time-series model, and where the two dimensions correspond to the first two estimated coefficients of the autoregressive model for a particular window. The model is fit in real time to the data every two seconds, and changes in coefficients reflect changes in the spectral signature of the motor current measurements.

The data in the lower plot of figure 9.4 show which data points belong to which condition (three groups, one normal and two fault conditions). Figure 9.5 is an illustrative example of the results of applying the K-means algorithm to clustering this data, using $K = 3$, and having removed the class labels (that is, using the data in the upper plot of figure 9.4 as input to the K-means algorithm). All three initial starting points for the algorithm are located in the center (normal) cloud, but after only four iterations (figure 9.5) the algorithm quickly converges to a clustering (the trajectory of the cluster means are plotted in figure 9.6). The final clustering after the fourth iteration (lower plot of figure

9.5) produces three groups that very closely match the known grouping shown in figure 9.4. For this data the grouping is relatively obvious, of course, in that the various fault conditions can be seen to be separated from the normal cloud (particularly the tachometer noise condition on the left). Nonetheless it is reassuring to see that the K-means algorithm quickly and accurately converges to a clustering that is very close to the true groups.

The complexity of the K-means algorithm is $O(KnI)$, where I is the number of iterations. Namely, given the current cluster centers $\mathbf{r}_k$, we can in one pass through the data compute all the Kn distances $d(\mathbf{r}_k, \mathbf{x})$ and for each $\mathbf{x}$ select the minimal one; then computing the new cluster centers can also be done in time $O(n)$.

A variation of this algorithm is to examine each point in turn and update the cluster centers whenever a point is reassigned, repeatedly cycling through the points until the solution does not change. If the data set is very large, we can simply add in each data point, without the recycling. Further extensions (for example, the ISODATA algorithm) include splitting and/or merging clusters. Note that there are a large number of different partition-based clustering algorithms, many of which hinge around adding or removing one point at a time from a cluster. Efficient updating formula been developed in the context of evaluating the change incurred in a score function by moving one data point in or out of a cluster—in particular, for all of the score functions involving $\mathbf{W}$ discussed in the last section.

The search in the K-means algorithm is restricted to a small part of the space of possible partitions. It is possible that a good cluster solution will be missed due to the algorithm converging to a local rather than global minimum of the score function. One way to alleviate (if not solve) this problem is to carry out multiple searches from different randomly chosen starting points for the cluster centers. We can even take this further and adopt a simulated annealing strategy (as discussed in chapter 8) to try to avoid getting trapped in local minima of the score function.

Since cluster analysis is essentially a problem of searching over a huge space of potential solutions to find whatever optimizes a specified score function, it is no surprise that various kinds of mathematical programming methods have been applied to this problem. These include linear programming, dynamic programming, and linear and nonlinear integer programming.

Clustering methods are often applied on large data sets. If the number of observations is so large that standard algorithms are not tractable, we can try to compress the data set by replacing groups of objects by succinct representations. For example, if 100 observations are very close to each other in a metric space, we can replace them with a weighted observation located at the centroid of those observations and having an additional feature (the radius of the group of points that is represented). It is relatively straightforward to modify some of the clustering algorithms to operate on such "condensed" representations.

9.5   Hierarchical Clustering

Whereas partition-based methods of cluster analysis begin with a specified number of clusters and search through possible allocations of points to clusters to find an allocation that optimizes some clustering score function, hierarchical methods gradually merge points or divide superclusters. In fact, on this basis we can identify two distinct types of hierarchical methods: the *agglomerative* (which merge) and the *divisive* (which divide). The agglomerative are the more important and widely used of the two. Note that hierarchical methods can be viewed as a specific (and particularly straightforward) way to reduce the size of the search. They are analogous to stepwise methods used for model building in other parts of this book.

A notable feature of hierarchical clustering is that it is difficult to separate the model from the score function and the search method used to determine the best clustering. Because of this, in this section we will focus on clustering algorithms directly. We can consider the final hierarchy to be a model, as a hierarchical mapping of data points to clusters; however, the nature of this model (that is, the cluster "shape") is implicit in the algorithm rather than being explicitly represented. Similarly for the score function, there is no notion of an explicit global score function. Instead, various local scores are calculated for pairs of leaves in the tree (that is, pairs of clusters for a particular hierarchical clustering of the data) to determine which pair of clusters are the best candidates for agglomeration (merging) or dividing (splitting). Note that as with the global score functions used for partition-based clustering, different local score functions can lead to very different final clusterings of the data.

Hierarchical methods of cluster analysis permit a convenient graphical display, in which the entire sequence of merging (or splitting) of clusters is shown. Because of its tree-like nature, such a display is called a *dendrogram*. We illustrate in an example below.

Cluster analysis is particularly useful when there are more than two variables: if there are only two, then we can eyeball a scatterplot to look for

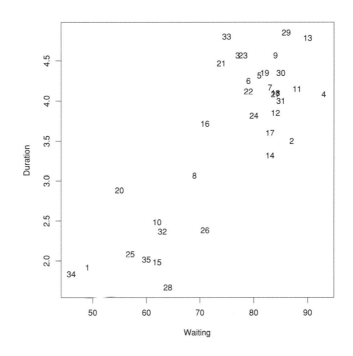

Figure 9.7   Duration of eruptions versus waiting time between eruptions (in minutes) for the Old Faithful geyser in Yellowstone Park.

structure. However, to illustrate the ideas on a data set where we can see what is going on, we will apply a hierarchical method to some two dimensional data. The data are extracted from a larger data set given in Azzalini and Bowman (1990). Figure 9.7 shows a scatterplot of the two-dimensional data. The vertical axis is the time between eruptions and the horizontal axis is the length of the following eruption, both measured in minutes. The points are given numbers in this plot merely so that we can relate them to the den-

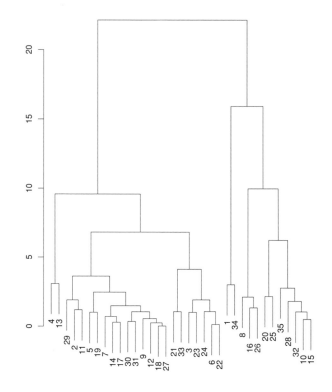

Figure 9.8   Dendrogram resulting from clustering of data in figure 9.7 using the criterion of merging clusters that leads to the smallest increase in the total sum of squared errors.

drogram in this exposition, and have no other substantive significance.

As an example, figure 9.8 shows the dendrogram that results from agglomerative merging the two clusters that leads to the smallest increase in within-cluster sum of squares. The height of the crossbars in the dendrogram (where branches merge) shows values of this score function. Thus, initially, the smallest increase is obtained by merging points 18 and 27, and from figure 9.7 we can see that these are indeed very close (in fact, the closest). Note that closeness from a visual perspective is distorted because of the fact that the x-scale is in fact compressed on the page relative to the y-scale. The next merger comes from merging points 6 and 22. After a few more mergers of individual pairs of neighboring points, point 12 is merged with the cluster consisting of the two points 18 and 27, this being the merger that leads to least increase in the clustering criterion. This procedure continues until the final merger, which is of two large clusters of points. This structure is evident from the dendrogram. (It need not always be like this. Sometimes the final merger is of a large cluster with one single outlying point—as we shall see below.) The hierarchical structure displayed in the dendrogram also makes it clear that we could terminate the process at other points. This would be equivalent to making a horizontal cut through the dendrogram at some other level, and would yield a different number of clusters.

9.5.1 Agglomerative Methods

Agglomerative methods are based on measures of distance between *clusters*. Essentially, given an initial clustering, they merge those two clusters that are nearest, to form a reduced number of clusters. This is repeated, each time merging the two closest clusters, until just one cluster, of all the data points, exists. Usually the starting point for the process is the initial clustering in which each cluster consists of a single data point, so that the procedure begins with the n points to be clustered.

Assume we are given n data points $D = \{\mathbf{x}(1), \ldots, \mathbf{x}(n)\}$, and a function $\mathcal{D}(C_i, C_j)$ for measuring the distance between two clusters C_i and C_j. Then an agglomerative algorithm for clustering can be described as follows:

> **for** $i = 1, \ldots, n$ let $C_i = \{\mathbf{x}(i)\}$;
> **while** there is more than one cluster left **do**
>   let C_i and C_j be the clusters
>   minimizing the distance $\mathcal{D}(C_k, C_h)$ between any two clusters;
> $C_i = C_i \cup C_j$;
>   remove cluster C_j;
> **end**;

What is the time complexity of this method? In the beginning there are n clusters, and in the end 1; thus there are n iterations of the main loop. In iteration i we have to find the closest pair of clusters among $n - i + 1$

clusters. We will see shortly that there are a variety of methods for defining the intercluster distance $\mathcal{D}(C_i, C_j)$. All of them, however, require in the first iteration that we locate the closest pair of objects. This takes $O(n^2)$ time, unless we have special knowledge about the distance between objects and so, in most cases, the algorithm requires $O(n^2)$ time, and frequently much more. Note also that the space complexity of the method is also $O(n^2)$, since all pairwise distances between objects must be available at the start of the algorithm. Thus, the method is typically not feasible for large values of n. Furthermore, interpreting a large dendrogram can be quite difficult (just as interpreting a large classification tree can be difficult).

Note that in agglomerative clustering we need distances between individual data objects to begin the clustering, and during clustering we need to be able to compute distances between groups of data points (that is, distances between clusters). Thus, one advantage of this approach (over partition-based clustering, for example) is the fact that we do not need to have a vector representation for each object as long as we can compute distances between objects or between sets of objects. Thus, for example, agglomerative clustering provides a natural framework for clustering objects that are not easily summarized as vector measurements. A good example would be clustering of protein sequences where there exist several well-defined notions of distance such as the *edit-distance* between two sequences (that is, a measure of how many basic edit operations are required to transform one sequence into another).

In terms of the general case of distances between sets of objects (that is, clusters) many measures of distance have been proposed. If the objects are vectors then any of the global score functions described in section 9.4 can be used, using the difference between the score before merger and that after merging two clusters.

However, local pairwise distance measures (that is, between pairs of clusters) are especially suited to hierarchical methods since they can be computed directly from pairwise distances of the members of each cluster. One of the earliest and most important of these is the *nearest neighbor* or *single link* method. This defines the distance between two clusters as the distance between the two closest points, one from each cluster;

$$\mathcal{D}_{sl}(C_i, C_j) = \min_{\mathbf{x}, \mathbf{y}}\{d(\mathbf{x}, \mathbf{y}) \mid \mathbf{x} \in C_i, \mathbf{y} \in C_j\},\qquad(9.22)$$

where $d(\mathbf{x}, \mathbf{y})$ is the distance between objects $\mathbf{x}$ and $\mathbf{y}$. The single link method is susceptible (which may be a good or bad thing, depending upon our objectives) to the phenomenon of "chaining," in which long strings of points are assigned to the same cluster (contrast this with the production of compact spherical clusters). This means that the single link method is of limited value for segmentation. It also means that the method is sensitive to small perturbations of the data and to outlying points (which, again, may be good or bad, depending upon what we are trying to do). The single link method also has the property (for which it is unique—no other measure of distance between clusters possesses it) that if two pairs of clusters are equidistant it does not matter which is merged first. The overall result will be the same, regardless of the order of merger.

The dendrogram from the single link method applied to the data in figure 9.7 is shown in figure 9.9. Although on this particular data set the results of single link clustering and that of figure 9.8 are quite similar, the two methods can in general produce quite different results.

At the other extreme from single link, *furthest neighbor,* or *complete link,* takes as the distance between two clusters the distance between the two most distant points, one from each cluster:

$$\mathcal{D}_{fl}(C_i, C_j) = \max_{\mathbf{x}, \mathbf{y}}\{d(\mathbf{x}, \mathbf{y}) \mid \mathbf{x} \in C_i, \mathbf{y} \in C_j\}, \tag{9.23}$$

where $d(\mathbf{x}, \mathbf{y})$ is again the distance between objects $\mathbf{x}$ and $\mathbf{y}$. For vector objects this imposes a tendency for the groups to be of equal size in terms of the volume of space occupied (and not in terms of numbers of points), making this measure particularly appropriate for segmentation problems.

Other important measures, intermediate between single link and complete link, include (for vector objects) the centroid measure (the distance between two clusters is the distance between their centroids), the group average measure (the distance between two clusters is the average of all the distances between pairs of points, one from each cluster), and Ward's measure for vector data (the distance between two clusters is the difference between the total within cluster sum of squares for the two clusters separately, and the within cluster sum of squares resulting from merging the two clusters discussed above). Each such measure has slightly different properties, and other variants also exist; for example, the median measure for vector data ignores the size of clusters, taking the "center" of a combination of two clusters to be the midpoint of the line joining the centers of the two components. Since we are seeking the novel in data mining, it may well be worthwhile to experiment with several measures, in case we throw up something unusual and interesting.

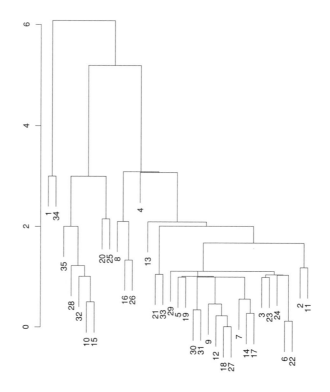

Figure 9.9   Dendrogram of the single link method applied to the data in figure 9.7.

9.5.2   Divisive Methods

Just as stepwise methods of variable selection can start with no variables and gradually add variables according to which lead to most improvement (analogous to agglomerative cluster analysis methods), so they can also start with all the variables and gradually remove those whose removal leads to least deterioration in the model. This second approach is analogous to divisive methods of cluster analysis. Divisive methods begin with a single cluster composed of all of the data points, and seek to split this into components. These further components are then split, and the process is taken as far as necessary. Ultimately, of course, the process will end with a partition in which each cluster consists of a single point.

Monothetic divisive methods split clusters using one variable at a time (so they are analogous to the basic form of tree classification methods discussed in chapter 5). This is a convenient (though restrictive) way to limit the number of possible partitions that must be examined. It has the attraction that the result is easily described by the dendrogram—the split at each node is defined in terms of just a single variable. The term *association analysis* is sometimes uses to describe monothetic divisive procedures applied to multivariate binary data. (This is not the same use as the term "association rules" described in chapter 5.)

Polythetic divisive methods make splits on the basis of all of the variables together. Any intercluster distance measure can be used. The difficulty comes in deciding how to choose potential allocations to clusters—that is, how to restrict the search through the space of possible partitions. In one approach, objects are examined one at a time, and that one is selected for transfer from a main cluster to a subcluster that leads to the greatest improvement in the clustering score.

In general, divisive methods are more computationally intensive and tend to be less widely used than agglomerative methods.

9.6   Probabilistic Model-Based Clustering Using Mixture Models

The mixture models of section 9.2.4 can also be used to provide a general framework for clustering in a probabilistic context. This is often referred to as *probabilistic model-based clustering* since there is an assumed probability model for each component cluster. In this framework it is assumed that the data come from a multivariate finite mixture model of the general form

$$f(\mathbf{x}) = \sum_{k=1}^{K} \pi_k f_k(\mathbf{x}; \theta_k), \tag{9.24}$$

where f_k are the component distributions. Roughly speaking, the general procedure is as follows: given a data set $D = \{\mathbf{x}(1), \ldots, \mathbf{x}(n)\}$, determine how many clusters K we want to fit to the data, choose parametric models for each of these K clusters (for example, multivariate Normal distributions

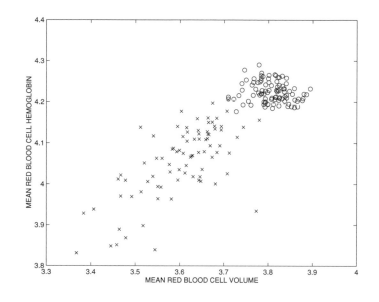

Figure 9.10 Red blood cell measurements (mean volume and mean hemoglobin concentration) from 182 individuals showing the separation of the individuals into two groups: healthy (circles) and iron deficient anemia (crosses).

are a common choice), and then use the EM algorithm of section 9.2.4 (and described in more detail in chapter 8) to determine the component parameters θ_k and component probabilities π_k from the data. (We can of course also try to determine a good value of K from the data, we will return to this question later in this section.) Typically the likelihood of the data (given the mixture model) is used as the score function, although other criteria (such as the so-called classification likelihood) can also be used. Once a mixture decomposition has been found, the data can then be assigned to clusters—for example, by assigning each point to the cluster from which it is most likely to have come.

To illustrate the idea, we apply the method to a data set where the true class labels are in fact known but are removed and then "discovered" by the algorithm.

Example 9.4 Individuals with chronic iron deficiency anemia tend to produce red blood cells of lower volume and lower hemoglobin concentration than nor-

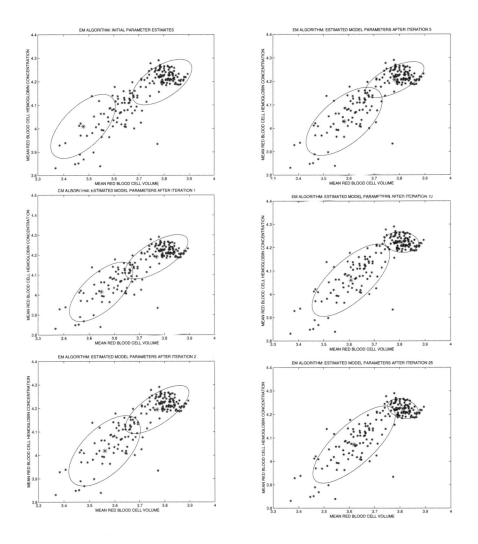

Figure 9.11   Example of running the EM algorithm on the red blood cell measurements of figure 9.10. The plots (running top to bottom, left first, then right) show the 3σ covariance ellipses and means of the fitted components at various stages of the EM algorithm.

mal. A blood sample can be taken to determine a person's mean red blood cell volume and hemoglobin concentration. Figure 9.10 shows a scatter plot of the bivariate mean volume and hemoglobin concentrations for 182 individuals with labels determined by a diagnostic lab test. A normal mixture model with $K = 2$ was fit to these individuals, with the labels removed. The results are shown in figure 9.11, illustrating that a two-component normal mixture appears to capture the main features of the data and would provide an excellent clustering if the group labels were unknown (that is, if the lab test had not been performed). Figure 9.2 verifies that the likelihood (or equivalently, log-likelihood) is nondecreasing as a function of iteration number. Note, however, that the rate of convergence is nonmonotonic; that is, between iterations 5 and 8 the rate of increase in log-likelihood slows down, and then increases again from iterations 8 to 12.

The red blood cell example of figure 9.11 illustrates several features of the probabilistic approach:

- The probabilistic model provides a full distributional description for each component. Note, for example, the difference between the two fitted clusters in the red blood cell example. The normal component is relatively compact, indicating that variability across individuals under normal circumstances is rather low. The iron deficient anemia cluster, on the other hand, has a much greater spread, indicating more variability. This certainly agrees with our common-sense intuition, and it is the type of information that can be very useful to a scientist investigating fundamental mechanisms at work in the data-generating process.

- Given the model, each individual (each data point) has an associated K-component vector of the probabilities that it arose from each group, and that can be calculated in a simple manner using Bayes rule. These probabilities are used as the basis for partitioning the data, and hence defining the clustering. For the red blood cell data, most individuals lie in one group or the other with probability near 1. However, there are certain individuals (close to the intersection of the two clouds) whose probability memberships will be closer to 0.5—that is, there is uncertainty about which group they belong to. Again, from the viewpoint of exploring the data, such data points may be valuable and worthy of detection and closer study (for example, individuals who may be just at the onset of iron deficient anemia).

- The score function and optimization procedures are quite natural in a probabilistic context, namely likelihood and EM respectively. Thus, there is a well-defined theory on how to fit parameters to such models as well as a large library of algorithms that can be leveraged. Extensions to MAP and Bayesian estimation (allowing incorporation of prior knowledge) are relatively straightforward.

- The basic finite mixture model provides a principled framework for a variety of extensions. One useful idea, for example, is to add a $(K + 1)$th noise component (for example, a uniform density) to pick up outliers and background points that do not appear to belong to any of the other K components; the relative weight π_{K+1} of this background component can be learned by EM directly from the data.

- The method can be extended to data that are not in p-dimensional vector form. For example, we can cluster sequences using mixtures of probabilistic sequence models (for example, mixtures of Markov models), cluster curves using mixtures of regression models, and so forth, all within the same general EM framework.

These advantages come at a certain cost. The main "cost" is the assumption of a parametric model for each component; for many problems it may be difficult a priori to know what distributional forms to assume. Thus, model-based probabilistic clustering is really only useful when we have reason to believe that the distributional forms are appropriate. For our red blood cell data, we can see by visual inspection that the normal assumptions are quite reasonable. Furthermore, since the two measurements consist of estimated means from large samples of blood cells, basic statistical theory also suggests that a normal distribution is likely to be quite appropriate.

The other main disadvantage of the probabilistic approach is the complexity of the associated estimation algorithm. Consider the difference between EM and K-means. We can think of K-means as a stepwise approximation to the EM algorithm applied to a mixture model with Normal mixture components (where the covariance matrices for each cluster are all assumed to be the identity matrix). However, rather than waiting until convergence is complete before assigning the points to the clusters, the K-means algorithm reassigns them at each step.

Example 9.5 Suppose that we have a data set where each variable X_j is 0/1 valued—for example, a large transaction data set where $x_j = 1$ (or 0) represents whether a person purchased item j (or not). We can apply the mixture modeling framework as follows: assume that given the cluster k, the variables

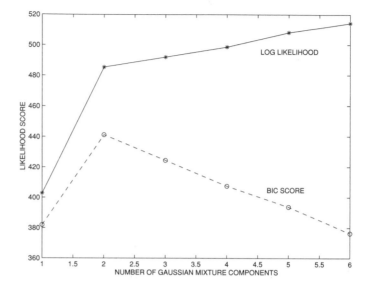

Figure 9.12   Log-likelihood and BIC score as a function of the number of Normal components fitted to the red blood cell data of figure 9.11.

are conditionally independent (as discussed in section 9.2.7); that is, that we can write

$$p_k(\mathbf{x};\theta_k) = \prod_{j=1}^{p} p_k(x_j;\theta_{kj}).$$

To specify a model for the data, we just need to specify the probability of observing value 1 for the jth variable in the kth component. Denoting this probability by θ_{kj}, we can write the component density for the kth component as

$$p_k(x_j;\theta_{kj}) = \theta_{kj}^{x_j}(1 - \theta_{kj})^{1-x_j}, \quad 1 \le k \le K,$$

which is a convenient way of writing the probability of observing value x_j in component k of the mixture model. The full mixture equation for observation $\mathbf{x}(i)$ is the weighted sum of these component densities:

$$
\begin{aligned}
p(\mathbf{x}(i)) &= \sum_{k=1}^{K} \pi_k p_k(\mathbf{x}(i);\theta_k) \\
&= \sum_{k=1}^{K} \pi_k \prod_{j} \theta_{kj}^{x_j(i)}(1 - \theta_{kj})^{1-x_j(i)}
\end{aligned}
$$

(9.25)

(9.26)

where $x_j(i)$ indicates whether person i bought product j or not.

The EM equations for this model are quite simple. Let $p(k|i)$ be the probability that person i belongs to cluster k. By Bayes rule, and given a fixed set of parameters θ, this can be written as:

$$p(k|i) = \frac{\pi_k \prod_j \theta_{kj}^{x_j(i)}(1 - \theta_{kj})^{1-x_j(i)}}{p(\mathbf{x}(i))}, \tag{9.27}$$

where $p(\mathbf{x}(i))$ is as defined in equation 9.26. Calculation of $p(k|i)$ takes $O(nK)$ steps since it must be carried out for each individual i and each cluster k. Calculation of these "membership probabilities" is in effect the E-step for this problem.

The M-step is simply a weighted estimate of the probability of a person buying item j given that they belong to cluster k:

$$\theta_{kj}^{\text{new}} = \frac{\sum_{i=1}^{n} p(k|i)x_j(i)}{\sum_{i=1}^{n} p(k|i)}, \tag{9.28}$$

where in this equation, observation $x_j(i)$ is weighted by the probability $p(k|i)$, namely the probability that individual i was generated by cluster k (according to the model). A particular product j purchased by individual i is in effect assigned fractionally (via the weights $p(k|i)$, $1 \le k \le K$) to the K cluster models. This M-step requires $O(nKp)$ operations since the weighted sum in the numerator must be performed over all n individuals, for each cluster k, and for each of the p parameters (one for each variable in the independence model). If we have I iterations of the EM algorithm in total we get $O(IKnp)$ as the basic complexity, which can be thought of as I times K times the size of the data matrix.

For really large data sets that reside on disk, however, doing I passes through the data set will not be computationally tractable. Techniques have been developed for summarizing cluster representations so that the data set can in effect be compressed during the clustering method. For example, in mixture modeling many data points "gravitate" to one component relatively early in the computation; that is, their membership probability for this component approaches 1. Updating the membership of such points could be omitted in future iterations. Similarly, if a point belongs to a group of points that always share cluster membership, then the points can be represented by using a short description.

To conclude our discussion on probabilistic clustering, consider the problem of finding the best value for K from the data. Note that as K (the number of clusters) is increased, the value of the likelihood at its maximum cannot decrease as a function of K. Thus, likelihood alone cannot tell us directly about which of the models, as a function of K, is closest to the true data generating process. Moreover, the usual approach of hypothesis testing (for example, testing the hypothesis of one component versus two, two versus three, and so forth) does not work for technical reasons related to the mixture likelihood. However, a variety of other ingenious schemes have been developed based to a large extent on approximations of theoretical analyses. We can identify three general classes of techniques in relatively widespread use:

Penalized Likelihood: Subtract a term from the maximizing value of the likelihood. The BIC (Bayesian Information Criterion) is widely used. Here

$$S_{BIC}(M_K) = 2S_L(\hat{\theta}_K; M_K) + d_K \log n \qquad (9.29)$$

where $S_L(\theta_K; M_K)$ is the minimizing value of the negative log-likelihood and d_K is the number of parameters, both for a mixture model with K components. This is evaluated from $K = 1$ up to some $K_{\max}$ and the minimum taken as the most likely value of K. The original derivation of BIC was based on asymptotic arguments in a different (regression) context, arguments that do not strictly hold for mixture modeling. Nonetheless, the technique has been found to work quite well in practice and has the merit of being relatively cheap to compute relative to the other methods listed below. In figure 9.12 the negative of the BIC score function is plotted for the red blood cell data and points to $K = 2$ as the best model (recall that there is independent medical knowledge that the data belong to two groups here, so this result is quite satisfying). There are a variety of other proposals for penalty terms (see chapter 7), but BIC appears to be the most widely used in the clustering context.

Resampling Techniques: We can use either bootstrap methods or cross-validated likelihood using resampling ideas as another approach to generate "honest" estimates of which K value is best. These techniques have the drawback of requiring significantly more computation than BIC—for example, ten times more for the application of ten-fold cross-validation. However, they do provide a more direct assessment of the quality of the models, avoiding the need for the assumptions associated with methods such as BIC.

Bayesian Approximations: The fully Bayesian solution to the problem is to estimate a distribution $p(K|D)$,—that is, the probability of each K value given the data, where all uncertainty about the parameters is integrated out in the usual fashion. In practice, of course, this integration is intractable (recall that we are integrating in a d_K-dimensional space) so various approximations are sought. Both analytic approximations (for example, the Laplace approximation about the mode of the posterior distribution) and sampling techniques (such as Markov chain Monte Carlo) are used. For large data sets with many parameters in the model, sampling techniques may be computationally impractical, so analytic approximation methods tend to be more widely used. For example, the AUTOCLASS algorithm of Cheeseman and Stutz (1996) for clustering with mixture models uses a specific analytic approximation of the posterior distribution for model selection. The BIC penalty-based score function can also be viewed as an approximation to the full Bayesian approach.

In a sense, the formal probabilistic modeling implicit in mixture decomposition is more general than cluster analysis. Cluster analysis aims to produce merely a partition of the available data, whereas mixture decomposition produces a description of the distribution underlying the data (that this distribution is composed of a number of components). Once these component probability distributions have been identified, points in the data set can be assigned to clusters on the basis of the component that is most likely to have generated them. We can also look at this another way: the aim of cluster analysis is to divide the data into naturally occurring regions in which the points are closely or densely clustered, so that there are relatively sparse regions between the clusters. From a probability density perspective, this will correspond to regions of high density separated by valleys of low density, so that the probability density function is fundamentally multimodal. However, mixture distributions, even though they are composed of several components, can well be unimodal.

Consider the case of a two-component univariate normal mixture. Clearly, if the means are equal, then this will be unimodal. In fact, a sufficient condition for the mixture to be unimodal (for all values of the mixing proportions) when the means are different is $| \mu_1 - \mu_2 | \le 2\min(\sigma_1, \sigma_2)$. Furthermore, for every choice of values of the means and standard deviations in a two-component normal mixture there exist values of the mixing proportions for which the mixture is unimodal. This means that if the means are close enough there will be just one cluster, even though there are two components. We can still use the mixture decomposition to induce a clustering, by assigning each data point to the cluster from which it is most likely to have come, but this is unlikely to be a useful clustering.

9.7   Further Reading

A general introduction to parametric probability modeling is Ross (1997) and an introduction to general concepts in multivariate data analysis is provided by Everitt and Dunn (1991). General texts on mixture distributions include Everitt and Hand (1981), Titterington, Smith, and Makov (1985), McLachlan and Basford (1988), Böhning (1998), and McLachlan and Peel (2000). Diebolt and Robert (1994) provide an example of the general Bayesian approach to mixture modeling. Statistical treatments of graphical models include those by Whittaker (1990), Edwards (1995), Cox and Wermuth (1996), and Lauritzen (1996). Pearl (1988) and Jensen (1996) emphasize representational and computational aspects of such models, and the edited collection by Jordan (1999) contains recent research articles on learning graphical models from data. Friedman and Goldszmidt (1996) and Chickering, Heckerman, and Meek (1997) provide details on specific algorithms for learning graphical models from data. Della Pietra, Della Pietra, and Lafferty (1997) describe the application of Markov random fields to text modeling, and Heckerman et al. (2000) describe use a form of Markov random fields for model-based collaborative filtering. Bishop, Fienberg, and Holland (1975) is a standard reference on log-linear models.

There are now many books on cluster analysis. Recommended ones include Anderberg (1973), Späth (1985), Jain and Dubes (1988), and Kaufman and Rousseeuw (1990). The distinction between dissection and finding natural partitions is not always appreciated, and yet it can be important and should not be ignored. Examples of authors who have made the distinction include Kendall (1980), Gordon (1981), and Späth (1985). Marriott (1971) showed that the criterion $K^2 tr(\mathbf{W})$ was asymptotically constant for optimal partitions of a multivariate uniform distribution. Krzanowski and Marriott (1995), table 10.6, give a list of updating formula for clustering criteria based on $\mathbf{W}$. Maximal predictive classification was developed by Gower (1974). The use of branch and bound to extend the range of exhaustive evaluation of all possible clusterings is described in Koontz, Narendra, and Fukunaga (1975) and Hand (1981). The K-means algorithm is described in MacQueen (1967), and the ISODATA algorithm is described in Hall and Ball (1965). Kaufman and Rousseeuw (1990) describe a variant in which the "central point" of each cluster is an element of that cluster, rather than the centroid of the elements. A review of early work on mathematical programming methods applied in cluster analysis is given by Rao (1971) with a more recent review provided by Mangasarian (1996).

One of the earliest references to the single link method of cluster analysis was Florek et al. (1951), and Sibson (1973) was important in promoting the idea. Lance and Williams (1967) presented a general formula, useful for computational purposes, that included single link and complete link as special cases. The median method of cluster analysis is due to Gower (1967). Lambert and Williams (1966) describe the "association analysis" method of monothetic divisive partitioning. The polythetic divisive method of clustering is due to MacNaughton-Smith et al. (1964). The overlapping cluster methods are due to Shepard and Arabie (1979).

Other formalisms for clustering also exist. For example, Karypis and Kumar (1998) discuss graph-based clustering algorithms. Zhang, Ramakrishnan, and Livny (1997) describe a framework for clustering that is scalable to very large databases. There are also countless applications of clustering. For a cluster analytic study of whiskies, see Lapointe and Legendre (1994). Eisen et al. (1998) illustrate the application of hierarchical agglomerative clustering to gene expression data. Zamir and Etzioni (1998) describe a clustering algorithm specifically for clustering Web documents.

Probabilistic clustering is discussed in the context of mixture models in Titterington, Smith, and Makov (1985) and in McLachlan and Basford (1987). Banfield and Raftery (1993) proposed the idea (in a mixture model context) of adding a "cluster" that pervades the whole space by superimposing a separate Poisson process that generated a low level of random points throughout the entire space, so easing the problem of clusters being distorted due to a handful of outlying points. More recent work on model-based probabilistic clustering is described in Celeux and Govaert (1995), Fraley and Raftery (1998), and McLachlan and Peel (1998). The application of mixture models to clustering sequences is described in Poulsen (1990), Smyth (1997), Ridgeway (1997), and Smyth (1999). Mixture-based clustering of curves for parametric models was originally described by Quandt and Ramsey (1978) and Späth (1979) and later generalized to the non-parametric case by Gaffney and Smyth (1999). Jordan and Jacobs (1994) provide a generalization of standard mixtures to a mixture-based architecture called "mixtures of experts" that provides a general mixture-based framework for function approximation.

Studies of tests for numbers of components of mixture models are described in Everitt (1981), McLachlan (1987), and Mendell, Finch, and Thode (1993). An early derivation of the BIC criterion is provided by Shibata (1978). Kass and Raftery (1995) provide a more recent overview including a justification for the application of BIC to a broad range of model selection tasks. The bootstrap method for determining the number of mixture model components was introduced by McLachlan (1987) and later refinements can be found in Feng and McCulloch (1996) and McLachlan and Peel (1997). Smyth (2000) describes a cross-validation approach to the same problem. Cheeseman and Stutz (1996) outline a general Bayesian framework to the problem of model-based clustering, and Chickering and Heckerman (1998) discuss an empirical study comparing different Bayesian approximation methods for finding the number of components K.

Different techniques for speeding up the basic EM algorithm for large data sets are described in Neal and Hinton (1998), Bradley, Fayyad, and Reina (1998), and Moore (1999).

Cheng and Wallace (1993) describe an interesting application of hierarchical agglomerative clustering to the problem of clustering spatial atmospheric measurements from the Earth's upper atmosphere. Smyth, Ide, and Ghil (1999) provide an alternative analysis of the same data using Normal mixture models, and use cross-validated likelihood to provide a quantitative confirmation of the earlier Cheng and Wallace clusters. Mixture models in haematology are described in McLaren (1996). Wedel and Kamakura (1998) provide an extensive review of the development and application of mixture models in consumer modeling and marketing applications. Cadez et al. (2000) describe the application of mixtures of Markov models to the problem of clustering individuals based on sequences of page-requests from massive Web logs.

The antenna data of figure 9.4 are described in more detail in Smyth (1994) and the red blood cell data of figure 9.10 are described in Cadez et al. (1999).

10 Predictive Modeling for Classification

10.1 A Brief Overview of Predictive Modeling

Descriptive models, as described in chapter 9, simply summarize data in convenient ways or in ways that we hope will lead to increased understanding of the way things work. In contrast, predictive models have the specific aim of allowing us to predict the unknown value of a variable of interest given known values of other variables. Examples include providing a diagnosis for a medical patient on the basis of a set of test results, estimating the probability that customers will buy product A given a list of other products they have purchased, or predicting the value of the Dow Jones index six months from now, given current and past values of the index.

In chapter 6 we discussed many of the basic functional forms of models that can be used for prediction. In this chapter and the next, we examine such models in more detail, and look at some of the specific aspects of the criteria and algorithms that permit such models to be fitted to the data.

Predictive modeling can be thought of as learning a mapping from an input set of vector measurements $\mathbf{x}$ to a scalar output y (we can learn mappings to vector outputs, but the scalar case is much more common in practice). In predictive modeling the training data D_{train} consists of *pairs* of measurements, each consisting of a vector $\mathbf{x}(i)$ with a corresponding "target" value $y(i), 1 \le i \le n$. Thus the goal of predictive modeling is to estimate (from the training data) a mapping or a function $y = f(\mathbf{x}; \theta)$ that can predict a value y given an input vector of measured values $\mathbf{x}$ and a set of estimated parameters θ for the model f. Recall that f is the functional form of the model structure (chapter 6), the θs are the unknown parameters within f whose values we will determine by minimizing a suitable score function on the data (chapter 7), and the process of searching for the best θ values is the basis for the actual data mining algorithm (chapter 8). We thus need to choose three things: a particular model structure (or a family of model structures), a score function, and an optimization strategy for finding the best parameters and model within the model family.

In data mining problems, since we typically know very little about the functional form of $f(\mathbf{x}; \theta)$ ahead of time, there may be attractions in adopting fairly flexible functional forms or models for f. On the other hand, as discussed in chapter 6, simpler models have the advantage of often being more stable and more interpretable, as well as often providing the functional components for more complex model structures. For predictive modeling, the score function is usually relatively straightforward to define, typically a function of the *difference* between the prediction of the model $\hat{y}(i) = f(\mathbf{x}(i); \theta)$ and the true value $y(i)$—that is,

$$
\begin{aligned}
S(\theta) & = \sum_{D_{train}} d\Big(y(i), \hat{y}(i) \Big) \\
& = \sum_{D_{train}} d\Big(y(i), f(\mathbf{x}(i); \theta) \Big)
\end{aligned}
\tag{10.1}
$$

where the sum is taken over the tuples $(\mathbf{x}(i), y(i))$ in the training data set D_{train} and the function d defines a scalar distance such as squared error for real-valued y or an indicator function for categorical y (see chapter 7 for further discussion in this context). The actual heart of the data mining algorithm then involves minimizing S as a function of θ; the details of this are determined both by the nature of the distance function and by the functional form of $f(\mathbf{x}; \theta)$ that jointly determine how S depends on θ (see the discussion in chapter 8).

To compare predictive models we need to estimate their performance on "out-of-sample data"—data that have not been used in constructing the models (or else, as discussed earlier, the performance estimates are likely to be biased). In this case we can redefine the score function $S(\theta)$ so that it is estimated on a validation data set, or via cross-validation, or using a penalized score function, rather than on the training data directly (as discussed in chapter 7).

We noted in chapter 6 that there are two important distinct kinds of tasks in predictive modeling depending on whether Y is categorical or real-valued. For categorical Y the task is called *classification* (or *supervised classification* to distinguish it from problems concerned with defining the classes in the first instance, such as cluster analysis), and for real-valued y the task is called *re-*

gression. Classification problems are the focus of this chapter, and regression problems are the focus of the next chapter. Although we can legitimately discuss both forms of modeling in the same general context (they share many of the same mathematical and statistical underpinnings), in the interests of organizational style we have assigned classification and regression each their own chapter. However, it is important for the reader to be aware that many of the model structures for classification that we discuss in this chapter have a "twin" in terms of being applicable to regression (chapter 11). For example, we discuss tree structures in the classification chapter, but they can also be used for regression. Similarly we discuss neural networks under regression, but they can also be used for classification.

In these two chapters we cover many of the more commonly used approaches to classification and regression problems—that is, the more commonly used tuples of model structures, score functions, and optimization techniques. The natural taxonomy of these algorithms tends to be closely aligned with the model structures being used for prediction (for example, tree structures, linear models, polynomials, and so on), leading to a division of the chapters largely into subsections according to different model structures. Even though specific combinations of models, score functions, and optimization strategies have become very popular ("standard" data mining algorithms) it is important to remember the general reductionist philosophy of data mining algorithms that we described in chapter 5; for a particular data mining problem we should always be aware of the option of tailoring the model, the score function, or the optimization strategy for the specific application at hand rather than just using an "off-the-shelf" technique.

10.2   Introduction to Classification Modeling

We introduced predictive models for classification in chapter 6. Here we briefly review some of the basic concepts. In classification we wish to learn a mapping from a vector of measurements $\mathbf{x}$ to a categorical variable Y. The variable to be predicted is typically called the *class variable* (for obvious reasons), and for convenience of notation we will use the variable C, taking values in the set $\{c_1, \ldots, c_m\}$ to denote this class variable for the rest of this chapter (instead of using Y). The observed or measured variables $X_1, \ldots, X_p$ are variously referred to as the features, attributes, explanatory variables, input variables, and so on—the generic term *input* variable will be used throughout this chapter. We will refer to $\mathbf{x}$ as a p-dimensional vector (that is, we take it to be comprised of p variables), where each component can be real-valued, ordinal, categorical, and so forth. $x_j(i)$ is the jth component of the ith input vector, where $1 \le i \le n$, $1 \le j \le p$. In our introductory discussion we will implicitly assume that we are using the so-called "0-1" loss function (see chapter 7), where a correct prediction incurs a loss of 0 and an incorrect class prediction incurs a loss of 1 irrespective of the true class and the predicted class.

We will begin by discussing two different but related general views of classification: the decision boundary (or discriminative) viewpoint, and the probabilistic viewpoint.

10.2.1 Discriminative Classification and Decision Boundaries

In the discriminative framework a classification model $f(\mathbf{x}; \theta)$ takes as input the measurements in the vector $\mathbf{x}$ and produces as output a symbol from the set $\{c_1, \ldots, c_m\}$. Consider the nature of the mapping function f for a simple problem with just two real-valued input variables X_1 and X_2. The mapping in effect produces a piecewise constant surface over the (X_1, X_2) plane; that is, only in certain regions does the surface take the value c_1. The union of all such regions where a c_1 is predicted is known as the *decision region* for class c_1; that is, if an input $\mathbf{x}(i)$ falls in this region its class will be predicted as c_1 (and the complement of this region is the decision region for all other classes).

Knowing where these decision regions are located in the (X_1, X_2) plane is equivalent to knowing where the *decision boundaries* or *decision surfaces* are between the regions. Thus we can think of the problem of learning a classification function f as being equivalent to learning decision boundaries between the classes. In this context, we can begin to think of the mathematical forms we can use to describe decision boundaries, for example, straight lines or planes (linear boundaries), curved boundaries such as low-order polynomials, and other more exotic functions.

In most real classification problems the classes are not perfectly separable in the $\mathbf{X}$ space. That is, it is possible for members of more than one class to occur at some (perhaps all) values of $\mathbf{X}$—though the probability that members of each class occur at any given value $\mathbf{x}$ will be different. (It is the fact that these probabilities differ that permits us to make a classification. Broadly speaking, we assign a point $\mathbf{x}$ to the most probable class at $\mathbf{x}$.) The fact that the classes "overlap" leads to another way of looking at classification problems. Instead of focusing on decision surfaces, we can seek a function $f(\mathbf{x}; \theta)$

that maximizes some measure of separation between the classes. Such functions are termed *discriminant functions*. Indeed, the earliest formal approach to classification, *Fisher's linear discriminant analysis method* (Fisher, 1936), was based on precisely this idea: it sought that linear combination of the variables in **x** that maximally discriminated between the (two) classes.

10.2.2 Probabilistic Models for Classification

Let $p(c_k)$ be the probability that a randomly chosen object or individual i comes from class c_k. Then $\sum_k p(c_k) = 1$, assuming that the classes are mutually exclusive and exhaustive. This may not always be the case—for example, if a person had more than one disease (classes are not mutually exclusive) we might model the problem as set of multiple two-class classification problems ("disease 1 or not," "disease 2 or not," and so on). Or there might be a disease that is not in our classification model (the set of classes is not exhaustive), in which case we could add an extra class c_{k+1} to the model to account for "all other diseases." Despite these potential practical complications, unless stated otherwise we will use the mutually exclusive and exhaustive assumption throughout this chapter since it is widely applicable in practice and provides the essential basis for probabilistic classification.

Imagine that there are two classes, males and females, and that $p(c_k)$, $k = 1, 2$, represents the probability that at conception a person receives the appropriate chromosomes to develop as male or female. The $p(c_k)$ are thus the probabilities that individual i belongs to class c_k if we have no other information (no measurements $\mathbf{x}(i)$) at all. The $p(c_k)$ are sometime referred to as the class "prior probabilities," since they represent the probabilities of class membership *before* observing the vector **x**. Note that estimating the $p(c_k)$ from data is often relatively easy: if a random sample of the entire population has been drawn, the maximum likelihood estimate of $p(c_k)$ is just the frequency with which c_k occurs in the training data set. Of course, if other sampling schemes have been adopted, things may be more complicated. For example, in some medical situations it is common to sample equal numbers from each class deliberately, so that the priors have to be estimated by some other means.

Objects or individuals belonging to class k are assumed to have measurement vectors **x** distributed according to some distribution or density function $p(\mathbf{x}|c_k, \theta_k)$, where the θ_k are unknown parameters governing the characteristics of class c_k. For example, for multivariate real-valued data, the assumed model structure for the **x** for each class might be multivariate Normal, and the parameters θ_k would represent the mean (location) and variance (scale) characteristics for each class. If the means are far enough apart, and the variances small enough, we can hope that the classes are relatively *well separated* in the input space, permitting classification with very low misclassification (or error) rate. The general problem arises when neither the functional form nor the parameters of the distributions of the xs are known a priori.

Once the $p(\mathbf{x}|c_k, \theta_k)$ distributions have been estimated, we can apply Bayes theorem to yield the *posterior probabilities*

$$p(c_k|\mathbf{x}) = \frac{p(\mathbf{x}|c_k, \theta)p(c_k)}{\sum_{l=1}^{m} p(\mathbf{x}|c_l, \theta_l)p(c_l)}, \quad 1 \leq k \leq m. \tag{10.2}$$

The posterior probabilities $p(c_k|\mathbf{x}, \theta_k)$ implicitly carve up the input space $\mathbf{x}$ into m decision regions with corresponding decision boundaries. For example, with two classes ($m = 2$) the decision boundaries will be located along the contours where $p(c_1|\mathbf{x}, \theta_1) = p(c_2|\mathbf{x}, \theta_2)$. Note that if we *knew* the true posterior class probabilities (instead of having to estimate them), we could make optimal predictions given a measurement vector $\mathbf{x}$. For example, for the case in which all errors incur equal cost we should predict the class value c_k that has the highest posterior probability $p(c_k|\mathbf{x})$ (is most likely given the data) for any given $\mathbf{x}$ value. Note that this scheme is optimal in the sense that no other prediction method can do better (with the given variables $\mathbf{x}$)— it does not mean that it makes no errors. Indeed, in most real problems the optimal classification scheme will have a nonzero error rate, arising from the overlap of the distributions $p(\mathbf{x}|c_k, \theta_k)$. This overlap means that the maximum class probability $p(c_k|\mathbf{x}) < 1$, so that there is a non-zero probability $1-p(c_k|\mathbf{x})$ of data arising from the other (less likely) classes at $\mathbf{x}$, even though the optimal decision at $\mathbf{x}$ is to choose c_k. Extending this argument over the whole space, and averaging with respect to $\mathbf{x}$ (or summing over discrete-valued variables), the *Bayes Error Rate* is defined as

$$p_B^* = \int (1 - \max_k p(c_k|\mathbf{x}))p(\mathbf{x})d\mathbf{x}. \tag{10.3}$$

This is the minimum possible error rate. No other classifier can achieve a lower expected error rate on unseen new data. In practical terms, the Bayes error is a lower-bound on the best possible classifier for the problem.

Example 10.1

Figure 10.1 shows a simple artificial example with a single predictor variable X (the horizontal axis) and two classes. The upper two plots show how the

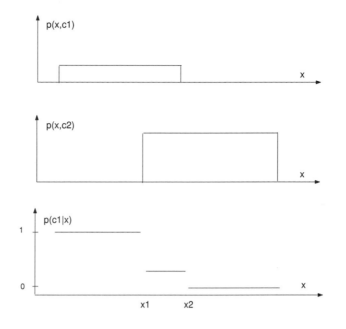

Figure 10.1   A simple example illustrating posterior class probabilities for a two-class one-dimensional classification problem.

data are distributed within class 1 and class 2 respectively. The plots show the joint probability of the class and the variable X, $p(x, c_k), k = 1, 2$. Each has a uniform distribution over a different range of X; class c_1 tends to have lower x values than class c_2. There is a region along the x axis (between values x_1 and x_2) where both class populations overlap.

The bottom plot shows the posterior class probability for class c_1, $p(c_1|x)$ as calculated via Bayes rule given the class distributions shown in the upper two plots. For values of $x \leq x_1$, the probability is 1 (since only class c_1 can produce data in that region), and for values of $x \geq x_2$ the probability is 0 (since only class c_2 can produce data in that region). The region of overlap (between x_1 and x_2) has a posterior probability of about $1/3$ for class c_1 (by Bayes rule) since class c_2 is roughly twice as likely as class c_1 in this region. Thus, class c_2 is the Bayes-optimal decision for any $x \geq x_1$ (noting that in the regions where $p(x, c_1)$ or $p(x, c_2)$ are *both* zero, the posterior probability is undefined). However, note that between x_1 and x_2 there is some fundamental ambiguity about which class may be present given an x value in this region; that is, although c_2

is the more likely class there is a $1/3$ chance of c_1 occurring. In fact, since there is a $1/3$ chance of making an incorrect decision in this region, and let us guess from visual inspection that there is a 20% chance of an x value falling in this region, this leads to a rough estimate of a Bayes error rate of about $\frac{20}{3} \approx 6.67\%$ for this particular problem.

Now consider a situation in which **x** is bivariate, and in which the members of one class are entirely surrounded by members of the other class. Here neither of the two X variables alone will lead to classification rules with zero error rate, but (provided an appropriate model was used) a rule based on both variables together could have zero error rate. Analogous situations, though seldom quite so extreme, often occur in practice: new variables add information, so that we can reduce the Bayes error rate by adding extra variables. This prompts this question: why should we not simply use many measurements in a classification problem, until the error rate is sufficiently low? The answer lies in the the bias-variance principle discussed in chapters 4 and 7. While the Bayes error rate can only stay the same or decrease if we add more variables to the model, in fact we do not know the optimal classifier or the Bayes error rate. We have to estimate a classification rule from a finite set of training data. If the number of variables for a fixed number of training points is increased, the training data are representing the underlying distributions less and less accurately. The Bayes error rate may be decreasing, but we have a poorer approximation to it. At some point, as the number of variables increases, the paucity of our approximation overwhelms the reduction in Bayes error rate, and the rules begin to deteriorate.

The solution is to choose our variables with care; we need variables that, when taken together, separate the classes well. Finding appropriate variables (or a small number of features—combinations of variables) is the key to effective classification. This is perhaps especially marked for complex and potentially very high dimensional data such as images, where it is generally acknowledged that finding the appropriate features can have a much greater impact on classification accuracy than the variability that may arise by choosing different classification models. One data-driven approach in this context is to use a score function such as cross-validated error rate to guide a search through combinations of features—of course, for some classifiers this may be very computationally intensive, since the classifier may need to be retrained for each subset examined and the total number of such subsets is combinatorial in p (the number of variables).

10.2.3 Building Real Classifiers

While this framework provides insight from a theoretical viewpoint, it does not provide a prescriptive framework for classification modeling. That is, it does not tell us specifically how to construct classifiers unless we happen to know precisely the functional form of $p(\mathbf{x}|c_k)$ (which is rare in practice). We can list three fundamental approaches:

1. **The discriminative approach:** Here we try to model the decision boundaries directly—that is, a direct mapping from inputs $\mathbf{x}$ to one of m class label $c_1, \ldots, c_m$. No direct attempt is made to model either the class-conditional or posterior class probabilities. Examples of this approach include perceptrons (see section 10.3) and the more general support vector machines (see section 10.9).

2. **The regression approach:** The posterior class probabilities $p(c_k|\mathbf{x})$ are modeled explicitly, and for prediction the maximum of these probabilities (possibly weighted by a cost function) is chosen. The most widely used technique in this category is known as logistic regression, discussed in section 10.7. Note that decision trees (for example, CART from chapter 5) can be considered under either the discriminative approach (if the tree only provides the predicted class at each leaf) or the regression approach (if in addition the tree provides the posterior class probability distribution at each leaf).

3. **The class-conditional approach:** Here, the class-conditional distributions $p(\mathbf{x}|c_k, \theta_k)$ are modeled explicitly, and along with estimates of $p(c_k)$ are inverted via Bayes rule (equation 10.2) to arrive at $p(c_k|\mathbf{x})$ for each class c_k, a maximum is picked (possibly weighted by costs), and so forth, as in the regression approach. We can refer to this as a "generative" model in the sense that we are specifying (via $p(\mathbf{x}|c_k, \theta_k)$) precisely how the data are *generated* for each class. Classifiers using this approach are also sometimes referred to as "Bayesian" classifiers because of the use of Bayes theorem, but they are not necessarily Bayesian in the formal sense of Bayesian parameter estimation discussed in chapter 4. In practice the parameter estimates used in equation 10.2, $\hat{\theta}_k$, are often estimated via maximum likelihood for each class c_k, and "plugged in" to $p(\mathbf{x}|c_k, \theta_k)$. There are Bayesian alternatives that average over θ_k. Furthermore, the functional form of $p(\mathbf{x}|c_k, \theta_k)$ can be quite general—any of parametric (for example, Normal), semi-parametric (for example, finite mixtures), or non-parametric

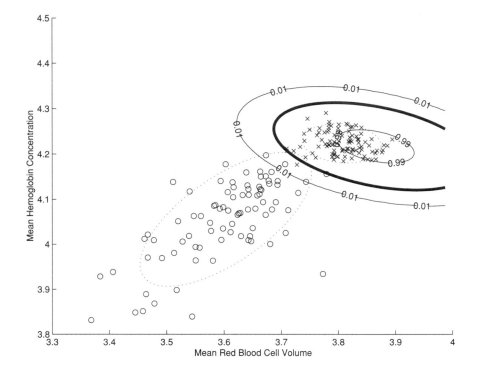

Figure 10.2 Posterior probability contours for $p(c_1|\mathbf{x})$ where c_1 is the label for the healthy class for the red blood cell data discussed in chapter 9. The heavy line is the decision boundary ($p(c_1|\mathbf{x}) = p(c_2|\mathbf{x}) = 0.5$) and the other two contour lines correspond to $p(c_1|\mathbf{x}) = 0.01$ and $p(c_1|\mathbf{x}) = 0.99$. Also plotted for reference are the original data points and the fitted covariance ellipses for each class (plotted as dotted lines).

(for example, kernels) can be used to estimate $p(\mathbf{x}|c_k, \theta_k)$. In addition, in principle, different model structures can be used for each class c_k (for example, class c_1 could be modeled as a Normal density, class c_2 could be modeled as a mixture of exponentials, and class c_3 could be modeled via a kernel density estimate).

Example 10.2 Choosing the most likely class is in general equivalent to picking the value of k for which the discriminant function $g_k(\mathbf{x}) = p(c_k|\mathbf{x})$ is largest, $1 \leq m$. It is often convenient to redefine the discriminants as $g_k(\mathbf{x}) =$

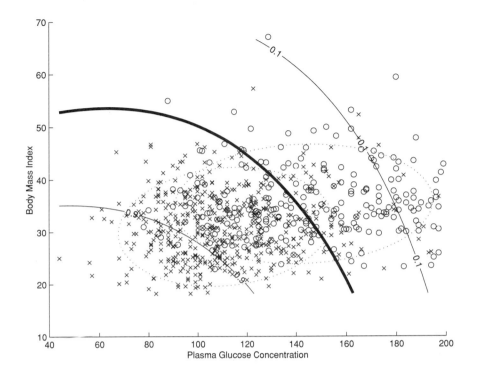

Figure 10.3 Posterior probability contours for $p(c_1|\mathbf{x})$ where c_1 is the label for the diabetic class for the Pima Indians data of chapter 3. The heavy line is the decision boundary ($p(c_1|\mathbf{x}) = p(c_2|\mathbf{x}) = 0.5$) and the other two contour lines correspond to $p(c_1|\mathbf{x}) = 0.1$ and $p(c_1|\mathbf{x}) = 0.9$. The fitted covariance ellipses for each class are plotted as dotted lines.

$\log p(\mathbf{x}|c_k)p(c_k)$ (via Bayes rule). For multivariate real-valued data $\mathbf{x}$, a commonly used class-conditional model is the multivariate Normal as discussed in chapter 9. If we take log (base e) of the Normal multivariate density function, and ignore terms that do not include k we get discriminant functions of the following form:

$$g_k(\mathbf{x}) = -\frac{1}{2}(\mathbf{x}-\mu_k)^T \Sigma_k^{-1}(\mathbf{x}-\mu_k) - \frac{p}{2}\log|\Sigma_k| - \log p(c_k) \quad 1 \le k \le m. \quad (10.4)$$

In the general case each of these $g_k(\mathbf{x})$ involve quadratics and pairwise products of the individual x variables. The decision boundary between any two classes k and l is defined by the solution to the equation $g_k(\mathbf{x}) - g_l(\mathbf{x}) = 0$

as a function of $\mathbf{x}$, and this will also be quadratic in $\mathbf{x}$ in the general case. Thus, a multivariate Normal class-conditional model leads to quadratic decision boundaries in general. In fact, if the covariance matrices Σ_k for each class k are constrained to be the same ($\Sigma_k = \Sigma$) it is straightforward to show that the $g_k(\mathbf{x})$ functions reduce to linear functions of $\mathbf{x}$ and the resulting decision boundaries are linear (that is, they define hyperplanes in the p-dimensional space).

Figure 10.2 shows the results of fitting a multivariate Normal classification model to the red blood cell data described in chapter 9. Maximum likelihood estimates (chapter 4) of $\mu_k, \Sigma_k, p(c_k)$ are obtained using the data from each of the two classes, $k = 1, 2$, and then "plugged in" to Bayes rule to determine the posterior probability function $p(c_k|\mathbf{x})$. In agreement with theory, we see that the resulting decision boundary is indeed quadratic in form (as indeed are the other plotted posterior probability contours). Note that the contours fall off rather sharply as one goes outwards from the mean of the healthy class (the crosses). Since the healthy class (class c_1) is characterized by lower variance in general than the anemic class (class c_2, the circles), the optimal classifier (assuming the Normal model) results in a boundary that completely encircles the healthy class.

Figure 10.3 shows the results of the same classification procedure (multivariate Normal, maximum likelihood estimates) but applied to a different data set. In this case two particular variables from the two-class Pima Indians data set (originally discussed in chapter 3) were used as the class variables, where problematic measurements taking value 0 (thought to be outliers, see discussion in chapter 3) were removed a priori. In contrast to the red blood cell data of figure 10.2, the two classes (healthy and diabetic) are heavily overlapped in these two dimensions. The estimated covariance matrices Σ_1 and Σ_2 are unconstrained, leading again to quadratic decision boundary and posterior probability contours. The degree of overlap is reflected in the posterior probability contours which are now much more spread out (they fall off slowly) than they were previously in figure 10.2.

Note that both the discriminative and regression approaches focus on the differences between the classes (or, more formally, the focus is on the probabilities of class membership conditional on the values of $\mathbf{x}$), whereas the class-conditional/generative approach focuses on the distributions of $\mathbf{x}$ for the classes. Methods that focus directly on the probabilities of class membership are sometimes referred to as *diagnostic* methods, while methods that focus on the distribution of the $\mathbf{x}$ values are termed *sampling* methods. Of course, all of the methods are related. The class-conditional/generative approach is related to the regression approach in that the former ultimately produces posterior class probabilities, but calculates them in a very specific manner (that is, via Bayes rule), whereas the regression approach is unconstrained in terms of how the posterior probabilities are modeled. Similarly, both the regression and class-conditional/generative approaches implicitly contain decision boundaries; that is, in "decision mode" they map inputs **x** to one of m classes; however, each does so within a probabilistic framework, while the "true" discriminative classifier is not constrained to do so.

We will discuss examples of each of these approaches in the sections that follow. Which type of classifier works best in practice will depend on the nature of the problem. For some applications (such as in medical diagnosis) it may be quite useful for the classifier to generate posterior class probabilities rather than just class labels. Methods based on the class-conditional distributions also have the advantage of providing a full description for each class (which, for example, provides a natural way to detect outliers—inputs **x** that do not appear to belong to any of the known classes). However, as discussed in chapter 9, it may be quite difficult (if not impossible) to accurately estimate functions $p(\mathbf{x}|c_k, \theta_k)$ in high dimensions. In such situations the discriminative classifier may work better. In general, methods based on the class-conditional distributions will require fitting the most parameters (and thus will lead to the most complex modeling), the regression approach will require fewer, and the discriminative model fewest of all. Intuitively this makes sense, since the optimal discriminative model contains only a subset of the information of the optimal regression model (the boundaries, rather than the full class probability surfaces), and the optimal regression model contains less information than the optimal class-conditional distribution model.

10.3   The Perceptron

One of the earliest examples of an automatic computer-based classification rule was the perceptron. The perceptron is an example of a discriminative rule, in that it focuses directly on learning the decision boundary surface. The perceptron model was originally motivated as a very simple artificial neural network model for the "accumulate and fire" threshold behavior of real neurons in our brain—in chapter 11 on regression models we will discuss more general and recent neural network models.

In its simplest form, the perceptron model (for two classes) is just a linear combination of the measurements in **x**. Thus, define $h(\mathbf{x}) = \sum w_j x_j$, where the $w_j, 1 \leq j \leq p$ are the weights (parameters) of the model. One usually adds an additional input with constant value 1 to allow for an additional trainable offset term in the operation of the model. Classification is achieved by comparing $h(\mathbf{x})$ with a threshold, which we shall here take to be zero for simplicity. If all class 1 points have $h(\mathbf{x}) > 0$ and all class 2 points have $h(\mathbf{x}) < 0$, we have perfect separation between the classes. We can try to achieve this by seeking a set of weights such that the above conditions are satisfied for all the points in the training set. This means that the score function is the number of misclassification errors on the training data for a given set of weights $w_1, \ldots, w_{p+1}$. Things are simplified if we transform the measurements of our class 2 points, replacing all the x_j by $-x_j$. Now we simply need a set of weights for which $h(\mathbf{x}) > 0$ for all the training set points.

The weights w_j are estimated by examining the training points sequentially. We start with an initial set of weights and classify the first training set point. If this is correctly classified, the weights remain unaltered. If it is incorrectly classified, so that $h(\mathbf{x}) < 0$, the weights are updated, so that $h(\mathbf{x})$ is increased. This is easily achieved by adding a multiple of the misclassified vector to the weights. That is, the updating rule is $\mathbf{w} = \mathbf{w} + \lambda \mathbf{x}_j$. Here λ is a small constant. This is repeated for all the data points, cycling through the training set several times if necessary. It is possible to prove that if the two classes are perfectly separable by a linear decision surface, then this algorithm will eventually find a separating surface, provided a sufficiently small value of λ is chosen. The updating algorithm is reminiscent of the gradient descent techniques discussed in chapter 8, although it is actually not calculating a gradient here but instead is gradually reducing the error rate score function.

Of course, other algorithms are possible, and others are indeed more attractive if the two classes are not perfectly linearly separable—as is often the case. In such cases, the misclassification error rate is rather difficult to deal with analytically (since it is not a smooth function of the weights), and the squared error score function is often used instead:

$$S(\mathbf{w}) = \sum_{i=1}^{n} \left(\sum_{j=1}^{p+1} w_j x_j(i) - y(i) \right)^2. \tag{10.5}$$

Since this is a quadratic error function it has a single global minimum as a function of the weight vector $\mathbf{w}$ and is relatively straightforward to minimize (either by a local gradient descent rule as in chapter 8, or more directly in closed-form using linear algebra).

Numerous variations of the basic perceptron idea exist, including (for example) extensions to handle more than two classes. The appeal of the perceptron model is that it is simple to understand and analyze. However, its applicability in practice is limited by the fact that its decision boundaries are linear (that is, hyperplanes in the input space $\mathbf{X}$) and real-world classification problems may require more complex decision surfaces for low error-rate classification.

10.4   Linear Discriminants

The linear discriminant approach to classification can be considered a "cousin" of the perceptron model within the general family of linear classifiers. It is based on the simple but useful concept of searching for the linear combination of the variables that best separates the classes. Again, it can be regarded an example of a discriminative approach, since it does not explicitly estimate either the posterior probabilities of class membership or the class-conditional distributions. Fisher (1936) presents one of the earliest treatments of linear discriminant analysis (for the two-class case). Let $\hat{\mathbf{C}}$ be the pooled sample covariance matrix defined as

$$\hat{\mathbf{C}} = \frac{1}{n_1 + n_2} \left(n_1 \hat{\mathbf{C}}_1 + n_2 \hat{\mathbf{C}}_2 \right), \qquad (10.6)$$

where n_i is the number of training data points per class, and $\hat{\mathbf{C}}_i$ are the $p \times p$ sample (estimated) covariance matrices for each class, $1 \leq i \leq 2$ (as defined in chapter 2). To capture the notion of separability along any p-dimensional vector $\mathbf{w}$, Fisher defined a scalar score function as follows:

$$S(\mathbf{w}) = \frac{\mathbf{w}^T \hat{\mu}_1 - \mathbf{w}^T \hat{\mu}_2}{\mathbf{w}^T \hat{\mathbf{C}} \mathbf{w}}, \qquad (10.7)$$

where $\hat{\mu}_1$ and $\hat{\mu}_2$ are the $p \times 1$ mean vectors for $\mathbf{x}$ for data from class 1 and class 2 respectively. The top term is the difference in projected means for each class, which we wish to maximize. The denominator is the estimated pooled variance of the projected data along direction $\mathbf{w}$ and takes into account the fact that the different variables x_j can have both different individual variances and covariance with each other.

Given the score function $S(\mathbf{w})$, the problem is to determine the direction $\mathbf{w}$ that maximizes this expression. In fact, there is a closed form solution for the maximizing $\mathbf{w}$, given by:

$$\hat{\mathbf{w}}_{lda} = \hat{\mathbf{C}}^{-1}(\hat{\mu}_1 - \hat{\mu}_2). \qquad (10.8)$$

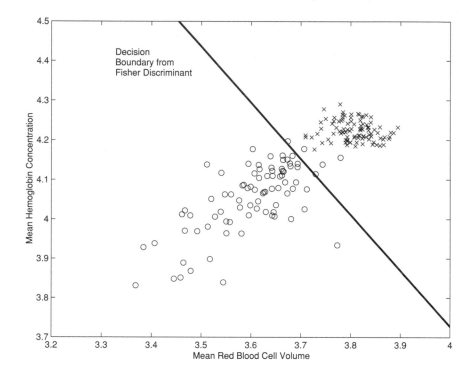

Figure 10.4   Decision boundary produced by the Fisher linear discriminant applied to the red blood cell data from chapter 9, where the crosses are the healthy class and the circles correspond to iron deficient anemia.

A new point is classified by projecting it onto the maximally separating direction, and classifying $\mathbf{x}$ to class 1 if

$$\mathbf{w}_{lda}^{T}\left(\mathbf{x} - \frac{1}{2}(\hat{\mu}_1 - \hat{\mu}_2)\right) > \log\frac{p(c_1)}{p(c_2)}, \qquad (10.9)$$

where $p(c_1)$ and $p(c_2)$ are the respective class probabilities.

Figure 10.4 shows the application of the Fisher linear discriminant method to the two class anemia classification problem discussed earlier. The linear decision boundary is not quite as good at separating the training data as the quadratic boundaries of example 10.2.

In the special case in which the distributions within each class have a multivariate Normal distribution with a common covariance matrix, this method yields the optimal classification rule as in equation 10.2 (and, indeed, it is optimal whenever the two classes have ellipsoidal distributions with equal quadratic forms). Note, however, that since $\mathbf{w}_{lda}$ was determined without assuming Normality, the linear discriminant methodology can often provide a useful classifier even when Normality does not hold. Note also that if we approach the linear discriminant analysis method from the perspective of assumed forms for the underlying distributions, the method might be more appropriately viewed as being based on the class-conditional distribution approach, rather than on the discriminative approach.

A variety of extensions to Fisher's original linear discriminant model have been developed. *Canonical discriminant functions* generate $m - 1$ different decision boundaries (assuming $m - 1 < p$) to handle the case where the number of classes $m > 2$. *Quadratic discriminant functions* lead to quadratic decision boundaries in the input space when the assumption that the covariance matrices are equal is relaxed, as discussed in example 10.2. *Regularized discriminant analysis* shrinks the quadratic method toward a simpler form.

Determining the linear discriminant model has computational complexity $O(mp^2 n)$. Here we are assuming that $n >> \{p, m\}$ so that the main cost is in estimating the class covariance matrices $\hat{\mathbf{C}}_i$, $1 \leq i \leq m$. All of these matrices can be found with at most two linear scans of the database (one to get the means and one to generate the $O(p^2)$ covariance matrix terms). Thus the method scales well to large numbers of observations, but is not particularly reliable for large numbers of variables, as the dependence (in terms of the number of parameters to be estimated) on p, the number of variables, is quadratic.

10.5   Tree Models

The basic principle of tree models is to partition (in a recursive manner) the space spanned by the input variables to maximize a score of class purity—meaning (roughly, depending on the particular score chosen) that the majority of points in each cell of the partition belong to one class. Thus, for example, with three input variables, $x, y,$ and z, one might split x, so that the input space is divided into two cells. Each of these cells is then itself split into two, perhaps again at some threshold on x or perhaps at some threshold on y or z. This process is repeated as many times as necessary (see below), with each branch point defining a node of a tree. To predict the class value for a new case with known values of input variables, we work down the tree, at each node choosing the appropriate branch by comparing the new case with the threshold value of the variable for that node.

Tree models have been around for a very long time, although formal methods of building them are a relatively recent innovation. Before the development of such methods they were constructed on the basis of prior human understanding of the underlying processes and phenomena generating the data. They have many attractive properties. They are easy to understand and explain. They can handle mixed variables (continuous and discrete, for example) with ease since, in their simplest form, trees partition the space using binary tests (thresholds on real variables and subset membership tests on categorical variables). They can predict the class value for a new case very quickly. They are also very flexible, so that they can provide a powerful predictive tool. However, their essentially sequential nature, which is reflected in the way they are constructed, can sometimes lead to suboptimal partitions of the space of input variables.

The basic strategy for building tree models is simplicity itself: we simply recursively split the cells of the space of input variables. To split a given cell (equivalently, to choose the variable and threshold on which to split the node) we simply search over each possible threshold for each variable to find the threshold split that leads to the greatest improvement in a specified score function. The score is assessed on the basis of the training data set elements. If the aim is to predict to which one of two classes an object belongs, we choose the variable and threshold that leads to the greatest average improvement to the local score (averaged across the two child nodes). Splitting a node cannot lead to a deterioration in the score function on the training data. For classification it turns out that using classification error directly is not a useful score function for selecting variables to split on. Other more indirect measures such as entropy have been found to be much more useful. Note that, for ordered variables, a binary split simply corresponds to a single threshold on the variable values. For nominal variables, a split corresponds to partitioning the variable values into two subsets of values.

Example 10.3 The entropy criterion for a particular real-valued threshold test T (where T stands for a threshold test $X_j > T$ on one of the variables) is defined as the average entropy after the test is performed:

$$H(C|T) = p(T = 0)H(C|T = 0) + p(T = 1)H(C|T = 1) \qquad (10.10)$$

where the conditional entropy $H(C|T = 1)$ is defined as

$$-\sum_{c_k} p(c_k|T = 1)\log_2 p(c_k|T = 1).$$

The average entropy is then the uncertainty from each branch ($T = 1$ or $T = 0$) averaged over the probability of going down each branch. Since we are trying to split the data into subsets where as many of the data points belong to one class or the other, this is directly equivalent to minimizing the entropy in each branch. In practice, we search among all variables (and all tests or thresholds on each variable) for the single test T that results in minimum average entropy after the binary split.

In principle, this splitting procedure can be continued until each leaf node contains a single training data point—or, in the case when some training data points have identical vectors of input variables (which can happen if the input variables are categorical) continuing until each leaf node contains only training data points with identical input variable values. However, this can lead to severe overfitting. Better trees (in the sense that they lead to better predictions on new data drawn from the same distributions) can typically be obtained by not going to such an extreme (that is, by constructing smaller, more parsimonious trees).

Early work sought to achieve this by stopping the growing process before the extreme had been reached (this is analogous to avoiding overfitting in neural networks by terminating the convergence procedure, as we will discuss in the next chapter). However, this approach suffers from a consequence of the sequential nature of the procedure. It is possible that the best improvement that can be made at the next step is only very small, so that growth stops, while the step *after* this could lead to substantial improvement in performance. The "poor" step might be necessary to set things up so that the next step can make a substantial improvement. There is nothing specific to trees about this, of course. It is a general disadvantage of sequential methods: precisely the same applies to the stepwise regression search algorithms discussed in chapter 11—which is why more sophisticated methods involving stepping forward and backward have been developed. Similar algorithms have evolved for tree methods.

Nowadays a common strategy is to build a large tree—to continue splitting until some termination criterion has been reached in each leaf (for example the points in a node all belong to one class or all have the same x vector)—and then to prune it back. That is, at each step the two leaf nodes are merged that lead to least reduction in predictive performance on the training set. Alternatively, measures such as minimum description length or cross-validation (for example, the CART algorithm described in chapter 5) are used to trade off goodness of fit to the training data against model complexity.

Two other strategies for avoiding the problem of overfitting the training set are also fairly widely used. The first is to average the predictions obtained by the leaves and the nodes leading to the leaves. The second, which has attracted much attention recently, is to base predictions on the averages of several trees, each one constructed by slightly perturbing the data in some way. Such *model averaging methods* are, in fact, generally suitable for all predictive modeling situations. Model averaging works particularly well with tree models since trees have relatively high variance in the following sense: a tree can be relatively sensitive to small changes in the training data since a slight perturbation in the data could lead to a different root node being chosen and a completely different tree structure being fit. Averaging over multiple perturbations of the data set (e.g., averaging over trees built on bootstrap samples from the training data) tends to counteract this effect by reducing variance.

The most common class value among the training data points at a given leaf node (the majority class) is typically declared as the predicted label for any data points that arrive at this leaf. In effect the region in the input space defined by the branch leading to this node is assigned the label of the most likely class in the region. Sometimes useful information is contained in the overall probability distribution of the classes in the training data at a given leaf. Note that for any particular class, the tree model produces probabilities that are in effect piecewise-constant in the input space, so small changes in the value of an input variable could send a data point down different branches (into a different leaf or region) with dramatically different class probabilities.

When seeking the next best split while building a large tree prior to pruning, the algorithm searches through all variables and all possible splits on those variables. For real-valued variables the number of possible positions for splits is typically taken to be $n' - 1$ (that is, one less than the number of data points n' at each node), each possible position being located halfway between two data points (putting them halfway between is not necessarily optimal, but has the virtue of simplicity). The computational complexity of finding the best splits among p real-valued variables will typically scale as $O(pn' \log n')$ if it is carried out in a direct manner. The $n' \log n'$ term results from having to sort the variable values at the node in order to calculate the score function: for any threshold we need to know how many points are above and below that threshold. For many score functions we can show that the optimal threshold for ordered variables must be located between two values of the variable that have different class labels. This fact can be used to speed up the search, particularly for large numbers of data points. In addition, various bookkeeping efficiencies can be taken advantage of to avoid resorting as we proceed from node to node. For categorical-valued variables, some form of combinatorial search must be conducted to find the best subset of variable values for defining a split.

From a database viewpoint, tree growing can be an expensive procedure. If the number of data points at a node exceeds the capacity of main memory, then the function must operate with a cache of data in main memory and the rest in secondary memory. A brute-force implementation will result in linear scans of the database for each node in the tree, resulting in a potentially very slow algorithm. Thus, when we use tree algorithms with data that exceeds the capacity of main memory, we typically either use clever tree algorithms whose data management strategy is tailored to try to minimize secondary memory access, or we resort to working with a random sample that can fit in main memory.

One disadvantage of the basic form of tree is that it is *monothetic*: each node is split on just one variable. Sometimes, in real problems, the class variable changes most rapidly with a combination of input variables. For example, in a classification problem involving two input variables, it might be that one class is characterized by having low values on both variables while the other has high values on both variables. The decision surface for such a problem would lie diagonally in the input variable space. Standard methods would try to achieve this by multiple splits, ending up with a staircaselike approximation to this diagonal decision surface. Figure 10.5 provides a simple illustration of this effect. The optimum, of course, would be achieved by using a threshold defined on a linear combination of the input variables—and some extensions to tree methods do just this, permitting linear combinations of the raw input variables to be included in the set of possible variables to be split. Of course, this complicates the search process required for building the tree.

10.6   Nearest Neighbor Methods

At their basic level, nearest neighbor methods are very straightforward: to classify a new object, with input vector **y**, we simply examine the k closest training data set points to **y** and assign the object to the class that has the majority of points among these k. *Close* is defined here in terms of the p-dimensional input space. Thus we are seeking those objects in the training data that are most similar to the new object, in terms of the input variables, and then classifying the new object into the most heavily represented class

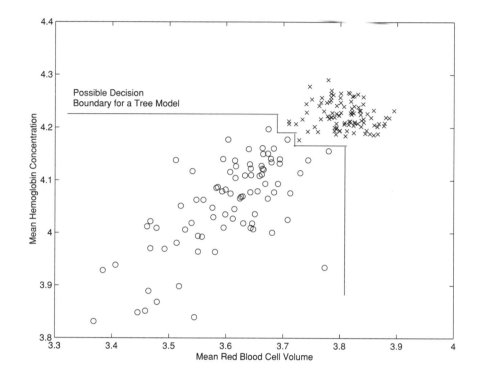

Figure 10.5 Decision boundary for a decision tree for the red blood cell data from chapter 9, composed of "axis-parallel" linear segments (contrast with the simpler boundaries in figure 10.4).

among these most similar objects.

In theoretical terms, we are taking a small volume of the space of variables, centered at $\mathbf{x}$, and with radius the distance to the kth nearest neighbor. Then the maximum likelihood estimators of the probability that a point in this small volume belongs to each class are given by the proportion of training points in this volume that belong to each class. The k-nearest neighbor method assigns a new point to the class that has the largest estimated probability. Nearest neighbor methods are essentially in the class of what we have termed "regression" methods—they directly estimate the posterior probabilities of class membership.

Of course, this simple outline leaves a lot unsaid. In particular, we must choose a value for k and a metric through which to define *close*. The most basic form takes $k = 1$, but this makes a rather unstable classifier (high variance, sensitive to the data), and the predictions can often be made more consistent by increasing k (reduces the variance, but may increase the bias of the method since there is more averaging). However, increasing k means that the training data points now being included are not necessarily very close to the object to be classified. This means that the "small volume" may not be small at all. Since the estimates are estimates of the average probability of belonging to each class in this volume, this may deviate substantially from the value at any particular point within the volume—and this deviation is likely to be larger as the volume is larger. The dimensionality p of course plays an important role here: for a fixed number of data points n we increase p (add variables) the data become more and more sparse. This means that the predicted probability may be biased from the true probability at the point in question.

We are back at the ubiquitous issue of the bias/variance trade-off, where increasing k reduces variance but may increase bias. There is theoretical work on the best choice of k, but since this will depend on the particular structure of the data set, as well as other general issues, the best strategy for choosing k seems to be a data-adaptive one: try various values, plotting the performance criterion (the misclassification rate, for example) against k, to find the best. In following this approach, the evaluation must be carried out on a data set independent of the training data (or else the usual problem of overoptimistic results ensues). However, for smaller data sets it would be unwise to reduce the size of the training data set too much by splitting off too large a test set, since the best value of k clearly depends on the number of points in the training data set. A leaving-one-out cross-validated score function is often a useful strategy to follow, particularly for small data sets.

Many applications of nearest neighbor methods adopt a Euclidean metric: if $\mathbf{y}$ is the input vector for the point to be classified, and $\mathbf{x}$ is the input vector for a training set point, then the Euclidean distance between them is $\sum_j (x_j - y_j)^2$. As discussed in chapter 2, the problem with this is that it does not provide an explicit measure of the relative importance of the different input variables. We could seek to overcome this by using $\sum_j w_j (x_j - y_j)^2$, where the w_j are weights. This seems more complicated than the Euclidean metric, but the appearance that the Euclidean metric does not require a choice of weights is illusory. This is easily seen simply by changing the units of measurement of one of the variables before calculating the Euclidean metric. (An exception to this is when all variables are measured in the same units—as, for example, with situations where the same variable is measured on several different occasions—so-called *repeated measures* data.)

In the two-class case, an optimal metric would be one defined in terms of the contours of probability of belonging to class c_1—that is, $P(c_1|\mathbf{x})$. Training data points on the same contour as $\mathbf{y}$ have the same probability of belonging to class c_1 as does a point at $\mathbf{y}$, so no bias is introduced by including them in the k nearest neighbors. This is true no matter how far from $\mathbf{y}$ they are, provided they are on the contour. In contrast, points close to $\mathbf{y}$ but not on the contour of $P(c_1|\mathbf{x})$ through $\mathbf{y}$ will have different probabilities of belonging to class c_1, so including them among the k will tend to introduce bias. Of course, we do not know the positions of the contours. If we did, we would not need to undertake the exercise at all. This means that, in practice, we estimate approximate contours and base the metrics on these. Both global approaches (for example estimating the classes by multivariate Normal distributions) and local approaches (for example iterative application of nearest neighbor methods) have been used for finding approximate contours.

Nearest neighbor methods are closely related to the kernel methods for density estimation that we discussed in chapter 6. The basic kernel method defines a cell by a fixed bandwidth and calculates the proportion of points within this cell that belong to each class. This means that the denominator in the proportion is a random variable. The basic nearest neighbor method fixes the proportion (at k/n) and lets the "bandwidth" be a random variable. More sophisticated extensions of both methods (for example, smoothly decaying kernel functions, differential weights on the nearest neighbor points according to their distance from $\mathbf{x}$, or choice of bandwidth that varies according to $\mathbf{x}$) often lead to methods that are barely distinguishable in practice.

The nearest neighbor method has several attractive properties. It is easy to program and no optimization or training is required. Its classification accuracy can be very good on some problems, comparing favorably with alternative more exotic methods such as neural networks. It permits easy application of the *reject option*, in which a decision is deferred if we are not sufficiently confident about the predicted class. Extension to multiple classes is straightforward (though the best choice of metric is not so clear here). Handling missing values (in the vector for the object to be classified) is simplicity itself: we simply work in the subspace of those variables that are present.

From a theoretical perspective, the nearest neighbor method is a valuable tool: as the design sample size increases, so the bias of the estimated probability will decrease, for fixed k. If we can contrive to increase k at a suitable rate (so that the variance of the estimates also decreases), the misclassification rate of a nearest neighbor rule will converge to a value related to the Bayes error rate. For example, the asymptotic nearest neighbor misclassification rate (the rate as the number of data points n goes to ∞) is bounded above by twice the Bayes error rate.

High-dimensional applications cause problems for all methods. Essentially such problems have to be overcome by adopting a classification rule that is not so flexible that it overfits the data, given the large opportunity for overfitting provided by the many variables. Parametric models of superficially restricted form (such as linear methods) often do well in such circumstances. Nearest neighbor methods often do not do well. With large numbers of variables (and not correspondingly large numbers of training data cases) the nearest k points are often quite far in real terms. This means that fairly gross smoothing is induced, smoothing that is not related to the classification objectives. The consequence is that nearest neighbor methods can perform poorly in problems with many variables.

In addition, theoretical analyses suggest potential problems for nearest neighbor methods in high dimensions. Under some distributional conditions the ratio of the distance to the closest point and the distance to the most distant point, from any particular $\mathbf{x}$ point, approaches 1 as the number of dimensions grows. Thus the concept of the nearest neighbor becomes more or less meaningless. However, the distributional assumptions needed for this result are relatively strong, and other more realistic assumptions imply that the notion of nearest neighbor is indeed well defined.

A potential drawback of nearest neighbor methods is that they do not build a model, relying instead on retaining all of the training data set points (for this reason, they are sometimes called "lazy" methods). If the training data set is large, searching through them to find the k nearest can be a time-consuming process. Specifically it can take $O(np)$ per query data point if performed in brute force manner, visiting each of the n training data points and performing p operations to calculate the distance to each. From a memory viewpoint, the method requires us to store the full training data set of size np. Both the time and storage requirements make the direct approach impractical for applications involving very large values of n and/or real-time classification (for example, real-time recommendation of a product to a visitor at a Web site using a nearest-neighbor algorithm to find similar individuals from a database with millions of customers).

A variety of methods have been developed for accelerating the search and reducing the memory demands of the basic approach. For example, branch and bound methods can be applied: if it is already known that at least k points lie within a distance d of the point to be classified, then a training set point is not worth considering if it lies within a distance d of a point already known to be further than $2d$ from the point to be classified. This involves preprocessing the training data set. Other preprocessing methods discard certain training data points. For example, *condensed nearest neighbor* and *reduced nearest neighbor* methods selectively discard design set points so that those remaining still correctly classify all other training data points. The *edited nearest neighbor* method discards isolated points from one class that are in dense regions of another class, smoothing out the empirical decision surface in this manner. The gains in speed and memory from these methods depend in general on a variety of factors: the values of n and p, the nature of the particular data set at hand, the particular technique used, and trade-offs between time and memory.

An alternative method for scaling up nearest neighbor methods for large data sets in high dimensions is to use clustering to obtain a grouping of the data. The data points are stored on disk according to their membership in clusters. When finding the nearest point for input point $\mathbf{y}$, the clusters nearest to $\mathbf{y}$ are located and search confined to those clusters. With high probability, under fairly broad assumptions, this method can produce the true nearest neighbor.

10.7   Logistic Discriminant Analysis

For the two-class case, one of the most widely used basic methods of classification based on the regression perspective is *logistic discriminant analysis*. Given a data point $\mathbf{x}$, the estimated probability that it belongs to class c_1 is

$$p\left(c_1|\mathbf{x}\right) = \frac{1}{1 + \exp\left(\beta'\mathbf{x}\right)}. \tag{10.11}$$

Since the probabilities of belonging to the two classes sum to one, by subtraction, the probability of belonging to class 2 is

$$p\left(c_2|\mathbf{x}\right) = \frac{\exp\left(\beta'\mathbf{x}\right)}{1 + \exp\left(\beta'\mathbf{x}\right)}. \tag{10.12}$$

By inverting this relationship, it is easy to see that the logarithm of the *odds ratio* is a linear function of the x_j. That is,

$$\log\frac{p\left(c_2|\mathbf{x}\right)}{p\left(c_1|\mathbf{x}\right)} = \beta'\mathbf{x}. \tag{10.13}$$

This approach to modeling the posterior probabilities has several attractive properties. For example, if the distributions are multivariate normal with equal covariance matrices, it is the optimal solution. Furthermore, it is also optimal with discrete x variables if the distributions can be modeled by log-linear models (mentioned in chapter 9) with the same interaction terms. These two optimality properties can combine, to yield an attractive model for mixed variables (that is, discrete and continuous) types.

Fisher's linear discriminant analysis method is also optimal for the case of multivariate normal classes with equal covariance matrices. If the data are known to be sampled from such distributions, then Fisher's method is more efficient. This is because it makes explicit use of this information, by modeling the covariance matrix, whereas the logistic method sidesteps this. On the other hand, the more general validity of the logistic method (no real data is ever exactly multivariate normally distributed) means that this is generally preferred to linear discriminant analysis nowadays. The word *nowadays* here arises because of the algorithms required to compute the parameters of the two models. The mathematical simplicity of the linear discriminant analysis model means that an explicit solution can be found. This is not the case for logistic discriminant analysis, and an iterative estimation procedure must be adopted. The most common such algorithm is a maximum likelihood approach, based on using the likelihood as the score function. This is described in chapter 11, in the more general context of *generalized linear models*.

10.8   The Naive Bayes Model

In principle, methods based on the class-conditional distributions in which the variables are all categorical are straightforward: we simply estimate the probabilities that an object from each class will fall in each cell of the discrete variables (each possible discrete value of the vector variable $\mathbf{X}$), and then use Bayes theorem to produce a classification. In practice, however, this is often very difficult to implement because of the sheer number of probabilities that must be estimated—$O(k^p)$ for p k-valued variables. For example, with $p = 30$ and binary variables ($k = 2$) we would need to estimate on the order of $2^{30} \approx 10^9$ probabilities. Assuming (as a rule of thumb) that we should have at least 10 data points for every parameter we estimate (where here the parameters in our model are the probabilities specifying the joint distribution), we would need on the order of 10^{10} data points to accurately estimate the required joint distribution. For m classes ($m > 2$) we would need m times this number. As

p grows the situation clearly becomes impractical.

We pointed out in chapters 6 and 9 that we can always simplify any joint distribution by making appropriate independence assumptions, essentially approximating a full table of k^p probabilities by products of much smaller tables. At an extreme, we can assume that all the variables are *conditionally independent*, given the classes—that is, that

$$p(\mathbf{x}|c_k) = p(x_1, \ldots, x_p|c_k) = \prod_{j=1}^{p} p(x_j|c_k), \quad 1 \le k \le m \tag{10.14}$$

This is sometimes referred to as the *Naive Bayes* or *first-order Bayes* assumption. The approximation allows us to approximate the full conditional distribution requiring $O(k^p)$ probabilities with a product of univariate distributions, requiring in total $O(kp)$ probabilities per class. Thus the conditional independence model is linear in the number of variables p rather than being exponential. To use the model for classification we simply use the product form for the class-conditional distributions, yielding the *Naive Bayes classifier*.

The reduction in the number of parameters by using the Naive Bayes model above comes at a cost: we are making a very strong independence assumption. In some cases the conditional independence assumption may be quite reasonable. For example, if the x_j are medical symptoms, and the c_k are different diseases, then it may (perhaps) be reasonable to assume that given that a person has disease c_k, the probability of any one symptom depends only on the disease c_k and not on the occurrence of any other symptom. In other words, we are modeling how symptoms appear, given each disease, as having no interactions (note that this does not mean that we are assuming marginal (unconditional) independence). In many practical cases this conditional independence assumption may not be very realistic. For example, let x_1 and x_2 be measures of annual income and savings total respectively for a group of people, and let c_k represent their creditworthiness, this being divided into two classes: good and bad. Even within each class we might expect to observe a dependence between x_1 and x_2, because it is likely that people who earn more also save more. Assuming that two variables are independent means, in effect, that we will treat them as providing two distinct pieces of information, which is clearly not the case in this example.

Although the independence assumption may not be a realistic model of the probabilities involved, it may still permit relatively accurate classification performance. There are various reasons for this, including: the fact that relatively few parameters are estimated implies that the variance of the es-

timates will be small; although the resulting probability estimates may be
biased, since we are not interested in their absolute values but only in their
ranked order, this may not matter; often a variable selection process has already been undertaken, in which one of each pair of highly correlated variables has been discarded; the decision surface from the naive Bayes classifier
may coincide with that of the optimal classifier.

Apart from the fact that its performance is often surprisingly good, there
is another reason for the popularity of this particularly simple form of classifier. Using Bayes theorem, our estimate of the probability that a point with
measurement vector $\mathbf{x}$ will belong to the kth class is

$$
\begin{aligned}
p(c_k|\mathbf{x}) &\propto p(\mathbf{x}|c_k)p(c_k) \\
&= p(c_k)\prod_{j=1}^{p} p(x_j|c_k) \quad 1 \leq k \leq m
\end{aligned}
\tag{10.15}
$$

by conditional independence. Now let us take the log-odds ratio and assume that we have just two classes c_1 and c_2. After some straightforward
manipulation we get

$$
\log\frac{p(c_1|\mathbf{x})}{p(c_2|\mathbf{x})} = \log\frac{p(c_1)}{p(c_2)} + \sum \log\frac{p(x_j|c_1)}{p(x_j|c_2)}.
\tag{10.16}
$$

Thus the log odds that a case belongs to class c_1 is given by a simple sum
of contributions from the priors and separate contributions from each of the
variables. This additive form can be quite useful for explanation purposes
since each term, $\log\frac{p(x_j|c_1)}{p(x_j|c_2)}$, can be viewed as contributing a positive or neg-
ative additive contribution to whether c_1 is c_2 is more likely.

The naive Bayes model can easily be generalized in many different directions. If our measurements x_j are real-valued we can still make the conditional independence assumption, where now we have products of estimated
univariate *densities*, instead of distributions. For any real-valued x_j we can
estimate $f(x_j|c_k)$ using any of our favorite density estimation techniques—
for example, parametric models such as a Normal density, more flexible
models such as a mixture, or a non-parametric estimate such as a kernel
density function. Combinations of real-valued and discrete variables can be
handled simply by products of distributions and densities in equation 10.15
above.

Despite the simplicity of the form of equations above, the decision surfaces
can be quite complicated and are certainly not constrained to be linear (e.g.,
the multivariate Normal naive Bayes model produces quadratic boundaries

in general), in contrast to the linear surfaces produced by simple weighted sums of raw variables (such as those of the perceptron and Fisher's linear discriminant). The simplicity, parsimony, and interpretability of the naive Bayes model has led to its widespread popularity, particularly in the machine learning literature.

We can generalize the model equally well by including *some but not all dependencies* beyond first-order. One can imagine searching for higher order dependencies to allow for selected "significant" pairwise dependencies in the model (such as $p(x_j, x_k | c_k)$, and then triples, and so forth). In doing so we are in fact building a general graphical model (or belief network—see chapter 6) for the conditional distribution $p(\mathbf{x} | c_k)$. However, the conventional wisdom in practice is that such additions to the model often provide only limited improvements in classification performance on many data sets, once again underscoring the difference between building accurate density estimators and building good classifiers.

Finally we comment on the computational complexity of the naive Bayes classifier. Since we are just using (in effect) additive models based on simple functions of univariate densities, the complexity scales roughly as pm times the complexity of the estimation for each of the individual univariate class-dependent densities or distributions. For discrete-valued variables, the sufficient statistics are simple counts of the number of data points in each bin, so we can construct a naive Bayes classifier with just a single pass through the data. A single scan is also sufficient for parametric univariate density models of real-valued variables (we just need to collect the sufficient statistics, such as the mean and the variance for Normal distributions). For more complex density models, such as mixture models, we may need multiple scans to build the model because of the iterative nature of fitting such density functions (as discussed in chapter 9).

10.9   Other Methods

A huge number of predictive classification methods have been developed in recent years. Many of these have been powerful and flexible methods, in response to the exciting possibilities offered by modern computing power. We have outlined some of these, showing how they are related. Many other methods also exist, but in just one chapter of one book it is not feasible to do justice to all of them. Furthermore, development and invention have not ended. Exciting work continues even as we write. Examples of methods that we have not had space to cover are:

- Mixture models and radial basis function approaches approximate each class-conditional distribution by a mixture of simpler distributions (for example, multivariate Normal distributions). Even the use of just a few component distributions can lead to a function that is surprisingly effective in modeling the class-conditional distributions.

- Feed-forward neural networks (as discussed in chapter 5 under the back-propagation algorithm and again to be discussed in chapter 11 for regression) are a generalization of perceptrons. Sometimes they are called *multi-layer perceptrons*. The first later generates h_1 linear terms, each a weighted combination of the p inputs (in effect, h_1 perceptrons). The h_1 terms are then non-linearly transformed (the logistic function is a popular choice) and the process repeated through multiple layers. The nonlinearity of the transformations permits highly flexible decision surface shapes, so that such models can be very effective for some classification problems. However, their fundamental nonlinearity means that estimation is not straightforward and iterative techniques (such as hill-climbing) must be used. The computational complexity of the estimation process means that such methods may not be particularly useful with large data sets.

- Projection pursuit methods can be viewed as a "cousin" of neural networks (we will return to them in the context of regression in chapter 11). They can be shown, mathematically, to be just as powerful, but they have the advantage that the estimation is more straightforward. They again consist of linear combinations of nonlinear transformations of linear combinations of the raw variables. However, whereas neural networks fix the transformations, in projection pursuit they are data-driven.

- Just as neural networks emerged from early work on the perceptron, so also did support vector machines. The early perceptron work assumed that the classes were perfectly separable, and then sought a suitable separating hyperplane. The best generalization performance was obtained when the hyperplane was as far as possible from all of the data points. Support vector machines generalize this to more complex surfaces by extending the measurement space, so that it includes transformations (combinations) of the raw variables. A linear decision surface that perfectly separates the data in this enhanced space is equivalent to a nonlinear decision surface that perfectly separates the data in the original raw measurement space. A distinct feature of this approach is the use of a unique score function, namely the "margin," which attempts to optimize the location of the linear decision boundary between the two classes in a manner that is likely to lead to the best possible generalization performance. Practical experience with such methods is rapidly improving, but estimation can be slow since it involves solving a complicated optimization problem that can require $O(n^2)$ storage and $O(n^3)$ time to solve.

Frequently in classification a very flexible model is fitted, and after that it is smoothed in some way to avoid overfitting (or the two processes occur simultaneously), and thus a suitable compromise between bias and variance is obtained. This is manifest in pruning of trees, in weight decay techniques for fitting neural networks, in regularization in discriminant analysis, in the "flatness" of support vector machines, and so on. A rather different strategy, that has proven highly effective in predictive modeling, is to estimate several (or many) models and to average their predictions, as with averaging multiple tree classifiers. This approach clearly has conceptual similarities to the Bayesian model-averaging approach of chapter 4, which explicitly regards the parameters of a model (or the model itself) as being uncertain and then averages over this uncertainty when making a prediction. Whereas model averaging has its natural origins in statistics, the similar approach of majority voting among classifiers has its natural origins in machine learning. Yet other ways of combining classifiers are also possible; for example, we can regard the output of classifiers as inputs to a higher level classifier. In principle, any type of predictive classification model can be used at each stage. Of course, parameter estimation will generally not be easy.

A question that obviously arises with the model averaging strategy is: how to weight the different contributions to the average—how much weight should each individual classifier be accorded? The simplest strategy is to use equal weights, but it seems obvious that there may be advantages to permitting the use of different weights (not least because equal weights are a special case of this more general model). Various strategies have been suggested for finding the weights, including letting them depend on the predictive performance of the individual model and on the relative complexity of the model. The method of *boosting* can also be viewed as a model averaging method. Here a succession of models is built, each one being trained on a data set in which points misclassified by the previous model are given more weight. This has obvious similarities to the basic error correction strategy used in early perceptron algorithms. Recent research has provided empirical and theoretical evidence suggesting that boosting can be a highly effective data-driven strategy for building flexible predictive models.

10.10 Evaluating and Comparing Classifiers

This chapter has discussed predictive classification models—models for predicting the likely class membership of a new object, based on a series of measurements on that object. There are many different methods available, so a perfectly reasonable question is "which particular method we should use for a given problem?" Unfortunately, there is no general answer to this question. Choice must depend on features of the problem, the data, and the objectives. We can be aware of the properties of the different methods, and this can help us make a choice, but theoretical properties are not always an effective guide to practical performance (the effectiveness of the independence Bayes model illustrates this). Of course, differences in expected and observed performance serve as a stimulus for further theoretical work, leading to deeper understanding.

If practical results sometimes confound the state of current understanding, we must often resort to empirical comparison of performance to guide our choice of method. There has been a huge amount of work on the assessment and evaluation of classification rules. Much of this work has provided an initial test bed for enhanced understanding in other areas of model building. This section provides a brief introduction to assessing the performance of classification models.

We have so far referred to the error rate or misclassification rate of classification models—the proportion of future objects that the rule is likely to incorrectly classify. We defined the Bayes error rate as the optimal error rate—the error rate that would result if our model were based on the true distribution functions underlying the data. In practice, of course, these functional forms must be selected a priori (or the alternative discriminative or regression approaches used, and their parameters estimated), so that the model is likely to depart from the optimal. In this case, the model has a *true* or *actual* error rate (which can be no smaller than the Bayes error rate). The true error rate is sometimes called the *conditional* error rate, because it is conditioned on the given training data set.

We will need ways to estimate this true error rate. One obvious way to do this is to reclassify the training data and see what proportion was misclassified. This is the *apparent* or *resubstitution* error rate. Unfortunately, this is likely to underestimate the future proportion misclassified. This is because the predictive model has been built so that it does well, in some sense, on the training data. (It would be perverse, to say the least, deliberately to choose a model that did poorly on the training data!) Since the training data is merely a sample from the distributions in question, it will not perfectly reflect these distributions. This means that our model may well reflect part of the data-specific aspects of the training data. Thus, if the training data are reclassified, a higher proportion will be correctly classified than would be the case for future data points.

We have already discussed this phenomenon in different contexts. Many ways have been proposed to overcome it. One straightforward possibility is to estimate future error rate by calculating the proportion misclassified in a new sample—a *test set*. This is perfectly fine—apart from the fact that, if a test set is available, we might more fruitfully use it to make a larger training data set. This will permit a more accurate predictive classification model to be constructed. It seems wasteful to ignore part of the data deliberately when we construct the model, unless of course n is very large and we are confident that training on (say) one million data points (keeping another million for testing) is just about as good as training on the full two million.

When our data size is more moderate, various cross-validation approaches have been suggested (see chapter 7 and elsewhere), in which some small portion (say, one tenth) of the data is left out when the rule is constructed, and then the rule is evaluated on the part that was left out. This can be repeated, with different parts of the data being omitted. Important methods based on this principle are:

- the *leaving-one-out* method, in which only one point is left out at each stage, but each point in turn is left out, so that we end up with a test set of size equal to that of the entire training set, but where each single point test set is independent of the model it is tested on. Other methods use larger fractions of the data for the test sets (for example, one tenth of the entire data set) but these are more biased than the leaving-one-out method as estimates of the future performance of the model based on the entire data set.

- *bootstrap* methods, of which there are several. These model the relationship between the unknown true distributions and the sample by the relationship between the sample and a *subsample* of the same size drawn, with replacement, from the sample. In one method, this relationship is used to correct the bias of the resubstitution error rate. Some highly sophisticated variants of bootstrap methods have been developed, and they are the most effective methods known to date. *Jackknife* methods are also based on leaving one training set element out at a time (as in cross-validation), but are equivalent to an approximation to the bootstrap approach.

There are many other methods of error rate estimation. The area has been the subject of several review papers—see the further reading section for details.

Error rate treats the misclassification of all objects as equally serious. However, this is often (some argue almost always) unrealistic. Often, certain kinds of misclassification are more serious than other kinds. For example, misdiagnosing a patient with a curable but otherwise lethal disease as suffering from some minor illness is more serious than the reverse. In this case, we may want to attach *costs* to the different kinds of misclassification. In place of simple error rate, then, we seek a model that will minimize overall loss.

These ideas generalize readily enough to the multiple-class case. Often it is useful to draw up a *confusion* matrix, a cross-classification of the predicted class against the true class. Each cell of such a matrix can be associated with the cost of making that particular kind of misclassification (or correct classification, in the case of the diagonal of the matrix) so that overall loss can be evaluated.

Unfortunately, costs are often difficult to determine. When this is the case, an alternative strategy is to integrate over all possible values of the ratio of one cost to the other (for the two-class case—generalizations are possible for more than two classes). This approach leads to what is known as the *Gini coefficient* of performance. This measure is equivalent to the test statistic used in the Mann-Whitney-Wilcoxon statistical test for comparing two independent samples, and is also equivalent to the area under a *Receiver Operating Characteristic* or *ROC* curve (a plot of the estimated proportion of class 1 objects correctly classified as class 1 against the estimated proportion of class 2 objects incorrectly classified as class 1). ROC curves and the areas under them are widely used in some areas of research. They are not without their interpretation problems, however.

Simple performance of classification models is but one aspect of the choice of a method. Another is how well the method matches the data. For example, some methods are better suited to discrete **x** variables, and others to continuous **x**, while others work with either type with equal facility. Missing values, of course, are a potential (and, indeed, ubiquitous) problem with any method. Some methods can handle incomplete data more readily than others. The independence Bayes method, for example, handles such data very easily, whereas Fisher's linear discriminant analysis approach does not. Things are further complicated by the fact that data may be missing for various reasons, and that the reasons can affect the validity of the model built on the incomplete data. The Further Reading section gives references to material discussing such issues.

In general, the assessment of classification models is an important area, and one that has been the subject of a huge amount of study.

10.11 Feature Selection for Classification in High Dimensions

An important issue that often confronts data miners in practice is the problem of having too many variables. Simply put, not all variables that are measured are likely to be *necessary* for accurate discrimination and including them in the classification model may in fact lead to a worse model than if they were removed. Consider the simple example of building a system to discriminate between images of male and female faces (a task that humans perform effortlessly and relatively accurately but that is quite challenging for an image classification algorithm). The colors of a person's eyes, hair, or skin are hardly likely to be useful in this discriminative context. These are variables that are easy to measure (and indeed are general characteristics of a person's appearance) but carry little information as to the class identity in this particular case.

In most data mining problems it is not so obvious which variables are (or are not) relevant. For example, relating a person's demographic characteristics to online purchasing behavior may be quite subtle and may not necessarily follow the traditional patterns (consider a hypothetical group of high-income PhD-educated consumers who spend a lot of money on comic books—if they exist, a comic-book retailer would like to know!). In data mining we are particularly interested in letting the data speak, which in the context of variable selection means using data-adaptive methods for variable selection (while noting as usual that should useful prior knowledge be available to inform us about which variables are clearly irrelevant to the task, then by all means we should use this information).

We have discussed this problem in a general modeling context in chapter 6, where we outlined some general strategies that we briefly review here:

Variable Selection: The idea here is to select a subset p' of the original p variables. Of course we don't know in advance what value of p' will work well or which variables should be included, so there is a combinatorially large search space of variable subsets that could be considered. Thus most approaches rely on some form of heuristic search through the space of variable subsets, often using a greedy approach to add or delete variables one at a time. There are two general approaches here: the first uses a classification algorithm that automatically performs variable selection as part of the definition of the basic model, the classification tree model being the best-known example. The second approach is to use the classifier as a "black box" and to have an external loop (or "wrapper") that systematically adds and subtracts variables to the current subset, each subset being evaluated on the basis of how well the classification model performs.

Variable Transformations: The idea here is to transform the original measurements by some linear or nonlinear function via a preprocessing step, typically resulting in a much smaller set of derived variables, and then to build the classifier on this transformed set. Examples of this approach include principal components analysis (in which we try to find the directions in the input space that have the highest variance, essentially a data compression technique—see chapters 3 and 6), projection pursuit (in which an algorithm searches for interesting linear projections—see chapters 6 and 11), and related techniques such as factor analysis and independent components analysis. While these techniques can be quite powerful in their own right, they suffer the disadvantage of not necessarily being well matched to the overall goal of improving classification performance. A case in point is principal component analysis. Figure 10.6 shows an illustrative example in which the first principal component direction (the direction in which the data would be projected and potentially used as input to a classifier) is completely orthogonal to the best linear discriminant for the problem—that is, it is completely in the wrong direction for the classification task! This is not a problem with the principal component methodology per se but simply an illustration of matching an inappropriate technique to the classification task. This is of course a somewhat artificial and pathological example; in practice principal component projections can often be quite useful for classification, but nonetheless it is important to keep the objectives in mind.

10.12 Further Reading

Fisher's original paper on linear discriminant analysis dates from 1936. Duda, Hart, and Stork (2001) (the second edition of the classic pattern recognition

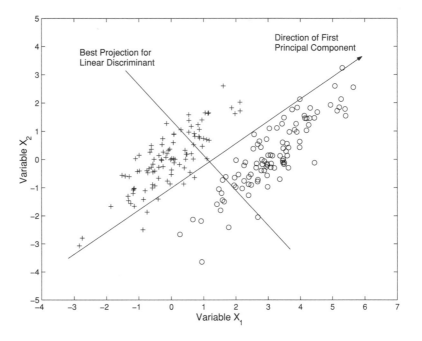

Figure 10.6 An illustration of the potential pitfalls of using principal component analysis as a preprocessor for classification. This is an artificial two-dimensional classification problem, with data from each class plotted with different symbols. The first principal component direction (which would be the first candidate direction on which to project the data if this were actually a high-dimensional problem) is in fact almost completely orthogonal to the best linear projection for discrimination as determined by Fisher's linear discriminant technique.

text by Duda and Hart (1973)) contains a wealth of detail on a variety of classification methods, with a particularly detailed treatment of Normal multivariate classifiers (chapter 3) and linear discriminant and perceptron learning algorithms (chapter 5). Statistically oriented reviews of classification are given by Hand (1981, 1997), Devijver and Kittler (1982), Fukunaga (1990), McLachlan (1992), Ripley (1996), Devroye, Gyorfi, and Lugosi (1996), and Webb (1999). Bishop (1995) provides a neural network perspective, Mitchell (1997) offers a viewpoint from artificial intelligence, and Witten and Frank (2000) provide a data-mining oriented introduction to classification.

Dasarathy (1991) contains many of the classic papers on nearest neighbor classification from the statistical pattern recognition literature and general descriptions of nearest neighbor methods, including outlines of methods for reducing the size of the retained set, may be found in Hand (1981) and McLachlan (1992). Choice of metric for nearest neighbor methods is discussed in Short and Fukunaga (1981), Fukunaga and Flick (1984), and Myles and Hand (1990). Hastie and Tibshirani (1996) describe an adaptive local technique for estimating a metric. Asymptotic properties of nearest neighbor rules are described in Devroye and Wagner (1982). The related kernel method is discussed in Hand (1982). The problem of the meaning of "nearest" neighbor in high dimensions is considered in Beyer et al. (1999) and Bennett, Fayad, and Geiger (1999), who also discuss the use of clustering for approximate searches.

One of the earliest descriptions of tree-based models is in Morgan and Sonquist (1963). The application of decision trees to classification was popularized in machine learning by Quinlan (1986, 1993). In statistics, the book by Breiman et al. (1984) describing the CART (*Classification And Regression Trees*) algorithm was highly influential in the widespread adoption and application of tree models. Chapter 7 of Ripley (1996) contains an extensive overview of the different contributions to the tree-learning literature from statistics, computer science, and engineering. A recent survey article is Murthy (1998). Scalable algorithms for constructing decision trees are considered in Shafer, Agrawal, and Mehta (1996), Gehrke, Ramakrishnan, and Ganti (1998), and Rastogi and Shim (1998). The Sprint method of Shafer, Agrawal, and Mehta (1996) operates in a very small amount of main memory but applies only to the CART splitting criterion. The RainForest framework of Gehrke, Ramakrishnan, and Ganti (1998) can be used to scale up a variety of splitting criteria, but its memory usage depends on the sizes of domains of the variables. The method of Rastogi and Shim (1998) interleaves tree building and pruning, thus preventing unnecessary access to the data. A nice survey of scalability issues is Ganti, Gehrke, and Ramakrishnan (1999).

Discussions of the independence Bayes method include Russek, Kronmal, and Fisher (1983), Hilden (1984), Kohavi (1996), Domingos and Pazzani (1997), and Hand and Yu (1999).

Descriptions of support vector machines are given by Vapnik (1995), Burges (1998), and Vapnik (1998). Scholkopf, Burges, and Smola (1999) is a collection of recent papers on the same topic, and Platt (1999) describes a useful technique for speeding up the training of these classifiers.

Techniques for combining classifiers, such as model averaging, are described in Xu, Krzyzak, and Suen (1992), Wolpert (1992), Buntine (1992), Ho, Hull, and Srihari (1994), Schaffer (1994), and Oliver and Hand (1996). Freund and Schapire (1996) describe the boosting technique; more recent theoretical treatments are provided by Schapire et al. (1998) and Friedman, Hastie, and Tibshirani (2000).

A detailed review of assessment and evaluation methods for classification algorithms is given in Hand (1997). Reviews of error rate estimation methods in particular are given in Toussaint (1974), Hand (1986), McLachlan (1987), and Schiavo and Hand (1999). The reject option is treated in detail in Devijver and Kittler (1982). MacMillan and Creelman (1991) provide an overview of ROC and related methods.

A seminal discussion of missing data, their different types, and how to handle them, is given in Little and Rubin (1987).

11 *Predictive Modeling for Regression*

11.1 Introduction

In chapter 6 we discussed the distinction between predictive and descriptive models. In chapter 10 we described in detail predictive models in which the variable to be predicted (the *response variable*) was a nominal variable—that is, it could take one of only a finite (and typically small) number of values and these values had no numerical significance, so that they were simply *class identifiers*. In this chapter we turn to predictive models in which the response variable does have numerical significance. Examples are the amount a retail store might earn from a given customer over a ten-year period, the rate of fuel consumption of a given type of car under normal conditions, the number of people who might access a particular Web site in a given month, and so on. The variables to be used as input for prediction will be called *predictor variables* and the variable to be predicted is the *response variable*. Other authors sometimes use the terms *dependent* or *target* for the response variable, and *independent, explanatory,* or *regressor* for the predictor variables. Other names used in the classification context were mentioned in chapter 10. Note that the predictor variables can be numerical, but they need not be. Our aim, then, is to use a sample of objects, for which both the response variable and the predictor variables are known, to construct a model that will allow prediction of the numerical value of the response variable for a new case for which only the predictor variables are known. This is essentially the same problem as in chapter 10, the only difference being the numerical instead of nominal nature of the response variable. In fact, as we will see later in this chapter, we can also treat prediction of nominal variables (that is, classification) within this general framework of regression.

Accuracy of prediction is one of the most important properties of such models, so various measures of accuracy have been devised. These measures may also be used for choosing between alternative models, and for choosing the values of parameters in models. In the terminology introduced earlier, these measures are *score* functions, by which different models may be compared.

Predictive accuracy is a critical aspect of models, but it is not the only aspect. For example, we might use the model to shed insight into which of the predictor variables are most important. We might even insist that some variables be included in the model, because we know they should be there on substantive grounds, even though they lead to only small predictive improvement. Contrariwise, we might omit variables that we feel would enhance our predictive performance. (An example of this situation arises in credit scoring, in which, in many countries, it is illegal to include sex or race as a predictor variable.) We might be interested in whether predictor variables interact, in the sense that the effect that one has on the response variable depends on the values taken by others. For obvious reasons, we might be interested in whether good prediction can be achieved by a simple model. Sometimes we might even be willing to sacrifice some predictive accuracy in exchange for substantially reduced model complexity. Though predictive accuracy is perhaps the most important component of the performance of a predictive model, this has to be tempered by the context in which the model is to be applied.

11.2   Linear Models and Least Squares Fitting

Chapter 6 introduced the idea of linear models, so called because they are linear in the parameters. The simplest such model yields predicted values, $\hat{y}$, of the response variable y, that are also a linear combination of the predictor variables x_j:

$$\hat{y} = a_o + \sum_{i=1}^{p} a_j x_j \tag{11.1}$$

In fact, of course, we will not normally be able to predict the response variable perfectly (life is seldom so simple) and a common aim is to predict the mean value that y takes at each vector of the predictor variables—so $\hat{y}$ is our predicted estimate of the mean value at $\mathbf{x} = (x_1, \ldots, x_p)$. Models of this form are known as *linear regression models*. In the simplest case of a single predictor variable (*simple regression*), we have a *regression line* in the space spanned by the response and predictor variables. More generally (*multiple regression*) we have a *regression plane*. Such models are the oldest, most important, and single most widely used form of predictive model. One reason for this is their evident simplicity; a simple weighted sum is very easy both to compute and to understand. Another compelling reason is that they often perform very well—even in circumstances in which we know enough to be confident that the true relationship between the predictor and response variables cannot be linear. This is not altogether surprising: when we expand continuous mathematical functions in a Taylor series we often find that the lowest order terms—the linear terms—are the most important, so that the best simple approximation is obtained by using a linear model.

It is extremely rare that the chosen model is exactly right. This is especially true in data mining situations, where our model is generally empirical rather than being based on an underlying theory (see chapter 9). The model may not include all of the predictor variables that are needed for perfect prediction (many may not have been measured or even be measurable); it may not include certain functions of the predictor variables (maybe x_1^2 is needed as well as x_1, or maybe products of the predictor variables are needed because they interact in their effect on y); and, in any case, no measurement is perfect; the y variable will have errors associated with it so that each vector $(x_1, \ldots, x_p)$ will be associated with a distribution of possible y values, as we have noted above.

All of this means that the actual y values in a sample will differ from the predicted values. The differences between observed and predicted values are called *residuals,* and we denote these by e:

$$y(i) = \hat{y}(i) + e(i) = a_o + \sum_{j=1}^{p} a_j x_j(i) + e(i), \quad 1 \leq i \leq n. \tag{11.2}$$

In matrix terms, if we denote the observed y measurements on the n objects in the training sample by the vector $\mathbf{y}$ and the p measurements of the predictor variables on the n objects by the n by $p + 1$ matrix $\mathbf{X}$ (an additional column of 1s are added to incorporate the intercept term a_0 in the model), we can express the relationship between the observed response and predictor measurements, in terms of our model, as

$$\mathbf{y} = \mathbf{X}\mathbf{a} + \mathbf{e}, \tag{11.3}$$

where $\mathbf{y}$ is an $n \times 1$ matrix of response values, $\mathbf{a} = (a_0, \ldots, a_p)$ represents the $(p+1) \times 1$ vector of parameter values, and the $n \times 1$ vector $\mathbf{e} = (e(1), \ldots, e(n))$ contains the residuals. Clearly we want to choose the parameters in our model (the values in the $p + 1$ vector **a**) so as to yield predictions that are as accurate as possible. Put another way, we must find estimates for the a_j that minimize the e discrepancies in some way. To do this, we combine the elements of **e** in such a way as to yield a single numerical measure that we can minimize. Various ways of combining the $e(i)$ have been proposed, but by far the most popular method is to sum their squares—that is, the sum of squared errors score function. Thus we seek the values for the parameter vector **a** that minimizes

$$\sum_{i=1}^{n} e(i)^2 = \sum_{i=1}^{n} \left(y(i) - \sum_{j=0}^{p} a_j x_j(i) \right)^2 \tag{11.4}$$

In this expression, $y(i)$ is the observed y value for the ith training sample point and

$$(x_0(i), x_1(i), \dots, x_p(i)) = (1, x_1(i), \dots, x_p(i))$$

is the vector of predictor variables for this point. For obvious reasons, this method is known as the *least squares method*. For simplicity, we will denote the parameter vector that minimizes this by $(a_0, \dots, a_p)$. (It would be more correct, of course, if we used some notation to indicate that it is an estimate, such as $(\hat{a}_0, \dots, \hat{a}_p)$, but our notation has the merit of simplicity.) In matrix terms, the values of the parameters that minimize equation 11.4 can be shown to be

$$\mathbf{a} = \left(\mathbf{X}^T \mathbf{X} \right)^{-1} \mathbf{X}^T \mathbf{y}. \tag{11.5}$$

In linear regression in general, the **a** parameters are called *regression coefficients*. Once the parameters have been estimated, they are used in equation 11.1 to yield predictions. The predicted value of y, $\hat{y}_k$, for a vector of predictor variables $\mathbf{x}_k$, is given by $\hat{y}_k = \mathbf{x}_k^T \mathbf{a} = \mathbf{a}^T \mathbf{x}_k$.

11.2.1   Computational Issues in Fitting the Model

Solving equation 11.5 directly requires that the matrix $\mathbf{X}^T \mathbf{X}$ be invertible. Problems will arise if the sample size n is small (rare in data mining situations) or if there are linear dependencies between the measured values of the predictor variables (not so rare). In the latter case, modern software packages normally issue warnings, and appropriate action can be taken, such as dropping some of the predictor variables.

A rather more subtle problem arises when the measured values of the predictor variables are not exactly linearly dependent, but are almost so. Now the matrix can be inverted, but the solution will be unstable. This means that slight alterations to the observed $\mathbf{X}$ values would lead to substantial differences in the estimated values of $\mathbf{a}$. Different measurement errors or a slightly different training sample would have led to different parameter estimates. This problem is termed *multicollinearity*. The instability in the estimated parameters is a problem if these values are the focus of interest—for example, if we want to know which of the variables is most important in the model. However, it will not normally be a problem as far as predictive accuracy is concerned: although substantially different a vectors may be produced by slight variations of the data, all of these vectors will lead to similar predictions for *most* $\mathbf{x}_k$ vectors.

Solving equation 11.5 is usually carried out by numerical linear algebra techniques for equation solving (such as the LU decomposition or the singular value decomposition (SVD)), which tend to have better numerical stability than that achieved by inverting the matrix $\mathbf{X}^T\mathbf{X}$ directly. The underlying computational complexity is typically the same no matter which particular technique is used, namely, $O(p^2 n + p^3)$. The $p^2 n$ term comes from the n multiplications required to calculate each element in the $p \times p$ matrix $\mathbf{C} = \mathbf{X}^T\mathbf{X}$. The p^3 term comes from then solving $\mathbf{Ca} = \mathbf{X}^T\mathbf{y}$ for $\mathbf{a}$.

In chapter 6 we remarked that the additive nature of the regression model could be retained while permitting more flexible model forms by including transformations of the raw x_j as well as the raw variables themselves. Figure 11.1 shows a plot of data collected in an experiment in which a subject performed a physical task at a gradually increasing level of difficulty. The vertical axis shows a measure on the gases expired from the lungs while the horizontal axis shows the oxygen uptake. The nonlinearity of the relationship between these two variables is quite clear from the plot. A straight line $y = a_0 + a_1 x$ provides a poor fit—as is shown in the figure. The predicted values from this model would be accurate only for x (oxygen uptake) values just above 1000 and just below 4000. (Despite this, the model is not grossly inaccurate—the point made earlier about models linear in x providing reasonable approximations is clearly true.) However, the model $y = a_0 + a_1 x + a_2 x^2$ gives the fitted line shown in figure 11.2. This model is still linear in the parameters, so that these can be easily estimated using the same standard matrix manipulation shown above in equation 11.5. It is clear that the predictions obtained from this model are about as good as they can be. The remaining inaccuracy in the model is the irreducible measurement error associated with the variance of y about its mean at each value of x.

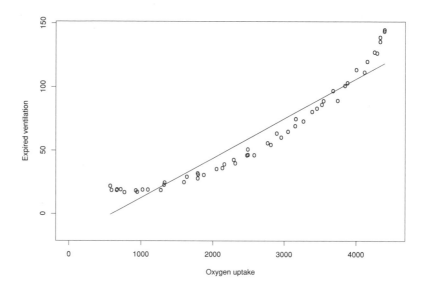

Figure 11.1 Expired ventilation plotted against oxygen uptake in a series of trials, with fitted straight line.

11.2.2 A Probabilistic Interpretation of Linear Regression

This informal data analytic route allows us to fit a regression model to any data set involving a response variable and a set of predictor variables, and to obtain a vector of estimated regression coefficients. If our aim were merely to produce a convenient summary of the training data (as, very occasionally, it is) we could stop there. However, this chapter is concerned with predictive models. Our aim is to go beyond the training data to predict y values for other "out-of-sample" objects. Goodness of fit to the given data is all very well, but we are really interested in fit to future data that arise from the same process, so that our future predictions are as accurate as possible. In order to explore this, we need to embed the model-building process in a more formal inferential context. To do this, we suppose that each observed value $y(i)$ is produced as a sum of weighted predictor variables $\alpha^T \mathbf{x}(i)$ and a random term $\epsilon(i)$ that follows a $N(0, \sigma^2)$ distribution independent of other values. (Note that implicit in this is the assumption that the variances of the random terms are all the same—σ^2 is the same for all possible values of the vector

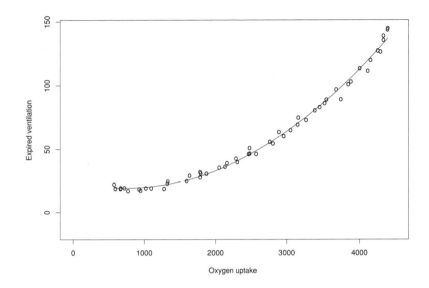

Figure 11.2　The data from figure 11.1 with a model that includes a term in x^2.

of predictor variables. We will discuss this assumption further below.) The $n \times 1$ random vector $\mathbf{Y}$ thus takes the form $\mathbf{Y} = \mathbf{X}\alpha + \epsilon$. The observed $n \times 1$ $\mathbf{y}$ vector in equation 11.3 is a realization from this distribution. The components of the $n \times 1$ vector ϵ are often called *errors*. Note that they are different from the residuals, e. An "error" is a random realization from a given distribution, whereas a residual is a difference between a fitted model and an observed y value. Note also that α is different from $\mathbf{a}$. α is represents the underlying and unknown truth, whereas $\mathbf{a}$ gives the values used in a model of the truth.

It turns out that within this framework the least squares estimate $\mathbf{a}$ is also the maximum likelihood estimate of α. Furthermore, the covariance matrix of the estimate $\mathbf{a}$ obtained above is $(\mathbf{X}^T\mathbf{X})^{-1}\sigma^2$, where this covariance matrix expresses the uncertainty in our parameter estimates $\mathbf{a}$. In the case of a single predictor variable, this gives

$$\left(1 + \frac{n\bar{x}^2}{\sum_i \left(x(i) - \bar{x} \right)^2} \right) \frac{\sigma^2}{n} \tag{11.6}$$

for the variance of the intercept term and

$$\frac{\sigma^2}{\sum_i \left(x(i) - \bar{x} \right)^2} \tag{11.7}$$

for the variance of the slope. Here $\bar{x}$ is the sample mean of the single predictor variable. The diagonal elements of the covariance matrix for $\mathbf{a}$ above give the variances of the regression coefficients—which can be used to test whether the individual regression coefficients are significantly different from zero. If v_j is the jth diagonal element of $(\mathbf{X}^T\mathbf{X})^{-1}\sigma^2$, then the ratio $a_j/\sqrt{v_j}$ can be compared with a $t(n - p - 1)$ distribution to see whether the regression coefficient is zero. However, as we discuss below, this test makes sense only in the context of the other variables included in the model, and alternative methods, also discussed below, are available for more elaborate model-building exercises. If $\mathbf{x}$ is the vector of predictor variables for a new object, with predicted y value $\hat{y}$, then the variance of $\hat{y}$ is $\mathbf{x}^T(\mathbf{X}^T\mathbf{X})^{-1}\mathbf{x}\sigma^2$. With one predictor variable, this reduces to $\sigma^2 \left(\frac{1}{n} + (x - \bar{x})^2 / \sum(x(i) - \bar{x})^2 \right)$. Note that this variance is greater the further $\mathbf{x}$ is from the mean of the training sample. That is, the least accurate predictions, in terms of variance, are those in the tails of the distribution of predictor variables. Note also that confidence intervals (see chapter 4) based on this variance are confidence values for the *predicted value* of y.

We may also be interested in (what are somewhat confusingly called) *prediction intervals,* telling us a range of plausible values for the observed y at a given value of x, not a range of plausible values for the predicted value. Prediction intervals must include the uncertainty arising from our prediction and also that arising from the variability of y about our predicted value. This means that the variance above is increased by an extra term σ^2, yielding $\sigma^2 \left(1 + \frac{1}{n} + (x - \bar{x})^2 / \sum(x(i) - \bar{x})^2 \right)$.

> **Example 11.1** The most important special case of linear regression arises when there is just one predictor variable. Figure 11.3 shows a plot of the record time (in 1984, in minutes) against the distance (in miles) for 35 Scottish hill races. We can use regression to attempt to predict record time from distance. A simple linear regression of the data gives an estimated intercept value of -4.83 and an estimated regression coefficient of 8.33. Most modern data analytic packages will give the associated standard errors of the estimates, along with significance tests of the null hypotheses that the true parameters that led to the data are zero. In this case, the standard errors are 5.76 and 0.62, respectively, yielding significance probabilities of 0.41 and < 0.01. From this we would conclude that there is strong evidence that the positive linear relationship is real, but

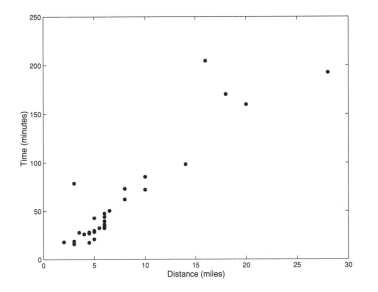

Figure 11.3   A plot of record time (in minutes) against distance (in miles) for 35 Scottish hill races from 1984.

no evidence of a non-zero intercept. The plot in figure 11.3 shows marked skewness in both variables (they become more sparsely spread towards the top and right of the figure). It is clear that the position of the regression line will be much more sensitive to the precise position of points to the right of the figure than it will be to the position of points to the left. Points that can have a big effect on the conclusion are called points of high *leverage*—they are points at the extreme values of estimated relative performance in figure 11.3. Points that actually do have a big effect are called *influential points*. For example, if the rightmost point in figure 11.3 had time of 100 (while still having distance around 28), it would clearly have a big effect on the regression line. The asymmetry of the leverage of the points in the figure might be regarded as undesirable. We might try to overcome this by reducing the skewness—for example, by log transforming both the variables before fitting the regression line.

11.2.3   Interpreting the Fitted Model

The coefficients in a multiple regression model can be interpreted as follows: if the jth predictor variable, x_j, is increased by one unit, while all the other predictor variables are kept fixed, then the response variable y will increase by α_j. The regression coefficients thus tell us the *conditional* effect of each predictor variable, conditional on keeping the other predictor variables constant. This is an important aspect of the interpretation. In particular, the size of the regression coefficient associated with the jth variable will depend on what other variables are in the model. This is clearly especially important if we are constructing models in a sequential manner: add another variable and the coefficients of those already in the model will change. (There is an exception to this. If the predictor variables are orthogonal, then the estimated regression coefficients are unaffected by the presence or absence of others in the model. However, this situation is most common in designed experiments, and is rare in the kinds of secondary data analyses encountered in data mining.) The sizes of the regression coefficients tell us the relative importance of the variables, in the sense that we can compare the effects of unit changes. Note also that the size of the effects depends on the chosen units of measurement for the predictor variables. If we measure x_1 in kilometers instead of millimeters, then its associated regression coefficient will be multiplied by a million. This can make comparisons between variables difficult, so people often work with standardized variables—measuring each predictor variable relative to its standard deviation.

We used the sum of squared errors between the predictions and the observed y values as a criterion through which to choose the values of the parameters in the model. This is the *residual sum of squares* or the *sum of squared residuals*, $\sum e(i)^2 = \sum (y(i) - \hat{y}(i))^2$. In a sense, the worst model would be obtained if we simply predicted all of the y values by the value $\bar{y}$, the mean of the sample of y values that is constant relative to the x values (thus effectively ignoring the inputs to the model and always guessing the output to be the mean of y). The *total sum of squares* is defined as the sum of squared errors for this worst model, $\sum (y(i) - \bar{y})^2$. The difference between the residual sum of squares from a model and the total sum of squares is the sum of squares that can be attributed to the regression for that model—it is the *regression sum of squares*. This is the sum of squared differences of the predicted values, $\hat{y}(i)$, from the overall mean, $\sum (\hat{y}(i) - \bar{y})^2$. The symbol R^2 is often used for the "multiple correlation coefficient," the ratio of the regression sum of squares to total sum of squares:

$$R^2 = \frac{\sum (\hat{y}(i) - \bar{y})^2}{\sum (y(i) - \bar{y})^2}. \tag{11.8}$$

A value near 1 tells us that the model explains most of the y variation in the data. The number of independent components contributing to each sum of

Source of variation	Sum of squares	Degrees of freedom	Mean square
Regression	$\sum \left(\hat{y}(i) - \bar{y} \right)^2$	p	$\sum \left(\hat{y}(i) - \bar{y} \right)^2 / p$
Residual	$\sum \left(y(i) - \hat{y}(i) \right)^2$	$n - p - 1$	$\sum \left(y(i) - \hat{y}(i) \right)^2 / (n - p - 1)$
Total	$\sum \left(y(i) - \bar{y} \right)^2$	$n - 1$	

Table 11.1   The analysis of variance decomposition table for a regression.

squares is called the number of *degrees of freedom* for that sum of squares. The degrees of freedom for the total sum of squares is $n - 1$ (one less than the sample size, since the components are all calculated relative to the mean). The degrees of freedom for the residual sum of squares is $n - 1 - p$ (although there are n terms in the summation, $p + 1$ regression coefficients are calculated). The degrees of freedom for the regression sum of squares is p, the difference between the total and residual degrees of freedom. These sums of squares and their associated degrees of freedom are usefully put together in an analysis of variance table, as in table 11.1, summarizing the decomposition of the totals into components. The meaning of the final column is described below.

11.2.4   Inference and Generalization

We have already noted that our real aim in building predictive models is one of inference: we want to make statements (predictions) about objects for which we do not know the y values. This means that goodness of fit to the training data is not our real objective. In particular, for example, merely because we have obtained nonzero estimated regression coefficients, this does not necessarily mean that the variables are related: it could be merely that our model has captured chance idiosyncrasies of the training sample. This is particularly relevant in the context of data mining where many models may be explored and fit to the data in a relatively automated fashion. As discussed earlier, we need some way to *test* the model, to see how easily the observed data could have arisen by chance, even if there was no structure in the population the data were collected from. In this case, we need to test whether the population regression coefficients are really zero. (Of course, this is not the only test we might be interested in, but it is the one most often required.) It can be shown that if the values of α_j are actually all zero (and still making the assumption that the $\epsilon(i)$ are independently distributed as $N(0, \sigma^2)$),

$$\frac{\sum(\hat{y}(i) - \bar{y})^2/p}{\sum(y(i) - \bar{y})^2/(n - p - 1)} \tag{11.9}$$

has an $F(p, n - p - 1)$ distribution. This is just the ratio of the two mean squares given in table 11.1. The test is carried out by comparing the value of this ratio with the upper critical level of the $F(p, n - p - 1)$ distribution. If the ratio exceeds this value the test is significant—and we would conclude that there is a linear relationship between the y and x_j variables (or that a very unlikely event has occurred). If the ratio is less than the critical value we have no evidence to reject the null hypothesis that the population regression coefficients are all zero.

11.2.5   Model Search and Model Building

We have described an overall test to see whether the regression coefficients in a given model are all zero. However, we are more often involved in a situation of searching over model space—or *model building*—in which we examine a sequence of models to find one that is "best" in some sense. In particular, we often need to examine the effect of adding a set of predictor variables to a set we have already included. Note that this includes the special case of adding just one extra variable, and that the idea is applied in reverse, it can also handle the situation of removing variables from a model.

In order to compare models we need a score function. Once again, the obvious one is the sum of squared errors between the predictions and the observed y values. Suppose we are comparing two models: a model with p predictor variables (model M) and the largest model we are prepared to contemplate, with q variables (these will include all the untransformed predictor variables we think might be relevant, along with any transformations of them we think might be relevant), model M^*. Each of these models will have an associated residual sum of squares, and the difference between them will tell us how much better the larger model fits the data than the smaller model. (Equivalently, we could calculate the difference between the regression sums of squares. Since the residual and regression sum of squares sum to the total sum of squares, which is the same for both models, the two calculations will yield the same result.) The degrees of freedom associated with the difference between the residual sums of squares for the two models is $q - p$, the extra number of regression coefficients computed in fitting the larger model, M^*. The ratio between the difference of the residual sums of squares and

Source of variation	Sum of squares	Degrees of freedom	Mean square
Regression Model 1	$SS(M)$	p	$SS(M)/p$
Regression Full Model	$SS(M^*)$	q	$SS(M^*)/q$
Difference	$SS(M^*) - SS(M)$	$q - p$	$\frac{(SS(M*)-SS(M))}{(q-p)}$
Residual	$SS(T) - SS(M^*)$	$n - q - 1$	$\frac{(SS(T)-SS(M^*))}{(n-q-1)}$
Total	$SS(T)$	$n - 1$	

Table 11.2 The analysis of variance decomposition table for model building.

the difference of degrees of freedom again gives us a mean square—now a mean square for the difference between the two models. Comparison of this with the residual mean square for model M^* gives us an F-test of whether the difference between the models is real or not. Table 11.2 illustrates this extension. From this table, the ratio

$$\left[\frac{(SS(M^*) - SS(M))}{(q - p)} \right] \Big/ \left[\frac{(SS(T) - SS(M^*))}{(n - q - 1)} \right]$$

is compared with the critical value of an $F(q - p, n - q - 1)$ distribution.

This is fine if we have just a few models we want to compare, but data mining problems are such that often we need to rely on automatic model building processes. Such automatic methods are available in most modern data mining computer packages. There are various strategies that may be adopted. A basic form is a *forward selection* method, mentioned in chapter 8, in which variables are added one at a time to an existing model. At each step that variable is chosen from the set of potential variables that leads to the greatest increase in predictive power (measured in terms of reduction of sum of squared residuals), provided the increase exceeds some specified threshold. Ideally, the addition would be made as long as the increase in predictive power was statistically significant, but in practice this is complicated to ensure: the variable selection process necessarily involves carrying out many tests, not all independent, so that computing correct significance values is a nontrivial process. The simple significance level based on table 11.2 does not apply when multiple dependent tests are made. (The implication of this is that if the significance level is being used to choose variables, then it is being used as a score function, and should not be given a probabilistic interpretation.)

We can, of course, in principle use any of the score functions discussed in chapter 7 for model selection in regression, such as BIC, minimum description length, cross-validation, or more Bayesian methods. These provide an alternative to the hypothesis-testing framework that measures the statistical significance of adding and deleting terms on a model-by-model basis. Penalized score functions such as BIC, and variations on cross-validation tailored specifically to regression, are commonly used in practice as score functions for model selection in regression.

A strategy opposite to that of forward selection is *backward elimination*. We begin with the most complex model we might contemplate (the "largest model," M^*, above) and progressively eliminate variables, selecting them on the basis that eliminating them leads to the least increase in sum of squared residuals (again, subject to some threshold). Other variants include combinations of forward selection and backward elimination. For example, we might add two variables, eliminate one, add two, remove one, and so on. For data sets where the number of variables p is very large, it may be much more practical computationally to build the model in the forward direction than in the backward direction. Stepwise methods are attempts to restrict the search of the space of all possible sets of predictor variables, so that the search is manageable. But if the search is restricted, it is possible that some highly effective combination of variables may be overlooked. Very occasionally (if the set of potential predictor variables is small), we can examine all possible sets of variables (although, with p variables, there are $(2^p - 1)$ possible subsets). The size of problems for which all possible subsets can be examined has been expanded by the use of strategies such as branch and bound, which rely on the monotonicity of the residual sum of squares criterion (see chapter 8).

A couple of cautionary comments are worth making here. First, as we have noted, the coefficients of variables already in the model will generally change as new variables are added. A variable that is important for one model may become less so when the model is extended. Second, as we have discussed in earlier chapters, if too elaborate a search is carried out there is a high chance of overfitting the training set—that is, of obtaining a model that provides a good fit to the training set (small residual sum of squares) but does not

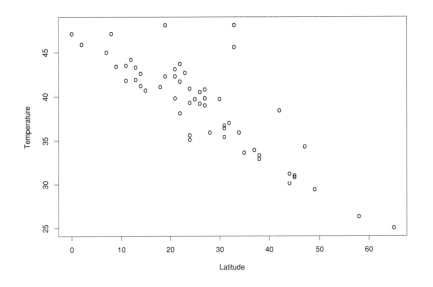

Figure 11.4   Temperature (degrees F) against latitude (degrees N) for 56 cities in the United States.

predict new data very well.

11.2.6   Diagnostics and Model Inspection

Although multiple regression is a very powerful and widely used technique, some of the assumptions might be regarded as restrictive. The assumption that the variance of the y distribution is the same at each vector $\mathbf{x}$ is often inappropriate. (This assumption of equal variances is called *homoscedasticity*. The converse is *heteroscedasticity*.) For example, figure 11.4 shows the normal average January minimum temperature (in deg F) plotted against the latitude (deg N) for 56 cities in the United States. There is evidence that, for smaller latitudes, at least, the variance of the temperature increases with increasing latitude (although the mean temperature seems to decrease). We can still apply the standard least squares algorithm above to estimate parameters in this new situation (and the resulting estimates would still be unbiased if the model form were correct), but we could do better in the sense that it is possible to find estimators with smaller variance.

To do this we need to modify the basic method. Essentially, we need to arrange things so that those values of $\mathbf{x}$ associated with y values with larger variance are weighted less heavily in the model fitting process. This makes perfect sense—it means that the estimator is more influenced by the more accurate values. Formally, this idea leads to a modification of the solution equation 11.5. Suppose that the covariance matrix of the $n \times 1$ random vector ϵ is the $n \times n$ matrix $\sigma^2 \mathbf{V}$ (previously we took $\mathbf{V} = \mathbf{I}$). The case of unequal variances means that $\mathbf{V}$ is diagonal with terms that are not all equal. Now it is possible (see any standard text on linear algebra) to find a unique nonsingular matrix $\mathbf{P}$ such that $\mathbf{P}^T \mathbf{P} = \mathbf{V}$. We can use this to define a new random vector $\mathbf{f} = \mathbf{P}^{-1}\epsilon$, and it is easy to show that the covariance matrix of $\mathbf{f}$ is $\sigma^2 \mathbf{I}$. Using this idea, we form a new model by premultiplying the old one by $\mathbf{P}^{-1}$:

$$\mathbf{P}^{-1}\mathbf{Y} = \mathbf{P}^{-1}\mathbf{X}\alpha + \mathbf{P}^{-1}\epsilon \qquad (11.10)$$

or

$$\mathbf{Z} = \mathbf{W}\beta + \mathbf{f}, \qquad (11.11)$$

now of the form required to apply the standard least squares algorithm. If we do this, and then convert the solution back into the original variables $\mathbf{Y}$, we obtain:

$$\mathbf{a} = \left(\mathbf{X}^T \mathbf{V}^{-1} \mathbf{X}\right) \mathbf{X} \mathbf{V}^{-1} \mathbf{y}, \qquad (11.12)$$

a *weighted* least squares solution. The variance of this estimated parameter vector $\mathbf{a}$ is $\left(\mathbf{X}^T \mathbf{V}^{-1} \mathbf{X}\right)^{-1} \sigma^2$.

Unequal variances of the y distributions for different $\mathbf{x}$ vectors is one way in which the assumptions of basic multiple regression can break down. There are others. What we really need are ways to explore the quality of the model and tools that will enable us to detect where and why the model deviates from the assumptions. That is, we require *diagnostic* tools. In simple regression, where there is only one predictor variable, we can see the quality of the model from a plot of y against x (see figures 11.1, 11.2, and 11.4). More generally, however, when there is more than one predictor variable, such a simple plot is not possible, and more sophisticated methods are needed. In general, the key features for examining the quality of a regression model are the residuals, the components of the vector $\mathbf{e} = \mathbf{y} - \hat{\mathbf{y}}$. If there is a pattern to these, it tells us that the model is failing to explain the distribution of the data. Various plots involving the residuals are used, including plotting the residuals against the fitted values, plotting standardized residuals (obtained

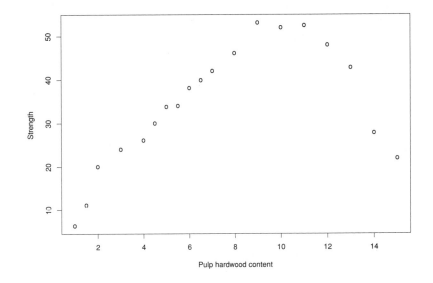

Figure 11.5 A plot of tensile strength of paper against the percentage of hardwood in the pulp.

by dividing the residuals by their standard errors) against the fitted values, and plotting the standardized residuals against standard normal quantiles. (The latter are "normal probability plots." If the residuals are approximately normally distributed, the points in this plot should lie roughly on a straight line.) Of course, interpreting some of the diagnostic plots requires practice and experience.

One general cautionary comment, applies to all predictive models: such models are valid only within the bounds of the data. It can be very risky to extrapolate beyond the data. A very simple example is given in figure 11.5. This shows a plot of the tensile strength of paper plotted against the percentage of hardwood in the pulp from which the paper was made. But suppose only those samples with pulp values between 1 and 9 had been measured. The figure shows that a straight line would provide quite a good fit to this subset of the data. For new samples of paper, with pulp values lying between 1 and 9, quite good prediction of the strength could legitimately be expected. But the figure also shows, strikingly clearly, that our model would produce predictions that were seriously amiss if we used it to predict the strength of paper with pulp values greater than 9. Only within the bounds of our data is the model trustworthy. We saw another example of this sort of thing in chapter 3, where we showed the number of credit cards in circulation each year. A straight line fitted to years 1985 to 1990 provided a good fit—but if predictions beyond those years were based on this model, disaster would follow.

These examples are particularly clear—but they involve just a few data points and a single predictor variable. In data mining applications, with large data sets and many variables, things may not be so clear. Caution needs to be exercised when we make predictions.

11.3   Generalized Linear Models

Section 11.2 described the *linear model*, in which the response variable was decomposed into two parts: a weighted sum of the predictor variables and a random component: $Y(i) = \sum_j \alpha_j x_j(i) + \epsilon(i)$. For inferential purposes we also assumed that the $\epsilon(i)$ were independently distributed as $N(0, \sigma^2)$. We can write this another way, which permits convenient generalization, splitting the description of the model into three parts:

(i) The $Y(i)$ are independent random variables, with distribution $N(\mu(i), \sigma^2)$.

(ii) The parameters enter the model in a linear way via the sum $\nu(i) = \sum \alpha_j x_j(i)$.

(iii) The $\nu(i)$ and $\mu(i)$ are linked by $\nu(i) = \mu(i)$.

This permits two immediate generalizations, while retaining the advantages of the linear combination of the parameters. First, in (i) we can relax the requirement that the random variables follow a normal distribution. Second, we can generalize the link expressed in (iii), so that some other *link* function $g(\mu(i)) = \nu(i)$ relates the parameter of the distribution to the linear term $\nu(i) = \sum \alpha_j x_j(i)$. These extensions result in what are called *generalized linear models*. They are one of the most important advances in data analysis of the last two decades. As we shall see, such models can also be regarded as fundamental components of feed forward neural networks.

One of the most important kinds of generalized linear model for data mining is *logistic regression*. We have already encountered this in chapter 10 in the form of logistic discrimination, but we describe it in rather more detail here, and use it as an illustration of the ideas underlying generalized linear models. In many situations the response variable is not continuous, as we have assumed above, but is a proportion: the number of flies from a given sample that die when exposed to an insecticide, the proportion of questions people get correct in a test, the proportion of oranges in a carton that are rotten. The extreme of this arises when the proportion is out of 1, that is, the observed response is binary: whether or not an individual insect dies, whether or not a person gets a particular one of the questions right, whether or not an individual orange is rotten. This is exactly the situation we discussed in chapter 10, though here we embed it in a more general context. We are now dealing with a binary response variable, with the random variable taking values 0 or 1 corresponding to the two possible outcomes. We will assume that the probability that the ith individual yields the value 1 is $p(i)$, and that the responses of different individuals are independent. This means that the response for the ith individual follows a Bernoulli distribution:

$$p\bigg(Y(i) = y(i)\bigg) = p(i)^{y(i)} \left(1 - p(i)\right)^{1-y(i)}, \tag{11.13}$$

where here $y(i) \in \{0, 1\}$. For logistic regression, this is the generalization of (i) above: the Bernoulli distribution is replacing the normal distribution.

Our aim is to formulate a model for the probability that an object with predictor vector $\mathbf{x}$ will take value 1. That is, we want a model for the mean value of the response, the probability $p(y = 1|\mathbf{x})$. We could use a linear model—a weighted sum of the predictor variables. However, this would not be ideal. Most obviously, a linear model can take values less than 0 and greater than 1 (if the $\mathbf{x}$ values are extreme enough). This suggests that we need to modify the model to include a nonlinear aspect. We achieve this by transforming the probability, nonlinearly, so that it can be modeled by a linear combination. That is, we use a nonlinear link function in (iii). A suitable function (not the only possible one) is a *logistic* (or *logit*) link function, in which

$$g\bigg(p(y = 1|\mathbf{x})\bigg) = \log \frac{p(y = 1|\mathbf{x})}{1 - p(y = 1|\mathbf{x})}, \tag{11.14}$$

where $g(p(y = 1|\mathbf{x}))$ is modeled as $\sum \alpha_j x_j$. As p varies from 0 to 1, $\log(p/1 - p)$ clearly varies from $-\infty$ to ∞, matching the potential range of $g(p) = \sum \alpha_j x_j(i)$. One of the advantages of the logistic link function over alternatives is that it permits convenient interpretation. For example:

- The ratio $\frac{p(y=1|\mathbf{x})}{1-p(y=1|\mathbf{x})}$ in the transformation is the familiar *odds* that a 1 will be observed and $\log \frac{p(y=1|\mathbf{x})}{1-p(y=1|\mathbf{x})}$ is the *log odds*.

- Given a new vector of predictor variables $\mathbf{x} = (x_1, \ldots, x_p)$, the predicted probability of observing a 1 is derived from $\log \frac{p(y=1|\mathbf{x})}{1-p(y=1|\mathbf{x})}$. The effect on this of changing the jth predictor variable by one unit is simply α_j. Thus the coefficients tell us the difference in log odds—or, equivalently, the log odds ratio resulting from the two values. From this it is easy to see that e^{α_j} is the factor by which the odds changes when the jth predictor variable changes by one unit (see the discussion of the effect of a unit change of one variable in the multiple regression case discussed in section 11.2).

Example 11.2 Two minutes into its flight on January 29, 1986, the space shuttle Challenger exploded, killing everyone on board. The two booster rockets for the shuttle are made of several pieces, with each of three joints sealed with a rubber "O-ring," making six rings in total. It was known that these O-rings were sensitive to temperature. Records of the proportion of O-rings damaged in previous flights were available, along with the temperatures on those days. The lowest previous temperature was 53degF. On the day of the flight the temperature was 31degF, so there was much discussion about whether the flight should go ahead. One argument was based on an analysis of the seven previous flights that had resulted in damage to at least one O-ring. A logistic regression to predict the probability of failure from temperature led to a slope estimate of 0.0014 with a standard error of 0.0498. From this, the predicted logit of the probability of failure at 31degF is 1.3466, yielding a predicted probability 0.206. The slope in this model is positive, suggesting that, if anything, the probability of failure is lower at low temperatures. However, this slope is not significantly different from zero, so that there is little evidence for a relationship between failure probability and temperature.

This analysis is far from ideal. First, 31degF is far below 53degF, so one is extrapolating beyond the data—a practice we warned against above. Secondly, there is valuable information in the 16 flights that had not resulted in O-ring damage. This is immediately obvious from a comparison of figure 11.6(a), which shows the numbers damaged for the seven flights above (vertical axis) against temperature (horizontal axis), and figure 11.6(b), which shows the number for all 23 flights. These 16 flights all took place at relatively high temperatures. The second figure suggests that the relationship might, in fact, have a negative slope. A logistic model fitted to the data in figure 11.6(b) gave a slope estimate of -0.1156, with a standard error of -2.46 (and an intercept estimate of 5.08 with standard error of 3.05). From this the predicted probability at 31degF is 0.817. This gives a rather different picture, one that could have been deduced before the flight if all the data had been studied.

Generalized linear models thus have three main features:

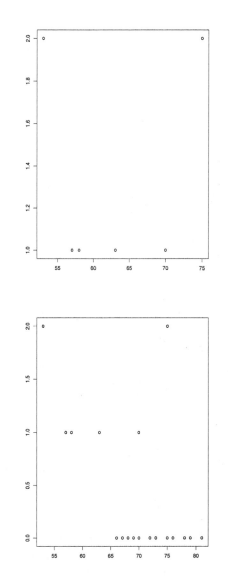

Figure 11.6 Number of O-rings damaged (vertical axis) against temperature on day of flight, (a) data examined before the flight, and (b) the complete data.

(i) The $Y(i), i = 1, \ldots, n$, are independent random variables, with the same exponential family distribution (see below).

(ii) The predictor variables are combined in a form $\nu(i) = \sum a_j x_j(i)$, called the *linear predictor*, where the a_js are *estimates* of the α_js.

(iii) The mean $\mu(i)$ of the distribution for a given predictor vector is related to the linear combination in (ii) through the link function $g\left(\mu(i)\right) = \nu(i) = \sum a_j x_j(i)$.

The *exponential family* of distributions is an important family that includes the normal, the Poisson, the Bernoulli, and the binomial distributions. Members of this family can be expressed in the general form

$$f(y; \theta, \phi) = e^{\frac{(y\theta - b(\theta))}{\alpha(\phi) + c(y, \phi)}}. \tag{11.15}$$

If ϕ is known, then θ is called the *natural* or *canonical* parameter. When, as is often the case, $\alpha(\phi) = \phi$, ϕ is called the *dispersion* or *scale* parameter. A little algebra reveals that the mean of this distribution is given by $b'(\theta)$ and the variance by $\alpha(\phi)b''(\theta)$. Note that the variance is related to the mean via $b''(\theta)$, and this, expressed in the form $V(\theta)$, is sometimes called the *variance function*. In the model as described in (i) to (iii) above, there are no restrictions on the link function. However (and this is where the exponential family comes in), things simplify if the link function is chosen to be the function expressing the canonical parameter for the distribution being used as a linear sum. For multiple regression this is simply the identity distribution and for logistic regression it is the logistic transformation presented above. For *Poisson regression,* in which the distribution in (i) is the Poisson distribution, the canonical link is the log link $g(u) = log(u)$.

Prediction from a generalized linear model requires the inversion of the relationship $g(\mu(i)) = \sum a_j x_j(i)$. The algorithms in least squares estimation were very straightforward, essentially involving only matrix inversion. For generalized linear models, however, things are more complicated: the non-linearity means that an iterative scheme has to be adopted. We will not go into details of the mathematics here, but it is not difficult to show that the maximum likelihood solution is given by solving the equations

$$\sum_{i=1}^{n} \frac{x_j(i)\left(y(i) - \mu(i)\right)}{a_i(\phi)\, V\left(\mu(i)\right) g'\left(\mu(i)\right)} = 0, \qquad j = 1, \ldots, p, \tag{11.16}$$

where the i indices for $a_i(\phi)$ and $\mu(i)$ are in recognition of the fact that these vary from data point to data point. Standard application of the Newton-Raphson method (chapter 8) leads to iteration of the equations

$$\mathbf{a}^{(s)} = \mathbf{a}^{(s-1)} - \mathbf{M}_{s-1}^{-1}\mathbf{u}_{s-1}, \tag{11.17}$$

where $\mathbf{a}^{(s)}$ represents the vector of values of $(a_1, \ldots, a_p)$ at the sth iteration, $\mathbf{u}_{s-1}$ is the vector of first derivatives of the log likelihood, evaluated at $\mathbf{a}^{(s-1)}$, and $\mathbf{M}_{s-1}$ is the matrix of second derivatives of the log likelihood, again evaluated at $\mathbf{a}^{(s-1)}$.

An alternative method, the method of "scoring" (this is a traditional name, and is not to be confused with our use of the word score in "score function," though the meaning is similar), replaces $\mathbf{M}_{s-1}$ by the matrix of expected second derivatives. The iterative steps of this method can be expressed in a form similar to the weighted version, equation 11.12, of the standard least squares matrix solution, equation 11.5:

$$\left(\mathbf{X'W}_{(s-1)}\mathbf{X}\right)\mathbf{a}^{(s)} = \mathbf{X'W}_{(s-1)}\mathbf{z}_{(s-1)}, \tag{11.18}$$

where $\mathbf{W}_{(s-1)}$ is a diagonal matrix with iith element $\partial\mu(i)/\partial\nu(i))^2/var(Y(i))$ evaluated at $\mathbf{a}^{(s-1)}$ and $\mathbf{z}_{(s-1)}$ is a vector with ith element $\sum_j x_j(i)a_j + (y(i) - \mu(i))\partial\nu(i)/\partial\mu(i)$ again evaluated at $\mathbf{a}^{(s-1)}$. Given the similarity of this to equation 11.12 it will hardly be surprising to learn that this method is called *iteratively weighted least squares*. We need a measure of the goodness of fit of a generalized linear model, analogous to the sum of squares used for linear regression. Such a measure is the *deviance* of a model. In fact, the sum of squares is the special case of deviance when it is applied to linear models. Deviance is defined as $D(M) = -2\left(\log L(M;Y) - \log L(M^*;Y)\right)$, essentially the difference between the log likelihood of model M and the log likelihood of the largest model we are prepared to contemplate, M^*. Deviance can be decomposed like the sum of squares to permit exploration of classes of models.

Example 11.3 In a study of ear infections in swimmers, 287 swimmers were asked if they were frequent ocean swimmers, whether they preferred beach or nonbeach, their age, their sex, and also the number of self-diagnosed ear infections they had had in a given period. The last variable here is the response variable, and a predictive model is sought, in which the number of ear infections can be predicted from the other variables. Clearly standard linear regression would be inappropriate: the response variable is discrete and, being a count, is unlikely to look remotely like a normal distribution. Likewise, it is not

	d.f.	deviance	mean deviance	deviance ratio
Regression	4	1.67	0.4166	0.42
Residual	282	47.11	0.1671	
Total	286	48.78	0.1706	
Change	-4	-1.67	0.4166	0.42

Table 11.3   Analysis of deviance table.

a proportion, it is not bounded between 0 and 1, so it would be inappropriate to model it using logistic regression. Instead, it is reasonable to assume that the response variable follows a Poisson distribution, with a parameter depending on the value of the predictor variables. Fitting a generalized linear model to predict the number of infections from the other variables, with the response following a Poisson distribution and using a log function for the link, led to the *analysis of deviance* table 11.3.

To test the null hypothesis of no predictive relationship between the response variable and the predictors, we compare the value of the regression deviance (1.67, from the top of the second column of numbers) with the chi-squared distribution with 4 degrees of freedom (given at the top of the first column of numbers). This gives a p-value of 0.7962. This is far from small, suggesting that there is little evidence that the response variable is related to the predictor variables. Not all data necessarily lead to a model that gives accurate predictions!

Before leaving this section, it is worth noting a property of equations 11.16. Although these were derived assuming that the random variables follow an exponential family distribution, examination reveals that these estimating equations make use of only the means $\mu(i)$, the variances $a_i(\phi)V(\mu(i))$, as well as the link function and the data values. There is nothing about any other aspect of the distributions. This means that even if we are not prepared to make tighter distributional assumptions, we can still estimate the parameters in the linear predictor $\nu(i) = \sum a_i x_j(i)$. Because no full likelihood has to be formulated in this approach, it is termed *quasilikelihood estimation*. Once again, of course, iterative algorithms are needed.

11.4   Artificial Neural Networks

Artificial neural networks (ANNs) are one of a class of highly parameterized statistical models that have attracted considerable attention in recent years (other such models are outlined in later sections). In the present context, we will be concerned only with *feed-forward neural networks* or *multilayer perceptrons*, as originally discussed in chapter 5. In this section, we can barely scratch the surface of this topic, and suitable further reading is suggested below. The fact that ANNs are highly parameterized makes them very flexible, so that they can accurately model relatively small irregularities in functions. On the other hand, as we have noted before, such flexibility means that there is a serious danger of overfitting. Indeed, early (by which is meant during the 1980s) work was characterized by inflated claims when such networks were overfitted to training sets, with predictions of future performance being based on the training set performance. In recent years strategies have been developed for overcoming this problem, resulting in a very powerful class of predictive models.

To set ANNs in context, recall that the generalized linear models of the previous section formed a linear combination of the predictor variables, and transformed this via a nonlinear transformation. Feedforward ANNs adopt this as the basic element. However, instead of using just one such element, they use multiple layers of many such elements. The outputs from one layer—the transformed linear combinations from each basic element—serve as inputs to the next layer. In this next layer the inputs are combined in exactly the same way—each element forms a weighted sum that is then nonlinearly transformed. Mathematically, for a network with just one layer of transformations between the input variables x and the output y (one *hidden* layer), we have

$$y = \sum_k w_k^{(2)} f_k \left(\sum_j w_j^{(1)} x_j \right). \tag{11.19}$$

Here the w are the weights in the linear combinations and the f_ks are the nonlinear transformations. The nonlinearity of these transformations is essential, since otherwise the model reduces to a nested series of linear combinations of linear combinations—which is simply a linear combination. The term *network* derives from a graphical representation of this structure in which the predictor variables and each weighted sum are nodes, with edges connecting the terms in the summation to the node.

There is no limit to the number of layers that can be used, though it can be proven that a single hidden layer (with enough nodes in that layer) is sufficient to model any continuous functions. Of course, the practicality of this will depend on the available data, and it might be convenient for other reasons (such as interpretability) to use more than one hidden layer. There are also generalizations, in which layers are skipped, with inputs to a node coming not only from the layer immediately preceding it but also from other preceding layers.

The earliest forms of ANN used threshold logic units as the nonlinear transformations: the output was 0 if the weighted sum of inputs was below some threshold and 1 otherwise. However, there are mathematical advantages to be gained by adopting differentiable forms for these functions. In applications, the two most common forms are logistic $f(x) = e^x/(1+e^x)$ and hyperbolic tangent $f(x) = \tanh(x)$ transformations of the weighted sums.

We saw, when we moved from simple linear models to generalized linear models, that estimating the parameters became more complicated. A further extra level of complication occurs when we move from generalized linear models to ANNs. This will probably not come as a surprise, given the number of parameters (these now being the weights in the linear combinations) in the model and the fundamental nonlinearity of the transformations. As a consequence of this, neural network models can be slow to train. This can limit their applicability in data mining problems involving large data sets. (But slow estimation and convergence is not all bad. There are stories within the ANN folklore relating how severe overfitting by a flexible model has been avoided by accident, simply because the estimation procedure was stopped early.) Various estimation algorithms have been proposed. A popular approach is to minimize the score function consisting of the sum of squared deviations (again!) between the output and predicted values by steepest descent on the weight parameters. This can be expressed as a sequence of steps in which the weights are updated, working from the output node(s) back to the input nodes. For this reason, the method is called *back-propagation*. Other criteria have also been used. When Y takes only two values (so that the problem is really one of supervised classification, as discussed in chapter 10) the sum of squared deviations is rather unnatural (since, as we have seen, the sum of squared deviations arises as a score function naturally from the log-likelihood for normal distributions). A more natural score function, based on log-likelihood for Bernoulli data, is

$$\sum_i \left[y(i) \log \frac{\hat{y}(i)}{y(i)} - (1 - y(i)) \log \frac{(1 - \hat{y}(i))}{(1 - y(i))} \right]. \tag{11.20}$$

As it happens, in practical applications with reasonably sized data sets, the precise choice of criterion seems to make little difference. The vast amount of work on neural networks in recent years, which has been carried out by a diverse range of intellectual communities, has led to the rediscovery of many concepts and phenomena already well known and understood in other areas. It has also led to the introduction of unnecessary new terminology.

Nonetheless, research in this area has also led to several novel general forms of models that we have not discussed here. For example, *radial basis function* networks replace the typical logistic nonlinearity of feedforward networks with a "bump" function (a radial basis function). An example would be a set of p-dimensional Gaussian bumps in **x** space, with specified widths. The output is approximated as a linear weighted combination of these bump functions. Model training consists of estimating the locations, widths, and weights of the bumps, in a manner reminiscent of mixture models described in chapter 9.

11.5   Other Highly Parameterized Models

The characterizing feature of neural networks is that they provide a very flexible model with which to approximate functions. Partly because of this power and flexibility, but probably also partly because of the appeal of their name with its implied promise, they have attracted a great deal of media attention. However, they are not the only class of flexible models. Others, in some cases with an approximating power equivalent to that of neural networks, have also been developed. Some of these have advantages as far as interpretation and estimation goes. In this section we briefly outline two of the more important classes of flexible model. Others are mentioned in section 11.5.2.

11.5.1   Generalized Additive Models

We have seen how the generalized linear model extends the ideas of linear models. Yet further extension arises in the form of *generalized additive models*. These replace the simple weighted sums of the predictor variables by weighted sums of *transformed* versions of the predictor variables. To achieve greater flexibility, the relationships between the response variable and the predictor variables are estimated nonparametrically—for example, by kernel or spline smoothing (see chapter 6), so that the generalized linear model form $g(\mu(i)) = \sum \alpha_j x_j(i)$ becomes $g(\mu(i)) = \sum \alpha_j f_j(x_j(i))$. The right-hand side here is sometimes termed the *additive predictor*. Such models take to the nonparametric limit the idea of extending the scope of linear models by transforming the predictor variables. Generalized additive models of this form retain the merits of linear and generalized linear models. In particular, how g changes with any particular predictor variable does not depend on how other predictor variables change; interpretation is eased. Of course, this is at the cost of assuming that such an additive form does provide a good approximation to the "true" surface. The model can be readily generalized by including multiple predictor variables within individual f components of the sum, but this is at the cost of relaxing the simple additive interpretation. The additive form also means that we can examine each smoothed predictor variable separately, to see how well it fits the data.

In the special case in which g is the identity function, appropriate smoothing functions can be found by a *backfitting* algorithm. If the additive model $y(i) = \sum \alpha_j f_j(x_j(i)) + \epsilon(i)$ is correct, then

$$f_k(X_k) = E\left(Y - \sum_{j \neq k} \alpha_j f_j(X_j(i)) | X_k\right).$$

This leads to an iterative algorithm in which, at each step the "partial residuals" $y - \sum_{j \neq k} \alpha_j f_j(x_j(i))$ for the kth predictor variable are smoothed, cycling through the predictor variables until the smoothed functions do not change. The precise details will, of course, depend on the choice of smoothing method: kernel, spline, or whatever.

To extend this from additive to generalized additive models, we make the same extension as above, where we extended the ideas from linear to generalized linear models. We have already outlined the iteratively weighted least squares algorithm for fitting generalized linear models. We showed that this was essentially an iteration of a weighted least squares solution applied to an "adjusted" response variable, defined by $\sum_j x_j(i)a_j + (y(i) - \mu(i)) \frac{\partial \eta(i)}{\partial \mu(i)}$. For generalized additive models, instead of the weighted linear regression we adopt an algorithm for fitting a weighted additive model.

Example 11.4 Sometimes blood pressure is deliberately lowered during surgery, using drugs. Once the operation is completed, and the administration of the drug discontinued, it is desirable that the blood pressure return to normal as soon as possible. The data in this example relate to how soon (in minutes) systolic blood pressure returned to 100 mm of mercury after the medication was discontinued. There are two predictor variables: the log of the dose of the particular drug used and the average systolic blood pressure of the patient

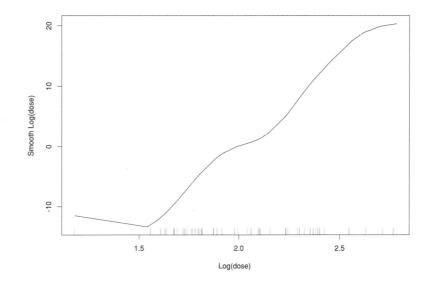

Figure 11.7   The transformation function of Log(dose) in the model for predicting time for blood pressure to revert to normal.

during administration of the drug. A generalized additive model was fitted, using splines (in fact, cubic B-splines) to effect the smoothing. Figures 11.7 and 11.8 show, respectively, a plot of the transformed Log(dose) against observed Log(dose) values and a plot of the transformed blood pressure during administration against the observed values. (There is some nonlinearity evident in both these plots—although that in the Log(dose) plot seems to be attributable to a single point.) Predictions to new data points are made by adding together the predictions from each of these components separately.

11.5.2   Projection Pursuit Regression

Projection pursuit regression models can be proven to have the same ability to estimate arbitrary functions as neural networks, but they are not as widely used. This is perhaps unfortunate, since estimating their parameters can have advantages over the neural network situation. The additive models of the last section essentially focus on individual variables (albeit transformed versions of these). Such models can be extended so that each

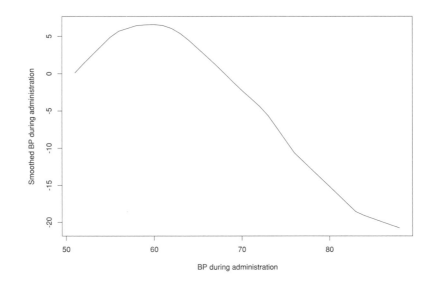

Figure 11.8   The transformation function of blood pressure during administration in the model for predicting time for blood pressure to revert to normal.

additive component involves several variables, but it is not clear how best to select such subsets. If the total number of available variables is large, then we may also be faced with a combinatorial explosion of possibilities. The basic projection pursuit regression model takes the form

$$Y = \alpha_0 + \sum f_k \left(\alpha_k^T \mathbf{X} \right) + \varepsilon. \qquad (11.21)$$

This has obvious close similarities to the neural network model—it is a linear combination of (potentially nonlinear) transformations of linear combinations of the raw variables. Here, however, the f functions are not constrained (as in neural networks) to take a particular form, but are usually found by smoothing, as in generalized additive models. This makes them a generalization of neural networks. Various forms of smoothing have been used, including spline methods, Friedman's "supersmoother" (which makes a local linear fit about the point where the smooth is required), and various polynomial functions. The term *projection pursuit* arises from the viewpoint that one is projecting $\mathbf{X}$ in direction α_k, and then seeking directions of projection that are optimal for some purpose. (In this case, optimal as components in a predictive model.) Various algorithms have been developed to estimate the parameters. In one, components of the sum are added sequentially up to some maximum value, and then sequentially dropped, each time selecting on the basis of least squares fit of the model to the data. For a given number of terms, the model is fitted using standard iterative procedures to estimate the parameters in the α_k vector. This fitting process is rather complex from a computational viewpoint, so that projection pursuit regression tends may not be practical for data sets that are massive (large n) and high-dimensional (large p).

11.6 Further Reading

Traditional linear regression is covered in depth in the classic book of Draper and Smith (1981), as well as in innumerable other texts. Furnival and Wilson (1974) describe the classic "leaps and bounds" algorithm, which efficiently searches for the best subset of predictors to include in a regression model. The seminal text on generalized linear models is that of McCullagh and Nelder (1989), and a comprehensive outline of generalized additive models is given in the book by Hastie and Tibshirani (1990). Projection pursuit regression (PPR) was introduced by Friedman and Stuetzle (1981), and theoretical approximation results are given in (for example) Diaconis and Shashahani (1984). A very flexible data-driven model for multivariate regression called MARS (Multivariate Adaptive Regression Splines) was introduced by Friedman (1991). Breiman et al. (1984) describe the application of tree-structure models to regression, and Weiss and Indurkhya (1995) describe related techniques for rule-based regression models. The technique of boosting, mentioned in chapter 10 in the context of classification, can also be usefully applied to regression. Regression can of course be cast in a Bayesian context, e.g., Gelman, Carlin, Stern, and Rubin (1995).

Techniques for *local regression*, analogous to kernel models for density estimation (chapter 9) and nearest neighbor methods for classification (chapter 10), rely on adaptive local fits to achieve a nonparametric regression function (for example, Cleveland and Devlin (1988) and Atkeson, Schall and Moore (1997)). Such techniques, however, can be quite computationally intensive and also are susceptible to the same estimation problems that plague local kernel methods in general in high dimensions.

Good introductions to neural networks are given by Bishop (1995), Ripley (1996), Golden (1996), Ballard (1997), and Fine (1999). Ripley's text is particularly noteworthy in that it includes an integrated and extensive discussion of many techniques from the fields of neural networks, statistics, machine learning, and pattern recognition (unlike most texts which tend to focus on one or two of these areas). Bayesian approaches to neural network training are described in MacKay (1992) and Neal (1996).

The computer CPU data set, the oxygen uptake data set, the ear infections in swimmers data set, and the blood pressure after surgery data are given in Hand et al. (1994). The temperature and latitude data are from Peixoto (1990). The space shuttle data are reproduced in Chatterjee, Hancock, and Simonoff (1995) and discussed in Lavine (1991).

12 *Data Organization and Databases*

12.1 Introduction

One of the features that distinguishes data mining from other types of data analytic tasks is the quantity of data. In many data mining applications (such as Web log analysis for example) there may be millions of rows and thousands of columns in the standard form data matrix, so that questions of efficiency of data analysis algorithms are very important. An algorithm whose running time scales exponentially in the number n of rows may be unusable for all but the smallest data sets. Examples of operations that can be carried out in time $O(n)$ or $O(n \log n)$ are counting simple frequencies from the data, finding the mode of a discrete variable or attribute, or sorting the data. Generally, such computations are feasible even for large data sets. However, even a linear time algorithm can be prohibitively costly to use if multiple passes through a data set are required.

If the number of rows n of a data set influences algorithm complexity, so also can the number of variables p. For some applications p is very small (less than 10, for example), but in others, like market basket analysis or analysis of text documents, we can encounter data sets with 10^5 or even 10^6 variables. In such situations we cannot use methods that involve, for example, operations as the $O(p^2)$ computation of pairwise measures of association for all pairs of attributes.

In any data analysis project it is useful to distinguish between two phases. The first is actually getting the data to the analysis algorithm, and the second is running the analysis method itself. The first phase might seem trivial, but it can often become the bottleneck. For example, in analyzing a set of data it may be necessary to apply an algorithm to many different subsets of the data. This means we have to be able to search and identify the members of each subset rapidly, and also to load that subset into main memory. Tree algorithms provide an obvious illustration of this, where the data set is progressively split into smaller subsets, each of which has to be identified before the tree can be extended. The purpose of *data organization* is to find methods for storing the data so that accessing subgroups of data is as fast as possible. Even in cases when all the data fit into main memory, data organization is important.

In addition to supporting efficient access to data for data mining algorithms, data organization plays an important role in the iterative and interactive nature of the overall data mining process. The aim of this chapter is to discuss briefly the memory hierarchy of modern computer and then present some index structures that database systems use to speed up the evaluation of queries. We then move to a discussion on relational databases and their query languages, as well as some special purpose database systems.

12.2   Memory Hierarchy

The memory of a computer is divided into several layers. These layers have different access times (where access time is the average time to retrieve a randomly selected byte of memory). Indeed, if disk storage were as fast as on-board cache, there would be no need to develop any sophisticated methods for data organization.

A general categorization of different memory structures is the following:

1. Registers of the processor. Typically there are fewer than 100 of these, and the processor can access data in the registers directly; that is, there is no slowdown associated with accessing a register.

2. On-processor or on-board cache. This is fast semiconductor memory implemented on the same chip as the processor or residing on the motherboard. Typical size is 16–1,000 kilobytes and access time is about 20 ns.

3. Main memory. Normal semiconductor memory, with sizes from 16 megabytes to several gigabytes, and access time about 70 ns.

4. Disk cache. Semiconductor memory implemented as an intermediate storage between main memory and disks.

5. Disk memory. Sizes vary from 1 gigabyte to hundreds or thousands of gigabytes for large arrays of disks. Typical access time is around 10 ms.

6. Magnetic tape. A magnetic tape can hold up to several gigabytes of data. Access time varies, but can be minutes.

The differences between the access times are truly large: in the 10 milliseconds needed for accessing a disk, we could perform up to a million accesses to fast cache. Another way to think about this is to pretend that access time is linearly proportional to actual distance. Thus, if we imagine main memory to be an effective distance of 1 meter away (within reach of your hand), the equivalent distance for disk memory is order of 10^5 times greater, i.e., 100 km!

Another major difference between main memory and disk is that individual bytes of main memory can be accessed, whereas for disk, whenever we access a byte, actually the whole disk page, about 4 kilobytes, containing that byte will be loaded to main memory. So if that page happens to contain information that can be used later, it will already be in fast memory. As an example, if we want to retrieve 1,000 integers, each taking 4 bytes to store, this can take between 1 and 1,000 disk accesses, depending on whether the integers are all stored in the same disk page or each on a page of their own.

The physical properties of the memory hierarchy lead to the following rules of thumb:

- If possible, data should be in main memory.

- In main memory, data items that are used together should be logically close to each other (that is, we should quickly be able to find the next element of a subset).

- On disk, data items that are used together should be also physically close to each other (that is, on the same disk page, if possible).

In practice, the user of a system typically has little control over the details of the way the data are placed in caches, or over the actual physical layout of data on disk. Normally, the systems try to load as much data as possible into main memory, and decide on their own how to deal the data objects onto disk pages. The user can influence the kinds of auxiliary structures that are created to access subgroups of the data. The next section describes in brief some of the data structures used for accessing large masses of data.

12.3   Index Structures

A primary goal of data organization is to find ways of quickly locating all the data points that satisfy a given selection condition. Usually the selection condition is a conjunction of conditions on individual attributes, such as "Age ≤ 40" and "Income $\leq 20,000$." We consider first data structures that are especially applicable to situations in which there is only one conjunct.

An *index* on an attribute A is a data structure that makes it possible to locate points with a given value of A more efficiently than by a sequential scan of the whole data set. Indices are typically built either by the use of B*-trees or by the use of hash functions.

12.3.1   B-trees

A *search tree* is probably the simplest index structure. Suppose we have a set S of data vectors $\{\mathbf{x}(1), \ldots, \mathbf{x}(n)\}$, and that we want to find all points having a particular value of an ordinal attribute (variable) A as quickly as we can. A search tree is a binary tree structure such that each node has a value of A stored into it, and each leaf has a pointer to an element of S. Moreover, the tree is structured so that all elements of S pointed to by leaves from the left subtree of a node u containing value a will have values of A which are less than or equal to a. Likewise, all elements of S pointed to by leaves in the right subtree of u have values for A that are greater than a.

Given a binary search tree for an attribute A, it is easy to find the data points from S that have a given value b for A. We simply start from the root of the tree, selecting the left or the right subtree by comparing b against the values stored in the nodes. When we get to a leaf, either we find a pointer to the record(s) with $A = b$, or we find that no such pointer exists.

It is also easy to find all the points from S that satisfy the condition $b \leq A \leq c$, a so-called "interval query." Simply locate the leaf where b should be (as above), locate the leaf where c should be, and the desired records are pointed to by the leaves between these two positions.

The time needed for finding the records with a given value for attribute A is proportional to the height of the tree plus the number of such records. In the worst case, the height of the tree is n, the number of points in the set S, but there are ways of ensuring that the height of the tree will be $O(\log n)$ (although they are beyond the scope of this text). In practice, binary search trees are relatively seldom used, since B*-trees, discussed below, are clearly superior for accessing data on a disk.

The basic idea for B*-trees is the same as for search trees: the pointers to the data objects are in the leaves of the tree, and interior nodes contain values of the attribute A that indicate where certain pointers are to be found. However, instead of having two children and one value for A per interior node, a B*-tree typically has hundreds of children and values.

In more detail, a B*-tree of degree M for set of values is a tree where

- all leaves are at the same depth;

- each leaf contains between $M/2$ and M keys (possible target values);

- each interior node (except possibly the root) has K children $C_1, \ldots, C_K$, where $M/2 \leq K \leq M$ and $K - 1$ values $a_1, \ldots, a_{K-1}$; for all i, all the key values stored in the leaves of subtree C_i are larger than a_{i-1} and at most as large as a_i.

Searching from a B*-tree is carried out in the same way as from a binary search tree: for each interior node of the tree, the values a_i are used to select the correct subtree.

A B*-tree differs from the basic binary search tree in that the height is guaranteed to be $O(\log n)$, since all leaves are on the same depth. Actually, the depth of the tree is bounded by $\log_{M/2} n$. Typically, the value of M is selected so that each node of the tree fits into a single disk page. If M is 100, then $(M/2)^5$ is over 300 million, and we find that for most realistic values of n, the number of elements in the set, the tree will have at most five levels: This means that finding a data point from 300 million points on the basis of the value of a single attribute can be done in three disk accesses, as the root node and the second level of the tree can be held in main memory. Most database management systems use B*-tree structures as one of their index structures.

12.3.2 Hash Indices

Suppose again that we have a set S of data points, and that we want to find all points such that attribute A has value a. If the set of possible values of A is small, we can do the following: for each possible value, construct a list of pointers to the data points with that value for A. Then, given the query "Find the points with $A = a$," we need only to access the list for a.

This method is not feasible, however, if there is a large number of potential values for A: we cannot maintain a list for each of the possible 2^{32} integers which can be represented by 32 bits, for example. What we can do is to apply a transformation to the A-values so as to reduce the range of possible values.

In more detail, let $Dom(A)$ be the set of possible values of A. A *hash function* is a function h from $Dom(A)$ to $\{1, \ldots, M\}$, where M is the size of the hash table r. For each $j \in \{1, \ldots, M\}$ we store into $r[j]$ a list of pointers to those records $\mathbf{x}_i$ in S whose A value a_i satisfies $h(a_i) = j$. When we want to find all the data points with $A = a$, we simply compute $h(a)$, go to location $r[h(a)]$ and traverse the list of data points, for each of them checking whether the value of A really was a, or whether it was another value b with the property that $h(b) = h(a)$ (this is called a *collision*).

A typical hash function is $a \bmod M$, when M is chosen to be suitable prime larger than n, the number of data points. If the hash function is well chosen and the hash table is sufficiently large, collisions are rare, and searching for the points with a given A value can be done in time essentially proportional to the number of such points. Hash indices, however, do not directly support interval queries.

12.4   Multidimensional Indexing

Traditional index structures such as hashing and B*-trees provide fast access to rows of tables on the basis of values of a given attribute or collection of attributes. In some applications, however, it is necessary to express selection conditions on the basis of several attributes, and normal index structures do not help. Consider, for example, the case of storing geographic information about cities. Suppose, for example, we wish to find all the cities with latitude between 30 N and 40 N, longitude between 60 W and 70 W, and population at least 1,000. Such a query is called a *rectangular range query*. Suppose the cities table is large, containing millions of city names. How should the query be evaluated? A B*-tree index on the latitude attribute makes it possible to find the cities that satisfy the conditions for that attribute, but for finding the rows that satisfy the conditions on longitude among these, we have to resort to a sequential scan. Similarly, an index on longitude does not help much. What is needed is an index structure that makes it possible to use directly the conditions on both attributes.

Multidimensional indexing refers to techniques for finding rows of tables on the basis of conditions on multiple attributes. One of the widely used methods is the R*-tree. Each node in the tree corresponds to a region in the underlying space, and the node represents the points within that region. For dimensions up to about 10, the multidimensional index structures speed up searches on large databases. Fast evaluation of range queries for data sets with larger numbers of dimensions (e.g., in the 100s) is still an open problem.

12.5 Relational Databases

In data mining we often need to access a particular subset of the data and compute a function from the values of certain attributes on that subset. We have discussed some data structures that can help in finding the relevant data points quickly. Relational databases provide a unified mechanism for fast access to selected parts of the data.

In database terminology, a *data model* is a set of constructs that can be used to describe the structure of data, plus a set of operations for manipulating the data. (Note that this use of the word *model* is rather different from that given earlier in the book. Here it is a structure imposed on the data by design, rather than a structure discovered existing within the data. The dual use of the word *model* is perhaps unfortunate, and arises because of the different disciplines that have contributed to data mining; in this case, statistics and database theory. Fortunately, confusion seldom arises; which of the two meanings is intended will generally be clear from the context). The *relational data model* is based on the idea of representing data in tabular form. A table header (*schema*) consists of the table name and a set of named columns; the column names are also called *attributes.* The actual *table* (an instance of the schema), also called a *relation*, is a named set of rows. Each table entry in the column for attribute A is a value from the domain $Dom(A)$ of A. Note that when the attributes are defined, the domain of each must also be specified. An attribute can be of any data type: categorical, numeric, etc. The order of the row and columns in a table is not significant.

We can put this more formally. A *relation schema* R is a set of attributes $\{A_1, \ldots, A_p\}$, where each attribute A_j has an associated domain $Dom(A_j)$. A row over the schema R is a mapping $t : R \rightarrow \cup_i Dom(A_j)$ where $t(A_j) \in Dom(A_j)$. A table or relation over the schema R is a collection of rows over R. A relational database schema $\mathbf{R}$ is a collection $\{R_1, \ldots, R_k\}$ of relation schemas (with possibly some constraints on the relation instances), and a relational database $\mathbf{r}$ over the schema $\mathbf{R}$ consists of a relation over R_i, for each $i = 1, \ldots, k$.

Example 12.1 Consider a retail outlet with barcode readers, or a Web site where we log each purchase by a customer. For each *customer transaction*, also called transactions

basket-id	chips	mustard	sausage	Pepsi	Coca-Cola	Miller	Bud
t_1	1	0	0	0	0	1	0
t_2	2	1	3	5	0	1	0
t_3	1	0	1	0	1	0	0
t_4	0	0	2	0	0	6	0
t_5	0	1	1	1	0	0	2
t_6	1	1	1	0	0	1	0
t_7	4	0	2	4	0	1	0
t_8	0	1	1	0	4	0	1
t_9	1	0	0	1	0	0	1
t_{10}	0	1	2	0	4	1	1

Figure 12.1 Representing market basket data as a table with an attribute for each product.

here a *basket*, we can collect information about which products the customer bought, and how many of each product. In principle, these data could be represented as a table, where there is an attribute for each product and a row for each transaction. For row t and attribute A the entry $t(A)$ in the matrix indicates how many As the customer bought. That is, for each attribute A the domain $Dom(A)$ is the set of nonnegative integers. See figure 12.1 for an example table, here called *transactions*.

As the product selection probably changes rapidly, encoding the names of products into attributes may not be a very good idea. An alternative representation would be to use a table such as the one called *baskets*, shown in figure 12.2, where the product names are represented as entries. This table has three attributes, **basket-id**, **product**, and **quantity**, and the domain of product is the set of all strings, while the domain of quantity is the set of nonnegative numbers. Note that there is no unique way of representing a given set of data as a relational database: both the transactions and baskets tables represent the same data set.

In addition to the data about the transactions, the retailer maintains information about the prices of individual products. This could be represented as a table such as the products table shown in figure 12.3.

The product data can be too detailed for useful summaries. Therefore, the retailer could use a classification of various products into larger product categories. An example is shown in figure 12.4.

baskets

basket-id	product	quantity
t_1	chips	1
t_1	Miller	1
t_2	chips	2
t_2	mustard	1
t_2	sausage	3
t_2	Pepsi	5
t_2	Miller	1
	. . .	

Figure 12.2   A more realistic representation of market basket data.

products

product	price	supplier	category
chips	1.00	ABC	food
Miller	0.55	ABC	drink
mustard	1.25	DEF	spices
sausage	2.00	DEF	food
Pepsi	0.75	ABC	drink
Coke	0.75	DEF	drink
	. . .		

Figure 12.3   Representing prices of products.

The table describes a hierarchy, in saying that Pepsi and Coke are soft drinks, and that soft drinks and beers are drinks.

The schemas of the tables in this example can be described succinctly by listing just the names of the tables and their attributes:

```
baskets(basket-id,product,quantity)
products(product,price)
product-hierarchy(product,category)
```

Thus the relational data model is based on the idea of tabular representation. The values in the cells may be arbitrary atomic values, such as real product-hierarchy

product	category
Pepsi	soft drink
Coke	soft drink
Budweiser	beer
Miller	beer
soft drink	drink
beer	drink
. . .	

Figure 12.4   Representing the hierarchy of products as a table.

numbers, integers, or strings; sets or lists of values are not allowed. This means that, if, for example, we want to represent information about people, their ages, and phone numbers, we cannot store multiple phone numbers in one attribute. If restricted in this way, the model is said to have *first normal form*.

The relational model is widely used in data management, and virtually all major database systems are based on it. Some systems provide additional functionality, such as the possibility of using object-oriented data modeling methods.

Even in relatively small organizations, relational databases can have hundreds of tables and thousands of attributes. Managing the schema of the database can, therefore, be a complicated task. Sometimes it is claimed that for data analysis purposes it suffices to combine all the tables into a massive observation matrix, or "universal table," and that therefore in data mining one does not have to care about the fact that the data are in a database. However, an examination of simple examples shows that this is not feasible: the universal table would be so large that operations on it would be prohibitively costly.

> **Example 12.2** Consider the example of products in a supermarket, and see what it would look like in a more realistic setting. Instead of having a table with attributes Product and Price only, we probably would have a table with at least attributes Product, Supplier, and Price, and an additional table about suppliers with attributes Supplier, Address, Phone Number, etc. If we wanted to combine the tables into one table, this table would have to include attributes Transaction ID, Product, Number, Supplier Address, Phone Number, Product

Price, etc. Furthermore, if each product belongs on the average to K different product groups, including the information from the Product-Hierarchy table would increase the size of the representation by a factor of K. For even a moderately sized database, this combining process would lead to a table that would be far too large to be stored explicitly.

12.6 Manipulating Tables

Being able to describe the structure of data and to store data using this structure is not sufficient in itself for data management: we also must be able to retrieve data from the database. We briefly describe two languages for manipulating collections of tables (that is, relational databases): relational algebra, in this section, and the Structured Query Language (SQL), in the next. Relational algebra is based on set-theoretic notation and is quite handy for theoretical purposes, while SQL is widely used in practice.

In the examples, we use r, s, etc. to refer to tables, and R, S, etc. to refer to the sets of attributes for those tables.

Relational algebra contains a set of basic operations for manipulating data given in tabular form, and several derived operations (operations that can be expressed as a sequence of basic operations) are also used. The operations include the three set operations—union, intersection, and difference—and the projection operation for removing columns, the selection operation for selecting rows, and the join and Cartesian product operations for combining rows from two tables.

> **Example 12.3** The operations of relational algebra are formally defined as follows: Assume r and s are tables over the set R of attributes,
>
> **Union** $r \cup s = \{t \mid t \in r \text{ or } t \in s\}$.
>
> **Intersection** $r \cap s = \{t \mid t \in r \text{ and } t \in s\}$.
>
> **Difference** $r \setminus s = \{t \mid t \in r \text{ and } t \notin s\}$.
>
> **Projection** Given $X \subseteq R$, then $r[X] = \{t[X] \mid t \in r\}$, where $t[X]$ is the row obtained from row t by leaving only the values in the columns of X.
>
> **Selection** Given a condition F on rows of table r,
>
> $$\sigma_F(r) = \{t \in r \mid t \text{ satisfies } F\}.$$
>
> **Join** $r \bowtie s = \{tu \mid t \in r, u \in s, t[A] = u[A] \text{ for all } A \in R \cap S\}$, where tu is the row obtained by pasting t and u together.

Set Operations

Tables are sets of rows, and all operations in the relational algebra are set-oriented: they take sets as arguments and produce a set as their result. This makes it possible to compose relational queries: the results of a query are relations, as are the arguments.

Conventional set operations are useful for manipulating tables. We shall include *union, intersection,* and *difference* (denoted by $r \cup s$, $r \cap s$, and $r \setminus s$, respectively) as the basic operations in relational algebra. The *union* operation combines two tables over the same set of attributes: the result $r \cup s$ contains all the rows that occur in r or s. The *intersection* operation $r \cap s$ results in the table containing those rows that occur in r and in s. The *difference* operation $r \setminus s$ gives the rows that occur in r but not in s. These operations all assume that r and s are tables over the same set of attributes.

As an example, suppose r is a table representing the prices of all soft drinks, and s is a table representing the prices of all products costing at most $2.00. Then $r \cup s$ is the table of all soft drinks and products costing less than $2.00, $r \cap s$ is the table of all soft drinks costing less than $2.00, and $r \setminus s$ contains one row for each soft drink that does not cost less than $2.00, i.e. that costs at least $2.00. The intersection operation could, of course, be defined using the union and difference operations: $r \cap s = (r \cup s) \setminus ((r \setminus s) \cup (s \setminus r))$.

Care must be taken to ensure that the resulting set is a table, in the sense that it has a schema. Therefore $r \cup s$, $r \cap s$ and $r \setminus s$ are defined only if r and s are tables over the same schema—that is, over the same set of attributes.

Intersection queries can be used in construction of rule sets, for example. (Algorithms for rule learning are discussed in chapter 13.) Suppose, we have computed a table r corresponding to the observations that satisfy a condition F, and similarly another table s that corresponds to the observations satisfying condition G. The intersection $r \cap s$ corresponds to those observations that satisfy both conditions; the cardinality of the intersection tells what the overlap between the conditions are. If r and s are computed from the same base table of observations, we can also achieve the same effect by using the conjunction $F \wedge G$ as the selection condition in the query. Intersection queries occur most naturally in situations in which we need to check whether the same value occurs in two tables.

Projection

The purpose of the projection operation is to trim a table so that only the data in specific columns of interest remain. Given a table r with attributes R, and $X \subseteq R$, the projection of r on X is obtained by removing from the table all the columns outside X. A side effect of projecting a table is that the number of rows, as well as the number of columns, may decrease. If the argument table over R is projected on a set of attributes X, and if table r over R contains two rows that agree on the X attributes, but differ on some attribute in $R \setminus X$, the projected rows would be identical. Such identical rows are commonly called *duplicates*. Since tables are sets, they cannot contain duplicates, and only one representative of each duplicate is retained. Because this feature is implicit in the concept of a set, it does not show up in the definition of the projection operation.

Commercial database systems often differ from the pure relational model on this point. In real implementations, tables are stored as files. Files, of course, *can* contain several identical records. Checking the uniqueness of records could take a lot of time. It is therefore customary that tables in commercial database management systems can contain duplicates.

The projection operation in relational databases is related to but not identical to the projection encountered in vector spaces. Both operations take points (called rows in databases) and produce points in a lower-dimensional space (rows with fewer attributes). In relational databases, we can project only to subspaces defined directly by the attributes; for vector spaces, projection can be defined for any subspace (that is, any linear combination of basis vectors (here attributes)).

Selection

The selection operation is used to select rows from a table. Given a Boolean condition F on the rows of a table r, the selection operation σ_F applied to r yields the table $\sigma_F(r)$ consisting of those rows of r that satisfy the condition.

Selection is probably the most frequently used operation of the relational algebra: each time we want to focus on a particular row or subset of rows in a table, we need to use selection. Selection occurs often in the implementation of data mining algorithms. For example, in building a decision tree we want a list of the observations that belong to a particular node of the tree. This set of observations is exactly the answer to a selection query, where the selection condition is the conjunction of the conditions appearing in the nodes from the root of the tree to the node in question. Similarly, if we want to implement association rule algorithms using the relational algebra, one has to execute several selection queries, each one that looks at the subset of observations satisfying the condition that each variable in a candidate frequent set has value 1.

In pure relational algebra, selections are based on exact equalities or inequalities. For data mining, we often need concepts of inexact or approximate matching. If a predicate `match` for approximate matching between attribute values is available, we can (at least in some database systems) use that directly in database operations to select rows that satisfy the approximate matching condition. (Chapter 14 discusses approximate matching in more detail.)

Cartesian Product and Join

Both projection and selection are used for removing data from a table. The *join* and *Cartesian product* operations are used for connecting data that are stored in two different tables. Given tables r and s with attributes R and S, respectively, and assuming that R and S are disjoint (that is, that no attribute name occurs in both) then the *Cartesian product* $r \times s$ of r and s is a table over the attributes $R \cup S$, and it contains all rows that can be obtained by pasting together a row from r and a row from s. Thus $r \times s$ will have $|r||s|$ rows, where $|r|$ is the number of rows in r.

The Cartesian product is needed for combining rows from different tables. It is seldom used by itself; more often, we use the *join* operation. Given a selection condition F, the *join* $r \bowtie_F s$ of r and s is obtained by selecting the rows satisfying F from $r \times s$. For example, we might compute the join of tables `baskets` and `products`, using the equality `baskets.product = products.product` as the join condition. The result of this operation is a table that has columns for the basket id, for the product name, quantity, and price. (To be precise, the result has two columns for the product name, one from each of the original tables; we might want to project one of them away.)

A typical application of the join in data mining algorithms is to combine different sources of information. If for example, we have data about customer demographics and customer purchase behavior, such data are usually stored in different tables. To combine the relevant pieces of data, we need to do a join operation.

12.7   The Structured Query Language (SQL)

Relational algebra is a useful and compact notation. In database management systems, SQL is the standard adopted by most database management system vendors. SQL implements a superset of the relational algebra. Here we introduce only the basic structure of SQL programs.

The basic statement of SQL is the "select-from-where" expression or query, which has the form

> **select** $A_1, A_2, \ldots, A_p$
> **from** $r_1, r_2, \ldots, r_k$
> **where**   list of conditions

Here each r_i is a table, and each A_j is an attribute. The intuitive meaning is that for each possible choice of rows $t_1, \ldots, t_k$ from the tables $r_1, \ldots, r_k$, we test whether the conditions are true. If they are, a row consisting of the values of the attributes A_j is output.

The second line of the query, the *from clause*, specifies the tables to which the SQL statement is applied. The third line, the *where clause*, specifies the conditions that the rows in those tables must satisfy to be accepted into the result of the statement. The first line, the *select clause*, then specifies which attributes of the participating tables should appear in the result. It corresponds to the projection operation of relational algebra (*not* the selection operation). The "where" clause is used for representing the selection conditions occurring in the selection and the join operations. For a selection operation, the selection conditions are simply listed in the list of conditions of the where clause, separated by the keywords **and, or,** and **not**.

Example 12.4 All products that cost more than 2.00 can be found by the query

> **select**   product
> **from**   products
> **where**   price > 2.00

Finding all transactions that included at least one product that cost more than 2.00 is achieved by

> **select**   basket-id, product, price
> **from**   baskets, products
> **where**   baskets.product = products.product and price > 2.00

If some tables in the "from" clause have common attributes, the attribute names must be prefixed by a dot and the name of the table when they appear in the "select" clause or "where" clause. If all attributes of participating tables should appear in the result, the list of attributes in the "select" clause can be replaced by a star.

Aggregation in database queries refers to the combination of several values into one, by the sum or maximum operators, for example. Relational algebra does not have operations for aggregation, but SQL does. An *aggregate* is in general a quantity computed from the database whose value depends on several rows of the database.

Example 12.5 The following queries show how aggregate queries relating to supermarket purchases can be described in SQL. First, we find for each product how many exemplars of it have been sold. To do this, we use the **group by** construct of SQL. This operation groups the rows of the input relation by the values of a certain attribute; the other operations in the SQL statement are performed separately for each clause.

```
select item, sum(quantity)
from baskets
group by item
```

The execution of this statement would proceed by first grouping the rows of the baskets relation according to the item attribute, and then for each group outputting the item name and the sum of the quantities for that group.

The next query finds the total sales for each product.

```
select item, sum(quantity)*price
from baskets, products
where item=product
group by item
```

Next we find total sales for each product belonging to soft drinks.

```
select item, sum(quantity)*price
from baskets, products, product-hierarchy
where item=product and products.product=product-hierarchy.product
    and class = "soft drink"
group by item
```

SQL was developed for traditional database applications such as generating reports and concurrent access and updating of transaction data by many users in real-time. Thus, it is not a big surprise that the language as such does not provide a very good platform for implementing data mining algorithms. There are two reasons for this: lack of suitable primitives and the need for efficiency.

Regarding the primitives, in SQL it is quite easy to do counting and aggregation. Therefore, for example, the operations needed for association rule algorithms are straightforward to implement by accessing the data using SQL. For building decision trees we need to be able to count the number of observations that fulfill the conditions occurring in the tree nodes from the root to the node in question. This is possible to do by selection and count queries. Where the primitives of SQL fail is in common statistical operations, such as matrix inversion, singular value decomposition (SVD), and so forth. Such operations would be extremely cumbersome to implement using SQL. This means that fitting complicated models is usually carried out outside the database system.

Even in cases when the SQL primitives are sufficient for expressing the operations in the data mining algorithm, there are reasons to implement the algorithm in a loosely-coupled manner, i.e., by downloading the relevant data to the algorithm. The reason is that the connection between a database management system and an application program typically enforces a large overhead for each query. Thus, while it is quite elegant to express the basic operations of association rule algorithms (for example) using SQL, such an implementation would typically be fairly slow. An additional cause for performance problems is that in association rule algorithms (for example) we must compute the frequency of a large number of candidate frequent sets. In a specialized implementation it is easy to do many of these counting operations in one pass through the data, whereas in an implementation based on using an SQL database management system, each candidate frequent set would cause a separate query to be issued.

12.8 Query Execution and Optimization

A query can be evaluated in various different ways. Consider, for example, the query

```
select t.product
from baskets t, baskets u
```

> **where** t.transaction = u.transaction
> and u.product = "beer"

Here the notation baskets t, baskets u means that, in the query, t and u refer
to rows of the baskets table. The notation is needed because we want to be
able to refer to two different rows of the same table. The query finds all the
products that have been bought in a transaction that also included beer.

The trivial method for evaluating such a query would be to try all possible
pairs of rows from the baskets table, to check whether they agree on the
basket-id attribute, and to test that the second row has "beer" in the product
attribute. This would require n^2 operations on rows, where n is the size of
the baskets table.

A more efficient method is to first locate the rows from the baskets table
that have "beer" in the product attribute and sort the basket-ids of those rows
into a list L. Then we can sort the baskets table using the basket-id attribute
as the sort key and extract the products from the rows whose basket-id appears in the list L. Assuming that L is a relatively short list, this approach requires $O(n)$ operations for finding the rows with beer, $O(n \log n)$ operations
for sorting the rows, and $O(n)$ operations for scanning the sorted list and
selecting the correct values; i.e., altogether $O(n \log n)$ operations are needed.
This is a clear improvement over the $O(n^2)$ operations needed for the naive
method.

Query optimization is the task of finding the best possible evaluation method
for a given query. Typically, query optimizers translate the SQL query into
an expression tree, where the leaves represent tables and the internal nodes
represent operations on the children of the nodes. Next, algebraic equalities
between operations can be used to transform the tree into an equivalent form
that is faster to evaluate. In the previous example, we have used the equa-
tion $\sigma_F(r \bowtie s) = \sigma_F(r) \bowtie s$, where F is a selection condition that concerns
only the attributes of r. After a suitable expression tree is found, evaluation
methods for each of the operations are selected. For example, a join operation can be evaluated in several different ways: by nested loops (as in the
trivial method above), by sorting, or by using indices. The efficiency of each
method depends on the sizes of the tables and the distribution of the values
in the tables. Thus, query optimizers keep information about such changing
quantities to find a good evaluation method. Theoretically, finding the best
evaluation strategy for a given query is an NP-hard problem, so that finding the best method is not feasible. However, good query optimizers can be
surprisingly effective.

Database management systems strive to provide good performance for a wide variety of queries. Thus, while for a single query it might be possible to write a program that computes the result more efficiently than a database management system would compute it, the strength of databases is that they provide fast execution for *most* of the queries. In data mining applications this is useful, as the queries are typically not known in advance (for example, in decision tree construction).

12.9   Data Warehousing and Online Analytical Processing (OLAP)

A retail database, with information about customers, transactions, products, prices, etc., is a typical example of an *operational database*: the database is used to conduct the daily operations of the organization, and the operations can rely quite heavily on it. Other examples of operational databases include airline reservation systems, bank account databases, etc. *Strategic databases* are databases that are used in decision making in the organization. The decision support viewpoint is quite closely aligned with the goal of data mining. Indeed one could say that a major goal of data mining is decision support.

Typically, an organization has several different operational databases. For example, a retail outlet might have a database about market baskets, a warehouse system, a customer database (or several), a payroll database, a database about suppliers, etc. Indeed, a diversified service company might even have several customer databases. Altogether, large organizations can have tens or hundreds of different operational databases. For decision support purposes one needs to combine information from various operational databases to find out overall patterns of activity within the company and with its customers. Building decision support applications that directly access the operational databases can be quite difficult.

Operational databases such as our hypothetical retail database, any customer database, or the reservation system of an airline, are most often used to answer well-defined and repetitive queries such as "What is the total price of the products in this basket," "What is the address of customer Smith," or "What is the balance of account 123456?" Such databases have to support a large number of transactions consisting of simple queries and updates on the contents of the data. This type of database usage is called *online transaction processing* (*OLTP*).

Decision support tasks require different types of queries: aggregation is far more important. A typical decision support query might be "Find the sales of all products by region and by month, and the difference compared to last year." The term *online analytical processing* (*OLAP*) refers to the use of databases for obtaining summaries of the data, with aggregation as the principal mechanism.

> **Example 12.6** The tables of the database of the retailer could have the following form:
>
> ```
> baskets(basket-id, item, quantity)
> products(product, price, supplier, category)
> product-hierarchy(product,category)
> basket-stores(basket-id,store,day)
> stores(store's name,city,country)
> ```
>
> Here we have added the table basket-stores that tells in which store and on what date a certain basket was produced. For decision support purposes a more useful representation of the data might be using the table
>
> ```
> sales(product,store,date,amount)
> ```
>
> for representing the amount of a product sold at a given store on a given date. We can add rows to this table by SQL statements
>
> ```
> insert into sales(product,store,date,amount)
> select item, store, date, sum(quantity)*price
> from baskets, basket-stores, products
> where baskets.basket-id = basket-stores.basket-id and item = product
> group by item, store, date
> ```
>
> After this, we can find the total dollar sales of all product categories by countries by giving the following query:
>
> ```
> select products.product, store.country, sum(amount)
> from sales, stores, dates, products
> where dates.year ≥ 1997
>        and sales.product=products.product
>        and sales.store=stores.store
>        and sales.date=dates.date
> group by products.category, store.country
> ```

OLTP and OLAP pose different requirements on the database management system. OLTP requires that the data are completely up to date, allows the queries to modify the database, allow several transactions to execute concurrently without interfering with each other, requires that responses be fast, and so forth. However, the OLTP queries and updates themselves are relatively simple. In contrast, in OLAP the queries can be quite complex, but normally only one of them executes at a given time. OLAP queries do not modify the data, and in finding out facts about last year's sales it is not crucial to have today's sale information. The requirements are so different that it makes sense to use different types of storage organizations for handling the two applications.

A *data warehouse* is a database system used to store information from various operational databases for decision support purposes. A data warehouse for a retailer might include information from a market basket database, a supplier database, customer databases, etc. The data in the payroll database might not be in the data warehouse if they are not considered to be crucial in decision support. A data warehouse is not created just by dumping the data from various databases to a single disk. Several integration tasks have to be carried out, such as resolving possible inconsistencies between attribute names and usages, finding out the semantics of attributes and values, and so on. Building data warehouses is often an expensive operation, as it requires much manual intervention and a detailed understanding of the operational databases.

The difference between OLTP, OLAP, and data mining is not always clear cut. We can in fact see a continuum of queries: find the address of a customer; find the sales of this product in the last month; find the sales of all products by region and month; find the trends in the sales; find what products have similar sales patterns; find rules that predict the sale of a certain product customer segmentation/clustering. The first query is typically carried out by using an OLTP query, the second is a typical OLAP query, and the last two might be called data mining queries. But it is difficult to define exactly where data mining starts and OLAP ends.

12.10   Data Structures for OLAP

OLAP requires the computation of various aggregates from large base tables. Since many aggregates will be needed over and over again, it makes sense to store some of them. The *data cube* is a clever technique for viewing the results of various aggregations in a tabular way.

The previous example showed the sales table with the schema

sales(product,store,date,amount).

A possible row from this table might be

sales(red wine, store 1, August 25, 17.25),

indicating that the sales of red wine at store number 1 on August 25 were $17.25. Inventing a new value **all** to stand for any product, we might consider rows like

sales(**all**, store 1, August 25, 14214.70),

with the intended meaning that the total sales of all products in store 1 on August 25 were $14,214.70. In statistical terms, this gives us the marginal of the table, summing over values of the first attribute.

The *data cube* for the sales table contains all rows

sales(a, b, c, d),

where a, b, and c, are either values from the domains of the corresponding attributes or the specific value **all**, and d is the corresponding sum. That is, the *data cube* consists of the raw table and all marginal tables: the one-dimensional ones, the two-dimensional ones, and so on up to those obtained by summing over each attribute individually.

12.11   String Databases

Interest in text and string-oriented databases has increased dramatically in recent years. Molecular biology is one of the reasons: modern biotechnology generates huge amounts of protein and DNA data sets that are often recorded as strings. Even more important has been the rise of the Web: search engines require efficient methods for finding documents that include a given set of terms. Relational databases are fine for storing data in a tabular form, but they are not well suited for representing and accessing large volumes of text. Recently, several commercial database systems have added support for the efficient querying of large text data fields.

Given a large collection of text, a typical query might be "find all occurrences of the word *mining* in the text." More generally, the problem is to find occurrences of a pattern P in a text T. The pattern P might be a simple string, a string with wildcards, or even a regular expression. The occurrence of P in T might be defined as an exact match or an approximate match, where errors are allowed.

The occurrences of the pattern P in text T can obviously be found by sequentially scanning the text and for each position testing whether P matches or not. Much more efficient solutions exist, however. For example, using the *suffix tree* data structure we can find the list of all occurrences of pattern p in time that is proportional to the length of p (and not dependent on the size of the text), and outputting the occurrences of p can be done in time $O(|p| + L)$, where L is the number of occurrences of p in the text. The suffix tree can be constructed in linear time in the size of the original text, and it is fast also in practice.

Schematically, a Web search engine might have two data structures: a relational table pages(page-address, page-text) and a suffix tree containing all the text of all the documents loaded into the system. When a user issues a query such as "find all documents containing the words *data* and *mining*," the suffix tree is used to find two lists pages: those containing the word *data* and those containing *mining*. Assuming the lists are sorted, it is straightforward to find the documents containing both words. Note, however, that the number of documents containing both *data* and *mining* is probably much less than the number containing one of the terms.

12.12   Massive Data Sets, Data Management, and Data Mining

So far in this chapter we have focused on database technology in a general sense. An important question remains as to how data mining and database technology interact. Our discussion of this interaction will be relatively brief, since there is no consensus to date among researchers and practitioners as to any "best" approach in terms of handling the interaction between data mining algorithms and database technology. At issue is the following: many massive data sets are either already stored in relational databases or could be more effectively managed and accessed during a data mining project if they were converted into relational database form. On the other hand, most data mining algorithms focus on the modeling and optimization aspects of the problem and effectively assume the data reside in a flat file in main memory. If the data to be mined are primarily on disk, and/or stored in a relational format (perhaps with an SQL interface), how then should we approach the question of interfacing our data mining algorithm to the data?

This is the issue of *data management,* which, as we briefly discussed in chapter 5, is typically not addressed explicitly in most descriptions of data mining algorithms. And perhaps this is indeed the most flexible approach, since the solutions we adopt in practice will be a function of various application factors, such as the amount of data, the amount of available main memory, how often the algorithm will need to be rerun, and so forth. Nonetheless, we can identify a few general approaches to this problem, which we discuss below.

12.12.1   Force the Data into Main Memory

The most obvious approach, and one that practitioners have used for years, is to see whether the data can in fact be stored in main memory and (subsequently) accessed efficiently by the data mining algorithm. As main memory technology allows random access memory sizes to grow into the gigabyte range, this approach can be quite practical for many "medium-sized" data analysis applications. Of course there are other applications, e.g., those with hundreds of millions of complex transactions, where we cannot hope to ever load the data into main memory in the forseeable future. In such cases we can hope to subselect parts of the data, perhaps by generating a random sample of records so that we have n' transactions instead of n to deal with (where n' is much smaller than n).

We could also select subsets of features in some manner. For example, one of the authors worked on a predictive modeling application involving on the order of 1,000 variables and 200,000 customers. Decision trees were built on random samples of 5,000 customers, and the union of variables from the resulting trees was then used to build models (using trees, nonlinear regression, and other techniques) on the entire set of 200,000 records. This is of course an entirely heuristic procedure, and an important variable might have been omitted from the trees as a result of the multiple random sampling during model building. Nonetheless, this is a fairly typical example of the type of "data engineering" that is often required in practice to obtain meaningful results in a reasonable amount of time. Note also that generating a random sample from a relational database can itself be a nontrivial process. There are, of course, numerous refinements to the basic idea of random sampling, e.g., taking an initial small sample to get a general idea of the "data landscape," then further refining this sample in some automated manner, and so forth.

Of course even if the data fit in main memory, we still must be careful. It may well be that we have to subsample the data even further to get our data mining algorithm to run in reasonable time. Furthermore, naive implementations of algorithms may create large internal data structures when they run (e.g., unnecessary copies of data matrices), which in turn may cause available memory to be exceeded. Thus, it goes without saying that efficient implementation from a memory and time viewpoint is still important, even when the data all reside in main memory.

12.12.2   Scalable Versions of Data Mining Algorithms

The term *scalable* is somewhat loosely used in the data mining literature, but we can think of it as referring to data mining algorithms that scale gracefully and predictably (e.g., linearly) as the number of records n and/or the number of variables p grow. For example, naive implementation of a decision tree algorithm will exhibit a dramatic slowdown in run-time performance once n becomes large enough that the algorithm needs to frequently access data on disk. In practice, research on scalability focuses more on the large n problem than on the large p problem: large p is inherently more difficult than large n.

One line of investigation in scalable data mining algorithms is to develop special-purpose scalable implementations of existing well-known algorithms that are guaranteed to return the same result as the original (naive) implementation, but that typically will run much faster on large data sets. An example of this general approach is that of Gehrke et al. (1999), who propose a family of algorithms called BOAT (Bootstrapped Optimistic Algorithm for Tree Construction). The BOAT approach uses two scans through the entire data set. In the first scan an "optimistic tree" is constructed using a small random sample from the full data (and that can fit in main memory). The second scan then takes care of any differences between the initial tree and the tree that would have been built using all of the data. The resulting tree is then the same tree that the naive algorithm would have constructed (in a potentially inefficient manner). The method involves various clever data structures to keep track of tree-node statistics. Gehrke et al. (1999) report fitting classification trees to nine-dimensional synthetically generated data sets with 10 million data vectors in about 200 seconds.

A related strategy is to derive new approximate algorithms that inherently have desirable scaling performance by virtue of relying on various heuristics based on a relatively small number of linear scans of the data. These algorithms typically return "good" solutions but are not necessarily in agreement

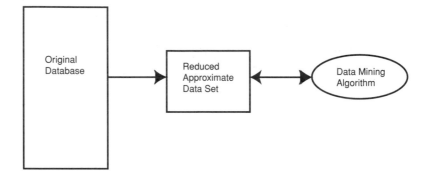

Figure 12.5 The concept of data mining algorithms which operate on an approximate version of the full data set.

with the original "nonscalable" version of the algorithm. For example, scalable clustering algorithms of this nature are described by Bradley, Fayyad, and Reina (1998) and Zhang, Ramakrishnan, and Livny (1997).

12.12.3   Special-Purpose Algorithms for Disk Access

Yet another approach to the problem of dealing with data on disk has been the development of new algorithms that are closely coupled with relational databases and transaction data. The best example in this context is that of association rule algorithms, which we have mentioned in chapter 5 and will discuss in more detail in chapter 13. The search component of association rule algorithms takes advantage of the typical sparsity of transaction data sets (i.e., most customers purchase relatively few items per transaction). At a high level, the algorithms typically involve breadth-first search strategies, where each level of the tree involves a single scan of the data that can be executed relatively easily. Agrawal et al. (1996) report results on synthetic data involving 1,000 items and up to 10 million transactions. They empirically demonstrate that the run-time of their algorithm scales up linearly on these data sets as a function of the number of transactions. Similar results have since been reported on a wide range of sparse transaction data sets and many variations of the basic algorithm have been developed (see chapter 13).

12.12.4   Pseudo Data Sets and Sufficient Statistics

Figure 12.5 illustrates another general idea that can be thought of as a generalization of random sampling. An approximate (and typically much smaller) data set is created that can then be accessed (e.g., in main memory) by the data mining algorithm instead of dealing with the full data (on disk). This general approach can, of course, only approximate the results we would have obtained had the algorithm been run on the full data. However, if the approximate data set is constructed in a clever enough manner, we can often get almost the same results on only a fraction of the data. It is often the case in practice that as part of the overall data mining process we will run our data mining algorithm many times, with different models, different variables, and so forth, in an exploratory manner, before finally settling on a final model. The use of an approximate data set for such exploratory modeling can be particularly useful (rather than having to deal with the full data set).

In this general context Du Mouchel et al. (1999) propose a statistically motivated methodology for "data-squashing" which amounts to creating a set of n' weighted "pseudo" data points, where n' is much smaller than the original number n, and where the pseudo data points are automatically chosen by the algorithm to mimic the statistical structure of the original larger data set. The general idea is to approximate the structure of the likelihood function as closely as possible, even without the functional form of the model being used in the data mining algorithm being specified. The method was empirically demonstrated to provide significant reduction in prediction error on a logistic regression problem compared to simple random sampling of a data set (Du Mouchel et al. (1999)).

On a related theme, for some data sets it may be sufficient simply to store the original data via a more efficient data structure than as a flat file or multiple tables in a relational database. The AD-Tree data structure proposed by Moore and Lee (1998) provides an efficient mechanism for storing multivariate categorical data (i.e., counts). Data mining algorithms can then quickly access counts and related statistics from the AD-Tree much more quickly than if the algorithm had to access the original data. Computational speed-ups of 50 to 5,000-fold on various classification algorithms (compared to naive implementation of the algorithms) have been reported (Moore (1999)).

In conclusion, we see that many different techniques can be used to implement data mining algorithms that are efficient in both time and space when we deal with very large data sets. Indeed there are several other approaches we have not even mentioned here, including the use of online algorithms that see each data point only once (useful for applications where data are arriving rapidly in a continuous stream over time) and more hardware-oriented solutions such as parallel processing implementations of algorithms (in cases when both the algorithm and the data permit efficient parallel approaches). Choice of a particular technique often depends on quite practical aspects of the data mining application—i.e., how quickly must the data mining algorithm produce an answer? Does the model need to be continually updated? and so forth. Research on scalable data mining algorithms is likely to continue for some time, and we can expect more developments in this area. The reader should be cautioned to be aware that, as in everything else, there is no free lunch! In other words, there are typically trade-offs involving model accuracy, algorithm speed and memory, and so forth. Informed judgment on which type of algorithm and data structures best suit your problem will require careful consideration of both algorithmic issues and application details about how the algorithm and model will be used in practice.

12.13   Further Reading

There are several high-quality yearly database conferences, such as ACM's SIGMOD Conference on Management of Data (SIGMOD), and the SIGACT-SIGMOD-SIGART Symposium on Principles of Database and Knowledge-base Systems (PODS), the Very Large Database Conference (VLDB), and the International Conference on Data Engineering (ICDE).

There are several fine database textbooks, including Ullman (1988), Abiteboul, Hull, and Vianu (1995), and Ramakrishnan and Gehrke (1999). A recent survey of query optimization is Chaudhuri (1998). The data cube is presented in Gray et al. (1996) and Gray et al. (1997). A good introduction to OLAP is Chaudhuri and Dayal (1997). Implementation of database management systems is described in detail in Garcia-Molina et al. (1999). A nice discussion of OLAP and statistical databases is given by Shoshani (1997). Issues in using database management systems to implement mining algorithms are considered in Sarawagi et al. (2000) and Holsheimer et al. (1995).

Madigan et al. (in press) discuss various extensions of the the original squashing approach. Provost and Kolluri (1999) provide an overview of different techniques for scaling up data mining algorithms to handle very large data sets. Provost, Jensen, and Oates (1999), and Domingos and Hulten (2000) give examples of sampling problems with very large databases in data mining.

13 *Finding Patterns and Rules*

13.1 Introduction

In this chapter we consider the problem of finding useful patterns and rules from large data sets. Recall that a pattern is a local concept, telling us something about a particular aspect of the data, while a model can be thought of as giving a full description of the data.

For a data set describing customers of a supermarket, a pattern might be "10 percent of the customers buy wine and cheese," and for a data set of telecommunication alarms a pattern could be "if alarms A and B occur within 30 seconds of each other, then alarm C occurs within 60 seconds with probability 0.5." For the Web log data set in chapter 1, an example pattern could be "if a person visits the CNN Web site, there is a 60% chance the person will visit the ABC News Web site in the same month." In each of these cases, the pattern is a potentially interesting piece of information about part of the data.

How do we find such patterns from data? Given some way of representing patterns and the set of all possible patterns in this representation, the trivial method is to try each pattern in turn and see whether it occurs in data and/or whether it is significant in some sense. If the number of possible patterns is small, then this method might be applicable, but typically it is completely infeasible. For example, in the supermarket example we could define a pattern for each possible subset of the set of all products. For 1,000 products this yields 2^{1000} patterns. In the case of images or sequences of alarms, there is a potentially infinite number of patterns.

If the patterns were completely unrelated to each other, we would have no other choice but to use the trivial method. However, the set of patterns typically has a great deal of structure. We have to use this structure of the patterns to guide the search. Typically, there is a generalization/specialization relation between patterns. A pattern α is more general than pattern β, if whenever β occurs in the data, α occurs too. For example, the pattern "At least 10 percent of the customers buy wine" is more general than the pattern "At least 5 percent of the customers buy wine and cheese." Use of such generalization relationships between patterns leads to simple algorithms for finding all patterns of a certain type that occur in the data.

In this chapter we present a number of methods for finding local patterns from large classes of data. We start from very simple pattern classes and relatively straightforward algorithms, and then discuss some generalizations. The basic theme in the chapter is the discovery of interesting patterns through the refinement of more general ones.

Scalability of pattern and rule discovery algorithms is obviously an important issue. The algorithms that we describe in this chapter typically carry out only a limited number of passes through the data, and hence they scale rather nicely for large data sets. In addition, if we are interested in finding only patterns or rules that apply to relatively large fractions of the data set, we can effectively use sampling. The frequency of a pattern in the sample will be approximately the same as in the whole data set, so pattern discovery from the sample produces reasonably good results. If our interest is in patterns that occur only rarely in the data, for example, finding very rare and unusual stars or galaxies among tens of millions of objects in the night sky, then sampling will be insufficient.

13.2   Rule Representations

A *rule* consists of a left-hand side proposition (the antecedent or condition) and a right-hand side (the consequent), e.g., "If it rains then the ground will be wet." Both the left and right-hand sides consist of Boolean (true or false) statements (or propositions) about the world. The rule states that if the left-hand side is true, then the right-hand side is also true. A *probabilistic rule* modifies this definition so that the right-hand side is true with probability p, given that the left-hand side is true—the probability p is simply the conditional probability of the right-hand side being true given the left-hand side is true.

Rules have a long history as a knowledge representation paradigm in cognitive modeling and artificial intelligence. Rules can also be relatively easy for humans to interpret (at least relatively small sets of rules are) and, as such, have been found to be a useful paradigm for learning interpretable knowledge from data in machine learning research. In fact, classification tree learning (discussed in chapters 6 and 10) can be thought of as a special case of learning a set of rules: the conditions at the nodes along the path to each leaf can be considered a conjunction of statements that make up the left-hand side of a rule, and the class label assignment at the leaf node provides the right-hand side of the rule.

Note that rules are inherently discrete in nature; that is, the left- and right-hand sides are Boolean statements. Thus, rules are particularly well matched to modeling discrete and categorical-valued variables, since it is straightforward to make statements about such variables in Boolean terms. We can, of course, extend the framework to real-valued variables by quantizing such variables into discrete-valued quanta, e.g., "if $X > 10.2$ then $Y < 1$" (this is precisely how classification trees handle real-valued variables, for example).

Typically the left-hand sides of rules are expressed as simple Boolean functions (e.g., conjunctions) of variable-value statements about individual variables (e.g., $A = a_1$ or $Y > 0$). The simplicity of conjunctions (compared to arbitrary Boolean functions) makes conjunctive rules by far the most widely used rule representation in data mining. For real-valued variables, a left-hand side such as $X > 1 \land Y > 2$ is defining a left-hand side region whose boundaries are parallel to the axes of the variables in (X, Y) space, i.e., a multidimensional "box" or hyperrectangle. Again, we could generalize to have statements about arbitrary functions of variables (leading to more complex left-hand side regions), but we would lose the interpretability of the simpler form. Thus, for handling real-valued variables in rule learning, simple univariate thresholds are popular in practice because of their simplicity and interpretability.

13.3   Frequent Itemsets and Association Rules

13.3.1   Introduction

Association rules (briefly discussed in chapters 5 and 12) provide a very simple but useful form of rule patterns for data mining. Consider again an artificial example of 0/1 data (an "indicator matrix") shown in figure 13.1. The rows represent the transactions of individual customers (in, for example, a "market basket" of items that were purchased together), and the columns represent the items in the store. A 1 in location (i, j) indicates that customer i purchased item j, and a 0 indicates that that item was not purchased.

We are interested in finding useful rules from such data. Given a set of 0,1

[htb]

basket-id	A	B	C	D	E		
t_1	1	0	0	0	0		
t_2	1	1	1	1	0		
t_3	1	0	1	0	1		
t_4	0	0	1	0	0		
t_5	0	1	1	1	0		
t_6	1	1	1	0	0		
t_7	1	0	1	1	0		
t_8	0	1	1	0	1		
t_9	1	0	0	1	0		
t_{10}	0	1	1	0	1		

Figure 13.1   An artificial example of basket data.

valued observations over variables $A_1, \ldots, A_p$, an association rule has the form

$$\left((A_{i_1} = 1) \wedge \cdots \wedge (A_{i_k} = 1) \right) \Rightarrow A_{i_{k+1}} = 1,$$

where $1 \leq i_j \leq p$ for all j. Such an association rule can be written more briefly as $\left((A_{i_1} \wedge \cdots \wedge A_{i_k}) \right) \Rightarrow A_{i_{k+1}}$. A pattern such as

$$(A_{i_1} = 1) \wedge \cdots \wedge (A_{i_k} = 1)$$

is called an *itemset*. Thus, association rules can be viewed as rules of the form $\theta \Rightarrow \varphi$, where θ is an itemset pattern and φ is an itemset pattern consisting of a single conjunct. We could also allow conjunctions on the right-hand side of rules, but for simplicity we do not.

The framework of association rules was originally developed for large sparse transaction data sets. The concept can be directly generalized to non-binary variables taking a finite number of values, although we will not do so here (for simplicity of notation).

Given an itemset pattern θ, its *frequency fr(θ)* is the number of cases in the data that satisfy θ. Note that the frequency $fr(\theta \wedge \varphi)$ is sometimes referred to as the *support*. Given an association rule $\theta \Rightarrow \varphi$, its *accuracy* $c(\theta \Rightarrow \varphi)$ (also sometimes referred to as the *confidence*) is the fraction of rows that satisfy φ

among those rows that satisfy θ, i.e.,

$$c(\theta \Rightarrow \varphi) = \frac{fr(\theta \wedge \varphi)}{fr(\theta)}.\tag{13.1}$$

In terms of conditional probability notation, the empirical accuracy of an association rule can be viewed as a maximum likelihood (frequency-based) estimate of the conditional probability that φ is true, given that θ is true. We note in passing that instead of a simple frequency-based estimate, we could use a maximum a posteriori estimate (chapter 4) to get a more robust estimate of this conditional probability for small sample sizes. However, since association rules are typically used in applications with very large data sets and with a large threshold on the size of the itemsets (that is, $fr(\theta)$ is usually fairly large), the simple maximum likelihood estimate above will be quite sufficient in such cases.

The frequent itemsets are very simple patterns telling us that variables in the set occur reasonably often together. Knowing a single frequent itemset does not provide us with a great deal of information about the data: it only gives a narrow viewpoint on a certain aspect of the data. Similarly, a single association rule tells us only about a single conditional probability, and does not inform us about the rest of the joint probability distribution governing the variables.

The task of finding frequent itemset patterns (or, *frequent sets*) is simple: given a frequency threshold s, find all itemset patterns that are frequent, and their frequencies. In the example of figure 13.1, the frequent sets for frequency threshold 0.4 are $\{A\}$, $\{B\}$, $\{C\}$, $\{D\}$, $\{AC\}$, and $\{BC\}$. From these we could find, for example, the rule $A \Rightarrow C$, which has accuracy $4/6 = 2/3$, and the rule $B \Rightarrow C$, with accuracy $5/5 = 1$.

Algorithms for finding association rules find all rules satisfying the frequency and accuracy thresholds. If the frequency threshold is low, there might be many frequent sets and hence also many rules. Thus, finding association rules is just the beginning in a data mining effort: some of these rules will probably be trivial to the user, while others may be quite interesting. One of the research challenges in using association rules for data mining is to develop methods for selecting potentially interesting rules from among the mass of discovered rules.

The rule frequency tells us how often a rule is applicable. In many cases, rules with low frequency are not interesting, and this assumption is indeed built into the definition of the association rule-finding problem. The accuracy of an association rule is not necessarily a very good indication of its interestingness. For example, consider a medical application where the rule is learned that pregnancy implies that the patient is female with accuracy 1! A rule with accuracy close to 1 could be interesting, but the same is true for a rule with accuracy close to 0. We will return later to this question of measuring how interesting a rule is to a user. (We discussed issues of data quality in chapter 2. With a large data set we might well find that pregnancy implies that the patient is female with accuracy less than 1. This does not mean that there are pregnant men running around, but merely that data are not perfect.)

The statistical significance of an association rule $A \Rightarrow B$ can be evaluated using standard statistical significance testing techniques to determine whether the estimated probability $p(B = 1|A = 1)$ differs from the estimated background probability of $B = 1$, and whether this difference would be likely to occur by chance. This is equivalent to testing whether $p(B = 1|A = 1)$ differs from $p(B = 1|A = 0)$ (e.g., see example 4.14).

Although such testing is possible, the use of significance testing methods to evaluate the quality of association rules is problematic, due to the multiple testing problem discussed in chapter 4. If we extract many rules from the data and conduct significance tests on each, then it is very likely, by chance alone, that we will find a rule that appears to be statistically significant, even if the data were purely random.

A set of association rules does not provide a single coherent model that would enable us to make inference in a systematic manner. For example, the rules do not provide a direct way of predicting what an unknown entry will be. Various rules might predict various values for a variable, and there is no central structure (as in decision trees) for deciding which rule is in force.

To illustrate, suppose we now obtain a further row for figure 13.1 with $A = 1$, $B = 1$, $D = 1$, and $E = 1$; then the set of rules obtained from that data could be used to suggest that (a) $C = 1$ with accuracy 2/3 (because of the rule $A \Rightarrow C$) or (b) $C = 1$ with accuracy 1 (because of the rule $B \Rightarrow C$). Thus the set of rules does not form a global and consistent description of the data set. (However, the collection of association rules or frequent sets can be viewed as providing a useful condensed representation of the original data set, in the sense that a lot of the marginal information about the data can be retrieved from this collection.)

Formulated in terms of the discussion of chapter 6, the model structure for association rules is the set of all possible conjunctive probabilistic rules. The score function can be thought of as binary: rules with sufficient accuracy and frequency get a score of 1 and all other rules have a score of 0 (only rules with a score of 1 are sought). In the next subsection we discuss search methods for finding all frequent sets and association rules, given pre-defined thresholds on frequency and accuracy.

13.3.2   Finding Frequent Sets and Association Rules

In this section we describe methods for finding association rules from large 0/1 matrices. For market basket and text document applications, a typical input data set might have 10^5 to 10^8 data rows, and 10^2 to 10^6 variables. These matrices are often quite sparse, since the number of 1s in any given row is typically very small, e.g., with 0.1% or less chance of finding a 1 in any given entry in the matrix.

The task in association rule discovery is to find all rules fulfilling given pre-specified frequency and accuracy criteria. This task might seem a little daunting, as there is an exponential number of potential frequent sets in the number of variables of the data, and that number tends to be quite large in, say, market basket applications. Fortunately, in real data sets it is the typical case that there will be relatively few frequent sets (for example, most customers will buy only a small subset of the overall universe of products).

If the data set is large enough, it will not fit into main memory. Thus we aim at methods that read the data as few times as possible. Algorithms to find association rules from data typically divide the problem into two parts: first find the frequent itemsets and then form the rules from the frequent sets.

If the frequent sets are known, then finding association rules is simple. If a rule $X \Rightarrow B$ has frequency at least s, then the set X must by definition have frequency at least s. Thus, if all frequent sets are known, we can generate all rules of the form $X \Rightarrow B$, where X is frequent, and evaluate the accuracy of each of the rules in a single pass through the data.

A trivial method for finding frequent sets would be to compute the frequency of all subsets, but obviously that is too slow. The key observation is that a set X of variables can be frequent only if all the subsets of X are frequent. This means that we do not have to find the frequency of any set X that has a non-frequent proper subset. Therefore, we can find all frequent sets by first finding all frequent sets consisting of 1 variable. Assuming these are known, we build candidate sets of size 2: sets $\{A, B\}$ such that $\{A\}$ is frequent and $\{B\}$ is frequent. After building the candidate sets of size 2, we find by looking at the data which of them are really frequent. This gives the frequent sets of size 2. From these, we can build candidate sets of size 3, whose frequency is then computed from the data, and so on. As an algorithm, the method is as follows.

$i = 0$;
$C_i = \{\{A\} \mid A \text{ is a variable }\}$;
while C_i is not empty **do**
    database pass:
        for each set in C_i, test whether it is frequent;
        let L_i be the collection of frequent sets from C_i;
    candidate formation:
        let C_{i+1} be those sets of size $i + 1$
            whose all subsets are frequent;
End.

This method is known as the APriori algorithm. Two issues remain to be solved: how are the candidates formed? and how is the frequency of each candidate computed? The first problem is easy to solve in a satisfactory manner. Suppose we have a collection L_i of frequent sets, and we want to find all sets Y of size $i + 1$ that possibly can be frequent; that is, all sets Y whose all proper subsets are frequent. This can be done by finding all pairs $\{U, V\}$ of sets from L_i such that the union of U and V has size $i + 1$, and then testing whether the union really is a potential candidate. There are fewer than $|L_i|^2$ pairs of sets in L_i, and for each one of them we have to check whether $|L_i|$ other sets are present. The worst-case complexity is approximately cubic in the size of L_i. In practice the method usually runs in linear time with respect to the size of L_i, since there are often only a few overlapping elements in L_i. Note that candidate formation is independent of the number of records n in the actual data.

Given a set C_i of candidates, their frequencies can be evaluated in a single pass through the database. Simply keep a counter for each candidate and increment the counter for each row that contains the candidate. The time needed for candidate C_i is $O(|C_i|np)$, if the test is implemented in a trivial way. Additional data structure techniques can be used to speed up the method.

The total time needed for the finding of the frequent sets is $O(\sum_i |C_i|np)$— that is, proportional to the product of the size of the data (np) and the number of sets that are candidates on any level. The algorithm needs k or $k + 1$ passes through the data, where k is the number of elements in the largest frequent set.

There exist many variants of the basic association rule algorithm. The methods typically strive toward one or more of the following three goals: minimizing the number of passes through the data, minimizing the number of candidates that have to be inspected, and minimizing the time needed for computing the frequency of individual candidates.

One important way of speeding up the computation of frequencies of candidates is to use data structures that make it easy to find out which candidate sets in C_i occur for each row in the data set. One possible way to organize the candidates is to use a tree-like structure with branching factor p (the number of variables). For each variable A, the child of the root of the tree labeled with A contains those candidates whose first variable (according to some ordering of the variables) is A. The child labeled A is constructed in a recursive manner.

Another important way of speeding up the computation of frequent sets is to use sampling. Since we are interested in finding patterns describing large subgroups, that is patterns having frequency higher than a given threshold, it is clear that just using a sample instead of the whole data set will give a fairly good approximation for the collection of frequent sets and their frequencies. A sample can also be used to obtain a method that with high probability needs only two passes through the data. First, compute from the sample the collection of frequent sets $\mathcal{F}$ using a threshold that is slightly lower than the one given by the user. Then compute the frequencies in the whole data set of each set in $\mathcal{F}$. This produces the exact answer to the problem of finding the frequent sets in the whole data set, unless there is a set Y of variables that was not frequent in the sample but all of whose subsets turned out to be frequent in the whole data set; in this case, we have to make an extra pass through the database.

13.4 Generalizations

The method for finding frequently occurring sets of variables can also be applied to other types of patterns and data, since the algorithms described above do not use any special properties of the frequent set patterns. What we used were (1) the conjunctive structure of the frequent sets and the monotonicity property, so that candidate patterns could be formed quickly, and (2) the ability to test quickly whether a pattern occurs in a row, so that the frequency of the pattern can be computed by a fast pass through the data.

Next we formulate the same algorithms in terms of more abstract notions.

Suppose that we have a class of *atomic patterns* $\mathcal{A}$, and our interest is in finding conjunctions of these atomic patterns that occur frequently. That is, the pattern class $\mathcal{P}$ is the set of all conjunctions

$$\alpha_1 \wedge \cdots \wedge \alpha_k,$$

where $\alpha_i \in \mathcal{A}$ for all i.

Let the data set D consist of n objects $d_1, \ldots, d_n$, and assume we can test whether a pattern α is true about an object d. A conjunction $\theta = \alpha_1 \wedge \cdots \wedge \alpha_k \in \mathcal{P}$ is true about d if all conjuncts α_i are true about d. Let σ be a threshold. The goal is to find those conjunctions of patterns that occur frequently:

$$\{\theta \in \mathcal{P} \mid \theta \text{ is true for for at least } \sigma \text{ objects } d \in D\}.$$

In the case of frequent itemsets, the atomic patterns were conditions of the form $A = 1$, where A is a variable, and the frequent sets like ABC were just shorthand notations for the conjunctions of form $A = 1 \wedge B = 1 \wedge C = 1$.

Suppose we can decide how many times each atomic pattern α occurs in the data. Then we can apply the above algorithm for finding all the patterns from $\mathcal{P}$ that occur frequently enough. We simply first find the atomic patterns that occur frequently enough, then build the conjunctions of two atomic patterns that can possibly occur frequently, test to see which of those occur frequently enough, build conjunctions of size 3, etc. The method works in exactly the same way as before. If the patterns are complex, we may have to do some clever processing to build the new candidates and to test for occurrence of patterns.

13.5   Finding Episodes from Sequences

In this section we present another application of the general idea of finding association rules: we describe algorithms for finding *episodes* from sequences.

Given a set of E of *event types*, an *event sequence* s is a sequence of pairs (e, t), where $e \in E$ and t is an integer, the occurrence time of the event of type e. An *episode* α is a partial order of event types, such as the ones shown in figure 13.2. Episodes can be viewed as graphs.

Given a window width W, the *frequency* of the episode α in event sequence S is the fraction of slices of width W taken from S such that the slice contains events of the types occurring in α in the order described by α. We now concentrate on the following discovery task: given an event sequence s, a set $\mathcal{E}$ of episodes, a window width *win*, and a frequency threshold *min_fr*, find the

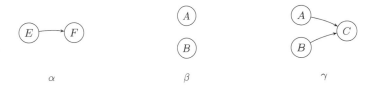

Figure 13.2   Episodes α, β, and γ.

collection $FE(\mathbf{s}, \textit{win}, \textit{min\_fr})$ of all episodes from the set that occur at least in a fraction of *min_fr* of all the windows of width *win* on the sequence s. The display below gives an algorithm for computing the collection of frequent episodes.

The method is based on the same general idea as the association rule algorithms: the frequencies of patterns are computed by starting from the simplest possible patterns. New candidate patterns are built using the information from previous passes through the data, and a pattern is not considered if any of its subpatterns is not frequent enough. The main difference compared to the algorithms outlined in the previous sections is that the conjunctive structure of episodes is not as obvious.

An episode β is defined as a *subepisode* of an episode α if all the nodes of β occur also in α and if all the relationships between the nodes in β are also present in α. Using graph-theoretic terminology, we can say that β is an induced subgraph of α. We write $\beta \preceq \alpha$ if β is a subepisode of α, and $\beta \prec \alpha$ if $\beta \preceq \alpha$ and $\beta \neq \alpha$.

Example 13.1 Given a set E of event types, an event sequence s over E, a set $\mathcal{E}$ of episodes, a window width *win*, and a frequency threshold *min_fr*, the following algorithm computes the collection $FE(\mathbf{s}, \textit{win}, \textit{min\_fr})$ of frequent episodes.

$$\mathcal{C}_1 := \{\alpha \in \mathcal{E} \mid |\alpha| = 1\};$$
$$l := 1;$$
while $\mathcal{C}_l \neq \emptyset$ **do**
    /* Database pass: */
    compute $\mathcal{F}_l := \{\alpha \in \mathcal{C}_l \mid \textit{fr}(\alpha, \mathbf{s}, \textit{win}) \geq \textit{min\_fr}\};$
    $l := l + 1;$
    /* Candidate generation: */
    compute $\mathcal{C}_l := \{\alpha \in \mathcal{E} \mid |\alpha| = l$ and for all $\beta \in \mathcal{E}$ such that $\beta \prec \alpha$
                 and $|\beta| < l$ we have $\beta \in \mathcal{F}_{|\beta|}\};$
end;
for all l **do output** $\mathcal{F}_l;$

The algorithm performs a levelwise (breadth-first) search in the class of episodes following the subepisode relation. The search starts from the most general episodes—that is, episodes with only one event. On each level the algorithm first computes a collection of candidate episodes, and then checks their frequencies from the event sequence.

The algorithm does at most $k + 1$ passes through the data, where k is the number of edges and vertices in the largest frequent episode. Each pass evaluates the frequency of $|\mathcal{C}_l|$ episodes. The computation of the frequency of an episode requires that we find the windows in the sequence in which the episode occurs. This can be done in time linear in the length of the sequence and the size of the episode. The running time of the episode discovery algorithm is thus $O(n \sum_{l=1}^{k} |\mathcal{C}_l| l)$, where n is the length of the sequence.

A similar approach can be used for any conjunctive class of patterns, as long as there are not too many frequent patterns.

13.6 Selective Discovery of Patterns and Rules

13.6.1 Introduction

The previous sections discussed methods that are used to find all rules of a certain type that fulfill simple frequency and accuracy criteria. While this task is useful in several applications, there are also simple and important classes of patterns for which we definitely do not want to see all the patterns. Consider, for example, a data set having variables with continuous values. Then, as in chapter 1, we can look at patterns such as

θ: if $X > x_1$ then $Y > y_1$ with probability p, and the frequency of the rule is q

Such a rule is a fine partial description of the data. The problem is that if in the data we have k different values of X and h different values of Y, there are kh potential rules, and many of these will have sufficient frequency to be interesting from that point of view. For example, from a data set with variables Age and Income we might discover rules

α: if Age>40 then Income>62755 (probability 0.34)
β: if Age>41 then Income>62855 (probability 0.33)

First, the user will not be be happy seeing two rules that express more or less the same general pattern. Thus, even if we found both of these rules, we should avoid showing them to the user, The second problem is that in this example the pattern α is more general than β, and there are very long sequences $\alpha_1, \alpha_2, \ldots$ of patterns such that α_i is more general than α_{i+1}. Hence the basic algorithmic idea in the previous sections of starting from the most general pattern, looking at the data, and expanding the qualified patterns in all possible ways does not work, as there are many specializations of any single pattern and the pattern space is too large.

All of this means that the search for patterns has to be pruned in addition to the use of frequency criteria. The pruning is typically done using two criteria:

1. interestingness: whether a discovered pattern is sufficiently interesting to be output;

2. promise: whether a discovered pattern has a potentially interesting specialization.

Note that a pattern can be promising even though it is not interesting. A simple example is any pattern that is true of all the data objects: it is not interesting, but some specialization of it can be. Interestingness can be quantified in various ways using the frequency and accuracy of the pattern as well as background knowledge.

13.6.2 Heuristic Search for Finding Patterns

Assume we have a way of defining the interestingness and promise of a pattern, as well as a way of pruning. Then a generic heuristic search algorithm for finding interesting patterns can be formulated as follows.

C = { the most general pattern };
while $C \neq \emptyset$ **do**
    E = all suitable selected specializations of
        elements of C;
    for $q \in E$ **do**
        if q satisfies the interestingness criteria **then** output q;
        if q is not promising **then** discard q **else** retain q
    End;
    additionally prune E;

```
        End;
    C = E;
end;
```

As instantiations of this algorithm, we get several more or less familiar methods:

1. Assume patterns are sets of variables, and define the interestingness and promise of an itemset X both by the predicate $fr(X) > \sigma$. Do no additional pruning. Then this algorithm is in principle the same as the algorithm for finding association rules.

2. Suppose the patterns are rules of the form

$$\alpha_1 \wedge \cdots \wedge \alpha_k \Rightarrow \beta,$$

where α_i and β are conditions of the form $X = c$, $X < c$, or $X > c$ for a variable X and a constant c. Let the interestingness criterion be that the rule is statistically significant in some sense and let the promise criteria be trivially true. The additional pruning step retains only one rule from E, the one with the highest statistical significance. This gives us a hill-climbing search for a rule with the highest statistical significance. (Of course, significance cannot be interpreted in a properly formal sense here because of the large number of interrelated tests.)

3. Suppose the interestingness criterion is that the rule is statistically significant, the promise test is trivially true, and the additional pruning retains the K rules whose significance is the highest. Above we had the case for $K = 1$; an arbitrary K gives us *beam search*.

13.6.3   Criteria for Interestingness

In the previous sections we referred to measures of interestingness for rules. Given a rule $\theta \Rightarrow \varphi$, its interestingness can be defined in many ways. Typically, background knowledge about the variables referred to in the patterns θ and φ have great influence in the interestingness of the rule. For example, in a credit scoring data set we might decide beforehand that rules connecting the month of birth and credit score are not interesting. Or, in a market basket database, we might say that the interest in a rule is directly proportional to the frequency of the rules multiplied by the prices of the items mentioned in the product, that is, we would be more interested in rules of high frequency that connect expensive items. Generally, there is no single method for automatically taking background knowledge into account, and rule discovery systems need to make it easy for the user to use such application-dependent criteria for interestingness.

Purely statistical criteria of interestingness are easier to use in an application-independent way. Perhaps the simplest criteria can be obtained by constructing a 2×2 contingency table by using the presence or absence of θ and φ as the variables, and having as the counts the frequencies of the four different combinations.

	φ	$\neg\varphi$
θ	$fr(\theta \wedge \varphi)$	$fr(\theta \wedge \neg\varphi)$
$\neg\theta$	$fr(\neg\theta \wedge \varphi)$	$fr(\neg\theta \wedge \neg\varphi)$

From the data in this table we can compute different types of measures of association between θ and φ, e.g., the χ^2 score. One particularly useful measure of interestingness of a rule $\theta \Rightarrow \varphi$ is the *J-measure*, defined as

$$J(\theta \Rightarrow \varphi) = p(\theta) \left(p(\varphi|\theta) \log \frac{p(\varphi|\theta)}{p(\varphi)} + (1 - p(\varphi|\theta)) \log \frac{1 - p(\varphi|\theta)}{1 - p(\varphi)} \right). \quad (13.2)$$

Here, $p(\varphi|\theta)$ is the empirically observed confidence (accuracy) of the rule, and $p(\varphi)$ and $p(\theta)$ are the empirically observed marginal probabilities of φ and θ respectively. This measure can be viewed as the cross-entropy between the binary variables defined by φ with and without conditioning on the event θ. The factor $p(\theta)$ indicates how widely the rule is applicable. The other factor measures how dissimilar our knowledge about φ is from only knowing about the marginal $p(\varphi)$, compared and with knowing that θ holds, i.e., the conditional probability $p(\varphi|\theta)$. The J-measure has the advantage that it behaves well with respect to specializations, that is, it is possible to prove bounds on the value of the J-measure for specializations of a given rule.

In practice it has been found that different score functions for interestingness will often return largely the same patterns, as long as the score functions obey some basic properties (such as the score monotonically increasing as the frequency of a pattern increases, with the accuracy remaining constant). General issues relating to the "interestingness" of patterns were also discussed in chapter 7.

13.7   From Local Patterns to Global Models

Given a collection of patterns occurring in the data, is there a way of forming a global model using the patterns? In this section we briefly outline two ways of doing this. The first method forms a decision list or rule set for a classification task, and the second method constructs an approximation of the probability distribution using the frequencies of the patterns.

Let B be, for simplicity, a binary variable and suppose that we have a discovered a collection of rules of the form $\theta_i \Rightarrow B = 1$ and $\eta_i \Rightarrow B = 0$. How would we form a decision list for finding out or predicting the value of B? (A decision list for variable B is an ordered list of rules of the form $\theta_i \Rightarrow B = b_i$, where θ_i is a pattern and b_i is a possible value of B.) The accuracy of such a decision list can be defined as the fraction of rows for which the list gives the correct prediction. The optimal decision list could be constructed, in principle at least, by considering all possible orderings of the rules and checking for each one that produces the best solution. However, this would take exponential time in the number of rules. A relatively good approximation can be obtained by viewing the problem as a weighted set cover task and using the greedy algorithm.

That is one way to use local patterns to obtain information about the whole data set. Here is another. If we know that pattern θ_i has frequency $fr(\theta_i)$ for each $i = 1, \ldots, k$, how much information do we have about the joint distribution on all variables $A_1, \ldots, A_p$? In principle, any distribution f that satisfies the pattern frequencies could have generated the observations $fr(\theta_i)$. However, a reasonable model to adopt would be one that made no further assumptions about the general nature of the distribution (since nothing further is known). This would be the distribution that maximizes the entropy, subject to the pattern frequencies that have been observed. This distribution can be constructed reasonably efficiently using the iterative proportional fitting algorithm. Roughly speaking, this algorithm operates as follows. Start with a random distribution $p(\mathbf{x})$ on the variables A_j, and then enforce the frequency constraint for each pattern θ_i. This is done by computing the sum of p over the states for which θ_i is true, and scaling these probabilities so that the resulting updated version of p has θ_i true in a set of measure $fr(\theta_i)$. The update step is carried out in turn for each pattern, until the observed frequencies of patterns agree with those provided by p. The method converges under fairly general conditions, and it is widely employed—for example, in statistical text modeling. The drawback of the method (at least if it is applied straightforwardly) is that it requires the construction of each of the states of the joint distribution, so that both the space and time complexity of the method are exponential in the number of variables.

13.8   Predictive Rule Induction

In this chapter we have so far focused primarily on association rules and similar rule formalisms. We began the chapter with a general definition of a rule, and we now return to this framework. Recall that we can interpret each branch of a classification tree as a rule, where the internal nodes on the path from the root to the leaf define the terms in the conjunctive left-hand side of the rule and the class label assigned to the leaf is the right-hand side. For classification problems the right-hand side of the rule will be of the form $C = c_k$, with a particular value being predicted for the class variable C.

Thus, we can consider our classification tree as consisting of a *set of rules*. This set has some rather specific properties—namely, it forms a mutually exclusive (disjoint) and exhaustive partition of the space of input variables. In this manner, any observation x will be classified by one and only one rule (namely the branch defining the region within which it lies). The set of rules is said to "cover" the input space in this manner.

We can see that it may be worth considering rule sets which are more general than tree-structured rule sets. The tree representation can be particularly inefficient (for example) at representing disjunctive Boolean functions. For example, consider the disjunctive mapping defined by $(A = 1 \wedge B = 1) \vee (D = 1 \wedge E = 1) \Rightarrow C = 1$ (and where $C = 0$ otherwise). We can represent this quite efficiently via the two rules $(A = 1 \wedge B = 1) \Rightarrow C = 1$ and $(D = 1 \wedge E = 1) \Rightarrow C = 1$. A tree representation of the same mapping would necessarily involve a specific single root-node variable for all branches (e.g., A) even though this variable is relevant to only part of the mapping.

One technique for generating a rule set is to build a classification tree (using any of the techniques described in chapter 10) and then to treat each of the branches as individual candidate rules. Visiting each such rule in turn, the rule-induction algorithm determines whether each condition on the left-hand side of each rule affects the accuracy of that rule on the data that it "covers." For example, we could assess whether the accuracy of the rule (which is equivalent to the estimated conditional probability) improves for the better (or indeed shows no significant change at all) when a particular condition is removed from the left-hand side. If it improves or shows no change, the condition can be deemed not necessary and can be removed to yield a simpler and potentially more accurate rule. The process can be repeated until all conditions in all rules are examined. In practice this method has often been found to eliminate a large fraction of the initial rule conditions, conditions that are introduced in the tree-growing process because of their *average* contribution in terms of model improvement, but that are not necessary for some particular branches.

The final rule set produced in this manner is then used for classification. Since the original rules carved up the input space in a disjoint manner, and we have removed a subset of the conditions defining these disjoint regions, the boundaries have been broadened (the rules have been generalized), and these regions may now overlap. Thus, we might have two rules of the form $A = 1 \Rightarrow C = 1$ and $B = 1 \Rightarrow C = 1$. The natural question is: how do we use two such rules to classify a new observation vector $\mathbf{x}$ where both $A = 1$ and $B = 1$? One approach would be to view the two rules as constraints on the overall joint distribution of $p(A, B, C)$ and to infer an estimate for $p(C = 1|A = 1, B = 1)$ using the maximum entropy approach described earlier in this chapter in section 13.7. However, since the maximum entropy approach is somewhat complex computationally, much simpler techniques tend to be used in practice. For example, we can find all the rules that "fire" (i.e., for which the conditions are satisfied) given the observation vector $\mathbf{x}$. If there is more than one rule, we can simply pick the one with the highest conditional probability. If no rules fire, we can simply pick the class value that is most likely a priori. Other more complex schemes are also possible, such as arranging the rules in an ordered decision list, or voting or averaging among multiple rules.

We might ask: why start with a classification tree and then produce rules, rather than search for the rules directly? One advantage of looking at classification trees is that it automatically quantizes any real-valued variables in a relatively simple and computationally efficient fashion during the tree-building phase (although, of course, these quanta need not necessarily be optimal in any sense in the context of the final rule set). Another advantage is the ease of implementing the technique; there are many efficient techniques for producing trees (both for data in main memory and in secondary memory, as discussed in chapter 10) and, thus, it is relatively straightforward to add the rule selection component as a "postprocessing" step.

Nonetheless, producing rules from trees imposes a particular bias on how we search for rules, and with this in mind, there has also been a great deal of work in machine learning and data mining on algorithms that search for rules directly, particularly for discrete-valued data. It is worth noting once again of course that the number of possible conjunctive rules is immense, $O(m^p)$ for p variables each taking m values. Thus, in searching for an optimal set of such rules (or even just the best single rule) we will usually resort to using some form of heuristic search through this space (as already pointed out in section 13.6 in the context of finding interesting sets of rules).

Note here that, in the context of classification, optimality should be defined as the set of rules that are most accurate on average on new data (or have the minimum average loss when classification costs are involved). However, just as with classification trees, classification accuracy on the training data need not be the best score function to guide in the selection of rules. For example, we could define a specific rule for each training example containing all of the variable values present in that example. Such a specific rule may have high accuracy (indeed, even accuracy 1 if all examples with the same variable values have the same class label), but may generalize poorly since it is so specific. Thus, score functions other than simple accuracy are often used in practice, particularly for selecting the next rule to add to the existing set, e.g., some trade-off between the coverage of the rule (the probability of the left-hand side expression) and the rule accuracy, such as the J-measure described earlier.

Having defined a suitable score function, the next issue is how to search for a set of rules to optimize this score on the training data. Many rule induction algorithms utilize a form of "general-to-specific" heuristic, of the same general form described earlier in searching for interesting rules, where now we replace the interestingness score function with a classification-related one. These algorithms start with a set containing the most general rule possible (that is, the left-hand side is empty) and proceed to add rules to this set in a greedy fashion by successively exploring more specific versions of the rules in the existing set. This can be viewed as a systematic search through the space of all subsets, starting from the null set and using an operator that can add only one condition to a rule at a time. A large variety of search techniques are applicable here, including any of the systematic heuristic search techniques (such as beam search) discussed in chapter 8. The opposite heuristic strategy of starting from the most specific rules and generalizing is also possible, although computationally this tends to be a bit more tricky, since it is not so obvious what set of rules to start from. For real-valued data we can either pre-quantize each real-valued variable into bins (for example by using a clustering algorithm on each variable), or quantize as one searches for rules. The latter option can be computationally quite demanding and tricky to implement; an interesting algorithm which operates in this manner is the

PRIM algorithm (Friedman and Fisher, (1999)), that gradually "shrinks" the rule regions starting from the full range of the data for each variable.

There is of course a trade-off between the more computationally (and memory) intensive search techniques which search more of the rule space, and the simpler techniques that can search only a smaller fraction of the space. In practice, as with classification trees, relatively simple greedy search techniques with simple operators often seem to perform almost as well empirically as the more complex methods and are quite popular as a result. As with classification trees, there is also the problem of deciding when to stop adding rules to the rule set (the familiar problem of deciding how complex the model should be—here we can interpret our set of rules as a "model" for the data). Once again, the technique of cross-validation can be quite useful in estimating the true predictive accuracy of a set of rules, but again it can be quite computationally intensive, particularly if it is invoked repeatedly at various stages of the rule search.

We conclude this discussion on predictive rules by mentioning a few notable extensions to the basic classification paradigm. The first extension is that, just as we can extend the ideas of classification trees to produce regression trees, so we can also perform *rule-based regression*. The left-hand side condition of a rule defines a particular region of the input space. Given this region we can then estimate a local regression model on the data in this region (it can be as simple as the best-fitting constant for example). If the rules are disjoint we get a piecewise local regression surface; if the rules overlap we must again decide how to combine the various rule predictions in the overlapping regions. One particular advantage of the rule-based regression framework is the ease of interpretability, particularly in high-dimensional problems, since only a small fraction of the variables are often selected as being relevant for inclusion in the rules.

The second notable extension to the basic rule induction paradigm is that of using relational logic as the basis for the rules. A discussion in any depth of this topic is beyond the scope of this text, but essentially the idea is to generalize beyond the notion of propositional logic statements ("Variable = value") to what are known as first-order relational logic statements such as "Parent$(X, Y) \wedge$ Male$(X) \Rightarrow$ Father (X, Y)." This type of learning is, in principle, extremely powerful, since it allows a much richer representational language to describe our data. A propositional version of a relational statement is typically quite awkward (and can be exponentially large), since there is no notion in the (simpler) propositional framework of objects and relations among objects. The extra representational power of relational logic comes at a cost of course, both in terms of reasoning with such rules and in terms of learning them from data. Algorithms for learning relational rules have been developed under the title "inductive logic programming," with some promising results, although largely on logical rather than probabilistic representations for data.

13.9 Further Reading

The association rule problem was introduced in Agrawal et al. (1993). The Apriori algorithm is independently due to Agrawal and Srikant (1994) and Mannila et al. (1994); see also Agrawal et al. (1996). There is an extensive literature on various algorithms for finding association rules; see, for example, Agrawal, Aggarwal, and Prasad (forthcoming), Brin et al. (1998), Fukuda et al. (1996), Han and Fu (1995), Holsheimer et al. (1995), Savasere et al. (1995), Srikant and Agrawal (1995, 1996), Toivonen (1996), and Webb (2000). Postprocessing of association rules is considered, for example, in Klemettinen et al. (1994) and Silberschatz and Tuzhilin (1996). The question of integrating association rule discovery into database systems is discussed in Imielinski and Mannila (1996), Mannila (1997), Meo et al. (1996), Imielinski et al. (1999), Imielinski and Virmani (1999), and Sarawagi et al. (1998). Algorithms for finding episodes in sequences are described in Mannila et al. (1997).

It is fair to say that there are far more papers published on algorithms to discover association rules than there are papers published on applications of association rules, i.e., at this point in time it is not yet clear what the primary applications of association rules are beyond exploratory data analysis. Nonetheless one interesting application of association rules is in cross-selling applications in a retail context, e.g., Brijs et al. (2000) and Lawrence et al. (2001).

Measures of interestingness for rules are discussed in Smyth and Goodman (1992), where the J-measure is introduced, and also in Silberschatz and Tuzhilin (1996).

A large number of different rule induction algorithms have been proposed in the machine learning literature, typically distinguished from each other in terms of the details of how the search is performed. The algorithm C4.5Rules (Quinlan (1987, 1993)) is the best-known method for deriving rules from classification trees. The CN2 algorithm (Clark and Niblett (1989)) uses an entropy-based measure to select rules by manner of a beam search. Other more recent rule induction algorithms, with demonstrated ability to provide accurate classification on large data sets, include RL (Clearwater and Stern (1991)), Brute (Segal and Etzioni (1994)) and Ripper (Cohen (1995)) — rule induction designers seem to have a preference for rather obscure names! The RISE algorithm (Domingos (1996)) is an interesting example of a rule-induction algorithm using a specific-to-general search heuristic. Holte (1993) describes an interesting study in which very simple classification rule models provide classification accuracies about as good as other more complex and widely used classifiers. Aronis and Provost (1997) discuss some practical tips on efficient implementation of rule induction algorithms for massive data sets.

An algorithmic framework for "bump-hunting" in high-dimensional data is described in Friedman and Fisher (1999) and is unusual in the rule induction literature in the following respects: it uses a "patient" search strategy rather than the more commonly used purely greedy strategy, it is cast in a general function approximation framework allowing both real-valued and categorical target variables, and it is motivated from a statistical perspective. Rule-based regression is described (for example) in Weiss and Indurkhya (1993) and in the commercial package known as Cubist from Rule-Quest (2000).

Quinlan's FOIL algorithm (1990) was one of the first relational rule induction programs. More recent work in relational rule learning (also known as inductive logic programming) is summarized in texts such as Lavrac and Dzeroski (1994) and Muggleton (1995).

14 *Retrieval by Content*

14.1   Introduction

In a database context, the traditional notion of a query is well defined, as an operation that returns a set of records (or entities) that exactly match a set of required specifications. An example of such a query in a personnel database would be [level = MANAGER] AND [age < 30], which (presumably) would return a list of young employees with significant responsibility. Traditional database management systems have been designed to provide answers to such precise queries efficiently as discussed in chapter 12.

However, there are many instances, particularly in data analysis, in which we are interested in more general, but less precise, queries. Consider a medical context, with a patient for whom we have demographic information (such as age, sex, and so forth), results from blood tests and other routine physical tests, as well as biomedical time series and X-ray images. To assist in the diagnosis of this patient, a physician would like to know whether the hospital's database contains any similar patients, and if so, what the diagnoses, treatments, and outcomes were for each. The difficult part of this problem is determining *similarity* among patients based on different data types (here, multivariate, time series and image data). However, the notion of an exact match is not directly relevant here, since it is highly unlikely that any other patient will match this particular patient exactly in terms of measurements.

In this chapter we will discuss problems of this nature, specifically the technical problems which must be addressed to allow queries to our data set of the following general form:

Find the k objects in the database that are most similar to either a specific query or a specific object.

Examples of such queries might be

- searching historical records of the Dow Jones index for past occurrences of a particular time series pattern,

- searching a database of satellite images of the earth for any images which contain evidence of recent volcano eruptions in Central America,

- searching the Internet for online documents that provide reviews of restaurants in Helsinki.

This form of retrieval can be viewed as *interactive* data mining in the sense that the user is directly involved in exploring a data set by specifying queries and interpreting the results of the matching process. This is in contrast to many of the predictive and descriptive forms of data mining discussed in earlier chapters, where the role of human judgment is often not as prominent.

If the data sets are annotated by content (for example, if the image database above had been manually reviewed and indexed based on visual content), the retrieval problem reduces to a standard (but potentially challenging) problem in database indexing, as discussed in chapter 12. We are interested here, however, in the more common case in practice in which the database is not preindexed. Instead, we have an example of what we are trying to find, namely, *the query pattern Q*. From the query pattern, we must infer which other objects in the data set are most similar to it. This approach to retrieval is known as *retrieval by content*. The best-known applications of such an approach are in text retrieval. Here the query pattern Q is usually quite short (a list of query words) and is matched with large sets of documents.

We will focus primarily on text document retrieval, since this is the most well-known and mature application of these ideas. However we will also discuss the generalization to applications in retrieval of image and time series data. The general problem can be thought of as having three fundamental components, namely:

- how to define a similarity measure between objects,

- how to implement a computationally efficient search algorithm (given a similarity measure), and

- how to incorporate user feedback and interaction in the retrieval process.

We will focus primarily on the first and third problems. The second problem typically reduces to an indexing problem (i.e., find the closest record in a database to a specific query) which was discussed in chapter 12.

Retrieval by content relies heavily on the notion of *similarity*. Throughout the discussion we will use both the terms *similarity* and *distance*. From a retrieval point of view it is not so important whether we use one or the other, since we can either maximize similarity or minimize distance. Thus, we will implicitly assume that, loosely speaking, these two terms are inverses of each other, and either can be used in practice.

We will see that across various applications (text, images, and so forth) it is common to reduce the measurements to a standard fixed-length vector format, and to then define distance measures using standard geometric notions of distance between vectors. Recall that in chapter 2 we discussed several standard distance measures such as Euclidean distance, weighted Euclidean distance, Manhattan distance, and so forth. It is worth keeping in mind that while these standard distance functions can be extremely useful, they are primarily mathematical constructs and, as such, may not necessarily match our human intuition about similarity. This will be particularly relevant when we discuss similarity in the context of data types such as text and images, where the retrieval performance of humans based on semantic content can be difficult to match using algorithms based on general domain-independent distance functions.

In section 14.2 we discuss a subtle issue: how to objectively evaluate the performance of a specific retrieval algorithm. The evaluation is significantly complicated by the fact that the ultimate judgment of performance comes from the subjective opinion of the user issuing the query, who determines whether the retrieved data is relevant.

For structured data (such as sequences, images, and text), solving the retrieval by content problem has an additional aspect, namely, determining the *representation* used for calculation of the similarity measure. For example, it is common to use color, texture, and similar features in representing images, and to use word counts in representing text. Such abstractions typically involve significant loss of information such as local context. Yet they are often essential, due to the difficulty of defining meaningful similarity measures at the pixel or ascii character level (for images and text respectively). Section 14.3 discusses retrieval by content for text data, focusing in particular on the vector-space representation. Algorithms for matching queries to documents, latent semantic indexing, and document classification are all discussed in this context. Section 14.4 introduces the topics of relevance feedback and automated recommender systems for modeling human preferences for one object over another. In section 14.5 we discuss representation and retrieval issues in image retrieval algorithms. General image retrieval is a difficult problem, and we will look at both the strengths and limitations of current approaches, in particular the issue of invariance. Section 14.6 reviews basic concepts in time series and sequence matching. As the one-dimensional analog of image retrieval, similar representational and invariance issues arise for sequential data as for image data. Section 14.7 and section 14.8 contain a summary overview and discussion of further reading, respectively.

14.2   Evaluation of Retrieval Systems

14.2.1   The Difficulty of Evaluating Retrieval Performance

In classification and regression the performance of a model can always be judged in an objective manner by empirically estimating the accuracy of the model (or more generally its loss) on unseen test data. This makes comparisons of different models and algorithms straightforward.

For retrieval by content, however, the problem of evaluating the performance of a particular retrieval algorithm or technique is more complex and subtle. The primary difficulty is that the ultimate measure of a retrieval system's performance is determined by the usefulness of the retrieved information to the user. Thus, retrieval performance in a real-world situation is inherently subjective (again, in contrast to classification or regression). Retrieval is a human-centered, interactive process, which makes performance evaluation difficult. This is an important point to keep in mind.

Although it may be very difficult to measure how useful a particular retrieval system is to an average user directly, there are nonetheless some relatively objective methods we can use if we are willing to make some simplifications. First we assume that (for test purposes) objects can be labeled as being relevant or not, relative to a particular query. In other words, for any query Q, it will be assumed that there exists a set of binary classification labels of all objects in the data set indicating which are relevant and which are not. In practice, of course, this is a simplification, since relevance is not necessarily a binary concept; e.g., particular articles among a set of journal articles can be individually more or less relevant to a particular student's research questions. Furthermore, this methodology also implicitly assumes that relevance is absolute (not user-centric) in the sense that the relevance of any object is the same for any pair of users, relative to a given query Q. Finally, it is assumed that somehow the objects have been labeled, presumably by a relatively objective and consistent human judge. In practice, with large data sets, getting such relevance judgments can be a formidable task.

Note in passing that one could treat the retrieval problem as a form of a classification task, where the class label is dependent on the query Q, i.e., "relevant or not to the query Q" and where the objects in the database are having their class labels estimated relative to Q. However, the retrieval problem has some distinguishing characteristics which make worthwhile to treat independently from classification. Firstly, the definition of the class variable is in the hands of the user (since the user defines the query Q) and can change every time the system is used. Secondly, the primary goal is not so much to classify all the objects in the database, but instead to return the set of most relevant objects to the user.

14.2.2 Precision versus Recall

Despite the caveats mentioned above, the general technique of labeling the objects in a large data set as being relevant or not (relative to a given set of predefined queries) is nonetheless quite useful in terms of providing a framework for objective empirical performance evaluation of various retrieval algorithms. We will discuss the issue of labeling in more detail in section 14.2.3. One practical approach is to use a committee of human experts to classify objects as relevant or nonrelevant.

Assume that we are evaluating the performance of a specific retrieval algorithm in response to a specific query Q on an independent test data set. The objects in the test data have already been preclassified as either relevant or irrelevant to the query Q. It is assumed that this test data set has not been used to tune the performance of this retrieval algorithm (otherwise the algorithm could simply memorize the mapping from the given query Q to the class labels). We can think of the retrieval algorithm as simply classifying the objects in the data set (in terms of relevance relative to Q), where the true class labels are hidden from the algorithm but are known for test purposes.

If the algorithm is using a distance measure (between each object in the data set and Q) to *rank* the set of objects, then the algorithm is typically parametrized by a threshold T. Thus, K_T objects will be returned by the algorithm, the ordered list of K_T objects that are closer than threshold T to the query object Q. Changing this threshold allows us to change the performance of the retrieval algorithm. If the threshold is very small, then we are being conservative in deciding which of the objects we classify as being relevant. However, we may miss some potentially relevant objects this way. A large threshold will have the opposite effect: more objects returned, but a potentially greater chance that (in truth) they are not relevant.

	Truth: Relevant	Truth: Not-Relevant
Algorithm: Relevant	TP	FP
Algorithm: Not Relevant	FN	TN

Table 14.1 A schematic of the four possible outcomes in a retrieval experiment where documents are labeled as being "relevant" or "not relevant" (relative to a particular query Q). The columns correspond to truth and rows correspond to the algorithm's decisions on the documents. TP, FP, FN, TN refer to true positive, false positive, false negative, and true negative respectively, where positive/negative refers to the relevant/nonrelevant classification provided by the algorithm. A perfect retrieval algorithm would produce a diagonal matrix with $FP = FN = 0$. This form of reporting classification results is sometimes referred to as a *confusion matrix*.

Suppose that in a test data set with N objects, a retrieval algorithm returns K_T objects of potential relevance. The performance of the algorithm can be summarized by table 14.1, where $N = TP + FP + FN + TN$ is the total number of labeled objects, $TP + FP = K_T$ is the number of objects returned by the algorithm, and $TP + FN$ is the total number of relevant objects. *Precision* is defined as the fraction of retrieved objects that are relevant, i.e., $TP/(TP + FP)$. *Recall* is defined as the proportion of relevant objects that are retrieved relative to the total number of relevant objects in the data set, i.e., $TP/(TP + FN)$. There is a natural trade-off here. As the number of returned objects K_T is increased (i.e., as we increase the threshold and allow the algorithm to declare more objects to be relevant) we can expect recall to increase (in the limit we can return all objects, in which case recall is 1), while precision can be expected to decrease (as K_T is increased, it will typically be more difficult to return only relevant objects). If we run the retrieval algorithm for different values of the threshold T, we will obtain a set of pairs of (recall, precision) points. In turn these can be plotted providing a recall-precision characterization of this particular retrieval algorithm (relative to the query Q, the particular data set, and the labeling of the data). In practice, rather than evaluating performance relative to a single query Q, we estimate the average recall-precision performance over a set of queries (see figure 14.1 for an example). Note that the recall-performance curve is essentially equivalent (except for a relabeling of the axes) to the well-known receiver-operating characteristic (ROC) used to characterize the performance of binary classifiers with variable thresholds.

Now consider what happens if we plot the recall-precision of a set of different retrieval algorithms relative to the same data set and set of queries. Very

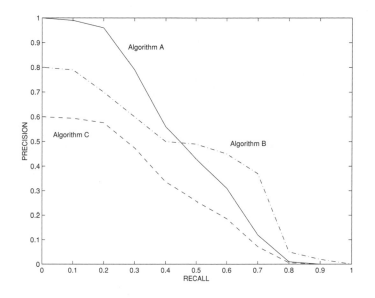

Figure 14.1 A simple (synthetic) example of precision-recall curves for three hypothetical query algorithms. Algorithm A has the highest precision for low recall values, while Algorithm B has the highest precision for high recall values. Algorithm C is universally worse than A or B, but we cannot make a clear distinction between A or B unless (for example) we were to operate at a specific recall value. The actual recall-precision numbers shown are fairly typical of current text-retrieval algorithms; e.g., the ballpark figures of 50% precision at 50% recall are not uncommon across different text-retrieval applications.

often, no one curve will dominate the others; i.e., for different recall values, different algorithms may be best in terms of precision (see figure 14.1 for a simple example). Thus, precision-recall curves do not necessarily allow one to state that one algorithm is in some sense better than another. Nonetheless they can provide a useful characterization of the relative and absolute performance of retrieval algorithms over a range of operating conditions. There are a number of schemes we can use to summarize precision-recall performance with a single number, e.g., precision at some fixed number of documents retrieved, precision at the point where recall and precision are equal, or average precision over multiple recall levels.

14.2.3   Precision and Recall in Practice

Precision-recall evaluations have been particularly popular in text retrieval research, although in principle the methodology is applicable to retrieval of any data type. The Text Retrieval Conferences (TREC) are an example of a large-scale precision-recall evaluation experiment, held roughly annually by the U.S. National Institute of Standards and Technology (NIST). A number of gigabyte-sized text data sets are used, consisting of roughly 1 million separate documents (objects) indexed by about 500 terms on average. A significant practical problem in this context is the evaluation of relevance, in particular determining the total number of relevant documents (for a given query Q) for the calculation of recall. With 50 different queries being used, this would require each human judge to supply on the order of 50 million class labels! Because of the large number of participants in the TREC conference (typically 30 or more), the TREC judges restrict their judgments to the set consisting of the union of the top 100 documents returned by each participant, the assumption being that this set typically contains almost all of the relevant documents in the collection. Thus, only a few thousand relevance judgments need to be made rather than tens of millions.

More generally, determining recall can be a significant practical problem. For example, in the retrieval of documents on the Internet it can be extremely difficult to accurately estimate the total number of potentially available relevant documents. Sampling techniques can in principle be used, but, combined with the fact that subjective human judgment is involved in determining relevance in the first place, precision-recall experiments on a large-scale can be extremely nontrivial to carry out.

14.3   Text Retrieval

Retrieval of text-based information has traditionally been termed information retrieval (IR) and has recently become a topic of great interest with the advent of text search engines on the Internet. Text is considered to be composed of two fundamental units, namely the *document* and the *term*. A *document* can be a traditional document such as a book or journal paper, but more generally is used as a name for any structured segment of text such as chapters, sections, paragraphs, or even e-mail messages, Web pages, computer source code, and so forth. A *term* can be a word, word-pair, or phrase within a document, e.g., the word `data` or word-pair `data mining`.

Traditionally in IR, *text queries* are specified as sets of terms. Although documents will usually be much longer than queries, it is convenient to think of a single representation language that we can use to represent both documents and queries. By representing both in a unified manner, we can begin to think of directly computing distances between queries and documents, thus providing a framework within which to directly implement simple text retrieval algorithms.

14.3.1 Representation of Text

As we will see again with image retrieval later in this chapter, much research in text retrieval focuses on finding general *representations* for documents that support both

- the capability to retain as much of the semantic content of the data as possible, and

- the computation of distance measures between queries and documents in an efficient manner.

A user who is using a text retrieval system (such as a search engine on the Web) wants to retrieve documents that are relevant to his or her needs in terms of semantic content. At a fundamental level, this requires solving a long-standing problem in artificial intelligence, namely, *natural language processing* (NLP), or the ability to program a computer to "understand" text data in the sense that it can map the ascii letters of the text into some well-defined semantic representation. In its general unconstrained form, this has been found to be an extremely challenging problem. *Polysemy* (the same word having several different meanings) and *synonmy* (several different ways to describe the same thing) are just two of the factors that make automated understanding of text rather difficult. Thus, perhaps not surprisingly, NLP techniques (which try to explicitly model and extract the semantic content of a document) are not the mainstay of most practical IR systems in use today; i.e., practical retrieval systems do not typically contain an explicit model of the meaning of a document.

Instead, current IR systems typically rely on simple term matching and counting techniques, where the content of a document is implicitly and approximately captured (at least in theory) by a vector of term occurrence counts. Assume that a set of terms t_j for retrieval, $1 \leq j \leq T$, has been defined a priori. The size of this set can be quite large (e.g., $T = 50,000$ terms or more).

	t1	t2	t3	t4	t5	t6
d1	24	21	9	0	0	3
d2	32	10	5	0	3	0
d3	12	16	5	0	0	0
d4	6	7	2	0	0	0
d5	43	31	20	0	3	0
d6	2	0	0	18	7	16
d7	0	0	1	32	12	0
d8	3	0	0	22	4	2
d9	1	0	0	34	27	25
d10	6	0	0	17	4	23

Table 14.2 A toy document-term matrix for 10 documents and 6 terms. Each ijth entry contains the number of times that term j appears in document i.

Each individual document D_i, $1 \leq i \leq N$, is then represented as a *term vector*:

$$D_i = (d_{i1}, d_{i2}, \ldots, d_{iT}) \tag{14.1}$$

where d_{ij} represents some information about the occurrence of the jth term in the ith document. The individual d_{ij}s are referred to as *term weights* (although, to be more precise, they are just the component values of the term vector).

In the *Boolean representation,* the term weights simply indicate whether certain terms appear in the document, i.e., $d_{ij} = 1$ if document i contains term j, and $d_{ij} = 0$ otherwise. In the *vector space representation* each term weight can be some real-valued number, e.g., a function of how often the term appears in the document, or (perhaps) the relative frequency of that term in the overall set of documents. We will look in more detail at term weights in section 14.3.2.

Note that when a document is represented as a T-dimensional term vector, not only has the word order of the original document been lost, but so also has syntactic information such as sentence structure. Despite this loss of information, term vectors can nonetheless be quite useful and effective in a variety of retrieval applications.

As an example, consider a very simple toy example with 10 documents and 6 terms, where the terms are

- t1 = database

- t2 = SQL

- t3 = index

- t4 = regression

- t5 = likelihood

- t6 = linear,

and we have a 10×6 document-term frequency matrix M as shown in table 14.2. Entry ij (row i, column j) contains the number of times term j is contained in document i. We can clearly see that the first five documents $d1$ to $d5$ contain mainly database terms (combinations of query, SQL, index) while the last five documents $d6$ to $d10$ contain mainly regression terms (combinations of regression, likelihood, linear). We will return to this example later in this chapter.

Given a particular vector-space representation, it is straightforward to define distance between documents as some simple well-defined function of distance between their document vectors. Most of the various distance measures we described in chapter 2 can be (and have been) used for document comparison. One widely used distance measure in this context is the *cosine distance*, which is defined as

$$d_c(D_i, D_j) = \frac{\sum_{k=1}^{T} d_{ik} d_{jk}}{\sqrt{\sum_{k=1}^{T} d_{ik}^2 \sum_{k=1}^{T} d_{jk}^2}}. \tag{14.2}$$

This is the cosine of the angle between the two vectors (equivalently, their inner product after each has been normalized to have unit length) and, thus, reflects similarity in terms of the *relative* distribution of their term components. There is nothing particularly special about this distance measure, however, it has been found historically to be quite effective in practical IR experiments.

Figure 14.2 shows in pixel form the distance matrices for the toy document-term frequency matrix of table 14.2. Both the Euclidean distance and cosine distance matrices are shown. For both distance matrices it is clear that there are two clusters of documents, one for database documents and one for regression, which show up as two relatively light subblocks in the figure. Conversely, the pairwise distances between elements of the two groups are relatively large (i.e., dark pixels). However, the cosine distance produces a better separation of the two groups. For example, documents 3 and 4 (in the database cluster) would be ranked as being closer to documents 6, 8, and 9

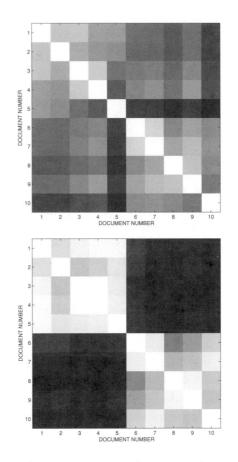

Figure 14.2   Pairwise document distances for the toy document-term matrix in the text, for Euclidean distance (top) and cosine distance (bottom). Brighter squares are more similar and darker squares are less similar, according to the relevant distance. For the Euclidean distance, white corresponds to zero (e.g., on the diagonals) and black is the maximum distance between any two documents. For the cosine distance brighter pixels correspond to larger cosine values (closer angles) and darker pixels correspond to smaller cosine values (larger angles).

(which are documents about regression) than to document 5 (which is another document about databases). This happens simply because the term vectors for documents 3 and 4 (and 6, 8, and 9) are close to the origin compared to document 5. By using angle-based distances, the cosine distance emphasizes the relative contributions of individual terms, resulting in the better separation evident in figure 14.2 (bottom).

Each vector D_i can be thought of as a *surrogate* document for the original document. The entire set of vectors can be represented as an $N \times T$ matrix. Typically this matrix is very sparse, for example with only about 0.03% of cells being nonzero for the TREC collections mentioned earlier. A natural interpretation of this matrix is that each row D_i (a document) of this matrix is a vector in T-dimensional "term space." Thus, thinking in terms of the data matrix we have used to described data sets in earlier chapters, the documents play the role of individual objects, the terms play the role of variables, and the vector entries represent "measurements" on the documents.

In a practical implementation of a text-retrieval system, due to the sparsity of the term-document matrix, the original set of text documents are represented as an *inverted file* structure (rather than as a matrix directly), i.e., a file indexed by the T terms where each term t_j points to a list of N numbers describing term occurrence (the d_{ij}, j fixed) for each document.

The process of generating a term-document matrix can by itself be quite nontrivial, including issues such as how to define terms, e.g., are plural and singular nouns counted as the same term? should very common words be used as terms? and so forth. We will not dwell on this issue except to point out that clearly there can be a substantial amount of "engineering" required at this level.

14.3.2 Matching Queries and Documents

Queries can also be expressed using the same term-based representation as that used for documents. In effect, the query is itself represented as a document, albeit one that typically contains very few terms (although we can, of course use a real document as a query itself, e.g., "Find documents that are similar to this one").

For the Boolean representation, a query is represented as a logical Boolean function on a subset of the available terms. Thus, for example, a typical query might be `data AND mining AND NOT(coal)`. The basic mechanism for retrieval in this context consists of scanning the inverted file to determine which documents *exactly* match the query specifications. Extensions of the basic Boolean query language are possible, such as adding weights to indicate the relative importance of certain terms over others. However, a general drawback of the Boolean representation is that there is no natural semantics for the notion of *distance* between queries and documents, and thus, no natural way to perform ranking of documents based on relevance. In addition, and perhaps somewhat surprisingly, humans often have great difficulty constructing Boolean queries that reflect precisely what they intend. Nonetheless, despite these drawbacks, the Boolean query method is popular in practical IR systems because of its efficiency and relative simplicity.

In the vector-space representation, a query can be expressed as a vector of weights. Terms not in the query are implicitly assigned zero weight. The simplest form of query assigns unit weight to each term in the query. More generally, individual weights can be assigned by the user to indicate the relative importance of each term (typically the weights are constrained to be between 0 and 1). In practice, it can be difficult for a user to know how to set the weights to effectively model his or her notion of relevance. Later we will see that a scheme called *relevance feedback* can be used to iteratively refine the weights over the course of multiple queries, but for now we will assume that the user provides the query as well as the weights for the terms in query.

Let the $Q = (q_1, \ldots, q_T)$ be a vector of query weights. In the simplest approach the query weights can be simply either 1 (the term is in the query) or 0 (the term is not in the query), or the same weighting scheme as used for document representation can be used (see below). As an example of the simple binary scheme consider three queries, each consisting of the single terms `database`, `SQL`, `regression`. For our toy example these three queries would be represented as three vectors: $(1, 0, 0, 0, 0, 0)$, $(0, 1, 0, 0, 0, 0)$, and $(0, 0, 0, 1, 0, 0)$. Using the cosine distance to match these three queries to our toy example data set of table 14.2 results in documents $d2, d3$, and $d9$ being ranked as closest, respectively.

To discuss more general concepts in matching queries to documents, we must first revisit briefly the idea of weights in the vector-space model. Let d_{ik} be the weight (or component value) for the kth term, $1 \leq k \leq T$ in document D_i. There have been many different (largely ad hoc) suggestions in the IR literature on how these weights should be set to improve retrieval performance. Ideally these terms should be chosen so that more relevant documents are ranked higher than less relevant ones. The Boolean approach of setting the weights to 1 if the term occurs anywhere in the document has been found to favor large documents (over relevant ones) simply because a larger documents is more likely to include a given query term somewhere in the document.

One particular weighting scheme, known as the TF-IDF weighting, has proven very useful in practice. TF stands for *term frequency* and simply means that each term component in a term vector is multiplied by the frequency by which that term occurs in the document. This has the effect of increasing the weight on terms that occur frequently in a given document. The toy document-term matrix of table 14.2 is expressed in TF form.

However, if a term occurs frequently in many documents in the document set, then using TF weights for retrieval may have little discriminative power, i.e., it will increase recall but may have poor precision. The *inverse-document-frequency* (IDF) weight helps to improve discrimination. It is defined as $\log(N/n_j)$, i.e., the log of the inverse of the fraction of documents in the whole set that contain term j, where n_j is the number of documents containing term j, and the total number of documents is N. The IDF weight favors terms that occur in relatively few documents; i.e., it has discriminative power. The use of the logarithm of IDF rather than IDF directly is motivated by the desire to make the weight relatively insensitive to the exact number of documents N.

The TF-IDF weight is simply the product of TF and IDF for a particular term in a particular document. As with the cosine distance measure (with which it is often used), there is no particularly compelling motivation for defining weights in this manner. However, it has been found to be generally superior in terms of precision-recall performance when it is compared to alternative weighting schemes. There are various enhancements to the basic TF-IDF method, but TF-IDF weighting as described above is still usually considered the default baseline method in evaluation experiments.

The same TF-IDF weights derived from the set of documents can be used to weight query terms as well. Another alternative for query-weighting is to use just IDF weights to emphasize query terms that are relatively rare. For example, if we were to issue the query Richard Nixon we would probably be happier to retrieve documents containing Nixon and not Richard than vice versa.

The document-term matrix of table 14.2 produces the following set of IDF weights (using natural logs): $(0.105, 0.693, 0.511, 0.693, 0.357, 0.693)$. Note, for example, that the first term *database* now receives a lower weight than the other terms, because it appears in more documents (i.e., is less discriminative). This results in the TF-IDF document-term matrix shown in table 14.3.

A classic approach to matching queries to documents is as follows:

2.53	14.56	4.60	0	0	2.07
3.37	6.93	2.55	0	1.07	0
1.26	11.09	2.55	0	0	0
0.63	4.85	1.02	0	0	0
4.53	21.48	10.21	0	1.07	0
0.63	0	0	11.78	1.42	15.94
0.21	0	0	22.18	4.28	0
0.31	0	0	15.24	1.42	1.38
0.10	0	0	23.56	9.63	17.33

Table 14.3   TF-IDF document-term matrix resulting from table 14.2

Document	TF distance	TF-IDF distance
d1	0.70	0.32
d2	0.77	0.51
d3	0.58	0.24
d4	0.60	0.23
d5	0.79	0.43
d6	0.14	0.02
d7	0.06	0.01
d8	0.02	0.02
d9	0.09	0.01
d10	0.01	0.00

Table 14.4   Distances resulting from a query containing the terms *database* and *index*, i.e., $Q = (1, 0, 1, 0, 0, 0)$, for the document-term matrix of table 14.2, using the cosine distance measure. Using the TF matrix, document $d5$ is closest; for the TF-IDF matrix, $d2$ is closest.

- represent queries as term vectors with 1s for terms occurring in the query and 0s everywhere else,

- represent term-vectors for documents using TF-IDF weights for the vector components, and

- use the cosine distance measure to rank the documents in terms of distance to the query.

Table 14.4 shows a simple example of a query comparing the TF and TF-IDF methods. Note that, unlike the exact match retrieval results of the Boolean case (where all matching documents are returned), here the distance measure produces a ranking of all documents that include at least one relevant term.

14.3.3 Latent Semantic Indexing

In the schemes we have discussed so far for text retrieval, we have relied exclusively on the notion of representing a document as a T-dimensional vector of term weights. A criticism of the term-based approach is that users may pose queries using different terminology than the terms used to index a document. For example, from a term similarity viewpoint the term `data mining` has nothing directly in common with the term `knowledge discovery`. However, *semantically*, these two terms have much in common and (presumably) if we posed a query with one of these terms, we would consider documents containing the other to be relevant. One solution to this problem is to use a knowledge base (a thesaurus or ontology) that is created a priori with the purpose of linking semantically related terms together. However, such knowledge bases are inherently subjective in that they depend on a particular viewpoint of how terms are related to semantic content.

An interesting, and useful, alternative methodology goes by the name of *latent semantic indexing* (LSI). The name suggests that hidden semantic structure is extracted from text rather than just term occurrences. What LSI actually does is to approximate the original T-dimensional term space by the first k principal component directions in this space, using the $N \times T$ document-term matrix to estimate the directions. As discussed in chapter 3, the first k principal component directions provide the best set of k orthogonal basis vectors in terms of explaining the most variance in the data matrix. The principal components approach will exploit redundancy in the terms, if it exists. Frequently in practice there is such redundancy. For example, terms such as `database`, `SQL`, `indexing`, `query optimization` can be expected to exhibit redundancy in the sense that many database-related documents may contain all four of these terms together. The intuition behind principal components is that a single vector consisting of a weighted combination of the original terms may be able to approximate quite closely the effect of a much larger set of terms. Thus the original document-term matrix of size $N \times T$ can be replaced by a matrix of size $N \times k$, where k may be much smaller than T with little loss in information. From a text retrieval perspective, for fixed recall, LSI can increase precision compared to the vector-space methods discussed earlier.

An interesting aspect of the the principal component representation for the document-term matrix is that it captures relationships among terms by creating new terms that may more closely reflect the semantic content of the document. For example, if the terms `database`, `SQL`, `indexing`, `query optimization` are effectively combined into a single principal component term, we can think of this new term as defining whether the content of a document is about database concepts. Thus, for example, if the query is posed using the term `SQL`, but the database-related documents in the set of documents contain only the term `indexing`, that set of database documents will nonetheless be returned by the LSI method (but would not be returned by a strictly term-based approach).

We can calculate a singular-value decomposition (SVD) for the document-term matrix $\mathbf{M}$ in table 14.2. That is, we find a decomposition $\mathbf{M} = \mathbf{U}\mathbf{S}\mathbf{V}^T$. Here $\mathbf{U}$ is a 10×6 matrix where each row is a vector of weights for a particular document, $\mathbf{S}$ is a 6×6 diagonal matrix of eigenvalues for each principal component direction, and the columns of the 6×6 matrix $\mathbf{V}^T$ provide a new orthogonal basis for the data, often referred to as the principal component directions.

The $\mathbf{S}$ matrix for $\mathbf{M}$ has diagonal elements

$$\lambda_1, \ldots, \lambda_6 = \{77.4, 69.5, 22.9, 13.5, 12.1, 4.8\}.$$

In agreement with our intuition, most of the variance in the data is captured by the first two principal components. In fact, if we were to retain only these two principal components (as two surrogate terms instead of the six original terms), the fraction of variance that our two-dimensional representation retains is $(\lambda_1^2 + \lambda_2^2)/\sum_{i=1}^6 \lambda_i^2 = 0.925$; i.e., only 7.5% of the information has been lost (in a mean-square sense). If we represent the documents in the new two-dimensional principal component space, the coefficients for each document correspond to the first two columns of the $\mathbf{U}$ matrix:

```
d1    30.8998    -11.4912
d2    30.3131    -10.7801
d3    18.0007     -7.7138
d4     8.3765     -3.5611
d5    52.7057    -20.6051
d6    14.2118     21.8263
d7    10.8052     21.9140
d8    11.5080     28.0101
d9     9.5259     17.7666
d10   19.9219     45.0751
```

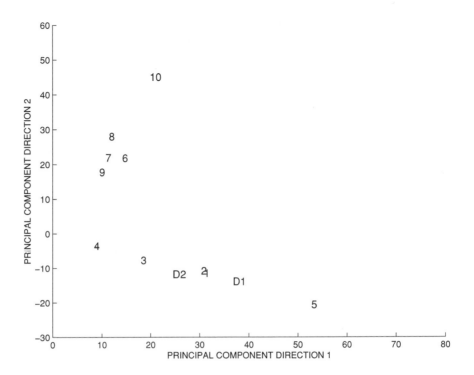

Figure 14.3   Projected locations of the 10 documents (from table 14.2) in the two dimensional plane spanned by the first two principal components of the document-term matrix M.

and we can consider these two columns as representing new *pseudo-terms* that are in effect linear combinations of the original six terms.

It is informative to look at the first two principal component directions:

$$\mathbf{v}_1 \quad = (0.74, 0.49.0.27, 0.28, 0.18, 0.19) \tag{14.3}$$

$$\mathbf{v}_2 \quad = (-0.28, -0.24, -0.12, 0.74, 0.37, 0.31). \tag{14.4}$$

These are the two directions (a plane) in the original six-dimensional term space where the data is most "spread out" (has the most variance). The first direction emphasizes the first two terms (*query, SQL*) more than the others: this is in effect the direction that characterizes documents relating to databases. The second direction emphasizes the last three terms *regression, likelihood, linear,* and can be considered the direction that characterizes documents relating to regression. Figure 14.3 demonstrates this graphically. We can see that the two different groups of documents are distributed in two different directions when they are projected onto the plane spanned by the first two principal component directions. Note that document 2 is almost on top of document 1, somewhat obscuring it. (Symbols D1 and D2 are discussed below.) The distances of the points from the origin reflect the magnitude of the term-vector (i.e., number of terms) for each document. For example, documents 5 and 10 have the most terms and are furthest from the origin. We can see here that the angle difference between documents is clearly a very useful indicator of similarity, since regression and database documents are each clustered around two different angles in the plane.

An advantage of principal components in this context can be seen by considering a new document D1 which contains, for example, the term *database* 50 times and another document D2, which contains the term *SQL* 50 times, and both documents contain none of the other terms. In a direct keyword representation, these two documents would not be considered similar since they contain no common terms (among the specific terms used in our toy example). However, if we instead represent D1 and D2 using the two principal component terms, they are projected into this space, as shown in figure 14.3, i.e., both are projected along the "database" direction even though each is missing two of the three terms associated with databases. The principal component approach has implicitly modeled the interrelationship between terms. This feature can be taken advantage of for querying. Imagine now that we pose a query using only the term *SQL*. If we use the principal component representation (e.g., the first two pseudo-terms) for our documents, we can also convert the query into the pseudo-term representation, where again the query will be closer (in angle) to the database documents than the regression documents, allowing retrieval of documents that do not contain the term *SQL* at all but are related in content.

From a computational viewpoint, directly computing the principal component vectors (by seeking the eigenvectors of the correlation or covariance matrix for example) is usually neither computationally feasible or numerically stable. In practice, the PCA vectors can be estimated using special-purpose sparse SVD techniques that are well-suited for high-dimensional sparse matrices.

There are many other variations of this basic framework outline. The application of principal components for text retrieval is often referred to as latent semantic indexing (LSI). Use of this general technique has been shown in certain cases to improve retrieval performance in systematic tests, based on its ability to match documents and queries with no terms in common.

We can also model the document-term matrix in a probabilistic manner as being generated by a mixture of simpler component models, where each component represents the distribution of words we would expect to see conditioned on a particular topic. Each of the component models can be (for example) conditional independence (naive Bayes) models or multinomials, and the EM algorithm for fitting mixtures, as described in chapter 9, can be applied directly and rather straightforwardly.

14.3.4   Document and Text Classification

It is clear from our discussion that the term-vector representation of documents provides a natural framework for classifying documents, where we can apply either the supervised classification framework of chapter 10 for documents that have labels preassigned, or the unsupervised learning (clustering) frameworks of chapter 9 for unlabeled documents. For example, a practical application of these ideas is that of automatically and accurately clustering Web documents into groups or taxonomies, for updating and maintaining the databases of large Web search engines.

Because of the fact that typical term-vectors are very high-dimensional (e.g., on the order of 10,000 or more terms is quite common), classifiers that are both accurate and efficient in high-dimensional spaces are usually the methods of choice in this context. For example, although classification trees can be useful for high-dimensional problems in general, for document classification the individual features (individual terms) may not be so informative. For documents in the class "sports" it is more likely to be the case that such documents contain some subset of words such as "score," "field," "stadium," "win," etc., rather than always containing any particular single word from this set. Thus, classification models such as the first-order Bayes classifier (naive Bayes) or linear combinations of weights (such as linear support vector machines) tend to work well for document representations, since they can combine evidence from many different features in a relatively simple (e.g., linear) manner. A feedforward neural network would not be a practical choice for most document modeling problems by virtue of the fact that it would be extremely complex, from the point of view of both the number of parameters in the model and the amount of time that it would take to train it.

Numerous interesting issues arise in the area of document classification that we will not dwell on here. For example, it makes sense to consider each document as belonging to multiple topics (classes) rather than just to a single class. Thus, instead of the usual framework where the class is considered to consist of mutually exclusive and exhaustive categories, for documents the classes need not be mutually exclusive. There are a number of different approaches to dealing with this "multiple membership" problem. One simple method is to train a binary classifier for each class separately, a method that is likely to be practical only if the total number of classes is relatively small.

14.4   Modeling Individual Preferences

14.4.1   Relevance Feedback

As mentioned earlier, retrieval algorithms tend to have a much more interactive flavor than most of the other data mining algorithms we have discussed in this book. In particular, a user with a particular query Q may be willing to iterate through a few sets of different retrieval "trials" by the algorithm, and provide user-based feedback to the algorithm by labeling the returned documents as relevant or nonrelevant from the user's viewpoint. We can use this idea with any retrieval system, not just text retrieval, but we will limit our discussion to text to keep things specific.

Rocchio's algorithm is particularly widely used in this context. The general idea is that relevance is essentially user-centric, i.e., if the user could (in theory) see all of the documents, he or she could in principle separate them into two sets, relevant R and irrelevant NR. Given these two sets, it can be shown that the optimal query (using a vector model) can be written as

$$Q_{optimal} = \frac{1}{|R|} \sum_{D \in R} D - \frac{1}{|NR|} \sum_{D \in NR} D. \tag{14.5}$$

where D denotes a term-vector representation for document whose labelings (by the user) are known.

In practice, of course, a particular user has not personally labeled all of the documents in the database. Instead the user starts out with a specific query $Q_{current}$, which can be presumed to be suboptimal relative to $Q_{optimal}$. The algorithm uses this initial query to return a small set of documents that are then labeled by the user as being relevant R' or not NR'. Rocchio's algorithm then refines the query in the following manner:

$$Q_{new} = \alpha Q_{current} + \frac{\beta}{|R'|} \sum_{D \in R'} D - \frac{\gamma}{|NR'|} \sum_{D \in NR'} D. \tag{14.6}$$

Thus, the query is modified by (in effect) moving the current query toward the mean vector of the documents judged to be relevant and away from the mean vector of of the documents judged to be irrelevant. The parameters α, β, and γ are positive constants (chosen heuristically) that control how sensitive the new query is to the most recent labeling of the documents, relative to the existing query vector $Q_{current}$. The process repeats; i.e., the new query Q_{new} is matched to the document set, and the user again labels the documents. Note that even if the initial query Q_0 is stated incorrectly by the user, the algorithm can in principle adapt and learn the implicit preferences of the user in terms of relevance. In principle, if the labelings at each iteration are consistent, Q_{new} gradually approaches $Q_{optimal}$.

Experimental evidence indicates that such user feedback does indeed improve precision-recall performance. In other words, incorporating feedback has been shown to be systematically effective for information retrieval. Of course, there are many details that must be specified to implement this approach in practice, such as the number of documents that should be presented to the user, the relative number of relevant and irrelevant documents to be used, the method used to choose the irrelevant documents, and so forth, leading to a large number of variations on this basic theme.

14.4.2 Automated Recommender Systems

Instead of modeling just the preferences of a single user, we can generalize to the case in which the database has information about multiple users and their preferences in terms of a large number of objects. The technique of *collaborative filtering* is a simple and well-known approach to leveraging this group information. For example, imagine you are interested in a certain musical group and buy a CD for this group at an online Web site. Several hundred other people also may have bought this particular CD, and it is likely that at least some of their general preferences in musical taste match yours. Thus, collaborative filtering in this context simply means that an algorithm running at the Web site can provide for you a list of other CDs purchased by people who bought the same CD as you. Clearly we can generalize the basic idea in various directions. For example, if we have a purchase history for each user and/or users are willing to provide more detailed information about their specific interests (in the form of user profiles), we can have a vector representation of each user, and the discussion earlier in the chapter about defining appropriate similarity metrics once again becomes quite relevant.

Collaborative filtering is in a sense an attempt to capture the expert judgment and recommendations of a large group, where the group is automatically selected to match the interests of a specific user. The algorithms generally work by first finding the subset of profiles of those users that are judged to be most similar to the target profile and then calculating a recommendation as a function of the properties of the matched set of profiles. The quality of the recommendation will depend on the quality and quantity of information that is known about each user and the size of the user database. The technique tends to work best with large numbers of users. Acquiring a large number of user profiles can be difficult in practice, since users are naturally reluctant to take the time to provide detailed personal information. Capturing users preferences by their actions (e.g., by what they buy, or by what Web pages they visit) is a less intrusive approach that implicitly tries to estimate user preferences, and it is commonly employed in Internet-based recommendation systems (for example). A common practical requirement (for example, in e-commerce applications) is that the recommendation must be generated by the algorithm in real time, e.g., in less than a second. If we have a very large database of users (e.g., order of millions), this can pose significant computational and data engineering challenges.

14.5   Image Retrieval

Image and video data sets are increasingly common, from the hobbyist who stores digital images of family birthdays to organizations such as NASA and military agencies that gather and archive remotely sensed images of the earth on a continuous basis. Retrieval by content is particularly appealing in this context as the number of images becomes large. Manual annotation of images is time-consuming, subjective, and may miss certain characteristics of the image depending on the specific viewpoint of the annotator. A picture may be worth a thousand words, but which thousand words to use is a nontrivial problem!

Thus, there is considerable motivation to develop efficient and accurate query-by-content algorithms for image databases, i.e., to develop interactive systems that allow a user to issue queries such as "find the K most similar images to this query image" or "find the K images which best match this set of image properties." Potential applications of such algorithms are numerous: searching for similar diagnostic images in radiology, finding relevant stock footage for advertising and journalism, and cataloging applications in geology, art, and fashion.

14.5.1 Image Understanding

Querying image data comes with an important caveat. Finding images that are similar to each other is in a certain sense equivalent to solving the general image understanding problem, namely the problem of extracting semantic content from image data. Humans excel at this. However, several decades of research in pattern recognition and computer vision have clearly shown that the performance of humans in visual understanding and recognition is extremely difficult to replicate with computer algorithms. (There is a direct analogy here to the NLP problem mentioned earlier in the context of text understanding.) Specific problems, such as face recognition or detection of airport runways, can be be successfully tackled, but general-purpose image understanding systems are still far off on the research horizon. For example, an infant can quickly learn to classify animals such as dogs of all sizes, colors, and shapes (including cartoon figures) in arbitrary scenes, whereas such completely unconstrained recognition is beyond the capability of any current vision algorithm. This ability to extract semantic content from raw image data is still relatively unique to the brain. Thus, not surprisingly, most current methods for image retrieval rely on relatively low-level visual cues.

14.5.2 Image Representation

For retrieval purposes, the original pixel data in an image can be abstracted to a feature representation. The features are typically expressed in terms of primitives such as color and texture features. As with text documents, the original images are converted into a more standard data matrix format where each row (object) represents a particular image and each column (variable) represents an image feature. Such feature representations are typically more robust to changes in scale and translation than the direct pixel measurements, but nonetheless may be invariant to only small changes in lighting, shading, and viewpoint.

Typically the features for the images in the image database are precomputed and stored for use in retrieval. Distance calculations and retrieval are thus carried out in multi-dimensional feature space. As with text, the original pixel data is reduced to a standard $N \times p$ data matrix, where each image is now represented as a p-dimensional vector in feature space.

Spatial information can be introduced in a coarse manner by computing features in localized subregions of an image. For example, we could compute color information in each 32×32 subregion of a $1,024 \times 1,024$ pixel image.

This allows coarse spatial constraints to be specified in image queries, such as "Find images that are primarily red in the center and blue around the edges."

As well as regular $m \times n$ pixel images of *scenes*, an image database can also contain specific images of *objects*, namely objects on a constant background (such as an image of a black chair on a white background). Thus, we can also extract primitive properties that are object-specific such as features based on color, size, and shape (geometry) of the object. Video images represent a further generalization of image data, where images (frames) are linked sequentially over time.

A well-known commercial example of a retrieval by content system for images is the *Query by Image Content* (QBIC) system developed by IBM researchers in the early 1990s. The system is based on the general ideas described in section 14.5, allowing users to interactively query image and video databases based on example images, user-entered sketches, color and texture patterns, object properties, and so forth. Queries are allowed on scenes, objects (parts of scenes), and sequences of video frames, or any combination of these. The QBIC system uses a variety of features and a variety of associated distance measures for retrieval:

- A three-dimensional color feature vector, spatially averaged over the whole image: the distance measure is simple Euclidean distance.

- K-dimensional color histograms, where the bins of the histogram can be selected by a partition-based clustering algorithm such as K-means, and K is application dependent. QBIC uses a Mahalanobis-type distance measure between color histogram vectors to account for color correlations.

- A three-dimensional texture vector consisting of features that measure coarseness/scale, directionality, and contrast. Distance is computed as a weighted Euclidean distance measure, where the default weights are inverse variances of the individual features.

- A 20-dimensional shape feature for objects, based on area, circularity, eccentricity, axis orientation, and various moments. Similarity is computed using Euclidean distance.

14.5.3   Image Queries

As with text data, the nature of the abstracted representation for images (i.e., the computed features) critically determines what types of query and retrieval operations can be performed. The feature representation provides a language for query formulation. Queries can be expressed in two basic forms. In query by example we provide a sample image of what we are looking for, or sketch the shape of the object of interest. Features are then computed for the example image, and the computed feature vector of the query is then matched to the precomputed database of feature vectors. Alternatively, the query can be expressed directly in terms of the feature representation itself, e.g., "Find images that are 50% red in color and contain a texture with specific directional and coarseness properties." If the query is expressed in terms of only a subset of the features (e.g., only color features are specified in the query), only that subset of features is used in the distance calculations.

Clearly, depending on the application, we can generalize to relatively sophisticated queries (given a feature representation), allowing (for example) various Boolean combinations of query terms. For image data, the query language can also be specialized to allow queries that take advantage of spatial relations (such as "Find images with object 1 above object 2") or sequential relations (such as "Find video sequences with soccer players taking shots at goal followed by images of players celebrating").

Representing images and queries in a common feature-vector form is quite similar to the vector-space representation for text retrieval discussed earlier. One important difference is that typically a feature for an image is a real number indicating (for example) a particular color intensity in a particular region of the image, while a term component in a term-vector is typically some form of weighted count of how often a term occurs in the document. Nonetheless, the general similarity of the retrieval-by-content problem for both problems has led to numerous applications of text retrieval techniques to image retrieval applications including (for example) the use of principal component analysis to reduce the dimensionality of the feature space and relevance feedback via Rocchio's algorithm to improve the image retrieval process.

14.5.4   Image Invariants

For retrieval by content with images, it is important to keep in mind that (with current techniques at least) we can realistically work only with a restricted notion of semantic content, based on relatively simple "low-level" measurements such as color, texture, and simple geometric properties of objects. There are many common distortions in visual data such as translations, rotations, nonlinear distortions, scale variability, and illumination changes (shadows, occlusion, lighting). The human visual system is able to handle many of these distortions with ease. For example, a human can view two scenes of the same object from completely different angles, with different lighting, and at different distances, and still easily attach the same semantic content to the scene (e.g., "It is a scene of my house taken after 1995").

However, the methods for content retrieval described here typically are *not* invariant under such distortions. Changes in scale, illumination, or viewing angle will typically change the feature measurements such that the distorted version of a scene is in a very different part of the feature space, compared to the original version of the scene. In other words, the retrieval results will not be invariant to such distortions, unless such distortion invariance is designed into the feature representation. Again, typically, distortion-invariant feature representations are currently known only for constrained visual environments, such as linear transformations of rigid objects, but not (for example) for general nonlinear transformations of nonrigid objects.

14.5.5   Generalizations of Image Retrieval

To conclude our discussion of image retrieval, we note that the term *image* can be interpreted much more broadly than the implicit interpretation as an image of a real-world scene (typically generated by a camera) as we have described it. More generally, image data can be embedded within text documents (such as books or Web pages). Other forms of images can include handwritten drawings (or text or equations), paintings, line drawings (such as in architecture or engineering), graphs, plots, maps, and so forth. Clearly, retrieval in each of these contexts needs to be handled in an application-specific manner, although many of the general principles discussed earlier will still apply. Video data also provides further challenges and opportunities in terms of automated indexing and interactive querying. For example, for a television news organization such as CNN, the ability to search through an archive of video footage to detect certain types of images would be quite useful.

14.6   Time Series and Sequence Retrieval

The problem of efficiently and accurately locating patterns of interest in time series and sequence data sets is an important and nontrivial problem in a wide variety of applications, including diagnosis and monitoring of complex systems, biomedical data analysis, and exploratory data analysis in scientific and business time series. Examples include

- finding customers whose spending patterns over time are similar to a given spending profile;

- searching for similar past examples of unusual current sensor signals for real-time monitoring and fault diagnosis of complex systems such as aircraft;

- noisy matching of substrings in protein sequences.

Sequential data can be considered to be the one-dimensional analog to two-dimensional image data. *Time series* data are perhaps the most well-known example, where a sequence of observations is measured over time, such that each observation is indexed by a time variable t. These measurements are often made at fixed time intervals, so that without loss of generality t can be treated as an integer taking values from 1 to T. The measurements at each time t can be multivariate (rather than just a single measurement), such as (for example) the daily closing stock prices of a *set* of individual stocks. Time series data are measured across a wide variety of applications, in areas as diverse as economics, biomedicine, ecology, atmospheric and ocean science, control engineering, and signal processing.

The notion of *sequential data* is more general than time series data in the sense that the sequence need not necessarily be a function of time. For example, in computational biology, proteins are indexed by sequential *position* in a protein sequence. (Text could, of course, be considered as just another form of sequential data; however, it is usually treated as a separate data type in its own right.)

As with image and text data, it is now commonplace to store large archives of sequential data sets. For example, several thousand sensors of each NASA Space Shuttle mission are archived once per second during the duration of each mission. With each mission lasting several days, this is an enormous repository of data (on the order of 10 Gbytes per mission, with order of 100 missions flown to date).

Retrieval in this context can be stated as follows: find the subsequence that best matches a given query sequence Q. For example, for the Shuttle archive, an engineer might observe a potentially anomalous sensor behavior (expressed as a short query sequence Q) in real time and wish to determine whether similar behavior had been observed in past missions.

14.6.1   Global Models for Time Series Data

Traditional time series modeling techniques (such as statistical methods) are largely based on *global linear* models, as discussed in chapter 6. An example is the Box-Jenkins autoregressive family of models where the current value $y(t)$ is modeled as a weighted linear combination of past values $y(t - k)$ plus additive noise:

$$y(t) = \sum_{i=1}^{k} \alpha_i y(t - i) + e(t) \tag{14.7}$$

where the α_i are the weighting coefficients and $e(t)$ is the noise at time t (typically presumed to be Gaussian with zero mean). The term *autoregression* is derived from the notion of using a regression model on past values of the same variable. Techniques that are very similar in spirit to the linear regression techniques of chapter 11 can be used to estimate the parameters α_i from data. Determination of the model structure (or order, k) can be performed by the usual techniques of penalized likelihood or cross-validation.

This type of model is closely linked to the spectral representation of y, in the sense that specifying the αs also specifies the frequency characteristics for a stationary time series process y. Thus it is clear that it only makes sense to consider the use of the autoregressive model for time series that can be well characterized by stationary spectral representations, i.e., a linear system whose frequency characteristics do not change with time.

A general contribution of the Box-Jenkins methodology has been to show that if a time series has an identifiable systematic nonstationary component (such as a trend), the nonstationary component can often be removed to reduce the time series to a stationary form. For example, economic indices such as annual gross domestic product or the Dow Jones Index contain an inherent upward trend (on average) which is typically removed before modeling. Even if the nonstationarity is not particularly simple, another useful approach is to assume that the signal is *locally stationary* in time. For example, this is how speech recognition systems work, by modeling the sequence of phoneme sounds produced by the human vocal tract and mouth as coming from a set of different linear systems. The model is then defined as a mixture of these systems, and the data are assumed to come from some form of switching process (typically Markov) between these different component linear systems.

Nonlinear global models generalize equation 14.7 to allow (for example) a nonlinear dependence of $y(t)$ on the past:

$$y(t) = g\left(\sum_{i=1}^{k} \alpha_i y(t-i)\right) + e(t) \qquad (14.8)$$

where $g(.)$ is a nonlinearity.

There are a large number of extensions of both the linear and nonlinear models of this general form. One key aspect they have in common is that, given an initial condition $y(0)$ and the parameters of the model, the statistics of the process (the distribution of y as a function of time) are completely determined, i.e., these models provide global aggregate descriptions of the expected behavior of the time series.

In terms of data mining, if we assume that such a global model is an adequate description of the underlying time series, we can use the model parameters (e.g., the weights above) as the basis for representing the data, rather than the original time series itself. For example, given a set of different time series (such as daily returns over time of various stocks), we could fit a different global model to each time series (i.e., estimate p parameters of a model) and then perform similarity calculations among the time series in p-dimensional parameter space. A problem arises here if the different time series are not all adequately modeled by the same model structure. One solution to this is to assume a nested model structure (i.e., where the model structures form a nested sequence of increasing complexity) and to simply fit the maximum-order model to all the time series.

By representing each time series as a vector of parameters, we have in essence performed the same trick as that used for representing documents and images in earlier sections of this chapter. Thus, in principle, we can define similarity measures in the vector space of parameters, define queries in this space for retrieval by content, and so forth.

One interesting application of data mining in this context is a technique known as *keyword spotting* in speech recognition. Consider, for example, a national security organization that monitors and records international telephone conversations (ignore the moral and legal ramifications!). From a security viewpoint the goal is to detect suspicious behavior. Naturally it is impossible for a human to monitor and listen to all of the hundreds of thousands of telephone conversations recorded daily. One automated approach to the problem is to build statistical models of specific keywords of interest. For example, we could construct (from training data) a different Markov linear-switching model (as mentioned earlier) for each specific word of interest. The incoming voice streams are run through each model in parallel, and if the likelihood of the observed audio data exceeds a certain threshold for any of the models, then that word is considered to be detected, and the voice stream can be tagged with the identified word and the location in time of that word. Naturally there are numerous practical engineering considerations for such a system, but the basic concept is to use a set of trained models to adaptively monitor a real-time stream of data to detect patterns of interest.

14.6.2   Structure and Shape in Time Series

Consider a real valued subsequence of time series values, $Q = [q(t), \ldots, q(t + m)]$, which we will call the query pattern, and a much larger archived time series $X = [x(1), \ldots, x(T)]$. The goal is find a subsequence within X that is most similar to Q. In reality X could be composed of many individual time series, but for simplicity imagine that they have all been concatenated into a single long series. In addition, for simplicity assume that both X and Q have been measured with the same time-sampling interval, i.e., the time units for one increment of t are the same for each. For example, Q could be a snapshot from an EEG monitor of a patient being monitored in real time, and X could be an archive of EEGs for patients who have already been diagnosed.

Clearly there is considerable latitude in how *similarity* is defined in this context. Note that the general approach of the last section provides only a global statistical characterization of a time series. In particular, there is no notion of local *shape* such as a peak in time. Global statistical models typically average out such local structural properties; i.e., they are not explicitly retained in the representation. However, many time series are more naturally described by their structural features. A good example is the S-T waveform in cardiac monitoring, which has a distinctive visual signature.

One approach is to perform a sequential scan of the query Q across the full length of the archival data X, moving the query Q along X one time point at a time, and calculating a distance metric (such as Euclidean distance) at each point. This is typically not only prohibitively expensive ($O(mT)$ for a brute-force approach) but also focuses on low-level sampled data points of the the signal rather than high-level structural properties such as peaks, plateaus, trends, and valleys. Direct Euclidean-distance matching is also very susceptible to slight deformations of the query Q or data X, e.g., a slight "stretching" along the time axis of the "ideal" query Q can result in a large increase in distance even though from the viewpoint of the human visual observer the query Q and the data X may appear to match well.

A popular approach in this context is to locally estimate shape-based features of both the query Q and the archived signal X, and to perform matching at the higher structural level. This can achieve a significant computational advantage in the matching process, since the abstraction is in essence a form of data compression, i.e., many irrelevant details of the signal can be ignored. More important, it can extract structural information in a form that is suitable for human interpretation. One example of this technique is to approximate a signal by piecewise linear (or polynomial) segments. The segmented series can now be represented as a list of locally parametrized curves, and structural features (such as peaks and valleys) can be directly calculated from the parametrized description. A probabilistic model can then be used to parametrize the expected shape and variability in terms of these features, allowing for a flexible family of deformable template models. Matching a query Q to a data archive X can be formulated as a search problem in terms of finding local regions in X that maximize the likelihood of the local data within that region given the probabilistic model for Q. This type of representation is particularly useful for the types of signals that are not easily handled by the global statistical models, i.e., nonstationary signals containing transients, step functions, trends, and various other shapelike patterns.

For discrete-valued sequences we can also look for subpatterns within a longer sequence, e.g., the occurrence of motifs in biological sequence data. A wide variety of techniques are used for these sorts of problems, ranging from relatively nonparametric edit-distance methods for matching two strings, to probabilistic model-based approaches using generative Markov (or hidden Markov) models.

14.7 Summary

Retrieval by content is an important problem for the interactive exploration of large databases. In particular, for data types such as images, text, and sequences, algorithms for retrieval by content have great potential utility across a variety of applications. However, in their full generality, such algorithms require the solution of several fundamental and long-standing problems in artificial intelligence and pattern recognition, such as the general NLP problem (for text) or the general image understanding problem (for images). In short, we are a long way from developing general-purpose methods for automatically extracting semantic content from data such as text or images in a manner that is competitive with the human brain.

Nonetheless, given that in many applications it is impossible to analyze the data manually because of its sheer volume, researchers have developed a variety of techniques for retrieval by content, largely relying on what we might term "low-level semantic content." Thus, for example, we retrieve images based on low-level features such as color or texture, and retrieve text based on word co-occurrences.

Across different data types, we can see that a common strategy for retrieval is often used, roughly following these steps:

1. Determine a robust set of features by which to describe the objects of interest.

2. Convert the original objects (text, images, sequences) into a fixed-length vector representation using these features.

3. Perform matching, distance calculations, principal component analysis, and so forth, in this vector-space, taking advantage of the wealth of theory that exists for multivariate data analysis.

We might term such systems as *first-generation retrieval by content systems.* Certainly they can be very useful, as is evidenced by Web search engines and the QBIC system, for example. However, it is clear that retrieval by content is far from being a solved problem, and there is considerable room for further advances.

14.8   Further Reading

The collected volume by Sparck Jones and Willett (1997) contains many of the classic papers in information (text) retrieval, with some very insightful and broad-ranging editorial discussion of central themes in retrieval problems and research. Van Rijsbergen (1979), Salton and McGill (1983), and Frakes and Baeza-Yates (1992) provide a more introductory coverage of the field. Salton (1971) contains many of the seminal early ideas on the vector-space representation and Raghavan and Wong (1986) provide a later perspective. Salton and Buckley (1988) is a brief but informative account of different term-weighting methods, with particular emphasis on the TF-IDF method. The TREC conferences are documented in Harman (1993–1999), and Harman (1995) provides a useful overview of the TREC experiments. A more recent treatment of general issues in evaluation in the context of text retrieval is in the special issue of the *Journal of the American Society for Information Science*

(1996). Witten, Moffat, and Bell (1999) provide an excellent account of many of the practical data engineering issues involved in storing and accessing large text document archives.

Deerwester et al. (1990) is one of the first papers to clearly demonstrate the utility of LSI in information retrieval. Landauer and Dumais (1997) provide a thought-provoking discussion of the general implications of the LSI approach for cognitive models of language and knowledge acquisition. Berry (1992) and Berry, Drmvac, and Jessup (1999) describe general numerical techniques for performing SVD computations on large sparse data sets such as term-document representations. Hofmann (1999) describes a probabilistic approach to dimension reduction in document-term matrices, based on mixture models, providing a general probabilistic framework for document modeling and demonstrating impressive empirical results.

"Text mining" is a phrase used to describe the application of data mining techniques to semi-automated discovery of new knowledge from text documents. An interesting line of work in this area is described in Swanson (1987) and Swanson and Smalheiser (1994, 1997) where automated text search algorithms were used to discover interesting relationships between seemingly unrelated sub-fields in the medical literature.

Rocchio (1971) introduced the original algorithm for relevance feedback. Salton and Buckley (1990) provide experimental evidence on the effectiveness of relevance feedback in improving recall-precision performance, and Buckley and Salton (1995) discuss optimality aspects of Rocchio's algorithm. Resnick et al. (1994) and Shardanand and Maes (1995) describe the initial work on collaborative filtering. Breese, Heckerman, and Cadie (1998) contains a more recent empirical evaluation of model-based collaborative filtering algorithms. Konstan and Riedl (in press) contains a useful recent overview of many of the practical factors involved in fielding automated recommender systems in e-commerce applications. Dumais et al. (1998) describe the use of support-vector machines for document classification.

The QBIC system is described in some detail in Faloutsos et al. (1994) and Flickner et al. (1995). The first paper contains a reasonably detailed discussion of the features, distance measures, and indexing schemes used, while the second paper focuses somewhat more on user interface issues. Other query by content systems for image and video retrieval are described in Kato, Kurita, and Shimogaki (1991), Smoliar and Zhang (1994), Pentland, Picard, and Sclaroff (1996), and Smith and Chang (1997). Rui et al. (1998) discuss the use of relevance feedback in an image-retrieval context. The edited collection by Maybury (1997) provides a useful overview of recent work in the general area of retrieval of multimedia objects such as images and video.

Box and Jenkins (1976) is a comprehensive and classic text on the fundamentals of linear global models for time series data. Chatfield (1989) provides a somewhat broader perspective and is particularly noteworthy as a gentle introduction to time series concepts for readers unfamiliar with the field in general. MacDonald and Zucchini (1997) provide a comprehensive description of statistical approaches to modeling discrete-valued time series, and Durbin et al. (1998) illustrate the application of sequence modeling and pattern recognition techniques to protein sequences and related problems in computational biology.

There are a large number of different techniques for efficient approximate subsequence matching for time series. The work of Faloutsos, Ranganathan, and Manolopolous (1994) is typical. Sequences are decomposed into windows, features are extracted from each window (locally estimated spectral coefficients in this case), and efficient matching is then performed using an R^*-tree structure in feature space. Agrawal et al. (1995) proposed an alternative approach that can handle amplitude scaling, offset translation, and "don't care" regions in the data, where distance is determined from the envelopes of the original sequences. Berndt and Clifford (1994) use dynamic time-warping approach to allow for "elasticity" in the temporal axis when a query Q is matched to a reference sequence R. Another popular approach is to abstract the notion of shape. Relational trees can be used to capture the hierarchy of peaks (or valleys) in a sequence, and tree-matching algorithms can then be used to compare two time series (Shaw and DeFigueiredo (1990); Wang et al., (1994)). Keogh and Smyth (1997) and Ge and Smyth (2000) illustrate the use of probabilistic deformable templates for flexible modeling and detection of time series shapes with applications to interactive analysis of Shuttle sensor data and online monitoring of semiconductor manufacturing data.

Appendix: Random Variables

A.1: Review of Univariate Random Variables

A univariate random variable is a single random variable X. If the domain of X is finite (or *denumerable*), we can characterize the uncertainty about X by listing for each possible value x of X—e.g., $x \in \{x_1, \ldots, x_m\}$—the probability that X has value x. We write this *probability distribution* of X as $p(X = x)$, or, to refer to the probability distribution of single values in general, $p(x)$. When the domain is finite, as in this case, the set of probabilities $\{p(x_1), \ldots, p(x_m)\}$ is often called a *probability mass function*. Note that the expression $p(X)$ refers to the set of m numbers $\{p(x_1), \ldots, p(x_m)\}$, and $p(x)$ refers to some (arbitrary) member of this set. The *cumulative distribution function* $P(x)$ of a random variable is the probability that it will take a value less than or equal to x (when the values x can be ordered).

Cumulative distribution functions can also be defined for continuous random variables (those that can take any value on an interval or the real line). In this case we will usually denote the cumulative distribution by $F(x)$ or $P(x)$, and the derivative of $F(x)$, the *probability density function* of x (often just "density function" for short), by $f(x)$ or $p(x)$. This function gives the probability that the observed value will lie in an infinitesimal interval surrounding x. Here, for the sake of simplicity, we will often provide descriptions only in terms of density functions, but analogous arguments apply to probability mass functions. Introductory texts on mathematical statistics provide more formal descriptions of these concepts, but these informal definitions will suffice for our purposes.

In terms of notation both $p(x)$ and $f(x)$ are often used to denote a probability density function on a continuous variable x. It should be clear from the context, depending on whether x is discrete or continuous, whether $p(x)$ is referring to a probability mass function or a probability density function for x.

The randomness of a random variable may arise for various reasons—essentially the sources of uncertainty: perhaps we have observed a randomly selected member of the population, perhaps there is measurement error associated with the value, perhaps X is not directly observable, and so on. We often approximate this randomness by assuming that the actual observed values have arisen from some well known distribution of possible values. Certain distributions are especially useful in data mining, and some of these are described in appendix A.2. They include the Normal (or Gaussian) distribution and the Poisson distribution.

We use the notion of the mean value (or *expected value,* or *expectation*) in chapter 2. For a sample (or finite population) the mean is the average value, obtained by dividing the sum of the values in the sample (or finite population) by the total number of values. More generally, suppose that value x occurs in the population with probability $p(x)$. Then the mean value of the variable X for the population is given by $\sum_x xp(x)$. However, if X can take a continuum of values, it is not meaningful to speak of the probability that any particular exact value x will occur, since exact values have zero probability of occurring. Instead we consider the probability that X lies in a small interval of width δx and find the limiting value of the sum $\sum_x xf(x)\delta x$ as this width decreases toward zero. This leads us to replace summation with integration. If the probability density function of the continuous variable X is $f(x)$, the expected value is $\int xf(x)dx$.

The notation E is often used to denote expectation, so that the expected value of a random variable X is $E[X]$. The Greek letter μ is also often used to denote a mean, or, if we need to make it clear that the random variable X is being discussed, μ_x may be used. More precisely, the expected value of X *with respect to* the density function $f(x)$ is denoted $E_{f(x)}[X]$. Note that we can define the expected value of a function of X, $g(x)$, with respect to $f(x)$, as $E_{f(x)}[g(x)] = \int g(x)f(x)dx$. If we let $g(x) = (x - E[x])^2$ we get the usual definition of variance σ_x^2.

Expectation is a linear operator. This is quite a useful general property. For example, it means that the expected value of a weighted sum of random variables is equal to the weighted sum of their expected values, regardless of whether the variables are dependent in any way (chapter 4 discusses more precisely what we mean by dependence of random variables).

The axioms of probability referred to above assign a probability of 0 to an event that cannot occur, and a probability of 1 to a certain event. If two events cannot occur together, the probability that one *or* the other will occur is the sum of their separate probabilities. Thus, in tossing a fair coin (with which the probability of obtaining a head is $1/2$) the probability of obtaining either a head or a tail is $1/2+1/2 = 1$. The situation starts to get more complicated—and more interesting—when events can occur together but are not certain to do so. This lead us to the notion of *multivariate* random variables, discussed in detail in chapter 4.

A.2: Some Common Probability Distributions

Above we discussed the general idea of a probability distribution. Here we describe some specific and important probability distributions that arise in data mining.

The Bernoulli distribution

The Bernoulli distribution has just two possible outcomes. Situations which might be described by such a distribution include the outcome of a coin toss (heads or tails) or whether a particular customer buys a particular product or not. Denoting the outcomes by 0 and 1, let p be the probability of observing a 1 and $(1-p)$ the probability of observing a 0. Then the probability mass function can be written as $p^x(1 - p)^{1-x}$, with x taking the value 0 or 1. The mean of the distribution is p and its variance is $p(1 - p)$. Note that this distribution has just a single parameter, namely p.

The Binomial Distribution

This is a generalization of the Bernoulli distribution, and describes the number x of "type 1 outcomes" (e.g., successes) in n independent Bernoulli trials, each with parameter p. The probability mass function has the form $\binom{n}{x}p^x(1 - p)^{n-x}$, where x can take integer values between 0 and n. The mean is np and the variance is $np(1 - p)$.

The Multinomial Distribution

The multinomial distribution is a generalization of the binomial distribution to the case where there are more than two potential outcomes; for example, there may be k possible outcomes, the ith having probability p_i of occurring, $1 \le i \le k$. The probabilities p_i sum to 1, and the model has $k - 1$ parameters $p_1, \ldots, p_{k-1}$ (since $p_k = 1 - \sum_i p_i$).

Suppose that n observations have been independently drawn from a multinomial distribution. Then the mean number of observations yielding the ith outcome is np_i and its variance is $np_i(1 - p_i)$. Note that, since the occurrence of one outcome means the others cannot occur, the individual outcomes must be negatively correlated. In fact, the covariance between the ith and jth $(i \neq j)$ outcome is $-np_i p_j$.

The Poisson Distribution

If random events are observed independently, with underlying rate λ, then we would expect to observe λt events on average in a time interval of length t. Sometimes, of course, we would observe none in time t, at other times we would observe 1, and so on. If the rate is low, we would rarely expect to observe a large number of events (unless t was large). A distribution which describes this state of affairs is the *Poisson distribution*. It has probability mass function $(\lambda t)^x e^{-\lambda t}/x!$. The mean and variance of the Poisson distribution are the same, both being λ.

Given a binomial distribution with large n and small p such that np is a constant, then this may be well approximated by a Poisson distribution .

The Normal (or Gaussian) Distribution

The probability density function takes the form

$$\frac{1}{\sigma\sqrt{2\pi}} exp\left(\frac{-1}{2\sigma^2}(x - \mu)^2\right)$$

where μ is the mean of the distribution and σ^2 is the variance. *The standard normal distribution* is the special case with zero mean and unit variance. The normal distribution is very important, partly as a consequence of the *central limit theorem*. Roughly speaking, this says that the distribution of the mean of a sample of n observations becomes more and more like the normal distribution as n increases, regardless of the form of the populations distribution from which the data are drawn. (Of course, mathematical niceties require this to be qualified for full rigor.) This is one reason why many statistical procedures are based on an assumption that various distributions are normal.

The normal distribution is symmetric about its mean, and 95% of its probability lies within ± 1.96 standard deviations of the mean.

The Student's *t*-distribution

Consider a sample from a normal distribution with known standard deviation σ. An appropriate test statistic to use to make inferences about the mean would be the ratio

$$\frac{\bar{x} - \mu}{\frac{\sigma}{\sqrt{n}}}$$

where $\bar{x}$ is the sample mean. Using this, for example, one can see how far the sample mean deviates from a hypothesized value of the unknown mean. This ratio will be normally distributed by the central limit theorem (see *Normal distribution* above). Note that here the denominator is a constant. Of course, in real life, one is more likely to be in a situation of making inferences about a mean when the standard deviation is *unknown*. This means that one would usually want to replace the above ratio by

$$\frac{\bar{x} - \mu}{\frac{s}{\sqrt{n}}}$$

where s is the sample estimate of the standard deviation. As soon as one does this the ratio ceases to be normally distributed—extra random variation has been introduced by the fact that the denominator now varies from sample to sample. The distribution of this new ratio will have a larger spread than that of the corresponding normal distribution—it will have fatter tails. This distribution is called the *t*-distribution. Note that there are many—they differ according to how large is the sample size, since this affects the variability in s. They are indexed by $(n - 1)$, known as the *degrees of freedom* of the distribution.

We can also describe this situation by saying that the ratio of two random variables, the numerator following a normal distribution and the square of the denominator following a chi-squared distribution (see below), follows a *t*-distribution.

The probability density function is quite complicated and it is unnecessary to reproduce it here (it is available in introductory texts on mathematical statistics). The mean is $n - 1$ and the variance is $(n - 1)/(n - 3)$.

The Chi-Squared Distribution

The distribution of the sum of the squares of n values, each following the standard normal distribution, is called the *chi-squared distribution with n degrees of freedom*. Such a distribution has mean n and variance $2n$. Again it seems unnecessary to reproduce the probability density function here—it can be readily found in introductory mathematical statistics texts it needed. The chi-squared distribution is particularly widely used in tests of goodness-of-fit.

The F Distribution

If u and v are independently distributed Chi-squared random variables with n_1 and n_2 degrees of freedom, respectively, then the ratio

$$F = \frac{u}{n_1} / \frac{v}{n_2}$$

is said to follow an F *distribution with n_1 and n_2 degrees of freedom.* This is widely used in tests to compare variances, such as arise in analysis of variance applications.

The Multivariate Normal Distribution

This is an extension of the univariate normal distribution to multiple random variables. Let $\mathbf{x} = (x_1, \ldots, x_p)$ denote a p component random vector. Then the probability density function of the multivariate normal distribution has the form

$$\frac{1}{(2\pi)^{\frac{p}{2}} |\Sigma|^{\frac{1}{2}}} e^{-\frac{1}{2}(\mathbf{x}-\mu)^T \Sigma^{-1} (\mathbf{x}-\mu)}$$

where μ is the p-dimensional mean vector of the distribution and Σ is the $p \times p$ covariance matrix.

Just as the univariate normal distribution plays a unique role in probabilistic modeling, so does the multivariate normal distribution. It has the property that its marginal distributions are normal, as also are its conditional distributions (the joint distribution of a subset of variables, given fixed values of the others). Note, however, that the converse is not true: just because the p marginals of a distribution are normal, this does not mean the overall distribution is multivariate normal.

References

Abiteboul, S., Hull, R., and Vianu, V. (1995) *Foundations of Databases*. Reading, MA: Addison-Wesley.

Adriaans, P., and Zantige, D. (1996) *Data Mining*. Harlow, UK: Addison-Wesley.

Agrawal, R., Aggarwal, C., and Prasad, V. (in press) A tree projection algorithm for finding frequent itemsets. *Journal of Parallel and Distributed Computing*.

Agrawal, R., Imielenski, T., and Swami, A. (1993) Mining association rules between sets of items in large databases. *Proceedings of the ACM SIGMOD Conference on Management of Data (SIGMOD'98)*, New York: ACM Press, pp. 207–216.

Agrawal, R., Lin, K.I., Sawhney, H.S., and Shim, K. (1995) Fast similarity search in the presence of noise, scaling, and translation in time-series databases. *Proceedings of VLDB-95*, pp. 490–501.

Agrawal, R., Mannila, H., Srikant, R., Toivonen, H., and Verkamo, A.I. (1996) Fast discovery of association rules. *Advances in Knowledge Discovery and Data Mining*, U.M., Fayyad, G., Piatetsky-Shapiro, P., Smyth, and Uthurasamy, R. (eds.). Menlo Park, CA: AAAI Press, pp. 307–328.

Agrawal, R., and Srikant, R. (1994) Fast algorithms for mining association rules in large databases. *Proceedings of the Twentieth International Conference on Very Large Data Bases (VLDB'94)*, pp. 487–499.

Akaike, H. (1973) Information theory and an extension of the maximum likelihood principle. In *Second International Symposium on Information The-*

ory, B.N. Petrov and F. Csaki (eds.), Academiai Kiado, Budapest, pp. 267–281.

Alon, N., and Spencer, J.H. (1992) *The Probabilistic Method*. New York: Wiley.

Anderberg, M.R. (1973) *Cluster Analysis for Applications*. New York: Academic Press.

Applebaum, D. (1996) *Probability and Information: An Integrated Approach*, Cambridge, U.K.: Cambridge University Press.

Aronis, J.M., and Provost, F.J. (1997) Increasing the efficiency of data mining algorithms with breadth-first marker propagation. *Proceedings of the Third International Conference on Knowledge Discovery and Data Mining*, Heckerman, D., Mannila, H., and Pregibon, D. (eds.). Menlo Park, CA: AAAI Press, pp. 119–122.

Asimov, D. (1985) The grand tour: a tool for viewing multidimensional data. *SIAM Journal of Scientific and Statistical Computing*, 6, pp. 128–143.

Atkeson, C.W., Schaal, S.A., and Moore, A.W. (1997) Locally weighted learning. *Artificial Intelligence Review*, 11, pp. 75–133.

Azzalini, A., and Bowman, A.W. (1990) A look at some data on the Old Faithful geyser. *Applied Statistics*, 39, pp. 357–365.

Babcock, C. (1994) Parallel processing mines retail data. *Computer World*, 6.

Ballard, D.H. (1997) *An Introduction to Natural Computation*. Cambridge, MA: MIT Press.

Banfield, J.D., and Raftery, A.E. (1993) Model-based Gaussian and non-Gaussian clustering. *Biometrics*, 49, pp. 803–821.

Barnett, V. (1982) *Comparative Statistical Inference*. Chichester, U.K.: Wiley.

Baum, L.E., and Petrie, T. (1966) Statistical inference for probabilistic functions of Markov chains. *Annals of Mathematical Statistics*, 37, pp. 1554–1563.

Bayardo, R.J., and Agrawal, R. (1999) Mining the most interesting rules. *Proc. 5th ACM SIGKDD International Conference on Knowledge Discovery and Data Mining (KDD-99)*. New York: ACM Press, pp. 145–154.

Becker, R.A., Cleveland, W.S., and Wilks, A.R. (1987) Dynamic graphics for data analysis. *Statistical Science*, 2, pp. 355–395.

Becker, R.A., Eick, S.G., and Wilks, A.R. (1995) Visualizing network data. *IEEE Transactions on Visualization and Computer Graphics*, 1(1), pp. 16–28.

Bennett, K., Fayyad, U., and Geiger, D. (1999) Density-based indexing for approximate nearest-neighbor queries. *Proceedings of the Fifth ACM SIG-KDD International Conference on Knowledge Discovery and Data Mining*, New York, NY: ACM Press, pp. 233–243.

Bernardo, J.M., and Smith, A.F.M. (1994) *Bayesian Theory*. New York, NY: Wiley.

Berndt, D.J., and Clifford, J. (1996) Finding patterns in time-series, a dynamic programming approach. *Advances in Knowledge Discovery and Data Mining*, Fayyad, U.M., Piatetsky-Shapiro, G., Smyth, P., and Uthurasamy, R. (eds). Menlo Park, CA: AAAI/MIT Press, pp. 229–248.

Berry, M.J.A., and Linoff, G. (1997) *Data Mining Techniques for Marketing, Sales, and Customer Support*. New York: Wiley.

Berry, M.J.A., and Linoff, G. (2000) *Mastering Data Mining*. New York: Wiley.

Berry, M.W. (1992) Large scale singular value computations. *International Journal of Supercomputer Applications* 6(1), pp. 13–49.

Berry, M.W., Drmvac, Z., and Jessup, E.R. (1999) Matrices, vector-spaces, and information retrieval, *SIAM Review*, 41(2), pp. 335–362.

Beyer, K., Goldstein, J., Ramakrishnan, R., and Shaft, U. (1999) When is "nearest neighbor" meaningful? *Proceedings of the 7th International Conference on Data Theory, ICDT'99*, Lecture Notes in Computer Science, LNCS, Number 1540. New York: Springer-Verlag, pp. 217–235.

Bhandari, I., Colet, E., Parker, J., Pines, Z., Pratap, R., and Ramanujam, K. (1997) Advanced Scout: data mining and knowledge discovery in NBA data. *Data Mining and Knowledge Discovery*, 1(1), pp. 121–125.

Bishop, C.M. (1995) *Neural Networks for Pattern Recognition*. Oxford, U.K.: Clarendon Press, 1995.

Bishop, Y.M.M., Fienberg, S.E., and Holland, P.W. (1975) *Discrete Multivariate Analysis*, Cambridge, MA: MIT Press.

Blasius, J., and Greenacre, M. (1998) *Visualization of Categorical Data.* San Diego, CA: Academic Press.

Blum, T., Keislaer, D., Wheaton, J., and Wold, E. (1997) Audio databases with content-based retrieval. *Intelligent Multimedia Information Retrieval,* Maybury, M. T. (ed.). Menlo Park, CA: AAAI Press, pp. 113–135.

Box, G.E.P., and Jenkins, G.M. (1976) *Time Series Analysis: Forecasting and Control.* Oakland, CA: Holden Day.

Box, G.E.P., Jenkins, G.M., and Reinsel, G.C. (1994) *Time Series Analysis: Forecasting and Control,* 3rd ed. Englewood Cliffs, NJ: Prentice Hall.

Bradley, P.S., Fayyad, U.M., and Mangasarian, O.L. (1999) Mathematical programming for data mining: formulation and challenges. *INFORMS Journal on Computing,* 11, pp. 217–238.

Bradley, P.S., Fayyad, U.M., Reina, C. (1998) Scaling clustering algorithms to large databases. In *Proceedings of the 4th International Conference on Knowledge Discovery and Data Mining,* R. Agrawal, P. Stolorz, and G. Piatetsky-Shapiro (eds.), Menlo Park, CA: AAAI Press, pp. 9–15.

Breese, J.S., Heckerman, D., and Kadie, C. (1998) Empirical analysis of predictive algorithms for collaborative filtering. *Proceedings 14th Conference on Uncertainty in Artificial Intelligence,* San Francisco, CA: Morgan Kaufmann, pp. 43–52..

Breiman, L., Friedman, J.H., Olshen, R.A., and Stone, C.J. (1984) *Classification and Regression Trees.* Belmont, CA: Wadsworth Statistical Press.

Brijs, T., Goethals, B., Swinnen, G., Vanhoof, K., and Wets, G. (2000) A data mining framework for optimal product selection in retail supermarket data: the generalized PROFSET model. *Proceedings of the ACM Seventh International Conference on Knowledge Discovery and Data Mining,* New York: ACM Press, pp. 300–304.

Brin, S., and Page, L. (1998) The anatomy of a large-scale hypertextual Web search engine. *Proceedings of the Seventh International World-Wide Web Conference,* Brisbane, Australia, pp. 107–117.

Brin, S., Motwani, R., and Silverstein, C. (1997) Beyond market baskets: generalizing association rules to correlations. *Proceedings of the ACM SIGMOD Conference on Management of Data (SIGMOD'97),* New York: ACM Press, pp. 265–276.

Brooks, S.P., and Morgan, B.J.T. (1995) Optimisation using simulated annealing. *The Statistician*, 44, pp. 241–257.

Buckley, C., and Salton, G. (1995) Optimization of relevance feedback weights. *Proceedings of the 18th Annual ACM 1995 SIGIR Conference*, pp. 351-356.

Buja, A., Cook, D., and Swayne, D.F. (1996) Interactive high-dimensional data visualization. *Journal of Computational and Graphical Statistics*, 5(1), 78–99.

Buntine, W. (1992) Learning classification trees. *Statistics and Computing*, 2, pp. 63–73.

Buntine, W., Fischer, B., and Pressburger, T. (1999) Towards automated synthesis of data mining programs. In *Proceedings of the Fifth ACM Conference on Knowledge Discovery and Data Mining*, S. Chaudhuri and D. Madigan (eds.), New York, NY: ACM Press, pp. 372–376.

Burges, C.J.C. (1998) A tutorial on support vector machines for pattern recognition. *Data Mining and Knowledge Discovery*, 2, pp. 121–167.

Burnham, K.P., and Anderson, D.R. (1998) *Model Selection and Inference: a Practical Information Theoretic Approach*. New York: Springer-Verlag.

Böhning, D. (1998) *Computer Assisted Analysis of Mixtures*, Boca Raton, FL: Chapman and Hall.

Cadez, I.V., McLaren, C.E., Smyth, P., and McLachlan, G.J. (1999) Hierarchical models for screening of iron-deficient anemia. *Proceedings of the 1999 International Conference on Machine Learning*, I. Bratko and S. Dzeroski (eds.), San Francisco, CA: Morgan Kaufmann, pp. 77–86.

Cadez, I.V., Heckerman, D., Meek, C., Smyth, P., and White, S. (2000) Visualization of navigation patterns on a Web site using model-based clustering. *Proceedings of the ACM Seventh International Conference on Knowledge Discovery and Data Mining*, New York, NY: ACM Press, pp. 280–284.

Card, S.K., MacKinlay, J.D., and Shneiderman, B. (eds.) (1999) *Readings in Information Visualization: Using Vision to Think*. San Francisco, CA: Morgan Kaufmann.

Carmines, E.G., and Zeller, R.A. (1979) *Reliability and Validity Assessment*. Beverly Hills, CA: Sage Publications.

Carr, D.B., Littlefield, R.J., Nicholson, W.L., and Littlefield, J.S. (1987) Scatterplot matrix techniques for large N. *Journal of the American Statistical Association,* 82(398), pp. 424–436.

Casti, J.L. (1990) *Searching for Certainty: What Scientists Can Know about the Future.* New York: Willam Morrow.

Celeux, G., and Govaert, G. (1995) Gaussian parsimonious clustering models. *Pattern Recognition,* 28, pp. 781–793.

Chambers, J.M., Cleveland, W.S., Kleiner, B., and Tukey, P.A. (1983) *Graphical Methods for Data Analysis.* Pacific Grove: Wadsworth and Brooks/Cole.

Chatfield, C. (1996) *The Analysis of Time Series: An Introduction.* London: Chapman and Hall.

Chatterjee, S., Handcock, M.S., and Simonoff, J.S. (1995) *A Casebook for a First Course in Statistics and Data Analysis.* New York: Wiley.

Chaudhuri, S. (1998) An overview of query optimization in relational systems. *Proceedings of the Seventeenth ACM SIGACT-SIGMOD-SIGART Symposium on Principles of Database Systems,* New York: ACM Press, pp. 34–43.

Chaudhuri, S., and Dayal, U. (1997) An overview of data warehousing and OLAP technology. *Proceedings of the 1997 ACM/SIGMOD Conference,* New York: ACM Press, pp. 65–75.

Cheeseman, P., and Stutz. J. (1996) Bayesian classification (AutoClass): theory and results. In *Advances in Knowledge Discovery and Data Mining,* U.M. Fayyad, G. Piatetsky-Shapiro, P. Smyth, R. Uthurusamy (eds.), Cambridge, MA: AAAI/MIT Press, pp. 153–180.

Cheng, X., and Wallace, J.M. (1993) Cluster analysis of the Northern Hemisphere wintertime 500-hPa height field: spatial patterns. *Journal of the Atmospheric Sciences,* 50, pp. 2674–2696.

Cherkassky, V.S., and Muller, F. (1998). *Learning from Data: Concepts, Theory, and Methods.* New York: Wiley.

Chernoff, H. (1973) The use of faces to represent points in k-dimensional space graphically. *Journal of the American Statistical Association,* 68, pp. 361–368.

Chickering, D.M., and Heckerman, D. (1997) Efficient approximations for the marginal likelihood of Bayesian networks with hidden variables. *Machine Learning*, 29(2/3), pp. 181–244.

Chickering, D.M., Heckerman, D., and Meek, C. (1997) A Bayesian approach to learning Bayesian networks with local structure. *Proceedings of Thirteenth Conference on Uncertainty in Artificial Intelligence*. San Francisco, CA: Morgan Kaufmann, pp. 80–89.

Chipman, H., George, E.I., and McCulloch, R.E. (1998) Bayesian CART model search (with discussion). *Journal of the American Statistical Association*, 93, pp. 935–960.

Clark, P., and Niblett, T. (1989) The CN2 induction algorithm. *Machine Learning*, 3(4), pp. 261–283.

Clearwater, S., and Stern, E. (1991) A rule-learning program in high-energy physics event classification. *Computational Physics Communications*, 67, pp. 159–182.

Cleveland, W.S., and McGill, M.E. (eds.) (1988) *Dynamic Graphics for Statistics*. Belmont, CA: Wadsworth and Brooks/Cole.

Cleveland, W.S., and Devlin, S.J. (1988) Locally-weighted regression: An approach to regression analysis by local fitting. *Journal of the American Statistical Association*, 83, pp. 597–610.

Cochran, W.G. (1977) *Sampling Techniques*. New York: Wiley.

Cohen, W. (1995) Fast effective rule induction. *Proceedings of the Twelfth International Conference on Machine Learning*, San Mateo, CA: Morgan Kaufmann, pp. 115–123.

Cook, R.D., and Weisberg, S. (1994) *An Introduction to Regression Graphics*. New York: Wiley.

Cook, R.D., and Weisberg, S. (1999) *Applied Regression Including Computing and Graphics*. New York: Wiley.

Cook, W.J., Cunningham, W.H., Pulleyblank, W.R., and Schrijver, A. (1998) *Combinatorial Optimization*. New York: Wiley.

Corman, T.H., Leiserson, C. E., and Rivest, R.L. (1990) *Introduction to Algorithms*. Cambridge, MA: MIT Press.

Cortes, C., and Pregibon, D. (1998) Giga-mining. In *Proceedings of the Fourth International Conference on Knowledge Discovery and Data Mining*, R. Agrawal and P. Stolorz (eds.), Menlo Park, CA: AAAI Press, pp. 174–178.

Cox D.R., and Wermuth, N. (1996) *Multivariate Dependencies: Models, Analysis, and Interpretation.* London: Chapman and Hall.

Cox, D.R., and Hinkley, D.V. (1974) *Theoretical Statistics.* London: Chapman and Hall.

Cox, T.F., and Cox, M.A.A. (1994) *Multidimensional Scaling.* London: Chapman and Hall.

Crawford, S.L. (1989) Extensions to the CART algorithm. *International Journal of Man-Machine Studies*, 31, pp. 197–217.

Cressie, N.A.C. (1981) *Statistics for Spatial Data*, New York: Wiley.

Crowder, M. J., and Hand, D. J. (1990) *Analysis of Repeated Measures.* London: Chapman and Hall.

Daly, F., Hand, D.J., Jones, M.C., Lunn, A.D., and McConway, K. (1995) *Elements of Statistics*, Wokingham, U.K.: Addison-Wesley.

Dasarathy, B.V. (ed.) (1991) *Nearest Neighbor (NN) Norms: NN Pattern Classification Techniques.* Los Alamitos, CA: IEEE Computer Society Press.

Davidson, M.L. (1983) *Multidimensional Scaling.* New York: Wiley.

Dawes, R.M., and Smith, T.L. (1985) Attitude and opinion measurement. In *The Handbook of Social Psychology*, Volume I (3rd edition), G. Lindzey and E. Aronson (eds.), New York: Random House, pp. 509–566.

Dawid, A.P. (1984) Statistical theory: The prequential approach (with discussion). *Journal of the Royal Statistical Society A*, 147, pp. 178–292.

Deerwester, S., Dumais, S.T., Furnas, G.W., Landauer, T.K., and Harshman, R. (1990) Indexing by latent semantic analysis. *Journal of the American Society for Information Science*, 41, pp. 391–407.

DeFinetti, B. (1974, 1975) *Theory of Probability*, Vols. 1 and 2. Chichester, U.K.: Wiley.

Della Pietra, S., Della Pietra, V., and Lafferty, J. (1997) Inducing features of random fields. *IEEE Transactions on Pattern Analysis and Machine Intelligence*, 19(4), pp. 380–393.

Dempster, A.P., Laird, N.M., and Rubin, D.B. (1977) Maximum likelihood from incomplete data via the EM algorithm (with discussion). *Journal of the Royal Statistical Society B*, 39, pp. 1–38.

Devijver, P.A., and Kittler, J. (1982) *Pattern Recognition: A Statistical Approach.* Englewood Cliffs, NJ: Prentice-Hall.

Devroye, L. (1984) *Nonparametric Density Estimation: the L1 View.* New York: Wiley.

Devroye, L., Gyorfi, L., and Lugosi, G. (1996) *A Probabilistic Theory of Pattern Recognition.* New York: Springer-Verlag.

Devroye, L.P., and Wagner, T.J. (1982) Nearest neighbor methods in discrimination. In *Handbook of Statistics,* vol. 2, P.R. Krishnaiah and L.N. Kanal, (eds.) Amsterdam: North-Holland, pp. 193–197.

Diaconis, P., and Shahshahani, M. (1984) On non-linear functions of linear combinations. *SIAM Journal of Scientific Computing*, 5, pp. 175–191.

Diebolt, J., and Robert, C.P. (1994) Bayesian estimation of finite mixture distributions. *Journal of the Royal Statistical Society B*, 56, pp. 363–375.

Dietterich, T.G. (1998) Approximate statistical tests for comparing supervised classification learning algorithms. *Neural Computation*, 10(7) pp. 1895-1924.

Digby, P., and Kempton, R. (1987) *Multivariate Analysis of Ecological Communities.* London: Chapman and Hall.

Diggle, P.J., Liang, K-Y., and Zeger, S.L. (1994) *Analysis of Longitudinal Data.* Oxford, U.K.: Clarendon Press.

Domingos, P. (1996) Unifying instance-based and rule-based induction. *Machine Learning*, 24, pp. 141–168.

Domingos, P. (1999) A general method for making classifiers cost-sensitive. *Proceedings of the Fifth ACM SIGKDD International Conference on Knowledge Discovery and Data Mining,* New York: ACM Press, pp. 155–164.

Domingos, P., and Hulten, G. (2000) Mining high-speed data streams. *Proceedings of the Sixth ACM SIGKDD International Conference on Knowledge Discovery and Data Mining*, New York: ACM Press, pp.71–80.

Domingos, P., and Pazzani, M. (1997) On the optimality of the simple Bayesian classifier under zero-one loss. *Machine Learning*, 29, pp. 103–130.

Draper, N.R., and Smith, H. (1981) *Applied Regression Analysis*, New York: Wiley.

Dryden, I.L., and Mardia, K.V. (1998) *Statistical Shape Analysis*. Chichester, UK: Wiley.

Du Mouchel, W., Volinsky, C., Johnson, T., Cortes, C., and Pregibon, D. (1999) Squashing flat files flatter. *Proceedings of the Fifth ACM SIGKDD International Conference on Knowledge Discovery and Data Mining*, New York: ACM Press, pp. 6–15.

Duda, R.O., and Hart, P.E. (1973) *Pattern Recognition and Scene Analysis*, New York: Wiley.

Duda, R.O., Hart, P.E., and Stork, D.J. (2001) *Pattern Recognition* New York: Wiley.

Dumais, S.T., Platt, J., Heckerman, D., and Sahami, M. (1998) Inductive learning algorithms and representations for text categorization. *Proceedings of the ACM Seventh International Conference on Information and Knowledge Management*, New York: ACM Press, pp. 148–155.

Dunn, G. (1989) *Design and Analysis of Reliability Studies*. London: Arnold.

Durbin, R., Eddy, S., Krogh, A., and Mitchison, G. (1998) *Biological Sequence Analysis: Probabilistic Models of Proteins and Nucleic Acids*. Cambridge, U.K.: Cambridge University Press.

Edwards, D. (1995) *Introduction to Graphical Modeling*. New York: Springer Verlag.

Edwards, A.W.F. (1972) *Likelihood*. Baltimore, MD: Johns Hopkins University Press, expanded edition.

Efron, B., and Tibshirani, R.J. (1993) *An Introduction to the Bootstrap*, New York: Chapman and Hall.

Ein-Dor, P., and Feldmesser, J. (1987) Attributes of the performance of central processing units: a relative performance prediction model. *Communications of the ACM*, 30, pp. 308–317.

Eisen, M.B., Spellman, P.T., Brown, P.O., and Botstein, D. (1998) Cluster analysis and display of genome-wide expression patterns. *Science*, 95(25), pp. 14863–68.

Elliott, R.J., Aggoun, L., and Moore, J.B. (1995) *Hidden Markov Models*. New York: Springer-Verlag.

Everitt, B.S. (1981) A Monte Carlo investigation of the likelihood ratio test for the number of components in a mixture of normal distributions. *Multivariate Behavioural Research*, 16, pp. 171–180.

Everitt, B.S., and Hand, D.J. (1981) *Finite Mixture Distributions*. London: Chapman and Hall.

Everitt, B.S., and Dunn, G. (1991) *Applied Multivariate Data Analysis*. New York: Halstead Press.

Everitt, B.S., Gourlay, A.J., and Kendell, R.E. (1971) An attempt at validation of traditional psychiatric syndromes by cluster analysis. *British Journal of Psychiatry*, 138, pp. 336–339.

Faloutsos, C., Barber, R., Flickner, M., Hafner, J., Niblack, W., Petkovic, D., and Equitz, W. (1994) Efficient and effective querying by image content. *Journal of Intelligent Information Systems*, 3, pp. 231–262.

Faloutsos, C., Ranganathan, M., and Manolopoulos, Y. (1994) Fast subsequence matching in time-series databases. *Proceedings of the 1994 Annual ACM SIGMOD Conference*, New York, NY: ACM Press, pp. 419–429.

Fan, J., and Gijbels, I. (1996) *Local Polynomial Modeling and its Applications*. London: Chapman and Hall.

Fawcett, T., and Provost, F. (1997) Adaptive fraud detection. *Data Mining and Knowledge Discovery*, 1(3), pp. 291–316.

Fayyad, U.M., Djorgovski S.G., and Weir N. (1996) Automating the analysis and cataloging of sky surveys. In *Advances in Knowledge Discovery and Data Mining* U.M. Fayyad, G. Piatetsky-Shapiro, P. Smyth, and R. Uthurusamy (eds.), Menlo Park, CA: AAAI Press, pp. 471–493.

Fayyad, U.M., Piatetsky-Shapiro, G., and Smyth, P. (1996) From data mining to knowledge discovery: an overview. In *Advances in Knowledge Discovery and Data Mining*, U.M. Fayyad, G. Piatetsky-Shapiro, P. Smyth, and R. Uthurusamy (eds.). Menlo Park, CA: AAAI Press. pp. 1–34.

Feller, W. (1968) *An Introduction to Probability Theory and its Applications*, Vol. 1 (3rd ed.) New York: Wiley.

Feng, Z.D., and McCulloch, C.E. (1996) Using bootstrap likelihood ratios in finite mixture models. *Journal of the Royal Statistical Society B*, 58(3), pp. 609–617.

Fenton, N.E. (1991) *Software Metrics*. London: Chapman and Hall.

Fine, T.L. (1999) *Feedforward Neural Network Methodology*. New York: Springer.

Fisher, R.A. (1936) The use of multiple measurements on taxonomic problems. *Annals of Eugenics*, 7, pp. 179–188.

Fletcher, R. (1987) *Practical Methods of Optimization*. New York: Wiley.

Flickner, M., Sawhney, H., Niblack, W., Ashley, J., Huang, Q., Dom, B., Gorkani, M., Hafner, J., Lee, D., Petkovic, D., Steele, D., and Yanker, P. (1995) Query by image and video content. *IEEE Computer*, 28(9), pp. 23–31.

Florek K., Lukasziwicz J., Perkal J., Steinhaus H., and Zubrzycki S. (1951) Sur la liaison et la division des points d'un ensemble fini. *Colloquium Mathematicum*, 2, pp. 282–285.

Frakes, W.B., and Baeza-Yates, R. (eds.) (1992) *Information Retrieval: Data Structures and Algorithms*, Englewood Cliffs, N.J.: Prentice Hall.

Fraley, C., and Raftery, A.E. (1998) How many clusters? Which clustering method? answers via model-based cluster analysis. *Computer Journal*, 41, pp. 578–588.

Freund, Y., and Schapire, R.E. (1996) Experiments with a new boosting algorithm. In *Proceedings of the Thirteenth International Conference on Machine Learning*, San Francisco, CA: Morgan Kaufmann, pp. 148–156.

Friedman, J. (1997) On bias, variance, 0/1 loss, and the curse of dimensionality. *Data Mining and Knowledge Discovery*, pp. 55–77.

Friedman, J.H. (1991) Multivariate adaptive regression splines (with discussion). *Annals of Statistics*, 19, pp. 1–141.

Friedman, J.H. and Stuetzle, W. (1981) Project pursuit regression. *Journal of the American Statistical Association*, 76, pp. 817–823.

Friedman, J.H., and Fisher, N.I. (1999) Bump hunting in high dimensional data (with discussion). *Statistics and Computing*, 9, pp. 123–162.

Friedman, J.H.F., Hastie, T., and Tibshirani, R. (2000) Additive logistic regression: a statistical view of boosting, *Annals of Statistics*, 28, 377–386.

Friedman, N., and Goldszmidt, M. (1996) Learning Bayesian networks with local structure. *Proceedings of Twelfth Conference on Uncertainty in Artificial Intelligence*, San Francisco, CA: Morgan Kaufmann, pp. 252–262.

Fukuda, T., Morimoto, Y., Morishita, S., and Tokuyama, T. (1996) Mining optimized association rules for numeric attributes. *Proceedings of the 15th ACM SIGACT-SIGMOD-SIGART Symposium on Principles of Database and Knowledgebase Systems (PODS'96)*, New York: ACM Press, pp. 182–191.

Fukunaga, K. (1990) *Introduction to Statistical Pattern Recognition*, San Diego, CA: Academic Press.

Fukunaga, K., and Flick, T.E. (1984) An optimal global nearest neighbor metric. *IEEE Transactions on Pattern Recognition and Machine Intelligence*, 6, pp. 314–318.

Furnival, G.M., and Wilson, R.W. (1974) Regression by leaps and bounds. *Technometrics*, 16, pp. 499–511.

Gaffney, S., and Smyth, P. (1999) Trajectory clustering with mixtures of regression models. In *Proceedings of the ACM 1999 Conference on Knowledge Discovery and Data Mining*, New York, NY: ACM Press, pp. 63–72.

Ganti, V., Gehrke, J., and Ramakrishnan, R. (1999) Mining very large databases. *IEEE Computer*, 32, pp. 38–45.

Garcia-Molina, H., Ullman, J.D., and Widom, J. (1999) *Database System Implementation*. Englewood Cliffs, NJ: Prentice Hall.

Ge, X., and Smyth, P. (2000) Deformable Markov model templates for time series pattern-matching. *Proceedings of the ACM Seventh International Conference on Knowledge Discovery and Data Mining*, New York: ACM Press, pp. 81–90.

Gehrke, J., Ganti, V., Ramakrishnan, R., and Loh, W-Y. (1999) BOAT—optimistic decision tree construction. *Proceedings of the 1999 ACM SIGMOD conference.* New York: ACM Press, pp. 169–180.

Gehrke, J.E., Ramakrishnan, R., and Ganti, V. (1998) RainForest—a framework for fast decision tree construction of large datasets. *Proceedings of the 24th International Conference on Very Large Databases (VLDB'98),* pp. 416–427.

Gelman, A., Carlin, J.B., Stern, H.S., and Rubin, D.B. (1995) *Bayesian Data Analysis,* London: Chapman and Hall.

Geman, S., Bienenstock, E., and Doursat, R. (1992) Neural networks and the bias-variance dilemma. *Neural Computation,* 4(1), pp. 1–58.

Gilks, W.R., Richardson, S., and Spiegelhalter, D.J. (1996) *Markov Chain Monte Carlo in Practice.* London: Chapman and Hall.

Gill, P.E., Murray, W., and Wright, M.H. (1981) *Practical Optimization.* New York: Academic Press.

Glymour, C., Madigan, D., Pregibon, D., and Smyth, P. (1997) Statistical themes and lessons for data mining. *Data Mining and Knowledge Discovery.* 1(1), pp. 11–28.

Goer, J.C. (1967) A comparison of some methods of cluster analysis. *Biometrics,* 23, pp. 623–628.

Golden, R.M. (1996) *Mathematical Methods for Neural Network Analysis and Design.* Cambridge, MA: MIT Press.

Goldstein, H. (1995) *Multilevel Statistical Models* (2nd ed.). London: Arnold.

Gordon, A. (1981) *Classification: Methods for the Exploratory Analysis of Multivariate Data.* London: Chapman and Hall.

Gower, J.C. (1974) Maximal predictive classification. *Biometrics,* 30, pp. 643–654.

Gower, J.C., and Hand, D.J. (1996) *Biplots.* London: Chapman and Hall.

Gray, J., Bosworth, A., Layman, A., and Pirahesh, H. (1996) Data cube: a relational aggregation operator generalizing group-by, cross-tab, and subtotals. *12th International Conference on Data Engineering (ICDE'96),* New Orleans, Louisiana, pp. 152–159.

Gray, J., Chaudhuri, S., Bosworth, A., Layman, A., Reichart, D., Venkatrao, M., Pellow, F., and Pirahesh, H. (1997) Data Cube: A relational aggregation operator generalizing group-by, cross-tab, and sub-totals. *Data Mining and Knowledge Discovery*, 1, pp. 29–53.

Grenander, U. (1996) *Elements of Pattern Theory*. Baltimore, MD: Johns Hopkins University Press.

Grimmett, G.R., and Stirzaker, D.R. (1992) *Probability and Random Processes*. (2nd ed.) Oxford: Clarenden Press.

Gusfield, D. (1997) *Algorithms on Strings, Trees and Sequences*. New York, NY: Cambridge University Press.

Hall, D.J., and Ball, G.B. (1965) ISODATA: A novel method of cluster analysis and pattern classification. Technical Report, Stanford Research Institute, Menlo Park, California.

Halstead, M.H. (1977) *Elements of Software Science*. New York: Elsevier.

Hamilton, J.D. (1994) *Time Series Analysis*. Princeton, NJ: Princeton University Press.

Hamming, R.W. (1991) *The Art of Probability for Scientists and Engineers*, Redwood City, CA: Addison-Wesley.

Han, J., and Fu, Y. (1995) Discovery of multiple-level association rules from large databases, *Proceedings of the Twenty First International Conference on Very Large Data Bases (VLDB'95)*, San Mateo, CA: Morgan Kaufmann, pp. 420–431.

Han, J., and Kamber, M. (2000) *Data Mining: Concepts and Techniques*, San Francisco, CA: Morgan Kaufmann.

Hand, D.J. (1981) *Discrimination and Classification*. Chichester, U.K.: Wiley.

Hand, D.J. (1982) *Kernel Discriminant Analysis*. Chichester, U.K.: Research Studies Press.

Hand, D.J. (1986) Recent advances in error rate estimation. *Pattern Recognition Letters*, 4, pp. 335–346.

Hand, D.J. (1996) Statistics and the theory of measurement (with discussion). *Journal of the Royal Statistical Society, Series A*, 159, pp. 445–492.

Hand, D.J. (1997) *Construction and Assessment of Classification Rules*. London: Wiley.

Hand, D.J., Blunt, G., Kelly, M.G., and Adams, N.M. (2000) Data mining for fun and profit. *Statistical Science*, 15, pp. 111-131.

Hand, D.J., and Crowder, M.J. (1996) *Practical Longitudinal Data Analysis*. London: Chapman and Hall.

Hand, D.J., Daly, F., Lunn, A.D., McConway, K.J., and Ostrowski, E. (eds.) (1994) *A Handbook of Small Data Sets*. London: Chapman and Hall.

Hand, D.J., McConway, K.J., and Stanghellini, E. (1997) Graphical models of applicants for credit. *IMA Journal of Mathematics Applied in Business and Industry*, 8, pp. 143–155.

Hand, D.J., and Yu, K. (1999) Idiot's Bayes—not so stupid after all? Working paper. Department of Mathematics, Imperial College, London.

Harman, D.K. (1993) The First Text Retrieval Conference (TREC-1), NIST SP 500-207, National Institute of Standards and Technology, Gaithersburg, Md.: (annual series, 1993–1999).

Harman, D.K., (1995) *Hypertext—Information Retrieval—Multimedia: Synergieeffekte Elektronischer Informationssysteme, Proceedings of HIM'95*, R. Kuhlen and M. Rittberger (eds.), Konstanz, Germany: Universitaetsforlag Konstanz, pp. 9–28.

Harrison, D. (1993) Backing up. *Neural Computing*, pp. 98–104.

Harvey, A.C. (1989) *Forecasting, Structural Time Series Models, and the Kalman Filter*. Cambridge, UK: Cambridge University Press.

Hastie, T., and Tibshirani, R.J. (1990) *Generalized Additive Models*. London: Chapman and Hall.

Hastie, T., and Tibshirani, R.J. (1996) Discriminant adaptive nearest neighbor classification. *IEEE Transactions on Pattern Analysis and Machine Intelligence*, 18, pp. 607–616.

Heckerman, D., Chickering, D.M., Meek, C., Rounthwaite, R., and Kadie, C. (2000) Dependency networks for inference, collaborative filtering, and data visualization. *Journal of Machine Learning Research*, 1, pp. 49–75.

Hendry, D.F. (1995) *Dynamic Econometrics*. New York: Oxford University Press.

Hilden, J. (1984) Statistical diagnosis based on conditional independence does not require it. *Computers in Biology and Medicine*, 14, pp. 429–435.

Hjort, J.S.U. (1993) *Computer Intensive Statistical Methods: Validation, Model Selection, and Bootstrap*. Boca Raton, FL: CRC Press.

Ho, T.K., Hull J.J., and Srihari, S.N. (1994) Decision combination in multiple classifier systems. *IEEE Transactions on Pattern Analysis and Machine Intelligence*, 16, pp. 66–75.

Hoffmann, T. (1999) Probabilistic latent sematic indexing. *Proceedings of the ACM SIGIR Conference 1999*, New York: ACM Press, pp. 50–57.

Holsheimer, M., Kersten, M., Mannila, H., and Toivonen, H. (1995) A perspective on databases and data mining. *Proceedings of the First International Conference on knowledge discovery and data mining*, Fayyad, U.M., and Uthurusamy, R. (eds.), Menlo Park, CA: AAAI Press, pp. 150–155.

Holte, R.C., (1993) Very simple classification rules perform well on most commonly used data sets. *Machine Learning*, 11, pp. 63–91.

Huba, G.J., Wingard, J.A., and Bentler, P.M. (1981) A comparison of two latent variable causal models for adolescent drug use. *Journal of Personality and Social Psychology*, 40, pp. 180–193.

Huber, P. (1985) Projection pursuit. *Annals of Statistics*, 13(2), pp. 435–475.

Huber, P.J. (1980) *Robust Statistics*. New York: Wiley.

Hunter, J.S. (1980) The national system of scientific measurement. *Science*, 210, 21 November 1980, pp. 869-874.

Hyvarinen, A. (1999) Survey on independent component analysis. *Neural Computing Surveys*, 2, pp. 94–128.

Imielinski, T., and Mannila, H. (1996) A database perspective on knowledge discovery. *Communications of the ACM*, 39(11), pp. 58–64.

Imielinski, T., and Virmani, A. (1999) MSQL: A query language for database mining. *Data Mining and Knowledge Discovery* 3(4), pp. 373–408.

Imielinski, T., Virmani, A., and Abdulghani, A. (1999) DMajor application programming interface for database mining. *Data Mining and Knowledge Discovery*, 3(4), pp. 347–372.

Jacoby, W.G. (1997) *Statistical Graphics for Univariate and Bivariate Data*. London: Sage Publications.

Jain, A., and Dubes, R. (1988) *Algorithms for Clustering Data.*, Englewood Cliffs, Prentice-Hall.

Jensen, F.V. (1996) *An Introduction to Bayesian Networks*. New York: Springer-Verlag.

Jolliffe, I.T. (1986) *Principal Component Analysis*. New York: Springer-Verlag.

Jordan, M.I. (1999) *Learning in Graphical Models*, Cambridge, MA: MIT Press.

Jordan, M.I., and Jacobs, R.A. (1994) Hierarchical mixtures of experts and the EM algorithm. *Neural Computation*, 6, pp. 181-214.

Journal of the American Society for Information Science (1996) Special Issue on Evaluation, 47:1–105.

Karypis, G., and Kumar, V. (1998) A parallel algorithm for multilevel graph partitioning and sparse matrix ordering. *Journal of Parallel and Distributed Computing*, 48(1), pp. 71–95.

Kass, R., and Raftery, A. (1995) Bayes factors. *Journal of the American Statistical Association*, 90, pp. 773–795.

Kato, T., Kurita, T., and Shimogaki, H. (1991) Intelligent visual interaction with image database systems—towards the multimedia personal interface. *Information Processing* (Japan), 14, pp. 134–143.

Kaufman, L., and Rousseeuw, P.J. (1990) *Finding Groups in Data: An Introduction to Cluster Analysis*. New York: Wiley.

Keim, D.A., and Kriegel, H.-P. (1994) VisDB: database exploration using multidimensional visualization. *IEEE Computer Graphics and Applications*, September 1994, pp. 40–49.

Kendall, M.G. (1980) *Multivariate Analysis* (2nd ed.). London: Griffin.

Keogh, E., and Smyth, P. (1997) A probabilistic approach to fast pattern matching in time series databases. *Proceedings of the 3rd International Conference on Knowledge Discovery and Data Mining,* Menlo Park, CA: AAAI Press, pp. 24–30.

Kim, C-J., and Nelson, C.R. (1999) *State-Space Models with Regime Switching: Classical and Gibbs Sampling Approaches with Applications.* Cambridge, MA: MIT Press.

Kirkpatrick, S., Gelatt, C.D. Jr., and Vecchi, M.P. (1983) Optimization by simulated annealing. *Science,* 220, pp. 671–680.

Kish, L. (1965) *Survey Sampling.* New York: Wiley.

Klemettinen, M., Mannila, H., Ronkainen, P., Toivonen, H., and Verkamo, A.I. (1994) Finding interesting rules from large sets of discovered association rules. *Proceedings of the Third International Conference on Information and Knowledge Management (CIKM'94),* New York: ACM Press, pp. 401–407.

Knight, K. (2000) *Mathematical Statistics,* Boca Raton, FL: Chapman and Hall.

Knuth, D. (1997). *The Art of Computer Programming: Fundamental Algorithms,* 3rd ed. Reading, MA: Addison Wesley.

Kohavi, R.(1996) Scaling up the accuracy of naive-Bayes classifiers: A decision-tree hybrid. *Proceedings of the Second International Conference on Knowledge Discovery and Data Mining.* Portland, OR: AAAI Press, pp. 202–207.

Koontz, W.L.G., Narendra, P.M., and Fukunaga, K. (1975) A branch and bound clustering algorithm. *IEEE Transactions on Computers,* 24, pp. 908–915.

Krantz, D.H., Luce, R.D., Suppes, P., and Tversky, A. (1971) *Foundations of Measurement, Volume 1: Additive and Polynomial Representations.* New York: Academic Press.

Krzanowski, W.J., and Marriott, F.H.C. (1995) *Multivariate Analysis vol. 2: Classification, Covariance Structures, and Repeated Measurements.* London: Arnold.

Lambert, J.M., and Williams, W.T. (1966) Multivariate methods in plant ecology IV: comparison of information analysis and association analysis. *Journal of Ecology,* 54, pp. 635–664.

Lance, G.N., and Williams, W.T. (1967) A general theory of classificatory sorting strategies: 1. Hierarchical systems. *Computer Journal, 9,* pp. 373–380.

Landauer, T.K., and Dumais, S.T., (1997). A solution to Plato's problem: The latent semantic analysis theory of acquisition, induction, and representation of knowledge. *Psychological Review,* 104(2), pp. 211–240.

Lange, K. (1995) A gradient algorithm locally equivalent to the EM algorithm. *Journal of the Royal Statistical Society B,* 57, pp. 425–437.

Lange, K. (1999) *Numerical Analysis for Statisticians.* New York: Springer-Verlag.

Lapointe, F.J., and Legendre, P. (1994) A classification of pure malt Scotch whiskies. *Applied Statistics,* 43, pp. 237–257.

Lauritzen, S.L. (1996) *Graphical Models.* Oxford: Clarendon Press.

Lavine, M. (1991) Problems in extrapolation illustrated with space shuttle O-ring data. *Journal of the American Statistical Association,* 86, pp. 919–922.

Lavrac, N., and Dzeroski, S. (1994) *Inductive Logic Programming: Techniques and Applications.* Ellis Horwood.

Lawrence, R.D., Almasi, G.S., Kotlyar, V., Viveros, M.S., and Duri, S.S. (2001) Personalization of supermarket product recommendations, *Data Mining and Knowledge Discovery,* to appear.

Leamer, E.E. (1978) *Specification Searches: Ad Hoc Inference with Experimental Data.* New York: Wiley.

Lee, P.M. (1989) *Bayesian Statistics: An Introduction.* London: Edward Arnold.

Lehmann, E.L. (1986) *Testing Statistical Hypotheses.* New York: Wiley.

Lehmann, E.L., and Casella, G. (1998) *Theory of Point Estimation,* New York: Springer-Verlag.

Leighton, G., and McKinlay, P.L. (1930) *Milk Consumption and the Growth of School Children.* London: HMSO.

Leinweber, D. (personal communication) Stupid data miner tricks: Overfitting the S&P 500.

Lewis, H.R., and Papadimitriou, C.H. (1998) *Elements of the Theory of Computation*, second edition. Upper Saddle River, NJ: Prentice-Hall.

Li, M., and Vitanyi, P. (1993) *An Introduction to Kolmogorov Complexity and Its Applications*. New York: Springer.

Lindsey, I. (1994) *Credit Cards: The Authoritative Guide to Payment and Credit Cards*. Leighton Buzzard: Rushmere Wynne.

Lindsey, J.K. (1996) *Parametric Statistical Inference*. Oxford, U.K.: Clarendon Press.

Lindsey, J.K. (1999) *Models for Repeated Measurements,* 2nd ed. Oxford, U.K.: Oxford University Press.

Lindsey, J.K. (1999) Relationships among sample size, model selection and likelihood regions, and scientifically important differences. *Journal of the Royal Statistical Society, Series D*, 48, pp. 401–411.

Linhart, H., and Zucchini, W. (1986) *Model Selection*. New York: Wiley.

Little, R.J.A., and Rubin, D.B. (1987) *Statistical Analysis with Missing Data*. New York: Wiley.

Looney, C.G. (1997) *Pattern Recognition Using Neural Networks*. Oxford, U.K.: Oxford University Press.

Lovell, M.C. (1983) Data mining. *Review of Economics and Statistics* 65(1), pp. 1–12.

Luce, R.D., Krantz, D.H., Suppes, P., and Tversky, A. (1990) *Foundations of Measurement, Volume 3: Representation, Axiomatization, and Invariance*. San Diego, CA: Academic Press.

Luenberger, D.G. (1984) *Introduction to Linear and Nonlinear Programming*. Menlo Park, CA: Addison-Wesley.

MacDonald, I.L., and Zucchini, W. (1997) *Hidden Markov and Other Models for Discrete-valued Time Series*. London: Chapman and Hall.

MacKay, D.J.C. (1992) A practical Bayesian framework for back-propagation networks. *Neural Computation*, 4, pp. 448–472.

MacMillan, N.A., and Creelman, C.D. (1991) *Signal Detection Theory: A User's Guide*, New York, NY: Cambridge University Press.

MacNaughton-Smith, P., Williams, W.T., Dale, M.B., and Mockett, L.G. (1964) Dissimilarity analysis. *Nature,* 202, pp. 1034–1035.

MacQueen, J. (1967) Some methods for classification and analysis of multivariate observations. In *Proceedings of the Fifth Berkeley Symposium on Mathematical Statistics and Probability,* L.M. Le Cam, and J. Neyman (eds.) Berkeley: University of California Press, pp. 281–297.

Madigan, D., Raghavan, N., DuMouchel, W., Nason, M., Posse, C., and Ridgeway, G. (in press) Likelihood-based data squashing: A modeling approach to instance construction. *Data Mining and Knowledge Discovery.*

Mangasarian, O. (1997) Mathematical programming in data mining. *Data Mining and Knowledge Discovery,* 1(2), pp.183–201.

Mannila, H. (1997) Inductive databases and condensed representations: Concepts for data mining. *International Logic Programming Symposium 1997,* Cambridge, MA: MIT Press, pp. 21–30.

Mannila, H., Toivonen, H., and Verkamo, A.I. (1994) Efficient algorithms for discovering association rules. *Knowledge Discovery in Databases: Papers from the AAAI-94 Workshop (KDD'94),* Menlo Park, CA: AAAI Press, pp. 181–192.

Mannila, H., Toivonen, H., and Verkamo, A.I. (1997) Discovery of frequent episodes in sequences. *Data Mining and Knowledge Discovery.* 1(3), pp. 259–290.

Maritz, J.S. (1981) *Distribution-Free Statistical Methods.* London: Chapman and Hall.

Marriott, F.H.C. (1971) Practical problems in a method of cluster analysis. *Biometrics,* 27, pp. 501-514.

Maybury, M.T. (ed.) (1997) *Intelligent Multimedia Information Retrieval.* Menlo Park, CA: AAAI Press.

McCullagh, P., and Nelder, J.A. (1989) *Generalized Linear Models,* 2nd ed. London: Chapman and Hall.

McKendrick, A.G. (1926) Applications of mathematics to medical problems. *Proceedings of the Edinburgh Mathematical Society,* 44, pp. 98–130.

McLachlan, G.J. (1987) Error rate estimation in discriminant analysis: recent advances. In *Advances in Multivariate Statistical Analysis*, A.K. Gupta, ed. The Netherlands: Reidel, pp. 233–252.

McLachlan, G.J. (1987) On bootstrapping the likelihood ratio test for the number of components in a normal mixture. *Applied Statistics*, 36, pp. 318–324.

McLachlan, G.J. (1992) *Discriminant Analysis and Statistical Pattern Recognition*. New York: Wiley.

McLachlan, G.J., and Basford, K.E. (1988) *Mixture Models: Inference and Applications to Clustering*. New York: Marcel Dekker.

McLachlan, G.J., and Krishnan, T. (1998) *The EM Algorithm and Extensions*. New York: Wiley.

McLachlan, G.J., and Peel, D. (1997) On a resampling approach to choosing the number of components in normal mixture models. In *Computing Science and Statistics (Vol 28)*, L. Billard, and N.I. Fisher (eds.). Fairfax Station, VA: Interface Foundation of North America, pp. 260–266.

McLachlan, G.J., and Peel, D. (1998) MIXFIT: An algorithm for the automatic fitting and testing of normal mixture models. *Proceedings of the 14th International Conference on Pattern Recognition*, vol. 1, Los Alamitos, CA: IEEE Computer Society, pp. 553–557.

McLachlan, G.J., and Peel, D. (2000) *Finite Mixture Models*. New York: Wiley.

McLaren, C.E. (1996) Mixture models in haematology: A series of case studies. *Statistical Methods in Medical Research*, 5, pp. 129–153.

Meilijson, I. (1989) A fast improvement to the EM algorithm on its own terms. *Journal of the Royal Statistical Society B*, 51, pp. 127–138.

Mendell, N.R., Finch, S.J., and Thode, H.C. (1993) Where is the likelihood ratio test powerful for detecting two component normal mixtures? *Biometrics*, 49, pp. 907–915.

Meo, R., Psaila, G., and Ceri, S. (1996) A new SQL-like operator for mining association rules. *Proceedings of the 22nd International Conference on Very Large Data Bases (VLDB'96)*, San Mateo, CA: Morgan Kaufmann.

Michell, J. (1986) Measurement scales and statistics: A clash of paradigms. *Psychological Bulletin*, 100, pp. 398–407.

Michell, J. (1990) *An Introduction to the Logic of Psychological Measurement.* Hillsdale: Lawrence Erlbaum.

Mitchell, M. (1997) *An Introduction to Genetic Algorithms.* Cambridge, MA: MIT Press.

Mitchell, T. (1997) *Machine Learning,* New York: McGraw-Hill.

Moore, A. (1999) Very fast EM-based mixture model clustering using multiresolution kd-trees. In *Advances in Neural Information Processing Systems 12,* San Francisco, CA: Morgan Kaufmann.

Moore, A.W. (1999) Cached sufficient statistics for automated discovery and data mining from massive data sources. Online white paper, Department of Computer Science, Carnegie Mellon University, Pittsburgh, PA.

Moore, A.W., and Lee, M. (1998) Cached sufficient statistics for efficient machine learning with large data sets. *Journal of Artificial Intelligence Research,* 8, pp. 67–91.

Morgan, B.J.T. (1981) Three applications of methods of cluster analysis. *The Statistician,* 30, pp. 205-223.

Morgan, J.N., and Sonquist, J.A. (1963) Problems in the analysis of survey data, and a proposal. *Journal of the American Statistical Association,* 58, pp. 415–434.

Mosteller, F. (1968) Nonsampling errors. In *International Encyclopedia of the Social Sciences*, 5, D.L. Sills (ed.), New York: MacMillan and Free Press, pp. 113–132.

Muggleton, S. (1995) *Foundations of Inductive Logic Programming,* Englewood Cliffs, NJ: Prentice Hall.

Murthy, S.K. (1998) Automatic construction of decision trees from data: A multi-disciplinary survey. *Data Mining and Knowledge Discovery,* 2, pp. 345–389.

Myles, J.P., and Hand, D.J. (1990) The multi-class metric problem in nearest neighbour discrimination rules. *Pattern Recognition,* 23, pp. 1291–1297.

Nakhaeizadeh, G., and Taylor, C.C. (eds.) (1997) *Machine Learning and Statistics*. New York: Wiley.

Neal, R. (1996) *Bayesian Learning for Neural Networks*. Lecture Notes in Statistics 118, New York: Springer.

Neal, R., and Hinton, G. (1998) A view of the EM algorithm that justifies incremental, sparse, and other variants. In *Learning in Graphical Models*, Jordan, M.I. (ed.), Cambridge, MA: MIT Press, pp. 355–371.

Nering, E.D., and Tucker, A.W. (1993) *Linear Programs and Related Problems*. Academic Press Inc.

Newcomb, S. (1886) A generalized theory of the combination of observations so as to obtain the best result. *American Journal of Mathematics*, 8, pp. 343–366.

Nightingale, F. (1858) *Notes on Matters Affecting the Health, Efficiency, and Hospital Administration of the British Army, founded chiefly on the Experience of the Late War*. London: Harrison.

Oliver, J.J., and Hand, D.J. (1996) Averaging over decision trees. *Journal of Classification*, 13, pp. 281–297.

Papadimitriou, C.H., and Steiglitz, K (1982) *Combinatorial Optimization— Algorithms and Complexity*. Englewood Cliffs, NJ: Prentice-Hall.

Park, J.S., Chen, M.S., and Yu, P.S. (1995) An effective hash-based algorithm for mining association rules. *Proceedings of the ACM SIGMOD Conference on Management of Data (SIGMOD'95)*, New York: ACM Press, pp. 175–186.

Pearl, J. (1984) *Heuristics: Intelligent Search Strategies for Computer Problem Solving*. Reading, MA: Addison-Wesley.

Pearl, J. (1988) *Probabilistic Reasoning in Intelligent Systems*, San Mateo, CA: Morgan Kaufmann.

Peixoto, J.L. (1990) A property of well-formulated polynomial regression models. *American Statistician*, 44, pp. 26–30.

Pentland, A., Picard, R.W., and Sclaroff, S. (1994) Photobook: Tools for content-based manipulation of image databases. *International Journal of Computer Vision*, 18, pp. 233–254.

Piatetsky-Shapiro, G. (1991) Discovery, analysis, and presentation of strong rules. In *Knowledge Discovery in Databases*. G. Piatetsky-Shapiro and W. Frawley (eds.), Menlo Park, CA: AAAI Press.

Piatetsky-Shapiro, G. (1999) The data-mining industry coming of age. *IEEE Expert*, 14(6), pp. 32–34.

Platt, J. (1999) Fast training of support vector machines using sequential minimal optimization. In *Advances in Kernel Methods—Support Vector Learning*, B. Scholkopf, C.J.C. Burges, and A.J. Smola (eds.), Cambridge, MA: MIT Press, pp. 185–208.

Poulsen, C.S. (1990) Mixed Markov and latent Markov modelling applied to brand choice behavior. *International Journal of Research in Marketing*, 7, pp. 5–19.

Press, W.H., Flannery, B.P., Teukolsky, S.A., and Vetterling, W.T. (1988) *Numerical Recipes in C: The Art of Scientific Computing*. Cambridge, UK: Cambridge University Press.

Provost, F., and Kolluri, V. (1999) A survey of methods for scaling up inductive algorithms. *Data Mining and Knowledge Discovery*, 3, pp. 131–169.

Provost, F., Jensen, D., and Oates, T. (1999) Efficient progressive sampling. *Proceedings of the Fifth ACM SIGKDD International Conference on Knowledge Discovery and Data Mining*, New York: ACM Press, pp. 23–32.

Quandt, R.E., and Ramsey, J.B. (1978) Estimating mixtures of normal distributions and switching regressions. *Journal of the American Statistical Association*, 73(364), 730–738.

Quinlan, J.R. (1986) Induction of decision trees. *Machine Learning*, 1, pp. 81–106.

Quinlan, J.R. (1987) Generating production rules from decision trees. *Proceedings of the Tenth International Joint Conference on Artificial Intelligence*, San Mateo, CA: Morgan Kaufmann, pp. 304–307.

Quinlan, J.R. (1990) Learning logical definitions from relations, *Machine Learning*, 5, pp. 239–266.

Quinlan, J.R. (1993) *C4.5: Programs for Machine Learning*. San Mateo, CA: Morgan Kaufmann.

Raghavan, V.V., and Wong, S.K.M. (1986) A critical analysis of the vector space model for information retrieval. *Journal of the American Society for Information Science,* 37(5), pp. 100–124.

Ramakrishnan, R., and Gehrke, J. (1999) *Database Management Systems,* Second Edition. New York: McGraw Hill.

Ramsey, J.O., and Silverman, B.W. (1996) *Functional Data Analysis.* New York: Springer-Verlag.

Randles, R.H., and Wolfe, D.A. (1979) *Introduction to the Theory of Nonparametric Statistics.* New York: Wiley.

Rao, M.R. (1971) Cluster analysis and mathematical programming. *Journal of the American Statistical Association,* 66, pp. 622–626.

Rastogi, R., and Shim, K. (1998) PUBLIC: A decision tree classifier that integrates building and pruning. *Proceedings of the 24th International Conference on Very Large Databases (VLDB'98),* pp. 405–415.

Redner, R.A., and Walker, H.F. (1984) Mixture densities, maximum likelihood, and the EM algorithm. *SIAM Review,* 26, pp. 195–239.

Resnick, P., Iacovou, N., Suchak, M., Bergstrom, P., and Riedl, J. (1994) GroupLens: An open architecture for collaborative filtering of netnews. *Proceedings of the ACM 1994 Conference on Computer Supported Cooperative Work,* Chapel Hill, N.C.: ACM Press, pp. 175-186.

Reyment, R., and Jöreskog K.G. (1993) *Applied Factor Analysis in the Natural Sciences,* Cambridge: Cambridge University Press.

Ridgeway, G. (1997) Finite discrete Markov process clustering. Technical Report TR 97-24, Microsoft Research, Redmond, WA.

Ripley, B.D. (1996) *Pattern Recognition and Neural Networks.* Cambridge, U.K.: Cambridge University Press.

Rissanen, J. (1987) Stochastic complexity (with discussion). *Journal of the Royal Statistical Society, Series B,* 49, pp. 223–239 and pp. 253–265.

Robbins, H., and Munro, S. (1951) A stochastic approximation method. *Annals of Mathematical Statistics,* 22, pp. 400–407.

Roberts, F.S. (1979) *Measurement Theory with Applications to Decision-making, Utility, and the Social Sciences.* Reading: Addison-Wesley.

Rocchio, J.J. (1971) Relevance feedback in information retrieval. *The SMART Retrieval System: Experiments in Automatic Document Processing,* Salton, G. (ed.). Englewood Cliffs, N.J.: Prentice Hall, pp. 313–323.

Ross, S.M. (1997) *Introduction to Probability Models.* San Diego, CA: Academic Press, 6th ed.

Rui, Y., Huang, T.S., Ortega, M., and Mehrotra, S. (1997) Relevance feedback: a power tool in interactive content-based image retrieval. *Proceedings of the IEEE Transactions on Circuits and Systems for Video Technology,* 8(5), pp. 644–655.

RuleQuest Research (2000) http://www.rulequest.com/cubist-info.html.

Russek, E., Kronmal, R.A., and Fisher, L.D. (1983) The effect of assuming independence in applying Bayes' theorem to risk estimation and classification in diagnosis. *Computers and Biomedical Research,* 16, pp. 537–552.

Salton, G. (ed.) (1971) *The SMART Retrieval System: Experiments in Automatic Document Processing.* Englewood Cliffs, N.J.: Prentice Hall.

Salton, G., and Buckley, C. (1988) Term-weighting approaches in automatic text retrieval. *Information Processing and Management,* 24:513-523.

Salton, G., and Buckley, C. (1990) Improving retrieval performance by relevance feedback. *Journal of the American Society of Information Science,* 41(4), pp. 288-297.

Salton, G., and McGill, M. (1983) *Introduction to Modern Information Retrieval,* New York: McGraw Hill.

Salzberg, S. (1997) On comparing classifiers: Pitfalls to avoid and a recommended approach. *Data Mining and Knowledge Discovery,* 1(3), pp. 317–327.

Salzberg, S. (1999) Gene discovery in DNA sequences. *IEEE Expert,* 14(6), pp. 44–48.

Sarawagi, S., Thomas, S., and Agrawal, R. (1998) Integrating mining with relational database systems: Alternatives and implications. *Proceedings of the ACM SIGMOD Conference on Mangement of Data (SIGMOD 1998),* New York: ACM Press, pp. 343–354.

Sarawagi, S., Thomas, S., and Agrawal, R. (2000) Integrating association rule mining with relational database systems: alternatives and implications. *Data Mining and Knowledge Discovery,* 4, pp. 89–125.

Savasere, A., Omiecinski, E., and Navathe, S. (1995) An efficient algorithm for mining association rules. *Proceedings of the 21st International Conference on Very Large Data Bases (VLDB'95),* San Mateo, CA: Morgan Kaufmann, pp. 432–444.

Schafer, J.B., Konstan, J., and Riedl, J. (in press) Electronic commerce recommender applications. *Data Mining and Knowledge Discovery.*

Schaffer, C. (1994) Cross-validation, stacking and bi-level stacking: Meta-methods for classification and learning. In *Selecting Models from Data: AI and Statistics IV,* P. Cheeseman and R.W. Oldford (eds.), New York: Springer-Verlag.

Schapire, R.E., Freund, Y., Bartlett, P., and Lee, W.S. (1998) Boosting the margin: A new explanation for the effectiveness of voting methods. *The Annals of Statistics,* 26(5), pp. 1651–1686.

Schervish, M.J. (1995) *Theory of Statistics.* New York: Springer-Verlag.

Schiavo, R., and Hand, D.J. (2000) Ten more years of error rate research. *International Statistical Review,* 68, pp. 295-310.

Scholkopf, B., Burges, C.J.C., and Smola, A.J. (eds.) (1999) *Advances in Kernel Methods—Support Vector Learning.* Cambridge, MA: MIT Press.

Schwarz, G. (1978) Estimating the dimension of a model. *Annals of Statistics,* 6, pp. 461–464.

Scott, D.F. (1992) *Multivariate Density Estimation: Theory and Visualization.* New York: Wiley.

Segal, R., and Etzioni, O. (1994) Learning decision lists using homogenous rules. *Proceedings of the Twelfth National Conference on Artificial Intelligence,* Menlo Park, CA: AAAI Press, pp. 619–625.

Shafer, G., and Pearl, J. (1990) *Readings in Uncertain Reasoning.* San Mateo: CA, Morgan Kaufman.

Shafer, J.C., Agrawal, R., and Mehta, M. (1996), SPRINT: A scalable parallel classifier for data mining. *Proceedings of the 22nd International Conference on Very Large Databases (VLDB'96)*, San Francisco, CA:Morgan Kaufmann, pp. 544–555.

Shardanand, U., and Maes, P., (1995) Social information filtering: Algorithms for automating "word of mouth." *Proceedings of CHI'95–Human Factors in Computing Systems*, pp. 210-217.

Shaw, S.W., Defigueiredo, R.J.P. (1990) Structural processing of waveforms as trees. *IEEE Transactions on Acoustic, Speech, and Signal Processing*, 38(2), pp. 328–338.

Shepard, R.N., and Arabie, P. (1979) Additive clustering: Representation of similarities as combinations of discrete overlapping properties. *Psychological Review*, 86, pp. 87–123.

Short, R.D., and Fukunaga, K. (1981) The optimal distance measure for nearest neighbor classification. *IEEE Transactions on Information Theory*, 27, pp. 622–627.

Shoshani, A. (1997) OLAP and statistical databases: Similarities and differences. *Proceedings of the Sixteenth ACM SIGACT-SIGMOD-SIGART Symposium on Principles of Database Systems*, New York: ACM Press, pp. 185–196.

Sibson, R. (1973) SLINK: An optimally efficient algorithm for the single link method. *Computer Journal*, 16, pp. 30–34.

Silberschatz, A., and Tuzhilin, A. (1996) What makes patterns interesting in knowledge-discovery systems, *IEEE Transactions on Knowledge and Data Engineering*, 8(6), pp. 970–974.

Silverman, B.W. (1986) *Density Estimation for Statistics and Data Analysis*. London: Chapman and Hall.

Simpson, C.H. (1951) The interpretation of interaction in contingency tables. *Journal of the Royal Statistical Society, Series B*, 13, pp. 238–241.

Smith, J.R., and Chang, S. (1997) Querying by color regions using VisualSEEk content-based visual query system. *Intelligent Multimedia Information Retrieval*, Maybury, M.T. (ed.). Menlo Park, CA: AAAI Press, pp. 23–41.

Smoliar, S., and Zhang, H. (1994) Content-based video indexing and retrieval. *IEEE Multimedia,* 1, pp. 62–72.

Smyth, P. (1994) Hidden Markov models for fault detection in dynamic systems. *Pattern Recognition,* 27(1), pp.149–164.

Smyth, P. (1997) Clustering sequences using hidden Markov models. In *Advances in Neural Information Processing 9,* M.C. Mozer, M.I. Jordan, and T. Petsche (eds.), Cambridge, MA: MIT Press, pp. 648–654.

Smyth, P. (1999) Probabilistic model-based clustering of multivariate and sequential data. In *Proceedings of the Seventh International Workshop on AI and Statistics,* D. Heckerman, and J. Whittaker eds., San Francisco, CA: Morgan Kaufman, pp. 299–304.

Smyth, P. (2000) Data mining: Data analysis on a grand scale? *Statistical Methods in Medical Research.* 9, pp. 309–327.

Smyth, P. (2000) Model selection for probabilistic clustering using cross-validated likelihood. *Statistics and Computing,* 9, pp. 63–72.

Smyth, P., and Goodman, R. (1992) An information-theoretic approach to rule induction from databases. *IEEE Transactions on Knowledge and Data Engineering,* 4(4), pp. 301–306.

Smyth, P., Ide, K., and Ghil, M. (1999) Multiple regimes in northern hemisphere height fields via mixture model clustering. *Journal of the Atmospheric Sciences,* 56(21), pp. 3704–3723.

Sparck Jones, K., and Willett, P. (1997) *Readings in Information Retrieval.* San Francisco: Morgan Kaufmann.

Späth, H. (1979) Clusterwise linear regression. *Computing,* 22(4), pp. 367–73.

Späth, H. (1985) *Cluster Analysis and Dissection.* Chichester, U.K.: Ellis Horwood.

Srikant, R., and Agrawal, R. (1995) Mining generalized association rules. *Proceedings of the 21st International Conference on Very Large Data Bases (VLDB'95),* San Mateo, CA: Morgan Kaufmann, pp. 407–419.

Srikant, R., and Agrawal, R. (1996) Mining quantitative association rules in large relational tables. *Proceedings of the ACM SIGMOD Conference on Management of Data (SIGMOD'96),* New York: ACM Press, pp. 1–12.

Srikant, R., Vu, Q., and Agrawal, R. (1997) Mining association rules with item constraints. *Proceedings of the Third International Conference on Knowledge Discovery and Data Mining (KDD'97)*, Heckerman, D., Mannila, H., and Pregibon, D. (eds.). Menlo Park, CA: AAAI Press, pp. 67–73.

Stone, M. (1974) Cross-validatory choice and assessment of statistical predictions (with Discussion). *Journal of the Royal Statistical Society, Series B,* 36, pp. 111–147.

Streiner, D.L., and Norman, G.R. (1995) *Health Measurement Scales*, second edition. Oxford: Oxford University Press.

Swanson, D.R. (1987) Two medical literatures that are logically but not bibliographically connected. *Journal of the American Society for Information Retrieval*, 38(4), pp. 228–233.

Swanson, D.R., and Smalheiser, N.R. (1994) Assessing a gap in the biomedical literature: Magnesium deficiency and neurologic disease. *Neuroscience Research Communications*, 15, pp. 1–9.

Swanson, D.R., and Smalheiser N.R. (1997) An interactive system for finding complementary literatures: A stimulus to scientific discovery. *Artificial Intelligence*, 91, pp. 183–203.

Suppes, P., Krantz, D.H., Luce, R.D., and Tversky, A. (1989) *Foundations of Measurement, Volume 2: Geometrical, Threshold, and Probabilistic Representations*. San Diego, CA: Academic Press.

Szalay, A.S., Kunszt, P., Thakar, A., and Gray, J. (1999) Designing and mining multi-terabyte astronomy archives: The Sloan Digital Sky Survey. Technical Report MS-TR-99-30, San Francisco, CA: Microsoft Research.

Thall, P.F., and Vail, S.C. (1990) Some covariance models for longitudinal count data with overdispersion. *Biometrics*, 46, pp. 657-671.

Thisted, R.A., (1988) *Elements of Statistical Computing*. London, Chapman and Hall.

Titterington, D.M., Smith, A.F.M., and Makov, U.E. (1985) *Statistical Analysis of Finite Mixture Distributions*. Chichester, U.K.: Wiley.

Toivonen, H. (1996) Sampling large databases for association rules, *Proceedings of the Twenty Second International Conference on Very Large Data Bases (VLDB'96)*, San Mateo, CA: Morgan Kaufmann, pp. 134–145.

Toussaint, G.T. (1974) Bibliography on estimation of misclassification. *IEEE Transactions on Information Theory,* 20, pp. 472–479.

Tsur, D., Ullman, J.D., Abiteboul, S., Clifton, C., Motwani, R., Nestorov, S., and Rosenthal, A. (1998) QueryFlocks: A generalization of association rule mining. *Proceedings of the ACM SIGMOD Conference on Management of Data (SIGMOD'98),* New York, NY: ACM Press, pp. 1–12.

Tufte, E.R. (1983) *The Visual Display of Quantitative Information.* Cheshire, CT: Graphics Press.

Tufte, E.R. (1990) *Envisioning Information.* Cheshire, CT: Graphics Press.

Tukey, J.W. (1977) *Exploratory Data Analysis.* Reading, MA: Addison-Wesley.

Ullman, J.D. (1988) *Principles of Database and Knowledge-Base Systems,* vol. 1. Rockville, MD: Computer Science Press.

Ullman, J.D., and Widom, J. (1997) *A First Course in Database Systems.* Upper Saddle River, NJ: Prentice-Hall.

van Laarhoven, P.J.M., and Aarts, E.H.L. (1987) *Simulated Annealing: Theory and Applications.* Dordrecht, Netherlands: D. Reidel.

Van Rijsbergen, C.J. (1979) *Information Retrieval.* London: Butterworth Press.

Vapnik, V. (1995) *The Nature of Statistical Learning Theory.* Berlin: Springer-Verlag.

Vapnik, V. (1998) *Statistical Learning Theory.* Chichester, U.K.: Wiley.

Wand, M.P., and Jones, M.C. (1995) *Kernel Smoothing.* London: Chapman and Hall.

Wang, J.T., Zhang, K., Jeong, K., and Shasha, D. (1994) A system for approximate tree matching. *IEEE Transactions on Knowledge and Data Engineering,* 6(4), 559–571.

Webb, A. (1999) *Statistical Pattern Recognition.* London: Arnold.

Webb, G. (2000) Efficient search for association rules. *Proceedings of the ACM Seventh International Conference on Knowledge Discovery and Data Mining,* New York, NY: ACM Press, pp. 300–304.

Wedel, M., and Kamakura, W.A. (1998) *Market Segmentation: Conceptual and Methodological Foundations.* Boston, MA: Kluwer.

Wegman, E.J. (1990) Hyperdimensional data analysis using parallel coordinates. *Journal of the American Statistical Association,* 85(411), pp. 664–675.

Weiss, S., and Indurkhya, N. (1993) Rule-based regression. *Proceedings of the International Joint Conference on Artificial Intelligence, IJCAI-93,* San Mateo, CA: Morgan Kaufmann, pp. 1072–1078.

Weiss, S., and Indurkhya, N. (1995) Rule-based machine learning methods for functional prediction. *Journal of Artificial Intelligence Research,* 3, pp. 383–403.

Weiss, S.M., and Indurkhya, N. (1998) *Predictive Data Mining: A Practical Guide.* San Francisco, CA: Morgan Kaufmann.

Whittaker, J. (1990) *Graphical Models in Applied Multivariate Statistics,* Chichester, U.K.: Wiley.

Wilkinson, L. (1999) *The Grammar of Graphics.* New York: Springer-Verlag.

Witten, I.H., and Franke, E. (2000) *Data Mining: Practical Machine Learning Tools and Techniques with Java Implementations.* San Francisco, CA: Morgan Kaufmann.

Witten, I.H., Moffat, A., and Bell, T.C. (1999) *Managing Gigabytes: Compressing and Indexing Documents and Images,* 2nd ed. San Francisco, CA: Morgan Kaufmann.

Xu, L., Krzyzak, A., and Suen, C.Y. (1992) Methods of combining multiple classifiers and their applications to handwriting recognition. *IEEE Transactions on Pattern Analysis and Machine Intelligence,* 22, pp. 418–435.

Zamir, O., and Etzioni, O. (1998) Web document clustering: A feasibility demonstration. *Proceedings of the 21st International ACM SIGIR Conference,* New York: ACM Press, pp. 46–54.

Zhang, T., Ramakrishnan, R., and Livny, M. (1997) BIRCH: an efficient data clustering method for very large databases. *Data Mining and Knowledge Discovery,* 1(2), pp. 141–182.

Index